D1548059

*Miracles, Convulsions, and Ecclesiastical Politics
in Early Eighteenth-Century Paris*

The deacon François de Pâris in prayer. From a drawing by Jean Restout. In Carré de Montgeron, La Vérité des Miracles (1737). Collection of B. Robert Kreiser.

Miracles, Convulsions,

AND

Ecclesiastical Politics

IN

Early Eighteenth-Century Paris

B. ROBERT KREISER

Princeton University Press

PRINCETON

1978

Copyright © 1978 by Princeton University Press
Published by Princeton University Press, Princeton, New Jersey
In the United Kingdom: Princeton University Press, Guildford, Surrey

All Rights Reserved

Library of Congress Cataloging in Publication Data will be
found on the last printed page of this book
This book has been composed in Linotype Janson
Designed by Bruce D. Campbell
Printed in the United States of America by Princeton
University Press, Princeton, New Jersey

*To Jeanette,
Joshua, and Deborah*

Contents

Preface

ON May 1, 1727, in the midst of the fierce controversies raging in France over the papal bull *Unigenitus* (1713), a saintly and revered Jansenist deacon named François de Pâris died in Paris. Two days later, when he was interred in the parish cemetery of Saint-Médard, crowds of worshipers from every station in society, but mostly from among the pious *menu peuple* living in and around the rue Mouffetard, began to flock to his grave. Here they witnessed the seemingly miraculous healings of apparently incurable ailments and diseases—ulcerous sores, cancerous tumors, persistent fevers, prolonged hemorrhaging, paralysis, blindness, deafness, rheumatism, arthritis—posthumously performed by this holy man. This dramatic proliferation of well-publicized supernatural phenomena soon occasioned the development of a full-scale, albeit unauthorized, religious cult and brought unanticipated notoriety to the obscure and generally squalid *faubourg* Saint-Marceau—one of the least likely places in Paris into which contemporary religious controversy might have been expected to intrude. In the following years the cult to the saintly deacon attracted crowds of adherents from all over Paris and even beyond, transforming the parish and *faubourg* into a major center of religious activity and focusing the attention of much of the kingdom upon this neglected corner of the capital. By the summer of 1731 the number of visitors frequenting the tomb, whether in search of miraculous cures or merely out of curiosity, had grown to unmanageable proportions. From the relatively calm and simple scene of pious devotions and occasional miracles, the situation at the cemetery had progressed—or degenerated—to the wilder, often frenzied spectacle of people in convulsions, people who claimed to be inspired by the Holy Spirit through the intercession of M. Pâris.

At the outset, these religious enthusiasts could hardly have posed a very serious threat to the established order, nor did they have any particular desire to do so. Their earliest miraculous cures seemed in no way different from others which the French populace had been experiencing at irregular intervals throughout the medieval and early modern period. The miracles and the religious observances which they occasioned at Saint-Médard were initially no more bizarre, notorious, or tinged with heterodoxy than were those which had occurred at a variety of other sanctuaries over the years. Such a situation, however, was not destined to last. Through an unusual combination of circumstances the cures attributed to the deacon Pâris were drawn into the stormy arena of contemporary ecclesiastical politics.

Since the late 1720s the opponents of the bull *Unigenitus* (the appellants or *anticonstitutionnaires*) had taken a considerable interest in the nascent Pâris cult. Frustrated in their efforts to overcome the Bull, many of these *anticonstitutionnaires*, like their Jansenist predecessors in the days of the Holy Thorn miracles, were eager to claim divine support and legitimation for their cause from the appellant deacon's posthumous cures. While Jansenist theologians began publishing numerous tracts exploiting the message of divine approval purportedly conveyed by the Pâris miracles, their coreligionists among the parish clergy encouraged the lay faithful—now including a broader cross section of the Parisian populace than at first—to participate in the devotions at M. Pâris' tomb. By these concerted actions, many of them at least tacitly supported by the lawyers and judges in the Parlement of Paris, the *anticonstitutionnaires* helped to swell the numbers of participants in the cult and, at the same time, to transform the events at Saint-Médard into a national *cause célèbre*.

While the issue of the Pâris cult reawakened the flagging hopes of the *anticonstitutionnaires*, its continued growth could not help arousing certain fears within the Church. The tradition-bound hierarchy considered itself the exclusive guardian and distributor of a particular number and kind of institutionalized signs of salvation and grace. To the post-Tridentine Church, eager to eliminate, or at least reduce, the parachristian beliefs and magical and "superstitious" practices of the *menu peuple*, an unsanctioned and expanding popular religious cult represented an automatic challenge to ecclesiastical authority and discipline—a sign of public disobedience and disrespect. The attempts of *anticonstitutionnaire* theologians and pamphleteers to draw out the doctrinal and political implications of the Pâris cures posed an even more ominous threat to the Church. At stake was not merely the acceptance of a papal bull, but also a number of other vexing questions concerning the fundamental nature and verifiability of miracles and the relationship between such prodigies and doctrinal orthodoxy. If the cures performed at Saint-Médard were indeed authentic miracles— and they were definitely well attested—then to deny their validity would have been tantamount to discrediting all miracles, the very basis upon which the Church had established the truth of Christian revelation and had frequently validated its pronouncements on doctrine and upheld its own legitimate claims to exclusive institutional authority.

By the summer of 1731, the civil and ecclesiastical establishment had begun to look upon the cult to François de Pâris as representing too great a public nuisance and too vexing a religious scandal to permit its adherents to continue their observances undisturbed. Various official measures were taken in an effort to impede or halt the activities at Saint-Médard, efforts which culminated in the government's promulgation of an edict on January 27, 1732, ordering the parish cemetery closed. Instead of stifling the cult, however, the royal ordinance left the convulsionaries (as the followers of M. Pâris had come to be called) more convinced than ever of the corruption and patent injustice pervading both Church and State and more determined than ever to pursue their spiritual services uninterrupted. Though forced to transfer their activities from the deacon's hallowed tomb, they simply went indoors and continued their unorthodox practices. At the same time, they began to believe with an absolutely unshakable conviction that they had received a divine mission of social and spiritual regeneration. It was the attempt to fulfill this mission that gave direction to their activities after January 1732, as Paris was swept by a wave of revivalism and millennialism.

A year later the crown formally proscribed even private manifestations of the convulsionary devotions. Yet even with a virtual monopoly of force at its disposal, the government never managed to bring the sect completely to its knees. Through political vicissitudes and despite the torments of official persecution and repression, the followers of M. Pâris clung tenaciously to their beliefs and practices. But the convulsionaries had no opportunity to realize all of their aspirations for spiritual renewal at this time. Driven by persecution and intimidation to ever more unconventional behavior, disgraced and discredited by the appearance in their very midst of two more activist and reputedly fanatical sects of convulsionaries, the followers of M. Pâris fell out of favor with many of their erstwhile *anticonstitutionnnaire* supporters, lay and clerical alike. The magistrates in the Parlement of Paris and a majority of the appellant clergy and theologians ultimately joined with the *constitutionnaire* bishops and the royal government to repudiate and to denounce the entire convulsionary movement. Hence, although the sect retained a certain degree of spiritual vitality throughout the century and persisted as an expression of popular disaffection with the established religious authorities, it was no longer a *cause célèbre* in contemporary ecclesiastical controversy.

Outside of an immediate circle of adherents and *anticonstitutionnaire* sympathizers, the Pâris cult and the convulsionaries of Saint-Médard have rarely received very favorable or thoughtful treatment, either from contemporaries or from later students of the subject. In the eighteenth century, "convulsionary" was a term of opprobrium almost synonymous with religious fanaticism. Both Catholics and "unbelievers" regarded the disciples of François de Pâris with utter disdain. This contemporary antipathy for the convulsionaries has survived in virtually all of the subsequent historical writing on the affair—what little there has been. With very few exceptions, historians have uncritically accepted and perpetuated eighteenth-century characterizations of the sect, viewing the entire Saint-Médard episode as proof of the alleged degeneration and decadence of Jansenism and hence a far cry from the spiritual beauty and grandeur of Port-Royal and its great figures.[1] These unsympathetic, indeed hostile, authors have also tended

[1] It was Sainte-Beuve who perhaps more than anyone else set the hostile tone which has prevailed in virtually all of the writings of the past century. At one point in his magistral *Port-Royal*, Sainte-Beuve bitterly explained that eighteenth-century Jansenism was for him "amaigri, séché, et comme un bras de fleuves détourné dans les sables et perdu dans les pierres." It was a subject where, "pour tout l'or du monde et toutes les promesses du ciel, on ne me ferait pas faire un pas." As he further observed elsewhere, "depuis que mon sujet est tombé en épilepsie (par les convulsions) je ne puis plus qu'en avoir dégoût, et on ne me fera pas passer pour un empire par ce cimetière misérable de St.-Médard" (cited and discussed in Raphaël Molho, *L'ordre et les ténèbres, ou, La naissance d'un mythe du 17ᵉ siècle, chez Sainte-Beuve* [Paris, 1972], p. 303). These animadversions have been echoed again and again by nearly every one of the leading historians of Jansenism, several of whom quote Sainte-Beuve's strictures approvingly: Augustin Gazier, *Histoire générale du mouvement janséniste depuis ses origines jusqu'à nos jours*, 2 vols. (Paris, 1922), I, 278, 296 (such phenomena "nous ont fait pénétrer dans un monde mystérieux où l'on n'ose pas s'aventurer de peur d'y perdre la raison"); Georges Hardy, *Le cardinal de Fleury et le mouvement janséniste* (Paris, 1925), p. 254; Edmond Préclin, *Les jansénistes du 18ᵉ siècle et la constitution civile du clergé* (Paris, 1929), p. iii ("Avec Sainte-Beuve nos contemporains, sauf les spécialistes de l'histoire médicale ou les esprits curieux des manifestations d'un mysticisme singulier, éprouvent quelque éloignement pour les 'absurdités et ignobles scènes des convulsions'"); and Joseph Dedieu, "L'agonie du jansénisme," *Revue d'histoire de l'Eglise de France*, 14 (1928), pp. 161-214, *passim*. Even so careful and objective a scholar as René Taveneaux has treated the convulsionaries rather contemptuously, as a peculiar form of religious extremism and a vulgarized version of Jansenism: *Le Jansénisme en Lorraine, 1640-1789* (Paris, 1960), pp. 728-29 ("ce jansénisme dégradé, superstitieux, populaire, tapageur, d'allure conspiratrice, qui fut le lot de beaucoup de régions françaises, notamment de la capitale. . . ." This Jansenism lacked "la dignité et la réserve de Port-Royal à ses débuts" and was overwhelmed by "les dégradations du merveilleux convulsionnaire"). To Ronald A. Knox, whose general study of religious enthusiasm is marked by a certain elitism, "It was . . . a singular retribution of Providence that bred a posterity of convulsionaries from the austere stock of Port-Royal" (*Enthusiasm: A Chapter in the History of Religion, with Special Reference to the*

to dismiss the convulsionaries as merely an odd sect of bizarre and fanatical Jansenists, whose "antics" and "crude spirituality" were thought to be of little or no consequence. Neglecting to give the convulsionary movement much careful or considered attention and content by and large to exploit the more sensational aspects of the clandestine convulsionary *séances*, most of them have failed to appreciate the nature and contemporary significance of this religious phenomenon or to explain the assumptions and fears of those civil and sacerdotal authorities concerned with its eradication. What is more, failing to comprehend the relationship of the Saint-Médard episode to the problems of the ecclesiastical history of the *ancien régime*, they have overlooked the opportunity of utilizing this episode to explore the character, complexities, and crucial importance of religious controversy in France during the last century before the Revolution.

A study of the convulsionaries of Saint-Médard is indeed instructive, for it reveals quite dramatically the close, almost inextricable connection between religion and politics in the *ancien régime* and discloses some of the major institutional conflicts and tensions which plagued the French monarchy and the Gallican Church during this period. Despite the growth of Bourbon absolutism, or perhaps because of it, the respective jurisdictions of the ecclesiastical and secular authorities were never very clearly delineated and were often hopelessly confused. In a world plagued with overlapping powers and only vaguely delimited jurisdictions, the result of centuries-old institutional accretions, nowhere was the confusion greater or more provocative of serious problems than in the religious sphere. Here various individuals and bodies—pope and king, royal councils and parlements, secular courts and episcopate, upper clergy and lower clergy, *curés* and churchwardens—vied with each other over competing legal claims and administrative prerogatives. So extensive was the interpenetration of Church and State that there were few important religious issues in which the secular authorities did not take an active interest. Saint-Médard involved precisely such a problem. At stake at the tomb of François de Pâris were not only issues of theology and Church governance, but also questions bearing directly upon the relationships between and within Church and State and upon the ability of the royal govern-

---

17th and 18th Centuries [Oxford, 1951], p. 374). Finally, and most recently, John McManners has dismissed the history of the convulsionary movement as "a subject that can hardly be looked at without either laughter or revulsion . . ." ("Jansenism and Politics in the 18th Century," in *Church, Society, and Politics*, ed. Derek Baker [Oxford, 1975], p. 263). But cf. Dominique Julia, "Problèmes d'historiographie religieuse," *18e siècle*, 5 (1973), esp. pp. 86-87.

ment to control the subjects of the king. At stake, too, was the question of the Church's capacity to fulfill its traditional function as an instrument of public discipline and social restraint. What is clear from the history of the Pâris cult is that, despite the existence of an extensive civil and ecclesiastical apparatus to provide intrusive surveillance, root out dissent, and reestablish conformity, the authorities were not always successful in regulating or controlling the religious beliefs and practices of the French people. What is also clear from the history of ecclesiastical politics in the 1720s and 1730s is that behind the façade of order, unity, and stability imposed from above, there were deep, fundamental divisions which threatened to rend the very fabric of the *ancien régime*.

Although I have devoted a substantial proportion of this book to the struggles over Jansenism and to the principal issues in dispute in the *Unigenitus* controversy, it has not been my intention to make the Jansenist problem the exclusive focus of this study. By the same token, although I have paid a great deal of attention to the experiences of popular piety associated with the name of François de Pâris, this book is not meant to be a study of eighteenth-century French popular religion. My purpose, rather, has been to weave together, and to make sense of, themes which were played out during this period at the intersection of these two realms. It is the interplay and convergence of events in what were normally two rather discrete and independent worlds—the world of ecclesiastical politics, with its almost perpetual confrontations among the political elite, its clashing and contradicting decrees, edicts, and ordinances, and the world of miracles and convulsions, a world of sometimes unorthodox, frequently unconventional religious activities—which is thus the central focus of this book. Setting out a narrative in an analytical framework, I have sought to examine the procedures and considerations (including problems of tactics and timing) involved in the formulation and execution of official policy on Jansenism and to analyze the ways in which that policy affected and was in turn affected by developments at Saint-Médard. This interweaving of large political issues and of very involved, technical maneuverings within the ecclesiastical establishment with the emergence of the Pâris cult, the accounts of miracles at Saint-Médard, and the subsequent development of the convulsionary movement has determined the organizational framework as well as the chronological limits of what follows.

May 1, 1977
Ithaca, N.Y.

Acknowledgments

No scholar can ever expect to discharge by a mere acknowledgment the enormous debts he incurs in undertaking a major research project. And yet this traditional form does at least allow an author to offer public expressions of appreciation to those persons (and institutions) whose varied contributions facilitated the completion of his book.

I am extremely grateful to the Woodrow Wilson Fellowship Foundation, the Newberry Library, the Folger Shakespeare Library, the American Philosophical Society, and the Universities of Chicago and Rochester for indispensable financial support which helped defray most of the research and travel expenses associated with the writing of this book. In addition, I am heavily indebted to the University of Rochester for generously granting me a year's leave of absence at a critical stage in the manuscript's preparation.

Two extraordinarily sympathetic and helpful chairmen, Eugene Genovese and Richard Kaeuper, assisted me with numerous kindnesses during the period I was working on this book and frequently found time in their own busy schedules to discuss various aspects of the manuscript with me. Many other friends and colleagues read all or parts of the manuscript in its diverse forms and made useful comments and suggestions. For their helpful criticism I should like to thank Theodore Brown, Stanley Engerman, Elizabeth Fox-Genovese, Richard Golden, Lionel Gossman, Emile Karafiol, Donald Kelley, Peter Linebaugh, William McGrath, Neil McMullin, Harvey Mitchell, Orest Ranum, John Salmon, Dale Van Kley, William H. Williams, and Perez Zagorin. I also received valuable aid from a number of French scholars, most notably François Furet and Julien Brancolini, who several years ago shared with me their own work on the miracles and convulsions of Saint-Médard. I am especially grateful to Joseph Klaits, who not only read two different versions of the manuscript with his usual painstaking care and offered many insightful observations, but also served as a close scholarly comrade throughout this project's long gestation.

My intellectual and personal debt to Keith Baker and John B. Wolf is immeasurable. In different ways they both helped initiate and sustain my early interest in the *ancien régime*; while providing a great deal of valuable advice and criticism along the way, they have also offered their warm support and encouragement. Thanks are also due Professor Baker for having suggested the subject of this study to me in the first place.

This book would not have been possible without the generous assistance of a host of resourceful archivists and librarians, in France, the Netherlands, and the United States. For special favors well beyond the call of official duty, I should like particularly to thank Mlle. Suzanne Solente, archivist at the Bibliothèque Nationale, and M. Paul Gazier, *bibliothécaire* and custodian of the superb collection at the Bibliothèque de la Société des Amis de Port-Royal. Gerri Martone, Sally Roche, and Ann Schertz of the University of Rochester's Interlibrary Loan Department cheerfully and efficiently bore with interminable requests for materials. Expressions of gratitude are likewise in order to Lorraine Frances Clark and Claire Sundeen for their help in the preparation of the typescript.

I owe a special word of appreciation to Lewis Bateman, former editor at Princeton University Press, whose friendly prodding and coaxing and invaluable editorial assistance have meant a great deal to me. In Eve Hanle I also had the benefit of an extremely diligent and conscientious copy editor. Gretchen Oberfranc was very helpful and reassuring as she guided the book (and its author) through the final stages of production.

My greatest debts of gratitude are personal, familial ones. Jeanette, whose patience and forbearance I have strained for too many years, has nevertheless continued to provide much-needed counsel and inspiration throughout the duration of this project. Josh and Deborah, who have likewise been forced to compete with this book for my attention and to endure its virtually constant intrusion into their lives, have also borne the frequent inconveniences almost without complaint. Their evident sense of release and relief has made the feelings associated with the manuscript's completion all the more pleasurable.

If I cannot repay any of these people for their much-appreciated support, cooperation, and understanding, I hope at least that the final version of this book is worthy of their assorted contributions.

Abbreviations

AAE	Archives du Ministère des Affaires Etrangères, Paris
AFA	Ancien Fonds d'Amersfoort, Rijksarchief, Utrecht
AN	Archives Nationales, Paris
BA	Bibliothèque de l'Arsenal, Paris
BHVP	Bibliothèque Historique de la Ville de Paris
BM	Bibliothèque Mazarine, Paris
BN	Bibliothèque Nationale, Paris
BPR	Bibliothèque de la Société des Amis de Port-Royal, Paris
C.P.	Correspondance Politique
DTC	*Dictionnaire de théologie catholique*
J.F.	Collection Joly de Fleury
L.P.	Collection Le Paige
M&D	Mémoires et Documents
MSS Fr.	Manuscrits Français
NAFr.	Nouvelles Acquisitions Françaises
NNEE	*Nouvelles ecclésiastiques*
P.R.	Port-Royal

*Miracles, Convulsions, and Ecclesiastical Politics
in Early Eighteenth-Century Paris*

CHAPTER I

Jansenism and the Problems of Ecclesiastical Politics in the Gallican Church, 1713-1729

INTRODUCTION

O F all the many religious struggles which preoccupied the authorities under the *ancien régime*, the Jansenist controversy was perhaps the most serious and vexing, for it was one which not only created a profound spiritual division within French Catholicism, but gradually came to engage all the traditional forces of early-modern ecclesiastical politics. Jansenism originated as but one manifestation of the intense, sometimes feverish religious revival which took place in France in the first half of the seventeenth century.[1] Save for Port-Royal, which served principally as a place of retreat, housing no more than a few dozen individuals at any one time, the Jansenist movement had no institutional or corporate existence and lacked any formal juridical or legal standing. Those who could be considered its adherents were united in free, voluntary association, essentially independent of any authority, royal, papal, or episcopal. Although self-styled "amis de la Vérité," defenders of the "fundamental and essential truths of the faith," they never really formed a cohesive or tightly organized sect or religious order and never subscribed to a uniform, undifferen-

---

[1] Studies of Jansenism, especially of its seventeenth-century manifestations, have been proliferating in recent years. The standard works on this subject, on which much of the following is based, include those by Augustin Gazier, Jean Orcibal, Louis Cognet, René Taveneaux, and Lucien Ceyssens, listed in the bibliography. Several outstanding doctoral dissertations on various aspects of the Jansenist question have also appeared in recent years: Kevin J. Hargreaves, "Cornelius Jansenius and the Origins of Jansenism" (Brandeis University, 1974); F. Ellen Weaver, "The Inner History of a Reform That Failed: The Monastery of Port-Royal (1674-1684)" (Princeton University, 1973); William R. Newton, "Port-Royal and Jansenism: Social Experience, Group Formation, and Religious Attitudes in 17th-Century France," 3 vols. (University of Michigan, 1974); and Richard M. Golden, "Godly Rebellion: Parisian *Curés* and the Religious Fronde, 1652-1662" (The Johns Hopkins University, 1974). Finally, Professor Alexander Sedgwick has recently published a major study, *Jansenism in 17th-Century France: Voices from the Wilderness* (Charlottesville, 1977).

tiated, or coherent set of beliefs.[2] In no sense constituting a single, monolithic party, at most they can be said to have shared an attitude of mind. In this sense Jansenism, whatever its various formulations,[3] was a rigidly austere and gloomily predestinarian doctrine, with an attendant concern for spiritual reform, a devotion to universal Christian charity, and a puritanical ideal of uncompromising virtue and saintliness for the perfection of the religious life. No matter how many changes in emphasis or direction the movement experienced during the seventeenth and eighteenth centuries, "Jansenism" remained throughout the *ancien régime* a severe and psychologically demanding form of Christianity and maintained its strict penitential discipline, its thoroughgoing gravity, its moral rigorism, and its pessimistic emphasis on the sinfulness and corruption of man and society. At the same time, Jansenism had very early on become a problem for both Church and State.

Certain of the leading Jansenists—men of a highly combative spirit, ardent, indefatigable controversialists, and fierce debaters—became embroiled in religious disputes almost from the first, managing in the process to arouse a great deal of hostility in influential circles. To a large degree, of course, the Jansenist movement represented a reaction to the aims, the outlook, and the theology of the Society of Jesus, their inveterate enemies. They regarded as scandalous the Society's Molinist position on the nature of grace and free will, its formal and mechanical practices of devotion and frequent communion, and its alleged laxity and casuistry in the confessional; they repeatedly accused the Jesuits of subverting all sound moral and religious principles. Indeed, to the extent that the Jansenists ever did constitute a "party," they did so principally on the basis of their bitter enmity toward the Jesuits, a feeling that was mutually shared. Born in opposition and nurtured in

[2] As Pierre Bayle once remarked, "Le jansénisme est une espèce d'hérésie que personne ne peut définir, mais qu'on impute à qui l'on veut, et dont on passe toujours pour convaincu dès qu'on a le malheur d'en être accusé . . ." (quoted by Jean Orcibal, *Louis XIV contre Innocent XI: Les appels au futur concile de 1688 et l'opinion française* [Paris, 1948], p. 62, n. 289). Cf. the observation of the maréchal d'Harcourt: "Un janséniste n'est souvent autre chose qu'un homme qu'on veut perdre à la cour" (cited by Georges Frêche, *Un chancelier gallican: D'Aguesseau* [Paris, 1969], p. 40).

[3] This period saw the development of several "Jansenisms," all related to one another but nevertheless distinguishable on one or more significant points. For a discussion of the problems of definition and an analysis of the seventeenth-century variants, see Orcibal, *Louis XIV contre Innocent XI*, p. 81, n. 366; *idem*, "Qu'est-ce que le jansénisme?" *Cahiers de l'Association internationale des études françaises*, 3-5 (1953), pp. 39-53; and Lucien Ceyssens, "Le jansénisme: Considérations historiques préliminaires à sa notion," *Analecta gregoriana*, 71 (1952), pp. 3-32.

controversy, the Jansenists, as self-proclaimed champions of evangelical piety and of a pure, uncorrupted form of Christianity, engaged in a long and frequently intemperate battle against the supposed innovations and deviations of the Jesuits—a battle which lasted until the Society's suppression in 1764.

Though perhaps their most implacable opponents, the Jesuits were certainly not the only ones among whom the Jansenists managed to arouse bitter hostility. In France and Rome the ecclesiastical authorities, who automatically feared any separatist movement within the Church, any suggestion of novelties, either dogmatic or spiritual, as a potential threat to the religious stability of France and to the unity of the Catholic faith, looked with great disfavor upon this Jansenist display of sect-like combativeness. Nor was it surprising that certain Jansenist principles—a respect for the sanctity of the autonomous conscience, an emphasis on the importance of the individual's interior disposition, a belief in the principles of efficacious grace and gratuitous predestination, and a resultant tendency to reduce the significance of the Church as the earthly mediator between God and man—should have aroused the enmity of influential members of the clerical establishment. But it was the Fronde which especially provoked the suspicion and hostility of the royal government toward Jansenism.

Perpetually haunted by memories of that abortive midcentury revolt, Louis XIV learned from Cardinal Mazarin to distrust Port-Royal and its various "friends" as a potentially subversive element, a center of general disaffection and unrest, a source of conspiracy and intrigue.[4] Despite their oft-repeated professions of loyalty to the crown, Louis came to suspect that the Jansenists were unfriendly to absolute monarchy and represented a stronghold of ideological opposition to the bureaucratic state which he and his ministers were working to create. Theologically benighted as well as politically prejudiced, the king never understood the thorny doctrinal problems of salvation and grace at issue with the Jansenists—nor did he care to. Rather, Louis' passionate and intrusive surveillance of religious affairs derived from a conception of his royal stewardship over Church and State and his concern for order and orthodoxy.[5] Rebellion against official doctrine he interpreted as rebellion against his divinely constituted temporal authority. Thus he also resented the Jansenists for arousing a divisive controversy in the Church, a controversy that he believed threatened

[4] Cf. Golden, esp. Ch. 4, and Paule Jansen, *Le Cardinal Mazarin et le mouvement janséniste français, 1653-1659* (Paris, 1967).

[5] See Paul Sonnino, *Louis XIV's View of the Papacy (1661-1667)* (Berkeley-Los Angeles, 1966).

the unity of his kingdom. By adopting a distinctive style of life and attitude toward the world and by advocating a religious position which most orthodox Catholics deemed suspect, the Jansenists were guilty of nonconformity, an intolerable incongruity in an absolute state and the very crime which the Sun King most hated. Their emphasis on the inviolable rights of individual conscience; their public rejection of the royal command to sign unequivocally the Formulary against the famous Five Propositions of Jansenius;[6] and their defiant actions in appealing to Pope Innocent XI in the *régale* affair—such attitudes and behavior made Louis even more resentful of Jansenist willfulness and "republican" independence.

Numerous efforts were thus made during the Sun King's reign to deal with this hated Jansenist "sect." Indeed, except for the ambiguous and tenuous Peace of the Church, that provisional settlement of 1669 which established a temporary and precarious truce in the controversy, these Jansenist dissenters were subjected throughout this period to fierce, if sporadic, persecution from both Church and State. But repeated condemnations issued in Rome, supported by the repressive measures of civil and ecclesiastical authorities in France, failed to stifle the Jansenists or extirpate their movement. In the meantime, the nature of Jansenism had begun to change markedly, and its concerns as well as its appeal began to broaden. Increasingly, Port-Royal became little more than the symbolic center of Jansenism, an institutional exemplar of the Jansenists' ideal of heroic unworldliness, while the developments occurring beyond its walls—both religious and political—assumed greater importance than ever.

For many of the Jansenists outside Port-Royal, for bishops and priests as well as for theologians and cloistered regulars, the period from the 1660s onward was one of intense and constructive activity, with a growing emphasis on devotional, pedagogical, and pastoral concerns.[7] To be sure, adherents of this so-called "second Jansenism" con-

---

[6] In 1660 the Assembly of the Clergy, which had previously confirmed the papal denunciations of five propositions extracted from Jansenius' *Augustinus*, imposed on all clergy, regular and secular, adherence to a Formulary condemning "Jansenism." On the widespread refusal to sign, see Orcibal, *Port-Royal entre le miracle et l'obéissance. Flavie Passart et Angélique de St.-Jean Arnauld d'Andilly* (Paris, 1957), and Gérard Namer, *L'abbé le Roy et ses amis: Essai sur le jansénisme extrémiste intramondain* (Paris, 1964).

[7] See Louis Pérouas, "La pastorale liturgique au 17ᵉ siècle," *Mélanges de science religieuse*, 23 (1966), pp. 30-44; Paul Broutin, *La réforme pastorale en France au 17ᵉ siècle: Recherches sur la tradition pastorale après le concile de Trente*, 2 vols. (Paris, 1956), *passim*; and Edmond Préclin and Eugène Jarry, *Les luttes politiques et doctrinales aux 17ᵉ et 18ᵉ siècles*, Vol. XIX of *Histoire de l'Eglise depuis les*

tinued by and large to conform to the fundamental moral and theological rigorism traditionally associated with Port-Royal. They also continued to turn out their share of apologetic and polemical tracts in defense of the "true faith." But these "new Jansenists" were no longer so exclusively preoccupied with weighty doctrinal matters or with plaintive jeremiads about the tragedy of the human condition and the corruption of the social order as the abbé de Saint-Cyran and certain of his immediate associates and successors had been and still were.[8] Less abstract and academic in their orientation, less detached and resigned in their outlook on the temporal order, many of them turned away from subtle theologizing and from an attitude of passive, ascetic withdrawal to become involved in much more practical tasks within the Church and the world at large.

The principal objective of much of the Jansenists' prolific activity in this period was to enable the laity to understand and appreciate more fully, more personally, the meaning of the faith.[9] Like Bérulle, François de Sales, Vincent de Paul, and other leading seventeenth-century French religious figures, these Jansenists were concerned to overcome what some regarded as the excessively dry, mechanical, and formal character of post-Tridentine devotions. In their effort to combat the supposedly superficial, uncomprehending piety of the faithful, they embarked in particular on a host of important projects designed to provide the uninstructed with vernacular translations of and pious commentaries on scriptural and liturgical texts.[10] One of the first—

---

origines jusqu'à nos jours, ed. J.-B. Duroselle and Eugène Jarry, 2 vols. (Paris, 1955-56), I, 206-207.

[8] Lucien Goldmann, *Le dieu caché. Etude sur la vision tragique dans les Pensées de Pascal et dans le théâtre de Racine* (Paris, 1955). Cf. Namer.

[9] The liturgical reforms of this period were designed to give a more active role to the faithful in the Mass: "Ne faisant qu'un même Corps avec J-C, ils doivent s'unir avec luy dans l'Offrande qu'il fait à Dieu de luy-même pour tout le Corps de son Eglise" (*Catéchisme ou doctrine chrétienne imprimé par ordre de Messeigneurs les évêques d'Angers, de La Rochelle et de Luçon, pour l'usage de leurs diocèses* [Paris, 1676], p. 348). The rationale for Jansenist liturgical innovations was developed more fully and explicitly in the eighteenth century. See, for example, Jean-Baptiste-Raymond de Pavie de Fourquevaux, *Catéchisme historique et dogmatique sur les contestations qui divisent maintenant l'Eglise*, 2 vols. (The Hague, 1729-30), II, 105-10. Cf. Bernard Plongeron, "Une image de l'Eglise d'après les *Nouvelles ecclésiastiques* (1728-1790)," *Revue d'histoire de l'Eglise de France*, 53 (1967), pp. 241-68; and Roger Mercier, *La réhabilitation de la nature humaine (1700-1750)* (Villemonble, 1960), pp. 142-45.

[10] See J. F. Crehan, "The Bible in the Roman Catholic Church from Trent to the Present Day," in *The Cambridge History of the Bible*, 3 vols. (Cambridge, Eng., 1963-70), III, 222-23. A survey of their efforts to provide the faithful with

and by far the most celebrated—of such devotional handbooks, a translation accompanied by annotations and commentary, was written by the Oratorian Father Pasquier Quesnel, whose book, entitled *Les Paroles de la Parole incarnée, Jésus-Christ, Notre Seigneur, tirées du Nouveau Testament* (1668), was eventually to attract an unanticipated renown and provoke a storm of controversy. The work, very different from the subtle and imposing theological tomes of Jansenius or Saint-Cyran, in that it was written in French and intended for laymen, was an immediate public success. Encouraged by the reception, Quesnel gradually expanded the book in a series of editions and by 1692 had also changed the title to *Le Nouveau Testament en français, avec des réflexions morales sur chaque verset, pour en rendre la lecture plus utile et la méditation plus aisée*. It was under a shortened version of the title, the *Réflexions morales*, that Quesnel's work gained its greatest notoriety.

It is noteworthy that the initial opposition within the Church to Quesnel's translations and commentaries was not based on theological grounds, for the Oratorian father had studiously avoided awakening the doctrinal controversies associated with the earlier Jansenists. In part, the religious authorities were disturbed by Quesnel's violation of their prohibition, only recently reiterated, against unauthorized translations, compilations, or commentaries.[11] Some Church officials had also argued that it was God's will that the reading of Scripture be reserved exclusively to priests and theologians. But the *Réflexions morales* represented an even more disquieting development in the area of ecclesiastical governance, a development very closely associated with certain other new tendencies of this "second Jansenism."

While attempting to present the spirit and message of Jansenism in terms more easily accessible to the laity and while advocating increased lay participation with the clergy in public worship, Quesnel and some

---

bons livres—missals, breviaries, and other manuals of popular devotion—in the vernacular is provided in Fourquevaux, II, 107-10; an extended justification of these activities is furnished in Antoine Arnauld, *De la lecture de l'Ecriture Sainte* (Antwerp, 1680), and in his *Défense des versions de l'Ecriture Sainte, des Offices de l'Eglise et des ouvrages des Pères et en particulier de la nouvelle traduction du Bréviaire* (Cologne, 1688). Cf. discussion in Henri-Jean Martin, *Livre, pouvoirs et société à Paris au 17ᵉ siècle (1598-1701)*, 2 vols. (Geneva, 1969), II, 775-97; and Julien Brancolini and Marie-Thérèse Bouyssy, "La vie provinciale du livre à la fin de l'ancien régime," in *Livre et société dans la France du 18ᵉ siècle* (Paris, 1970), II, 3-37.

11 See Antoine Adam, *Du mysticisme à la révolte* (Paris, 1968), pp. 285-87; and Pierre Blet, *Le clergé de France et la monarchie: Etude sur les Assemblées Générales du Clergé de 1615 à 1666*, 2 vols. (Rome, 1959), II, 292-315.

of his colleagues had also begun to advance the claims of the "second order" of the clergy for a greater role in the Church polity.[12] The adoption of antihierarchical ideas widely attributed to the celebrated theologian Edmond Richer[13]—himself inspired by the Gallican Gerson —would have been all but unthinkable to the "first Jansenists," several of whom had explicitly condemned "Richerism" earlier in the century.[14] But this was in many ways a new generation of Jansenists, one which depended increasingly for its numerical strength as well as its spiritual force upon the adherence of members of the lower clergy. Indeed, the required signature of the Formulary had had the unintended effect of further diffusing the Jansenist controversy into every corner of the realm and of allowing, in fact, forcing, even the most obscure parish priest to voice his opinion on a matter about which he was not ordinarily consulted or especially concerned.[15] Though not yet the prominent voice that they were to become in the eighteenth-century struggles over "Jansenism," the lower clergy had already begun making a significant contribution to the movement. Beginning with the so-called religious Fronde of the 1650s and the publication of Pascal's highly successful *Lettres provinciales*, a growing number of parish clergy was attracted—out of a mixture of spiritual, ecclesiastical, theological, and political motives—to the Jansenist camp.[16] Many of them refused to sign the Formulary, insisting that a higher duty to individual conscience took precedence over the requirements of silent submission and humble obedience. From the 1660s onward, their uncompromising protests, broadened into a general defense of ecclesiastical "liberties," came to have a significant influence in shaping and transforming the Jansenist movement's dominant ideology.[17]

Reflecting this changing character of Jansenist support and ideology, Quesnel, in the course of revising his *Réflexions morales*, devoted increasing attention to questions concerning Church governance and the

[12] See, for example, Jacques Boileau, *De antiquo juro presbyterorum in regimine ecclesiastico* (Taurini, 1676). For a discussion of these "Richerist" developments, see the opening chapters of Edmond Préclin, *Les jansénistes*. For the earlier period, see also Pierre-Edouard Puyol, *Edmond Richer: Etude historique et critique sur la rénovation du gallicanisme au commencement du 17ᵉ siècle*, 2 vols. (Paris, 1876).

[13] On Richer, see Préclin, "Edmond Richer (1559-1631): Sa vie, son oeuvre, le richérisme," *Revue d'histoire moderne*, 5 (1930), pp. 241-69, 321-36.

[14] See, for example, Orcibal, "Jansénius et Rome" (paper presented at the Academica Belgica de Rome, Louvain, November 1973).

[15] Robert Mandrou, "La fille aînée de l'Eglise," in *La France au temps de Louis XIV* (Paris, 1966), pp. 192-93.

[16] See Golden, Ch. 4.   [17] See Namer, esp. pp. 162-66.

nature of the priesthood. In succeeding editions of the work he championed the cause of the lower clergy, emphasizing the idea that ecclesiastical authority resided in the entire body of the Church and invoking the legendary traditions of the primitive Church to uphold his position in defense of an independent parochial ministry with claims to consultation in diocesan affairs. The lower clergy no doubt derived considerable aid and comfort from the Quesnelist exaltation of their dignity and status in the Church hierarchy and their central role in both ecclesiastical governance and the cure of souls. But these ideas, widely denounced as "presbyterian," were fraught with dangerous implications for the discipline and even the organization of the Gallican Church. Though the precise manner of their diffusion and their degree of influence remain unclear, it is certain that the writings of Quesnel, like those of several of his followers, were becoming ever more disturbing to the ecclesiastical authorities by the end of the seventeenth century.[18]

Toward the Bull "Unigenitus"

As the work of Quesnel and the bold writings and activities of other like-minded colleagues helped place Jansenism further beyond the pale, the attitude of both Church and State turned from mistrust to open hostility. Between 1695 and 1703 a series of political and theological controversies, exacerbated by very bitter antagonisms and rivalries—personal as well as corporate—strained and complicated matters immeasurably. In the spirit of faction and polemic which had come to characterize much of French religious life, various groups and individuals with vested interests to protect and axes to grind became involved in the renewed struggles over Jansenism.[19]

But Louis XIV, for all his antipathy toward the Jansenists, remained somewhat reluctant to engage in the religious confrontations which over the years had seen his government's authority compromised. It took the unexpected discovery of Quesnel's private papers to induce the crown to act. Though Quesnel had been in self-imposed exile since his refusal to sign the Formulary in 1684, he had not lost his considerable reputation and influence among the Jansenists in France, as well as those in the Low Countries and in Rome, with whom he had for a number of years been maintaining an extensive correspondence.[20] The

[18] Préclin, *Les jansénistes*, pp. 27-28, *et passim*. Cf. J.A.G. Tans, "Les idées politiques des jansénistes," *Neophilologus*, 40 (1956), pp. 1-18.

[19] Adam, pp. 296-308; H. G. Judge, "Church and State under Louis XIV," *History*, 45 (1960), pp. 229-33.

[20] See Albert Le Roy, *Le Gallicanisme au 18ᵉ siècle: La France et Rome de*

religious authorities had for some time regarded the Oratorian father as the head of the supposed "Jansenist party," Quesnel's protestations to the contrary notwithstanding. The seizure of his private correspondence when he was arrested in Brussels in 1703 suggested that official suspicions had been correct. Quesnel's papers revealed an intricate and far-reaching secret network of "Jansenists," extending even to high places in the papal court. They also offered apparent substantiation of Jesuit charges that the Jansenists constituted an active, organized movement of subversives who posed an imminent threat to both Church and State. Alarmed at this turn of affairs and already obsessed with a fear of theological cabals, the king and his government decided that the hour had come to resolve the doctrinal questions that had been shuttled back and forth across the Alps since the days of Richelieu and to crush the Jansenist dissenters once and for all. Having previously patched up most of his differences with the papacy,[21] Louis was persuaded by his ultramontane advisers to appeal to Rome for help in restoring orthodoxy, confessional unity, and order to the Gallican Church.

The bull *Vineam Domini*, promulgated by Pope Clement XI in July 1705, renewed several earlier papal decrees against the Jansenists and condemned all exceptions and restrictions brought to the signature of the Formulary.[22] But *Vineam Domini* did not meet with the success in France which Louis XIV had promised Rome. Although the bull was accepted by the Assembly of the Clergy and the various theological faculties, published by virtually all the bishops, and even registered by the Parlement of Paris, its prescriptions were widely defied in the years that followed. Among those who persisted in their opposition were the handful of nuns still at Port-Royal-des-Champs. They

---

1700 à 1715 (Paris, 1892); J.A.G. Tans, *Pasquier Quesnel et les Pays-Bas* (Paris, 1960); Mme. Albert Le Roy (ed.), *Un janséniste en exil: Correspondance de Pasquier Quesnel sur les affaires politiques et religieuses de son temps*, 2 vols. (Paris, 1900); Lucien Ceyssens, "Les papiers de Quesnel saisis à Bruxelles et transportés à Paris en 1703 et 1704," *Revue d'histoire ecclésiastique*, 44 (1949), pp. 508-51; and Albert C. de Veer, "Le 'Grand recueil' dans les papiers de Quesnel saisis à Bruxelles et transportés à Paris en 1703 et 1704," *ibid.*, 46 (1951), pp. 187-91.

[21] On the crisis in Franco-papal relations, especially during the pontificate of Innocent XI, see Orcibal, *Louis XIV contre Innocent XI*. Most of the relevant documents are in Léon Mention (ed.), *Documents relatifs aux rapports du clergé avec la royauté*, 2 vols. (Paris, 1893-1903), I, 27-83. On the resolution of the conflict see Jean Meuvret, "Les aspects politiques de la liquidation du conflit gallican, 1691-92," *Revue d'histoire de l'Eglise de France*, 33 (1947), pp. 257-70.

[22] The Latin text of the bull is in Mention, I, 163-75.

soon paid a heavy penalty for their intransigence. In July 1709 Louis XIV, encouraged by his new confessor, the rabidly anti-Jansenist Father Le Tellier, obtained papel authorization for the suppression of what little remained of the convent. In late October the lieutenant-general of police, Voyer d'Argenson, accompanied by 200 archers, carried out orders for the dispersal of the miserable remnant of aged and infirm nuns. Less than two years later, a royal decree ordered the buildings and cemetery at Port-Royal-des-Champs razed, thereby shattering the communal symbol of the Jansenist movement. The news of the military operation conducted against the sisters at Port-Royal offended even Fénelon, archenemy of the Jansenists for over a decade, who also expressed the fear that, "A stroke of authority such as that which has just been executed . . . can only arouse public sympathy for these women and bitter resentment toward their persecutors."[23] Indeed, a campaign of pamphlets on behalf of the nuns' plight brought them widespread compassion, while the considerable public indignation greatly strengthened the Jansenist movement in its disaffection. This excessively brutal and destructive act on the part of the secular authorities thus proved to be a serious miscalculation.

In the meantime, there was mounting pressure in France and at Rome to obtain the censure and denunciation of Quesnel's *Réflexions morales*. Until this time, no outstanding condemnation had cited the work for doctrinal unorthodoxy. Indeed, the devotional manual had received the praise of more than a generation of ecclesiastics, including Cardinal Albani, some years before his election to the papacy as Clement XI in 1700. It was not through any fault or conscious effort on Quesnel's part that the *Réflexions morales* became embroiled in a stormy controversy. Notwithstanding the conclusions drawn from the seizure of his private papers in 1703, the exiled septuagenarian had generally held himself aloof from the recent polemical debates surrounding the "Jansenist question." His orthodoxy—and that of his book—was first seriously contested largely as a consequence of peripheral clerical intrigues and animosities which had been agitating the Gallican Church for more than a decade.[24]

In the course of a complicated and envenomed conflict, during which the *conseil d'état* prohibited further publication of the *Réflexions*

[23] Letter to the duc de Chevreuse, Nov. 24, 1709, cited in Lilian Rea, *The Enthusiasts of Port-Royal* (London, 1912), pp. 327-38. Cf. the poignant description in [Jérôme Besoigne], *Histoire de l'abbaye de Port-Royal*, 6 vols. (Cologne, 1752-53), III, 192ff.

[24] Jacques-François Thomas, *La querelle de l'Unigenitus* (Paris, 1949), pp. 45-53; Jean Carreyre, "Quesnel et le Quesnellisme," *DTC*, XIII², cols. 1,519-35; and Adam, pp. 317-18.

morales (November 11, 1711), the king became convinced of the need to turn again to Rome, this time for a definitive condemnation of Quesnel's work. However, Louis did not find Clement XI in a very acquiescent mood. Having suffered a humiliating experience with the widespread opposition to his previous bull, he was reluctant to issue another one and run the risk of further embarrassment by the Gallican Church. It thus took the tireless political maneuvering on the part of the Jesuits and their allies and considerable diplomatic pressure from Versailles (including promises of the crown's all-out support) to secure the appointment of a commission charged with studying the now-suspect *Réflexions morales* and preparing the papal decree. Though heavily biased against Quesnel, whom it refused to hear in person, the commission nevertheless required almost two years of intensive examination and careful deliberation to produce the report which the pope received in the summer of 1713. On September 8, 1713, Clement XI promulgated the famous bull, or constitution, *Unigenitus.*[25]

The Bull began with a general attack on the aged Quesnel, whom the pope described as a false prophet, master of artifice and deceit, and purveyor of dangerous doctrines. These virulent opening remarks were followed by the major part of the Bull: the formal condemnation of 101 propositions allegedly extracted—and frequently wrenched out of context—from the *Réflexions morales*, which the pope branded as the latest compendium of pernicious Jansenist error. The intention was that the careful selection and methodical arrangement of the Quesnel propositions would constitute a comprehensive summary of what was adjudged to be typical Jansenist positions. But this selection was not in all cases satisfactory. A significant number dealt with doctrinal matters, grace and free will, universality of redemption—questions which did, indeed, hark back to the old, so-called "first Jansenism," but which were no longer the exclusive, or even the principal, concern of the newest generation of Jansenists, particularly those associated with the Oratorian Quesnel. In addition, although some of these propositions, as well as others on moral discipline, could be regarded as more or less specifically "Jansenist," many of the most prominent ones seemed to be innocuous, indeed perfectly orthodox, doctrinal formulae currently accepted among even non-Jansenist theologians. In certain cases Quesnel had actually contradicted and implicitly rejected the views of

---

[25] The complete text of the Bull may be found in several places, including Mention, II, 2-40; J.-F. Thomas, pp. 24-34; and Augustin Gazier, *Histoire générale du mouvement janséniste depuis ses origines jusqu'à nos jours,* 2 vols. (Paris, 1922), II, 303-34. I have used the copy in Gazier, which contains the so-called *édition janséniste* of 1741.

Jansenius. Even more striking, several of the condemned propositions appear to have been straightforward French translations of passages taken directly from the New Testament or the Church Fathers. Most of the remaining propositions reflected recent developments of the so-called "second Jansenism." These included statements about the nature of the Church, defined as the entire body of the faithful; a series of proposals to make Holy Scripture freely available in the vernacular to the laity; and others to effect innovations in the liturgy —notions and reforming tendencies which were foreign, indeed antithetical, to the spirit of the established hierarchical Church and regarded as subversive of traditional ecclesiastical authority. Despite the wide variety of themes contained in this selection, all of the propositions were anathematized as being respectively

> false, captious, shocking, capable of offending pious ears, scandalous, pernicious, rash, harmful to the Church, insulting to the secular powers, seditious, impious, blasphemous, suspected of heresy, smacking of heresy, favorable to heretics, to heresies, and to schism, erroneous, approaching heresy, and often condemned; finally, as heretical and as renewing diverse heresies, principally those which are contained in the famous propositions of Jansenius, taken in the sense in which they have been condemned.[26]

But Clement's complete and uncompromising censure of "Quesnelism" was not to be the last word on the subject. Although Louis XIV had guaranteed the pope a favorable reception for his decree, the Bull soon evoked a fierce outcry from several quarters—not just the "Jansenists"—for much more was at stake in the denunciation of Quesnel's book than simply "Jansenist" theological and moral doctrines.

In taking their joint stand against the *Réflexions morales*, Rome and Versailles had not only rejected a particular doctrine of grace and a general program of spiritual and ecclesiastical reform, but had also taken a position on two of the most vexing and passionately contested issues of *ancien-régime* religious politics. The Bull raised—and seemed unequivocally to have answered—a number of very serious questions concerning the perennial problems of internal Church governance and the relationship between the ecclesiastical and secular authorities, both within France and between France and Rome. To many observers the sum of the denunciations contained in *Unigenitus* amounted to a triumph of pope over king, bishops over parish clergy, and the spiritual power over the temporal—a situation which raised great fears and deep

[26] *Ibid.*, II, 333.

resentments among various individuals and groups all over France. The Bull was supposed to be the final blow in the more than half-century battle which the papacy and the French government had waged intermittently against an elusive Jansenist enemy. Instead, it marked the beginning of one of the longest and most impassioned conflicts of the *ancien régime*—a conflict that was to occupy a place of central importance in religious politics during much of the eighteenth century.

Almost from the outset, political and personal partisanship embittered the dispute surrounding the Bull, making its enforcement a serious problem for the government of Louis XIV. Nor were the crown and papacy entirely without responsibility for this difficult state of affairs. Though Clement XI was careful to state that the Bull had been prepared at the king's request and drawn up in consultation with representatives of the French Church, he had nevertheless failed to take the customary action of forwarding to Versailles an advance draft of the document so that the king's advisers might examine it for offensive remarks before the crown proposed it for formal publication. The government might have actually forestalled—or at least tempered—a good deal of the subsequent opposition to *Unigenitus* had the royal ministers and the *gens du roi* at the Paris Parlement been consulted before its promulgation. At this point, however, Louis XIV could hardly repudiate the papal bull, whatever its shortcomings. Indeed, in his zeal for restoring the purity of the faith, the king seemed to believe that he had a more compelling obligation to fulfill his promise to the pope and stifle all opposition to the Bull than to adhere to the letter of the Gallican tradition.

From the time that *Unigenitus* reached him at Fontainebleau in late September 1713, Louis did his utmost to enforce it.[27] Seeking episcopal support for the papal decree, the king convoked an "extraordinary assembly" of the clergy, consisting of those nonresident bishops who happened to be in the vicinity of Paris at the time as well as a handful of others who could presumably be counted on to side with the crown.[28]

[27] For a firsthand discussion of the complicated maneuvering and discussions which took place in the fall of 1713, see the "Journal historique de Guillaume de Lamoignon, avocat-général au Parlement de Paris, 1713-1718," ed. Henri Courteault, *Annuaire-Bulletin de la Société de l'Histoire de France*, 47 (1910), pp. 246-49.

[28] *Ibid.*, pp. 249-51. With the crown possessing a virtual monopoly on the distribution of important benefices, and with the First Estate very much dependent on the royal government both for ecclesiastical preferment and for the protection of its prerogatives, the monarchy had usually been able to count on having a loyal and accommodating clientele, especially among the upper clergy. These men were reluctant to challenge government policy on important issues for fear

In all, forty-nine prelates were summoned. Yet despite the character of the gathering, the bishops could not be persuaded to accept the Bull by acclamation, as the king had hoped and expected. Indeed, from the outset the discussions revealed some deep divisions within the assembly. Aside from the handful of ardent ultramontanes who were willing to receive the Bull "purely and simply," without reservations or explanations, the overwhelming majority were not quite so anxious to relinquish their traditional right to review its contents. Though they strongly favored acceptance of the decree, they insisted that this acceptance be accompanied by a pastoral instruction containing explanations and qualifications of each of the condemned propositions, in order to temper some of the Bull's most offensive features and to clarify the numerous ambiguities. In late January 1714, forty bishops, including the original "pure acceptants," agreed to sign the model pastoral letter (known as the "Instruction des Quarante"), which was intended for circulation to all the French bishops who had not attended the assembly and designed to justify the Bull to them and encourage their adherence. Finally, the forty *constitutionnaire* prelates, anxious not to offend the pope by having presumed to impose their own explanations upon the Bull, joined together in signing a letter to Clement XI. While declaring their "respect and obedience" for papal authority and their admiration for "this excellent and solemn Constitution," they also announced their intention of ensuring its reception all over France.[29]

Under the leadership of Cardinal Noailles, archbishop of Paris, a minority of nine (later reduced to eight) bishops declined to sign any of these documents. They argued, in the first place, that the preparation of the Bull constituted a violation of the principles of episcopal Gallicanism. By turning to Rome for papal definitions of doctrinal orthodoxy on Quesnel's work, the king had in effect renounced the rights and privileges of the bishops to resolve such matters on their own and to regulate the affairs of the French Church without papal or royal interference.[30] Respectful of the pope's primacy of honor and

---

that their orthodoxy as well as their dedication to the king might be suspect at Versailles.

[29] Mention, II, 41-44. The bishops' own arguments in justification of their pastoral instruction suggest how ambiguous and disputable the Bull really was (see *ibid.*, p. 42).

[30] Only nine years earlier, the General Assembly of the Clergy, meeting in 1705, had hedged its reception of the bull *Vineam Domini* with its own rather strong reassertion of episcopal Gallicanism: "(1) Bishops have the right, by divine institution, to judge matters of doctrine. (2) Papal constitutions are binding on

jurisdiction, Noailles and the other prelates were nevertheless suspicious of papal pretensions to absolute and unlimited authority within the Church. They insisted that all bishops were equal successors of the Apostles and that their authority, of divine origin, was shared with the pope. Consequently, they refused to be treated as mere executors of the pontiff's decrees. The *anticonstitutionnaire* prelates also opposed *Unigenitus* on doctrinal grounds. Aside from the frequent equivocations and ambiguities with which they insisted the Bull was filled, the bishops charged that the pope had wrongfully denounced propositions of unexceptionable orthodoxy and, amid the deluge of epithets and ignominious adjectives, had condemned some of the most striking truths of the Church. They did not deny that the censured propositions were present in the *Réflexions morales*, for, unlike the earlier struggles over the famous Five Propositions of Jansenius, the issue now lay not with the *fait* but with the *droit*. The bishops disputed the pope's right to condemn these propositions and contended, moreover, that the pope had erred in the faith. They denied that the Bull could be regarded as a "rule of faith" or considered as an "irreformable judgment of the Church." As a result, they announced their refusal to accept Clement's decree "purely and simply" unless the pope himself offered explanations and qualifications. Challenging implied papal claims to infallibility on doctrinal issues and appealing to the pope "better informed," they insisted with Noailles that Clement "provide the means for clearly allaying [the fears of] alarmed consciences . . . and preserving the peace in the churches."[31] Finally, when these *anticonstitutionnaire* bishops resolved to address the pope directly, the king intervened. He refused to permit them to communicate with Rome, banished Noailles from court, and exiled the cardinal-archbishop's episcopal allies to their respective dioceses.

Neither banishments nor exiles could obscure the fact that Louis XIV had been unable to obtain unanimous support for the Bull—even from a specially chosen segment of the French episcopate. Nevertheless, the king was anxious to proceed to registration and called his representatives in the Parlement of Paris, the *procureur-général* Henri-François Daguesseau and the *avocat-général* Guillaume-François Joly de Fleury, for consultation. More concerned than Louis with conforming to the legalities of the Gallican tradition, the *gens du roi* cautioned him

the entire Church [only] when they are accepted by the body of pastors. (3) This acceptance on the part of the bishops is always made as a matter of [episcopal] judgment" (cited by Adam, p. 312).

[31] Cited by Mention, II, 45.

against attempting to register the Bull at this time.[32] They argued, in the first place, that an assembly of bishops summoned fortuitously and arbitrarily could not pronounce a binding and infallible judgment on the Bull and therefore could not give it legal force within the kingdom.[33] According to the Gallican Articles of 1682, a papal constitution did not become a law of the French Church until the episcopate first accepted it—a requirement which, despite the king's own hopes and expectations, the assembly of 1713-1714 had not adequately fulfilled.[34] At the same time, since the bull *Unigenitus* could not yet be considered a "law of the Church," it could not become a law of the State, registered by the Paris Parlement and issued with letters patent.[35] The king's legal advisers also raised some serious objections to the substance of *Unigenitus*. They observed that the Bull's condemnation was so strong and comprehensive that its unqualified acceptance would constitute a triumph of papal absolutism and hence a threat to the Gallican liberties. They found especially offensive and pernicious the pope's denunciation of proposition XCI, the rather strongly regalist principle that "the fear of an unjust excommunication must never prevent us from doing our duty: One never leaves the Church, even when it appears that one is banished from it by the spitefulness of men, [provided that] one is devoted to God, to Jesus Christ, and to the Church itself through charity." They charged that the condemnation of this proposition, according to which the pope asserted an unrestricted right to excommunicate the king and to lift from his subjects their duty of obedience, represented an implicit repudiation of the first of the four Gallican Articles of 1682[36] and

[32] Daguesseau privately described the Bull as "la croix non seulement des théologiens mais des premiers magistrats de ce royaume" (A. Gazier [ed.], "Fragment inédit des Mémoires du chancelier Daguesseau," *Bulletin philologique et historique (jusqu'à 1715) du Comité des travaux historiques* [1917], p. 26).

[33] On the views of the *gens du roi* regarding bishops' rights with respect to papal bulls, see *ibid.*, pp. 38-39; and "Journal historique de Lamoignon," pp. 246, 252-54.

[34] See especially Article IV of the decree of 1682, which declared that, although the pope should retain the primary role in matters of faith, his decisions were to become irrevocable only if the whole Church consented to ratify them (Mention, I, 31).

[35] J. H. Shennan, "The Political Role of the Parlement of Paris, 1715-1723," *Historical Journal*, 8 (1965), p. 184.

[36] This first article, by far the most controversial, stipulated that the king was "not subject to any ecclesiastical power in temporal matters by the order of God," that he could not be deposed (excommunicated) "either directly or indirectly by the authority of the Keys of the Church," and that his subjects could not for any reason be absolved from their obligations of loyalty and obedience to the crown (Mention, I, 27-28).

established the right of the Roman pontiff to encroach upon the temporal sovereignty of the French crown and the spiritual independence of the French Church. As such, it constituted a potentially dangerous threat to the security and tranquillity of the kingdom.[37]

Though no doubt offered in the monarchy's own best interest, the objections raised by the *gens du roi* infuriated the king[38] and served to reopen some vexing ecclesiastical questions which the royal government had claimed to resolve more than two decades earlier. The perplexing questions at issue centered on the monarchy's concept of Gallicanism[39] and the ambiguous relationship which existed between crown and papacy. Never consistent or predictable, repeatedly shifting with changes in political climate and conflicts of interest, Versailles' relations with Rome had always been a major cause of tension and uncertainty for the Gallican Church and were forever complicating the French monarch's role in religious matters.[40] Much of this uncertainty derived from the traditionally ambivalent ecclesiastical stance of the king of France, who was unable either unequivocally to embrace the Gallican (regalist) position or wholly to repudiate the ultramontane point of view. As titular head of the French Church, jealous of his overriding prerogatives and his prestige, he claimed the right and the duty to defend the venerable tradition of independent Gallican liberties against papal efforts to dictate French ecclesiastical policy. Indeed, during the anointing at his coronation, the monarch swore a

[37] See "Fragments des Mémoires de Daguesseau," p. 38. In another area, the *gens du roi* also questioned the wisdom of the pope's censure of propositions concerned with the reading of Scripture, arguing that such a censure would make a bad impression on the pious faithful, especially those newly converted to Catholicism (*ibid.*).

[38] For a firsthand account of the heated discussions between Louis XIV, his ministers, and the *gens du roi* concerning a proposal to submit the Bull to the Parlement of Paris at this time, see "Journal historique de Lamoignon," pp. 251-56.

[39] "Gallicanism" is a term which covers a wide variety of political, theological, and ecclesiastical tendencies, as well as judicial and administrative practices and procedures. For an analysis of its various meanings and of its several *ancien-régime* manifestations—royal, parlementary, and episcopal—see Victor Martin, *Le gallicanisme politique et le clergé de France, 1615-1682* (Paris, 1929); *idem, Les origines du gallicanisme*, 2 vols. (Paris, 1939); Aimé-Georges Martimort, *Le gallicanisme* (Paris, 1973); Marc Dubruel, "Gallicanisme," *DTC*, VI[1], cols. 1,096-137; *idem* and Henri-Xavier Arquillière, "Gallicanisme," *Dictionnaire apologétique de la foi catholique*, II, cols. 193-273; and Joseph Lecler, "Qu'est-ce que les libertés de l'Eglise gallicane?" *Recherches de science religieuse*, 23 (1933), pp. 385-410, 542-68; 24 (1934), pp. 47-85.

[40] The Concordat of Bologna continued to define royal-papal ecclesiastical dealings throughout the *ancien régime*. While the doctrinal decrees of the Council of Trent had been formally accepted in France, those on discipline and Church government had not.

sacred oath which confirmed his assumption of this solemn responsibility and established him as "bishop from outside" with legitimate authority over the Gallican Church in disciplinary and temporal matters. However, as "Most Christian King," accountable to God, he was the sworn and inflexible defender of religious orthodoxy, which was established and maintained by Rome. From this perspective the papacy represented not a potential rival, but the principal symbol and instrument of unity and order in the Catholic Church, an authority with which he was in general duty-bound to cooperate. Not surprisingly, therefore, the king and his ministers found it necessary to pursue an opportunistic policy, their posture toward Rome usually determined by the nature of the question at issue as well as by all accompanying political circumstances, particularly the crown's ability to obtain support for its program from influential elements within the kingdom. The royal government could thus unite with the pope against common enemies, such as the Jansenists, or engage Rome in spectacular conflicts, as in the celebrated affair of the regalian rights.

While the crown may have sought to remain flexible and pragmatic in its dealings with the papacy, it was not always free to shift policies at will. Any drift toward ultramontanism, for example, ran the risk of arousing the ire of the magistrates in the Parlement of Paris, the highest royal court in the kingdom. On matters affecting the Gallican liberties, the position of the Parlement had been rather clear and consistent for some time.[41] Indeed, as the royal government had frequently discovered to its regret, the magistrates were much more outspoken and intransigent Gallicans (and regalists) than even the king. It was traditional with the Parlement of Paris to insist on the absolute, irrevocable independence of the monarchy in relation to the pope in temporal affairs and to regard itself as responsible for protecting the king's inalienable sovereign authority and the dignity of the lay estate from the challenge of papal encroachment. Vigilant guardians of the royal prerogatives, inherently suspicious of papal policy, the judges had also assumed the additional responsibility of defending the autonomy of the French clergy from any Roman intrusion, denying the pope competence to intervene directly in matters of concern to the Gallican Church and refusing to allow papal bulls to enter France unless they had been previously requested by the crown after direct consultation with the Gallican episcopate.[42]

[41] On the origins and early development of parlementary Gallicanism see, in addition to the works cited above in n. 39, J. H. Shennan, *The Parlement of Paris* (Ithaca, 1968), pp. 166-87.

[42] Even when these requirements had been fulfilled, the Parlement was frequently still reluctant to register papal decrees.

Not unexpectedly, therefore, the judges in the Parlement of Paris were offended by the opportunistic alliance which the crown had once again effected with the papacy in obtaining the bull *Unigenitus*. The magistrates reacted to the Bull with a vehemence and defiance that was to be characteristic of their involvement in the eighteenth-century mêlée over "Jansenism." They deeply resented Louis XIV's inconsistent and arbitrary violation of the very Gallican liberties which they were duty-bound to preserve and which the king had himself fought so hard to secure in his controversy with Innocent XI over the *régale*. In his single-minded determination to punish the Jansenists, and in his zeal to enforce the papal bull condemning them, the king appeared to have willingly sacrificed all assured guarantees of royal and ecclesiastical independence vis-à-vis the papacy. Like the *gens du roi*, the judges regarded the acceptance of the papal denunciation of proposition XCI as tantamount to accepting the pope as the supreme and infallible arbiter of all questions affecting the French Church and subjecting the crown and episcopate to ultramontane pressure and caprice.[43]

But the magistrates' vehement opposition to the Bull could not withstand the king's determination to obtain its registration. Even so, the Parlement did not accept the Bull "purely and simply," as the king had wished. The court insisted on qualifying its registration of the letters patent—on Louis' behalf, if contrary to his wishes—with the stipulation that it be "without prejudice to the liberties of the Gallican Church, rights and preeminence of the Crown, power and jurisdiction of the bishops of the Kingdom. . . ."[44]

While serious opposition to the Bull was being voiced in episcopal circles and especially within the Paris Parlement, similar objections were also being expressed by a substantial proportion of the theologians in the Sorbonne.[45] The prestigious Faculty of Theology of the University of Paris was a bastion of ecclesiastical Gallicanism, upholding a centuries-long tradition of ardent resistance both to the claims of the papacy to sovereignty over the French Church and to the attempts of the regalists (particularly the Parlement of Paris) to control or encroach upon the spiritual power. Like Noailles and his episcopal allies, many of the Paris doctors objected to the Bull on both theo-

---

[43] Nor was the magistrates' concern about an "unjust papal excommunication" entirely unreasonable or without historical precedent. Innocent XI's threatened excommunication of Louis XIV and his ministers in 1688 was no doubt familiar to them (see Orcibal, *Louis XIV contre Innocent XI*, pp. 75-88).

[44] Mention, II, 49-50, n. 1.

[45] On the diverse meanings of the term, "Sorbonne," and the possible confusions in its use, see Roland Mousnier, *Paris au 17ᵉ siècle* (Paris, 1961), pp. 313-14.

logical and ecclesiastical grounds, and, like the bishops, called upon Rome to offer explanations or clarifications before they would accept the papal decree. However, the king, having staked his own reputation as absolute monarch upon the universal acceptance of *Unigenitus* within the realm, could no more abide this challenge to his authority than that of the Paris Parlement. A stormy debate between theologians and crown officials lasted for almost a week, during which several doctors were exiled from Paris. Despite their strong resentment against the Bull, the Faculty succumbed to the pressure of strict royal orders and signed a formula of acceptance on March 5.[46]

The success of Louis' government in forcefully imposing the Bull upon the Parlement of Paris and the Sorbonne did not mark the end of the controversy. Far from it. A passionate debate was carried on in both religious and secular circles through the publication of a very large number of books and pamphlets, more than two hundred tracts appearing in 1714 alone.[47] Nor was the opposition confined to magistrates, theologians, and bishops. Just as portentous as the opposition which the Bull had provoked among these groups, but perhaps even more ominous, was the hostile response which it aroused among certain elements of the lower clergy, increasingly resentful of a growing "episcopal despotism" which they had detected within the Gallican Church—a resentment that was not without foundation.

During the reign of Louis XIV, the government's concessions to the authority of the bishops had reinforced the principle of episcopal primacy in the governance of the Church and further enshrined the "first order" of the clergy in a position of indisputable preponderance within the diocese. This trend toward the institutional subordination of the "second order," accomplished through the active collaboration of Church and State, had culminated in two important developments in 1695. On January 17, 1695, desperate for funds to pay for its war effort, the crown announced the imposition of the *capitation* on all of the king's subjects. This new tax became the subject of a lively discussion at the quinquennial Assembly of the Clergy, the bishops angrily charging the king with violating the traditional fiscal privileges and immunities of the Church. Negotiations with the government produced a "compromise": in return for clerical exemption from the *capitation* and an implicit recognition of both the contractual nature

[46] On the conflicts between crown and Faculty, see Charles-Marie-Gabriel-Bréchillet Jourdain, *Histoire de l'Université de Paris au 17ᵉ et 18ᵉ siècles* (Paris, 1862-66), pp. 302-304; see also *Relation des délibérations de la Faculté de théologie de Paris au sujet de l'acceptation de la bulle "Unigenitus"* (N.p., 1714).

[47] Louis Cognet, *Le jansénisme* (Paris, 1961), p. 101.

of its fiscal obligations to the State and the inviolability of the Church's temporals, the Assembly voted to offer the government an extraordinary *don gratuit* of four million *livres* annually throughout the duration of the war. The bishops' success in purchasing their way out of the *capitation* was accomplished at the expense of the lower clergy, most of them poor priests whose financial plight was notorious. By helping to perpetuate the outrageously inequitable assessment of clerical taxes, the government's acquiescence in the corporate independence of the First Estate produced considerable distress among certain segments of an already harassed and frequently overburdened "second order" and was the source of much subsequent protest.

A few weeks after the compromise over the *capitation*, which served to sanction the maldistribution of wealth inside the Church, the bishops obtained an additional concession from the royal government—this one perhaps of greater consequence than the first. In April 1695, in the famous edict "regulating ecclesiastical jurisdiction,"[48] the Assembly of the Clergy received the support of the crown in strengthening the administrative and judicial power of the episcopate over the whole French Church. The lengthy edict, which tied the cause of the upper clergy more closely than ever to that of the crown, was intended to codify previous decrees and ordinances in order to establish throughout France a more consistent and uniform system of jurisdictions, both within the Church and between the secular and ecclesiastical authorities, and to prevent thereby "the disorders which [jurisdictional conflicts and confusions] could produce to the detriment of ecclesiastical discipline."[49] In those provisions having to do with internal Church governance, the royal decree placed the priest in the position of a mere auxiliary, a simple delegate of the bishop, whose discretionary authority was made virtually limitless. The edict gave the bishops extensive inspection and disciplinary power throughout the diocese and commanded parish officials to execute promptly and obediently all episcopal orders. It affirmed episcopal control over the lower clergy's right to preach, to administer the sacraments, and to hear confessions by requiring that every priest, regular and secular, other than parish priests, first obtain special authorization from his bishop. Finally, the edict granted the bishop the exclusive right of determining the spiritual qualifications of all candidates for sacerdotal office and of conferring on them the *visa* of occupancy—a "license" the bishop was empowered to modify or revoke at any time, without having to indicate his reasons and without permitting further legitimate appeal.[50]

---

[48] Mention, I, 114-50.

[49] Preamble, *ibid.*, p. 114.

[50] See Arts. 11-16, *ibid.*, pp. 118-19.

In effect, the edict of 1695 seemed to establish the bishop as the permanent judge and censor of all priestly activities. In the next five years additional pronouncements were made which further consecrated the subordination of the parish priests to their diocesan superiors and restricted the role of the second order in ecclesiastical government. A royal declaration issued on December 15, 1698, gave bishops the authority to order any disobedient priest into retreat in a seminary for as long as three months—without requiring the prelate to justify his action.[51] If this temporary suspension proved an inadequate form of discipline, the government made *lettres de cachet* readily available to the bishop to enable him to deal with those priests who remained recalcitrant. Not content with limiting the independence of the activities of the priests within the diocese, the meeting of the General Assembly of the Clergy in 1700 denied the delegates from the second order the right to participate as full members in the deliberations of that body.[52] Indeed, though they represented an overwhelming majority of the clergy, these "mere priests" were virtually excluded—with government sanction—from active participation in all subsequent General Assemblies convoked during the remainder of Louis XIV's reign. With the official approval of the crown, the patrician bishops were encouraged to wield their administrative and judicial authority without restraint and to continue to treat the plebeian "second order" as an inferior and entirely dependent caste.

Humiliated and frustrated anew, some embittered members of the lower clergy and their various spokesmen made various protests, but these protests, still isolated and therefore without much impact, were either condemned or ignored. Not until the promulgation of the bull *Unigenitus* did the "second order" have an issue around which its members could unite and an opportunity to hurl a concerted challenge at the Church establishment. In condemning the propositions which dealt with the role of the lower clergy within the hierarchy, the Bull had struck a blow in defense of the established ecclesiastical order and against all attempts at restructuring it and redistributing sacerdotal power in a more "democratic" direction. A small but growing segment of the "second order" found these sections of the Bull particularly offensive and was anxious to reassert its claims to a more

[51] "Déclaration pour l'établissement des Séminaires dans les Diocèses où il n'y en a point, et pour exécuter les Ordonnances des Archevêques et Evêques dans leurs visites," in Daniel Jousse, *Commentaire sur l'édit du mois d'avril 1695, concernant la juridiction ecclésiastique*, 2 vols. (Paris, 1764), II, 269-71. For other legislation issued in this period in clarification or amplification of provisions of the April 1695 edict, see *ibid.*, pp. 239-42, 261-68, 271-73, and 275-77.

[52] See Préclin, *Les jansénistes*, p. 30.

elevated status and a more substantial role in the governance of the Church. Resentful of subjection to their episcopal masters, whose sovereignty they were eager to challenge, and supported by a handful of canonists, theologians, and lawyers, the *curés* seized on this occasion to reaffirm the presbyterian theses of Edmond Richer which had been enunciated during the course of the seventeenth century and been recently expanded and given forceful expression in Quesnelist circles.[53] While acknowledging the distinctions in practical duties and administrative functions which differentiated them from the bishops, the *curés* proclaimed themselves inherently equal to the "first order" of the clergy as judges of the faith. The spiritual authority of the priesthood, like that of the episcopate, they argued, was of divine, not human, institution, having been established immediately by Jesus Christ Himself: just as the bishops were the successors of the Apostles, it was asserted, the *curés* were the direct descendants of the seventy-two disciples, commissioned by Christ independently of the Apostles to preach the Gospel. Believing themselves thus possessed of an innate dignity and an inalienable authority which not even their episcopal superiors could abrogate, the *curés* felt justified in insisting on a reassessed equality of power and respect befitting their honorable status. The importance of the lower clergy's claims and associated protests still lay in the future, however, when the increasingly radical elements of the "second order" became allied with other groups which shared some of their grievances toward the established authorities. But the very existence of these protests—some of them quite audacious and uncompromising in tone—was symbolic of the widespread ecclesiastical discontent aroused by the Bull. Indeed, they were a further demonstration that the policies of Louis XIV's government with regard to the "Jansenist problem" had ultimately been a failure.

In a sometimes obsessive pursuit of the "Jansenist sect" neither the king nor his religious advisers seems to have fully appreciated the important changes which Jansenism had undergone in the course of the seventeenth century and the complex and sensitive issues involved in its condemnation. In a fateful misperception of political and ecclesiastical realities, Louis' government continued to deceive itself into believing that it would be able to stamp out the Jansenists by resorting to traditional expedients of repression—papal bulls and royal decrees—which had never really achieved more than limited success before. To be sure, except for the exiled Quesnel, the Jansenists no longer had any outstanding leaders, and with the destruction of Port-Royal they had lost their symbol of unity. Clearly, the policy of repression had had

[53] *Ibid.*, pp. 31-34.

a modicum of success. All that was needed, therefore, was one more papal decree. The bull *Unigenitus* was designed to be the final solution to the "Jansenist problem."

However, Louis XIV and his advisers had gravely miscalculated the nature and strength of the opposition which the pope's attack on "Jansenism" would call forth. In the process of attempting to deal the Jansenist remnant its final death blows, the royal government had been midwife to another and more ominous development. The resistance which Louis' ecclesiastical policies had encountered in the seventeenth century was nothing by comparison with the battle that erupted after September 1713. The action of the crown in brutally destroying Port-Royal had already inspired a considerable public outcry and helped to perpetuate the legendary significance and the spiritual presence of the monastery for succeeding generations. But the promulgation of the bull *Unigenitus* provoked throughout the kingdom a swelling chorus of outspoken dissent, the most widespread agitation and criticism that Louis XIV had witnessed since the days of the Fronde. By its sponsorship of the papal decree, the crown provided the occasion for a regrouping of dissident forces. The result was the transformation of what had been merely a diversified hodgepodge of unorganized and unfocused opposition into an increasingly active and vocal resistance movement, more explicitly and alarmingly political in character and language, centered on the issue of the Bull, and marshaled by a newly revived and truculent Parlement of Paris. Having become in the eighteenth century the rallying cry for an ever-expanding disaffection with pontifical, royal, and episcopal absolutism, "Jansenism" now gathered under its banner a rather motley coalition of lay and clerical allies and included a confused, but formidable, combination of tendencies—spiritual and theological, ethical and juridical, political and constitutional. With all these discontented elements both within and without the Gallican Church thus taking up the cause of "Jansenism," each with a different perception of the principal issues at stake, the "Jansenist movement" had truly become an ideology of opposition and a force to be reckoned with—one which represented an open and potentially dangerous challenge to throne and episcopate alike.

The Legacy of Louis XIV: From the Regency to the Ministry of Cardinal Fleury

With the passing of Louis XIV and the coming of the Duke of Orléans as Regent, a severe and heavy-handed religious policy of repression gave way to an almost lax and indifferent one of moderate toleration. Orléans does not seem to have been very much concerned with establishing rigorous orthodoxy throughout the realm. Like Louis, to be sure, the Regent wished to put an end to the quarrels surrounding the bull *Unigenitus* and to inaugurate an era of religious peace. But whereas the Sun King would brook no opposition, the Duke of Orléans deemed it more profitable to take a conciliatory approach to the affair.

The Regency government began by reversing the strategy and tactics followed by the late king and adopting a policy of accommodation toward—if not one of outright support for—the *anticonstitutionnaires*. Noailles, exiled from court in 1714, returned to favor under Orléans, who named him to head the newly created *conseil de conscience*.[54] The council, which bore responsibility for directing official ecclesiastical policy, consisted entirely of Gallicans, as the Regent made a conscious effort to remove from positions of influence the ultramontane Jesuits who had dominated Louis XIV during the last years of his reign[55] In addition, the Regent freed those whom Louis had imprisoned for their opposition to the Bull and permitted the banished Sorbonne doctors to resume their functions. However, fearing the consequences of a public break with Rome, he shrank from giving outright support to the dissidents, attempting instead to strike a delicate equilibrium between the two sides.

Despite the Regent's irenic intentions, he had misperceived the religious temper of France at this time. The controversy had already become too heated and the opposing camps too divided to expect a policy of peaceful coexistence to succeed.[56] The partisans of the Bull,

[54] Decree in Isambert, XXI, 71-73. Shortly after his appointment, Noailles issued an order to all the clergy in his diocese forbidding them, "under pain of *ipso facto* suspension," to accept the Bull without his authorization.

[55] The other members of the council were the abbé Claude Fleury, author of numerous works in ecclesiastical history, who had recently replaced the Jesuit Father Le Tellier as royal confessor; Daguesseau, former *procureur-général*, who had opposed the promulgation of *Unigenitus* from the first and who was now named chancellor; and the abbé Antoine Dorsanne, Noailles' trusted confidant, who was appointed secretary. Another indication of the Jesuits' fall from power under the Regency may be seen in Cardinal Noailles' episcopal ordinance of Nov. 12, 1716, by which he deprived the Company of its powers to preach, to hear confession, or to conduct catechism instruction in the diocese.

[56] The bitter debate may be conveniently followed in Jean Carreyre, *Le jansénisme durant la Régence*, 3 vols. (Louvain, 1929-33); *idem*, "Unigenitus," *DTC*, xv², cols. 2,061-78; Henri Leclercq, *Histoire de la Régence pendant la minorité de Louis XV*, 3 vols. (Paris, 1921-22); and Jacques Parguez, *La bulle "Unigenitus" et le Jansénisme politique* (Paris, 1936). See also Emile Appolis, *Le "tiers parti" catholique au 18e siècle, entre Jansénistes et Zelanti* (Paris, 1960), esp. pp. 49-153.

who remained an overwhelming majority of the Church, scorned his appeals for moderation as well as his attempts at personally arbitrating the dispute. They persisted in giving their unreserved support to *Unigenitus* as "the true doctrine of the Church" and clamored for its complete acceptance by the entire French clergy. With strong encouragement from Rome, they published strident episcopal decrees and polemical tracts, some of them containing provocative attacks on various *anticonstitutionnaire* individuals and groups, especially the Sorbonne and the Parlement of Paris.[57] In addition, a substantial number of *constitutionnaire* bishops ordered all priests under their jurisdicton to accept the Bull or face severe reprisals (including possible excommunication). For its part, the papacy, in no mood for compromise, remained adamant in refusing to offer qualifications to the Bull.

The *anticonstitutionnaires*, however, were not to be denied a hearing. Though Louis XIV had stifled the dissenters, he had not converted them. Encouraged by the Regent's relaxation of authority and his implied assurances that the royal government would not take action against them, they quickly responded to their *acceptant* enemies, releasing energies long pent up under the late king's authoritarian rule. They launched a strong and skillful propaganda campaign of their own, directing most of their polemical attacks against the Jesuits and others who were suspected of subverting the Gallican liberties. Nor was that all. One by one the several groups which Louis XIV had intimidated into accepting the Bull recanted without much interference from the Orléans government. The Faculty of Theology of Paris declared in early 1716 that it had originally received the Bull only under duress and now wished to disavow its acceptance. In this retractation it was soon followed by the faculties of Reims and Nantes. By the beginning of 1717 the Parlement of Paris, enjoying a resurgence of independent corporate power with its right of prior remonstrance restored in 1715, had followed the lead of the various faculties and was joined by several other sovereign courts in revoking previously extorted acceptances.

It was for a variety of motives that the judges in the Paris Parlement had begun to play an increasingly active role in determining the direction of religious politics during this period.[58] Arguing that

[57] See, for example, *Les Tocsins avec les écrits et les arrêts publiés contre ces libelles violentes et séditieux, avec un recueil des mandements et autres pièces qui ont rapport aux écrits précédents* (Paris, 1716).

[58] See James Hardy, *Judicial Politics in the Old Regime: The Parlement of Paris During the Regency* (Baton Rouge, 1967); and Shennan, "Parlement of Paris, 1715-23."

issues of Church authority were properly within their juridical competence, the magistrates claimed to have a compelling obligation to take a public stand against the Bull. At the same time, although they had perfectly justifiable traditions and legal precedents upon which to base their opposition, the magistrates also sought to enhance their own judicial authority and prestige, to curry popular favor, and to stake out a position for themselves in affairs of state from which Louis XIV had regularly barred them. They were also kept very busy suppressing ultramontane tracts and issuing prohibitions against episcopal efforts to receive or to execute papal decrees without royal authorization. In the process the court managed to renew its longstanding feud with the Gallican episcopate over the frontiers of their respective jurisdictions.

Throughout the protracted struggles which had engaged Parlement and episcopate, the magistrates had repeatedly sought to challenge the corporate autonomy of the bishops and the power, both theoretical and real, which these prelates claimed to exercise in their dioceses. The perennial debate was no less virulent in the early decades of the eighteenth century than it had been in times past. In the view of the magistrates, the recent controversy over the bull *Unigenitus* and the ongoing struggle with Rome over the nature of ultimate authority in the Church were only part of a larger, more fundamental jurisdictional conflict between the spiritual and temporal powers. While bishops and *parlementaires* had often been able to make common cause in their mutual opposition to "papal absolutism," agreeing on the need to keep the French Church independent of Rome, there was much less room for agreement on the broader issue of Church-State relations. The magistrates had already provoked considerable resentment on the part of the Church by frequently suggesting that the French clergy was not only subordinate to the king, but also dependent upon the protection of the monarch and his sovereign courts for the preservation of the Gallican liberties.

Even more disturbing to the First Estate, the Parlement of Paris had claimed responsibility for upholding and protecting the supremacy and autonomy of the secular power from clerical incursions of any kind, episcopal as well as papal. The magistrates even claimed the authority to intervene in Church affairs whenever they believed that the clergy had violated the so-called fundamental laws and maxims of the kingdom. Concerned with restricting episcopal exemptions and immunities and with restraining potential "episcopal despotism," they had been seeking for some time to establish their own courts as the supreme

29

arbiter in a wide range of religious matters, with the right to override rulings of ecclesiastical courts (*officialités*) by means of the procedure known as the *appel comme d'abus*.

The legal process of the *appel comme d'abus*—one of the most fundamental but least explored or understood juridical concepts of medieval and early modern France—allowed complaints to be brought before the parlements on behalf of the victim of a decision rendered by an ecclesiastical judge who had allegedly exceeded or abused his authority.[59] The secular courts would generally take up such judicial appeals when the ecclesiastical decisions "involved judicial irregularities, threatened the jurisdiction of the secular courts, or in some way violated the liberties of the Gallican Church."[60] To be sure, rulings handed down in these cases were not definitive or final judgments, but only provisional and suspensive ones, requiring additional hearings and deliberations. Even so, the parlements' willingness to examine an *appel comme d'abus* effectively resulted in a stay of execution of the original ecclesiastical decision until final adjudication of the case—a situation which most French bishops saw as a usurpation of their prerogatives and a challenge to their disciplinary authority.

Not surprisingly, the hierarchy of the Gallican Church, fearing the ominous prospect of unconditional clerical subjection to the royal courts, took great exception to this growing secular intrusion into areas it regarded as its exclusive domain. In seeking to protect their independence and jurisdictional competence from further erosion, the beleaguered French bishops had frequent recourse to the crown. For decades episcopal representatives to the quinquennial General Assemblies, supported by a succession of Agents-General of the Clergy, had been complaining about a conspiracy formed between the aggressive magistrates in the secular courts and large numbers of disobedient lower clergy throughout France to encroach upon or abrogate the bishops' traditional autonomy and jealously guarded prerogatives within their own dioceses. Excessive recourse to and alleged misuse of the *appel comme d'abus* procedure—in contravention of existing royal decrees—were especially irritating to these prelates, who in recent years had turned repeatedly to the royal councils for the nullification, suspen-

---

[59] The *appel comme d'abus* was first instituted in the fourteenth century and was originally limited to extraordinary cases, though its scope had been expanded considerably in subsequent years. For an extended analysis of the appeal procedure, see Robert Génestal, *Les origines de l'appel comme d'abus* (Paris, 1950).

[60] Dale Van Kley, *The Jansenists and the Expulsion of the Jesuits from France, 1757-1765* (New Haven, 1975), p. 128.

sion, or reversal of civil court decisions.[61] For most of Louis XIV's reign—a reign that was itself marked by the gradual expansion of the crown's role as director and initiator of ecclesiastical policy and by the increasing subordination of the Church's judicial authority to that of the king—the government's formal replies to these innumerable clerical remonstrances and petitions were limited to conciliar interventions, "stop-gap expedients involving specific cases."[62] It was not until the April 1695 edict on ecclesiastical jurisdiction that the royal administration issued its first full-scale response to such episcopal complaints. Although somewhat ambiguous on the issue of the *appel comme d'abus*, as on other debatable jurisdictional questions, the royal edict definitely appeared to favor the bishops over the parlements.[63] Without attempting to restrict the competence of the magistrates too specifically or to weaken their authority too severely, the government placed important limitations on the right of the sovereign courts to take cognizance of Church affairs or to interfere with the legitimate exercise of episcopal authority—a source of subsequent bitter clashes between the Parlement of Paris and the royal councils during much of the eighteenth century.[64]

In its apparent concern to protect what remained of the Church's independence from relentless encroachment by the belligerent sov-

---

[61] On the various mechanisms, both formal and informal, available to the Church for appeals to the crown, see Louis S. Greenbaum, *Talleyrand: Statesman-Priest. The Agent-General of the Clergy and the Church of France at the End of the Old Regime* (Washington, 1970); and Cynthia A. Dent, "The Council of State and the Clergy During the Reign of Louis XIV: An Aspect of the Growth of French Absolutism," *Journal of Ecclesiastical History*, 24 (1973), pp. 245-66. For the clerical complaints see *Recueil des actes, titres et mémoires concernant les affaires du clergé de France*, ed. Pierre Lemerre, 14 vols. (Paris, 1768-71), VII, cols. 1,515-1,602.

[62] Dent, p. 257.

[63] See esp. Arts. 30, 34-39 (Mention, I, 127-31). Cf. declaration of March 29, 1696, in *Recueil des actes du clergé*, VII, cols. 1,538-39.

[64] Much of the trouble resulted from the fact that the crown had difficulty adhering to a consistent policy in its dealings with the sovereign court and was simultaneously pulled in opposite directions. On the one hand, the judges could frequently be useful allies in the monarchy's relationships with Rome or with an obstreperous hierarchy; on the other hand, the magistrates were often capable of obstructing royal legislation and riding roughshod over the independence of the Gallican Church. Hence, as one writer has observed, "the crown's efforts to restrain the sovereign courts were designed neither to strengthen the church nor to weaken the royal courts" (Dent, "Changes in the Episcopal Structure of the Church of France in the 17th Century as an Aspect of Bourbon State-Building," *Bulletin of the Institute of Historical Research*, 48 [1975], p. 214).

ereign courts, the royal government had succeeded in tying the cause of the upper clergy more closely than ever to that of the crown— an ironic situation for the Church, one which underscored the fundamental weakness of its position in relation to the State and seemed ultimately to deny the corporate autonomy of the clerical estate. In addition, the success of the bishops in obtaining continued crown support was achieved only at the expense of further alienating the magistrates and the lower clergy from both the king and his bishops. To the Parlement of Paris the declaration of April 1695, like similar legislation issued in the following years, threatened, at least by implication, the court's legitimate judicial prerogatives and responsibilities.[65] The judges maintained that they were duty-bound to protect all individuals, clergy as well as laity, from ecclesiastical injustice, and that, in pronouncing favorable judgments on behalf of the complainants who came before them, they were simply acting to thwart the hierarchy's illicit enterprises. Consequently, in spite of various legal restrictions on its jurisdictional competence, the Parlement continued to receive *appels comme d'abus*, the number of which had begun to mount since the promulgation of the bull *Unigenitus*.

While the Paris Parlement may have actually encouraged refractory priests to present appeals over the heads of their diocesan superiors even in cases where no grave abuses were at issue, and while the court may have also sought to exploit this priestly litigiousness for its own political purposes, the appellate process was nevertheless a necessary one to prevent powerful clergy from tyrannizing their subordinates. In this connection, a critical test case came before the magistrates in late April 1716, brought by six priests and canons from the diocese of Reims. Almost a year earlier, their archbishop, the zealous *constitutionnaire* Cardinal François de Mailly, had ordered all priests in his diocese to publish his pastoral letter on *Unigenitus* and to accept the Bull as a sign of obedient respect for papal, episcopal, and royal authority. The six ecclesiastics who refused to submit were excommunicated, whereupon they presented an *appel comme d'abus* to the magistrates in the Paris Parlement. The suit attracted considerable public attention during a month of judicial deliberations which ended on May 28. The judges annulled Mailly's decree as "abusive and erroneous" and condemned the influential cardinal-archbishop for exceeding

[65] As a consequence, although the ostensible purpose of the edict had been not to innovate, but merely to regularize existing laws and practices, the magistrates in the Paris Parlement nevertheless found it a pernicious document. In an unwonted display of independence during Louis XIV's reign, the *Grand'Chambre* refused to register the decree until the king ordered them to do so.

his episcopal authority. Although the Regent eventually set aside the court's ruling, the magistrates had already established an extremely significant precedent and clearly signaled their intention of protecting *anticonstitutionnaire* members of the lower clergy within the court's resort from arbitrary episcopal reprisals. In the future, any bishops who attempted to force adherence to *Unigenitus* in their dioceses might find themselves faced with the prospect of a similar confrontation with the magistrates.[66]

In the meantime, while the vicious and almost unabated pamphlet war continued to aggravate an already tense situation, disorder and dissension had penetrated into all parts of the realm. The Regent's continuing attempts at accommodation were repeatedly rebuffed, as the recalcitrants on both sides refused to compromise. Throughout the conflict the opposition clergy remained but a beleaguered minority confronted by a *constitutionnaire* majority much too numerous and inflexible to be coerced into meaningful or substantive concessions. It appeared, therefore, that if the split were to be healed, it could be managed only through a capitulation on papal terms, which meant adherence to the Bull. Such a conclusion was entirely unsatisfactory to the Jansenist party.

After several years of unsuccessful attempts to resolve these difficulties, four *anticonstitutionnaire* bishops,[67] exasperated by the pope's refusal to offer explanations on *Unigenitus* and alarmed that the Bull had caused irreparable damage to the "Truth," interrupted all efforts at reconciliation with an act which rendered the rift permanent. Amid protestations of their unswerving loyalty to Rome and their undiminished respect for papal authority, the bishops appealed against the bull *Unigenitus* and from the pope misinformed "to a future general council legitimately assembled in a safe place, to which they or their representatives might freely and securely go."[68] Claiming that they were acting "For the glory of Almighty God, for the preservation and exaltation of the Catholic faith and traditional doctrine, for the peace and tranquility of the Church and the realm, for the defense of the

[66] One may follow the case in a series of contemporary tracts: BN, Salle des Imprimés, LD-4 773-74, 800-802, 844. See also discussion in J. Hardy, pp. 57-60.

[67] Charles-Joachim Colbert de Croissy of Montpellier (nephew of Louis XIV's great minister), Jean Soanen of Senez, Pierre de la Broue of Mirepoix, and Pierre de Langle of Boulogne.

[68] "Acte d'appel interjeté le 1er mars 1717," reproduced in Parguez, pp. 203-10. For an analysis of the appeal and its connection with the royal appeal of 1688, which appears to have served as an important precedent, see Orcibal, *Louis XIV contre Innocent XI*, pp. 75-88.

rights of the episcopate and the liberties of the Gallican Church,"[69] they deposited a notarized act of appeal in the Sorbonne on March 5, 1717. The next day they left a similar document with the abbé Antoine Dorsanne, *official* in the diocese of Paris, who formally inscribed it on his registers. By their action the bishops provided the disparate forces of opposition with a more concrete issue around which to unite.[70]

A considerable number of lay and clerical supporters quickly rallied behind the four prelates. Lists of these "appellants" were published and widely circulated throughout France. One of them bore the names of 97 out of the 110 Sorbonne doctors present when the bishops delivered their act of appeal. Across the country, ecclesiastics of every rank added their signatures. Many members of the lower clergy eagerly seized upon the appeal, in some cases as an opportunity to challenge or to defy the authority of their superiors, in others, as a means of reasserting their independent priestly prerogatives, in still others, as a way of protesting the dogmatic and spiritual implications of the Bull.[71] In Paris supporters of the four bishops rushed to record their names in the registers of the *officialité*. Indeed, with some three-quarters of the Paris clergy openly adhering to the appeal, the capital and its suburbs were the strongest bastion of appellant sentiment in the country. Cardinal Noailles himself, frustrated in his many attempts to reach an accommodation with Rome, signed an act of appeal on April 3, which he had inscribed in the diocesan registers, but which he did not make public until some eighteen months later. Many university faculties, cathedral chapters, and religious orders and congregations gave their approval as well, while the several parlements of the realm looked with great favor upon the appeal as a means of rendering the Bull ineffective. At its height the appeal eventually attracted the support of approximately 3,000 of the 100,000 members of the French clergy, among them more than a dozen bishops.[72] Though numerically never more than a very small minority, the appellants were still a very active, troublesome, and tenacious force, especially in Paris, where the archiepiscopal authorities openly welcomed even laymen, whatever their status or condition, to enter their names in the lists. The op-

[69] "Acte d'appel," in Parguez, pp. 203-204.

[70] The four prelates were all banished to their respective dioceses by order of the Regent, who also sent to the Bastille the notary who had received their appeal.

[71] According to Orcibal (*Louis XIV contre Innocent XI*, p. 83), some of these parish priests were clearly Molinist in their theological tendencies—another indication of the extent to which the opposition to the Bull cut across ideological lines. Cf. Pierre Deyon, *Amiens, capitale provinciale: Etudes sur la société urbaine au 17ᵉ siècle* (Paris-The Hague, 1967), pp. 372-73.

[72] Cognet, p. 105.

ponents of the Bull had thus staked out their position on the basis of a formal appeal which was clearly within the Gallican tradition.[73]

As might have been expected, the appeal was accompanied by a marked increase in the number and intensity of the polemics from both sides, with parish priests, bishops, lawyers, and theologians all entering the fray. The escalation of the conflict deeply disturbed the Regent, who became more anxious than ever to restore peace and tranquility to the Gallican Church. In early October 1717, with the concurrence of the Parlement of Paris, he issued a declaration enjoining silence on all parties to the dispute, in order to give the government's representatives in Rome time to negotiate with the pope. Neither side, however, would abide by the royal declaration. Nor was Clement XI any less adamant than before in his refusal to offer qualifications to his bull. Indeed, relations between France and the papacy, already strained by the widespread opposition to *Unigenitus*, had deteriorated rapidly as a consequence of the appeal. For a time Clement refused to send bulls of investiture to consecrate bishops for vacant French sees. Though he resumed his confirmations in April 1718, the pope was still in no mood for compromise. Having repeatedly rebuffed various attempts by the Regent, Noailles, and others to obtain "explanations" that might temper certain aspects of the Bull and thereby quiet the controversy, Clement now issued a scathing denunciation of the appeal in his famous apostolic letters, *Pastoralis officii*.

These highly provocative letters were promulgated on September 8, 1718, the fifth anniversary of the appearance of *Unigenitus*. Attacking the appeal as a threat to the integrity of the Church and declaring the Bull clear to the eyes of all good Catholics, the pope commanded the faithful to accept his original decree or face the possibility of disciplinary action. He further ordered all *anticonstitutionnaire* bishops to renounce their adherence to the appeal or suffer the penalty of excommunication. Clement's latest pronouncement reminded the opponents of *Unigenitus* of the *excommunication injuste* referred to in the condemned proposition XCI and immediately provoked another stormy controversy in France. The magistrates in the Parlement of Paris charged that the pope, in claiming the authority to force French bishops to execute his decrees and in constituting himself judge of the Gallican episcopate's conduct, was not only abusing his papal authority, but also presuming himself infallible—a presumption which the magistrates clearly could not abide. They declared the papal letters in blatant violation of the Gallican liberties and refused to allow them

[73] See Art. 2 of the Declaration of 1682, which announced that general councils were superior to the authority of the pope in spiritual matters (Mention, I, 29).

to be published in France. They also suppressed a series of ultra-montane tracts written in support of the pope's pronouncements.[74]

Far from stifling the appellant bishops, the pope's latest action served only to strengthen their will to resist the Roman intrusion. On January 14, 1719, convinced that explanations would never be forthcoming from Rome, Cardinal Noailles published a massive *Mandement sur la Constitution Unigenitus*, a volume of almost 300 pages. The pastoral decree contained a clear and strong justification of Quesnel's *Réflexions morales* and of propositions condemned in the Bull and offered a vigorous defense of the appeal. Though immediately placed on the Index, Noailles' *mandement* was widely applauded by his fellow appellants in Paris and throughout the kingdom, and put the Regent in an even more difficult position.

Embroiled in a war with Spain, Orléans could not afford continued strained relations with Rome. Nor for that matter could he risk losing control over the religious situation in France. Despite recent developments, the Regent had not abandoned all efforts at compromise and was still hopeful of negotiating the question with Rome. In an effort to implement this policy of reconciliation, the government again sought to impose official silence throughout the kingdom. But the royal declaration of June 5, 1719, though reinforced by the government's renewal of previous censorship legislation, proved no more effective than the earlier one. Undaunted, Orléans renewed his earlier peace overtures to Rome and undertook an active campaign to mend the religious rift. At the end of 1719 he commissioned a group of clergy, including Cardinal Noailles, to draw up a compromise document on the Bull, the *corps de doctrine*, or *accommodement*, which would be acceptable to all the parties concerned. While satisfactory to the moderates in both camps, the accommodation did not please the intransigent. The zealous *constitutionnaires*, supported by the pope, continued to insist that the Bull had to be accepted purely and simply, without further qualifications or explanations. The ardent appellants claimed that they were still awaiting a general council for a decision in the matter. The debate went on, as heated as ever.

In its efforts to mend the religious rift, the Regency government had tried the way of compromise and found it wanting. Though still sympathetic to the Gallican position, Orléans could no longer afford to tolerate the dissidence of the appellants. By now the duke had come under the sway of the ambitious abbé Dubois, who turned him in-

---

[74] In this they were joined by their colleagues in the provincial parlements, who had also suppressed a series of *constitutionnaire* pastoral letters which threatened unrepentant appellants with excommunication.

creasingly toward the *constitutionnaire* view. Dubois, once the Regent's tutor, convinced his former pupil of the need for religious uniformity, not so much to ensure orthodoxy as to guarantee peace and order. Under Dubois' prodding, the Regent determined to eliminate all dissent by according the conciliatory *corps de doctrine* the royal imprimatur. The compromise document, already granted qualified approval by Cardinal Noailles, was embodied in the "Déclaration du Roy touchant la conciliation des Evêques du Royaume à l'occasion de la Constitution *Unigenitus*," which the Regent presented to the Parlement of Paris for registration on August 4.[75]

The royal declaration began with a long preamble in which the Regent expressed his heartfelt wish for a complete and total reconciliation within the Church and happily announced that most of the French bishops had accepted the *corps de doctrine* upon which the government had placed its "seal of authority." He went on to declare that "all suitable precautions" would be taken to stifle those whose "false zeal and partisan spirit" had been responsible for fomenting discord and dissension throughout the kingdom and to reestablish in the Church "a subordination as just as it is necessary." The first article, intended in part to mollify ruffled papal feelings, confirmed the letters patent of February 1714 and stated that the Parlement's *arrêts d'enregistrement* regarding the bull *Unigenitus* would be universally and uniformly executed and observed. It also prohibited the expression or publication of any opinions against the Bull. The second article gave further satisfaction to the pope and to the *constitutionnaire* bishops by declaring —in the name of "order and canonical discipline"—that all appeals from the Bull to a council would be "of no effect." However, the government included an important stipulation, reaffirming the inviolability of "the rules of the Church and the maxims of the realm regarding the right to appeal to a future council." Article three condemned in general terms what the government described as a widespread disregard of royal, episcopal, and papal decrees and disrespect for civil and ecclesiastical authority and renewed previous ordinances concerning "the police, ecclesiastical discipline, and the execution of judgments of the Church in matters of doctrine." The fourth article renewed Article XXX from the royal edict of April 1695 on ecclesiastical jurisdiction, reaffirming the independence and supremacy of the episcopate in doctrinal matters and commanding the parlements to cease violating the bishops' prerogatives in such questions. The fifth, and final, article expressly forbade all the king's subjects to call anyone a Jansenist, a schismatic, or a heretic.

[75] The text of the declaration is in Mention, II, 52-60.

While the Regent had attempted in various ways to avoid rekindling old hostilities or blatantly offending the sensibilities of the Gallican parlements, the declaration of August 4 nevertheless represented a rather clear-cut defeat for the opponents of the Bull. Yet *anticonstitutionnaire* agitation did not thereby cease. Only the lukewarm fell away. On September 10, the four original appellant bishops, ignoring the compromise settlement which Noailles seemed about to accept, defiantly renewed their appeal. This time, however, the government quickly condemned the renewed appeal, though not before it had attracted substantial, if diminished, support. In the meantime, Orléans was encountering considerable difficulty from the magistrates in the Parlement of Paris, who were adamantly refusing to register the royal declaration. A long and bitter debate ensued, during which the Regent threatened the sovereign court, already exiled to Pontoise for its obstructionist behavior in the Law affair, with further banishment. It was not until December that he finally managed to force the Parlement to register the decree. Even so, the court's registration was not simply a capitulation, since the magistrates, as in the enforced registration originally obtained by Louis XIV in 1714, carefully hedged their acceptance with important qualifications intended to protect the Gallican liberties. Although the Regent had managed to heal the split with Rome and successfully averted and postponed for a decade a much more serious confrontation between crown and Parlement, the quarrel over the Bull was far from settled.

In the last three years of the Regency, the government sought to enforce the declaration of August 4. Faced with continued defiance on the part of a dwindling, but tenacious, group of ecclesiastical dissidents and exasperated by the basic failure of most of his efforts at peaceful reconciliation, the Duke of Orléans was forced to resort to harsh measures of exile and imprisonment in order to end the struggle. The number of *lettres de cachet* issued against those who violated the royal declaration multiplied quickly, resuming the policy of the previous reign. But by the time he died in December 1723, the Regent had managed to induce submission from only the least ardent of the *anticonstitutionnaires*, without dramatically affecting a rather substantial number of reappellants both among the lower clergy and in various religious orders and congregations. Despite the vacillation of its cardinal-archbishop, the diocese of Paris, the most influential and prestigious see in the kingdom, remained the center of an increasingly dangerous *anticonstitutionnaire* agitation. The Regency government had thus failed to bring either the country or the capital much nearer to the religious settlement Orléans had been seeking intermittently since September 1715. What is more, royal authority had in the meantime been compromised and severely weakened. The restoration of religious tranquility and of respect for the crown was the task which fell next to the young king's tutor, Bishop André-Hercule de Fleury of Fréjus.

CARDINAL FLEURY AND THE ENFORCEMENT OF THE BULL "UNIGENITUS"

Though he did not become the unofficial first minister of France until June 1726, Fleury had already wielded considerable influence over ecclesiastical affairs under both the Regent and the Duke of Bourbon. While a dominant figure and active member, first of the *conseil de conscience*, and then of the more informal *conseil* (or *chambre*) *ecclésiastique*,[76] Fleury acquired virtual control over appointments to the Gallican Church, through the so-called *feuille des bénéfices*.[77] Gradually the future cardinal also became the main architect and director of the government's anti-Jansenist policy. After 1726, as Fleury gained the absolute confidence of the king, his own authority and power prerogatives expanded accordingly. He took over the reins of government almost completely and surrounded himself with a host of capable advisers and subordinates to counsel him in the formulation and execution of government policy. For the first decade of Fleury's ministry the problems of ecclesiastical politics would continue to occupy a major part of his attention and that of his team of colleagues and creatures at Versailles and in Paris.[78]

More a pragmatic minister of state than a zealous or dogmatic partisan, Fleury, like Richelieu and Mazarin before him, favored a religious policy that was more political than religious, anti-Jansenist without being ultramontane. His attitude toward the *anticonstitutionnaires* did not derive so much from doctrinal considerations, which hardly interested him, nor from any profound ideological commitment to the Bull, as from an abiding conviction that the various opponents

---

[76] Which replaced the former after the polysynodal system of government had been abandoned.

[77] For a brief discussion of the nature of this office, see Norman Ravitch, *Sword and Mitre: Government and Episcopate in France and England in the Age of Aristocracy* (The Hague, 1966), pp. 56-57.

[78] On the composition and responsibilities of Fleury's "conseil des affaires ecclésiastiques" during the early years of the cardinal's ministry, see Michel Antoine, *Le conseil du roi sous le règne de Louis XV* (Geneva, 1970), pp. 128-30; cf. Louis-Hector, duc de Villars, *Mémoires*, 6 vols. (Paris, 1884-1904), IV, 278. For a somewhat later period see J.M.J. Rogister, "New Light on the Fall of Chauvelin," *English Historical Review*, 83 (1968), pp. 314-30, *passim*.

of *Unigenitus* constituted a distinct threat to public order and stability, civil and ecclesiastical. Consequently, in place of Orléans' hesitations and ineffective accommodations, Fleury (for the while undisturbed by the Parlement of Paris) substituted a more rigorous and less compromising policy of enforced subscription and adherence to the Bull. He was willing to be conciliatory on occasion, but only on his own terms, firmly refusing to make the kinds of concessions, in the name of "peace," which tended to undermine the integrity of Church and State.

Though possessed of no grand scheme or program, Fleury aimed at weakening the opposition to the Bull in several ways. One method was to bar from ecclesiastical preferment all adherents to the appeal. In his capacity as dispenser of Church patronage, Fleury began systematically to deny vacant benefices to all appellants, hoping thereby to purge the hierarchy. Nominations to bishoprics, abbeys, and canonries under his jurisdiction were reserved for *constitutionnaires*, that is, "persons who were committed to sound doctrine."[79] Such a procedure, while virtually guaranteed success in the long run, would necessarily take some time and affect only a limited, if influential, segment of the opposition. Impatient to eliminate the Jansenist threat more quickly and thoroughly, Fleury adopted additional more rigorous and authoritarian measures for reducing *anticonstitutionnaire* strength. Through severe censorship legislation, affecting pamphleteers, printers, and hawkers alike, the cardinal-minister tried to put an end to all publications hostile to the Bull and prevent the Jansenist opposition from propagating its views.[80] He strictly enforced the royal declaration of July 11, 1722, which had enjoined bishops and universities to require all candidates for orders and degrees to sign "purely and simply" the Formulary against the Five Propositions of Jansenius. With the aid of *constitutionnaire* bishops he dismissed numerous appellants from places in universities, *collèges*, and seminaries throughout the kingdom. He also attempted to force those congregations and religious orders, male and female, which were reputedly sympathetic to the appeal to submit to the Bull by holding the threat of suspension and exile over their members' heads and by restricting their recruitment of new pension-

[79] Fleury to Clement XII, Oct. 23, 1730, AAE, C.P., Rome, MS 715, fols. 400ff. The cardinal-minister was reluctant, however, to appoint *acceptant* zealots to such posts, fearing that they might exacerbate the tensions within the Church (see Ravitch and Appolis, both *passim*).

[80] Isambert, XXI, 304-305. The number of persons arrested for printing or distributing *anticonstitutionnaire* tracts increased dramatically throughout this period. See François Ravaisson (ed.), *Archives de la Bastille*, 19 vols. (Paris, 1866-1904), XIV, 1-11, 65-76, 143-46, 168-91, 238-40.

aries, novices, and postulants. A torrent of *lettres de cachet*[81] constrained many contumacious clergy to silence and obedience and intimidated others into renouncing their former opposition. Many of those who refused to capitulate were deprived of their benefices, confined in a monastery or a seminary, immured in a dungeon, or banished from the country. Still others fled abroad (particularly to the Netherlands) to avoid capture.

In Paris, where hostility toward the Bull was strongest and where, because of the prestige and dominant influence of the capital,[82] such opposition was potentially the most dangerous, Fleury faced his most serious challenge, especially since he could not count on a cooperative archbishop to assist him. Indeed, the persistent refusal of Cardinal Noailles to accept the Bull would remain for years a major stumbling block to the government's efforts to pacify the city. Moreover, the continued indulgence of the cardinal-archbishop toward *anticonstitutionnaire* priests exiled from other dioceses who sought refuge in Paris had helped swell the number of priestly activists in the capital. With Noailles' benevolent encouragement, proscribed clergy flocked to the city. Some of these fugitives attached themselves to particular parishes as *prêtres habitués* and there assumed various sacerdotal responsibilities. Others found shelter or took up posts in seminaries and *collèges* that were then under Jansenist directorship. Still others helped staff the free charity schools (modeled on the *petites écoles* of Port-Royal) which several lay and clerical benefactors had established in predominantly appellant parishes scattered throughout the city.[83]

[81] An estimated 40,000 *lettres de cachet* were issued during Cardinal Fleury's seventeen-year ministry (Cécile Gazier, *Histoire de la Société et de la Bibliothèque de Port-Royal* [Paris, 1966], p. 9).

[82] On the central importance of Paris, see the essays by Adrien Friedmann and Roland Mousnier in *Paris, fonctions d'une capitale* (Paris, 1962), esp. pp. 29, 36, 39-41. See also Dent, "Changes in Episcopal Structure," which deals in passing with "the great increase in power of the see of Paris in the formulation and execution of ecclesiastical policy" (p. 214).

[83] A. Gazier, "Les écoles de charité du faubourg Saint-Antoine, école normale et groupes scolaires, 1713-1887," *Revue internationale de l'enseignement*, 51 (1906), pp. 217-37, 314-26; C. Gazier, *Après Port-Royal: L'ordre hospitalier des Soeurs de Sainte-Marthe de Paris, 1713-1918* (Paris, 1923), pp. 14-20, 39-40; *idem, Histoire de la Société et de la Bibliothèque de Port-Royal* (Paris, 1966). See also Joseph Dedieu, "Le désarroi janséniste pendant le période du quesnellisme," *Introduction aux études d'histoire ecclésiastique locale*, ed. Victor Carrière, 3 vols. (Paris, 1934-40), III, 567-73; and François de Dainville, "La carte du jansénisme à Paris en 1739 d'après les papiers de la Nonciature," *Bulletin de la Société de l'Histoire de Paris et de l'Ile de France*, 96 (1969), pp. 113-24. Numerous private foundations and generous bequests, many of them secret and anonymous, helped sustain the

Fleury's principal method of handling the Jansenist problem in Paris was to attack the *anticonstitutionnaires* from the top down. He thus expended considerable energy in a secret campaign to convert Cardinal Noailles, whose position as putative leader of the appellant clergy seemed to make his capitulation a necessity. To convert Noailles to the orthodox camp, Fleury believed, would effectively reduce the strength of the party.

Nor did the cardinal-minister have any hesitations about resorting to the Paris police,[84] then under the direction of the resourceful and energetic lieutenant-general, René Hérault, former *intendant* of Tours. Since the days of Louis XIV, the police of Paris, with Versailles' blessing, had come to assume an ever-expanding role in a variety of urban affairs, including supervision over certain matters of religious conformity and discipline. Under Fleury's government, the considerable responsibilities of the police were extended even further, as the position of lieutenant-general—the city's principal administrator and the chief executor of royal policy in Paris—was elevated to virtually ministerial status. Indeed, the loyal Hérault was one of Fleury's closest, most reliable collaborators throughout this period, particularly in dealing with questions of ecclesiastical politics, an area in which the police lieutenant frequently received special assignments. The cardinal-minister, who always liked to be kept fully and accurately informed of current affairs in the capital, ordinarily held regular weekly meetings with Hérault at Versailles and maintained a direct private correspond-

---

adherents of the Jansenist cause throughout the eighteenth century and beyond. The number, amounts, and management of these gifts remain shrouded in mystery and merit further careful study.

[84] It should be understood that the term, "police," when used in an eighteenth-century context, does not denote what it does in most present-day usage. In the *ancien régime* the word designated a very broad set of undifferentiated judicial and administrative functions and activities—focused principally on the enforcement of laws and regulations and the preservation of public order—rather than an entity, an agency, or an identifiable company of men. On the Paris police in the eighteenth century, its duties, and its relationship to other, rival institutions in the capital, see Jean-Lucien Gay, "L'administration de la capitale entre 1770 et 1789," *Mémoires de la Fédération des Sociétés historiques et archéologiques de Paris et de l'Ile de France*, 8 (1956), pp. 299-370; 9 (1957-58), pp. 283-363; 10 (1959), pp. 181-247; 11 (1960), pp. 363-403; 12 (1961), pp. 135-218; Marc Chassaigne, *La Lieutenance-Générale de Police de Paris* (Paris, 1906); and esp. Alan J. Williams, "The Police of Paris, 1718-1789" (Ph.D. Dissertation, Yale University, 1974). See also Jacques Saint-Germain, *La Reynie et la police au grand siècle* (Paris, 1962); and Marc Raeff, "The Well-Ordered Police State and the Development of Modernity in 17th- and 18th-Century Europe: An Attempt at a Comparative Approach," *American Historical Review*, 80 (1975), pp. 1,221-43.

ence with him for more than a decade.[85] To help ferret out, intimidate, arrest, and prosecute the more suspicious or troublesome enemies of the Bull, the lieutenant of police and his inspectors employed a network of paid spies, informers, and undercover agents (variously known as *mouches*, *sous-inspecteurs*, and *observateurs*).[86] Recruited from many social settings, this force of auxiliaries was established all over Paris, including the area known as the Montagne Sainte-Geneviève, long a Jansenist stronghold, where they insinuated their way into public and private gatherings alike, obtaining intelligence which enabled the police to keep abreast of any hint of discontent. The lieutenant of police and his supporting personnel thus assumed an indispensable role in the crown's efforts to stifle the Jansenist opposition.[87]

By separating Cardinal Noailles from his *anticonstitutionnaire* lower clergy, by applying incessant pressure on other centers of Jansenist resistance, individual and group, and by frequently employing *lettres de cachet* against the unruly and recalcitrant, the authorities hoped to splinter the appellant coalition and thereby bring the party to its knees. By early spring 1727 Fleury seemed to be making progress in his efforts to force a capitulation from Noailles. He had managed to put a halt to the negotiations with Rome by which the cardinal-archbishop had been attempting to obtain papal ratification of twelve articles that "explained" and clarified certain especially ambiguous and disputed propositions in the Bull. But in April, just when Noailles seemed on the verge of retracting his pastoral instruction of 1719 and

[85] On the Fleury-Hérault relationship, see Georges Hardy, *Le Cardinal de Fleury et le mouvement janséniste* (Paris, 1925), pp. 117, 348; and Frances Phipps, "Louis XV: A Style of Kingship, 1710-1757" (Ph.D. Dissertation, The Johns Hopkins University, 1973), p. 176. Hostile contemporaries depicted Hérault as "le grand arc-boutant du parti des molinistes, jésuites, évêques, hypocrites et ambitieux," and as "l'âme damnée, le valet, le bras droit" of Cardinal Fleury (see Claude-Henri Feydeau de Marville, *Lettres de M. de Marville, lieutenant-général de police, au ministre Maurepas (1742-1747)*, ed. A. de Boislisle, 3 vols. [Paris 1896-1905], I, xlii-xliii). His unmediated correspondence with Fleury—from whom he took most of his orders and to whom he generally looked for direction—conferred upon Hérault great authority and independence and enhanced his position vis-à-vis the other elements of the royal government possessing administrative jurisdiction over Paris.

[86] On the use of *mouches* and other such covert observers and informants, see Williams, pp. 160-73, 369-74; Evelyn Cruickshanks, "Public Opinion in Paris in the 1740s: The Reports of the Chevalier de Mouhy," *Bulletin of the Institute for Historical Research*, 27 (1954), pp. 54-68; and Robert Darnton, "The Grub Street Style of Revolution: J.-P. Brissot, Police Spy," *Journal of Modern History*, 40 (1968), p. 320.

[87] For examples of police harassment and persecution, see *NNEE*, Supplément pour 1728, pp. 290-304, *passim*.

disavowing the twelve articles, a brief anonymous pamphlet appeared on the streets of Paris. Although the growing irresolution of the archbishop was already well known, the *Relation fidèle de ce qui s'est passé, tant à Rome que de la part du cardinal de Noailles, sur l'affaire de la Constitution depuis l'exaltation de N.S.P. le pape Benoît XIII* served to expose and at the same time to denounce the devious methods and secret maneuvers by which Cardinal Fleury had sought to take advantage of him. These widely circulated revelations were an embarrassment to the royal government and, much more important, provoked a strong reaction from influential elements among the *anticonstitutionnaire* clergy of Paris.[88]

In mid-May, thirty *curés* from the diocese, alarmed by reports that Cardinal Noailles had reached a secret agreement with Rome and Versailles, addressed him an importunate, but respectful *mémoire*, urging their archbishop to persist in his refusal to accept the Bull.[89] In their *mémoire*, originally composed more than three months earlier but not delivered until after the publication of the *Relation fidèle*, the *curés* insisted that the Bull remained full of ambiguities and errors on crucial doctrinal, spiritual, and ecclesiastical matters. They further contended that the Bull could not be regarded as a universal judgment of the Church, inasmuch as that body had never given the papal decree its unanimous approval. But these *anticonstitutionnaire* priests were not satisfied with merely reaffirming their usual objections to the Bull. Their immediate concerns went beyond the contents of the Bull, beyond official attempts to enforce adherence. The *curés* of Paris, better educated, better organized, and more vocal and contentious than their counterparts elsewhere in France, and possessed of a long tradition of concerted agitation,[90] had increasingly become one of the most formidable and cohesive forces of opposition in the entire kingdom. Yet

[88] See discussion in G. Hardy, pp. 57-59.

[89] *Mémoire présentée par trente curés de la ville de Paris à S. E. Msgr. le cardinal de Noailles leur archevêque, au sujet du bruit qui s'est répandu d'une prochaine acceptation de la bulle Unigenitus.* See also Antoine Dorsanne, *Journal*, 2 vols. (Rome, 1753), II, 386. This was not the first time that rumors of Noailles' capitulation had stirred the *anticonstitutionnaire* Paris clergy to bring pressure to bear on the archbishop. Similar efforts in late 1716 and early 1717—just before the formal appeal to a council—had seen hundreds of ecclesiastics, regular and secular, from throughout the diocese, along with an overwhelming majority of the Sorbonne faculty, join in a letter-writing campaign exhorting Noailles not to submit (see Fourquevaux, II, 184, 239-41, and BN, Salle des Imprimés, LD-4 851, 857, 890, 897).

[90] Paul de Crousaz-Crétat, *Paris sous Louis XIV*, 2 vols. (Paris, 1922-23), II, 23-25; and Jeanne Ferté, *La vie religieuse dans les campagnes parisiennes (1622-1695)* (Paris, 1962), pp. 26-27, 194-95. See also Golden, *passim*.

they were still denied corporate status and hence deprived of the dignity, autonomy, legal standing, and rights and privileges which accompanied such status in the corporate society of the *ancien régime*.[91] The resentment and frustration at their continued subordination to episcopal authority and at their lack of corporate autonomy had been building for years. The *mémoire* provided them with an opportunity to give vent to some of this discontent and to reassert their presumed right of collective assembly. While renewing previous arguments on behalf of a council as the only sure means of reaching an accord on the Bull, they demanded the convocation of a general diocesan synod, to be presided over by their archbishop, in which all the members of the "second order" might legitimately make their voices heard with full authority and on a broad range of issues.[92] In subsequent weeks these disaffected *curés* engaged in an active propaganda campaign in parish after parish, soliciting new ecclesiastical adherents to their *mémoire*, which was now circulating in a printed version throughout the diocese. By early June, over 500 parish clergy, including 120 *curés* and 78 doctors in the Sorbonne, had countersigned a letter accompanying the manifesto, thus giving it even wider distribution and publicity.[93]

As the voices of ecclesiastical opposition grew ever stronger and more strident, the most important diocese in the kingdom seemed on the verge of a priests' revolt not unlike that which had confronted Mazarin in the 1650s. Fleury was understandably alarmed. Rebuffed in his efforts to obtain an *arrêt* from the Parlement of Paris suppressing the *mémoire*, the cardinal-minister turned to the *conseil d'état*. A royal decree of June 14 condemned the manifesto and ordered the lieutenant-general of police to confiscate all copies and to arrest those responsible for composing, printing, or distributing the work. But the council's

[91] See Pierre Blet, "L'ordre du clergé au 17e siècle," *Revue d'histoire de l'Eglise de France*, 54 (1968), p. 16. Legislation issued in 1659 had specifically denied the *curés* the right to constitute themselves into a separate body or to convoke assemblies on their own authority. Such a privilege, it was argued, had never been accorded them and would, in any event, have been an affront to the authority of their episcopal superior.

[92] By the 1720s the diocesan synod had actually been reduced to a meeting of the *curés* of Paris and *faubourgs*, presided over by the *official*, and its competence was narrowly restricted to questions of internal discipline (R. Besnier, "Les synodes du diocèse de Paris de 1715 à 1790," in *Etudes d'histoire du droit canonique dédiées à Gabriel Le Bras*, 2 vols. [Paris, 1965], I, 40). Such calls for rights of assembly were not limited to Paris, of course, and became more audacious as the century wore on (see Préclin, *Les jansénistes*, *passim*; and Taveneaux, *La vie quotidienne*, pp. 118-19).

[93] *NNEE*, Aug. 23, 1727, p. 171.

action did not silence the *curés*. On the contrary, for on September 5 they responded to the government's suppression of their *mémoire* by sending Fleury their *Très-humbles Remontrances au roi*, a tract which was notably assertive, almost defiant, in tone.[94] While denying the police any competence in ecclesiastical matters, the *curés* claimed both the right to address their archbishop with impunity and the duty to defend "the honor and the dignity of the priesthood, the interest of the Truth, and the doctrine of the Church."[95] They went on to reiterate their unequivocal condemnation of the Bull and their adherence to the appeal. Finally, they reaffirmed their independent corporate status and their right of corporate association, while insisting on a more substantial role in the governance of the diocese by means of regular conferences and synodal meetings with their archbishop.

Not surprisingly, when the *Remontrances* of the *curés* appeared in print and began circulating around Paris, Fleury had the work suppressed. In a decree dated October 11, the *conseil d'état* condemned its "spirit of revolt and independence" and denounced the *curés* for their insubordination toward and defiance of royal and ecclesiastical authority in claiming "to form a corporate body with the right to present remonstrances to the king."[96] This time the *curés*, who pretended to disavow the tract, decided not to offer a direct reply. Having resolutely and audaciously made their protests known to both their archbishop and their king, the priests did not choose to pursue this matter any further—at least not for the present. In any case, other developments had in the meantime already overtaken them.

As if the defiant actions of the Paris *curés* were not challenge enough for Cardinal Fleury, the year 1727 brought still other difficulties. In January the septuagenarian Bishop Jean Soanen of Senez, one of the four original appellants, widely revered as one of the most pious and virtuous of French prelates, published an incendiary pastoral instruction which he had originally delivered the previous August.[97] In his

[94] *Les très-humbles Remontrances des curés de Paris qui ont présenté à Son Eminence Msgr. le cardinal de Noailles un Mémoire . . . , lequel a été supprimé par Arrêt du Conseil d'Etat du roi. . . .* Excerpts from the text and discussion in Dorsanne, II, 390-93.

[95] *Ibid.*, p. 390.

[96] See brief discussion of *arrêt* in Mathieu Marais, *Journal et mémoires sur la Régence et le règne de Louis XV (1715-1737)*, ed. A. M. de Lescure, 4 vols. (Paris, 1863-68), III, 255 (Oct. 13, 1727).

[97] *Instruction pastorale de monseigneur l'évêque de Senez, dans laquelle, à l'occasion des bruits qui se sont répandus de sa mort, il rend son clergé et son peuple dépositaires de ses derniers sentiments sur les contestations qui agitent l'Eglise* (Paris, 1727).

instruction, which was to serve as a kind of personal spiritual testament, Soanen issued a blistering denunciation of the bull *Unigenitus* and even went so far as to exhort the faithful to read Quesnel's proscribed work. As Noailles had come more and more to submit to Fleury, the venerable Soanen, along with his fellow controversialist and colleague in the appeal, Bishop Colbert of Montpellier, had assumed a position of symbolic leadership within the *anticonstitutionnaire* party. The publication of this latest pastoral instruction, circulated far beyond the small, remote, and inconsequential diocese of Senez, reopened hostilities and led to the resumption of a bitter pamphlet war throughout France.[98] Eager to punish Soanen for his temerity and to teach all the appellants a memorable lesson, Cardinal Fleury advised the bishop's metropolitan, the notorious *constitutionnaire* Archbishop Tencin of Embrun, to convoke a provincial council. The Council of Embrun, which opened in mid-August, lasted for a month and a half and handed down a very harsh sentence. It severely condemned Soanen and suspended him from his episcopal functions. A *lettre de cachet* issued at Versailles permanently exiled the deposed bishop to the monastery of Chaise-Dieu in the Auvergne. What is more, in addition to passing sentence on Soanen, the council asserted flatly that the bull *Unigenitus* was a "dogmatic judgment of the Church" and as such not subject to qualification or appeal. In a brief of December 17, 1727, the pope eagerly confirmed these decisions.

From the standpoint of reestablishing religious peace, the Council of Embrun proved a serious blunder, for its findings were provocative in the extreme and served mainly to exacerbate an already difficult situation, especially in Paris. As on previous occasions, the *anticonstitutionnaire* reactions, originating from several quarters, were swift and sharp. Ignoring the strict censorship laws, Jansenist propagandists produced a new barrage of pamphlets. In a polemical atmosphere of intense and turbulent agitation, they attempted to win over public sympathy, in

[98] For what follows see Ch. de Labriolle, "Le concile d'Embrun de 1727, révélateur de la société du 18ᵉ siècle," *Bulletin de la Société d'études des Hautes-Alpes* (1966), pp. 143-56; Marcel Laurent, "Jean Soanen, évêque de Senez, devant le 'Concile' d'Embrun (1727)," *Revue d'Auvergne*, 82 (1968), pp. 94-112; Charles Juge-Chapsal, "L'épiscopat de Jean Soanen," *Bulletin historique et scientifique de l'Auvergne*, 75 (1955), pp. 33-67; Agnès de la Gorce, "Joute d'évêques à Embrun en 1727," *Miroir de l'histoire*, No. 38 (March 1953), pp. 167-72; abbé L. Ventre, "A propos d'un centenaire, 1740-1940: Jean Soanen, évêque janséniste de Senez," *Bulletin de la Société scientifique et littéraire des Basses-Alpes*, 28 (1940-41), pp. 7-50, 181-95, 291-316; 29 (1942), pp. 40-53, 158-65; Jean Carreyre, "Le Concile d'Embrun (1727-1728)," *Revue des questions historiques*, 14 (1929), pp. 47-106, 318-67; and Jean Sareil, *Les Tencin* (Geneva, 1969), pp. 157-83.

part by portraying themselves as an unjustly persecuted sect.[99] In innumerable tracts, *chansons frondeuses*, prayers, canticles, and hymns composed on Soanen's behalf, they emphasized the bishop's undoubted moral authority and dedication, his ascetic manner, and his indefatigable religious zeal. Contemporary engravings depicted him with the nimbus of a haloed martyr, and Soanen began referring to himself as "the prisoner of Jesus Christ." Utilizing caricatures, epigrams, and other satirical media, Soanen's supporters dubbed the council which had condemned and persecuted him the *Brigandage* or *Conciliabule* of Embrun and reviled and ridiculed its members, especially Tencin.[100] The severity of the decision against Soanen led to accusations that the councilors had acted arbitrarily and as tools of the Jesuits. The spirited and defiant *anticonstitutionnaire* reaction to the council was an attack that at once encompassed the Bull, the pope, the king, and Fleury, in addition to the direct perpetrators of the supposed *brigandage*. As usual, Fleury responded with police measures, instructing Hérault to round up the guilty parties and toss them into the Bastille.

To escape the eyes of the censors and to continue to spread their message of opposition, the *anticonstitutionnaires* had to find new ways of cleverly concealing and disseminating the ideas and information of their party. For years they had been making use of a fairly extensive system of pseudonymous and anonymous correspondence and of private news sheets, and would continue to do so,[101] but they found such exclusive exchanges of letters and manuscripts among fellow *amis de la Vérité* to be a limited and inexpedient method for making an impact on contemporary religious affairs. Likewise, though they had managed to publish an extraordinary number of polemical tracts and pamphlets in opposition to the dreaded bull *Unigenitus*, their various propaganda pieces had remained for the most part but ephemeral *livres de circonstance*, appearing irregularly, on diverse subjects, and without any continuity of themes or uniformity of opinions; moreover, they were addressed primarily to the educated elite of the *anticonstitutionnaire*

---

[99] With the possible exception of the destruction of Port-Royal, the Council of Embrun contributed more than any other previous event to "rendre le jansénisme populaire et le faire pénétrer, ce qui n'était jamais arrivé au temps de Port-Royal, dans les couches profondes de la société française" (Gazier, *Histoire générale*, I, 272).

[100] For an example of the scurrilous songs produced for the occasion, see Labriolle, p. 150; see also Emile Raunié (ed.), *Chansonnier historique du 18ᵉ siècle*, 10 vols. (Paris, 1879-84), V, 111-22, 166-67. Raunié also provides a sample of songs composed in defense of the council (*ibid.*, pp. 133-41).

[101] See Taveneaux, *La vie quotidienne*, pp. 227-34. Cf. Hérault to Fleury, November 1726, in Ravaisson, XIV, 73.

party, persons who were already committed to the appellant cause. Largely in response to the Embrun affair, therefore, a group of Paris appellants, indignant at the treatment of Bishop Soanen and anxious to present their views to a wider audience, embarked on a project designed to be far more effective—and daring—than private correspondence or occasional treatises in presenting their point of view to the public at large. In February 1728, with the financial backing of the wealthy and influential brothers Desessarts, this group undertook the publication of a clandestine journal, the *Nouvelles ecclésiastiques, ou Mémoires pour servir à l'histoire de la Constitution "Unigenitus."*[102] It was the avowedly propagandistic aim of the directors of the new Paris-based weekly to overcome the public's indifference to the vital issues associated with the notorious bull *Unigenitus* and to arouse as many of the faithful as possible to an awareness of the "great evils of the Church" which were "the bitter fruit" of the papal decree.[103] The message of the *Nouvelles ecclésiastiques* was ostensibly intended even for the simple faithful and priced accordingly at only three *sous* per issue. The journal was to serve as a kind of clearinghouse on the moral, theological, spiritual, and ecclesiastical issues of the day, receiving opinion and information and diffusing them to thousands of interested readers throughout the kingdom. It contained all the latest news about the activities of the *anticonstitutionnaire* party (its adherents depicted as the only true guardians of religious orthodoxy in France) as well as reviews of important books and theses and frequent reports of Jesuit and other *constitutionnaire* "misdeeds." Despite the staunchly partisan character and polemical tone of the journal, it remained a generally accurate and reliable source for information on the development of eighteenth-century ecclesiastical politics.

The *Nouvellistes'* entire operation, from composition to printing to distribution, eventually came to depend on a vast network of friends and accomplices all over Paris and in other parts of France who were

---

[102] For what follows, see Françoise Bontoux, *'Nouvelles ecclésiastiques,' parlement de Paris et parlementaires (1730-1762)* (Diplôme d'études supérieures d'histoire, Paris, 1955); *idem*, "Paris janséniste au 18e siècle: *Les Nouvelles ecclésiastiques*," *Mémoires de la Fédération des Sociétés historiques et archéologiques de Paris et de l'Ile de France*, 7 (1955), pp. 205-20; Cyril B. O'Keefe, *Contemporary Reactions to the Enlightenment, 1728-1762* (Geneva-Paris, 1974), pp. 9-11; and Taveneaux, *La vie quotidienne*, pp. 234-40. Cf. Plongeron, "Une image de l'Eglise." Most of those involved in establishing the journal had some association, either as students or as instructors, with the Oratorian seminary of Saint-Magloire.

[103] *NNEE*, "Preliminary Discourse" (i.e., editorial) for 1728, pp. 1-3. See also *ibid.*, Feb. 24, 1731, pp. 37-38; and Nicolas Le Gros, *Discours sur les "Nouvelles ecclésiastiques"* (1735), p. 1.

all in secret and active collaboration. The continued success of the enterprise was the result of many factors: the ingenuity and audacity of unidentified "informants" or "correspondents," who brought or smuggled their manuscript copy to the editor and his anonymous aides; the complicity of numerous printers courageous enough to risk their livelihoods; the multiplicity of secret presses, many of them small and easily portable, located in back rooms and hidden alcoves, in barns, in cellars, and even in boats docked along the Seine; and a clever and intricately decentralized system of circulation, involving an underground of women, children, and priests as colporteurs and messengers. By means of such ploys and devices the crusading journal was able to maintain regular, almost uninterrupted weekly service and to avoid the interference of Fleury, Hérault, and their successors for almost three-quarters of a century—one of the marvels of clandestine printing under the *ancien régime*. In open violation of the laws, the forbidden paper was circulated in the streets of Paris and beyond, reaching to the most isolated religious communities and obscure villages in provincial France and joining together all who aspired to be "defenders of the Truth." The government's repeated attempts to outlaw this "subversive" *organe de combat*, beginning with the royal declaration of May 29, 1728, met with embarrassingly little success. For every writer or colporteur arrested, for every printing press confiscated or destroyed, there were several replacements readily available. The authorities were never even able to discover the identity of the editor, the outspoken and energetic Jacques Fontaine de la Roche, who supervised the operation from late 1728 and throughout this period, or to penetrate the intricate code system by which he kept it functioning so smoothly. As a result of de la Roche's dedicated efforts and those of his countless collaborators, the *Nouvelles ecclésiastiques* quickly became one of the most effective polemical weapons available to the *anticonstitutionnaires* in their counteroffensive against the Council of Embrun and in subsequent battles waged against the *constitutionnaire* forces in Church and State.

While the *Nouvellistes* were launching their campaign against the authorities responsible for Embrun, there was continued agitation against the *brigandage* from still other quarters. Some 1,500 to 2,000 ecclesiastics, most of them members of the lower clergy, signed petitions against the council.[104] At the same time, a group of twelve bishops, headed by Cardinal Noailles, issued its own public protest against the sentencing of Soanen. In an indignant letter addressed to the king

[104] Préclin, *Les jansénistes*, p. 123.

in late October 1727 and published the following March, they complained that the council, by denouncing a French bishop in the name of ultramontane doctrines, had violated "the most sacred laws and most holy liberties of the realm."[105] In Paris, where more than eight hundred priests signed petitions on behalf of Soanen, thirty-two *curés* wrote Noailles a public letter, applauding him and his eleven episcopal colleagues for "a wise and necessary action."[106] The king returned the bishops' letter, however, and severely rebuked them for their audacity and misplaced zeal. Undaunted, they replied with a second letter. This time the government responded with *lettres de cachet* which exiled them all to their respective dioceses. Though several of them persisted in their protests, most of the prelates, including Noailles, were finally prevailed upon to retract their signatures from the earlier letters to the king.[107]

In the meantime, perhaps the strongest and most notable opposition to the council—and indirectly to Fleury's religious policies—came from a group of staunchly Gallican *avocats* in the Parlement of Paris, a group which included some of the most experienced and erudite members of the bar, honored and respected by their colleagues and closely allied with several prominent Jansenist theologians.[108] A writ of the *conseil d'état*, issued even before Embrun, had forbidden the magistrates in the sovereign court to receive any *appels comme d'abus* against decisions of the council; but the writ did not keep the *avocats* from voicing their own protests. On October 30, 1727, fifty of them signed a legal *Consultation* which denounced the verdict against Soanen as null and void on the grounds of procedural irregularities, the council's incompetence to judge, and the absolute innocence of the accused.[109] The *avocats*, who were establishing themselves as spokesmen for the Gallican position and as defenders of persecuted *anticonstitutionnaires*, understood the far-reaching implications of the council's decisions, particularly its conclusions regarding the Bull. Marshaling an array of legal and scriptural arguments, they responded by denying

---

[105] *Lettre de 12 évêques au roi, pour la défense de M. l'évêque de Senez condamné par le saint Concile d'Ambrun.*

[106] *Lettre de 32 curés de la ville, faubourgs et banlieue de Paris à S. Em. monseigneur le cardinal de Noailles (16 mars 1728).* Text and discussion in Dorsanne, II, 426-27; cf. *NNEE*, April 24, 1728, p. 59, and June 3, 1728, pp. 90-91.

[107] Dorsanne, II, 437-42.

[108] Principally, Laurent Boursier and Nicolas Petitpied, who helped compose a number of the *avocats'* tracts (Préclin, *Les jansénistes*, pp. 119-20, 122).

[109] *Consultation de MM. les avocats du parlement de Paris, au sujet du jugement rendu à Ambrun contre M. l'évêque de Senez.* Excerpts and discussion in Parguez, pp. 66-74.

the assertion that *Unigenitus* was a law of the Church and insisting on the legitimacy and canonicity of the appeal. The *Consultation*, which appeared originally in manuscript, went through four editions in published form and stirred up a stormy controversy of its own. A papal brief condemned the work on June 9, 1728, as did a special assembly of *constitutionnaire* prelates meeting in Paris.[110] Finally, when the Parlement of Paris refused to suppress the *consultation* (with which they no doubt felt great sympathy), Fleury obtained yet another decree from the *conseil d'état* on July 3, 1728.[111] But from the cardinal-minister's point of view the damage had already been done, for the *avocats* had not only issued a vigorous reassertion of the Gallican position but had also staked out their claim to an active and conspicuous role in contemporary ecclesiastical politics, thereby setting a precedent for subsequent interventions on behalf of the Jansenist cause.[112] What is more, in the process, their action had served to bring the debates of ecclesiastical politics back into the purview of the magistrates in the Parlement of Paris, who were increasingly prepared to follow the lead of their influential professional colleagues responsible for pleading cases before the court. Although the judges did not choose to intervene at this time, they were to find in the writings of the *avocats* much of the legal foundation upon which they would establish their own judicial opinions on the ecclesiastical controversies of the day.

Despite these apparent setbacks, Fleury's staunch refusal to accommodate *anticonstitutionnaire* demands, supported by a series of re-

[110] In a letter to the king written on May 4, 1728, twenty-six bishops accused the *avocats* of regarding the Church "comme une république populaire dont toute l'authorité législative et coactive réside dans la société entière et dans le consentement exprès ou présumé de la multitude" (cited by Préclin, *Les jansenistes*, p. 121). Denouncing the pretensions of the "second order," the bishops countered these "subversive views" with the argument that spiritual authority resided exclusively in the episcopate, who vested the priests with the keys in the ceremony of ordination.

[111] Edmond-Jean-François Barbier, *Chronique de la régence et du règne de Louis XV (1718-1763)*, 8 vols. [Paris, 1857], II, 36 [February 1728]). A contemporary song, "Sur la Consultation des avocats au sujet du concile d'Embrun," ridiculed the lawyers for presuming to take the role of theologians, a role that was allegedly beyond their intellectual capacity and their jurisdictional competence (*ibid.*, pp. 32-35).

[112] As Fleury later confided to Pope Clement XII on the *avocats*, ". . . comme ils sont d'ordinaire plus instruits que le commun des magistrats, ils ont pris l'ascendant sur eux et sont devenus les maîtres absolus du Parlement" (Oct. 23, 1730, AAE, C.P., Rome, MS 715, fols. 400ff.). For their role in the midcentury struggles with the Society of Jesus, see Van Kley.

sounding royal, papal, and episcopal condemnations of the dissenters, served to put an immediate, if only temporary, halt to their open resistance to the Council of Embrun. Indeed, for all his substantial difficulties with *curés*, *avocats*, and a handful of bishops, the cardinal-minister had still been making considerable progress with his policy of trying to win over important individuals and groups from the enemy. In an edict of May 1728, the government renewed the harsh restrictions on appellant publications, charging the authors of such tracts with displaying a lack of respect for the pope and the bishops.[113] Numerous arrests followed in the wake of this decree. At the same time, a significant number of clergy was forced, under penalty of dismissal, to sign the Formulary and submit to the Bull. But Fleury's crowning achievement, not without its own problems, was the apparent conversion of Cardinal Noailles.[114]

On October 11, 1728, Noailles, aged and sick, long pressed by Fleury and besieged by confidential friends and officious relatives, retracted his pastoral instruction of 1719 and everything else he had published in opposition to the Bull and allowed a "pure and simple" acceptance of *Unigenitus* to appear in his name.[115] A month later the formal inscription of the archbishop's *mandement* in the diocesan registers seemingly made his acceptance official.[116] By the time he died on May 4, 1729, Noailles had apparently effected a final reconciliation with the Holy See, though no one ever knew for certain whether he had actually persevered in his opposition to the end.[117] The archbishop's death was

[113] See Isambert, xxi, 312-15.

[114] For details on the long and tortuous discussions between Noailles and various representatives of the cardinal-minister, see Barbier, II, 54-56 (October 1728), *et passim*; Dorsanne, II, 441-48; and Fourquevaux, II, 418-26. For an analysis of these developments see G. Hardy, esp. pp. 114-29.

[115] *Mandement de S. E. monseigneur le cardinal de Noailles, archevêque de Paris, pour l'acceptation et publication de la constitution de N.-S.-P. le pape Clément XI, du 8 septembre 1713.* On the protracted negotiations to get Noailles' *mandement* issued, see AAE, M&D, France, MS 1261, *passim*; MS 1262, fols. 1-125; MS 1263, fols. 74-197, 200-201; and MS 1264, *passim*.

[116] Between October and November, Fleury had been busily working to replace various diocesan officials who had all been Noailles' appointees and had remained loyal Gallicans strongly committed to the appeal and very much opposed to their archbishop's submission. It became necessary, therefore, for Fleury to find an excuse for replacing them with ecclesiastics who would do his bidding. One by one he revoked their charges and made new appointments, all of them *constitutionnaires* (Fourquevaux, II, 425-26; *NNEE*, Dec. 4, 1728, pp. 247-49).

[117] Disputes about Noailles' final position regarding the Bull continued to rage for many months after the cardinal-archbishop's death. See *NNEE*, Nov. 28, 1729, pp. 203-204; AAE, M&D, France, MS 1264, fols. 231-58, 303-304; Fourquevaux II, 418, 423-25.

not the occasion for deep or prolonged mourning.[118] Ever since his arrival in Paris in 1695, Noailles had found himself caught in the cross-currents of contemporary religious politics, repeatedly forced to choose sides on an endless series of ecclesiastical controversies. Naturally mild of temperament and disposition, occasionally vacillating and unclear about what to do, the cardinal-archbishop must have possessed a great deal of resilience—and considerable political skills—to have survived in this tense atmosphere for so long. To friends and enemies alike, however, he had frequently given the impression of timorousness, of being weak in his resolves—unable to act with firmness and decision and incapable of resisting political pressures for any length of time. Yet despite his reputation for constant equivocation and interminable wavering,[119] Noailles had remained throughout his career a staunch defender of the Gallican liberties and, by the influence of his see and the prestige of his name, had probably contributed as much as any of the other *anticonstitutionnaire* bishops to prolonging the resistance to the Bull and to the ecclesiastical policies of Cardinal Fleury. In a certain sense, of course, his conversion had by this time become more or less an afterthought of little consequence. But Noailles' apparent capitulation and subsequent death had considerable symbolic significance. With his loss, the public submission of several more appellant bishops, the exile of Soanen, and the succession of *constitutionnaire* prelates to formerly Jansenist sees, episcopal opposition, which had originally been in the forefront of the appeal, had all but come to an end. Though other formidable bastions of dissent still remained, especially in clerical and legal-judicial circles in Paris, and though Noailles' rather inconclusive reconciliation with the Holy See by no means relieved the underlying stresses and tensions within the diocese, the appointment of a loyal *acceptant* archbishop to this vital see was expected to remedy even those problems before too long.

A NEW ARCHBISHOP IN PARIS

In mid-May a courier arrived at Versailles bearing a letter for Cardinal Fleury from his long-time friend and fellow septuagenarian, Archbishop

[118] The *NNEE* provided only a brief and not terribly laudatory obituary on the cardinal-archbishop (May 9, 1729, p. 62).

[119] Noailles' vacillations were memorialized in a piece of typical Parisian doggerel: "Ci-gît Louis Cahin-Caha/ Qui dévotement appela;/ De oui, de non s'entortilla;/ Puis dit ceci, puis dit cela;/ Perdit la tête et s'en alla" (cited by Henri Carré, *Le règne de Louis XV (1715-1774)*, Vol. VIII² of *Histoire de France depuis les origines jusqu'à la Révolution*, ed. Ernest Lavisse, 9 vols. [Paris, 1903-11], p. 112). Cf. similar satirical verses in Raunié, v, 149-60, 170-71.

Vintimille of Aix. Having just learned that Cardinal Noailles was near death, and being mindful of the religious turmoil that had been disturbing the capital for years, Vintimille wrote to advise Fleury regarding the appointment of a successor to the embattled Paris see. What is needed, he recommended, is "someone of an age to be able to occupy the position for some time, firm in his faith, but extremely wise and prudent, and attentive to profit from your salutary counsel, in order that Your Eminence may have more peace and tranquility in Church affairs than heretofore."[120] It is clear from the tone and contents of this letter and from his subsequent behavior that Vintimille was certainly not touting himself for the vacancy. Ironically, however, only five days earlier, in a letter which presumably crossed Vintimille's in the post, an exultant Cardinal Fleury had already notified Vintimille that

> the Cardinal de Noailles died tonight . . . and as soon as the King learned this news, he named you . . . as the person most capable of filling this important position.
>
> I wish you heartfelt congratulations on your appointment. What pleases me most is that we will be able to finish our last days together, after having spent the better part of our lives in the closest friendship. Do not be frightened by the burden. I am persuaded that with your wisdom and with the support of the King you will acquit yourself with success. . . . I await your arrival impatiently.[121]

But Vintimille must have had some qualms about accepting the appointment, for on May 16 Fleury found it necessary to write again in an effort to overcome his friend's reservations. Appealing to Vintimille's duty "to serve the Church and the King" and to "support the good cause," the cardinal-minister succeeded in persuading him to leave his relatively peaceful see in Provence and take up the new post.[122] Even as he began preparations for the long journey north, Vintimille no doubt continued to harbor misgivings about his fateful decision, about the awesome responsibilities he had agreed to assume, and about his own strength and capacity to handle the grave difficulties that would soon confront him.

The new archbishop-elect, who belonged to an illustrious family originally from Italy,[123] had long been a man of some influence within

---

[120] May 9, 1729, BM, MS 2357, pp. 12-13.

[121] May 4, 1729, *ibid.*, pp. 13-14; cf. Villars, v, 173.

[122] BM, MS 2357, pp. 14-15.

[123] According to G. Hardy, Charles-Gaspard-Guillaume de Vintimille du Luc

the Gallican Church. An experienced ecclesiastical politician, Vintimille had held the confidence of a succession of royal governments and been invited to attend every General Assembly and Extraordinary Assembly of the Clergy convoked for the past half-century—a testimony not only to his longevity but also to his capacity to remain throughout his career well in the mainstream of official Church policy. In his long tenure as bishop of Marseille and then archbishop of Aix, he had also acquired the reputation of being a capable administrator, with an ability to attract loyal and dedicated subordinates to help govern the diocese.[124]

But it was more than friendship, family connections, or political and administrative skills which had commended Vintimille to Cardinal Fleury. What especially inclined the cardinal-minister to name Vintimille to the archbishopric of Paris were the prelate's personal qualities and, above all, his religious views. By temperament and outlook he appeared to be an excellent choice. According to various contemporary estimates, Vintimille was an amiable and pleasant sort, a moderate, and a conciliator. Though he had displayed a certain timidity in the face of theological disputes and an inclination to shrink away from confrontations of any sort, Vintimille had also shown that he was willing and able to take strong, rigorous action when necessary. Ideologically as well, Vintimille seemed a reasonably good candidate for accomplishing the government's goal of pacifying the diocese of Paris. The ecclesiastical philosophy of the new archbishop very much resembled that of his friend Fleury. Like the cardinal-minister, he had a deep and abiding concern with reestablishing peace and stability in the Church, without at the same time being a fanatic in his defense of the Bull or of the *constitutionnaire* cause.[125] Like Fleury, too, Vintimille held an exalted view of episcopal authority, which he seemed prepared to defend against clerical and parlementary challenges. Order and subordination were his principal watchwords: the Church was a society in which an obedient submission to the decisions of the hierarchy was the first and most important duty of every Christian.

But congeniality of outlook with the king's first minister would obviously not be sufficient for the major task Vintimille had now agreed to assume. Whether he was indeed emotionally equipped or

---

"s'apparentait aux Conrad, empereurs et rois d'Italie et aux Lascaris, empereurs de Constantinople" (p. 171).

[124] On Vintimille's career in Marseille and especially in Aix, see *NNEE*, Oct. 30, 1729, pp. 187-88; and Paul Ardoin, *La bulle Unigenitus dans les diocèses d'Aix, Arles, Marseille, Fréjus, Toulon*, 2 vols. (Marseille, 1936), I, 45-46, *et passim*.

[125] *NNEE*, Feb. 22, 1729, pp. 15-16.

mentally prepared for the gruelling battles in which he would shortly find himself embroiled remained uncertain, for his capacity to handle a disaffected parish clergy and other powerful dissidents had never really been tested. Nevertheless, Cardinal Fleury was hopeful that Vintimille's character and personal qualities—"his moderation, his experience in Church government, and his affability"—might bring a "mild and peaceful rule" to the diocese and put an end to the "dangerous intrigues" which had been disrupting the capital.[126]

The succession of Fleury's creature to his new archiepiscopal see marked the beginning of a renewed assault on the Jansenists in Paris. Even before Vintimille's arrival in the city, he and the cardinal-minister had begun to discuss plans for taking concerted action to purge the diocese of these "troublesome fanatics."[127] Proceeding firmly but cautiously, Vintimille attempted, with Fleury's assistance and encouragement, to make substantial inroads among the *anticonstitutionnaires*. Early in September, as if to commemorate Vintimille's own formal installation, the Chapter of Notre-Dame became the first of several major corporate religious bodies in Paris to withdraw its appeal and adhere to the Bull, which a majority of its members agreed to accept "purely and simply."[128] Buoyed by the almost complete submission of the Chapter and assured of the support of his metropolitan church, Vintimille turned to the much more difficult task of subduing the diocese itself. On September 29, 1729, he published his first ordinance and pastoral instruction, in which he sought to persuade his new flock to accept *Unigenitus*.[129] He portrayed the Bull as an innocuous document, perfectly consonant with Catholic tradition and offensive neither to the purity of dogma and morals nor to the liberties of the Gallican Church. Only the factious, he insisted, continued to resist, with the result that all discipline and order were lost, the pope was insulted, the authority of bishops was ignored, and a spirit of hatred, insubordi-

126 Fleury to the Dean of the Chapter of Notre-Dame, May 5, 1729, cited *ibid.*, Sept. 30, 1729, p. 166.

127 Fleury to Vintimille, Aug. 19, 1729, BM, MS 2357, p. 20. The two friends had already embarked on a regular correspondence that was to continue throughout most of their remaining years and which happily provides the historian with a rare firsthand glimpse into the discussion and formulation of official ecclesiastical policy during this turbulent period.

128 AAE, M&D, Fonds divers (Rome), MS 58, fols. 69-75. See also *NNEE*, Sept. 15, 1729, pp. 152-53. The *Nouvellistes'* report indicates that there was a vocal minority in the Chapter who remained adamantly opposed to the Bull. Cf. Vintimille to Fleury, Nov. 17, 1729, BM, MS 2357, pp. 27-29, and Fleury to Vintimille, Nov. 17, 1729, *ibid.*, pp. 30-31.

129 *Ordonnance et instruction pastorale de monseigneur l'archevêque de Paris, au sujet de la constitution "Unigenitus."*

nation, and revolt was rampant. Despite the querulous and accusatory character of certain passages, the tone of the pastoral letter was basically moderate and conciliatory.[130] The problem, however, was to ensure that the archbishop's ordinance obtained a favorable reception throughout the diocese.

In late October, Fleury, Dean of the Sorbonne since Noailles' death, forced the Faculty of Theology to submit to Vintimille's pastoral instruction by threatening with expulsion all doctors who had adhered to the renewed appeal since the royal declaration of August 4, 1720, withdrawn their signatures of the Formulary or signed it with the prohibited reservations (the famous "respectful silence"), or supported the cause of the deposed Bishop Soanen. Armed with *lettres de cachet*, the syndic Romigny (another Fleury creature) obtained the dismissal from the Faculty's councils of forty-eight refractory doctors.[131] By the end of the year, threatened with further intimidation and reprisals, the most prestigious theological faculty in France had renewed its original acceptance of 1714 as a "free, legitimate, and authoritative act." While recognizing the Bull as "a dogmatic judgment of the universal Church," it formally revoked and disavowed the appeal of 1717 and barred from its ranks all who still refused to submit. The rump faculty also addressed a circular letter to the other universities in the kingdom, notifying them of these decisions and encouraging them to follow suit.

Even as the *anticonstitutionnaires* were deploring the Sorbonne's purge and capitulation, the authorities were taking similar repressive measures against some of the recalcitrant religious orders and congregations. In this area, as in other matters of ecclesiastical discipline, Vintimille and Fleury worked in close collaboration with the lieutenant-general of police, René Hérault, whom the *Nouvelles ecclésiastiques* contemptuously described as the archbishop's "faithful coadjutor."[132]

---

[130] *Too* moderate and conciliatory, according to the view in some quarters. Although the pope congratulated Vintimille "pour son zèle et le succès de sa vigilance pastorale à ramener les errans à la connoissance de la vérité, et à l'obéissance qui est due à la Constitution *Unigenitus*" (*NNEE*, January 1730, pp. 19-20), the archbishop's inclusion of the fairly strong Gallican statement that "La bulle est devenue loi de l'Eglise par l'approbation du corps des pasteurs," prevented his pastoral instruction from receiving formal papal approval (see Eugène Grisselle, "Vers la paix de l'Eglise de France, d'après des lettres inédites du négociateur le cardinal de Polignac (1725-1732)," *Revue d'histoire de l'Eglise de France*, 2 [1917], p. 417).

[131] Jourdain, II, 351-52; Barbier, II, 83-84 (November 1729).

[132] Nov. 28, 1729, p. 204; cf. Dorsanne, II, 495-96. Remarkably enough, Hérault's term as lieutenant of police (1725-40) and Vintimille's as archbishop (1729-46) coincided roughly with each other and with Fleury's tenure of power (1726-43).

Under Hérault's direction, the police had continued to harass and arrest numerous Jansenist priests.[133] But Hérault himself had also been delegated several special *ad hoc* assignments of his own. With the police lieutenant acting as representative of the royal council (*commissaire du conseil*) and authorized to intervene in meetings of various chapters-general, *constitutionnaire* superiors were installed in suspect orders and appellants were systematically excluded from leading roles in congregational assemblies.[134] At the same time, the government undertook to suspend or close down a number of Jansenist *collèges* and seminaries, transferring the direction of these institutions to *acceptant* administrators and arresting or dispersing their faculty and students.[135] Like the "corrupted" religious orders and congregations, which Fleury aimed at "changing, weakening, and diminishing as much as possible,"[136] the *collèges* and seminaries had provided fertile soil for the training and recruitment of numerous priests and confessors of *anticonstitutionnaire* outlook and had served to expand the network of active collaborators in the publication and distribution of the *Nouvelles ecclésiastiques*.[137] By "gradually destroying all the schools where error is taught," the cardinal-minister hoped to reduce the party's institutional base and finally "arrest the progress of the [Jansenist] malady."[138]

With the opponents of the Bull having lost most of their formerly "impregnable forts" to the enemy camp, and with appellant ecclesiastical ranks thereby markedly depleted, *anticonstitutionnaire* prospects

[133] *NNEE*, Feb. 25, 1729, pp. 17-18; March 15, 1729, pp. 30-32; April 4, 1729, p. 61; May 9, 1729, pp. 62-63; July 10, 1729, p. 113. This represents only a portion of the arrests and acts of harassment reported by the *Nouvellistes* in 1729 alone.

[134] On the interference with the Oratory's meeting at Saint-Honoré, see *ibid.*, Sept. 20, 1729, pp. 159-61, and Sept. 30, 1729, p. 168. Several excluded Oratorian fathers countered with a protest manifesto: *Mémoire dressé par les députés de l'Oratoire exclus, . . . où l'on prouve la nullité des assemblées générales de l'Oratoire depuis 1723*. On the earlier harassment of the Fathers of the Christian Doctrine, see *NNEE*, July 1 and 20, 1729, pp. 107-108, 121-25. Cf. discussion in G. Hardy, pp. 182-84.

[135] *NNEE*, Oct. 9 and 26, 1730, pp. 220, 225-32; Fourquevaux, II, 452. Cf. Dainville, pp. 115-20; Joseph Dedieu, "Le désarroi janséniste pendant la période du quesnellisme," in *Introduction aux études d'histoire ecclésiastique locale*, ed. Victor Carrière, 3 vols. (Paris, 1934-40), III, 569-73; and C. Gazier, "Un apôtre oublié du 17e siècle: Claude Bernard et le Séminaire des Trente-Trois," *Le Correspondant*, 314 (1929), pp. 906-908.

[136] Fleury to Pope Clement XII, Oct. 23, 1730, AAE, C.P., Rome, MS 715, fols. 400ff.

[137] Dedieu, "Désarroi janséniste," III, 567-73; Préclin, *Les jansénistes*, pp. 87, 215-17.

[138] Fleury to Clement XII, Oct. 23, 1730, AAE, C.P., Rome, MS 715, fols. 400ff.

now appeared bleaker than ever.[139] Under the circumstances, Cardinal Fleury could hardly be blamed for expressing cautious optimism about this turn of events.[140] From the viewpoint of the established authorities, spiritual as well as secular, the situation looked most encouraging. At last religious peace seemed about to be restored in Paris. Yet Fleury was seriously mistaken if he interpreted the series of recent successes as proof that total victory was imminent. Even his own archbishop already seemed to have told him otherwise. Vintimille's pastoral letter of September 29, which contained a gloomy portrait of conditions in his diocese, should have dispelled any mood of overconfidence on Fleury's part. While the archbishop acknowledged with great satisfaction that many opponents of the Bull had indeed returned to the fold, he was at the same time greatly concerned that large numbers obstinately continued to remain outside. He was also appalled at the breakdown of discipline and loss of respect for episcopal and papal authority among his distracted and disobedient flock, much of which he traced to the recent defiant actions and audacious statements of appellant parish priests. Indeed, the capacity of the *anticonstitution-naire* movement in Paris to survive the massive onslaught from civil and religious authorities depended more than ever on the efforts of the lower clergy, as the focus of resistance to the Bull shifted more and more to the parish level. Although these priests were now without the benign indulgence of a sympathetic archbishop and had lost the support of many of the principal corporate religious bodies in Paris, their voices were far from silenced. As Vintimille quickly discovered to his profound regret, these resurgent priests, especially the appellant *curés* among them, were far less tractable than the Chapter of Notre-Dame, the Faculty of Theology, and the other ecclesiastical bodies in Paris had been.

Led by a group of outspoken militants, the *curés* were well aware of the considerable potential power they had to wield, so long as they acted in concert, coordinated a common strategy, and maintained a united front—even if it was illegal for them to do so. A substantial number of these priests refused unequivocally to renounce their adherence to the appeal. On September 23, within three weeks of Vintimille's formal installation, and more than two weeks before the actual appearance of his first ordinance and pastoral instruction, a deputation of five *curés* personally delivered an importunate letter to their new

[139] *NNEE*, Dec. 6, 1720, p. 207.

[140] See Fleury to Cardinal Corradini, Sept. 13, 1729, AAE, M&D, Fonds divers (Rome), MS 58, fols. 81-91.

superior.[141] In their letter, also countersigned by some two dozen of their colleagues, the *curés* repeated the usual attacks on the Bull for its alleged violations of Christian morality and its supposed contravention of the doctrines of the Church, the teachings of the Holy Fathers, and the Gallican liberties. But they expressed their greatest concern about the widespread and apparently well-founded rumors that "certain persons" were urging Vintimille to withdraw the authority to preach and hear confessions from "a multitude of worthy and respected priests" in their parishes whom Cardinal Noailles had originally welcomed into the diocese. They alleged that the new archbishop was planning to reserve such revocations and dismissals for opponents of the Bull, while leaving untouched "those ministers [i.e., the Jesuits] whose conduct and doctrine are reprehensible." The *curés* argued that such rumors were causing great alarm among their parishioners, who feared the loss of priests in whom they had long placed great trust and confidence. They also charged that Vintimille's anticipated actions represented an interference with their parochial autonomy, especially with their supposed right to appoint their own catechists, confessors, and other clerical subordinates. Finally, they contended that the archbishop, by proceeding as rumored, would undermine discipline and foment discord within their parishes, thereby lighting the fires of schism and giving aid and comfort to the libertines and the impious.

Despite the reproachful and rather presumptuous tone of the *curés'* letter and despite Cardinal Fleury's recommendation that the archbishop reprimand them very harshly for their temerity,[142] Vintimille contented himself with making a fairly mild, circumspect reply. Summoning the five principal *curés* to his archiepiscopal palace, he rebuked them for having failed to come to him individually to discuss their various complaints in private. He also charged them with having violated the laws of the kingdom against unauthorized corporate associations and with thus complicating his efforts "to restore calm to this city and this diocese." Even though he insisted that the actions of these refractory priests were "clearly against the rules" and demonstrated a "blatant disrespect for their archbishop," Vintimille preferred

141 *Lettre d'un grand nombre de curés de la ville, faubourgs et banlieue de Paris, à Msgr. l'Archevêque, pour lui demander que l'opposition à la bulle "Unigenitus" ne serve pas de prétexte pour ôter les pouvoirs aux ecclésiastiques qui travaillent avec fruit dans le diocèse.* Excerpts and brief discussion in Dorsanne, II, 486-87, and *NNEE*, Sept. 30, 1729, p. 167. The five *curés* involved in delivering the letter were those of Sainte-Marguerite, Saint-Séverin, Saint-Jean-en-Grève, Saint-Josse, and Saint-André-des-Arts.

142 Fleury to Vintimille, Sept. 25, 1729, BM, MS 2357, p. 26.

to deal with their disobedience in a "spirit of charity and patience." By treating them in this manner and by speaking to them "as a friend and not as a superior," he was hopeful of winning the *curés* over to his views or at least of establishing a more amicable working relationship with them. As a sign of his good faith, the archbishop reassured them that he had no plans for dismissing large numbers of *anticonstitutionnaire* priests en masse.[143]

In a further effort to avoid unduly provoking the already suspicious parish clergy, Vintimille had prudently refrained from issuing an ultimatum ordering them to accept the Bull immediately and unconditionally. What is more, in issuing his pastoral instruction of September 29, the archbishop had also sought to avert yet another confrontation with the *curés* over its publication; rather than order it to be announced from the parish pulpits, Vintimille addressed it directly to the Paris faithful and on October 12 had it posted all over the city. Instead of placating the dissidents, however, the prelate's relatively moderate ways and conciliatory gestures appear to have been taken in some quarters as signs of weakness and indecision. Vintimille was soon faced with a series of additional *anticonstitutionnaire* challenges.[144]

On October 16 a group of *curés* from several rural parishes in the archdiocese addressed a formal petition to Vintimille protesting his pastoral instruction.[145] On that same day there appeared an anonymous *libelle* which not only condemned Vintimille's ordinance but also contained a vicious personal attack against the archbishop himself.[146] Within the next few weeks the clandestine *anticonstitutionnaire* presses had turned out still another anonymous brochure, the *Réflexions abrégées sur l'Ordonnance de M. l'archevêque de Paris, du 29 septembre 1729*, followed by the *Suite des réflexions abrégées* less than

---

[143] Vintimille to Fleury, September 1729, *ibid.*, pp. 21-23. Cf. *NNEE*, Sept. 30, 1729, p. 167, and Oct. 7, 1729, pp. 170-71. For Fleury's reaction to Vintimille's handling of the *curés*, see the cardinal-minister's letter of Sept. 29, 1729 (BM, MS 2357, pp. 25-26).

[144] Most of the documents for what follows may be found in BPR, L.P. 444, Nos. 74-82, 85.

[145] *Requête des curés de la campagne du diocèse de Paris, adressée à Msgr. l'archevêque, au sujet de son Ordonnance et instruction pastorale du 29 septembre 1729.*

[146] *Remontrances des fidèles du diocèse de Paris à Msgr. leur Archevêque, sur son instruction pastorale du 29 septembre 1729.* This work was eventually condemned, suppressed, and burned by the Parlement of Paris on Feb. 23, 1730. For a long, critical discussion of the Parlement's action, see *NNEE*, March 4, 1730, p. 46. For Cardinal Fleury's views of the work in question, see his letter to the *gens du roi*, Feb. 18, 1730 (AAE, M&D, Fonds divers [Rome], MS 58, fols. 507-508).

two weeks later. Efforts on the part of the police to discover the printing establishments responsible for these abusive works proved entirely fruitless, and the opponents of the archbishop remained free to carry on their vituperative attacks.[147]

In the meantime, in early November Vintimille published an order throughout Paris enjoining all confessors and preachers from the city and suburbs to present themselves within the space of four months for an official archdiocesan examination into their fitness and competence to retain their spiritual powers.[148] The appearance of this order, though it fully conformed with normal procedures in effect throughout the Gallican Church on the accession of a new prelate, convinced many *anticonstitutionnaires* that the authorities intended to make the acceptance of the bull *Unigenitus* and the signature of the Formulary "the touchstone for determining the purity of a priest's faith," and that a wholesale purge of the diocese was imminent.[149] In fact, however, Vintimille deprived only thirty ecclesiastics of their positions. These included the most "troublesome," "arrogant," and "unworthy" priests in the city, many of them former exiles from other dioceses who had flocked to Paris during the reign of Cardinal Noailles. At the same time, the archbishop confirmed all of the others, including large numbers of clerics who still refused to accept his pastoral instruction of September 29.

Despite the rather lenient and forbearing treatment which Vintimille had accorded most of his staunchly *anticonstitutionnaire* clerical subordinates, the archbishop soon confronted another barrage of critical tracts. A series of anonymous pieces appeared on the streets of Paris in mid-November which denounced the prelate's action in depriving even thirty priests of their functions.[150] More than a month later, on December 29, twenty-three *curés* published their own direct attack on Vintimille's ordinance and pastoral instruction. In a blistering letter and *mémoire*[151] they depicted the Paris of M. Vintimille as "covered with grief (*afflictions*) and darkness (*ténèbres*)." Protesting anew the archbishop's interdiction of thirty confessors, they charged him with depriving his diocese "of all its worthy ministers" and with surrendering his flock "to blind and lax guides." These same *curés*, some of whom had been among the group of doctors excluded from the Sor-

---

[147] See discussion of these works in *NNEE*, Dec. 14, 1729, pp. 212-14, and Dec. 22, 1729, pp. 223-24.

[148] BPR, L.P. 444, No. 73.   [149] *NNEE*, Nov. 12, 1729, pp. 195-96.

[150] Dorsanne, II, 485-89; *NNEE*, Jan. 30, 1730, p. 21.

[151] AAE, M&D, Fonds divers (Rome), MS 58, fols. 285-89; see discussion in *NNEE*, Jan. 24, 1730, p. 16.

bonne, also added their voices to the swelling chorus of *anticonstitutionnaires* who formally denounced the government's purge of the Faculty of Theology and its interference with that body's freedom of deliberation.[152] They joined in a futile attempt to get the Parlement of Paris to reverse Cardinal Fleury's action, going so far as to present a petition to the sovereign court through the abbé René Pucelle, the most articulate and widely respected opponent of the Bull in the Parlement.[153] But the cardinal-minister, by evoking the case to the royal council, quickly put a halt to the affair before the magistrates could even consider the petition.[154] Even so, the *curés* and their *anticonstitutionnaire* compatriots had again served notice that they were not easily to be cowed nor were they prepared simply to acquiesce in offensive royal or episcopal decisions.

These "unpriestly" actions, along with others that were not so well publicized, deeply disturbed Vintimille and threatened to compromise the earlier successes that he and Cardinal Fleury had managed to accomplish.[155] Not that the stepped-up agitation of the Paris *curés* against official ecclesiastical policy should have come as any surprise to either the archbishop or the cardinal-minister. In large measure, of course, the *curés'* insubordinate attitude toward the *constitutionnaire* Vintimille derived from their longstanding antipathy for the Bull and to their archbishop's command that they accept it. As we have seen, however, the question of accepting *Unigenitus* had become inextricably bound up with a host of other ecclesiastical issues. The refusal of these dissident priests to obey the directives of their superior was probably as much an expression of opposition to episcopal autocracy as it was an indication of intractable *anticonstitutionnaire* sentiment. To be sure, so long as the appellant Noailles was still archbishop and did not prevent his ecclesiastical subordinates from expressing their strong views on the Bull, the priests had remained generally obedient on other matters of Church governance. But even under Noailles' sympathetic, if sometimes vacillating, direction, they had shown growing signs of independence, a growing consciousness of their role as a vital force in the life of the Church, the edicts of 1695 and 1698 on ecclesiastical au-

---

[152] For the protest of the excluded theologians, see AAE, M&D, Fonds divers (Rome), MS 58, fols. 175-77.

[153] A group of 67 Gallican *avocats* drew up a legal brief demonstrating the "injustices and irregularities" of the Sorbonne's recent purge (Fourquevaux, II, 452).

[154] On the Parlement's role see BN, J.F., MS 129, fols. 80-158. Cf. discussion in *NNEE*, Dec. 6, 1729, pp. 207-11, and Dec. 16, 1729, pp. 216-21.

[155] Vintimille to Fleury, Dec. 9, 1729, BM, MS 2357, pp. 33-34.

thority notwithstanding. Resentful of their subordinate status, they had recently begun clamoring to get their voices heard in ecclesiastical debates and asserting claims for much broader powers and responsibilities within the diocese—claims that they were increasingly impatient to realize. Their protests, now put forward with renewed fervor, underscored the deep gulf between bishop and *curé* and the persistent —and, in Paris, mounting—difficulty in achieving a properly functioning relationship between the hierarchy and the parish. If, in clamoring for their rights in Church affairs and in questioning the validity of decisions made without their participation or consultation, the *curés* had pretensions of wresting some degree of power from their archbishop, they could not have hoped to succeed in the face of the authorities massed against them. On the other hand, neither their words nor their deeds could be lightly dismissed, especially since, having adopted the role of neighborhood agitators, they had managed to achieve considerable success in winning over their parishioners to the *anticonstitutionnaire* cause.[156]

Jansenism and Parisian Ecclesiastical Politics in 1729

From the outset of the dispute over the Bull, the opponents of *Unigenitus* had been making appeals for lay support at all levels of society. The pope's condemnation of certain propositions (79-85) which referred to the laity's right to read Scripture in the vernacular and to participate actively in the liturgy represented one of the most unpopular sections of a generally unpopular decree, and the *anticonstitutionnaire* propagandists had used the issue to great advantage.[157] In a spate of virulent pamphlets, circulating clandestinely, as well as in countless public sermons, lectures on Holy Scripture, and theological conferences they had firmly denounced the injustice of such proscriptions. At the same time, a host of anonymous versifiers and satirists, including the author of a popular "board game," the *jeu de la constitution*, all

---

[156] See Barbier, II, 18 (September 1727). As early as 1717, contemporaries had begun to note the decidedly *anticonstitutionnaire* character of Parisian public opinion (see discussion in H. Leclercq, II, 43-44).

[157] Fourquevaux, II, 269; *Entretiens sur les miracles* (1732), pp. 53, 87, *et passim*. On the development of Jansenist ecclesiology in the eighteenth century and the expanded role which certain *anticonstitutionnaire* clergy advocated for the laity in the Church polity, see Plongeron, "Une image de l'Eglise." Cf. Elisabeth Germain, *Langages de la foi à travers l'histoire. Mentalités et catéchèse: Approche d'une étude des mentalités* (Paris, 1972), esp. pp. 103-107; and Préclin, *Les jansénistes*, pp. 180-97, *et passim*.

sought to discredit the *constitutionnaire* position through ridicule or scorn.[158] More than any pamphleteer, journalist, or clever wit, however, it was the parish clergy who bore the primary responsibility for diffusing the *anticonstitutionnaire* message among the lay populace. The various functions of the parish priest—spiritual guide, director of conscience, and purveyor of social services—kept him in constant, even intimate, contact with the faithful and thus presumably in a position to exert tremendous influence.[159] While the pulpit was certainly the most important vehicle for the priest to communicate directly with his flock, he no doubt mixed in a healthy dose of propaganda with his catechism instruction as well. But preaching alone—even with the support of a vast array of printed propaganda, some of it "à la portée des simples fidèles"—was an inadequate means of mobilizing public opinion or of overcoming popular indifference, particularly since the Jansenist cause was not one to which the unsophisticated were ordinarily willing or able to make a commitment.

Ironically, the government itself may have been the most effective agent for converting Parisians to the *anticonstitutionnaire* side. The revolting scene of destruction at Port-Royal had already aroused widespread public indigation over the crown's brutal persecution of pious nuns, whose only "crime" was their staunch opposition to an official religious policy which they judged as misguided and a perversion of the true faith. The rigged Council of Embrun, which deposed and exiled the devout Soanen, had likewise given the Jansenists yet another weapon for their political arsenal and an additional opportunity to pose as the oppressed victims of a powerful, Jesuit-led, and Rome-inspired cabal—an image they attempted to exploit in order to demonstrate that they not only needed protection but were also worthy of support.[160] However, the repressive actions taken against *anticonstitutionnaire* priests and confessors, many of them forcibly banished from their posts, had the most direct and unsettling impact on the lives of these people, taking a profound emotional toll and making them more acutely con-

---

[158] Excerpts from the several thousand verses which comprise the *Essai du nouveau conte de ma mère l'oie, ou Enluminures du jeu de la Constitution* (1722), generally attributed to Louis Debonnaire, are in Raunié, IV, 156-61. See discussion in Carreyre, *Jansénisme durant la Régence*, II, 114-18; Taveneaux, *La vie quotidienne*, pp. 210-11, 279, n. 10; and Deyon, *Amiens*, p. 424. Cf. also *Poésies sur la Constitution Unigenitus* (Villefranche, 1724).

[159] Ravaisson, XIII, 502-503, *et passim*. The government was afraid that they were teaching unorthodox doctrine and were inculcating sentiments opposed to the decisions of the Church. Deeply disturbed by the sermons of these appellant preachers, Fleury had many of them placed under close surveillance.

[160] See *NNEE*, "Preliminary Discourse" for 1728, pp. 1-3.

scious than ever of the authoritarian abuses of power of which the architects and executors of official ecclesiastical policy were capable. The involvement of this segment of the laity in the *Unigenitus* controversy and their professed hostility to the Bull was thus motivated primarily by personal rather than by doctrinal or ideological considerations, arising out of their devoted attachment to worthy pastors unaccountably removed from their midst and not out of any particular commitment to a Richerist ecclesiology, to the doctrine of efficacious grace, or to the moral austerity and dark theological tendencies of Port-Royal.[161]

How many of the Paris faithful were ultimately drawn to the Jansenist side by these various means—whether or not they really understood or even cared about the issues at stake—cannot be determined with any certainty. If we may trust the rather sardonic observations of the watchful *avocat*-diarist Barbier, *anticonstitutionnaire* success among the traditionally volatile Parisian populace must have been considerable. And even if one discounts as greatly exaggerated his contention that "all the second order of the clergy and the greater part of the bourgeoisie, the magistrates, the women, and the common people" were Jansenist,[162] it seems fair to conclude that by the late 1720s a large, increasingly vocal, and steadily growing body of sentiment had begun to range itself quite passionately against the Bull, which obtained a veritable *succès de scandale* in the capital, especially in the parishes around the perimeter of the University.[163] Nevertheless, whatever the proportion of the Paris population already won over to the *anticonstitutionnaire* cause during the first two decades of the controversy, their numbers were to swell in the early 1730s. With the outbreak of miracles which occurred all over France through the intercession of various

[161] See, for example, the storm of public protest at Saint-Etienne-du-Mont in October 1728 when the police, armed with *lettres de cachet*, removed a popular Jansenist priest from the parish (*ibid.*, Supplément pour 1728, pp. 295-96). Concern for the plight of such vulnerable clergy found expression in raucous demonstrations on their behalf among parish faithful throughout Paris and beyond (see *ibid.*, 1728-29, *passim*). Cf. discussion in Deyon, *Amiens*, pp. 423-25; and Dainville, esp. p. 121.

[162] Vol. II, 21 (October 1727). The notion that Paris was "janséniste de la tête aux pieds" was a theme heard in a constant refrain in Barbier's journal (II, 29-30 [January 1728]; II, 47 [July 1728]; II, 202 [October 1732]. Cf. similar remarks made by Bishop Massillon of Clermont to P. Mercier, November 1724, *Correspondance inédite* (Bar-le-Duc, 1869), pp. 256-57.

[163] Gazier, *Histoire générale*, I, 250; Dainville, *passim*; and Dedieu, "Le désarroi janséniste," pp. 558-65. For the hostile public reaction which greeted the news of Cardinal Noailles' capitulation on *Unigenitus*, see Barbier, II, 54-57 (October-November 1728); Fourquevaux, II, 418-21; and Dorsanne, II, 444-45.

Jansenist thaumaturges, first in 1725, more numerous after 1727, the opponents of the Bull had a tailor-made issue for recruiting a new crowd of adherents from among the uncommitted laity and for remedying thereby the widespread loss of support and deficiency of highly placed ecclesiastical allies which Fleury's efforts had been costing them. The miracles performed by appellants, some of whom had died while still opposed to *Unigenitus*, did not involve any abstruse theological mysteries or incomprehensible political machinations but served as an easy means of assuring even the simplest of the populace which side had the blessings of God. With the growing incidence of miracles, the appellants could readily seek full vindication of their claim to be defenders of truth and righteousness. Indeed, in the eyes of many of the pious faithful the Jansenists, already the party of holiness and sanctity, would soon become the party of Truth as well.

To a society which still accepted the possibility of direct divine intervention in human affairs and attached great significance to such interventions, the potential propaganda value of the miracles extended beyond enlisting stronger lay support for the *anticonstitutionnaire* cause. While enabling the appellants to take their case more effectively to the public, the miracles also provided them with an important source of polemical and apologetic arguments to hurl against the government and the *constitutionnaire* bishops and theologians. Such providential signs and prodigies gave the party new hope and were to encourage the *anticonstitutionnaires* in their resistance. Indeed, the miracles were eventually to enable the opponents of the Bull to pose as agents of God, Whose direct testimony and support they could invoke in their continued defiance of official ecclesiastical policy. For many appellants, proof by miracles would become an accepted part of their counteroffensive and would remain in their polemical repertoire so long as this "weapon" was useful to the cause.

The *anticonstitutionnaires*' open appeal to the supernatural marked the beginning of a new chapter in the development of Jansenism from a narrowly elitist and aristocratic movement to a much more popular and even vaguely "democratic" one. It also marked the transformation of the Jansenist problem from a semiprivate doctrinal controversy among a handful of theologians into an increasingly public dispute over such vital questions of ecclesiastical politics as the nature of Church governance, the relationship between secular and sacerdotal authority, and the role of the laity in religious affairs—questions which posed a potentially serious challenge to the government of Louis XV and threatened to undermine the fundamental structure of the Gallican Church. Official efforts to eliminate the "Jansenist problem" by administrative proscription continued to prove unavailing. By early 1730, although the crown had ruthlessly broken much of the nationwide resistance to the bull *Unigenitus*, there were still signs, in Paris at least, that *anticonstitutionnaire* fortunes were far less bleak than Cardinal Fleury might have imagined. In their smoothly functioning, clandestine *Nouvelles ecclésiastiques* the opponents of the Bull had already developed a sophisticated apparatus for the dissemination of party news and propaganda, to go along with the endless stream of broadsides, placards, *libelles*, songs, verses, and *estampes* which were the traditional methods of purveying information, opinion, and rumor in the *ancien régime*. In the forefront of *anticonstitutionnaire* agitation was a militant and increasingly confident group of *curés*, in control of some two dozen parishes in the capital and anxious to assert the prerogatives of the "second order" of clergy. Making common cause with non-clerical elements of society, they had found in the *avocats* of the Paris Parlement not only fellow exponents of Gallican opposition to ultramontane encroachments within the French Church but also welcome allies in the battle against the arbitrary power of episcopal "despotism." In addition, from exile or seclusion, a handful of outspoken theologians, some of them recently purged from the Sorbonne, continued to work faithfully for the *anticonstitutionnaire* cause, producing scores of tracts, treatises, and letters which circulated regularly, if secretly, through the streets of Paris. Finally, and perhaps most ominously for Fleury's administration, influential magistrates in the Parlement were becoming increasingly disturbed by the government's efforts to impose the dreaded Bull with a heavy hand. While this formidable association of civil and ecclesiastical allies was stiffening in its resistance to the bull *Unigenitus*, and in the midst of this widespread restiveness and turmoil, a new popular religious cult burst onto the scene.

CHAPTER II

Jansenist Miracles: From the Holy Thorn to the Origins of the Cult to François de Pâris

T HE appeal to, and ideological exploitation of, miracles in times of political adversity had a long history in the Jansenist controversy, dating back to the mid-seventeenth century.[1] Throughout this stormy period there had been a large number of miraculous cures as well as a variety of other "supernatural" signs and portents associated with Port-Royal, all of which served to sustain the Jansenists' sense of themselves as a specially chosen religious elite. Recourse to the miraculous and appeal for supernatural aid—whether for cures of specific physical disabilities or out of a need for celestial comfort in the face of official persecution—became an almost daily occurrence in certain Jansenist circles. Increasingly, the miracle, which bore direct and unequivocal witness to the divine presence, came to constitute perhaps the most important vehicle of expression available to the persecuted Jansenist faithful. The miracle was God's way of giving "voice" to the previously stifled and frustrated partisans of the "Truth," of enabling them not only to "speak out" but to do so effectively, with a "language" of extraordinary force and conviction. It thus provided the Jansenists with a powerful apologetic weapon and afforded them a means of fending off the suspicions of the civil and ecclesiastical authorities.[2]

Of all the miracles claimed by and for Port-Royal none was more cherished than the famous cure of Pascal's young niece, Marguerite Perrier, on March 24, 1656, just three months after her uncle had published the first of his *Lettres provinciales*. Mlle. Perrier had been suffering for a long time from a serious and disfiguring lachrymal fistula in the corner of one eye. She was suddenly healed when a Holy Thorn

---

[1] For a broad discussion of the Jansenists' attitude toward the miraculous and the role of intercessionary prayers (individual and collective) in Jansenist theology, see Taveneaux, *La vie quotidienne*, pp. 126-27, 179-90. Cf. R. C. Finucane, "The Use and Abuse of Medieval Miracles," *History*, 60 (1975), pp. 1-10.

[2] Such providential signs and interventions also served to encourage the Jansenists in their resistance to these same authorities. Cf. Willem Frijhoff, "La fonction du miracle dans une minorité catholique: Les Provinces-Unies au 17ᵉ siècle," *Revue d'histoire de la spiritualité*, 48 (1972), pp. 151-77.

recently presented to the sisters of Port-Royal-des-Champs, where she was a pensionary, was simply touched to her ulcerous sore. Despite vehement Jesuit denunciations and attempts to explain it away, the miracle, supported by substantial medical evidence and duly authenticated a short time later by the diocesan authorities, made a profound impression on the public. So great was the impact of this extraordinary event that the queen mother herself accepted the cure as miraculous and allegedly induced Mazarin to hold off the persecution of the Jansenists for another five years because of it. Within a few months the cures and other miracles attributed to the Holy Thorn multiplied to fourteen, and afterwards to eighty.[3]

Deeply impressed by these incidents, various Jansenist apologists were inspired to pious meditations on the nature of miracles, the means of verifying them, and their significance in times of religious controversy. Pascal, in particular, was moved to a series of long and fruitful reflections on the miracles of the Old and New Testaments and a discussion of the relationship between miracles and religious truth. In notes compiled for a pamphlet (never completed) dealing with the miracle worked upon his little niece, he argued, among other things, that the principal purpose of miracles since the time of the Apostles had always been to discern true doctrine from false—an argument that would be taken up again in the eighteenth century.[4] Residents and friends of Port-Royal, following Pascal, confidently looked upon the Perrier miracle and the other Holy Thorn cures not simply as evidence that they possessed an authentic relic but rather as a demonstration that their defense of efficacious grace had the blessing of God. Accused of a revolt against Church and State, they claimed that these miracles were divine justification of the righteousness of their cause.[5]

---

[3] [Jérôme Besoigne], *Histoire de l'abbaye de Port-Royal*, 6 vols. (Cologne, 1752), I, 364-89, *et passim*; [Dom Charles Clémencet], *Histoire générale de Port-Royal*, 10 vols. (Amsterdam, 1755-57), III, 370-404, IV, 18-22; and [Nicolas Fontaine], *Mémoires pour servir à l'histoire de Port-Royal*, 2 vols. (Utrecht, 1736), II, 131-43. For a series of contemporary verses on the Holy Thorn miracles, see BN, NAFr., MS 1702, fols. 34-48, 191-92. For a hostile contemporary assessment, see René Rapin, *Mémoires sur l'Église et la société, la cour, la ville et le jansénisme, 1644-1669*, ed. Léon Aubineau, 3 vols. (Paris, 1865), II, 418-23. See also Charles-Augustin Sainte-Beuve, *Port-Royal*, Gallimard ed., 3 vols. (Paris, 1953-55), II, 176-89, 196-98.

[4] Blaise Pascal, *Pensées*, ed. Louis Lafuma, trans. John Warrington (London, 1960), pp. 247-63; see also "Pensées" 365, 474, 478, 728, 743, *et passim*.

[5] Marguerite Perrier's survival to 1733, several years after "God had renewed his prodigies" at Saint-Médard and elsewhere in France, and at a time when Jansenist fortunes were similarly bleak, was later to be accounted another sure sign of divine favor. By then Mlle. Perrier had become committed to the *anticonstitu-*

While the Holy Thorn miracles were undoubtedly the most striking and widely publicized "supernatural" phenomena associated with Port-Royal and the Jansenists in the seventeenth century, they were by no means the only ones.[6] Numberless other miracles were also attributed to the intercession of a host of Jansenist heroes, lay and clerical, beginning with Saint-Cyran and including Mère Angélique Arnauld, the duchess de Longueville, the abbé de Pontchâteau, and several "saintly bishops" who had devoted themselves to the cause of Port-Royal (Pavillon, Vialart, and Choart de Buzenval among them).[7] Their mortal remains and a variety of their relics were carefully preserved, usually at the monastery, as objects of profound veneration and sources of continual protection and spiritual sustenance.[8] Most of the miraculous cures the "saints" performed were, like those attributed to the Holy Thorn, confined to the limited circle of the "société de Port-Royal." Occasionally, however, as in the cases of Pontchâteau and Bishop Vialart of Châlons, the alleged cures were operated in public arenas and gave rise to popular devotions not unlike those which developed around the deacon Pâris in the eighteenth century.[9] They also gave rise to an important split within the Jansenist camp.

The expectation of miracles and other supernatural signs had become almost an integral part of the Jansenist world view by the end of the seventeenth century, a source of profound psychological consolation,

---

tionnaire cause and was a dedicated admirer of François de Pâris and of the convulsionaries. She thus represented a real link between Port-Royal and Saint-Médard, and when she died in 1733, she was flanked by the portraits of Pascal and the deacon Pâris on either side of her bed. Surely, it was argued, God had prolonged her life to the extraordinary age of eighty-seven in order to establish the connection between the two causes—Port-Royal and the appeal—and the miracles by which He justified both of them. See Bishop Colbert to Father Guerrier, Feb. 8, 1733, in Charles-Joachim Colbert de Croissy, *Oeuvres*, 3 vols. (Cologne, 1740), III, 568; see also several letters written by Mlle. Perrier to various correspondents, 1725-32 (AFA, P.R. 2954, 3095, 3182, 4182).

[6] Jean Orcibal, *Port-Royal entre le miracle et l'obéissance: Flavie Passart et Angélique de St.-Jean Arnauld d'Andilly* (Paris, 1957); *idem*, "La signification du miracle et sa place dans l'ecclésiologie pascalienne," *Chroniques de Port-Royal*, Nos. 20-21 (1972), pp. 83-95.

[7] References abound in Besoigne, Clémencet, and Fontaine, as well as in Claude Lancelot, *Mémoires touchant la vie de M. de Saint-Cyran*, 2 vols. (Cologne, 1738).

[8] On the passion for relics see Besoigne, II, 209, and Lancelot, I, 254-58. See also Orcibal, *Port-Royal entre le miracle et l'obéissance*, *passim*.

[9] On Pontchâteau see Besoigne, IV, 641-44, and Clémencet, VIII, 206-209, as well as the discussion in Sainte-Beuve, III, 247-49. On Vialart see Ruth Clark (ed.), *Lettres de Germain Vuillart, ami de Port-Royal, à M. de Préfontaine (1694-1700)* (Geneva-Lille, 1951), especially letters of Nov. 29, 1698 (p. 167), Dec. 13, 1698 (p. 172), and May 6, 1699 (p. 222).

and a means of achieving symbolic victory in the teeth of imminent or actual defeat. Some Jansenists had grown accustomed to finding providential meaning even in perfectly normal-seeming events. But there was an important body of opinion among the party's theologians which denied the significance of the supposed portents and questioned the very reality of some of the alleged cures and their usefulness to the faithful. Though this skeptical position was expressed initially by Saint-Cyran himself, it received its strongest statement in the works of Pierre Nicole. Nicole's skepticism, directed particularly at the "public, visible" miracles associated with Pontchâteau and others, was a reflection of the growing rationalist critique of the supernatural within the post-Tridentine Catholic Church at large, part of a reaction against what one writer has termed "the credulity, the impostures, the lack of critical intelligence" displayed by large numbers of the faithful.[10] Other writers, stressing the need for austerity and discipline in religious practice and for an interior mortification of the senses, were likewise wary of emphasizing in any way the "magical" side of religion, which they saw as a gross deviation from the spirituality of Port-Royal and from the pure message of the Gospel.[11] Though they never rejected the cult of the Virgin or the veneration of saints, they, like Nicole, especially distrusted the proliferation of unauthorized popular devotions and the "superstitious follies" such devotions helped foster and perpetuate.[12]

This questioning attitude toward the miraculous, born of a vague mixture of suspicion and skepticism, would remain strong in certain Jansenist circles throughout the eighteenth century and was to play a complicating role in the *anticonstitutionnaires'* response to the miracles attributed to François de Pâris. Nevertheless, despite the reservations expressed by these Jansenists toward the movement's recourse to the supernatural—reservations which would be reiterated with even greater force in the 1730s—the justificatory miracle, like the symbolic portent, continued to play a significant role in much of the party's apologetic literature until the very end of the reign of Louis XIV. This special receptivity to, indeed craving for, the miraculous, and the presence

[10] E. D. James, *Pierre Nicole, Jansenist and Humanist: A Study of His Thought* (The Hague, 1973), pp. 68-73. See also Sainte-Beuve, III, 248n. On the more generalized *crise du miracle* in Western Christian thought, see Paul Hazard, *The European Mind, 1680-1715*, trans. J. Lewis May (New York, 1963), pp. 155-79. See also Ch. IV below.

[11] Namer, p. 152; Orcibal, *Port-Royal entre le miracle et l'obéissance*.

[12] Louis Cognet, "La dévotion mariale à Port-Royal," in *Maria: Etudes sur la Sainte Vierge*, ed. Hubert Du Manoir, 8 vols. (Paris, 1949-71), III, 119-51; Paul Hoffer, *La dévotion à Marie au déclin du 17ᵉ siècle. Autour du jansénisme et des "Avis salutaires de la B. V. M. à ses dévots indiscrets"* (Paris, 1938).

within the movement of several uncanonized popular saints, constituted important, though generally overlooked, elements of the cultural baggage bequeathed to the eighteenth-century heirs of the tradition of Port-Royal. By recognizing the reality and significance of this "dévotion affective au merveilleux" within seventeenth-century Jansenism,[13] we may discover that the line from Port-Royal to Saint-Médard is not as tenuous or obscure as has usually been thought.[14]

The condition of the appellants in the 1720s, following Cardinal Fleury's rise to power, was reminiscent of the situation that had obtained in the 1650s—prior to the Holy Thorn miracles—when the initial persecution of the Jansenists was imminent and the fortunes of Port-Royal were similarly bleak. The post-Regency period, like the period of Mazarin's rule, witnessed a sudden and dramatic proliferation of reputedly miraculous cures—this time associated with and performed by a series of worthy appellant clergy. In May 1725 the first in a long series of such cures took place in the parish of Sainte-Marguerite in Paris and began vaguely and almost imperceptibly to reawaken the flagging hopes of the *anticonstitutionnaire* party. On May 31, during the procession of the Holy Sacrament through the parish, a certain Madame Lafosse, wife of a cabinetmaker from the *faubourg* Saint-Antoine, was suddenly cured of a partial paralysis and considerable hemorrhaging which had severely enfeebled her for a long time.[15] The news of the event spread quickly through Paris, and within a short time Cardinal Noailles appointed a commission to investigate the cure and compile an extensive dossier. After carefully reviewing the results of the commission's inquiry, the archbishop published the details of the findings in a celebrated pastoral letter of August 10, 1725.[16] On the basis of testimony taken from some fifty witnesses to the prodigy, among them Voltaire himself,[17] as well as the depositions of several medical experts, Noailles certified that the cure was a real miracle

[13] The terminology is Taveneaux's: *La vie quotidienne*, Ch. 10.

[14] See n. 5 above.

[15] Barbier, I, 390-92 (June 1725); Marais, III, 192 (June 5, 1725), and 199-200 (June 24, 1725).

[16] *Mandement . . . à l'occasion du miracle opéré dans la paroisse de Sainte-Marguerite, le 31 mai, jour du saint sacrement* (Paris, 1725). See also Marais, III, 216-27 (August 1725). Additional accounts of the miracle, and even a portrait of Mme. Lafosse, may be found in the BN, Salle des Imprimés, especially LD-4 1399-1405, 1407.

[17] Voltaire's involvement in this affair is perhaps one of the most curious episodes in his long and involved career. See Augustin Gazier, "Le frère de Voltaire," *Revue des deux mondes*, 5th per., 32 (1906), pp. 618-20.

which "Providence had just accomplished in order to confound the libertines and the Protestants, both enemies of the Real Presence."[18]

A public celebration of the miracle took place later in August, shortly after Noailles had issued his pastoral letter. Once again the Holy Sacrament of the parish Sainte-Marguerite was carried in a procession through the *faubourg* Saint-Antoine. Noailles took part, while Madame Lafosse walked behind holding a candle in her hand. The following Sunday, parishioners from Sainte-Marguerite came in a procession to the cathedral of Notre-Dame along with persons from all over the *faubourg*;[19] as before, Madame Lafosse walked at the rear, candle in hand. Finally, she was even presented to the king.[20]

The matter might have ended there as a brief and simple episode of early modern popular piety. It might have, but it did not. The *curé* who had originally consecrated the host and borne the Corpus Christi was the pious Jean-Baptiste Goy,[21] a doctor of theology in the Sorbonne and an avowed appellant, as were most of the clergy who served under him at Sainte-Marguerite. Thus the miracle soon assumed a much greater significance for the partisans of the appeal. Indeed, it was to provoke an exchange of theological polemics which might be regarded as a small-scale dress rehearsal for the later debates over Saint-Médard.

[18] To the cardinal-archbishop, then embroiled in fruitless discussions with Rome and Versailles over the bull *Unigenitus*, the miracle also had a quite personal meaning: "si le sacré Collège m'abandonne, le Dieu de toute consolation ne m'abandonne pas. Il a fait ces jours-ci dans une paroisse de Paris un miracle qui . . . fait bien voir que le Diocèse de Paris n'est pas pour J. C. un Diocèse prohibé" (Noailles to Father Gravezon, June 11, 1725, AAE, M&D, Fonds divers [Rome], MS 54, fol. 110; cf. Noailles to Gravezon, June 18, 1725, *ibid.*, fols. 143-44).

[19] The quarter had recently been beset by bread riots—a fact that may account in part for the great popular enthusiasm with which news of this "supernatural event" was greeted. Evidence of the public craving at this time for signs of divine favor was by no means limited to the Lafosse miracle and its aftermath. See Barbier, I, 394-400 (June-July 1725), 402-403 (August 1725), 410 (September 1725); Marais, III, 198 (June 17, 1725), 202-203 (June 27-July 5, 1725). See also Steven Kaplan, "Religion, Subsistence, and Social Control: The Uses of Saint-Geneviève in Eighteenth-Century France" (forthcoming), *passim*. I am grateful to Professor Kaplan for permitting me to read a typescript of his article in advance of its publication in *Societas: A Review of Social History*.

[20] Barbier, I, 404 (August 1725); Marais, III, 358 (Sept. 1, 1725); Ludwig von Pastor, *History of the Popes*, trans. Ernest Graf, 40 vols. (St. Louis, 1923-53), XXXIV, 276, n. 2.

[21] Goy, who had an outstanding reputation for charitable activities within his parish, had been instrumental in sustaining the educational work of the Frères du faubourg Saint-Antoine (C. Gazier, *Après Port-Royal*, pp. 38-39). He died in 1738, reportedly "in the odor of sanctity" (BA, MS 11606, fol. 229).

The "supernatural" precedents of the seventeenth century, especially the Holy Thorn miracles, and the commentaries of Pascal and others were not lost on an important group of *anticonstitutionnaires*. Exultant, they seized upon the Lafosse cure as a striking sign not only of the truth and righteousness of their opposition to the Bull but also of the divine protection gracing their cause and justifying their conduct. Noailles had been reluctant to go so far in his decree, but with him such hesitation was not uncommon. In his public pronouncements, the cardinal-archbishop had limited himself to citing the testimony of the miracle in order to enlighten the faithful; according to his *mandement*, the miracle was neither more nor less than a proof of the Real Presence.[22] Others, however, were prepared to go much further.

Bishop Colbert of Montpellier, one of the four original appellants, was particularly eager to extend Noailles' analysis in order to exploit the occasion for the *anticonstitutionnaire* party. In a pastoral letter dated October 1725, which first appeared in 1726, Colbert went beyond his colleague's attack on the libertines and the Protestants to assail the proponents of the Bull for preaching "revolt, schism, and division."[23] He argued that the miracle represented both God's approval of the appellants and His condemnation and repudiation of their opponents. Regarding the specific case of Sainte-Marguerite, Colbert claimed that prior to the miracle the *acceptants* had successfully turned many of M. Goy's parishioners against him, to the point where the faithful were even refusing to receive the sacraments from his hands. Divine intercession, according to Colbert, had preserved the *curé*'s reputation from the discrediting calumnies of his enemies.[24] Following Pascal, Colbert further asserted that miracles had a general application in times of controversy, as the means by which God discerned the true doctrine from the false. In the case of the Bull, God had evidently declared that the supporters of the appeal, though in the minority, were the righteous preservers of the faith.[25]

Predictably, the *constitutionnaires* were not prepared to let these pretensions to justification go unchallenged for very long. Bishop Jean-Joseph Languet de Gergy of Soissons (later archbishop of Sens), one

[22] Valentin Durand, *Le jansénisme au 18e siècle et Joachim Colbert, évêque de Montpellier* (Toulouse, 1907), p. 168.

[23] *Lettre pastorale . . . adressée aux fidèles de son diocèse à l'occasion du miracle opéré à Paris* (Paris, 1726), pp. 6-9.

[24] *Ibid.*, p. 9.

[25] *Ibid.*, p. 10. Colbert received warm expressions of appreciation for his pastoral instruction from both of the principals involved in the miracle of Saint-Marguerite, the abbé Goy (Feb. 5 and Aug. 24, 1726, AFA, P.R. 5166), and Mme. Lafosse herself (Jan. 28, 1726, *ibid.*, P.R. 5249).

of the most prolific and vitriolic pamphleteer-theologians in his party, responded to Colbert in a pastoral letter of April 1726.[26] The irrefutable evidence collected by Noailles in favor of the Lafosse cure made any challenge to its authenticity appear fruitless. Languet's approach, therefore, was to attack as unwarranted the inferences which Colbert had drawn from it in the controversy over the bull *Unigenitus*. Languet argued that miracles are not always an indubitable proof of the purity of faith, but rather a demonstration of the omnipotence and goodness of God, Who performs miracles when He chooses to do so and for reasons known only to Himself. To be sure, Languet conceded, although miracles once were a means of separating truth from error, this had been the case principally in the days of the Apostles. But after the Church had been firmly established, it alone was entrusted with the task of interpreting the faith. Hence, the only guaranteed source of revealed truth was to be found in the teachings of the Church. Furthermore, he argued, it is doctrine which "discerns the miracles" and not the other way around. The body of bishops, united with the pope, has the apostolic authority to judge. The bull *Unigenitus* had been declared by them to be official doctrine of the Church. Therefore, the cure, allegedly operated on behalf of those who had challenged official doctrine, could not have been a true miracle. Such an argument was, of course, begging the question, since the notion that the Bull was a "judgment of the Church" was precisely the issue upon which neither side could agree.[27]

From a most unexpected quarter there came yet another rebuke to Colbert for his pastoral letter. The Parlement of Paris, despite its sympathy for the bishop's espousal of the appellant cause, issued an *arrêt* on April 15, 1726, ordering the letter suppressed. On the urging of the royal administration, the court reproached Colbert (in the words of the *avocat-général*) for "turning a true miracle to partisan account."[28] But the Parlement's action, aimed at stopping the episcopal quarrel between Colbert and Languet before it went any further, did not prevent the indefatigable bishop of Montpellier from issuing more letters denouncing the "schismatic ardor" of his opponents. Not surprisingly, Languet, joined by Bishop Belsunce of Marseille among others, continued to match Colbert statement for statement, in number if not in

---

[26] *7ᵉ Lettre pastoral . . . donnée à l'occasion de divers écrits* (Paris, 1726). Cf. the anonymous *Lettre d'un théologien à Mgr. l'évêque de Montpellier sur sa lettre pastorale. . . .*

[27] For a discussion of Languet's pastoral letter and the controversy with Colbert, see Durand, pp. 170-72.

[28] *NNEE*, April 19, 1726, p. 138.

audacity or persuasiveness.[29] By 1727, when François de Pâris died, the parties to the *Unigenitus* controversy were only just beginning to skirmish on their new battleground. But the polemical broadsides which they exchanged over the Lafosse miracle were already setting the main lines and terms of the theological controversy that was later to surround the Pâris miracles at Saint-Médard. Furthermore, Colbert and Languet also established the bitter, uncompromising tone which marked the debate that raged in the ensuing years.[30]

There is no reason to believe, as some of their *acceptant* enemies alleged, that the appellants had actually staged the Lafosse cure in the interests of their propaganda campaign.[31] Indeed, the miracle had been so well confirmed that even the pope was reported to have approved of Noailles' findings.[32] Nevertheless, many of the *constitutionnaires* in France continued to suspect that their opponents were practicing pious frauds, thereby causing the faith incalculable harm. Nor were their suspicions allayed when other allegedly miraculous cures, all supposedly performed through the intercession of critics of the Bull, followed upon the Lafosse miracle.

For all of Colbert's polemical efforts, one miracle could hardly have vindicated the claims of the appellants to divine justification of their cause. In subsequent months, however, numerous additional cures, unconnected with that of Madame Lafosse, were reportedly taking place throughout Paris and gave heightened significance to the miracle of Sainte-Marguerite. In July 1725, miracles occurred in the church of Sainte-Geneviève, then in the hands of appellant canons. About the same time, relics of the late Father Quesnel were said to be producing still other miracles all over the diocese.[33] Soon the cures were more widespread. In late 1725 several occurred at the tomb of a certain M. Sauvage, an obscure Jansenist priest from Boulogne.[34] In March 1727, in Lyons, the Oratorian Father Celoron, another ardent appellant,

---

29 See, in particular, *3e Lettre de monseigneur l'évêque de Montpellier à monseigneur l'évêque de Soissons, au sujet de la 7e Lettre pastorale de ce prélat . . .* (1727), and *Lettre de monseigneur l'évêque de Soissons à monseigneur l'évêque de Montpellier, en réponse aux deux Lettres de ce prélat . . .* (1727). Cf. discussion in Orcibal, "La signification du miracle," pp. 93-95. It was at this time (February 1727) that Colbert arranged the publication of Pascal's *pensées* on miracles, which until then had circulated only in manuscript.

30 Durand, pp. 172-75.

31 Marais, III, 199-200 (June 24, 1725), and 352 (Aug. 1, 1725). Allegations repeated in Michel-Pierre-Joseph Picot's rabidly anti-Jansenist *Mémoires pour servir à l'histoire ecclésiastique pendant le 18e siècle*, 3rd ed., 7 vols. (Paris, 1853-57), II, 43.

32 Durand, p. 168.   33 Pastor, XXXIV, 277.

34 Colbert, *Oeuvres*, III, 194n.

worked a miracle on a three-year-old child who had been stricken blind from smallpox. Celoron later attested himself to the restoration of the boy's sight.[35]

Nor were these phenomena confined to France. In January 1727, Amsterdam was the scene of the sudden cure of a forty-five-year-old woman named Agathe Leenders-Stouthandel, who for twelve years had been afflicted with several maladies deemed incurable by three doctors. The event occurred after she had received the Eucharist from the hands of Archbishop Barchman of Utrecht, kissed his priestly vestments, and obtained his benediction. The archbishop, installed in his episcopal see more than a year earlier, had seen the canonicity of his election and the validity of his consecration—performed by the suspended French missionary bishop of Babylone, Dominique Varlet—called into question at Rome because of his own Jansenist affiliations. The miracle, attested to by 170 witnesses, including several doctors and many non-Catholics, thus stood for his supporters as divine legitimation of the prelate's elevation.[36]

It was in the diocese of Reims, however, that these miracles first aroused a public stir great enough to involve the authorities. The controversy developed around the Jansenist priest, Gérard Rousse, a pious canon in the royal abbey of Avenay, who died on May 9, 1727. His *constitutionnaire curé* had refused Rousse the last sacraments because of his adherence to the appeal and also denied him the right of burial in holy ground. Upon hearing of Rousse's plight, the sympathetic *curé* of a nearby parish administered the last rites and provided a resting place in his chapel.[37] Shortly afterward, M. Rousse was temporarily raised from obscurity when, in the space of less than a year, two miraculous cures occurred at his tomb.

The first cure took place in early July. The poverty-stricken Anne Augier, paralyzed for twenty-two years, suddenly recovered the full use of her limbs while lying on Rousse's tomb.[38] In spite of a decree from the *grands vicaires* which dismissed the event, the miracle, witnessed by dozens of spectators, won the support of thirty-two *curés*

[35] *NNEE*, April 8, 1727, pp. 153-54; April 4, 1729, pp. 57-59. Discussion in Justin Godart, *Le jansénisme à Lyon: Benoît Fourgon (1687-1773)* (Paris, 1934), pp. 113-18.

[36] BN, Collection Clairambault, MS 558, fols. 46-53; *NNEE*, Jan. 29, 1727, p. 143; Feb. 10, 1727, p. 147; Feb. 28, 1728, pp. 30-31. See also J. Carreyre, "Utrecht (Eglise d')," *DTC*, xv², esp. cols. 2,401-407.

[37] *NNEE*, June 10, 1728, p. 100.

[38] *Ibid.*, Jan. 10, 1728, p. 5. For details see *Relation du miracle arrivé à Avenay . . . en la personne d'Anne Augier . . .* (1727) and *Mémoire et pièces justificatives touchant le miracle . . .* (1728).

of the diocese, ten of whom were not even appellants. Acting in accordance with prescribed canonical procedure, the priests called upon the diocesan authorities to undertake a full-scale examination of the cure to determine if it were an authentic miracle. But their superiors refused the request.[39]

Once the Augier case was made public, however, a great number of sick persons began to flock to Rousse's grave to pray for relief from their infirmities.[40] The *curé* of Avenay had already warned the duke of Rohan, archbishop of Reims, who immediately forbade the faithful to make any pilgrimage to the tomb or even to invoke Rousse's name in their prayers. These prohibitions, supported by the strictures of *constitutionnaire* parish confessors, served to force the submission of the more timid and weak.[41] But some refused to be cowed.

During May 1728 a certain Madame Jeanne Stapart, wife of a notary, defied the prohibition and went to Rousse's tomb. There she was cured of a severe paralysis and also had the sight restored to her left eye after eleven years of blindness originally occasioned by an attack of apoplexy.[42] The *curés* of Reims once again requested a canonical investigation, this time of both the Augier and the Stapart cures. As before, they were refused.[43] A pastoral letter published by Bishop Colbert of Montpellier on behalf of the Stapart miracle did not change the situation either.[44] Other efforts were similarly unsuccessful, for the authorities, alarmed at the lack of discipline on the part of clergy and laity alike, were already preparing to suppress the newly formed Rousse cult. An order of October 1728 from Chauvelin, Keeper of the Seals, to the intendant in Champagne, directed the latter to take precautions against the followers of M. Rousse and assist the archbishop of Reims in putting a stop to their "superstitious pilgrimages."[45] The intendant, who believed that the proposal to stifle the cult would only

[39] *NNEE*, Jan. 10, 1728, p. 5.   [40] *Ibid.*, June 10, 1728, p. 100.
[41] *Ibid.*

[42] *Ibid.*, June 3, 1728, pp. 96-98; June 10, 1728, pp. 99-101. For details see *Recueil de pièces justificatives du miracle arrivé à Avenay . . . en la personne de mademoiselle Marie-Jeanne Gaulard, épouse de M. François Stapart, notaire royale à Epernay* (1729). The Stapart cure as well as that of Anne Augier was popularized and immortalized by the artist Jean Restout, who illustrated the famous work of Carré de Montgeron (see Ch. IX below). The *NNEE* (Feb. 5, 1728, pp. 19-20) reported a third Rousse miracle, operated on an "incurable" nine-year-old mute paralytic, but for some reason this cure did not attract as much notice as the other two.

[43] *Ibid.*, Aug. 26, 1728, p. 180.

[44] *Ibid.*, July 22, 1728, p. 162. See also Colbert to François Stapart, husband of the *miraculée*, June 27, 1728 (*ibid.*, July 22, 1728, p. 162).

[45] *Ibid.*, Sept. 30, 1729, p. 165.

encourage larger crowds to worship at Rousse's tomb, objected stren-
uously. After a considerable delay, the government finally ordered
archers placed at the entrance to the chapel where the abbé's tomb
was located.[46] Despite the intendant's misgivings, these repressive measures, combined with earlier ecclesiastical threats of excommunication
for those who continued to practice the prohibited devotions, proved
quite successful. Indeed, in fairly short order and without too much
difficulty, royal officials acting in concert with the vigilant Church
authorities in Reims effectively put a halt to the popular observances
before they could become too unmanageable. Now proscribed, the
nascent cult briefly associated with Gérard Rousse appears to have
come to an abrupt and rather undramatic end.

For more than two years the various appellant miracles we have
been describing had remained essentially sporadic, isolated phenomena.
With the notable exception of the Lafosse cure, they had attracted
relatively little attention beyond the localities in which they had taken
place and produced no longstanding or far-reaching repercussions. In
the one case—Reims—where the incidence of miracles had given rise
to an unsanctioned religious cult, fairly prompt and forceful intervention on the part of the authorities had succeeded in bringing the situation completely under control. Within a short time, therefore, the
names of Rousse, Goy, Celeron, and the other Jansenist worthies who
had "performed" assorted miracles since 1725 had sunk back into historical oblivion. To be sure, the cures which had reportedly been
effected through their intercession—for the present of only limited
propaganda potential for the appellant party—were not entirely without symbolic importance. In subsequent years, when the opponents
of the bull *Unigenitus* began to elaborate the full doctrinal and political
implications of the Saint-Médard miracles for the *anticonstitutionnaire*
cause, they were to interpret these first miracles as a divine anticipation
of those which were accomplished through the intercession of the appellant François de Pâris. But it was around the tomb of this originally
obscure Jansenist deacon, the most prolific miracle-worker of the age,
that there developed what was ultimately to become the most controversial religious cult to emerge during the *ancien régime*. It is to
the initial formation and early development of this Pâris cult that we
must turn our attention in the remainder of this chapter.

The special character of his life and the particular nature of his activities, both private and public, determined in large part the emergence
of the popular cult associated with François de Pâris. Resembling many

---

[46] *Ibid.*

a saintly martyr of the primitive Church, this deacon with an amazingly fortunate name for a folk hero, appears to have been the model
of a perfect Christian—a man of consummate piety, humility, penitence, and liberality toward the poor. Regrettably, almost the only
detailed sources available to us about him are the three pious biographies published four years after his death in the midst of the controversies raging over the miracles performed at his tomb.[47] As a consequence, it is very difficult to say how much of what we know about
his life is the product of partisan or hagiographic mythologizing, and
how much is historically factual. In any event, what is recorded in
those accounts of Pâris' life and in a handful of other extant documents
is the stuff of which popular legends are made, legends from which
the Catholic faithful would draw much spiritual sustenance.

Born in Paris on June 30, 1690, François was the elder son of Nicolas
de Pâris, a wealthy counselor in the Parlement of Paris from the second
chamber of *enquêtes*, who had nearly two centuries of "robe nobility"
behind him, but no particularly strong or notable religious convictions
or affiliations. Nor except for an uncle was the rest of young Pâris'
family especially committed to or involved in spiritual affairs. Despite
this background, or perhaps because of it, François demonstrated from
an early age a strong predisposition for the religious life. Even as a
youth he gave himself over to frequent mortifications, exercises of piety,
and solitary prayer. Once he had completed his education at the *collège* Mazarin, however, he had to confront the problem of selecting a
vocation. His parents, who had decided long before that he would
eventually succeed to his father's charge as magistrate, were appalled
when he announced his firm intention to follow an ecclesiastical career. They adamantly insisted that he begin the study of law, in preparation for an official career. Reluctantly deferring to their wishes,
François pursued his legal courses with considerable success until 1711.
Now twenty-one years of age, and believing that he had sufficiently
complied with the demands of his parents, he renewed his intention
of entering the clergy. Two years later, in spite of their continued
resistance, he entered the celebrated Oratorian seminary of Saint-
Magloire. There he came under the influence of some of the leading

[47] [Pierre Boyer], *La Vie de M. de Pâris, diacre* (Brussels, 1731); [Barbeau de
la Bruyère], *La Vie de M. François de Pâris, diacre* (Paris, 1731), which was derived from the Boyer; and [Barthélemy Doyen], *Vie de M. Pâris, diacre du
diocèse de Paris* (Paris, 1731). See also Paul Valet, "Le diacre Pâris et les convulsionnaires de Saint-Médard," *Bulletin de la Montagne Sainte-Geneviève et ses
abords*, 1 (1896), pp. 343-420, and Albert Mousset, *L'étrange histoire des convulsionnaires de Saint-Médard* (Paris, 1953), pp. 33-43.

Jansenist theologians and controversialists of the time and made the acquaintance of numerous other Jansenist worthies, including Bishop Jean Soanen of Senez. There, too, he became increasingly committed to the Jansenist point of view—a personal commitment to the sect's austere and demanding form of Christianity and to the wide range of spiritual, charitable, pastoral, and educational enterprises with which the school of Port-Royal had come to be associated. In addition to his own daily prayer, work, and religious studies at the seminary, he managed to find time to give catechism instruction to the children from the parish of Saint-Jacques-du-Haut-Pas, where he attracted some attention both by his impressive eloquence and by his generosity in distributing books of piety. So outraged was Nicolas de Pâris by his son's disobedience that in 1714, just before his death, he partially disinherited him, reducing François' portion substantially and leaving the remainder to a younger son, Jérôme-Nicolas, to whom the father also bequeathed his judicial post. Ever humane and charitable, the biographers tell us, François converted a great part of his inheritance into alms and personally distributed to the less fortunate some of the cloth and linen that had been left to him.

Thus freed from most of his temporal cares, François de Pâris gave himself over passionately to his religious studies. Though he demonstrated little talent for original thought or theological subtlety,[48] he devoted long hours to the study of Scripture and the Church Fathers; he learned several ancient languages to facilitate his task of understanding these original sources of the faith and to make himself more thoroughly conversant with sacred and ecclesiastical history. By June 1715 he had received Minor Orders and in 1717 left Saint-Magloire. After much coaxing, he reluctantly agreed to be ordained subdeacon in 1718, but when he was appointed deacon in December 1720, he humbly refused to assume the position on the grounds that he was a sinful creature, unworthy of holding so exalted an office.[49]

At the same time, François did not abstain from involvement in the debate over the bull Unigenitus. Quite the contrary, he gloried in the

[48] The theological writings which he did manage to produce—all published posthumously—were essentially derivative works that follow closely the thought of the Jansenist Gaspard Juénin. See Alphonse Adhemar d'Alès, "La théologie du diacre Pâris," Recherches de science religieuse, 10 (1920), pp. 373-87.

[49] This exaggerated sense of unworthiness about assuming priestly office was characteristic of many Jansenists at this time. Cf. the case of Henri de Roquette, later an active convulsionary, who also remained a "simple clerc tonsuré" (P. Lepaysant, Le Port-Royal de Normandie. Saint-Himer-en-Auge et son prieur: Henri de Roquette, 1699-1789 [Paris, 1926], p. 8). See also L.-J. Rogier et al., Nouvelle histoire de l'Eglise, 5 vols. (Paris, 1963-75), III, 417-18.

fact that he had adhered to the appeal in 1717 and had been one of the first to sign the renewed appeal in 1720, acts which were to have posthumous repercussions.[50] Nor had he ever hidden his unequivocal disapproval of the Bull, which he regarded as the work of the devil, and which he believed was "as much opposed to the rights of the king as to those of God."[51] However, in his activities on behalf of the appellant cause, Pâris did not become directly involved in the polemical debates. Instead, he proffered charitable assistance to a number of fellow *anticonstitutionnaires* who had been forced into exile and obliged to relinquish their inheritances or forfeit their benefices. More important, though, were his efforts to do penance for the evils of the Church. According to his biographers, it was M. Pâris' contention that, whereas others had been blessed with talent to defend the Church with their writings, he had been specially called to defend it "with his prayers and his tears, and to win for it God's benediction and protection through the practices of poverty [and] mortifications and the rigors of penitence" to which he began submitting himself.[52] His task, as he conceived it, was to offer himself to God as an expiatory victim. This was his personal effort to appease God's anger, which had allegedly been aroused by the decline of spirituality within the contemporary Church and especially by the acts of persecution which the *constitutionnaires* had committed against the party of "Truth."[53] "He would have consented to being martyred," observed one of his biographers, "asking that God's wrath be extinguished in and through him."[54]

Despite M. Pâris' avowedly *anticonstitutionnaire* affiliations, his name was proposed for the vacant place as *curé* of Saint-Côme in Paris. But François declared that he could not in good conscience sign the Formulary against the Five Propositions that had been required of all Gallican clergy since the 1660s. From then on a sacerdotal career was closed to him, which was just as well, for he had already resolved to spend the rest of his days in poverty and virtual seclusion. In 1722, reportedly disillusioned by the turmoil within the Church, he retired to the notoriously squalid *faubourg* Saint-Marceau—first the rue de l'Arbalète, subsequently the rue des Bourguignons (the present boulevard Port-

50 Doyen, p. 105.

51 Letter to his brother, undated, cited in Valet, p. 354. Despite the break with his father, the deacon remained faithful to his heritage in matters of ecclesiastical politics and upheld the senior Pâris' traditional robe defense of the Gallican position. Cf. his letter written to "un ami de Province" in 1723, reprinted in *NNEE*, June 27, 1731, p. 126.

52 *Ibid.*, July 22, 1728, p. 158; Doyen, p. 92.

53 *Ibid.*, pp. 88-91, 103-104.   54 *Ibid.*, p. 90.

Royal), not far from Val-de-Grâce—to lead a simple life of austere renunciation and exemplary piety, all for the glory of God.

There were at least two principal reasons why François de Pâris had chosen to settle in this area of the capital. The first, and perhaps most important, reason had to do with the religious associations that area had for the Jansenists. Saint-Marceau was located in the heart of the legendary Montagne Sainte-Geneviève, long a stronghold of Jansenist agitation, and probably the most "priest-infested" and overwhelmingly *anticonstitutionnaire* district in the city. It was also an area filled with monastic houses and religious congregations as well as numerous educational and printing establishments, many of them of Jansenist inspiration.[55] In addition, it was here that the ongoing effort to preserve the traditions of Port-Royal had continued to receive much of its energetic direction. The organization of pilgrimages to the ruins of the sacred monastery,[56] the collection and preservation of relics, the production and distribution of innumerable *estampes* and *gravures*, the publication of important works of seventeenth-century Jansenists left in manuscript form by their authors, the composition of pious biographies, and the compilation of necrologies—all were part of the large-scale project to recapture the glorious Jansenist past to which many appellants devoted themselves throughout this period.[57] This was the environment in which François de Pâris (for whom Port-Royal likewise served as a subject of constant meditation) was determined to do his part to sustain the memory of the monastery and to resurrect its spiritual ideals of piety and interior religiosity.[58]

Having committed himself to a life of heroic unworldliness, Pâris thus found Saint-Marceau the perfect setting for accomplishing his purpose. Before long he was joined by three or four like-minded ascetics of his acquaintance, and together, in a modest apartment they found on the rue des Bourguignons,[59] they established a small religious "community" consciously patterned on the model of the Solitaries of Port-Royal. They lived there in relatively peaceful seclusion, sharing

[55] These did a thriving business and helped to sustain party cohesion by turning out works of theology and piety along with large quantities of propaganda. See Dainville, "La carte du jansénisme," pp. 113-24.

[56] See Restout's *estampe*, "Le pèlerinage de piété," which depicts François de Pâris and Father Firmin Tournus, his confessor, going to pray together at the ruins of Port-Royal-des-Champs.

[57] See C. Gazier, *Après Port-Royal*.

[58] Louis Cognet, "Le mépris du monde à Port-Royal et dans le jansénisme," *Revue d'ascétique et de mystique*, 41 (1965), pp. 400-402.

[59] The house in which their apartment was located remained standing until 1868 (Mousset, p. 36).

various domestic tasks. Though they were subject to no religious vows, they adhered voluntarily to a rigorous *règlement de vie* which François de Pâris had drawn up for their mutual use, a "rule" which defined the different spiritual exercises to be performed, individually and collectively, as well as the strict order to be followed in their daily lives. They hoped thereby to emulate, albeit on a very small scale, the fraternal and collegial spirit, the austere piety, and the penitential discipline of their seventeenth-century ancestors.[60] Despite a fundamental *mépris du monde*, however, their flight from worldly distractions and temptations was not intended as a total escape or withdrawal. As with most of the Jansenists at Port-Royal, separation was primarily of an interior sort and did not involve a complete refusal of all contact with the society at large.[61] Nor did it imply an attitude of spiritual passivity or indifference, especially toward the plight of the poor, the unfortunate, or the religiously benighted. On the contrary, for the life of Christian perfection, as the Jansenists had generally conceived it, involved an obligation to perform good works, particularly acts of charity, on behalf of others. It was in this sacred injunction to minister to Christ's poor—an injunction of course incumbent upon all Christians, but in this period taken perhaps more seriously by the Jansenists than by many of their fellow Catholics—that François de Pâris found a second compelling reason for moving to Saint-Marceau. There he would have more than ample opportunity to fulfill this Christian duty.

The *faubourg* Saint-Marceau was an area of considerable poverty and very high population density.[62] An old and notably grubby quarter, Saint-Marceau included some of the poorest, most overcrowded, and most depressed districts in the capital. The *faubourg* was one of the traditional centers of Parisian artisanal activity, primarily in the brewing and tanning industries. But it also housed a wide range of other wage earners as well as small property owners: shopkeepers, small manufacturers and retail merchants, traders and peddlers, hired laborers and odd-job men and women, and a motley horde of unskilled and semi-skilled workers in the lower trades and crafts. Even in the best of times many of these people lived in relatively precarious ma-

[60] An excerpt from the *règlement* is quoted in Doyen, pp. 71-72. The outlook expressed here resembles that of the seventeenth-century Solitary, Antoine Le Maître (see Taveneaux, *La vie quotidienne*, pp. 45-46).

[61] On this question see the Cognet article cited above, n. 58, pp. 387-402; and Taveneaux, *La vie quotidienne*, esp. Chs. 3 and 8.

[62] Marcel Brongniart, *La paroisse Saint-Médard au faubourg Saint-Marceau* (Paris, 1951), p. 6; Jeffry Kaplow, *The Names of Kings: The Parisian Laboring Poor in the Eighteenth Century* (New York, 1972), p. 8.

terial circumstances. However, in the wake of the financial debacle of Law's System, countless hundreds, perhaps thousands, had no doubt suffered especially severe economic and social dislocation, thereby swelling the numbers of laboring poor living on the very brink of destitution.[63] It was to this milieu that the pious and compassionate deacon Pâris had determined to move and where he was destined to live out his last years. François de Pâris was in his element in Saint-Marceau. His neighbors, many of them poverty-stricken like him, though not by choice, knew him only by the name of M. François and until his death were to remain unaware of his real identity. During most of this period not even his own brother knew his whereabouts.

Though he loved his solitude and remained for long periods in his chamber without company, M. François devoted many hours daily to the performance of some pious or charitable act on behalf of his less fortunate neighbors.[64] Seeking to render himself as useful as possible to his fellow man, he not only bestowed all he had on the poor, thereby providing their material necessities, but frequently purchased religious books to distribute among them, thus attempting to satisfy their spiritual needs as well. He paid frequent visits to his fellow appellants or to poor parishioners to see if there was anything he could do for them. Kind, considerate, and attentive to their various needs, he also shared in an endless variety of menial tasks and services around the *faubourg*, from cleaning the streets and paths to carrying buckets of water.[65] To avoid becoming financially dependent on others and to enable him better to serve the needs of the poor, Pâris purchased a trade and began to make woolen stockings.[66] He gave most of them away and sold the rest to persons who could afford to buy them. He thus earned enough money to sustain his own simple requirements while obtaining additional funds for his charitable benefactions.

This boundless generosity and indefatigable charity he displayed toward the poor residents of the parish and *faubourg* were no doubt initially responsible for drawing popular attention to François de Pâris. No less important, however, for the saintly reputation he was

[63] Earl Hamilton, "Prices and Wages at Paris under John Law's System," *Quarterly Journal of Economics*, 51 (1936-37), pp. 42-70.

[64] On the tradition of Jansenist charity toward the poor, see Taveneaux, *La vie quotidienne*, pp. 149-55.

[65] *Ibid.*, p. 192.

[66] In a number of contemporary engravings, Pâris is shown seated at a wooden frame weaving the stockings. These *estampes*, depicting the deacon as "artisan," vied in popularity with those which showed him in a more purely spiritual pose and setting.

later to acquire was the nature of the penitential discipline, physical and spiritual, which he practiced during the last four or five years of his life. Material goods and possessions having already become a matter of little concern to him, Pâris had determined to live in extremely austere circumstances and at a level of bare subsistence. But the extraordinary degree of deprivation to which he eagerly subjected himself amazed even some of his fellow penitents and those of his neighbors who occasionally visited him. The deacon's miserable living quarters were starkly drab, without even the most elementary of creature comforts. There was little or no furniture, an overturned armoire serving as his bed. Nor was there anything else in the little room to distract from an atmosphere of unrelieved, almost morbid, gloom. As for food, Pâris' single daily meal—usually taken early in the evening—generally consisted of a piece of bread, a bit of rice, and some cabbage soup, and only rarely included any meat.

Despite this regimen of extreme self-denial, François continued his tireless activities on behalf of his fellow parishioners, all the while seeking ever more severe forms of mortification with which to torture his body. During Lent in 1724 he fasted completely. So incredibly rigorous was his abstention that he was reduced to a state of severe nervous exhaustion, which ultimately reached the point of convulsive agitations notably similar to those that were to occur at his grave some years later.[67] At the same time, the bodily penances and frequent macerations went on unabated—and were even redoubled. To the hairshirt which he had worn all along he added a plate or sheet of bristling iron wires which tore into his flesh and sometimes caused the blood to flow. Nor was that all. When his confessor ordered him to remove the spiked metal belt which until then he had also kept tied around his body, he found yet other macabre torture devices with which to replace it.[68]

Exceedingly scrupulous about his own interior disposition and possessed of an overly sensitive conscience and an exaggerated sense of unworthiness, Pâris also felt driven to extremes of spiritual self-denial and self-degradation. Not satisfied with refusing, out of humility, the various clerical charges offered to him, he voluntarily abstained for two years from receiving communion or fulfilling his Easter duties. Only after a formal order had come from his spiritual director and from the curé of Saint-Médard did François consent to take communion again.

---

[67] One of his biographers suggested that this "extraordinarily violent state" was intended to presage the convulsionaries and to justify them in advance. By God's grace, he added, François de Pâris could endure "des jeûnes si extraordinaires en confirmation de la justice de la cause qu'il défend" (Doyen, p. 51).

[68] Taveneaux, *La vie quotidienne*, p. 192.

But the attitude of almost obsessive submission to God, the sense of fear and trembling in His awesome presence, persisted as before.

By 1725, despite the care M. Pâris had taken to preserve his anonymity, his assiduous devotions, his innumerable benefactions toward the poor, and the public instruction he gave at Saint-Médard attracted the admiring and respectful attention of the parish *curé*, the appellant Nicolas Pommart. At Pentecost in that year, M. Pommart, with assistance from Pâris' confessor, finally overcame François' resistance to donning the surplice that had rightfully been his since his elevation to the diaconate in 1720.[69] What is more, the *curé* put him officially in charge of giving catechism lessons to the children of the parish and also made him clerical superior. In this latter capacity he had the task of instructing the young clerics in their duties, and in the process profoundly impressed them and the rest of the parish clergy not only with his wisdom and his piety but with the humility and simplicity which formed his character.

While continuing to carry out these various duties at Saint-Médard and to perform frequent acts of charity for his neighbors throughout the quarter, Pâris also continued his intense mortifications and bodily penances. Such physical tortures could not fail to have had a debilitating effect on the deacon's already weakened constitution.[70] A number of short, but enervating pilgrimages taken in 1726 and early 1727 further exhausted him and sapped his declining strength.[71] In April 1727, after quietly suffering for over a month from a large tumor on the knee, he was finally bedridden with a fever and various gastrointestinal difficulties. As he languished in bed for many days, his condition steadily deteriorated. On May 1, 1727, the abbé Pommart, accompanied by a number of clergy from Saint-Médard, was called to administer the last rites. Legend has it that after writing or dictating his last testament[72] and making arrangements on behalf of those persons, lay and ecclesiastic, whom he had been assisting, François de Pâris asked for one final time to be given the opportunity to state publicly his unshakable opposition to the Bull. "It is not necessary to explain your-

---

[69] This capitulation was only temporary, however, for Pâris was not to wear the surplice again for another two years, and then only because he was on his deathbed and about to receive the last sacrament.

[70] A contemporary portrait by Restout reveals "les visages osseux, vieilli prématurément [qui] indique les jeûnes et les macérations" (Lepaysant, p. 56).

[71] In 1726 he traveled to Villeneuve-le-Roi to meet with the exiled appellant abbé d'Asfeld, his unofficial spiritual adviser since his days at Saint-Magloire. A letter reporting their meeting, held because Pâris was seeking advice about undertaking an even more thorough "retreat," is in Doyen, pp. 131-34.

[72] A portion is cited in Valet, p. 362. See also BN, MSS Fr., MS 11431, fol. 9.

self further," interrupted Father Pommart, "your views are well known."[73] Serene and composed, François de Pâris now received extreme unction. Although he continued for hours to struggle against his impending death and even temporarily regained some strength, the deacon eventually succumbed that evening, a *suicide religieux*, two months before his thirty-seventh birthday.[74]

As the news of his death quickly circulated throughout the parish, the public reaction was overwhelming. A huge crowd of people, shopkeepers, artisans, and others from the *faubourg*, flocked to M. François' house to pay their last respects and to view the body, which rested in state in a very simple coffin. Many of them, once they had said their prayers and implored the deacon to intercede with God on their behalf, touched the corpse with rosaries, garments, religious icons, and devotional books, hoping to sanctify the object by direct bodily contact with one whom they already regarded as "Blessed" (*bienheureux*).[75] Some cut off his nails or bits of his hair, while still others tried to satisfy their desire for some holy relic either by ripping off a tiny piece of the cloth shirt which M. François had been wearing when he died or by taking a splinter of wood from the overturned armoire which had served as his deathbed.[76] The first posthumous "supernatural phenomenon" associated with the deacon was reported at this time: those who filed past the bier declared that Pâris seemed to be only sleeping, for his face appeared to have retained the rosy color of life.[77]

Two days later François de Pâris was buried as he had wished, in a very simple grave in one of the little cemeteries, usually reserved for poor parishioners, which at that time flanked the church of Saint-Mé-

[73] Cited by Valet, p. 362. On the previous day, Pâris had already dictated a "profession of faith" to the abbé Paul Collard, one of the ecclesiastics who lived with him: "Le diacre Pâris . . . lui recommanda de dénoncer les Jésuites comme auteurs des maux de l'Eglise et de propager l'oeuvre de Port-Royal . . ." (BN, MSS Fr., MS 11431, fol. 9).

[74] Doyen, pp. 167-68.   [75] *Ibid.*, p. 173.

[76] The public's craving for relics was simply astounding. According to one observer, "La dévotion qui dans les commencements avoit attiré dans sa maison un concours infini de personnes de toutes conditions et de tout sexe a fait disparoître en entier . . . un bas qu'il avait commencé pendant sa maladie et que la piété du peuple a enlevé. Il en auroit été aussi de même de l'armoire qui luy servoit de lit si les parens de M. Pâris n'eussent fait enlever les restes de cette armoire et le gros pavé qu'on a trouvé auprès et qui probablement luy avoit servi de chevet lorsqu'il couchoit par terre. La piété du peuple a pareillement enlevé un arbre qui se trouvoit auprès de l'endroit où il est enterré" (BHVP, C.P. 3522, "Réflexions générales").

[77] Valet, p. 364.

dard.[78] Though only a modest ceremony, the funeral attracted a large throng of mourners from every station in society and from all over Paris—a situation which thoroughly astonished M. François' poor neighbors, who were overwhelmed to see such distinguished company present at the burial of someone whom they had always believed to be their social equal.[79]

Those who had known and admired him, including his archbishop and fellow appellant, Cardinal Noailles, and others who had merely heard stories of this saintly man, came to offer their prayers for his soul.[80] François de Pâris had already begun to obtain posthumously the very notoriety and renown that he had rather successfully shunned most of his life. But it was only the beginning.

A dramatic incident occurred on the day of interment, an event which first established François de Pâris' reputation for thaumaturgic powers. An elderly and illiterate woolworker, the widow Louise-Madeleine Reigney (or Beigney), who had met M. François several times in the parish and had watched him admiringly at the church of Saint-Médard as he stood in solitary meditation and prayer, went to the services to pay her respects to the deacon for having been such a great friend of the poor and the unfortunate. But she also had another reason for attending. Despite frequent and sincere invocation of divine power, she had until then been unable to obtain a cure for her arm, paralyzed for nearly twenty years. She hoped God might heal the arm this time if she prayed for M. François' intercession. Approaching the bier, full of trust, she fell down on her knees, recited some prayers, embraced and kissed the deacon's feet—and went away cured![81] This supposedly miraculous cure was but a foretaste of many

[78] For descriptions of the cemetery, see J. Hillairet, *Les 200 cimetières du vieux Paris* (Paris, 1958), pp. 84-85; A. Gazier, *Histoire générale*, I, 279; and Mousset, pp. 49-50, 72. According to Marcel Brongniart, "Il n'y a que les plus pauvres qui sont enterrés au cimetière. Dès qu'il s'agit d'un marchand, l'inhumation se fait dans l'église et presque toujours le plus près possible du banc où le défunt avait l'habitude d'assister aux offices" (p. 99).

[79] Doyen, pp. 172-73. See also BHVP, C.P. 3522, "Réflexions générales."

[80] For examples of the prayers dedicated to M. Pâris' memory, see BA, MS 2054, fols. 82, 133-38; MS 5346, fols. 167-83; MS 5351, fols. 140-42; and MS 6884, fol. 449. See also "Prière composée par M. Pâris et récitée par lui tous les jours" (BA, MS 5351, fol. 142v°).

[81] Details of this cure may be found in an account which the widow Reigney presented to the notaries at the Châtelet on Dec. 5, 1733, and had published in the *Relation du premier miracle opéré subitement dans la maison du bienheureux François de Pâris.* She claimed to have made her declaration "pour rendre gloire à Dieu et témoignage à la sainteté de son serviteur, et en conserver la mémoire à la postérité . . . ," but who composed the "relation" for her and why she waited

others to come, most of them far more remarkable, and a prelude to the almost unimaginable drama that was to be played at Saint-Médard.

During his lifetime, François de Pâris had won the love and veneration of his fellow parishioners, for whom he had been a truly heroic, indeed charismatic, figure. Long before the deacon's death, his neighbors—those who had benefited directly from his kindness and charity and others who knew of him and his works only by reputation—had proudly exchanged stories about the extraordinary devotions and acts of piety that he had been performing daily in their very midst. In an age lacking in religious heroes, here was an inspirational figure whose ascetic life seemed beyond ordinary human capability and equivalent to martyrdom, whose qualities of saintliness appeared to match those of other celebrated exemplars of humanity, including Pâris' own great medieval namesake. Like Saint Francis, he had renounced all wealth, property, privileges, and status and had identified himself with the meek and the humble, in whose well-being he had taken a special interest. Having led a life that no doubt conformed to popular expectations of how a holy man should live, this generous "victime de la pénitence" thus left a vivid impression upon the people of Saint-Médard, who were already much moved by his death.[82] But the dramatic cure of Mme. Reigney immediately captured their imagination, serving to confirm them in their exalted view of M. François and demonstrating that he was endowed with extraordinary intercessionary powers. When news of the miracle spread beyond the parish and throughout the city, a virtual army of sick people, pious believers, and devout pilgrims was drawn to Saint-Médard from all corners of Paris, some to pray for the cure of diseases which had baffled the doctors, others to obtain a relic from among the various effects left by or associated with M. Pâris.[83] As his reputation grew, these people, possessed of sufficient and conclusive proof of his sanctity and too impatient to await an official judgment from the Church, were quick to canonize their deacon, "dead in the odor of sanctity."[84] The

more than six years after the event to come forward and issue such a statement remain unclear. Excerpts cited by P.-F. Mathieu, *Histoire des miraculés et des convulsionnaires de Saint-Médard* (Paris, 1864), pp. 117-20.

[82] According to an eyewitness account, "les pauvres et les enfans qu'il avoit catéchisés pleuroient à hautte voix à son enterrement et pendant le service" (BHVP, C.P. 3522, "Réflexions générales").

[83] Doyen, p. 174.

[84] "Pendant le convoy les pauvres qui bordoient les rues apostrophoient Mr de Pâris le cons^r sans le connoître, en luy disant, Monsr., si vous êtes frère de M^r

largely popular cult which developed in the ensuing years bore witness to this extraordinary reverence for and confidence in François de Pâris and, especially among the most miserable and distressed, may have satisfied a craving for some new spiritual outlet, some other-worldly consolation or compensation for material afflictions suffered in this life.

Within a year of the burial, Jérôme-Nicolas de Pâris erected a tomb in his brother's memory. The modest monument consisted of a large rectangular slab of black marble, raised slightly above the ground by four stone supports. There was just enough space left for a person, crawling on his stomach, to fit between the marble and the grave—an exercise which many were to perform in subsequent years. Jérôme-Nicolas also commissioned a certain Jaudin, doctor of theology at the Sorbonne, to engrave on the tombstone a long Latin epitaph summarizing the life and merits of M. François.[85] The epitaph received the express approval of Cardinal Noailles, who had been among the admirers present when the deacon was buried.

Noailles, who had apparently looked favorably upon the nascent Pâris cult from the outset, played a crucial role in its early development and in the establishment of its legitimacy and respectability. The cardinal-archbishop did not hesitate to acknowledge and extol the saintly character of the deacon's life or to grant M. François the appellation of *bienheureux* which the *menu peuple* had already bestowed upon him.[86] More significantly, as a consequence of his exalted ecclesiastical position and in accordance with the Tridentine legislation governing the veneration of saints, Noailles was soon called upon to

l'abbé de Pâris vous pouvez être assuré que vous avez un frère dans le ciel" (BHVP, C.P. 3522, "Réflexions générales"). For a brief discussion of the process of popular "canonization," see Augustin Gazier, "Jean Restout et les miracles de M. Pâris," *Revue de l'art chrétien*, 62 (1912), p. 117; and James F. Hitchcock, "Popular Religion in Elizabethan England" (Ph.D. Dissertation, Princeton University, 1965), pp. 75-77. For a more extended analysis, see Gabriele De Rosa, "Santeté, clergé et peuple dans le Mezzogiorno italien au milieu du 18ᵉ siècle," *Revue d'histoire de la spiritualité*, 52 (1976), pp. 245-64.

[85] The original Latin version, along with a French transcription, is in BA, MS 2054, fols. 139-42; they are also reprinted in Mousset, pp. 40-43.

[86] *NNEE*, May 20, 1729, p. 77; Dorsanne, II, 470. See also Louis Figuier, *Histoire du merveilleux dans les temps modernes*, 2 vols. (Paris, 1860-61), I, 345-46. When it was objected that the deacon Pâris had not yet been beatified, Noailles allegedly replied that "the word of God, as expressed through the prodigies occurring at Saint-Médard, was worth more than that of men."

deal with the subject of the Pâris cures. In the spring of 1728, aware of Pâris' reputation for thaumaturgic powers and impressed by the number and notoriety of the cures the deacon was said to have performed at Saint-Médard, Cardinal Noailles initiated plans for an official examination of these allegedly miraculous phenomena. Following the formal juridical procedures prescribed by the Church, he appointed the abbé Achille Thomassin, his vicegerent (administrative deputy) in the ecclesiastical court of the archdiocese, to undertake a careful preliminary study of these cures, in order to determine whether there was sufficient evidence to warrant a full-scale episcopal investigation. After an intensive, three-month probe, Thomassin concluded that a substantial number of seemingly authentic miracles was involved and that the entire affair was clearly worthy of the archbishop's immediate and direct attention. Once apprised of these preliminary findings, Noailles issued an episcopal order, published on June 15, 1728, naming Father Thomassin to head an official commission of inquiry. He empowered the vicegerent to review with deliberate and painstaking thoroughness all the previous testimony given by the *miraculés* and their assorted witnesses (relatives, friends, neighbors, employers or employees, colleagues, priests, doctors); to evaluate the notarized depositions of medical experts; to examine the character and evaluate the credibility of all persons called to testify; to take further testimony from additional witnesses wherever such supplementary evidence was believed necessary; and, finally, to continue to gather together all relevant information on any other cures reported or discovered in the interim.[87]

By the end of August the commission had heard numerous persons who claimed to have been miraculously cured, taken depositions from scores of witnesses to these cures, and compiled a series of voluminous dossiers. The initial results of this intensive, probing inquest were striking. A report submitted to Noailles at this time singled out for particular consideration four of the dozen or so cures that had been under investigation, most of them on persons from outside the parish of Saint-Médard.[88] Pierre Lero, thirty-five-year-old *marchand fripier*

---

[87] *Requête présentée au parlement par 23 curés de . . . Paris, 5 mai 1735* (Paris, 1735), pp. 3-4; *NNEE*, July 1, 1728, p. 130. On the procedures involved in such an investigation, see Henri Platelle, *Chrétiens face au miracle: Lille au 17ᵉ siècle* (Paris, 1968), especially pp. 32-37. It would be very interesting to know who bore the considerable expense involved in the Thomassin inquest. Unfortunately, none of the surviving records gives any indication of what party or parties acted as benefactor(s).

[88] BN, MSS Fr., MS 22245, fols. 3-34.

from the parish of Saint-Eustache, had been cured in September 1727 of an ulcerated leg that had incapacitated him for more than a year and a half. Marie-Jeanne Orget, fifty-seven-year-old *maîtresse couturière* from Saint-Louis-en-l'Ile, had been cured in March 1728 of acute erysipelas on the leg which had plagued her intermittently for over thirty years. Elisabeth de la Loë, twenty-five-year-old woman from the parish of Bonnes Nouvelles and a recent convert from Protestantism, had been cured in July 1728 of a severe swelling of the breast first experienced some eighteen months earlier. Finally, Marie-Madeleine Mossaron, twenty-seven-year-old daughter of the *agent des affaires* of the Grand Duke of Tuscany, residing in the parish of Saint-Eustache, had been cured in late July 1728 of convulsions, apoplexy, and a virtual paralysis of the left side of her body suffered since January 1727.[89] Though none of these four cures had been effected instantaneously, each appeared to be so well substantiated that only the authorization of the archbishop was needed to publish the commission's findings and to declare that the phenomena in question were indeed "true and miraculous." Just as Noailles seemed on the point of doing so, however, Versailles intervened.

Alarmed by what the Saint-Médard affair might portend in the debate over the Bull, and concerned that Noailles' public approbation would immediately increase the credibility and the fame of these miracles and endow the tales of Pâris' thaumaturgic powers with the requisite prestige, the government sought to squelch the proceedings. As early as June, Chauvelin had written a rather patronizing letter to Noailles, recommending that the archbishop terminate the inquest because it was displeasing to Cardinal Fleury.[90] Later that same month, after apparently obtaining Noailles' assurance of compliance, Chauvelin sent another, much more forceful letter to Father Thomassin, urging him not to carry out his charge. "In times like these," Chauvelin insisted, "it is important to do nothing which might give rise to new controversies and new pamphlets."[91]

Refusing to be intimidated by the government's coercive tactics, Thomassin had resolved to fulfill his assignment and to make a full report to Noailles. But by this time, the aged archbishop was failing in health and apparently losing touch with reality. Vacillating more and more in his stand on the Bull and related issues of theology and

[89] A long account of this cure and copies of the medical certificates are in *NNEE*, July 22, 1728, pp. 155-58.

[90] *Ibid.*, p. 158; Dorsanne, II, 439, contains the text of Chauvelin's letter, along with a brief commentary.

[91] Text of letter, *ibid.*, pp. 439-40.

ecclesiastical politics, he had come increasingly under the influence of his family, who were working in concert with Fleury to convert him to the *constitutionnaire* side. Despite the positive findings of Thomassin's commission, despite the growing crowds of the faithful throughout his diocese who were flocking to Saint-Médard, and despite his own express support for the Pâris cult, Noailles no longer had either the strength or the courage to stand up publicly to the mounting resistance from Versailles. When in October 1728 Fleury's allies in Paris managed to force the resignation of Thomassin and other appellants who had long held positions of authority in the diocese and replaced them all with *constitutionnaire* officials loyal to the government, the cardinal-archbishop found himself virtually alone.[92] Hoping to effect a reconciliation of all parties, and on the verge of an apparent capitulation to Fleury and the pope over the Bull, Noailles was prevailed upon not to publish the Thomassin *procès-verbaux*. But though he may have acquiesced in Fleury's demand that he remain silent on the matter and not make any public statement regarding the miracles, the enfeebled archbishop seems to have still had enough presence of mind to take certain steps to ensure that the results of his former vicegerent's investigation would not be lost. In order that the *procès-verbaux* might be preserved for possible future use under the appropriate circumstances, Noailles, within a month before his death, had the dossiers secretly conveyed to the Oratorian Father Charles-Armand Fouquet, former superior in the seminary of Saint-Magloire and a friend of the late deacon Pâris.[93] Events were later to prove how shrewd and foresighted a precaution this was.

Although the miracles of Saint-Médard had thus been denied formal episcopal consecration, the secret maneuverings over the *procès-verbaux* did not materially affect the public observances of the cult. The tomb of François de Pâris had become a hallowed sanctuary to which the pious and the sick in ever greater numbers—most of them oblivi-

[92] According to the *curés* of Paris, "sans les changements qui survinrent à l'Archevêché au mois d'Octobre 1728, . . . il y auroit eu dès lors plus de 20 Miracles examinés par une information juridique" (*Requête présentée au parlement par 23 curés de . . . Paris, 5 mai 1735*, p. 4).

[93] According to the terms of the *Acte de décharge* given to the abbé Thomassin on April 12, 1729, Noailles stipulated that his vicegerent "remettra au porteur les minutes des Procès-verbaux, qu'il a faits en vertu de la Commission que je lui ai donnée, sur les Miracles de M. l'abbé Pâris de sainte mémoire, *sans en rien dire à personne*" (*ibid.*, my italics). The secrecy with which the disposition of the papers was handled later gave rise to a series of bitter disputes regarding Noailles' precise sentiments on the issue of Saint-Médard and his actual orders to Father Thomassin.

ous to the turbulent debates of ecclesiastical politics swirling about the diocese and unaware of or little concerned about M. François' appellant affiliations—continued to make their pilgrimages.[94] For at least two more years the government would make no serious attempt to oppose or even to disturb these religious devotions, concentrating its attention for the time being on more pressing matters. Perhaps Fleury was satisfied at having successfully squelched Noailles' attempt to give official recognition to the nascent cult. Or perhaps he was not sure that these developments at Saint-Médard posed a very serious problem. Whatever the reasons, by the time of Noailles' death in May 1729 neither civil nor ecclesiastical intervention seems to have been under consideration.

Government and church indifference or inaction would not last indefinitely, however. At Saint-Médard the unofficial, unauthorized popular religious cult associated with François de Pâris had already succeeded in attracting many adherents. Though deprived of ecclesiastical legitimation, the cult had obtained at least the tacit approval of Cardinal Noailles before his death. What is more, it had acquired the explicit support of the *curé* of Saint-Médard himself, who was one of its earliest and most ardent promoters. Indeed, in the parish of Saint-Médard local enthusiasm for the cult—lay and clerical—was considerable, as the presence of a saintly hero in the very midst of this poor, generally obscure, and frequently overlooked quarter no doubt evoked a strong sense of communal pride and excitement. When the *constitutionnaire* Vintimille succeeded to the archbishopric of Paris, he was bent on restoring order and discipline throughout the diocese. Saint-Médard, which had by then become a place of pilgrimage for many of the Paris faithful, was shortly to become a source of deep disquiet for Vintimille. But, as we shall see, once the new archbishop found it necessary to intervene against the Pâris cult, there was a sudden recrudescence of miracles at the cemetery. This new development came at a time of increasingly militant and vocal challenges to his episcopal authority from magistrates, *avocats*, and parish clergy alike. Pursued relentlessly by a formidable political and ecclesiastical opposition, declining in strength and needful of allies, the Jansenist party was once more to find its most eloquent and forceful apology in a direct intervention of God. Utilizing their extensive and well-functioning propaganda apparatus, the clerical opponents of the Bull were ultimately

[94] Miracles attributed to Pâris' intercession were already being reported at some distance from the capital (Jérôme-Nicolas de Pâris to Mme. Chevalier, July 4, 1727, BN, NAFr., MS 5096, fols. 20-22).

to seize on the Pâris cult as an incontrovertible justification of the *anticonstitutionnaire* cause and as a live, exploitable political issue. The result of the ensuing confrontation was to transform the Saint-Médard observances from a local phenomenon to a diocesan and eventually a national *cause célèbre* and to draw the popular cult into the turbulent sphere of ecclesiastical politics.

CHAPTER III

◗✖ℰ◗✖ℰ◗✖ℰ◗✖ℰ◗✖ℰ◗✖ℰ

Ecclesiastical Politics in the Diocese of Paris and the Miracles of François de Pâris, 1730-1731

ALTHOUGH by the summer of 1930 François de Pâris and other appellant thaumaturges all over France had already been credited with working dozens of miraculous cures, the number of *anticonstitutionnaires* who paid them much attention remained relatively small. The opponents of the Bull continued to turn out their numerous and tirelessly repetitious polemics and theological tracts, with scarcely a reference to the events going on in public forums at Saint-Médard and elsewhere.[1] Save for an occasional passing mention of specific miracles, the *Nouvelles ecclésiastiques* evinced little abiding interest in the popular observances that were daily taking place around the grave of the deacon Pâris. Indeed, it would appear that most appellants either did not at first envisage or did not care to contemplate the propaganda potential which the Pâris miracles might afford their cause. For one thing, even as late as 1730 the cures were still only isolated and occasional events. For another, many leading *anticonstitutionnaire* theologians continued to believe that these cures were superfluous and indeed irrelevant to the defense of the appeal; as the party of "Truth," they felt certain of sustaining their position by means of constitutional and theological arguments alone, without recourse to any popular cult or supernatural phenomena.[2]

On the *constitutionnaire* side, in the meantime, official expressions of concern regarding Saint-Médard remained virtually nonexistent. Neither Vintimille nor Fleury, both preoccupied with more immediately pressing religious matters, showed much interest in the events occurring at Pâris' tomb. By the following spring, however, the relative indifference exhibited by both sides was to change dramatically.

---

[1] Bishop Colbert of Montpellier was, of course, the most notable exception (see Ch. II above), though even he had paid relatively scant attention thus far to the Pâris miracles.

[2] *Pensées sur les prodiges de nos jours* (*1734*), p. 3. There was also a certain degree of skepticism behind these reservations. Cf. the attitude of Nicole and other seventeenth-century Jansenists, discussed in Ch. II above.

After March 1731, the miracles of François de Pâris came increasingly to be identified with and exploited by the appellant party. Shortly thereafter the ecclesiastical and civil authorities, faced with this latest propaganda thrust, were forced to respond in turn. To understand this dramatic change—in large part a carefully calculated political act, consciously conceived by certain *anticonstitutionnaires* as a challenge to official religious policy—requires an understanding of the principal developments in national and Parisian ecclesiastical politics in 1730 and the first half of 1731. The history of the growing association between the Pâris cult and the opposition to *Unigenitus* began after the royal government stepped up its efforts to impose the Bull on the entire kingdom and, in collaboration with the civil and religious authorities in Paris, attempted to stifle all *anticonstitutionnaire* resistance throughout the capital.

Within a short time after Vintimille's accession to the archbishopric of Paris in 1729, Cardinal Fleury and his new episcopal creature resolutely embarked on an ambitious campaign to reduce to submission the reputedly weakened, leaderless, and demoralized Jansenist party in the diocese. Fleury's goal, unchanged since the beginning of his ministry, was to reestablish religious peace and uniformity throughout France on the basis of the Bull's full and unqualified acceptance. The rigor and method were not new, but the cardinal-minister had not previously been able to count on cooperation or assistance from the archbishop of Paris. By the end of 1729, Fleury and Vintimille, working closely together with Lieutenant of Police Hérault, had achieved a rapid and marked success in stifling the opposition of several corporate religious bodies, including the Faculty of Theology and a number of suspect congregations and regular orders. Nevertheless, as we have already seen,[3] despite these initial successes, the tensions and strains between the archbishop and the *anticonstitutionnaire* partisans had grown rather than diminished. Challenges to his episcopal authority, particularly at the parish level, were rife. The agitation of the lower clergy, who had gained the open support and protection of sympathetic *avocats* and magistrates in the Paris Parlement, was more vocal and audacious than ever. Unauthorized assemblies of *curés*, organized for the purpose of resisting Vintimille's pronouncements, met frequently throughout this period.[4] Jansenist priests and confessors all over the capital continued with considerable success to encourage the faithful in their spiritual care to oppose the Bull. Capable and prolific propagandists, including the mysterious editor of the *Nouvelles ec-*

[3] See Ch. 1 above.   [4] Préclin, *Les jansénistes*, p. 132, n. 92.

clésiastiques, persisted in their frequent attacks, some of them quite vicious, against the policies and the very person of the archbishop. The resistance confronting Vintimille in the early weeks of 1730 thus seemed every bit as serious as it had been on his arrival in Paris less than six months before.

His earlier hopes of immediately restoring peace and tranquility to his embattled diocese all but dashed, Vintimille felt increasingly overwhelmed by a sense of utter helplessness. As he fretfully, but perceptively, observed in a letter to Cardinal Fleury, it was "impractical in the present circumstances" to attempt to discipline those *curés* who were most responsible for this state of affairs, not only because the procedure involved would be too time-consuming, but also because it would have potentially dangerous consequences, arousing further resentment among the *curés* and their faithful parishioners and provoking these same *curés* and the Gallican *avocats* to bring an *appel comme d'abus* before the Parlement.[5] Frustrated at his inability to find any other way of remedying "the deplorable condition" of his diocese, and disturbed at charges of indifference and inaction which some of his fellow bishops had made against him, Vintimille determined "for the good of the State as well as that of the Church" to appeal directly to the king for assistance.[6]

In a letter composed with Fleury's assistance and sent to Louis XV with the cardinal-minister's approval, Vintimille began by bemoaning the state of religious affairs in Paris—"the sad consequences of parochial resistance." The archbishop went on to express his belief that a firmer, more rigorous policy was needed to bring the recalcitrant to heel, "so that, by a perfect union of the sacerdotal and temporal powers, anyone who causes trouble or disorder may be punished according to canonical and civil procedures."[7] In his reply, the king, through Fleury, promised to support Vintimille "with all his authority if [the archbishop] could not win back these stubborn individuals by moderate methods."[8] In addition, the cardinal-minister authorized Vintimille

---

[5] Vintimille to Fleury, Jan. 21, 1730, BM, MS 2357, pp. 51-52.

[6] Vintimille to Fleury, Feb. 8, 1730, *ibid.*, pp. 55-56.

[7] *Lettre de M. l'archevêque de Paris au roi (8 février 1730)*, BPR, L.P. 444, No. 83. Cf. similar complaints made in a letter written to the pope about the same time: Vintimille to Clement XII, Feb. 6, 1730, excerpt quoted in *NNEE*, May 1, 1731, p. 91.

[8] *Lettre du roi, écrite de la propre main de Sa Majesté, en réponse à la Lettre de M. l'archevêque de Paris (15 février 1730)*, BPR, L.P. 444, No. 83. Cf. the anonymous *Justification de MM les Curés de Paris contre la Lettre de M. l'Archevêque au Roi en datte du 28 février 1730*, dated April 1730 but published later in the year (*NNEE*, Jan. 19, 1731, p. 16).

to publish the two letters and circulate them in the streets of Paris, in the hope that they might at least have a favorable impact upon the public, even if their implied threat had little effect upon the obdurate *curés*.[9] No sooner had the letters appeared in print than Vintimille, as if to demonstrate that he meant business, proceeded to add some sixty to seventy priests and confessors to the list of those already suspended from their functions.[10] But even this unwonted show of strength on the part of the archbishop proved unavailing. What was required in Vintimille's view was that the royal government itself take decisive action in proscribing *anticonstitutionnaire* opposition once and for all.

Vintimille's desperately urgent entreaties to Fleury and the king, coming as they did from the principal diocese in the realm and from the cardinal-minister's own creature and close friend, made a most compelling case for prompt and dramatic royal intervention. Nor was the archbishop of Paris alone in his appeals. Indeed, for months various representatives of the Holy See as well as numerous *constitutionnaire* clergy all over France, including a particularly zealous and influential faction at court, had been exerting pressure upon Fleury's administration to intervene once more against the opponents of the Bull. Personally predisposed to following a moderate course and fearful, like Vintimille, of the possibly dangerous consequences of resorting to "violent or extreme remedies" which might exacerbate old tensions or provoke new ones, Fleury was determined to proceed cautiously. In mid-February he summoned his lay and clerical advisers to a meeting at Versailles. After prolonged discussions which continued for the next several weeks, it was decided that the king would issue a formal declaration recognizing the bull *Unigenitus* unequivocally as a law of the State.[11]

Prepared in consultation with the *procureur-général*[12] and with several influential judges from the Parlement of Paris—an obvious effort to forestall potential opposition from that quarter—the royal declaration was published on March 24.[13] More political than religious, con-

---

[9] Fleury to Vintimille, Feb. 18, 1730, BM, MS 2357, p. 59.

[10] *NNEE*, March 25, 1730, pp. 63-64, and April 2, 1730, pp. 68-70.

[11] G. Hardy, pp. 185-91. As Michel Antoine has demonstrated, it was at this time that the *Conseil des Dépêches* began taking principal responsibility for coordinating the government's parlementary and anti-Jansenist policies. See his *Le Conseil du Roi sous le règne de Louis XV* (Geneva, 1970), pp. 442, 445; and his "Le Conseil des Dépêches sous le règne de Louis XV," *Bibliothèque de l'Ecole des Chartes*, 111 (1953), pp. 166-72.

[12] See extensive correspondence exchanged between Chancellor Daguesseau and Joly de Fleury, BN, J.F., MS 84, fols. 71ff.

[13] "Déclaration par laquelle le roi explique de nouveau ses intentions sur l'exé-

cerned with reestablishing law and order and restoring discipline and respect for legitimate authority, the declaration was consistent with Fleury's longstanding religious policy.[14] It was a rather comprehensive piece of legislation, containing two major sets of provisions. In the first place, after bitterly complaining of the bad faith and perverse intractability of the refractory clergy and decrying the disturbances which the Jansenists had allegedly caused in the kingdom, the declaration attempted to define the sense in which the bull *Unigenitus* was to be understood and interpreted. Renewing previous royal declarations on the subject, it empowered the clergy to instruct the faithful in their obligations to receive the Bull. It further pronounced *Unigenitus* to be not only a dogmatic judgment of the universal Church—in consequence of "the general consent of the episcopate"—but also a law of the State, which could not be subject to qualifications or restrictions nor attacked with impunity. Another series of provisions in the decree appeared to sanction and even to encourage *constitutionnaire* bishops to pursue those contumacious clergy who persisted in their adherence to the appeal. All priests or candidates for canonical functions were required to sign the Formulary on Jansenism and also to accept the Bull "purely and simply." Those who failed to do so would neither receive ordination nor be endowed with benefices. What is more, ecclesiastics suspended from their functions or refused canonical institution could not have recourse to the secular courts, since *appels comme d'abus* were denied the power of suspension in all cases enunciated in the law. In any event, according to explicit provisions of the declaration concerning its enforcement, there could no longer be a question of abuse of authority in those cases.

In empowering the bishops to debar appellant priests from their functions while denying such dismissed clergy the right to turn to the parlements for redress, the royal government expected to deplete the Jansenist ranks still further and reestablish religious uniformity more completely throughout the kingdom. Indeed, applied in all its uncompromising rigor, the new declaration would have forcibly imposed the Bull on the entire realm and rendered the *anticonstitutionnaire* opposition, still quite formidable in Paris, totally impotent. But if the decree was designed to ensure respect for Vintimille and other be-

---

cution des bulles des papes données contre le jansénisme, et sur celle de la constitution *Unigenitus*," in Mention, ii, 62-69.

[14] For a brief summary and justification of the declaration, offered by one of its principal authors, see Daguesseau to M. de Polinchove (First President of the Parlement of Flanders), April 14, 1730, BN, MSS Fr., MS 6822, fols. 122-23.

leaguered *constitutionnaire* prelates and to put an end to all debate surrounding the bull *Unigenitus*, it quickly proved a serious miscalculation on the part of Fleury's administration. In Paris at least, far from restoring religious peace, the government's action merely increased tensions. Interpreting the administration's policies as both provocative and authoritarian, a substantial number of the magistrates and *avocats* in the Parlement as well as many of the lower clergy in the diocese refused to acquiesce in the government's latest ecclesiastical initiative. Both groups—sometimes acting separately, sometimes working in concert—vigorously resisted the implementation of the declaration.

The Parlement of Paris, which was responsible for registering all royal legislation, would have the first opportunity to respond. Under the Regency, the sovereign court had acquired greater institutional powers, regained the right of prior remonstrance with all its unmeasured possibilities, further developed the techniques (and the rhetoric) of protest and of appeal to public opinion, and reestablished the patterns of political confrontation with the royal government over major issues of state policy that extended far beyond ordinary judicial administration. In the name of the Gallican liberties, and often through the vehicle of *appels comme d'abus*, the court had penetrated freely into the domain of ecclesiastical politics. To be sure, the magistrates had not been engaged in any serious conflict with the crown or the Church since 1720, when they were exiled to Pontoise in the Law affair, nor had they offered a single remonstrance over any issue since 1725.[15] During a decade of only modest participation in affairs of state, they had not been in a militant or outspoken mood. Indeed, they had remained conspicuously silent throughout the heated disputes occasioned by the Council of Embrun. Nevertheless, the court had continued to watch over religious affairs and given abundant evidence of its undiminished hostility to the Bull, its sensitivity to the slightest ultramontane encroachment on the Gallican liberties, and its vigilant opposition to alleged episcopal abuses of authority.[16] It was as a direct

[15] Jules Flammermont (ed.), *Remontrances du Parlement de Paris au 18ᵉ siècle*, 3 vols. (Paris, 1888-98), I, xv, 187-219.

[16] The Parlement's activities in this period in defense of the appellant cause are admiringly chronicled in the *NNEE* (*passim*, but see, in particular, Feb. 15, 1729, pp. 19-20). The most spectacular conflict in 1729, involving *anticonstitutionnaires* all over France, concerned the "legend of Gregory VII." The dispute may be followed most conveniently *ibid.*, June 25, 1729, p. 94; July 10, pp. 113-14; July 30, pp. 130-31; Sept. 15, pp. 149-50; Sept. 20, pp. 158-59; Oct. 7, p. 171; March 4, 1730, pp. 45-46; and March 8, pp. 49-54. See also G. Hardy, pp. 162-70, for an analysis of the controversy.

consequence of the royal declaration, therefore, that the Parlement awoke from its fairly prolonged political lethargy.

Although the militant *anticonstitutionnaires* among the magistrates were clearly in the minority during this period, they represented the most active, persuasive, and perhaps best-disciplined group of judges within the court.[17] The putative leader of this hard core of aggressive *anticonstitutionnaires* was the abbé René Pucelle, an experienced hand in the struggles of ecclesiastical politics, whose vehement harangues and eloquent diatribes had won the esteem of his fellow counselors and of innumerable Gallican allies beyond the Palais de Justice as well as the grudging respect (and fear) of Cardinal Fleury's administration.[18] Functioning in a world where internal squabbling and factionalism were recurrent phenomena—with splits along personal and ideological lines, quarrels about strategy and tactics, divisions over questions of rank and seniority—and where corporate strife and disunity frequently precluded the court's opposing the crown with consistent force, Pucelle and the so-called *parti janséniste* nevertheless managed to exert great influence over their colleagues and hence on the course of parlementary behavior, repeatedly mobilizing the court against objectionable royal policies. Their corporate opposition to the declaration, as to the bull *Unigenitus* itself, was motivated by a variety of judicial, institutional, and political considerations. The new declaration, they argued, jeopardized the legal tradition of regalist Gallicanism which the Parlement had historically upheld and protected. In addition, it threatened to limit the jurisdictional competence of the court and, by reducing the magistrates' prerogatives, to restrict their influence in public affairs. Furthermore, the judges, who had been engaged in a longstanding debate with the episcopate over the position of the semiautonomous Church in relation to the State, believed that the declaration's provisions would only further abet the hierarchy in its

[17] For a perceptive analysis and discussion of the question of parlementary Jansenism, albeit for a later period, see Van Kley, pp. 20-30, 37-61. See also Françoise Bontoux, "*Nouvelles ecclésiastiques,*" *parlement de Paris et parlementaires (1730-1762)* (Diplôme d'études supérieures d'histoire [Paris, 1955]), pp. 141-42.

[18] Fleury himself had shown considerable appreciation for Pucelle's standing within the sovereign court. In a letter delivered to Pucelle in December 1729, he tried to convince the abbé—and through him the Parlement—to withdraw his support from the appellant cause. But Fleury's efforts at reaching a truce proved unavailing, his arguments making no impact whatever on the subsequent opposition to the March 24 declaration. See AAE, M&D, France, MS 1265, fols. 15-20; and *ibid.*, MS 1266, fol. 10. Cf. discussion in G. Hardy, pp. 189-91.

continued abuse of spiritual power and harm the "true interests" of the crown. The sovereign court, they concluded, could not countenance such egregious violations of "fundamental law" nor allow its jurisdiction in ecclesiastical matters to be hedged by the crown and the First Estate, and they determined to put up a strong resistance.

On March 28, 1730, Fleury had the royal declaration presented to the Parlement for examination and registration. Despite the cardinal-minister's explicit assurances that the declaration would not impair the Gallican liberties—assurances that were even embodied in the declaration itself[19]—his "guarantees" did not appease the magistrates. In the stormy scenes which marked that day's assembly, the court quickly demonstrated its formidable opposition to the document. At the *lit de justice*, for which the king came all the way to Paris on April 3, several magistrates voiced vehement objections both to the decree and to the heavy-handed procedures used by the government to obtain its registration. Although eventually forced to register the law, the Parlement demonstrated by its subsequent behavior that it did not accept the declaration as a *fait accompli*.[20] Indeed, for the next two years the court would utilize its considerable institutional prerogatives and its imposing authority and prestige to frustrate the royal will. This date thus marks the beginning of a period of renewed agitation in the Palais de Justice—a period which found the sovereign court in persistent antagonism to and confrontation with the crown and the Church hierarchy.[21]

While Fleury was occupied with the Parlement of Paris over the registration of the royal declaration, Vintimille and other *constitutionnaire* prelates throughout the realm were already taking the offensive against the *anticonstitutionnaires*. Acting under the declaration's formal authorization and exploiting the powers of episcopal review of sacer-

[19] These assurances were contained in the introductory portion of the declaration (see Mention, II, 62-63). Actually, the Paris Parlement had twice previously registered royal declarations on the Bull, in 1714 and in 1720, though each time with important restrictions and qualifications regarding the independence of the Gallican Church and the preeminence of civil over ecclesiastical authority.

[20] For details on the conflict over registration and on the ensuing struggles, which continued throughout the spring, see AAE, M&D, France, MS 1266, fols. 212-15, 238-47, 253-56, 262-63, 269-70, 287-91. One can also follow the debate in NNEE, *passim* (including verbatim reports of speeches given within the chambers of the Parlement); Barbier, II, 102-21 (March-May 1730); and Marais, IV, 117-27 (April 8-24, 1730).

[21] It was, moreover, a struggle in which the public was to take an increasingly active interest. Indeed, the stand which the Parlement had adopted won considerable popular support (see Barbier, II, 108 [April 1730]).

dotal competence already guaranteed them in the edict of 1695, they began systematically to purge their dioceses of refractory ecclesiastics. In succeeding months they revoked the powers of preaching and hearing confession from an increasing number of appellant priests and religious and replaced them with reliable clergy who had already accepted the Bull and who might be expected to win the straying faithful back to the *constitutionnaire* fold. Some prelates, however, were not content with dismissing simple priests (*prêtres habitués*) or suspending them from their duties—administrative actions for which there were clearly established precedents.[22] These bishops, among them the newly emboldened archbishop of Paris, went so far as to initiate legal proceedings within their diocesan courts against certain especially troublesome *curés*. In a few extreme instances they even suspended some *curés* from benefices to which they had been canonically confirmed. Since such suspensions were the equivalent of outright dismissals—and hence were not indisputably within the bishops' rightful authority—they left the prelates open to potential judicial appeals.[23]

In spite of the recent prohibitions against *appels comme d'abus*, a number of dissident *curés*, especially those from dioceses within the resort of the Parlement of Paris, responded to these episcopal assaults on their prerogatives by turning to their benevolent guardians in the sovereign court. Armed with long, carefully reasoned legal *consultations* prepared by *avocats* sympathetic to their plight,[24] they called upon the magistrates to overturn the rulings of the diocesan courts. The *curés'* appeals usually found a receptive audience among the magistrates in the Parlement, who openly welcomed these unauthorized cases and suspended the judgments of several diocesan tribunals.[25]

[22] In particular, the edict of 1695 on ecclesiastical jurisdiction, esp. Articles 10 and 11 (Mention, I, 117-18). Measures adopted for removing dissident priests were frequently accompanied by episcopal orders prohibiting the access of the *anticonstitutionnaire* laity to sympathetic confessors outside their parishes and limiting irremovable appellant priests to hearing confession exclusively from their own parishioners. Such restrictions gave rise to still other controversies (see Préclin, *Les jansénistes*, pp. 217-18).

[23] Daniel Jousse, *Traité du gouvernement spirituel et temporel des paroisses* (Paris, 1769), pp. 263ff. See also Alcime Bachelier, *Le jansénisme à Nantes* (Paris, 1934), pp. 202-203.

[24] See, for example, "Consultation pour les Pères Sallart, curé de La Villette, Blondel, de Saint-Etienne-du-Mont, et Pommart, de Saint-Médard," Dec. 22, 1730, BA, MS 10178.

[25] The first case of this type, and one of the most complicated and prolonged of this period, involved Bishop Fleuriau of Orléans and several of his clergy whom he had deprived of their priestly functions for refusing to publish his

Deliberately ignoring the provisions of the March declaration, they contended that such petitions were not only clearly within their customary judicial competence, but remained the sole means by which the secular courts could watch over the victims of allegedly unwarranted and arbitrary episcopal attacks. The Parlement's actions could not help provoking a bitter response from the other side, thereby placing Fleury's government once again in the exceedingly awkward position of trying to mediate between episcopate and sovereign court.[26]

To the bishops attending the quinquennial Assembly of the Clergy in Paris at this time, the Parlement's attempts to prevent the enforcement of episcopal sanctions against opponents of the Bull were a blatant and intolerable infringement of their traditional jurisdiction. In their view, episcopal suspensions and interdictions—legitimately imposed for willful acts of disobedience to the commands of clerical superiors or for failure to perform spiritual duties properly—were purely ecclesiastical matters over which the Church exercised exclusive competence. The Parlement's action in receiving appeals from insubordinate clerics in disputed ecclesiastical cases was said to be not only in direct contravention of the royal declaration of March 24, but also in violation of earlier royal legislation on ecclesiastical jurisdiction, and threatened to destroy the autonomy of the First Estate.[27] Speaking on behalf of his fellow prelates, the bishop of Boulogne complained that the court's suspensive *arrêts* tended to undermine discipline within the Church, "reverse the hierarchical order, . . . and cause scandal,

---

pastoral letter against Soanen. See *NNEE* for 1729 and 1730, *passim*; also discussion in G. Hardy, esp. pp. 151-59.

[26] Sympathetic to the interests of the *constitutionnaire* bishops, the cardinal-minister was nevertheless concerned to prevent their taking any drastic or precipitous action without first consulting Versailles (see Fleury to Vintimille, May 23, 1730, BM, MS 2357, p. 126).

[27] *Recueil des actes, titres, et mémoires concernant les affaires du clergé de France*, ed. Pierre Lemerre, 14 vols. (Paris, 1768-71), XIII, col. 1,653. Though he was unable to attend the Assembly's meetings in Paris, Cardinal Fleury was kept completely informed of all its deliberations through the almost daily correspondence maintained between Chauvelin (at Versailles) and Archbishop Lavergne de Monthenard de Tressan of Rouen (at Paris), one of Fleury's closest advisers and confidants (AAE, M&D, France, MS 1267, fols. 164-66, 168-71, 198-200, 204-205, 211, 225-26, 234-35, 239-40, 242-43, 248-50, and 263-65). It was also through the archbishop of Rouen that the royal government was able to exercise a substantial influence over the Assembly and keep its sessions generally calm and peaceful (cf. *ibid.*, fols. 227-33). Vintimille also reported to Fleury on the activities of the Assembly, over which he was the presiding officer (see Fleury to Vintimille, Aug. 18, 1730, BM, MS 2357, pp. 229-30; Vintimille to Fleury, Aug. 22, 1730, *ibid.*, p. 231; and Vintimille to Fleury, Aug. 29, 1730, *ibid.*, pp. 233-35).

confusion, and division."[28] In remonstrances to the king that were drawn up near the conclusion of the Assembly in mid-September, the bishops emphasized the dangerous consequences arising from the coalition between *curés* and *parlementaires* and from the complicity of the latter in the insubordination of the former:

> The independence and revolt of the *curés* are openly protected, the most sacred rights of the bishops are contested, and their ministry is rendered useless; laymen constitute themselves judges of doctrine, and, what is still more distressing, the spirit of schism is gradually being introduced into your Estates. These, Sire, are the sad consequences and ominous results of the continual usurpations made by the secular tribunals upon the spiritual authority.[29]

The Assembly concluded with an urgent appeal to the royal government to remedy the "deplorable state" in which the French Church found itself.

Even before the opening of the Assembly, Cardinal Fleury had resolved to take steps to halt the Parlement's reception of *appels comme d'abus*.[30] A projected royal declaration on the subject was actually drawn up, but no formal decree was ever promulgated.[31] Instead, the crown preferred to deal with the problem case by case. On each occasion that an appeal came before the sovereign court, the royal government responded by evoking the matter to the *conseil d'état*, thereby effectively depriving the magistrates of jurisdiction. All through the summer of 1730, as the crown repeatedly resorted to acts of evocation, the judges became more and more frustrated. If they resented the continued restrictions placed on their right of remonstrance against the original declaration, they were even more sensitive to Fleury's interference with their administration of justice. In the matter of the *appel comme d'abus* they shared a common interest with the "second order" of clergy as well as with the barristers who pleaded cases before the court. On this occasion, as on so many others during this turbulent period, the *avocats* were the first to reply.

On October 3, forty lawyers publicly challenged Fleury's policy of evocations by circulating a legal brief, originally written in July, entitled *Mémoire pour les sieurs Samson, curé d'Olivet; . . . et autres*

[28] *Recueil des actes du clergé*, XIII, col. 1,655.

[29] *Très-humbles remontrances présentées au Roi par le Clergé, assemblé en l'année 1730 au sujet de quelques arrêts donnés par le parlement de Paris* (*ibid.*, col. 1,651).

[30] See Fleury to Vintimille, May 23, 1730, BM, MS 2357, p. 126.

[31] AAE, M&D, France, MS 1267, fols. 278-82.

ecclésiastiques de différents diocèses, appellants, comme d'abus, contre M. l'évêque d'Orléans et autres archevêques et évêques de différents diocèses, intimés, sur l'effet des arrêts des parlements, tant provisoires que définitifs, en matière d'appel, comme d'abus, des censures ecclésiastiques. In this *Mémoire*, which contained a series of quite radical assertions, the *avocats* expressed their views not only with respect to the exercise of episcopal authority, but also as to the jurisdiction and prerogatives of the crown. The Parlement, they insisted, bore exclusive responsibility for rendering justice in the king's name and exercised a sovereign jurisdiction over all individuals and corporate bodies, lay or ecclesiastical, within its province. What is more, neither the king nor the bishops could reserve to their own jurisdiction cases that rightfully belonged to the Parlement. As members of a "sovereign tribunal" and as "constitutional assessors of the throne," with the ultimate duty of overseeing all the laws of the kingdom, the magistrates could legitimately intervene even in matters of ecclesiastical discipline. Indeed, all judgments reached before ecclesiastical courts were properly within the magistrates' competence and were an integral part of the Parlement's administrative control over the *police générale* of the kingdom. The Church in and of itself possessed no rights or jurisdictional competence beyond purely spiritual matters and had at its disposal no penalties other than those of a spiritual nature. It was, consequently, the prerogative—indeed, the responsibility—of the magistrates to protect the members of the lower clergy from the authoritarian abuses of their episcopal superiors and to issue judicial decrees suspending the execution of oppressive ecclesiastical sentences until the disputed case could finally be adjudicated. Since the deposed priests from Orléans and other dioceses had obtained *arrêts de défense*, they were entitled to resume their functions, notwithstanding any ecclesiastical or royal judgments to the contrary.[32]

In articulating this exaggerated and expanded version of parlementary constitutional claims and in attempting severely to circumscribe the jurisdictional competence of both crown and episcopate, the *Mémoire* went considerably beyond any opinions the magistrates themselves had publicly expressed in recent years. Not surprisingly, the work produced an immediate stir. During a meeting of the *conseil des dépêches* held on October 30, it was decided to issue an *arrêt* suppressing the *consultation* for containing propositions which were "disrespectful

[32] For a sympathetic *anticonstitutionnaire* view of the lawyers' provocative *consultation*, see *NNEE*, Aug. 20, 1730, pp. 182-83, and Oct. 9, 1730, pp. 218-19. G. Hardy also provides a useful discussion, pp. 224-26.

of royal authority, seditious, and dangerous to public order."[33] The government instructed Hérault to confiscate and destroy every copy of it his officers could find and to prohibit the printer from producing any more, although by the time the police lieutenant received his orders the *Mémoire* was circulating all over Paris.[34] The *avocats* were ordered to disavow or retract the document within a month or face possible suspension from the Parlement and ultimate disbarment. Prevailed upon by Fleury and by some two hundred of their more moderate fellow lawyers, they reluctantly capitulated, issuing their retraction in the form of a brief explanatory memorandum.[35] A conciliar *arrêt* of November 25, which described the *avocats* as "faithful defenders of the rights of the crown," acquitted them of all charges of rebellion and acknowledged the government's satisfaction with their apology and disavowal.[36]

The affair did not end there, however. Several of the *constitutionnaire* bishops, including Vintimille, remained dissatisfied; although the *avocats* had disavowed their attacks on the rights and supremacy of the crown, they had not retracted their assaults upon ecclesiastical authority.[37] Indeed, in their explanatory memorandum to the king the *avocats* had renewed their earlier charges against the bishops, accusing them of taking despotic advantage of their authority. The *avocats* had also reasserted both the legitimacy of *appels comme d'abus* against episcopal edicts and the priority of parlementary over ecclesiastical decrees. Despite Fleury's attempts to keep the bishops from taking any provocative action, a number of them issued blistering manifestoes condemning the original *Mémoire* and attacking both the lawyers and the magistrates in the Paris Parlement for their arbitrary and improper interference in spiritual and ecclesiastical affairs.[38] But it fell to Vinti-

[33] BN, MSS Fr., MS 22090, fols. 301-302. Text also cited in *NNEE*, Nov. 23, 1730, p. 246.

[34] Barbier, II, 132-33 (November 1730).

[35] *Mémoire des avocats au Roi*, AAE, M&D, Fonds divers (Rome), MS 60, fols. 21-25.

[36] BN, MSS Fr., MS 22090, fols. 389-90. See also Barbier, II, 133-37 (November 1730).

[37] Vintimille to Fleury, Nov. 29, 1730, BM, MS 2357, pp. 261-62.

[38] See, in particular, the *Mandement de monseigneur l'évêque-duc de Laon* [Etienne-Joseph de La Fare] *sur la soumission due à la constitution 'Unigenitus', sur la fidélité indispensable des sujets envers leur souverain, et sur les droits sacrés de l'épiscopat*, and the *Mandement de monseigneur l'archevêque-prince d'Embrun* [Guérin de Tencin], *portant condamnation d'un écrit signé par 40 avocats, et intitulé: "Mémoire pour les sieurs Samson. . . ."*

mille to deal directly with the *avocats*, for, as Paris faithful, they came under his immediate jurisdiction.

In recent months Vintimille's fellow *constitutionnaire* bishops had repeatedly reproached him for his failure to respond publicly to the numerous provocative actions and pronouncements emanating from the Palais de Justice. In addition, papal representatives in Paris and Rome—where the *avocats'* *Mémoire* had already been ordered burned —had criticized him for failing immediately to censure the lawyers for their *consultation*. Having sat silently by for nearly a year, watching the constant legal and judicial challenges to his authority, Vintimille could remain silent no longer. At stake, he wrote Fleury in late December, were not only the spiritual health of Paris and of the entire kingdom, but also his own personal honor and reputation among his colleagues as well as the trust and confidence of his flock.[39] In a pastoral decree composed after careful deliberation with Cardinal Fleury and the *conseil ecclésiastique* at Versailles, and dated January 10, 1731, though not published until a month later, a deeply embittered Vintimille struck back.[40] The archbishop began by reasserting the autonomy of the episcopate in its judicial character and the right of the bishops to legislate in matters of discipline and doctrine, faith and morals, and to enforce their enactments with ecclesiastical penalties, without any meddling or encroachment by the secular courts. But Vintimille did not stop there. He accused the *avocats* of making a determined effort to undermine all constituted authority in Church and State and to bring dishonor and discredit upon the diocese of Paris. Even more serious, he went on to charge them with fomenting widespread disorder and confusion and with favoring presbyterianism and other schismatic or heretical principles—strong charges he would soon have cause to regret.[41]

The Parlement of Paris, which took particular exception to these

[39] Vintimille to Fleury, Dec. 27, 1730, BM, MS 2357, pp. 276-78, and Dec. 30, 1730, pp. 278-80. In the space of one month, between late November and late December, Fleury and Vintimille had exchanged more than half a dozen letters dealing with the question of the *avocats* (*ibid.*, pp. 261-80).

[40] *Ordonnance et instruction pastorale de monseigneur l'archevêque de Paris, portant condamnation d'un écrit qui a pour titre: "Mémoire pour les sieurs Samson. . . ."* A principal reason for the delay in the formal publication was the fact that Chancellor Daguesseau was worried about the Parlement's reaction (Daguesseau to Fleury, Feb. 6, 1731, AAE, M&D, France, MS 1269, fols. 53-58). The chancellor's recommendation that Vintimille not publish his pastoral instruction for the time being was not adopted.

[41] Even Barbier, who was usually unsympathetic to the views of the more radical of his fellow *avocats*, was angered by Vintimille's indictment (II, 147-48 [February 1731]).

various ecclesiastical censures issued by Vintimille and his *constitutionnaire* colleagues, had already reentered the fray on another related matter. On January 9, 1731, the magistrates, chafing at the evocations by which Fleury's administration had interfered with the court's jurisdiction throughout the previous year, presented remonstrances to the king protesting the government's ecclesiastical policies.[42] Overshadowed by the *avocats* in recent months and perhaps embarrassed by, if not envious of, the lawyers' display of courageous independence in speaking on the court's behalf and negotiating directly with the royal administration, the judges were eager to reassert their own prerogatives. Though quite moderate in tone and limited to challenging the legality of conciliar evocations, their remonstrances were nevertheless harshly denounced by the chancellor.[43] Undeterred, they effectively continued their attack on crown policy by redirecting most of their animosity at the *constitutionnaire* bishops, who had been the principal beneficiaries of the evocations and other government rulings on major ecclesiastical and jurisdictional issues. In a series of *arrêts* issued in January and February, the Parlement suppressed several incendiary pastoral letters and episcopal decrees from *constitutionnaire* pens.[44] But the court took its most significant and dramatic action when it proceeded against the archbishop of Paris. On March 5, 1731, the Parlement, coming to the defense of the *avocats* whom Vintimille had so harshly rebuked in his January *mandement*, received the *procureur-général* as an *appelant comme d'abus*.[45] The sovereign court, which found an "abuse of power" in the ordinance and pastoral instruction of M. Vintimille, ordered it immediately withdrawn from circulation —an action which left the archbishop, the putative "patriarch of the Gallican Church," once again stunned and outraged.[46]

With the *constitutionnaire* bishops issuing decrees in defense of

[42] Flammermont, I, 232-40.

[43] *Ibid.*, pp. 240-42. In substantiation of its claim that the evocations had been "presque continuelles," the court appended a list of those that had been issued since 1718—a total of over 40 (*ibid.*, pp. 645-51).

[44] *Arrêts* of Jan. 29 and Feb. 20, 1731 quashed the *mandements* of three leading *constitutionnaire* prelates (the archbishop of Embrun, the former bishop of Apt, and the bishop of Laon) and denounced their pastoral instructions as "rash, seditious, and tending to disturb the tranquility of both Church and State." It was these actions, already anticipated when he wrote Fleury in early February (see n. 40, above), which Daguesseau had in mind in counseling delay of Vintimille's *ordonnance*.

[45] BN, MSS Fr., MS 22090, fols. 374-75. Two government *mémoires*, or position papers, were prepared at this time to examine ways of dealing with this latest ecclesiastical crisis (AAE, M&D, France, MS 1269, fols. 71-79, 90-92).

[46] See Vintimille to Fleury, March 9 and 12, 1731, BM, MS 2357, pp. 325-28.

episcopal privileges, the parlements suppressing these manifestoes and receiving *appels comme d'abus* from dissident priests and others, and the *avocats* resolving to defend themselves against their archbishop's calumnious allegations, Fleury was now farther than ever from the tranquility he had hoped to restore to the realm. What is more, the cardinal-minister had himself come under attack from the zealous *constitutionnaires*, who went so far as to charge him with indifference toward their plight and with abandoning the interests of the Church.[47] Appeals to both sides for calm and prudence went unheeded. Consequently, it was decided to impose general and absolute silence on all parties, this time including the *constitutionnaire* bishops whom the declaration of March 1730 had (to Fleury's regret) left legally free to express their intemperate opinions. A royal decree enjoining silence was issued on March 10, 1731.[48] It proscribed all assemblies, deliberations, acts, requests, and writings which dealt with the contested issues. In an effort to resolve the jurisdictional disputes raging between Parlement and episcopate, the decree further provided that the determination of "the extent, the nature, and the respective limits of the secular and spiritual powers" would thereafter be reserved to the king alone.[49] In transmitting the *arrêt* to all the bishops of the realm, the government sent an accompanying circular letter in which the crown not only guaranteed the Church's traditional prerogatives and exclusive authority on questions of a purely spiritual nature, but also confirmed all the rights and privileges previously accorded the First Estate. At the same time, the king appointed an "extraordinary commission" of lay and clerical advisers to whom he delegated responsibility for seeing to the execution of the decree and for taking the necessary measures to maintain the "inviolable rights" of both the spiritual and the temporal powers.[50]

Despite all these precautions, the order of silence had little effect.

[47] Fleury to Vintimille, March 8, 1731, *ibid.*, pp. 320-24.

[48] *Arrêt du conseil à l'occasion des disputes qui se sont élevées au sujet des deux puissances*, in Isambert, XXI, 354-56. See also *NNEE*, April 13, 1731, p. 73, and Barbier, II, 150-51 (March 1731).

[49] Cf. Fleury to Vintimille, March 12, 1731, BM, MS 2357, p. 329.

[50] In "appointing" this commission, the king gave formal, *de jure* status to a body that had already been in existence, if only informally, for some time. The commission included the Cardinals Fleury, Rohan, and Bissy, the archbishop of Rouen, Chancellor Daguesseau, Keeper of the Seals Chauvelin, and two *conseillers d'état*, one of whom was the comte d'Argenson. Cf. d'Argenson's voluminous dossier: "Papiers, mémoires et recherches concernant l'exécution de l'arrest du 10 mars 1731, rendu à l'occasion des disputes qui se sont élevées au sujet des 2 puissances, pour l'exécution duquel j'ay été nommé commissaire" (BA, MS 3053, fols. 276-362).

That it proved inadequate to restore religious peace was chiefly the fault of several uncompromising *constitutionnaire* prelates. Just as they had been determined to disregard all judgments by the Parlement in ecclesiastical affairs, responding to parlementary decrees with more virulent pastoral letters, these bishops, encouraged by influential allies at Versailles and in Rome, were also of the opinion that they could not be prohibited from speaking out. They also insisted that the declaration of March 10 had not included them under its restrictions of silence. Their attitude put Fleury in an awkward position, particularly since the magistrates and lawyers in the Parlement of Paris, who were no more inclined than the bishops to heed such an injunction, were prepared to escalate the conflict once more. Forced to choose sides on several occasions between March and July, Fleury could do nothing but support the interests of his fellow bishops, especially those of Archbishop Vintimille. The cardinal-minister had thus implicitly construed the "general and absolute silence" as excluding the defenders of the bull *Unigenitus*. Once again overtly tolerated, they would derive great encouragement from Fleury's actions.[51] Four months after the decree of silence, the disputes it was supposed to stifle were as bitter as ever.

In the meantime, while polemics, remonstrances, and *arrêts* continued to fly back and forth, important developments had been taking place within the diocese of Paris—developments which helped focus the attention of all the disputants increasingly upon the cemetery of Saint-Médard, where the cult observances associated with François de Pâris had been flourishing for some time. It was not the actual events occurring at Pâris' tomb so much as it was the purge of troublesome Parisian *curés* being carried on by Vintimille that ultimately prompted the *anti-constitutionnaire* party to "adopt" the cult as a political issue. This chapter in the politicization of the miracles and cult of the deacon Pâris began with Vintimille's suspension of the aged appellant *curé* of Saint-Barthélemy, the abbé Guillaume Lair.

Almost from his very accession to the Paris see, Vintimille had been keeping a watchful eye on Saint-Barthélemy, a parish that had long been regarded as one of the most troublesome in the capital. The *curé*, Father Lair, had for several years been in the forefront of *anti-constitutionnaire* agitation within the diocese and was consequently one of several parish priests the archbishop had been especially eager to discipline. Vintimille's opportunity to do so came in the summer of 1730. For months Lair was rumored to have committed serious irregularities in the daily performance of his spiritual duties, including

[51] G. Hardy, pp. 238-39.

numerous errors and omissions both in the celebration of Mass and in the administration of the sacraments. In addition, Lair had been charged with repeatedly refusing to allow into Saint-Barthélemy priests whom Vintimille had appointed to the parish without the *curé*'s consent or approval.[52] Despite the seriousness of the charges, Vintimille was initially hesitant about proceeding against Lair for fear of arousing hostilities at the Palais de Justice.[53] He cautiously proposed to send the *curé* into temporary retreat at a seminary and in the interim to name another, more reliable priest to the vacant parish—a mild, but meaningful, punishment, in conformity with provisions of late seventeenth-century legislation intended for just such cases and hence unlikely to agitate the Parlement or occasion a dreaded *appel comme d'abus*.[54] But the archbishop, who was then at his summer residence in Conflans, had not counted on the imprudent zeal of his *official* (judicial vicar), the staunch *constitutionnaire*, Urbain Robinet.

Believing that a harsh sentence meted out to Lair might serve as a useful example to those *curés* who continued to flaunt their superior's orders, Robinet was eager to pursue the charges against the aged priest. In early July, after the *promoteur* had conducted an investigation into these allegations and found that they had some basis in fact, Robinet summoned Lair to a hearing before the *officialité*.[55] The interrogations lasted only a short time before the diocesan court had judged the case and determined the sentence. Acting on his own authority, without conferring with Vintimille or obtaining an opinion from the archbishop's legal counsel, the *official* suspended the *curé* from his functions.[56] The precipitous suspension of Father Lair—the first time the archdiocesan authorities had taken such drastic action against any Parisian *anticonstitutionnaire* with the status of a beneficed *curé*—provoked a stormy reaction from every side in the dispute over the Bull and once again plunged the entire diocese into a massive controversy.

Following the lead of other *curés* previously subjected to similar treatment, Father Lair appealed the sentence to the Parlement of Paris. In support of his petition to the court, Lair submitted a *mémoire*

[52] *NNEE*, August 8, 1730, p. 171; cf. Préclin, *Les jansénistes*, pp. 217-18. According to reports of the *Nouvellistes*, there were dozens of other cases in which interdictions of *anticonstitutionnaire* clergy had been obtained on the basis of allegedly faulty performance in the Mass (see esp. April 2, 1730, pp. 68-70).

[53] Vintimille to Fleury, July 10, 1730, BM, MS 2357, p. 176.

[54] Vintimille to Fleury, July 20, 1730, *ibid.*, p. 194.

[55] An excerpt from Robinet's "Décret d'ajournement personnel contre le Sr Lair" may be found in AAE, M&D, Fonds divers (Rome), MS 59, fols. 260-61.

[56] Vintimille to Fleury, July 20 and 23, 1731, BM, MS 2357, pp. 191-94, 196-98.

justificatif in which he attempted to refute the *official*'s charges.[57] Concerning the supposed omissions in his performance of his holy functions, the venerable priest contended that they could only have occurred—if they had occurred at all—during moments of distraction or preoccupation, or as a result of temporary lapses occasioned by his advanced age. In that case, he argued, they could not be construed as an indictable offense and were surely not grounds for removal unless it could be proved that they had been done purposely, "out of contempt for the faith, out of impiety, or out of willful negligence," allegations which none of his accusers had even made. Lair also refuted the second grounds for complaint. His refusal to admit into his parish appointees of the archbishop was, he contended, the traditional right of the *curé*, recognized by the clause *de consensu Pastoris*, and could hardly be considered a crime.[58]

Near the end of July the Parlement, ignoring Fleury's representations to the *gens du roi* to ignore the case, agreed to receive M. Lair's appeal along with a supporting legal *consultation* signed by eight *avocats*.[59] On July 26 the court issued an *arrêt de défense* prohibiting the *official* from carrying out the sentence and threatening stiff fines and other reprisals against anyone who attempted to contravene its order. In addition, instead of remanding the case to the diocesan court for a new hearing, the magistrates, acting on their own authority, returned Lair to his post.[60] The following day an overwhelming number of his parishioners joyously welcomed the *curé* back to the pulpit from which he had been temporarily suspended. But their joy was short-lived.[61]

No sooner had the abbé Lair resumed his priestly duties than the *officialité* issued its own *mémoire justificatif*, which attempted to explain the conduct of M. Robinet and to prove that the Parlement's "intolerable intervention" had unnecessarily "stirred up trouble in the parish."[62] Despite the extended justifications and complaints contained

[57] BPR, L.P. 448, No. 74.   [58] *NNEE*, Aug. 8, 1730, p. 171.
[59] The *NNEE* summarized the contents of the *consultation* in its issue of Aug. 20, 1730, pp. 182-83.
[60] For Daguesseau's report on First President Portail's explanation of the Parlement's action, see the chancellor's letter to Fleury, July 27, 1730, AAE, M&D, France, MS 1267, fols. 145-46. "Par tout ce qu'il m'a dit sur ce sujet," recalled Daguesseau, "je vois que l'unique fondement de l'arrest est que l'imbecillité n'est pas un crime, et que toutes les fautes d'un curé n'en estant qu'une suitte, elles ne devoient pas servir de matière à une procédure criminelle" (fol. 145); for another copy of this letter see AAE, M&D, Fonds divers (Rome), MS 59, fols. 265-67.
[61] *NNEE*, Aug. 20, 1730, p. 182.
[62] The *Nouvellistes* dismissed these as false allegations, typical of "la calomnie

in Robinet's *mémoire*, the entire affair—again pitting priestly and parlementary prerogatives against archiepiscopal authority—had once more placed Vintimille in a difficult position. While regretting the developments in the Lair case, a turn of events for which he had not himself been responsible, the unfortunate archbishop could hardly have disavowed his *official*'s suspension of the troublesome *curé*.[63] Indeed, he felt compelled to defend Robinet's imprudent decision in order to secure his own position and protect the interests of his "poor, desolate, and scorned Church."[64] The Parlement's *arrêt*, he complained to Fleury, "will further embolden all the disobedient priests in the diocese" and help "turn their willful independence into outright, criminal insolence."[65] "I feel useless, defenseless, scorned, and abused," the archbishop lamented. "This diocese has become virtually ungovernable and will remain so until a way is found to prevent these stubborn ecclesiastics from obtaining parlementary support in the future."[66] Hinting vaguely that he might resign "unless some prompt remedy [was] found for resolving the present crisis," Vintimille appealed to Fleury to evoke the Lair case to the royal council immediately.[67] Nor was Vintimille alone. The Lair case had already come before the quinquennial Assembly of the Clergy, then meeting in Paris (Vintimille presiding), which sought to bring its corporate pressure to bear upon the royal government to act quickly. Indeed, a number of the *constitutionnaire* prelates in attendance had previously reproached both Vintimille and Fleury for failing to take forceful action much sooner; they even went so far as to charge the archbishop of Paris with "a criminal indolence" in his handling of the affair.[68] Appalled at the "scandalous impudence" of *curés* and magistrates, the Assembly charged that the Parlement had illegally arrogated to itself the right to reinstate a suspended priest. The court, they maintained, had vio-

---

grossière et la mauvaise foi dans l'exposition des faits" they had come to expect from the *constitutionnaires* (*ibid.*).

[63] On Vintimille's regret about Robinet's precipitous action and the archbishop's sense of personal embarrassment and chagrin, see the following letters to Fleury (all in BM, MS 2357): July 20, 1730, pp. 191-94; July 23, 1730, pp. 196-98; July 28, 1730, pp. 205-207; Aug. 3, 1730, p. 212; and Aug. 10, 1730, p. 223.

[64] Vintimille to Fleury, July 28, 1730, *ibid.*, p. 206.

[65] Vintimille to Fleury, July 27, 1730, *ibid.*, p. 204, and Aug. 6, 1730, *ibid.*, p. 218.

[66] Vintimille to Fleury, July 20, 1730, *ibid.*, p. 193; July 28, 1730, *ibid.*, p. 206; and Aug. 6, 1730, *ibid.*, pp. 217-18.

[67] Vintimille to Fleury, July 20, 1730, *ibid.*, p. 193, and July 28, 1730, *ibid.*, p. 207.

[68] Vintimille to Fleury, Aug. 3, 1730, *ibid.*, p. 213.

lated the discretionary authority of the archbishop to judge sacerdotal competence and to suspend or revoke errant or unworthy clergy and had thereby contravened the canonical rules and hierarchical order of the Church.[69] The assembled bishops joined Vintimille in calling for the royal council to suppress the Parlement's *arrêt* and evoke the case to the king.[70]

Cardinal Fleury, who was as concerned as Vintimille and the Assembly about the danger posed by the alliance between Parlement and *curés*, attempted to reassure his episcopal colleagues that the royal government had the matter under study and was preparing a response in support of their position.[71] In a letter addressed to Chancellor Daguesseau on August 1, a troubled Fleury spoke of the urgency of finding a solution to this vexed problem:

> In truth all the human patience and discretion in the world fail in the face of what the Parlement is doing daily, openly raising the standard of revolt against the authority of the Church and the King. A firm commitment has been made to destroy episcopal jurisdiction, and you are too well informed . . . not to be able to envisage the frightful consequences. The archbishop of Paris has a justifiable complaint, as does the Church itself. We cannot hope to change the minds of men who follow only their passions and who lead astray those who would be reasonable. . . . The only thing which is certain is that Church authority is lost if we do not do anything, and that in doing something we will still have considerable difficulty protecting it from its destruction.[72]

The cardinal-minister was determined not to act too precipitously on the matter; so serious and delicate an issue demanded careful and ex-

---

[69] *Recueil des actes du clergé*, XIII, cols. 1,654-56, 1,658-64.

[70] Vintimille to Fleury, Aug. 22, 1730, BM, MS 2357, p. 231. Even before the Lair affair, Vintimille was already expressing great concern about his standing with the other bishops in the forthcoming General Assembly of the Clergy (see letter to Fleury, May 22, 1730, *ibid.*, p. 121). For the cardinal-minister's repeated assurances of support, see his letters of May 23 and July 22, 1730, *ibid.*, pp. 125-26, 198.

[71] Fleury to Vintimille, Aug. 1 and 5, 1730, *ibid.*, pp. 211-12, 215-16. Fleury, who had actually approved of Lair's suspension from the start (cf. letters of July 14 and 18, 1730, *ibid.*, pp. 177, 183), cautioned Vintimille against making his feelings of discouragement too public, for in doing so the archbishop might bring great joy to the Jansenist camp—something to be avoided if at all possible.

[72] AAE, M&D, France, MS 1267, fol. 155. This letter was sent in response to Daguesseau's of July 27, cited in n. 60 above. For additional government discussion of the Lair problem, see AAE, M&D, France, MS 1267, fols. 153-54, 164-65, 168-69, 226-33, 239, 263.

tended deliberation. Fleury instructed the chancellor to draw up a legal memorandum on the subject of evocations and conducted his own intensive discussions of the Lair case with his various advisers. Rumors began circulating around the Palais de Justice in early September that the government was preparing to announce a general evocation of all *appels comme d'abus* from the Parlement of Paris.[73] In fact, the crown had decided upon a much more limited resolution of the affair. On September 23, just two weeks after the Parlement had begun its annual vacation, the *conseil d'état* issued an *arrêt* which nullified that of the court, evoked Father Lair's appeal to the king, and once again forbade the *curé* of Saint-Barthélemy to assume his sacerdotal duties.[74] Fleury had the well-timed *arrêt* published in the streets of Paris on October 4, the same day on which Vintimille appointed the abbé Gouffé, doctor in the Sorbonne, as *desservant* (officiating priest) to replace Lair.[75] With the Parlement already in recess, the magistrates, whether or not they were inclined to do so, were in no position to pursue the subject any further at this time.[76] The matter was at last closed—or so it must have seemed to all concerned.

While the political and juridical implications of the Saint-Barthélemy affair were no doubt of considerable significance for the various individuals and corporate bodies involved in the case, it was M. Lair's devoted parishioners as well as his loyal clergy who had been the ones most directly and personally affected by his dismissal. In depriving them of their beloved *curé* for a second time, the authorities had dealt them an especially severe blow. If all the customary channels for the redress of ecclesiastical grievances were closed, then the people, ordinarily without recourse in such circumstances, would have to suffer their loss in disgruntled silence. But these were extraordinary times, and at least some of Lair's faithful parish clergy and parishioners were not ready to give up quite so easily. One of these pious parishioners, a hitherto obscure woman named Anne Lefranc, was particularly distraught over her *curé*'s suspension and found the opportunity to do something about it at the tomb of François de Pâris. By her action she unwittingly[77] helped transform the Pâris cult and the observances at Saint-Médard into a national *cause célèbre*.

---

[73] Journal of De Lisle (*greffier* in the Parlement of Paris), September 1730, AN, U-374.

[74] The text of the royal *arrêt* is reproduced in *NNEE*, Oct. 9, 1730, p. 218.

[75] *Ibid.*   [76] *Ibid.*, Jan. 13, 1731, pp. 9-12.

[77] Probably the most difficult problem with which one is faced on a subject of this sort is to try to make a determination of what was "contrived" and what was "real"; who went to the cemetery out of pure spiritual motives and who was prompted by appellants or others; who had real "cures" and, later, real

For nearly thirty years Anne Lefranc had been suffering from a variety of ailments, including blindness in one eye and partial paralysis, deemed incurable by several doctors who had attended her at different times. The sickly spinster had led a rather dull and lonely existence, a life torn by family strife and personal misfortune. A woman apparently without much ambition or purpose in life, she had found in the aged abbé Lair a figure whom she could trust, someone who cared deeply about her welfare. Before his dismissal Father Lair had many times administered to her spiritual needs and consoled her about her numerous infirmities. Since Lair's suspension Mlle. Lefranc had come under the influence of a new confessor, the *anticonstitutionnaire* abbé Desvaux, a close adviser of the deposed *curé* and long a hostile critic of Vintimille's policies.[78] Desvaux had reportedly attempted to persuade her that she had a special role to play in helping to return Father Lair to his rightful place in the parish and that she had been specifically chosen to go to Saint-Médard to bear divine witness for her beloved *curé* and to help reinstate him in his parish.[79] Mlle. Lefranc does not seem to have needed much persuading. Having already heard the marvelous tales about M. Pâris and his reputed healing powers, she resolved to go to the deacon's grave to seek a cure from God, not for herself, but rather to "make manifest the justice of the cause of her legitimate pastor."[80] In early November, full of hope and confidence, she went to Saint-Médard, where she offered prayers to God, through François

---

"convulsions" and who merely pretended to have them; and, in all these cases— why? These and other questions associated with the thorny problem of motivation are ones with which contemporaries also wrestled and over which disputes raged long and loud. They are perhaps insoluble. While there must have been a considerable amount of earnest prompting and urging throughout this entire Saint-Médard episode, especially after political considerations became involved, unless fraud or deception was clearly in evidence (which seems undeniable in some cases), I have assumed that, whatever their actual cause, "real" cures and "real" convulsions occurred at Pâris' tomb, and that most of the people who frequented the cemetery or the church of Saint-Médard did so out of sincere conviction and faith in the thaumaturgic powers of François de Pâris.

[78] Vintimille described him as "l'âme et le conseil du curé de Saint-Barthélemy" (Vintimille to Fleury, June 19, 1731, BM, MS 2357, p. 394).

[79] The charge that Desvaux had been responsible for Anne Lefranc's going to pray at Pâris' tomb comes from hostile sources, including Vintimille and Mlle. Lefranc's own brother (see especially letter cited above, n. 78). It has not been possible to verify the charge through other, more independent, sources. This matter bears on the discussion above, n. 77. It is worth noting, incidentally, that Desvaux was later suspended from his post, apparently on the grounds of his involvement in the Lefranc affair (*NNEE*, June 14, 1731, p. 110).

[80] *Ibid.*, June 4, 1731, p. 109.

de Pâris, that He might restore her to good health. Within a few days she had experienced a remission of symptoms: her paralysis and blindness as well as most of her other physical disabilities were reportedly gone. God, it was believed, had answered her prayers, acknowledging through this miraculous cure that M. Lair had been unjustly removed from his benefice and unfairly dismissed from his parish.[81] To obtain a similar acknowledgment from the authorities, however, was an entirely different matter.

In the next several months some anonymous parties requested that Vintimille open an official, canonical investigation into the cure.[82] Receiving no response from the archbishop or any of his administrative subordinates, they proceeded to gather the relevant information themselves. In early March of 1731, having already waited five months for the ecclesiastical authorities to undertake an inquest, they secretly published their findings with abundant supporting testimony, including the copies of 22 notarized certificates bearing the names of 120 witnesses, some of whom had known Mlle. Lefranc since the onset of her infirmities. The Anne Lefranc cure was thus the first Pâris miracle of which a detailed account circulated in public. More important, however, in conjunction with the printed *Relation* of the cure, purportedly written and signed by Anne Lefranc herself, her anonymous spokesmen issued an explosive thirty-three-page tract, the famous *Dissertation sur les miracles, et en particulier sur ceux qui ont été opérés au tombeau de M. de Pâris, en l'église de S.-Médard de Paris.*

The *Dissertation sur les miracles* was the first, and perhaps the most important, of many tracts and treatises written on the same general subject. In addition to providing a detailed analysis of the Lefranc cure, which served as the focus of the work, the anonymous author—believed to have been the noted Jansenist theologian, Nicolas Petitpied[83]—offered extended reflections on the broad religious and political implications of the Pâris miracles as they applied to the Lair case and to the entire controversy over the Bull. His arguments, reminiscent of the ones adduced by some of his seventeenth-century Jansenist predecessors and by Bishop Colbert in the 1720s,[84] emphasized the belief that the working of a miracle was a direct expression of the divine will, a visible sign of God's continuing presence and His special favor, a means by which a distant, remote *Dieu câché* revealed Himself to the faithful. It was Petitpied's contention that if the archbishop of Paris intended to remain silent, then the friends of Anne Lefranc had to

---

[81] *Ibid.*   [82] *Ibid.*, June 27, 1731, p. 125.

[83] Vintimille to Fleury, May 19, 1731, BM, MS 2357, p. 365.

[84] See Ch. II, above.

act on their own. "The works of God must not be ignored," he insisted, especially when He has intended that they should be the decisive means of leading the faithful away from the "party of error" to the "party of Truth."[85] The significance of these "works of God" was clear, he explained, part of a divine plan to rescue the Church from error and iniquity.[86] "In the present circumstances, when the excesses were reaching their height, God wanted to appear in order to defend His cause . . . and to teach all the faithful that those who attack the opponents of the Bull are really attacking Him."[87] In according to François de Pâris the ability to work miracles, God wished not only to demonstrate that He held the deacon in particular esteem, but also to provide irrefutable confirmation of the saintliness of Pâris' life, the purity of his faith, and the orthodoxy of his doctrine.[88] Thus the miracles attributed to M. Pâris' intercession also stood as divine affirmation that his conduct in the *Unigenitus* controversy was entirely above reproach and far from "criminal, schismatic, seditious, or rebellious toward the king," as various civil and ecclesiastical authorities had charged.[89] What is more, these miracles, when taken together with those "performed" since 1725 by other appellant thaumaturges all over France, clearly manifested the divine purpose and unequivocally testified to the same truth: "the cause of the appeal is the cause approved by God."[90]

After taking some pains to refute various *constitutionnaire* objections to the general authority of miracles in resolving dogmatic disputes,[91] Petitpied went on to include extended remarks in defense of the *anticonstitutionnaire* resistance to the Bull. He attacked the "arbitrary and irresponsible measures" which the authorities had adopted to ensure the Bull's reception in France. In particular, he denounced them for "ravaging the churches of the realm" by dismissing many worthy priests and confessors while appointing ignorant or debauched clergy

---

[85] *Dissertation sur les miracles*, p. 9.   [86] *Ibid.*, p. 20.
[87] *Ibid.*, p. 21.   [88] *Ibid.*, pp. 9-11.
[89] *Ibid.*, pp. 11-12. The *anticonstitutionnaires* also took pains to point out that M. Pâris had died in the bosom of the Church, enjoying to his very last days the full rights of a Catholic in good standing, including the right of burial in consecrated ground.
[90] *Ibid.*, pp. 11-23.
[91] The appellants, he argued, were not using the miracles to challenge the authority and decisions of the Church, nor were they questioning whether or not one must submit to the Church when it has pronounced on a matter of faith. Rather, their recourse to the miracles served as a demonstration that the bull *Unigenitus* was not, in fact, a doctrinally valid pronouncement of the Church, all *constitutionnaire* claims to the contrary notwithstanding.

to fill their places.[92] Petitpied also condemned the royal government for its interference with the Paris Parlement's reception of *appels comme d'abus*. By attempting to limit the magistrates' jurisdiction, he complained, the authorities had deprived the "innocent oppressed" among the lower clergy of any other means of redress and had left the way open for the enemies of the faith to overturn "all the laws of the realm and the very precious maxims of the French Church."[93] Finally, in a concluding peroration, Petitpied hurled a challenge at his opponents:

> [In] vain do the *constitutionnaires* boast of their numbers and of their authority to oppress the defenders of the truth. The promises of God are immutable. He will always preserve in His Church a sufficient number of witnesses of His truth; He will protect them, and the very punishments with which their enemies [seek to] overwhelm them will only serve to increase their strength.

"You may gather together in great numbers," the author warned his *constitutionnaire* enemies, drawing loosely upon Isaiah (Chapter 8),

> [but] you will be no less vanquished, and the report of your defeat will resound across the land. . . . [You may] prepare yourselves for combat, and revive your courage, [but you will] be overthrown. . . . Compose ordinances in prejudice to the truth, in order to destroy it here on earth, and they will not be executed in spite of all your threats, because God is with us, and He manifests His goodness by means of miracles.[94]

In the months ahead, such warnings, arguments, and assertions—further embellished and more extensively developed in a succession of theological and political discourses—came to be a fundamental weapon in the *anticonstitutionnaire* polemical arsenal. By attempting to exploit the miracles of François de Pâris both to oppose royal and episcopal policies on the Bull and to justify the general cause of the appeal as well as the specific causes of M. Lair, the *curés*, and the *avocats* and magistrates in the Parlement of Paris, the *Dissertation sur les miracles* marked the beginning of a new Jansenist offensive. To be sure, not all the *anticonstitutionnaires* were quick to embrace either the Lefranc *Relation* or the Petitpied *Dissertation*. A number of influential Jansenist theologians, recalling the earlier arguments of Pierre Nicole and others, remained somewhat skeptical.[95] The editor of the *Nouvelles ecclésiastiques*, reflecting this initial hesitancy and uncer-

---

[92] *Dissertation sur les miracles*, pp. 30-32.
[93] *Ibid.*, p. 32. [94] *Ibid.*, p. 33. [95] See n. 2, above.

tainty, reacted rather cautiously at first, waiting quite a few months before he even provided any news of the Lefranc cure. With the issue of June 4, 1731, however, the *Nouvellistes* suddenly broke their silence. Without any prior announcement or mention of the matter, without any previous expression of sentiments akin to those found in the *Dissertation*, the newspaper, in its lead article from Paris, provided a brief synopsis of the miracle along with some highly favorable comments on behalf of Mlle. Lefranc and her *Relation*.[96] The editor also demonstrated his high regard for the position enunciated in the *Dissertation*, by warmly recommending the work to his readers.[97] The principles of this first pamphlet on the miracles thereafter became the principles espoused by the journal as well. Thus by late spring of 1731 an important segment of *anticonstitutionnaire* opinion had definitely "adopted" the miracles of and cult to François de Pâris and, by transforming the observances at Saint-Médard into a political *cause célèbre*, had created a new problem for Fleury and Vintimille.

For a long time, while the Pâris cult was continuing to attract adherents, the authorities—at Versailles, in Rome, and even in the archdiocese—had remained notably silent. Although they were fundamentally distrustful of such spiritual novelties and may have thus found the unsanctioned observances at Saint-Médard disconcerting, they had made no effort to interfere with or disrupt the proceedings. In fact, the subject of the Pâris cult had not been raised even once in the regular correspondence exchanged between Vintimille and Fleury or that between the crown and the Holy See. However, the publication of the Anne Lefranc *Relation* and the accompanying *Dissertation* changed all that quite dramatically. The appellants' artful attempt to draw the cult into the controversy over the bull *Unigenitus* gave a new dimension to the entire Saint-Médard affair, thereby provoking a strong reaction from the established authorities.

According to legislation promulgated at the Council of Trent, a miracle could be published only after an investigation by, and with the express permission of, the ordinary. Not surprisingly, therefore, Vintimille was "appalled, chagrined, and outraged" that the *anticonstitutionnaire* authors of the *Relation* and the *Dissertation* had blatantly contravened his archiepiscopal authority: it was yet another example of the "spirit of audacity and insubordination" which had been causing "confusion and division and disrupting the tranquility of the diocese" since his arrival nearly two years earlier.[98] Having received copies of

[96] *NNEE*, June 4, 1731, p. 109.   [97] *Ibid.*
[98] Vintimille to Fleury, May 19, 1731, BM, MS 2357, pp. 365-67, and May 22, 1731, *ibid.*, p. 373.

the two tracts in mid-May, the archbishop began almost immediately to discuss with Cardinal Fleury, the lieutenant of police, Hérault, and his own *grands-vicaires* an appropriate response to the *anticonstitution-naires'* latest offensive. Acknowledging the seriousness of the matter, Fleury likewise called a high-level strategy session at Versailles to consider the royal government's reaction.[99] Both the archbishop and the cardinal-minister shared the view that Vintimille was no longer free to remain silent; indeed, he had a duty to act to counter this latest challenge to his authority and that of the Church. But both men were also aware that the situation was a delicate one, demanding cautious, deliberate reflection.[100] For several weeks, with Hérault and Vintimille's confidant, the abbé de Cosnac, serving as intermediaries and messengers, various proposals were relayed back and forth between Paris and Versailles. It was finally decided that Vintimille would order his *promoteur* (M. Le Blanc) and his *official* (M. Robinet) to conduct an inquest into the Lefranc cure and eventually publish their findings —already presumed to be unfavorable to Mlle. Lefranc—along with a refutation of the *Dissertation sur les miracles*, in a major pastoral decree.[101]

The diocesan officials conducting the inquest called 40 of the original 120 witnesses to Anne Lefranc's "miraculous cure," as well as a number of other persons, to appear before their commission. After subjecting the collected testimony to careful scrutiny, they arrived at conclusions widely at variance with those contained in the *Relation*. Perhaps the most damaging testimony in the case came from members of Anne Lefranc's own immediate family. Her brother, whose deposition was to be printed separately and eventually circulated all over Paris, accused her and especially her confessor of perpetrating a hoax, contending that the abbé Desvaux had taken advantage of his sister's credulity in order to recruit new adherents to the Pâris cult. He further asserted, with support from his mother, that Anne's various afflictions had by no means been completely cured.[102] With the testimony of her relatives and that of other hostile witnesses the case against Mlle. Lefranc was already quite substantial. Before closing the investigation, however, Robinet, on the advice of Chancellor Daguesseau,

<hr>

[99] Fleury to Vintimille, May 21, 1731, *ibid.*, pp. 367-68. Cf. Fleury to Hérault, May 25, 1731, BA, MS 10196.

[100] Vintimille to Fleury, May 22, 1731, BM, MS 2357, pp. 370-71.

[101] Fleury to Vintimille, June 11, 1731, *ibid.*, pp. 382-83.

[102] *Déclaration du sieur abbé Le Franc, frère de la demoiselle Anne Le Franc* (1731).

called several medical experts to give their opinions on the case.[103] The seven doctors and surgeons brought in for consultation, basing their judgments on the accounts given in the *Relation* and in the supporting certificates, were virtually unanimous in their testimony. After analyzing the nature of Anne Lefranc's principal infirmity, they dismissed it as an *affection histérique* having to do with menstrual irregularity. Indeed, they claimed that all of her "ailments" were a consequence of this problem and that no miracle whatever was involved in her cure. They further contended that her various "afflictions" should never have been classified as incurable in the first place and that, moreover, her "cure" was not nearly so sudden as she had claimed.[104]

By early July, satisfied that a strong case had been established for denying the alleged miracle, Vintimille's theologians completed work on a projected *mandement*. The archbishop submitted the proposed decree, along with his *official*'s conclusions, to an eagerly expectant Cardinal Fleury. Within a few days Fleury returned the *mandement* to Vintimille with a few suggestions and corrections.[105] By mid-July, despite a few remaining problems, the pastoral decree, the first official and public pronouncement against the miracles and cult of François de Pàris, was in press.[106]

Vintimille's *mandement* combined both pastoral and ecclesiastical censure. He began by asserting two principal objections to recent *anticonstitutionnaire* activities at Saint-Médard:

> In the first place, in contempt of the laws of the Church and those of this diocese, [the appellants] have undertaken the publication of miracles which we have not officially recognized; and secondly, by an abuse which might have very dangerous consequences, they have sought to authorize a religious cult which the Church has not approved.[107]

Vintimille argued further that, since the Church must take precautions against all impostures and protect itself from the libertines and nonbelievers who seek to discredit true miracles, it has traditionally defined precise rules regarding the recognition of miracles and saints.

[103] Vintimille to Fleury, June 24, 1731, BM, MS 2357, pp. 399-400, and June 30, 1730, *ibid.*, p. 403.

[104] See appendix to Vintimille's *mandement* of July 15, 1731, especially pp. 31-34.

[105] Vintimille to Fleury, July 2, 1731, BM, MS 2357, p. 418; Fleury to Vintimille, July 5, 1731, *ibid.*, p. 426.

[106] *Mandement de monseigneur l'archévêque de Paris, au sujet d'un écrit qui a pour titre: "Dissertation sur les miracles . . ." (15 juillet 1731).*

[107] *Ibid.*, p. 4.

The laity has ignored these teachings, he contended, while mere priests have loudly protested in public against archiepiscopal authority and against a judgment of the Church.[108]

In the next section of his decree Vintimille attempted to demonstrate that the Jansenists were using a faked miracle to dupe the pious faithful into believing in François de Pâris and therefore in their partisan cause.[109] Anne Lefranc was a simple, ignorant girl, he reminded his flock. The style and contents of the *Relation*, reflecting considerable sophistication and a deep involvement in the religious disputes, were obviously not hers—proof "that another hand guided that of Anne Lefranc."[110] What is more, the supposedly miraculous cure was no miracle at all:

> A cure may be regarded as miraculous only when the malady was incurable or when the afflicted person has recovered his health in a manner so perfect and so sudden that it is clear that such a change could not possibly be attributed to a natural cause; without one of these two circumstances no cure, however surprising it may appear, can be regarded as a true miracle, because nature keeps hidden within its bosom the principles of such an effect.[111]

Judged from these criteria, Vintimille asserted, Anne Lefranc's alleged cure was nothing more than "a succession of suppositions, deceptions, and lies."[112] Many of the certificates included in support of the *Relation* had been "either obtained by fraud or extorted through persistent solicitation," while others "were altered and falsified in essential parts."[113] There were no doctors' certificates to attest to the nature of the disease or the quality of the cure. Even Mlle. Lefranc's own mother and brother testified that she had never been partially blind in one eye, as she had claimed.[114] Moreover, though the paralysis had been authentic, she still could not walk several months after the "cure."[115] Claiming the responsibility as archbishop to protect the credulous faithful from being seduced by such fraudulent shams, Vintimille maintained that he was obliged to forbid the publication of the supposed miracle and to prohibit the popular observances of the cult to M. Pâris.

Vintimille concluded his decree with a resounding denunciation of the *anticonstitutionnaires*, a denunciation which matched the final peroration of the *Dissertation* in its strident tone. After declaring the Anne

---

[108] *Ibid.*, p. 5.
[111] *Ibid.*, p. 9.
[114] *Ibid.*, pp. 13-16.

[109] *Ibid.*, p. 25.
[112] *Ibid.*, p. 16.
[115] *Ibid.*, p. 20.

[110] *Ibid.*, pp. 8-9.
[113] *Ibid.*, p. 12.

Lefranc cure to be "false and contrived," he went on to forbid the publication of new miracles without his permission and without a prior canonical examination. He issued a formal prohibition against "worshiping M. Pâris, revering his tomb, [or] . . . having Masses celebrated in his honor." Finally, he condemned the *Dissertation sur les miracles* for "tending to seduce the faithful, insulting the pope and the episcopate, and favoring errors condemned by the Church," and he forbade the faithful to read it or even to possess a copy.[116] Although initially inclined to order the *mandement* to be published from the pulpit of every parish in the city and to subject to disciplinary action any *curé* who contravened this order, Vintimille was prevailed upon to adopt a less provocative approach.[117] As a precaution against widespread parochial agitation and in order to forestall yet another dangerous confrontation with his parish clergy, the archbishop, with some reluctance, decided to limit its formal publication to the parishes of Saint-Médard and Saint-Barthélemy, the ones which were most directly affected by its contents.

Despite having restricted the *mandement*'s publication within the diocese, Vintimille, in issuing such a strongly worded decree, guaranteed that the battle over the miracles, first inaugurated by the appellants in their *Dissertation sur les miracles*, would not be quickly settled. In the same way that the *Dissertation* had demonstrated influential *anticonstitutionnaire* sentiment in favor of the miracles and cult of M. Pâris, Vintimille's declaration, composed with the express approval of Cardinal Fleury himself, made it very clear that the civil and ecclesiastical authorities were going to stand firmly against the cult. Consequently, by early summer of 1731 the lines of division between *constitutionnaires* and *anticonstitutionnaires* over this issue were being drawn more sharply than ever. Both sides now saw Saint-Médard as a significant, decidedly volatile, and potentially explosive political issue, which no one could afford to ignore any longer. Nor could anyone remain oblivious to its long-range implications and its possible consequences. Before considerations of ecclesiastical politics began to intrude upon the observances at Saint-Médard, the Pâris cures had constituted the center of a rather ordinary, if unsanctioned, popular cult of only minor importance and posed no very serious threat to the established authorities. However, the Anne Lefranc affair changed the character

---

[116] *Ibid.*, pp. 29-30.

[117] Vintimille to Fleury, July 2, 1731, BM, MS 2357, p. 419, and July 13, 1731, *ibid.*, pp. 427-28; Fleury to Vintimille, July 14, 1731, *ibid.*, p. 431. In fact, the printed version of the *mandement* did contain an injunction that the decree be "read, published, and posted" throughout the diocese (p. 30).

of the problem in spectacular fashion. The appellant action in publishing the *Dissertation sur les miracles* had challenged Vintimille's authority, among other things, and forced him to take an uncompromising position in response. Not too surprisingly, the archbishop's reply called forth additional challenges of various kinds from the other side. Newly begun, the conflict over the miracles now escalated rapidly.

While certain Jansenists may have shared Vintimille's skepticism toward, if not his contempt of, the Lefranc cure and the Saint-Médard observances, most of them very decidedly did not. Indeed, most of the party took great offense at the archbishop's pastoral decree. A group of leading *anticonstitutionnaire* polemicists and pamphleteers, their pens ever at hand, were the first to respond. The editor of the *Nouvelles ecclésiastiques*, for example, believed that Vintimille's pastoral decree was of such great significance that he felt obliged to publish a special number of the newspaper and to go beyond the normal limits of a simple extract. Within a week after the *mandement*'s publication at Saint-Médard and Saint-Barthélemy, the *Nouvellistes* had given over almost an entire issue to the subject.[118] The editor denounced Vintimille's appointed commission for the "highly questionable procedures" it had followed in investigating Anne Lefranc's cure and condemned the archbishop for the hostile and insensitive tone he had adopted toward those who were participating in religious observances at Saint-Médard. The newspaper also challenged the validity of the inquest's conclusions regarding the Lefranc cure. Acknowledging that he had not exhausted all that was "reprehensible" in the decree, the editor appealed to others to join him in carrying on the battle.[119]

Without waiting for the *Nouvellistes'* call to action, other *anticonstitutionnaire* controversialists were quick to join in the attack upon Vintimille's pastoral decree. In fact, two anonymous tracts—the *Lettre de M*** à un de ses amis, touchant les informations qui se font à l'officialité de Paris au sujet du miracle arrivé, le 3 novembre 1730, en la personne d'Anne Lefranc* and the *Lettre d'un théologien à son ami, au sujet du dernier Mandement de Monseigneur l'archevêque*—were already being hawked in the streets of Paris even before the special edition of the *Nouvelles ecclésiastiques* had rolled off the presses. The first "letter," dated June 30, actually anticipated by three weeks the formal publication of Vintimille's *mandement* and was originally written to warn of the archbishop's impending condemnation of the Lefranc miracle. The second, dated July 26, reiterated the arguments

[118] July 29, 1731, pp. 149-52.   [119] *Ibid.*, p. 152.

and assertions originally developed in the *Dissertation sur les miracles* in an effort to rebut the arguments on which Vintimille had based his interdiction of the Pâris cult. The controversy became even more intense when Vintimille's *constitutionnaire* defenders also entered the fray. Within a short time, scores of broadsides, *libelles*, tracts, and treatises devoted to the Saint-Médard observances and the Pâris miracles were circulating all over France. Yet for all the intensity of these polemical exchanges, the most significant response to Vintimille's decree, the response which eventually attracted the most attention and created perhaps the greatest furor, was that of the Parisian *curés*.

On August 13, 1731, twenty-three *curés* from Paris and vicinity—among them most of those who had challenged Vintimille several times before—addressed to their archbishop a *requête* on the subject of the miracles[120] and hired a courier to deliver it to him at his summer retreat in Conflans.[121] Their petition, accompanied by a large quantity of documents, including excerpts from the *procès-verbaux* compiled by the abbé Achille Thomassin in 1728, called on Vintimille to reopen the investigation of the cures that had originally been examined under Cardinal Noailles. Since Noailles had never formally certified these cures as miraculous, the *curés* now sought Vintimille's official authorization to present them to the faithful, in order thereby "to contribute to their edification and consolation."[122] In addition, the *curés* further petitioned the archbishop to look into numerous other miracles that had been attributed to the intercession of François de Pâris since the ones initially examined three years earlier. They even offered to provide Vintimille with the necessary proofs for those which had taken place in their own parishes, so that the diocesan authorities might verify them more easily.[123] All these facts, they asserted, "concern the glory of God, the faith, the salvation of the people, and in particular the Church and the city of Paris."[124]

Another letter addressed to Vintimille on that same day and written on the same subject came from the *curé* of Saint-Pierre-des-Arcis, Claude-François Thomassin, former *promoteur* in the archdiocese and brother of Noailles' vicegerent.[125] Drawing on the experience

---

[120] *Requête présentée à monseigneur l'archevêque par les curés de Paris, au sujet des miracles qui s'opèrent au tombeau de M. l'abbé de Pâris.*

[121] Vintimille to Fleury, Aug. 13, 1731, BM, MS 2357, p. 477.

[122] *Requête*, p. 4.

[123] See Vintimille to Fleury, Aug. 13, 1731, BM, MS 2357, pp. 476-77.

[124] *Requête*, p. 5.

[125] BN, MSS Fr., MS 22245, fols. 159-60; another copy in BA, MS 4852, fol. 153. Cf. *NNEE*, Aug. 10, 1731, p. 160.

of twenty-seven years in beatification procedures, Thomassin, who had been unable to sign his colleagues' original petition, began by trying to persuade Vintimille to authorize the public observances at Pâris' tomb. "Neither the Holy See nor the Bishops," he argued, "have ever prevented the gathering of people at the tombs of those who, like [M. Pâris], have died in the odor of sanctity; indeed, in times past, this was the only procedure that was required in order to arrive at their canonization." As for the *procès-verbaux* compiled by his brother, Thomassin reminded Vintimille that it was his responsibility, as archbishop, to issue a definitive ruling: "all of Paris is impatiently awaiting your decision," he observed.

The tone of the *curés'* petition, like that of Thomassin's letter, was comparatively mild and deferential. Nowhere did they make any mention of the bull *Unigenitus*; nowhere did they refer to the fact that François de Pâris had been an appellant. In fact, though it had been composed in consultation with the noted *anticonstitutionnaire* controversialist, Laurent Boursier,[126] the *curés'* petition was remarkably free of any partisan comment whatsoever. But their efforts were clearly not without partisan intent. To the *anticonstitutionnaire* Paris clergy, Vintimille's latest pastoral decree was only the most recent example of the continuing official harassment being carried out against the opponents of the Bull. Vintimille's refusal to approve the Lefranc cure —and, indeed, his insistence on denying its miraculous character and condemning the entire Pâris cult—had, at least for the time being, deprived the parish priests of a striking propaganda victory. If the archbishop had acknowledged that Anne Lefranc's cure had been a true miracle—an acknowledgment that was clearly unthinkable under the circumstances—there could have been no confusion as to its meaning. The *curés*, especially the abbé Lair, would have been able to claim that their affirmation of the prerogatives of the "second order" and their resistance to episcopal authority had received divine legitimation. In the miracles of François de Pâris, the advocates of episcopal preeminence within the Church, like the proponents of the bull *Unigenitus*, were faced with yet another formidable challenge. And the Paris *curés*, for all the circumspection and deference displayed in their petition, seemed eager to flaunt that challenge directly at Vintimille. Without waiting for a reply from their archbishop, they published

---

[126] This fact was disclosed by the *Nouvellistes* only after Boursier's death, in the gazette's long obituary on him (*ibid.*, Oct. 23, 1749, p. 170). This entire obituary contains a very revealing description of Boursier's role on behalf of the appeal and, in particular, his active involvement on the side of the *curés* in their frequent squabbles with Vintimille.

their *requête* along with Thomassin's letter and all the supporting documents from the inquest of 1728.

Even before these materials had appeared in print and joined the other anonymous *anticonstitutionnaire* publications circulating through the streets of Paris, Vintimille was beside himself with rage. Though he did take the time to look through the various documents which the *curés* had presented to him and to read over their petition, he had no intention of acceding to their request. On the contrary, in a fit of pique he dashed off a letter to Cardinal Fleury in which he denounced the "audacity and presumptuousness" of these parish priests and pleaded once again for his friend's assistance in dealing with this latest act of defiance.[127] The cardinal-minister, who described himself as similarly "astonished, dismayed, and shocked" to see "the seduction, bad faith, and treachery of the Jansenists reach such heights," sought to console Vintimille and offered him promises of renewed support.[128] But the archbishop was inconsolable. "It is both sad and cruel," he lamented to Fleury a week later, "to see oneself daily exposed to the impudence and insolence of such persons. I cannot punish them myself nor can I take action against them through an appeal to the Parlement (as they can against me). I am consequently made to feel useless, impotent, and contemptible in my own diocese."[129] Although he was eager to strike down the most fractious and have them removed by royal *lettres de cachet*, the archbishop understood the serious disadvantages to such a procedure.[130] In the end, it was decided to do nothing: to offer no response to the *curés'* petition and to leave those responsible untouched. But while Vintimille may have chosen to ignore the *requête*, he could not ignore the fact that these priests, by acting in concert and placing their own considerable prestige and authority behind the Pâris cult, had made his problem more difficult than ever. Nor were these tenacious ecclesiastics likely to give up this latest fight very easily.

Indeed, though their petition had gone largely unheard, the *curés* were by no means deterred. On October 4, after waiting impatiently for several weeks for word from the archdiocesan authorities, twenty-two *curés*[131] signed a second *requête* on the subject of miracles, which they had a messenger present to Vintimille at his archiepiscopal palace

[127] Vintimille to Fleury, Aug. 13, 1731, BM, MS 2357, p. 477.
[128] Fleury to Vintimille, Aug. 13, 1731, *ibid.*, p. 478.
[129] Vintimille to Fleury, Aug. 20, 1731, *ibid.*, p. 479.
[130] Vintimille to Fleury, Aug. 20, 1731, *ibid.*, p. 480.
[131] For an explanation of the discrepancy in the number of *curés* who signed this second petition as compared with those who had adhered to the previous one, see *NNEE*, Dec. 15, 1731, p. 242.

in Paris.[132] In the month and a half which had intervened since they made their first request, the *cures* had observed a considerable number of additional cures, "some sudden and perfect, others gradual and incomplete," which had been occurring in the view of all Paris and even in some nearby parishes outside the city. The accounts of thirteen such cures, along with abundant supporting testimony, accompanied their second *requête*. Claiming as before to be acting only in the best interests of the faith and citing various theological arguments and historical precedents to buttress their case, the *cures* appealed to Vintimille not to reject their latest petition out of hand:

> These cures are so substantial in themselves, so evidently certified by a large number of witnesses of undoubted sincerity, and invested with such striking character that [we] hope that Your Grace will be prepared to look into them and that, after having conducted a juridical inquest into these facts, you will then continue the investigations of all the others.[133]

Once again the *cures* offered to assist the archdiocesan authorities in conducting the investigations and administering the necessary tests prescribed for proper canonical procedure.

But the second petition proved no more successful than the first one had been in obtaining archiepiscopal authorization for the Pâris cult. This time, however, the *cures* did manage to evoke a public response from Vintimille. Shortly after receiving the document, the harassed archbishop replied with a ringing denunciation that underscored the profoundly political character which the Saint-Médard affair had by now assumed. "Messieurs," he haughtily addressed his refractory clergy,

> prove to me in good faith that M. Pâris did not die an adherent to the appeal against the Bull or that a willful appeal is not a schismatic act against the visible authority [of the Church] established by Jesus Christ. If [you can] not, [then] cease pleading with me to verify and publish some supposed miracles accomplished through the intercession of this deacon. . . . [B]y the incontestable rules of the faith, . . . a man who dies in revolt against the decisions of the Church dies a schismatic. Do not de-

---

[132] *Seconde Requête présentée à monseigneur l'archevêque par les curés de Paris . . . au sujet des miracles qui s'opèrent tous les jours au tombeau de M. l'abbé de Pâris.* As with the first petition, the *cures* did not present this second one to Vintimille themselves, for fear of *lettres de cachet* charging them with unlawful association—a charge which the archbishop had leveled at them many times (*NNEE*, Dec. 15, 1731, p. 241).

[133] *Seconde Requête*, p. 4.

lude yourselves [, therefore,] into thinking that I would permit
or [even] willingly tolerate that he should be honored as a saint
in my diocese. Do not suppose, either, that I will undertake an
examination of your alleged miracles: it is not done, it cannot be
done, for such a subject and for such a cause.[134]

In subsequent discussions with Cardinal Fleury, the frustrated Vintimille, fearing that he was becoming "the mere plaything of a growing
fanaticism," once again threatened to take prompt and firm action
against the *curés* for their "intolerable impudence." As before, however, the archbishop did nothing more than threaten and bluster, the
unstable conditions within the diocese convincing him that any drastic
measures he might adopt would only cause the situation to deteriorate
still further.[135]

For the second time in less than two months, the *anticonstitutionnaire curés* had forced Vintimille into taking an uncompromising stand
over the miracles and cult of François de Pâris. While perhaps understandable, the archbishop's adamant rebuke of the *curés*, like his earlier
condemnations of Anne Lefranc and the *Dissertation sur les miracles*,
was hardly calculated to win back the diocese to his side or to put a
halt to the activities at Saint-Médard—particularly since the authorities
had chosen thus far not to impose any additional sanctions upon the
cult's adherents. On the contrary, his various actions and statements
had a quite opposite effect. Although the opponents of the Bull had
themselves been the instigators in transforming the popular phenomena
at Saint-Médard into a major issue of religious politics, Vintimille's
own pronouncements served to exacerbate the controversy, helping
to raise a spiritual and theological problem into an ecclesiastical and
judicial *cause célèbre*.

To make matters worse, the efforts of the ecclesiastical authorities
to suppress the Pâris cult drew several prominent *avocats* from the
Parlement of Paris—and eventually the sovereign court itself—into the
fray. Within a short time after Vintimille had published his *mandement*
on the Anne Lefranc case, a group of *avocats* acting on behalf of
Mlle. Lefranc presented the magistrates with an *appel comme d'abus*
against the archbishop's pastoral decree.[136] In their petition for a hear-

---

134 BPR, L.P. 480, No. 33.

135 Vintimille to Fleury, Oct. 6, 1731, BM, MS 2357, pp. 519-21, and Oct.
[10?], 1731, *ibid.*, p. 526.

136 *Requête présentée au parlement par Anne Le Franc, appelante, comme
d'abus, du Mandement de M. l'archevêque de Paris en date du 15 juillet 1731.*
Cf. the *Acte d'appel au parlement, interjeté par Anne Le Franc, du Mandement
de M. l'archevêque de Paris du 15 juillet 1731 (20 août).*

ing before the court, the lawyers, still smarting from their as yet un-resolved confrontation with Vintimille earlier in the year, raised sev-eral objections to the investigations carried on under his auspices. They were particularly concerned about alleged abuses of procedure and about the seemingly biased character of the information gathered by the archdiocesan authorities. They complained, in the first place, that M. Robinet, the *official* who conducted the inquest, had never called Anne Lefranc to testify on her own behalf, and that the various medical experts on whose reports Vintimille based much of his decree had never examined her directly.[137] They further objected that the arch-bishop had ignored most of the 120 certificates originally published in substantiation of the cure, including the notarized depositions taken from over 30 of the most distinguished and irreproachable ecclesias-tics and lay officials from the parish of Saint-Barthélemy. The lawyers also alleged that the inquest had agreed to hear testimony only from those witnesses whom the archbishop could induce to refute the mira-cle and had studiously ignored the rest.[138] Finally, the *avocats* took strong exception to the decree's conclusions for defaming the pious faithful, Mlle. Lefranc among them, who believed in the miracles which God was performing at Saint-Médard.[139] The lawyers called upon the Parlement to take prompt action, asking that the magistrates order the investigation of the Lefranc cure to be reopened and conducted in accordance with fair and proper canonical procedures, and that, in the meantime, the court require the archbishop immediately to with-

---

[137] *Requête présentée par Anne Le Franc*, pp. 3-4. The *Nouvellistes* charged that these doctors had been chosen "dans le même esprit et avec la même par-tialité que les témoins" (*NNEE*, July 29, 1731, p. 150). In addition, according to the *avocat* Marais, the doctors' "indelicate" discussion of Mlle. Lefranc's medical symptoms, which Vintimille appended to his *mandement* (pp. 31-34), caused quite an uproar in some circles (*Journal et mémoires*, IV, 262 [July 29, 1731]). The report also gave rise to a dispute within the Parisian medical community. See, for example, *Lettre d'un chirurgien de St-Cosme à un autre chirurgien de ses amis, au sujet du certificat . . . joint au Mandement de M. l'archevêque de Paris . . . (8 septembre 1731)*. The question of eighteenth-century medical views toward the miracles and convulsions of Saint-Médard is a subject that merits fur-ther study (cf. Owsei Temkin, *The Falling Sickness: A History of Epilepsy from the Greeks to the Beginnings of Modern Neurology* [Baltimore, 1945], *passim*).

[138] *Requête présentée par Anne Le Franc*, pp. 4-5. The appellants also alleged that Anne's brother, an ardent *constitutionnaire* priest, had been prevailed upon to bear witness against his sister in order to protect his religious standing and enhance his chances of clerical advancement (*Entretiens sur les miracles* [1732], p. 11).

[139] *Requête présentée par Anne Le Franc*, p. 5. Arguments similar to these were made in *NNEE*, July 29, 1731, pp. 149-52.

draw his *mandement* from circulation.[140] In so acting, the *avocats* contended, the judges would not be undertaking to establish or verify a miracle—a matter which was in any event beyond the Parlement's jurisdictional competence. Rather, the court would be trying to "make a thorough study of the archbishop's charge that a fraudulent miracle had been conjured up to seduce the faithful—a charge which, if proved true, represents a source of [potential] trouble for the State and hence a matter for the Parlement to suppress."[141]

As early as July 29 a four-man council of *avocats*, led by the distinguished Jansenist barrister, Jacques-Charles Aubry,[142] had agreed to present the *appel comme d'abus* to the Parlement. The appeal was accompanied by a statement from Anne Lefranc herself, in which she again attested to the veracity of the facts contained in her original *Relation* and declared her willingness to testify to these facts at any time. On August 3 the *Grand'Chambre* appointed the counselor Delpech *rapporteur* to review the case and present his findings to the court.[143]

Within a week after the appeal had been presented to the Parlement, Vintimille, stung by this dramatic and unexpected *coup d'éclat*, wrote several times to Cardinal Fleury once again mourning his unhappy fate and soliciting his friend's support. "It is shocking and appalling," the indignant archbishop complained, "that a man of my character and occupying a position of such honor should be exposed to a legal proceeding involving a wretched woman from the dregs of society."[144] As he had done so many times before, he reminded the cardinal-minister of earlier promises of continued royal protection: "You must admit, My Lord, that I would not have experienced such misadventures had I remained in Aix; it might have been better for me to have stayed there and less sad for you to have drawn me here with assurances that I could count on the king's authority."[145] Following the familiar litany of plaintive jeremiads, Vintimille appealed to Fleury to head off the Lefranc *appel comme d'abus*. After discussing the case with the chancellor, Fleury promised to do all he could to protect the archbishop and prevent the appeal from reaching the court. "I do not know where this crisis will end," he observed, "but rest assured that

[140] *Requête présentée par Anne Le Franc*, p. 6.
[141] *Ibid.*, p. 7.
[142] He had also been the author of Anne Lefranc's *Requête* (*NNEE*, Dec. 19, 1739, p. 198).
[143] "Nouvelles du temps, 1-4 Août 1731," Journal of De Lisle, AN, U-376.
[144] Vintimille to Fleury, Aug. 5, 1731, BM, MS 2357, pp. 465-66.
[145] Vintimille to Fleury, Aug. 1, 1731, *ibid.*, pp. 461-62.

you will be supported and that we will not abandon you." Of course, he added, "if everyone had followed my advice and sent Anne Lefranc off to a convent on the very day that you published your *mandement*, we would have avoided much of this problem."[146]

The government, however, seemed unwilling or unable to prevent the Parlement from considering Mlle. Lefranc's appeal. On September 3 the counselor Delpech delivered his report to the *Grand'Chambre*, whereupon the petition was communicated to the *procureur-général* for his disposition of the case. That same day printed copies of the relevant legal documents, including Anne Lefranc's petition and her *appel comme d'abus*, were being publicly hawked in the streets of Paris.[147] These developments prompted a series of hastily called conferences and frantic exchanges of letters between Paris and Versailles, all involved with attempting to delay or postpone the Parlement's formally admitting the petition, which had yet to be read or reported *au parquet*.[148] With Chancellor Daguesseau and the *gens du roi* at the center of most of these discussions, along with the presidents of several of the court's principal chambers, the government was hopeful of at least "reaching September 8," the date on which the Parlement suspended normal judicial operations for its annual vacation. Indeed, by a succession of dilatory tactics the *procureur-général* and the First President managed to prevent the magistrates from hearing the appeal at this time, deferring the case until the court's next term. The hope was that the press of new business on their return from recess might convince the magistrates to leave the Lefranc appeal pending indefinitely.

Although the arrival of the recess had forced the Parlement to leave the suit of Anne Lefranc pending, the authorities at Versailles and in the archdiocese of Paris could hardly have felt relieved. The entrance of the Palais de Justice into the fray meant that all the old embattled forces of Parisian ecclesiastical politics—magistrates and *avocats*, *curés* and priests, theologians and pamphleteers—had now become embroiled to one extent or another in the Saint-Médard affair. The previous chal-

---

[146] Fleury to Vintimille, Aug. 6, 1731, *ibid.*, pp. 466-67.

[147] Marais, IV, 295 (Sept. 17, 1731). See also *ibid.*, IV, 291-92 (Sept. 8, 1731), and *NNEE*, Sept. 9, 1731, p. 176.

[148] Chauvelin to Daguesseau, Sept. 3 or 4, 1731, BPR, L.P. 480, No. 23 (copy); Daguesseau to Joly de Fleury, Sept. 4, 1731, BN, J.F., MS 107, fol. 25; Joly de Fleury to Daguesseau, Sept. 4, 1731, *ibid.*, fol. 159; Daguesseau to Portail (First President in the Parlement of Paris), Sept. 5, 1731, BPR, L.P. 480, No. 27 (copy); Daguesseau to Joly de Fleury, Sept. 5, 1731, BN, J.F., MS 107, fol. 26; Joly de Fleury to Daguesseau, Sept. 5, 1731, BPR, L.P. 480, No. 25 (copy); and Joly de Fleury to Daguesseau, Sept. 6, 1731, *ibid.*, No. 26 (copy).

lenges to his authority, which had already left Vintimille a thoroughly dispirited man, were almost nothing by comparison with the series of setbacks he had experienced in the wake of his pastoral decree condemning the Pâris cult. What is more, the various attacks on his decree which were launched by the *Nouvellistes*, the *curés*, the *avocats*, and the other groups and individuals with experience in the game of ecclesiastical politics were not the only responses to greet the *mandement*. Indeed, perhaps the most complete and effective challenge the archbishop would have to face came at Saint-Médard itself. The months following the publication of the order saw a dramatic increase in the number of worshipers at Pâris' tomb and an extraordinary proliferation of miraculous cures attributed to the deacon. It was the devoted followers of M. Pâris, seeking to make their own voices heard loudly and clearly, who were ultimately most responsible for rendering Vintimille's decree totally ineffectual.

CHAPTER IV

From Miracles to Convulsions

WHILE the *anticonstitutionnaire* party—lawyers and judges, priests and theologians—was raising serious questions about Vintimille's treatment of the Anne Lefranc case and attempting to combat his *mandement* in various ways, a strong and unfavorable public outcry against the decree was beginning to be heard in the streets of Paris. Beyond the world of erudite controversy, legalistic maneuvering, and polemical encounters, scurrilous satires and vicious lampoons were appearing which attacked the archbishop for his alleged insensitivity to the spiritual needs of the Paris faithful, for his failure to provide true pastoral care. Sarcastic songs and verses were recited or posted on walls all over the city.[1] Not that Vintimille had ever been held in very high esteem among his Parisian flock, who continued to compare him—unfavorably—to his predecessor, the pious Cardinal Noailles. Indeed, on his very arrival in the capital in 1729, some anonymous wit, alluding to the girth and the reported gluttony of the new prelate, scribbled some graffiti on the door of the archbishop's palace: "Saint Antoine [i.e., Noailles] est mort, il nous a laissé son cochon." Another wag added: "On ne trouvera pas un archevêque comme le cardinal, en *vent-il mille*."[2] Mocking references to "Archbishop Ventre-mille" had also abounded since Vintimille's first days in Paris. In addition to the mounting abuse being heaped upon him by his resentful flock, there were growing fears

[1] BA, MS 2056, "Pièces des vers sur le mandement de l'archevêque de Paris qui défend de croire aux miracles," *passim*. See also verses cited by Charles-Henri Manneville, "Une vieille église à Paris: Saint-Médard," *Bulletin de la Montagne Sainte-Geneviève et ses abords*, 4 (1903-1904), p. 226.

[2] Barbier, II, 82-83 (October 1729). For satires which greeted Vintimille's accession to the archdiocese of Paris, see BN, MSS Fr., MS 12800, fols. 340-44, and BPR, L.P. 444, Nos. 55-56, 79. Some of these have been published in Raunié, v, 172-76. Cf. also the famous *Sarcellades, ou Recueils de poésies burlesques sous le nom des habitans de la paroisse de Sarcelles, dans le diocèse de Paris*, a series of devastating lampoons, written in a local patois, which appeared in both manuscript and print at various intervals beginning in 1729; they were ostensibly prompted by the archbishop's dismissal of the Jansenist *curé* of Sarcelles (see BN, MSS Fr., MS 25564). The police *gazetins* (BA, MS 10161) also contain passing satirical references to Vintimille.

that Vintimille, not satisfied with interdicting the Pâris cult through a pastoral decree, was preparing to interfere more directly with the popular devotions at Saint-Médard by having the body of François de Pâris exhumed and reburied at the Hôtel-Dieu. Furthermore, according to a rumor circulating on the evening of July 25, the day after the formal publication of his decree at the parishes of Saint-Barthélemy and Saint-Médard, the police were under orders to wall up the entire cemetery during the night.[3] Although these rumors proved entirely groundless, they were yet further indication of what the people— dependent on the gossip mills for much of their news—were prepared to believe of Vintimille and the Paris authorities in the wake of the archbishop's recent pronouncement. A political and ecclesiastical *cause célèbre* to the *anticonstitutionnaires*, the Pâris cult was now to become a spiritual *cause célèbre* to the pious lay faithful whose religious values and expectations the archbishop of Paris had apparently violated and challenged.

Although from the perspective of François de Pâris' devoted followers Vintimille's decree may have appeared to be a callous and unconscionable act, from the archbishop's vantage point and from that of the Church his decree was perfectly consistent with official doctrine and episcopal practice. The Council of Trent, in the course of reaffirming as articles of faith the existence of saints and the importance and efficacy of venerating them, had also sought to regulate hagiological devotion.[4] It had granted to the episcopate principal responsibility for "instruct[ing] the faithful diligently in matters relating to [the] intercession and invocation of the saints, the veneration of relics, and the legitimate use of images." Concerned that cults accorded to unorthodox, unworthy, or even mythical figures be uprooted, that "all superstition . . . be removed, all filthy quest for gain eliminated, and all lasciviousness avoided," and that "the celebration of saints and the visitation of relics" be conducted in the proper spirit and with the appropriate sense of decency and decorum, the council stipulated that "such zeal and care should be exhibited by the bishops with regard to these things that nothing may appear that is disorderly or unbecoming and confusedly arranged, nothing that is profane, nothing disrespectful. . . ." To forestall or eradicate any such abuses and to ensure that its orders were "faithfully observed," the council decreed

[3] Journal of De Lisle, July 1731, AN, U-376.

[4] H. J. Schroeder, *Canons and Decrees of the Council of Trent* (London, 1941), pp. 215-17 (Session xxv, Dec. 3-4, 1563).

that no one is permitted to erect or cause to be erected in any place or church, howsoever exempt, any unusual image unless it has been approved by the bishop; also that no new miracles be accepted and no relics recognized unless they have been investigated and approved by the same bishop, who, as soon as he has obtained any knowledge of such matters, shall, after consulting theologians and other pious men, act thereon as he shall judge consonant with truth and piety.

Thus, as Vintimille protested on many occasions, in pronouncing against the Pâris cult, he was only fulfilling his episcopal duty and carrying out a responsibility spelled out explicitly in the Tridentine canons and decrees. Like many bishops before him, however, Vintimille was to find that any attempt to overturn popular modes of belief and practice was fraught with serious difficulties.

For over a century and a half since Trent, the Gallican Church had been preoccupied with establishing doctrinal orthodoxy and uniformity of religious practice, with codifying the official worship of the Catholic faith, and with eliminating all challenges to its undisputed sway as exclusive depository, interpreter, and dispenser of the divine mysteries. Through pastoral decrees, episcopal ordinances, and synodal statutes the bishops of France had undertaken a major campaign to purge the faith of all "profane" or "superstitious deviations" and to denounce all unauthorized, excessive, or ambiguous manifestations of popular devotion, individual and especially collective. With the sanction of the civil authority, they also attempted to impose on all the faithful a system of prescribed duties and periodic religious obligations, while suppressing certain "unorthodox" rituals, placing restrictions on pilgrimages, denying the veneration of uncanonized saints, and in general "turning collective Christians into individual ones."[5] This process of regularization and purification (or "Christianization") was accompanied by a large-scale effort to raise the moral and intellectual level of the clergy, to reform the liturgy, to reconstruct and improve the condition of the

[5] John Bossy, "The Counter-Reformation and the People of Catholic Europe," *Past and Present*, No. 47 (May 1970), p. 62. Writing of analogous developments in early modern England, E. P. Thompson speaks of the Church's efforts to "impose upon the people . . . a rigmarole best calculated to inculcate the values of deference and order . . . to enforce that particular ritual method of living which makes the people most serviceable and least disobedient to their masters" ("Anthropology and the Discipline of Historical Context," *Midland History*, 1 [1971-72], p. 51). In these efforts the Church received considerable support from the crown, as, for example, with the edict of 1671, which upheld the authority of the bishop to forbid the laity to go on pilgrimage without his express permission.

churches, and to undertake evangelizing missions among the benighted populations in the kingdom.[6]

In addition to trying to extend the Church's control over every sphere of religious life and to elevate the spiritual tone of its message and the quality of its messengers, a principal goal in all these efforts had been to overcome popular "ignorance" and "credulity," to transform the popular religious consciousness, and to foster a new sense of the sacred as well as a new order and respectability in popular religious activity. There was never any thought in all this of trying to eliminate all the "magic" from the Catholic faith. On the contrary, for in claiming dignity for itself and in seeking to justify its institutional authority, the Church had always pointed to its own comprehensive system of supernatural aids and its own peculiarly powerful and successful forms of magic, and it would continue to do so.[7] However, in the process of attempting to suppress the extraecclesiastical sources of magic, of which it naturally disapproved, the clerical establishment displayed a certain psychological insensitivity to the practical concerns and aspirations of large numbers of the faithful. While the Church continued to sanction and dispense various "supernatural remedies" of its own, the ecclesiastical authorities had become less adaptable, less accommodating, less open to the myriad (but frequently uncontrolled and undisciplined) forms of popular devotion which over the centuries had helped sustain the ordinary believer during times of hardship and adversity. Although recent studies have shown that the official religion of the eighteenth century was not so cold, formal, or barren as has frequently been alleged, nevertheless, the Church of that period did provide less room for the kinds of para-liturgical spiritual activities which had traditionally appealed to the masses of Christians.[8] As the Church tried to sub-

[6] Louis Pérouas, "La pastorale liturgique au 17ᵉ siècle," *Mélanges de science religieuse*, 23 (1966), pp. 30-44. See also the same author's "Missions intérieures et missions extérieures françaises pendant les premières décennies du 17ᵉ siècle," *Parole et mission*, 7 (1964), pp. 644-59; *Grignion de Montfort, les missions* (Paris, 1966); and *Ce que croyait Grignion de Montfort et comment il a vécu sa foi* (Paris, 1973).

[7] For an extended discussion of Catholic "magic," see Keith Thomas, *Religion and the Decline of Magic* (New York, 1971), pp. 25-50. Cf. also the debate between Hildred Geertz, "An Anthropology of Religion and Magic, I," *Journal of Interdisciplinary History*, 6 (1975), pp. 71-89; and Thomas, "An Anthropology of Religion and Magic, II," *ibid.*, pp. 91-109.

[8] Pérouas speaks of "Une Eglise qui se sclérose" (*Ce que croyait Grignion*, pp. 10-12), while Pierre Deyon emphasizes the "contraste entre le dynamisme de l'Eglise catholique dans la première moitié du 17ᵉ siècle et son engourdissement au 18ᵉ!" (*Amiens, capitale provinciale: Etude sur la société urbaine au 17ᵉ siècle* [Paris-The Hague, 1967], p. 425).

stitute a more formal, regularized religion for the one which these people lived and esteemed, as its institutionalized forms of worship became increasingly dissociated from popular forms of piety, the "moods of festivity and joyful ecstasy" as well as the spirit of creativity and spontaneity which characterized much popular observance were all but eliminated from "the religious life of official post-Tridentine Catholicism."[9]

The post-Tridentine Church no doubt achieved great success in its efforts to institute a whole range of liturgical, educational, and administrative reforms, to establish a more orderly, uniform system of worship, to create a more effective, centralized, and better disciplined hierarchical structure, and to impose on the people a stricter code of religious behavior and a system of parochial conformity.[10] In general, however, the Catholic Reformation, accomplished principally by and for a spiritual, cultural, and social elite and placing particular emphasis on legislative, administrative, and institutional matters, had not fully penetrated the traditionalist popular mentality. Indeed, though the Church, supported by the intrusive surveillance of the secular power, did manage to establish a higher level of outward conformity to certain of its behavioral prescriptions, the ecclesiastical authorities encountered great difficulty in attempting to wean the people away from their customary patterns of religious observance.[11] Efforts to legislate changes in religious attitudes and to impose on the people new forms of thought and behavior went largely unheeded, not simply out of a spirit of defiance or perverse obstinacy on the part of the masses (though active,

[9] Natalie Zemon Davis, "Some Tasks and Themes in the Study of Popular Religion," in *The Pursuit of Holiness in Late Medieval and Renaissance Religion*, ed. Charles Trinkaus with Heiko A. Oberman, Vol. x of *Studies in Medieval and Reformation Thought* (Leiden, 1974), p. 309.

[10] Jean Delumeau, *Le Catholicisme entre Luther et Voltaire* (Paris, 1971), pp. 256-92, provides a very useful summary and assessment of the Church's efforts at "Christianization." See also Louis Trénard, "Le catholicisme au 18e siècle, d'après les travaux récents," *L'information historique*, 26 (1964), pp. 53-65; and *idem*, "La vie religieuse au 17e siècle," *ibid.*, 31 (1969), pp. 23-29, 66-72.

[11] Delumeau, *Catholicisme*, pp. 323-30; *idem*, "Au sujet de la déchristianisation," *Revue d'histoire moderne et contemporaine*, 22 (1975), pp. 52-60; and *idem*, "Ignorance religieuse et mentalité magique sous l'ancien régime" (Paper presented before the annual meeting of the Society for French Historical Studies, Ottawa, March 1972). On the vexed subject of "dechristianization," see also Gabriel Le Bras, "Déchristianisation: Mot fallacieux," *Cahiers d'histoire*, 9 (1964), pp. 92-97; René Rémond "La déchristianisation: Etat présent de la question et des travaux en langue française," *Concilium*, 7 (1965), pp. 131-36; and Michel Vovelle, "Etude quantitative de la déchristianisation au 18e siècle: Débat ouvert, tabou ou dépassé?" *18e siècle*, 5 (1973), pp. 163-72.

purposive resistance to the Church's strictures was certainly not uncommon), but largely because these people did not always comprehend the revised message now being preached to them and because they
were fundamentally unprepared for the radical intellectual and psychological reorientation demanded of them. Despite the Church's efforts to
define, to regulate, and to discipline all religious beliefs and practices,
the lines dividing the orthodox from the heterodox, the sacred from the
profane, piety from superstition, faith from credulity, tended to remain
blurred and indistinct. The longstanding tensions—the cultural discrep-
ancies—within Christianity between "popular" and "official" religion
remained unresolved. Old beliefs and old routines continued to exercise
a powerful grip on the popular mind, both rural and urban, well into
the eighteenth century.[12]

The popular "style of religion," like the popular "world view," was
never consciously articulated or formulated and never developed into
a fully integrated or unified system.[13] Though not always or even neces-

[12] Cf. Deyon, *Amiens*, pp. 385-90, 424-25, *et passim*; Kaplow, pp. 111-20; and
Jeanne Ferté, *La vie religieuse dans les campagnes parisiennes (1622-1695)* (Paris,
1962), pp. 336-69. Among contemporary works on popular "superstition" the
following are especially useful: [Jacques d'Autun], *L'incrédulité sçavante et la
crédulité ignorante, au sujet des magiciens et des sorciers* (Lyon, 1671); Jean-
Baptiste Thiers, *Traité des superstitions selon l'Ecriture sainte, les décrets des
conciles et les sentiments des saints et des théologien*, 2nd ed., 4 vols. (Paris,
1697-1704); and Pierre Lebrun, *Histoire critique des pratiques superstitieuses*
(Rouen, 1702).

[13] But cf. Thompson, pp. 51-55. In the absence of any single work of synthesis
that provides for early modern France the integrated view of popular religious
beliefs that Keith Thomas does for Tudor-Stuart England, one must piece together any analysis from various partial studies. In addition to the works cited
above, nn. 7-12, the following have been particularly useful in dealing with this
subject: Hervé Barbin and Jean-Pierre Duteil, "Miracle et pèlerinage au 17e
siècle," *Revue d'histoire de l'Eglise de France*, 61 (1975), pp. 246-56; Marie-
Hélène Froeschle-Chopard, "La dévotion populaire d'après les visites pastorales:
Un exemple, le diocèse de Vence au début du 18e siècle," *ibid.*, 60 (1974), pp.
85-99; Thérèse-Jean Schmitt, *L'organisation ecclésiastique et la pratique religieuse
dans l'archidiaconé d'Autun de 1650 à 1750* (Autun, 1957); Louis Trénard, "L'histoire des mentalités collectives. Les pensées et les hommes. Bilans et perspectives,"
Revue d'histoire moderne et contemporaine, 16 (1969), pp. 652-62; *idem* and
Yves-Marie Hilaire, "Idées, croyances et sensibilité religieuses du 18e siècle au
19e," *Bulletin de la Section d'Histoire moderne et contemporaine du Comité des
travaux historiques et scientifiques*, fasc. 5 (1964), pp. 7-27; M. Vovelle, *Piété
baroque et déchristianisation en Provence au 18e siècle* (Paris, 1973); François
Lebrun, *Les hommes et la mort en Anjou aux 17e et 18e siècles. Essai de démographie et de psychologie historiques* (Paris-The Hague, 1971); Alain Lottin,
Vie et mentalité d'un Lillois sous Louis XIV (Lille, 1968); Robert Sauzet, "Miracles et Contre-Réforme en Bas-Languedoc sous Louis XIV," *Revue d'histoire*

sarily incompatible with the "official" modes of belief, "popular religion" provided an alternative, and often more satisfying, means of dealing with the mysterious forces—malign and benevolent—in an uncertain, incomprehensible universe, an approach which could and frequently did bypass the institutional Church entirely and often disregarded its theology as altogether irrelevant. More (and perhaps less) than a formal creed or code, the religion of the masses represented the faith of living persons, a religion which they themselves experienced and which they ordinarily transmitted and preserved through oral tradition and daily practice. It was a religion which possessed its own logic and coherence and which they found particularly appropriate to their lives and to their way of apprehending the world. Involving a characteristic mixture of orthodox and "superstitious" (that is, para-Christian and pagan) activities and beliefs, this syncretic Catholicism corresponded to the spiritual aspirations and psychological needs of a people who did not always derive full emotional satisfaction from the formal

de la spiritualité, 48 (1972), pp. 179-91; idem, "Pèlerinage panique et pèlerinage de dévotion: Notre-Dame de Rochefort au 17ᵉ siècle," Annales du Midi, 77 (1965), pp. 375-97; Marc Soriano, Les contes de Perrault: Culture savante et traditions populaires (Paris, 1968); Victor-Lucien Tapié et al., Retables baroques de Bretagne et spiritualité du 17ᵉ siècle: Etude sémiographique et religieuse (Paris, 1972); P. Deyon, "Mentalités populaires, un sondage à Amiens au 17ᵉ siècle," Annales: Economies, Sociétés, Civilisations, 17 (1962), pp. 448-58; André Latreille, "Pratique, piété, et foi populaire dans la France moderne au 19ᵉ et 20ᵉ siècles," in Popular Belief and Practice, ed. G. J. Cuming and Derek Baker, Vol. 8 of Studies in Church History (Cambridge, Eng., 1972), pp. 277-90; Jean Chatelus, "Thèmes picturaux dans les appartements de marchands et artisans parisiens au 18ᵉ siècle," 18ᵉ siècle, 6 (1974), pp. 309-24; R. Lecotté, "Méthodes d'enquêtes pour les cultes populaires," Revue de synthèse, 78 (1957), pp. 367-89; Gérard Bouchard, Le village immobile: Sennely-en-Sologne au 18ᵉ siècle (Paris, 1972); Emmanuel Le Roy Ladurie, Les paysans de Languedoc (Paris, 1966); Robert Mandrou, De la culture populaire aux 17ᵉ et 18ᵉ siècles: La Bibliothèque bleue de Troyes (Paris, 1964); idem, "Littérature de colportage et mentalités paysannes aux 17ᵉ et 18ᵉ siècles," Etudes rurales, 15 (1964), pp. 72-85; idem, "Spiritualité et pratique catholique au 17ᵉ siècle," Annales: Economies, Sociétés, Civilisations, 16 (1961), pp. 136-46; Geneviève Bollème, La bibliothèque bleue: Littérature populaire en France du 17ᵉ au 19ᵉ siècles (Paris, 1971); idem, Les almanachs populaires au 17ᵉ et 18ᵉ siècles: Essai d'histoire sociale (Paris, 1969); idem, "Littérature populaire et littérature de colportage au 18ᵉ siècle," in Livre et société dans la France du 18ᵉ siècle (Paris, 1965), pp. 61-92; Alphonse Dupront, "Formes de la culture de masses: De la doléance politique au pèlerinage panique (18ᵉ-20ᵉ siècles)," in Niveaux de culture et groupes sociaux (Paris-The Hague, 1967), pp. 149-70; idem, "Problèmes et méthodes d'une histoire de la psychologie collective," Annales: Economies, Sociétés, Civilisations, 16 (1961), pp. 3-11; Henri Platelle, Les Chrétiens face au miracle. Lille au 17ᵉ siècle (Paris, 1968); and Bernard Groethuysen, Origines de l'esprit bourgeois en France: L'Eglise et la bourgeoisie (Paris, 1927).

services of the Church and the prescribed forms of liturgy they were authorized to practice. The fact that the official doctrine did not generally approve of their brand of Catholicism rarely deterred them. With remarkable earnestness and tenacity, and with great respect and reverence for supernatural power, they clung to a wide range of devotional activities, many of them initiated by the laity and practiced independently of any priestly sanction or mediation. They purchased their little books of piety (especially those which circulated in the famous *Bibliothèque bleue*),[14] recited a great variety of prayers and formulae, participated in a comprehensive range of religious processions, rituals, and ceremonies, and collected relics, crosses, images, and other holy objects reputedly consecrated by prayers and benediction. In their attempt to maintain their religion of symbols, gestures, and actions— a religion of tactile, visual, and aural experiences and sensations—such items served as palpable objects of the faith, indicating, so to speak, the "real presence" of their belief, their direct contact or encounter with God.

For all the efforts of the post-Tridentine Church to channel the religious energies of the faithful in more orthodox directions, the *menu peuple* (even the most loyal, compliant, and conscientiously docile among them) had thus managed to cling to their own special sense of the sacred, a *crédulité ignorante* through which they expressed their aspirations as well as their profound disquietude. By means of such frequent reaffirmations of their faith, they could also feel hopeful of God's continuous protection, especially when they were faced with great danger, frustration, or misfortune. In a world that was penetrated and suffused with unseen supernatural influences, a world where regular medical practitioners were frequently unavailable or ineffectual and "incurable" illnesses and incapacitating disabilities were rife, recourse to the saints—wonder-working heroes both past and present —continued to be an especially important part of the popular religious culture. Indeed, as in the case of François de Pâris, the *menu peuple* continued with unbounded faith to venerate a whole host of individuals who had died in the odor of sanctity but who had not yet been beatified or canonized—except by popular acclaim—and hence had no status within the Church. To these pious folk the saints were familiar and easily accessible celestial friends, powerful and benevolent pro-

---

[14] Among other things the *Bibliothèque bleue*, which included a substantial number of canticles, sermons, saints' lives, and descriptions of pilgrimages and processions in its stock of popular literature, defined for the use of the lower classes the corpus of a religion reduced to simplified prescriptions and requirements. See the works of Mandrou and Bollème cited in n. 13, above.

tectors, whose intercession they felt confident of obtaining. To them, moreover, sainthood still needed but one proof: the miracle, a phenomenon which had always exercised a tremendous fascination on the popular mentality and one which many of them claimed to have experienced themselves or at least to have witnessed with their very own eyes. Through the years certain shrines and sanctuaries acquired a popular reputation as sacred places where miraculous cures and other supernatural favors could be obtained by persons who declared their unbounded faith in God and their devotion to the individual saint who represented Him here on earth. The pilgrimage to these widely scattered holy sites, many of which had never obtained official consecration, was a principal outlet for popular piety and one of the most common examples of collective devotion in this period. Under the circumstances, therefore, most of the faithful regarded the formal canonization procedures of the Church as unnecessary, if not utterly irrelevant, to the establishment and acclamation of a true saint and to his or her continued veneration. What is more, they had demonstrated more than once that they were prepared to oppose episcopal efforts to stifle their devotions and to resist clerical encroachments upon the autonomy of their religious universe.

Such views, attitudes, and habits of mind were no doubt shared, at least in part, by a substantial proportion of the participants in the Pâris cult. It is hardly surprising, therefore, that the faithful should have regarded Vintimille's *mandement* enjoining further observances at Saint-Médard as an unwarranted and disquieting intrusion on a sacred activity. It is no less surprising that the archbishop's decree should have failed to deter the deacon's legion of followers from proceeding with their devotions uninterrupted. The stage had been set for a major confrontation between two competing, and increasingly incompatible, modes of religious sensibility. Vintimille's particular concerns, even as revealed in his pronouncement of July 15, 1731, seem to have been focused on the need to preserve and protect his episcopal authority, including his responsibilities as supreme arbiter and "censor" of the faith of his flock—responsibilities which he saw being challenged. Only indirectly, if at all, did he reveal much concern for the spiritual or emotional requirements of those in his charge.[15] His experience,

---

[15] Throughout his long and extensive correspondence with Cardinal Fleury, Vintimille rarely expressed any concern about the pastoral duties of his office or about his possible failure to deal adequately with the spiritual requirements of the faithful. Respect, order, honor, obedience—these were what had continued to preoccupy the archbishop almost exclusively ever since his arrival in Paris. Cf. the indictment of Vintimille contained in the *IVe Sarcellade* (1736), BN, MSS Fr., MS 25564, fol. 330.

outlook, and temperament had left him unprepared to cope with what he encountered at Saint-Médard. As the archbishop was to discover, however, such solid commitment as the people at Pâris' grave had already exhibited was not easily shaken. Indeed, the most direct and dramatic evidence of the popular attitude toward the decree—and, indirectly, toward Vintimille's precious authority—came at Saint-Médard itself, where the *mandement* had the exact opposite of its intended effect.

Whereas no more than two dozen alleged miracles had taken place between May 1727 and the spring of 1731, that is, between the death of François de Pâris and the appearance of the Anne Lefranc *Relation*, their number and their publicity increased dramatically in late July and August. Indeed, some seventy miracles reportedly took place in the course of 1731 alone, most of them occurring after the publication of Vintimille's controversial decree, which served to give Pâris' thaumaturgic powers greater notoriety than ever.[16] A "general practitioner," the deacon had gradually acquired the reputation of being able to cure a wide variety of functional as well as organic disorders, including many diseases of an obviously somatic nature, none of which had responded to available medical treatment. The physical ills which he apparently healed or at least alleviated ranged from several kinds of nervous disorders and psychomotor disturbances to serious and debilitating diseases or infections, disfigurements from accidents, ill-mended fractures or dislocations, hideous sores and lingering cancers, blindness and deafness (complete as well as partial), and various degrees of contracture or paralysis. Relatively rare was the individual whose malady or disability was of quite recent origin. Many of M. Pâris' "patients" had been afflicted with their debilities from birth or at least since childhood; most had suffered for anywhere from several months to a few years. From the data that have survived, however, there appears to be no correlation between the duration of a person's reported affliction and the time required to obtain a cure. Although some patients were cured immediately the first time they appeared at Saint-Médard, and others required a few months, generally the times varied from several days to three or four weeks, the cures taking effect only by degrees or perhaps after a certain delay. Of course, many unfortunate people (how many we shall never know, since only the suc-

16 See *NNEE, passim*; BPR, L.P. 482, No. 2; and various *recueils des miracles* published throughout the 1730s. What follows is based primarily on these sources as well as on a large number of *anticonstitutionnaire* tracts and treatises.

cesses were recorded) were not cured at all, despite long and earnest supplications, while even among those who were "cured" the results were not always permanent. Neither the speed of the cure nor its completeness mattered very much to the faithful, however. A gradual improvement in the patient's condition over a long interval of time was often accounted a miracle. Some claimed to be cured when they had experienced only a temporary or partial remission of symptoms. These individuals remained convinced of the "cure" even after they had suffered a relapse. To be sure, certain of the ailments from which they had been suffering were what modern medical science would describe as self-limiting debilities, ones from which a natural or spontaneous recovery might ordinarily have been expected.[17] Some were clearly chronic or periodic maladies, normally subject to intermittent or temporary remissions. Others were no doubt psychosomatic in nature.[18] At a time when medical treatment frequently consisted of "bleeding, blistering, purging, cupping, [and] cauterizing," it is perhaps not surprising that some patients left alone as incurable by their doctors eventually recovered their health.[19] Such retrospective observations and

[17] Some contemporary medical writers were already ascribing many of these phenomena to natural causes (at times for polemical purposes, that is, in order to deny the "miraculous" character of the cures that did take place). See, for example, *Dissertation physique sur les miracles de M. Pâris, dans laquelle on prouve que les guérisons qui se font à son tombeau ne sont que les effets des causes purement naturelles, et qu'elles n'ont aucun caractère des vrais miracles* (n.d.).

[18] On the general problem of "faith cures," see Louis Rose, *Faith Healing* (Harmondsworth, 1971). On the specific question of the Saint-Médard cures, see the interesting, though dated, analyses in Jean-Martin Charcot, "La foi qui guérit," *Revue hebdomadaire*, 7 (December 1892), pp. 112-32, and Julien Noir, "La foi qui guérit à Saint-Médard. A propos d'un portrait du diacre Pâris," *Bulletin de la Montagne Sainte-Geneviève et ses abords*, 6 (1909-12), pp. 69-82. Noir's article is based on an examination of an *estampe* of 1731 or 1732 showing a portrait of M. Pâris surrounded by a bay wreath with forty-one leaves, on each of which was related a brief account of a miracle obtained at the tomb. For an analysis of miraculous cures in various medieval contexts, see the articles by Finucane; Pierre-André Sigal, "Maladies, pèlerinages et guérisons au 12e siècle. Les miracles de saint Gibrien à Reims," *Annales: Economies, Sociétés, Civilizations*, 24 (1969), pp. 1,522-39; and Ernest Wickersheimer, "Les guérisons miraculeuses du cardinal Pierre de Luxembourg (1387-1390)," *Comptes rendus du 2e Congrès international de l'histoire de la médecine* (Evreux, 1922), pp. 371-89.

[19] Renée Haynes, *Philosopher-King: The Humanist Pope, Benedict XIV* (London, 1970), p. 123. Haynes's book contains an illuminating discussion of the monumental efforts of Cardinal Prospero Lambertini (Benedict's name before his elevation to the papacy) to codify Church doctrine and procedures on the questions of miracles and canonization (*ibid.*, pp. 96-150). Lambertini's efforts, which acquired a special urgency as a result of the phenomena then being observed at Saint-Médard, culminated in his famous *De servorum Dei beatificatione et bea-*

diagnoses are of course pretty much beside the point.[20] A whole range of illnesses and infirmities which had heretofore baffled the doctors had in fact been more or less cured at the deacon Pâris' grave, and to the average, unsophisticated mind of the eighteenth century, it was perfectly reasonable to account such cures as miraculous.

But the quantity and quality of these supposed cures left many observers, especially among the cult's numerous *constitutionnaire* detractors, more than just a little skeptical. Indignant opponents of these phenomena criticized the incomplete, partial, and gradual character of many of them. More significantly, they charged that the alleged cures were pious inventions, consciously contrived impostures.[21] The frequency and seriousness of such charges, already made by Archbishop Vintimille in the Anne Lefranc case, prompted *anticonstitutionnaire* supporters of the cult to be scrupulously careful to check on all reports first before recording or announcing them.[22] To protect themselves still further against accusations of fraud or excessive bias and credulity, they established in the sacristy of the church at Saint-Médard a "bureau of verifications," composed of a dozen or more medical experts who were assisted by various lay officials from the parish and by priests from the diocese. This panel of doctors and surgeons provided constant on-the-spot examinations to ascertain the nature of the disability when the sufferers arrived and to determine the character of the cure (if any) before they departed.[23] Though their activities were

---

torum canonizatione, 4 vols. (Bologna, 1734-38). Cf. also the analysis of Jean-Denys-Bernard Gorce, *L'oeuvre médicale de Prospero Lambertini (Pape Benoît XIV), 1675-1758* (Bordeaux, 1915).

[20] As Keith Thomas has observed, "The historian who attempts to investigate the working of the magical healers of an earlier age is . . . led into the paths of speculative psychology in which his competence must necessarily fail him." The study of the "mental and perceptual processes" involved in these supposed miracles "must be left to the psychologist and the psychic researcher." "But it is clear that these healing agencies were not necessarily ineffective or fraudulent" (*Religion and Decline of Magic*, pp. 211, 595). For a discussion of some of these issues, see the works cited in n. 18 above; see also the works cited in Finucane, p. 6, n. 36.

[21] Cf. the views of the nineteenth-century critic, Picot, I, 235-36.

[22] *Histoire des miracles et du culte de M. Pâris. Avec les persécutions suscitées à sa mémoire et aux malades qui ont eu recours à lui. Pour servir de suite à la Vie de ce saint diacre*, rev. ed. (1734), p. 140.

[23] Police reports of Aug. 6 and 15 and Sept. 24, 1731 (BA, MS 10196); [Poncet Desessarts], *XIIe Lettre de M.*** à un de ses amis, au sujet de la Consultation contre les convulsions* (1735), p. 25. Though the abbé Desessarts claimed that the unidentified "medical experts" were honest, conscientious, and completely disinterested observers, it is hard to believe they were not sympathetically predis-

denounced by the authorities,[24] those in charge of this makeshift, unofficial operation continued to carry out their responsibilities with great care, registering only those cures which appeared authentic and certain. They took depositions from as many eyewitnesses as they could find and even did follow-up investigations of the supposed *miraculés* after they left the cemetery—precautions which enabled them to dismiss all cases where there was any evidence of imposture and which also lent greater credibility to those that they did authenticate.[25]

Little wonder that the crowds in attendance at Saint-Médard had begun to swell, that—*constitutionnaire* strictures notwithstanding—the expectation of miracles was more marked than ever.[26] More importantly, however, these crowds had also begun to change somewhat in their basic character. Most of the people who went to Pâris' tomb during the first years of the cult had come from various parts of Paris, especially from the parishes surrounding Saint-Médard. In addition, although bedridden invalids from nearby *faubourgs* were usually carried there on litters, many of the deacon's prospective patients, if their physical condition permitted, made their way to the cemetery alone and unaided. But in an increasing majority of cases the patient was

---

posed. The critical role of "medical expertise" in certifying cases of miraculous cures (or of witchcraft) is a subject that merits further study. The remarks of Michel de Certeau, "Une mutation culturelle et religieuse: Les magistrats devant les sorciers du 17ᵉ siècle," *Revue d'histoire de l'Eglise de France*, 55 (1969), pp. 300-19, esp. pp. 309-10, are pertinent here: "Partisan ou critique, le médecin devient le recours. C'est l'homme de la 'science' et de l' 'expérience'—les deux ne faisant qu'un. Devant le diabolique, comme devant le miracle, son 'témoignage' ou son 'attestation' est nécessaire, et contre lui on fait appel non au théologien, mais à un autre médecin." Cf. Platelle, pp. 35-37.

[24] Duval (*prêtre habitué* at Saint-Médard) to Hérault or Fleury, Aug. 11, 1731, BA, MS 10196.

[25] See the abbé d'Etemare to Fouillou, Sept. 30, 1733, *ibid.*, MS 5784, p. 30. Cf. the remarks of A. Gazier, "Le frère de Voltaire," p. 634. Unfortunately neither these registrars nor the later compilers and publishers of the miracles ever indicated the nature of the criteria under which they were operating in their efforts to determine the authenticity of various cures. Hence it is impossible to know what proportion of the cures were actually recorded and how many were eliminated as nonmiraculous (or for what reasons); similarly we do not know how many would-be *miraculés* M. Pâris failed to satisfy and thus what proportion of the whole his successful "patients" represented.

[26] "Il y va plus de malades que dans un hôpital," remarked Marais in late August (IV, 272 [Aug. 22, 1731]). According to Barbier, on July 25, 1731, the day after Vintimille's decree was actually published, the crowds were so great that, "dès 4 heures du matin, on ne pouvoit pas entrer dans l'église de Saint-Médard, ni dans le petit cimetière où est le tombeau (II, 170 [July 1731]).

now coming in the company of others, often in large entourages of fellow pilgrims, including family, friends, even acquaintances, who offered assistance where needed and also provided moral support and the strength of additional prayers. By midsummer, moreover, as word of François de Pâris' thaumaturgic powers spread beyond the capital and as the saintly deacon came to achieve a national reputation, substantial numbers of worshipers and would-be *miraculés* were arriving from ever greater distances, sometimes accompanied by a local notable or two. A few of those who undertook long and arduous journeys to reach the shrine were actually cured en route.[27]

The changes at Saint-Médard were by no means merely quantitative. The posthumous activities of the deacon had also come to attract an increasingly diverse group of people, many of them in no particular need of a cure or in any way associated with individuals who were. Persons of quality and wretched commoners, the notable and the anonymous, rich and poor, young and old, men and women, the able-bodied and the crippled, the healthy and the sick, Parisians and provincials—all rubbed elbows with one another, most of them joining in common prayer and devotion and bearing public witness to their faith. To be sure, not all of those present at the cemetery had come for purely spiritual reasons or out of genuine religious conviction. Some people, no doubt dissatisfied with the drab, predictable, often miserable existence they led, must have welcomed the opportunity to add an element of novelty or excitement to their lives. In addition, they were very likely happy for the chance to see and to mingle with elements of French society that they rarely encountered, except at a distance. Like certain of the *menu peuple*, many of the individuals of rank and quality who attended and left their carriages blocking the adjacent streets came only as spectators.[28] Attendance at Saint-Médard was becoming the fashionable pastime for these people, many of whom, for want of something better to do, perhaps saw it as an entertaining distraction, a means of diversion from their ordinarily dull routines; here they could examine at first hand the spectacle about which all Paris had been buzzing. In addition to these curiosity-seekers, however, there were quite a few nobles and other individuals of social or professional standing who became devout participants in the Pâris cult.

[27] In addition to the sources cited in n. 16 above, see the daily police reports issued from Saint-Médard throughout this period; BA, MS 10196.

[28] The princess de Rohan, the duchess de Montbazon, and the count de Rome-nez were in attendance on September 29. At various other times such additional social luminaries as the countess de Grignan, the duchess d'Antin, the marchioness de la Branche, the duchess de la Trémoille, and the marquis de Seignelay made appearances at Saint-Médard (*ibid., passim*).

Some, perhaps like des Grieux in Prévost's *Manon Lescaut* (published just at this time), had embarked on a quest for values and meaning in a world without established norms or ultimate values and may have thought to find these in the religious observances at Pâris' tomb. Others, already Jansenist or *anticonstitutionnaire* by conviction, had rather different reasons for partaking of the devotions. Whatever their motives or pretexts, the presence of these *gens de condition* was duly noted by those in attendance and lent a certain air of respectability and a special kind of excitement to the proceedings.

A number of these pious "persons of rank and quality" made significant contributions to the religious activities at the cemetery. The count de Clermont, for example, purchased dozens of portraits of François de Pâris that were being sold by local vendors and had them distributed to the faithful worshiping alongside him.[29] Several of his fellow nobles as well as numerous magistrates and lawyers from the Parlement of Paris assisted various patients who needed transportation to Saint-Médard or who required help once they got there. Many of them also served as witnesses to the cures effected at the deacon's grave.[30] Of all the important personages to participate in these services, however, perhaps the most notable was Marie-Thérèse de Bourbon, princess de Conti. The princess, who had been suffering for the past four or five years from progressive blindness which had not responded to medical treatment, made several appearances at Saint-Médard in the confident hope of obtaining a cure. On one occasion over four hundred people reportedly crowded around her as she leaned against the tomb; they all knelt with the princess, adding their prayers to hers.[31] Although the cure they collectively besought through Pâris' intercession was not forthcoming, these visits of Mme. de Conti proved to be a moving ex-

[29] Police report of July 29, 1731 (*ibid.*).

[30] In fact, a very substantial number of the witnesses were persons of some social or professional standing. Among the some 370 notarized certificates referred to in the second *recueil des miracles*—which contains accounts of thirteen cures effected in 1730-31—nearly 40 percent are from individuals who may be characterized as *Noblesse, Clergé*, or *Professions libérales*. Another 40 percent can be described as *Maîtres et marchands* or *Bourgeois de Paris, roturiers sans profession* (the socio-professional categories are those developed in Adeline Daumard and François Furet, *Structures et relations sociales à Paris au milieu du 18ᵉ siècle* [Paris, 1961]). Unfortunately, it is not possible to determine what proportion of all witnesses to the Pâris miracles—or of active participants in the cult—these figures represent; there were obvious propaganda advantages to including testimony from a disproportionate number of prominent or high-status individuals in documents such as these printed *recueils*.

[31] See esp. the police report of Aug. 17, 1731, BA, MS 10196. See also Barbier, II, 177 (August 1731).

perience for those in attendance and were later commemorated in a popular *estampe* sold around the parish and throughout the streets of Paris.[32]

Even though personal attendance at the shrine was generally believed to be more beneficial (if not always fruitful), one did not necessarily have to be present at Saint-Médard to obtain a cure through the deacon Pâris. Some persons, totally incapacitated and unable to reach the cemetery under any circumstances, had friends or relatives go to the shrine and invoke the intercession of M. Pâris on their behalf. Others who could attend only briefly or irregularly actually "hired" residents from the parish (usually old women) to say daily novenas for them for a prescribed period of time—and for a specified sum of money.[33] Nor did one have to content oneself with utilizing these various surrogates or proxies, successful though they sometimes were. The ready availability of relics and other reputedly holy objects associated with the saintly deacon meant that M. Pâris could be spiritually present at great distances from his grave and could work his restorative powers on the lame and the infirm anywhere, provided they touched these various items to the affected parts of their bodies. Indeed, as the relics became more widely dispersed, the cult quickly spread offshoots throughout the kingdom, and miracles were soon being reported from Brittany to Provence.[34]

Many devotees of the Pâris cult naturally had little or no choice but to avail themselves of these various alternative procedures for obtaining the deacon's assistance. Nevertheless, for most of his adherents Saint-Médard and its sacred shrine remained the center of interest, the site where the miraculous cures continued to proliferate and the faithful continued to congregate. Here they shared and sometimes exchanged various relics, manuals of piety, portraits of M. Pâris, and other assorted religious objects.[35] They scrawled prayers to and invocations

[32] BA, MS 2056, fol. 328.

[33] See, for example, the case of Pierre Lero, who was one of M. Pâris' first successful *miraculés*. According to Lero's own testimony, he paid "12 sols à une pauvre femme demeurante sur l'étendue de la paroisse Saint-Médard . . . de faire des prières pour lui . . . sur le tombeau . . . pendant 9 jours" (*1er Recueil des miracles*).

[34] See *Tables raisonnées et alphabétiques des "Nouvelles ecclésiastiques" depuis 1728 jusqu'en 1760 inclusivement*, ed. abbé de Bonnemare, 2 vols. (Paris, 1767), s.v. "Miracles."

[35] BA, MS 10196, *passim*. On August 2 the police reported that several priests were distributing—free of charge—bits of wool that had allegedly come from Pâris' mattress and pieces of wood from his bed (*ibid.*; see also BN, MSS Fr., MS 22245, fol. 186).

of the deacon, often on little scraps of paper, and posted them on the walls of both the church and the cemetery. They sang psalms, chanted hymns, or read aloud from pious books. They regaled one another with wondrous stories of cures already effected—stories which served as a source of renewed hope for those still suffering from their afflictions—or joined together in beseeching their beloved saint to work one on them. Finally, they gathered around the tomb with its raised marble slab, under which a few people would manage to crawl and on top of which several would usually be seated. Throughout most of the summer and fall, even when the crowds were tightly packed and access to the tomb became rather difficult, these remained generally orderly gatherings. The atmosphere of course was frequently tense with expectation, and great joy and excitement descended over the assembly whenever a cure was announced. People rushed to see the person cured and a chorus of worshipers chanted *Te Deums* in celebration of the miracle. Such cures, which had had a much more personal character prior to July 1731, now came to be regarded as collective accomplishments, achieved in response to collective prayers. Indeed, one of the most significant, albeit unintended, consequences of Vintimille's decree seems to have been to unite the cult's adherents more closely together and to instill in them an increased sense of sharing in a common purpose and a common experience.

The abandoned crutches and bandages and the dozens of candles burning in the church of Saint-Médard—the votive offerings of grateful devotees—bore mute testimony to the great works which "Saint" François de Pâris had accomplished and would continue to accomplish for some time to come. M. Pâris did not, however, confine his posthumous activities exclusively to the alleviation of bodily afflictions, even though these healing events represented his primary field of action and received the greatest amount of attention. He was also credited with effecting the sudden, unexpected conversions of "dead souls," of atheists like Boindin de Boisbessin, skeptics like the counselor Carré de Montgeron, and libertines like the Chevalier de Folard.[36] Some of these nonbelievers had gone, like many others, merely out of curiosity but stayed on to become devoted participants in the cult. The "admirable

---

[36] On Boindin de Boisbessin, see *ibid.*, MS 12800, fols. 390-91, and his own *Lettre . . . par laquelle il rend compte à M*** de la manière dont Dieu l'a appelé du pyrrhonisme à la véritable religion, à l'occasion des merveilles opérées au tombeau de M. de Pâris (12 février 1734)*. On Carré de Montgeron, see Ch. ix below. On Folard, see BN, MSS NAFr., MS 11635, fols. 157, 160, *et passim*, and Jean Godefroy, "Le chevalier de Folard et les Bénédictins de Saint-Germain-des-Près," *Revue Mabillon*, 26 (1936), pp. 114-33, 154-66.

renewal of piety and faith" represented in these various conversions to "the cause of Truth," noted one *anticonstitutionnaire* writer, was "an edifying and consoling spectacle" for the crowds gathered around the deacon's tomb.[37]

In addition to the miraculous cures and conversions, Saint-Médard was also the scene of "miraculous punishments" meted out to certain individuals who had come to deride the cult and its devoted practitioners. One case in particular produced an extraordinary sensation. On the afternoon of August 4, Gabrielle Gautier, sixty-year-old widow of Pierre Delorme, visited the cemetery "in a spirit of mocking incredulity." Feigning paralysis, Mme. Delorme placed herself upon the tomb and pretended to solicit the intercession of François de Pâris. Her action was almost immediately punished, as she was suddenly struck down with real paralysis of the entire right side of her body. Carried off to the Hôtel-Dieu in the midst of a large and excited crowd, who spread the news of this novel portent throughout the parish and beyond, Mme. Delorme quickly repented of her blasphemy. Three days later she confessed her sins in a declaration made before two notaries and in the presence of twenty-six witnesses, including three counselors from the Parlement of Paris, two canons of Notre-Dame, and her own confessor, the avowed Molinist, abbé Chaulin. While printed copies of the declaration were soon circulating in the streets of Paris and large crowds were paying daily visits to the paralyzed widow, Vintimille intervened "to arrest this confusion." The archbishop revoked Chaulin's powers of preaching and hearing confession in the diocese on the grounds that the priest had authorized Mme. Delorme's declaration in patent disobedience of contrary orders given by the superiors at the Hôtel-Dieu. For her part, the widow Delorme was placed under arrest and kept imprisoned until the following April when, under duress, she was forced to retract her declaration. By that time, however, the published documents had already reached several editions and made a tremendous impact on the public.[38]

[37] *Entretiens sur les miracles*, p. 110.
[38] *Déclaration faite par Gabrielle Gautier, veuve de Pierre De Lorme, des dispositions dans lesquelles elle est allée au tombeau de M. de Pâris (7 août 1731); Relation de la manière dont Gabrielle Gautier . . . a été frappée d'une paralysie subite . . . , avec un détail des circonstances les plus singulières qui ont précédé et suivi cet événement, recueillies par M. Chaulin, prêtre, docteur en théologie de la Faculté de Paris, confesseur de la malade (4 décembre 1731)*; Barbier, II, 171-76 (August 1731); Marais, IV, 268 (Aug. 13, 1731), IV, 272 (Aug. 22, 1731). Vintimille's secondhand account of this entire incident differs markedly from the generally accepted one (letters to Fleury, Aug. 8 and 10, 1731, BM, MS 2357, pp. 469-74).

Although additional *punitions miraculeuses* (or "countermiracles") of varying degrees of severity were visited upon a number of others who sought to defame the memory of M. Pâris,[39] none was to achieve the notoriety of the Delorme case. In the meantime, while God was supposedly showing His great displeasure with these acts of blasphemous mockery, the deacon's devoted adherents, too impatient to await divine justice in other cases of irreverence or profanity, were taking their own direct action against several of the cult's more troublesome detractors. The faithful were unwilling to tolerate any slurs whatsoever on their saint's holy name and engaged in many a lively public dispute on this matter.[40] Anyone who dared to challenge the authenticity of the miracles ran the risk of a physical beating at the hands of Pâris' more zealous followers. Indeed, on more than one occasion they demonstrated quite graphically the fierceness with which they were prepared to defend their cult. Most of these incidents took place at Saint-Médard and involved hostile ecclesiastics, several of whom suffered rather severe thrashings and barely escaped serious bodily harm.[41] In the most spectacular incident, this one at the Palais de Justice, an abbé who had uttered some disparaging remarks against M. Pâris found himself beaten up and his priestly cloak torn off before he was chased away amid loud hoots and jeers.[42]

The faithful made it clear that they did not appreciate the presence of unfriendly elements at Saint-Médard. Nor did they take very kindly to the presence of the police in their midst. Almost from the beginning of the Pâris cult the activities occurring in and around Saint-Médard had attracted the attention of Hérault's men and even that of the lieutenant-general himself.[43] Since 1729, in addition to the regular contingent of officers and spies who patrolled the neighborhood along the rue Mouffetard and adjacent streets, at least one guard had been stationed near the cemetery and assigned the task of reporting daily on all

---

[39] See *Lettre écrite au sujet de la mort surprenante du garçon chirurgien de Monsieur Lombard, nommé Jean de la Croix* (*16 janvier 1732*). The sudden, unexplained death of the young surgeon's aide was widely attributed to his "outrageously blasphemous mockery" of the Pâris cult. Other somewhat less spectacular incidents occurred between 1731 and 1737 (see Mathieu, pp. 405-11).

[40] See, for example, police report for Jan. 13, 1732, BA, MS 10196.

[41] Reports for Aug. 3, 5, and 6, and Sept. 24, 1731 (*ibid.*); Journal of De Lisle, July 11, 1731, AN, U-376. One incident involving a Capuchin priest gave rise to a series of pointed satirical verses (Mathieu, p. 222 and n. 1).

[42] Barbier, II, 185 (August 1731). In recounting this incident the *Nouvelles ecclésiastiques* observed, no doubt with some relish: "ce n'est point là l'esprit des Défenseurs de la Vérité; mais qui peut retenir ce qu'on appelle le peuple!" (Oct. 2, 1731, p. 186).

[43] Dorsanne, II, 499.

that happened, identifying those in attendance, and indicating whether they were participants in the religious services or just curious on-lookers. Yet, even though the police continued throughout this period to exercise an intrusive surveillance of local activities, their impact had remained rather limited. For months now the handful of guards posted at the cemetery had faithfully discharged their responsibility —as they would for years to come—but with little or no discernible effect on the religious observances. To be sure, so long as the royal government did not attempt to enforce with legal sanctions Vintimille's July 15 proscription of the cult (the only official pronouncement to date), and so long as the public assemblies at the cemetery remained basically orderly and peaceful, there was not much the police could do. For the time being, therefore, their continued surveillance and occasional harassment remained little more than a minor irritant to the faithful, a ubiquitous and unpleasant reminder of the official attitude of disapproval toward the cult activities. But the mere presence of these officers failed to interrupt the routine of the people worshiping at M. Pâris' tomb.

One function which did keep Hérault's men somewhat busy during this period was the occasional arrests of individuals who hawked various proscribed articles in the cloisters and environs of Saint-Médard.[44] Although there is no evidence of actual manipulation of the cult for financial gain, the religious devotions had in fact given rise to a certain degree of commercial exploitation.[45] A host of shrewd and enterprising peddlers installed themselves just outside the cemetery and at other strategic locations in the neighborhood, selling a wide variety of merchandise. A number of these vendors specialized in the sale of assorted relics, some of which they claimed to have obtained from M. Pâris' very deathbed. Others peddled *estampes*, hymns or canticles, Jansenist pamphlets, and, when it became available in midsummer, copies of a pious biography of the saintly deacon.[46] Still others sold small packets of

---

[44] Arrests are reported, for example, in BA, MS 11154, fols. 207-11, 213-17, 307-24; Ravaisson, xiv, 285, 306, *et passim; NNEE*, Jan. 24, 1732, p. 15, March 5, 1732, p. 44, *et passim;* Barbier, ii, 168-69 (July 1731), and ii, 212 (November 1731); and Marais, iv, 314 (Oct. 31, 1731).

[45] BA, MS 10196, *passim*, but esp. reports for July 30, and Aug. 4, 6, and 7, 1731.

[46] An excellent collection of contemporary *estampes* may be found in BA, MS 2056. Most of the books being sold at Saint-Médard (and circulated all over the kingdom) were inexpensive pocket-size works, specifically intended for popular consumption. None of these, of course, had been regulated for their orthodox content, since every step in the production of such works—from composition to publication to distribution—involved a clandestine operation.

dirt taken from around François de Pâris' grave or containers of water supposedly drawn from a well at the deacon's last residence on the rue des Bourguignons. One resourceful scribe, later joined by two other copyists, set up a table inside the cemetery on which he composed and tirelessly wrote out dozens of prayers; he sold these to the faithful at prices scaled according to the length and quality of the particular prayer. Although the police subjected many of these hawkers to occasional harassment and intimidation and even took some of them into custody while confiscating their wares, most of these vendors no doubt still turned a tidy profit for their efforts.[47]

These assorted salesmen were not the only ones to benefit financially from the money which the masses of pilgrims brought into the community. The nearby cafés and cabarets swarmed with people eager for something to eat or drink and a convenient place to sit down and talk. Shopkeepers in the area likewise did a thriving business, as did those with rooms to rent to the weary pilgrims who had traveled considerable distances to visit the shrine. This sudden prosperity also proved a great boon to the church of Saint-Médard, its coffers now filled as never before. However, although vast numbers of the local population rejoiced in the notoriety and spiritual and financial benefits the cult had thus conferred upon the parish and its residents, the ecclesiastical officials at Saint-Médard did not share in this general enthusiasm. On the contrary, for the observances at M. Pâris' tomb had for many months been taking place in an atmosphere of mounting parochial tensions and embittered relations between the *curé* and his parishioners—a situation which the astonishing success of the Pâris cult had served only to exacerbate.

The trouble at Saint-Médard, initially unrelated to the observances of the Pâris cult, began in October 1730, when, as part of his campaign to purge the diocese of "subversive" and "insubordinate" parish priests, Archbishop Vintimille obtained the dismissal of the abbé Pommart, *curé* of Saint-Médard, along with two of his colleagues, the abbés Blondel of Saint-Etienne-du-Mont and Sallart de Lormois of La Villette. All three priests, whom Cardinal Fleury reportedly described as members "of a cabal which was [acting] no less against the State than against the Church,"[48] were canons-regular in the Congregation of Sainte-Geneviève, from which they had originally been appointed to

---

[47] Not all vendors were arrested since, as Barbier pointed out, some were "femmes des soldats aux gardes [qui] . . . n'avoient rien à craindre des archers du faubourg Saint-Marceau, par suite de leurs maris" (II, 169 [July 1731]).

[48] *NNEE*, Nov. 17, 1730, p. 244.

their respective benefices. Their formal dismissal had thus devolved upon their superior, the abbot of Sainte-Geneviève, who was initially reluctant to do the archbishop's bidding.[49] Prodded and pressured by Fleury and by Secretary of State Maurepas, who commanded him to cooperate with Vintimille, the abbot finally agreed to discharge the three curés and to name three other members of his congregation to fill their places.[50] The archbishop, in concert with the abbot, then exiled the priests to three separate monasteries, without even formally charging them.

While Pommart and his colleagues were protesting the legality of these revocations, Vintimille and the abbot of Sainte-Geneviève were busy examining candidates for the three vacant posts. After several génovéfain priests under consideration as replacements for the deposed curés declined to accept the appointments,[51] three men were finally found who agreed to serve. The priest selected to replace Pommart at Saint-Médard was the abbé Jacques Coëffrel, formerly curé of Saint-Georges-sur-Loire, a staunch and imperious constitutionnaire who was expected to bring order and respect for authority back to the beleaguered parish.[52] However, the almost universally hostile public reaction which greeted this whole affair, from Pommart's dismissal to Coëffrel's appointment, guaranteed that these expectations were not to be realized.

Father Pommart's faithful parishioners resented what they regarded as the unjust and arbitrary removal of their legitimate pastor, to whom they felt a strong attachment. The worthy Pommart, curé since July 1723, had worked very hard on behalf of the appeal, had been close to François de Pâris in the deacon's last years, and had enthusiastically supported the Pâris cult. More important, perhaps, he had also been a dedicated priest and a model pastor, one whom the Nouvelles ecclésiastiques later singled out for his deep devotion to the moral, spiritual, and material welfare of his flock.[53] It was this dedication which seems to have won him the love and respect of most of the faithful in his charge, who refused to recognize the new appointee as their rightful curé and declined to attend his installation ceremonies, which took place in early December.[54] In this opposition they received strong en-

---

[49] Vintimille to Fleury, Oct. 20, 1730, BM, MS 2357, pp. 241-42.

[50] NNEE, Nov. 17, 1730, p. 244.

[51] A certificate of refusal from Fr. Simon de Lespine, curé of Nanterre, may be found among the pièces justificatives published with the miracle of Louise Coirin (Louis-Basile Carré de Montgeron, La Vérité des Miracles [1737], I, v-vi).

[52] Brongniart, pp. 73-74.

[53] See his obituary, July 17, 1754, p. 114.

[54] Even more dramatic evidence for the popular attitude on this matter may be found in an undated report from the police officer Pillerault: "Un particulier

couragement from the sacristan and the *marguilliers* (churchwardens) of the parish. The outspoken Collet Desroches, elected in February 1726 to the office of sacristan, a post which involved responsibility for taking care of the church and its sacred furnishings, was in the fore-front of the resistance to Pommart's dismissal from the very first. While encouraging the faithful to boycott Coëffrel's formal investi-ture, which had to be conducted by clergy from outside the parish, he went so far as to refuse to provide the new *curé* with the vestments for the performance of Mass.[55] The sacristan was to persist in these and other obstructive tactics for some time to come, causing Coëffrel more than a little inconvenience and discomfiture.

In addition to the resistance from the parish faithful and the sacristan, Coëffrel was also faced with opposition from several holdover priests, most of them *anticonstitutionnaires*, who likewise felt a keen sense of loyalty to the abbé Pommart and who resented having to take orders from a superior whose views on ecclesiastical matters were diamet-rically opposite to theirs.[56] But by far the most hostile reception ac-corded the new *curé* came from the churchwardens, or lay adminis-trators, of Saint-Médard. As was common in the *ancien régime*, certain leading families with long ties to the parish and with strong feelings of common interest and a self-conscious sense of solidarity had estab-lished virtual dynasties on the *conseil de fabrique* (lay council or ves-try). The influential Bouillerot family, an old, established line of modest, respectable master tanners, with strongly Jansenist leanings, dominated the *fabrique* of Saint-Médard at this time and led the resistance to Coëffrel's accession.[57] Offended at Vintimille's having dismissed Father Pommart without consulting with them or giving them any prior warning, they attacked the revocation as invalid and contrary to the

---

nommé le Sr. Moreau, maître fourreur, est venu dans le corps de garde à Saint-Médard, dire au Sr. Guignard, sergant et ces gardes en se railland de M. le Curé, nous navon que faire de curé ny prestres dans notre paroisse, car nous avons résolus entre nous danvoyer nos confessions par lettre à M. Paumard notre curé et il nous renvoye de mesme l'absolution de la pénitence" (BA, MS 10196).

[55] Brongniart, p. 74.

[56] A number of these *prêtres habitués*, including the abbés Le Leu and Le Clerc, canon and *curé*, respectively, from the diocese of Laon, had taken up residence in the parish of Saint-Médard after having originally been banished by their own bishops (Vintimille to [Hérault ?], Jan. 17, 1731, BA, MS 10196).

[57] Of the some fifty to sixty current or former churchwardens who comprised the *conseil de fabrique* as of 1731, eight were members of the Bouillerot family. On the role of the *fabrique* in the *ancien régime*, see Bernard Plongeron, *La vie quotidienne du clergé français au 18ᵉ siècle* (Paris, 1974), pp. 149-52.

rights of the parish and the parishioners.[58] They also insisted that they would continue to recognize M. Pommart as their legitimate pastor and would always regard the abbé Coëffrel as an intruder and a usurper.[59] Finally, they announced their determination to go about the business of administering the temporal affairs of the parish as if the post of *curé* were vacant. Nor were these merely idle threats. Within a short time of Coëffrel's installation the *marguilliers*, in violation of longstanding ecclesiastical procedures, refused to provide him with an inventory of the parish holdings. A few weeks later, on December 26, they convoked a general assembly of the *fabrique* at which they elected a new *commissaire des pauvres* without involving Coëffrel in their decision. The *curé*, who was celebrating a High Mass at the time, had not even been informed that such a meeting was scheduled to take place.[60] The *marguilliers* followed this highly irregular procedure a month later with still another one, when, on January 21, 1731, they elected several new members to their company without inviting Coëffrel to participate in any of their discussions.[61] Though the *curé* appealed for assistance to Vintimille and, through the archbishop, to police lieutenant Hérault and Cardinal Fleury, there was little that the authorities outside the parish could do to stop the Bouillerots and their colleagues, who had only just begun to fight.

Not long after making this series of defiant gestures toward Coëffrel, the *marguilliers* took the dramatic step of lodging a complaint with the *Grand Conseil*, formally protesting the "arbitrary and despotic" dismissal of the abbé Pommart and calling on the council to reinstate him in the parish. The churchwardens' *appel comme d'abus* was supported by a legal brief drawn up the previous December by a panel of nine *avocats* who, basing their arguments on two conciliar *arrêts* of 1679, denied the authority of the archbishop of Paris and the abbot of Sainte-Geneviève to remove a canonically installed *curé* without specifying the grounds for the dismissal or revocation.[62] Vintimille him-

---

[58] Petitions to that effect were circulated throughout the parish and obtained widespread support from the faithful (BA, MS 10171).

[59] BA, MS 10178 (no fol.); "Mémoire à M. le Lieutenant de Police," Dec. 28, 1730," *ibid.*, MS 10171, 5ᵉ Dossier. Cf. the attitude of the churchwardens of Saint-Etienne (*NNEE*, Nov. 17, 1730, p. 244).

[60] This action incensed both Coëffrel and Vintimille, the latter appealing to Hérault to "faire bâtonner et biffer la délibération prise" (Dec. 31, 1730, BA, MS 10196; see also Vintimille to Hérault or Maurepas, Jan. 17, 1731, *ibid.*). The police lieutenant, of course, did no such thing.

[61] This action did win them a stiff reproach from Hérault (*NNEE*, Feb. 18, 1731, p. 35).

[62] The *consultation* had actually been prepared on behalf of all three deposed

self took offense at this appeal and the challenge to authority which it represented. Deeply disturbed at the spirit of "defiance, indiscipline, and disorder" that was rampant in Saint-Médard and concerned about the disrespectful and insubordinate attitude displayed toward Coëffrel, the archbishop demanded that Cardinal Fleury intervene in the case on behalf of the *curé*.[63] After extended discussion, the *Grand Conseil* eventually rejected the *marguilliers'* petition. Nevertheless, despite repeated royal commands that they acknowledge the legitimacy of Coëffrel's position and "show him the proper respect and deference owing to someone of his rank,"[64] the churchwardens persisted in their refusal to do so. They continued relentlessly to challenge the decisions of the authorities, royal, diocesan, and parochial, and even risked prison rather than relinquish their autonomy or abandon what they saw as their rights.[65]

Although the *marguilliers* had lost their appeal, they did not give up the struggle. Their conflict with Coëffrel over various issues of parochial governance was thus to rage on virtually unabated for the next several years,[66] embittering relations within the parish and eventually becoming caught up in the other fierce debates which had already begun swirling throughout the capital and especially around the tomb of François de Pâris. Indeed, Coëffrel's attitude toward the Pâris cult contributed in no small measure to exacerbating the parochial tensions at Saint-Médard and to elevating the local "tempête sous un clocher" to diocesan, even national, significance.

Almost from the outset, Coëffrel had demonstrated his opposition to the religious devotions at M. Pâris' tomb. Shortly after his arrival the new *curé* expressed the view to his parishioners that "there would soon be an order to close the cemetery."[67] This barely veiled threat, like others made throughout 1731, was not carried out for quite some time. Nevertheless, the churchwardens and a large proportion of the parish faithful would not abide this ecclesiastical intruder's interference with the observances at "their" holy shrine. Their opposition to Coëffrel on this score was no doubt motivated largely by spiritual considerations: they were concerned primarily with the threatened disruption

curés from Sainte-Geneviève and contained a strongly Richerist defense of the rights of the "second order" (BA, MS 10178). Cf. discussion in *NNEE*, Nov. 29, 1730, p. 252, and that in Brongniart, p. 73.

[63] Vintimille to Fleury, April 18, 1731, BM, MS 2357, p. 350, and Vintimille to Fleury, June 9, 1731, *ibid.*, pp. 381-82.

[64] *Arrêt du Grand Conseil*, June 11, 1731, BA, MS 2056.

[65] Brongniart, p. 79.

[66] *Ibid.*, pp. 79-81; Mousset, pp. 81-92; and Manneville, pp. 74-76.

[67] Cited by Mousset, p. 83.

of the worship services which the *curé*'s offensive remarks seemed to betoken. But a significant element of parochial chauvinism was also clearly involved here. Save for an almost forgotten (and unpleasant) incident in the early days of the religious wars, the parish of Saint-Médard had no prior claims to fame or notoriety. An obscure backwater in a poor, generally overlooked corner of Paris, it had not previously been a pilgrimage center nor was it a site where miraculous cures were known to have taken place. By obvious implication, the parish owed its sudden emergence from obscurity to François de Pâris, whose presence in their midst evoked a strong sense of local excitement and communal pride among the faithful. From the first these people had eagerly rallied around their saint, proudly revered him as a local folk hero, and enthusiastically embraced the cult established in his honor—as they would continue to do for a long time to come.

In addition to experiencing a tremendous sense of local pride and spiritual uplift, feelings which they must have been anxious to sustain, the people of Saint-Médard were no doubt also eager to retain the assorted monetary benefits which had recently begun accruing to the parish. As we have seen, the influx of worshipers into the area had made a major impact on the economic well-being of many individuals in the *faubourg* Saint-Marceau. Shopkeepers, café-owners, vendors, and a whole host of other residents had profited materially from the cult. Like these various private citizens, the churchwardens recognized the pecuniary rewards the cult had bestowed upon Saint-Médard. As administrators of the temporal affairs of the parish, with particular responsibility for overseeing its usually overburdened finances, the churchwardens looked upon the cult as a fiscal godsend. So long as the many hundreds of pilgrims continued to make their way daily to the shrine, the collection boxes in the church would remain filled, and the parish would be solvent and hence better able to handle its numerous financial obligations.[68]

The parishioners and churchwardens of Saint-Médard thus had a major stake, material as well as spiritual, in the continued survival of the Pâris cult and in preventing either Father Coëffrel or Archbishop Vintimille from interfering with the services at the cemetery. Consequently, they continued to ignore official strictures against the cult and to publicize their deacon's celestial achievements, while promoting the

---

[68] There were some critics who charged that the *marguilliers'* support of the cult was motivated by pure cupidity. See "Le chef d'oeuvre d'un inconnu ou chanson nouvelle sur l'air des pendus," verse 6, in Hyacinthe Bougeant, *Relation des miracles de saint Pâris avec un abrégé de la vie du saint et un dialogue sur les neuvaines* (1731); and Ravaisson, XIV, 286n.

unauthorized observances at his tomb. In this effort they had the tire-less support of Collet Desroches, Coëffrel's arch-nemesis. Deliberately disregarding the *curé*'s instructions, the sacristan persisted in encour-aging and receiving Mass stipends or honorariums—fees paid for the celebration of Mass for the individual intention of the donor—which he registered at the sacristy. Even after Coëffrel had obtained Des-roches' dismissal in late June for insubordination,[69] the *marguilliers* managed to replace him with another like-minded officer. During the months of July and August the new sacristan, following the proce-dures of his defiant predecessor, was reported to have registered some 500 to 650 requests for Masses daily.[70] He also took a major role in the conduct of the devotional services, in the registration of miracu-lous cures, and in the maintenance of an orderly routine at both the church and the cemetery. In short, given the official parochial opposi-tion at Saint-Médard to these observances, the actions of this handful of proud and tenacious local notables who stood up to the abbé Coëf-frel did much to sustain the life of the Pâris cult.

However important, even indispensable, were the efforts of the churchwardens and sacristans at Saint-Médard, their actions would cer-tainly not have been enough to maintain the cult's existence in the face of concerted official hostility had it not been for the resolute and ener-getic support of the *anticonstitutionnaire* parish clergy. Indeed, the continued activities at the deacon's tomb, conducted in open and de-liberate defiance of Vintimille's decree and Coëffrel's animadversions, had the explicit encouragement of a substantial number of *curés* and parish priests from throughout the diocese of Paris. Though the devo-tees of the Pâris cult still comprised a formally leaderless body, the Paris clergy had come to play a central role in publicizing and sanc-tioning their activities. In authorizing the veneration of M. Pâris and thereby giving credibility to his thaumaturgic powers, these priests undoubtedly helped strengthen the hope of patients seeking cures through the deacon's intercession and ensured that the number of pil-

[69] Vintimille himself had become quite concerned with Collet Desroches' ac-tivities at Saint-Médard and had been trying for some time to get the govern-ment to expel the sacristan from the parish (see Vintimille to Hérault, May [23], 1731, BA, MS 10196, and Vintimille to Fleury, June 9, 1731, BM, MS 2357, p. 381). Despite an initial reluctance, Cardinal Fleury finally agreed to do so, and Desroches was banished from Paris (Fleury to Vintimille, June 11, 1731, BM, MS 2357, p. 383; and Vintimille to Fleury, June 19, 1731, *ibid.*, p. 395).

[70] Anonymous, undated letter to Hérault, cited in Mousset, p. 84. Novenas had also become so numerous that they were now being registered at the sacristy as well, along with the Masses.

grims continued to swell.[71] Nor did the parish clergy limit their encouragement to mere words. Many ecclesiastics went to the cemetery
themselves, often accompanying their parishioners to the shrine.[72] To
judge from the daily police reports from Saint-Médard, the clergy of
Paris, both regular and secular, figured very prominently among the
participants in the devotions at the deacon's tomb.[73] Those present,
sometimes as many as forty or fifty at a time, met together regularly
in the sacristy or under the charnel house, where they discussed various
spiritual matters.[74] Fulfilling their role as priests, they frequently led
their fellow worshipers in reciting prayers on behalf of would-be
miraculés who besought God, through M. Pâris, to work a cure on
their wretched bodies. In addition, some celebrated Mass in the church.
Others delivered sermons extolling the virtues of the saintly deacon
and exhorting the faithful to model their lives after his. Still others became involved with the verification and registration of cures which
Pâris by his intercession had already managed to obtain.[75]

To be sure, much of the vitality of the Pâris cult continued to derive
from the dedication and initiative of its lay adherents, many of whom
had required little or no priestly prompting before they became devoted adherents of the deacon. Nevertheless, the active, legitimating
presence of these numerous ecclesiastics probably served to inspire
attendance at the cemetery by additional faithful from Paris and vicinity who might otherwise have hesitated to come because of the
refusal of their local priests to grant them permission to do so. The
mere presence at Saint-Médard and throughout the diocese of large
numbers of sympathetic clergy must have given many such people the

[71] Several *miraculés* testified that their *curés* had specifically urged them to
invoke the deacon Pâris (see, for example, the cases of Marie-Anne Tridan,
Jeanne-Marguerite Dutilleux, and Marguerite Giroust, found in the third and
fourth *Recueils des miracles*, published in 1732).

[72] The *NNEE* cited the remarks of one Paris *curé*, M. Penet of Saint-Landry,
who spoke to his flock in glowing—even hyperbolic—terms of the "truly edifying spectacle" he had witnessed at Saint-Médard: "Ces miracles sont si déclarés
et en si grande abondance," he observed, "que l'on ne voit rien de pareil depuis
le commencement de l'Eglise, et que cet événement nous retrace ce que Jésus-
Christ faisoit de son temps. Quoique ce Bienheureux ne soit pas encore canonisé,
il paroît qu'il a une grande puissance auprès de Dieu: C'est pourquoi *je vous ex-
horte à avoir confiance en lui, et à aller à son Tombeau*" (Aug. 10, 1731, p. 159;
italics added).

[73] See, in particular, the police reports of July 27, July 31, and Aug. 3, 1731,
BA, MS 10196.

[74] Police report of Aug. 18, 1731, *ibid.*

[75] On these and other priestly activities at Saint-Médard, see *ibid., passim.*

courage to withstand the intimidations of hostile *curés* and confessors. As a result, some actually went to Saint-Médard in blatant defiance of their parish clergy's admonitions against participating in the observances conducted there. A group of disobedient pilgrims from the town of Saint-Denis, for example, issued a blistering attack on their *curé* shortly after he had delivered a sermon denouncing the miracles and person of François de Pâris:

> We who are writing to you are neither theologians nor philosophers. Thank God, we know neither Greek nor Latin. But we do know French; and it is [precisely] because we understand it well that we are extremely shocked by your harangues against the memory of a man whose holiness God has manifested by so many prodigies. We complain all the more about your blindness because it is completely willful. Only the hardhearted can possibly oppose the marvels which are bursting forth at the present time.
>
> You say that M. Pâris is damned. It is not enough to assert it; you must prove it. Have you had direct communication from God, or were you present when He judged M. Pâris, so that you can say so assuredly and in such an audacious tone that he is damned? Where do you get such temerity? . . . It is an [act of] cruelty, inhumanity, and barbarity to damn men whom the Church has not yet separated from its communion. . . .
>
> [No matter what you say,] we shall continue to go to Saint-Médard, while waiting for the Archbishop to join us there.[76]

Although the defiant insolence of this letter would be difficult to match in any other document from this period, these people from Saint-Denis were by no means alone in their disobedience. The parish clergy at Saint-Sulpice, a *constitutionnaire* stronghold in Paris, had reportedly threatened to withhold absolution from anyone who went to pray at M. Pâris' tomb. Their parishioners, however, do not seem to have heeded these warnings. Similar results obtained elsewhere in the city. At Saint-Barthélemy (Anne Lefranc's parish), when M. Gouffé, Lair's replacement as *curé*, denounced the deacon Pâris as a heretic and therefore unworthy of reverence and went on to declare Saint-Médard off limits to his parishioners, they simply ignored him.[77] As Barbier observed, "the people, once impressed, are not easily turned

---

[76] Letter to M. Lenoir, *curé* of Saint-Michel, Oct. 12, 1731, *ibid.*, MS 2056, fols. 204-205.

[77] Journal of De Lisle, July 20 and 22, 1731, AM, U-376. But cf. Vintimille to Fleury, July 22, 1731, BM, MS 2357, pp. 443-44.

around,"[78] especially, he might have added, since there were refractory priests in abundance all over the city who were eager to support them in their disobedience.

The crucial role which the *anticonstitutionnaire* Paris clergy played in stimulating and sustaining interest in the Pâris cult and in effectively nullifying Vintimille's *mandement* of July 15 is undeniable. But in all of their quite substantial activity on behalf of the Saint-Médard devotions, these priests were by no means acting as wholly disinterested observers or without any thought of partisan advantage. Indeed, although there is little question as to the sincerity of their support for and participation in the cult, and although any suggestion of conscious demagoguery would be difficult to document, one cannot ignore the fact that there was enormous political capital to be made from encouraging the faithful to worship at Pâris' tomb and from publicizing the miracles which took place there. And these ecclesiastics, frustrated by their long and fruitless sparring with Vintimille over the archbishop's refusal to recognize the Pâris miracles, had determined to exploit these phenomena to the full. Much of their "propaganda" campaign came to be centered on the parish level and was directed at the large body of faithful who, though involved in the Pâris cult, had not yet associated the cause of M. Pâris with the *anticonstitutionnaire* point of view.

The great majority of those who continued, despite many obstacles, to make their way to Saint-Médard were still not especially preoccupied with or even capable of understanding the various doctrinal and ecclesiastical questions that had been exercising their more learned and more sophisticated fellow Catholics for the previous two decades. Popular devotion to the memory of François de Pâris began innocently enough and remained essentially independent of any strong or particularly noticeable attachment to the appellant cause to which the deacon had dedicated his last years. To the worshipers at his grave, who from the outset were only vaguely, if at all, aware of Pâris' political persuasions, the cemetery would always remain first and foremost a place of pilgrimage, a source of joyous renewal and vital spiritual sustenance. For them, attendance at Saint-Médard represented a response to the spiritual appeal made by M. François from beyond his grave. They saw the deacon's tomb as the site where miraculous cures performed by their great *ami des pauvres* served as infallible testimony to his saintliness, even though he had not obtained formal canonization. For many of these people the deacon's miracles would never lose their "nonpar-

---

[78] II, 170 (July 1731). Referring to M. Pâris, Barbier had earlier remarked that "le peuple le sanctifiera sans cour de Rome, si cela continue" (II, 167).

tisan" character; for them the impulse behind the public observances would continue to be primarily, if not exclusively, a deeply religious one. As we have seen, however, the Paris faithful were by no means oblivious to the ecclesiastical controversies raging throughout the diocese, even if they still did not comprehend many of the issues in dispute. For some years their *anticonstitutionnaire* parish priests had been endeavoring to open their eyes to the seriousness of the debate while trying to win popular sympathy for the appellant cause.[79] The growing incidence of miracles, along with Vintimille's ill-advised decisions to ignore and then to suppress the Pâris cult without a full-scale inquest, had enabled the appellant clergy to modify and expand its campaign of popular politicization. These *anticonstitutionnaire* ecclesiastics, while they were preaching their sermons to captive congregations, hearing confessions, offering spiritual counsel to those afflicted with various physical ailments, and encouraging attendance at Saint-Médard,[80] also undertook to "translate" the Pâris cult into political terms for their parishioners, to demonstrate the close connection between the miraculous cures and the deacon's staunch opposition to the bull *Unigenitus*, and in general to raise the level of popular political consciousness.[81] Their task proved to be an easy one, for they appear to have found a most willing and susceptible audience among the large numbers who had already embraced the Pâris cult.[82] These people were well prepared to view the miracles as a proof for the Jansenist cause, to see Saint-Médard as the place where God manifested His holy truth, and to identify *their* François de Pâris, the saintly *ami des pauvres*, with the *anticonstitutionnaire* François de Pâris, *défenseur de la foi et martyr pour la Vérité*.[83] While the miracles worked through the dea-

[79] See, in particular, the *Avis aux fidèles de l'Eglise de Paris, sur ce qu'ils ont à craindre de la part des confesseurs qui acceptent la Constitution "Unigenitus"* (1730), a tract which was so outspoken in its attack on the *constitutionnaires* that the *Grand'Chambre* issued an *arrêt* on Jan. 12, 1731, ordering it suppressed (extended summary and comment in *NNEE*, Jan. 7 and 19, 1731, pp. 7-8, 14-15). Cf. discussion in Chs. I and III, *passim*, above.

[80] See, for example, police interrogation of Marie Tassiaux, Jan. 18, 1732, BA, MS 11210, fols. 253-54.

[81] Several priests argued the need to "discerner les abus de l'autorité d'avec l'autorité toujours sainte et respectable. . . . Il faut obéir à Dieu plutôt qu'aux hommes" ([Philippe Boucher], *Lettres de M. l'abbé De L'Isle à un ami de Paris, sur les miracles qui s'opèrent par l'intercession de M. de Pâris*, 2nd ed. [Utrecht, 1732], p. 160).

[82] As Marais observed, "Ceux qui vont à son tombeau disent que c'est le tombeau de la Constitution" (IV, 272 [Aug. 22, 1731]).

[83] *Histoire des miracles et du culte de M. Pâris*, pp. iv-v. See also Fourquevaux, IV, 372, and *Réflexions sur les miracles que Dieu opère au tombeau de M. Pâris* (n.d.), p. 33.

con's intercession continued to serve the simple, straightforward functions of curing diseases and ailments, of relieving pain and discomfort, and of providing hope and consolation to the faithful believers, these cures, like the cult being observed to Pâris' memory, had also begun to assume in the popular mind a very definite ideological coloration.[84]

While the *anticonstitutionnaire* parish priests were working to convert parishioners to their cause, and while sizable crowds continued to attend Pâris' tomb, Jansenist theologians and pamphleteers began redoubling their efforts to sustain the propaganda campaign first announced in the *Dissertation sur les miracles*. Indeed, through both pulpit and press the opponents of the Bull stepped up their efforts to exploit the miracles and to give them greater publicity throughout Paris and in the provinces. Having already blatantly violated Vintimille's interdiction of the cult, they now proceeded to ignore other provisions of the archbishop's July 15 decree. Unauthorized accounts of various cures, accompanied by copies of the signed and notarized testimony of witnesses, started to appear in print in considerable numbers. News of the miracles was thus spread more quickly than ever and the *anticonstitutionnaire* message broadcast to the general reading public along with it.

The publication of Vintimille's *mandement* also prompted the *Nouvelles ecclésiastiques* to display considerably more interest than before in the miracles of François de Pâris. At first, as with the Anne Lefranc affair, the editor had hesitated before reporting any detailed news of the miraculous cures, in large part because certain leading Jansenist theologians continued to harbor serious doubts and reservations, refus-

---

[84] One has only to look at the various prayers being offered in François de Pâris' honor to get a sense of how successfully the *anticonstitutionnaires* had "politicized" the cult. One worshiper beseeched the Lord to have pity on "votre Eglise affligée de tant de maux, tourmentée de tant de persécutions, agitée de tant de disputes" (cited in Manneville, p. 223). Another referred to the "Vérités de foy pour la déffense desquelles votre bienheureux serviteur s'est immolé comme une victime de la pénitence" (BA, MS 10196). Other examples may be found in the *3ᵉ Recueil des miracles*, pp. 43-44, 53, 58, and in the *4ᵉ Recueil des miracles*, p. 29. A number of popular songs and verses also demonstrated the ever closer alliance being effected between the followers of M. Pâris and the opposition to the bull *Unigenitus*. On Aug. 30, 1731, for example, the following poem appeared on the doors of parish churches throughout the capital: "Humble et vrai pénitent au sortir du berceau/ Pâris ne peut que prier et se taire./ De la Bulle il pleura le ténébreux mystère,/ Pour elle, à Dieu, s'offrit victime volontaire./ De la Bulle appelant descendit au tombeau,/ Mais un prodige nouveau/ Sa cendre aujourd'hui salutaire/ De la Bulle devient le terrible fléau" (cited in Manneville, p. 225). For an anti-Pâris verse composed in response to this one and posted the next day on the deacon's tomb, see *ibid*.

ing to see in the manifestations at Saint-Médard any definitive sign
from God in justification of their appeal and in some cases doubting
the miraculous character of the cures reportedly being effected there.
Not until late June, when the journal enthusiastically announced the
publication of the first biography of M. Pâris and pronounced it "very
edifying for the appellant cause," did the editor overcome his own
hesitations and begin to take cognizance of the miracles.[85] Cautiously
he announced his intention of publishing information on the cures
"once they have been cleared up and confirmed."[86] By August the
journal, now seconded by an impressive array of notable *anticonstitutionnaires*, including the venerable Bishops Colbert and Soanen,[87]
was positively exultant:

> . . . here is [the] most efficacious and most complete refutation
> of the *mandement* [of Msgr. Vintimille]. God himself is providing
> it by means of the miracles which He has not ceased operating at
> the tomb of the Saintly Deacon and which He has seemed to in-
> crease all the more because of the efforts to hinder them.[88]

What is more, while clandestine Jansenist presses in Paris and elsewhere had already begun publishing detailed "relations" of miracles,
the gazette now for the first time followed suit. In one issue devoted
almost entirely to the subject, the *Nouvellistes* reported a summary
of nineteen miracles, "proofs of which had come to [the editor's] attention since the previous May."[89] The journal was nevertheless still
determined to proceed cautiously. Aware that some might yet balk
at the idea of invoking such phenomena in support of the *anticonstitutionnaire* cause, the editor felt obliged to stress the well-attested
character of the miracles and to reassure "those who are too far away
to enter into this discussion" that they need not "suspect us of having
wished to deceive them inasmuch as the events under consideration

---

[85] June 27, 1731, p. 125.   [86] *Ibid.*, p. 126.

[87] The first reference to the Pâris miracles in Colbert's correspondence occurred
in a letter to Bishop Caylus of Auxerre, July 12, 1731 (*Oeuvres*, III, 497). In subsequent letters to virtually every one of his correspondents, the bishop of Montpellier dwelled on this subject at some length; in the process he struck a note of
increasingly heightened optimism, displaying a sense of impending victory over
the *constitutionnaires*. Like Colbert, Soanen had become extremely enthusiastic,
indeed eloquent, in extolling the miracles and praising their utility for the cause
of the appeal (see, for example, his letter to Colbert, July 10, 1731, *Vie et lettres*,
I, 472). See also the letters from an unknown Paris correspondent to the abbé
Joubert, Colbert's *grand-vicaire*, especially those of June 30, 1731, and Aug. 12,
1731, BA, MS 5307, fols. 64-65, 66-67.

[88] *NNEE*, Aug. 26, 1731, p. 165.   [89] *Ibid.*

had been occurring in full public view and were known all over Paris."[90] The miracles reported in that number of the gazette took up virtually the entire four pages. Brief reports of other cures continued to appear sporadically in succeeding issues, usually couched in terms that made the editorial point of view of the *anticonstitutionnaire* party quite clear. The awesome tales which had until then been disseminated by word of mouth or by separate "relations," would thereafter be recounted in the pages of the most important organ of Jansenist propaganda and were thereby transmitted throughout the kingdom. If the archbishop of Paris and his *constitutionnaire* colleagues were determined to place their authority and that of the Church against these divine manifestations, then the *Nouvellistes* were not about to shrink from the challenge.

In the meantime, as the political ferment continued to increase, the progress of events at Saint-Médard had begun to take a new and far more fantastic course. In mid-July, shortly before Vintimille's ineffectual prohibition of pilgrimages to M. Pâris' tomb, dramatic things had started happening at the cemetery. Until then the manifestations which had been occurring since the deacon's death, though unauthorized, had not been especially unusual or extraordinary. Popular cults and miraculous cures were not totally foreign even to the "enlightened" eighteenth century. Large-scale public outbreaks of convulsions, however, were quite another matter. The first convulsive agitations at the shrine occurred quite unexpectedly, in the very midst of the miracles, although for some time prior to their outbreak several cures had been accompanied or preceded by painful or distressing movements and sensations (*vives douleurs*), which occasionally persisted even after the apparent healings had been effected.[91] How and when the actual convulsions began cannot be determined with certainty. It is nevertheless possible to follow their early development.

The first recorded instance of convulsions seems to have been those of a certain Aimée Pivert, who came to Saint-Médard already suffering from some kind of nervous disorder, perhaps epilepsy, for which she sought a cure.[92] On July 12, 1731, when placed on Pâris' tomb, she

---

[90] *Ibid.* Cf. letter to abbé Joubert, Jan. 25, 1732, BA, MS 5307, fols. 68-69.

[91] *Recherche de la vérité, ou Lettres sur l'oeuvre des convulsions* (1733), p. 5.

[92] Individual fits and seizures of various kinds were apparently a not uncommon feature of *ancien-régime* culture, leading one historian to suggest that "a profound hysteroid tendency [may have been] characteristic of the Old Regime, at least in the lower classes" (Jean-Pierre Peter, "Disease and the Sick at the End of the 18th Century," in Robert Forster and Orest Ranum (eds.), *Biology of Man in History* [Baltimore, 1975], p. 117). Peter's suggestion needs—and merits—

experienced involuntary spasms or convulsions and amazing contortions of her limbs, almost, some claimed, as if she were possessed. Her agitations recurred every day with the same intensity until August 3, when she went away perfectly "cured."[93] A few weeks later, in mid-August, the same strong, uncontrollable movements appeared in two young Parisian girls and in a deaf-mute from Versailles named Cathérine Bigot.[94] Mlle. Bigot reportedly experienced a partial recovery of both her hearing and her speech as a result of the convulsions—a claim which was subjected to an immediate challenge.[95] In any event, in the days and weeks that followed, a handful of other individuals—some of them no doubt epileptics—were similarly overcome by spontaneous paroxysms of the body. But the convulsions did not become more widespread until the end of August, when the most famous of the early convulsionaries (as they came to be called), the abbé Bescherand of Montpellier, made his first appearance at Saint-Médard.

Perhaps more than anyone else, Bescherand was responsible for turning the cemetery into the *lieu de supplice*[96] for which it has since been so notorious. Afflicted from youth with a severe atrophy of the left leg, Bescherand went by carriage twice a day to Saint-Médard in order to pray for a cure, whereby he might demonstrate both the reality of the miracles and the injustice of Vintimille's recent decree.[97] After he lay down on M. Pâris' tomb, and while those present prayed fervently on his behalf, Bescherand was seized with sudden and violent convulsions, made contorted grimaces, uttered occasional exclamations or screams of pain, and sometimes foamed at the mouth. Along with these frenzied writhings of his whole frame, witnesses reported seeing his entire body "forcibly lifted into the air," despite the efforts of several attendants who grasped him firmly by the arms and endeavored to hold him down. These various movements, or "hysterical attacks," usually continued for hours on end. Those persons assisting Bescherand and attending to his needs asked him from time to time to indicate the

---

further investigation; what bearing, if any, his observation has on the subject of the convulsionaries of Saint-Médard also remains to be explored.

[93] *Recherche de la vérité*, p. 5.   [94] *Ibid.*

[95] See Montgeron, "Idée de l'oeuvre des convulsions," II, 5-21 (along with sixteen pages of *pièces justificatives*). The challenge was made by Hérault (letter to Fleury or Chauvelin, Sept. 10, 1731, AAE, M&D, France, MS 1270, fol. 259).

[96] Jacques-Antoine Dulaure, *Histoire physique, civile et morale de Paris*, 6th ed., 8 vols. (Paris, 1837-39), V, 36.

[97] Augustin Noyon, "Un miracle du diacre Pâris: La guérison de l'abbé de Bécherand (1731-1732)," *Etudes*, 156 (1918), pp. 412-32. On Bishop Colbert's own view of his much-disputed role in prompting Bescherand to go to Saint-Médard, see letter to Mme. de Coetquen, Oct. 5, 1731, *Oeuvres*, III, 506.

different areas of his body where he felt pain, and they would rub dirt from Pâris' grave all over the affected parts to relieve his discomfort.[98] The bewildered police agents stationed at the cemetery to ensure that law and order prevailed made frequent reports on the abbé's "startling and extravagant performances" and commented almost daily on his "terrifying," "scandalous," or "diabolical" demonstrations.[99] Bescherand regularly submitted himself to medical examinations in the sacristy, and several sympathetic doctors declared that he had derived great benefit from his efforts, that "the sinews had recovered their natural elasticity."[100] Partisan claims that Bescherand's cure was progressing slowly, but surely,[101] were hotly disputed by the *constitutionnaires*, who derided the abbé's "indecent and obscene cavorting" as a "kind of farce" and an "illusion."[102] They also pointed out that Bescherand was still lame, and that he limped around as much as ever. Whatever the truth of the matter, the abbé continued for months to make his twice-daily appearances. Almost oblivious to changes in the weather, he persisted in his regular "spectaculars" even into the winter. Indeed, so assiduous was he in his attendance and so adept did he seem in his "performances," that the spectators began to wonder whether they were watching a saint or someone possessed.[103] Diabolical or divine, his convulsions soon proved "contagious."

During the rapid diffusion of this behavior, crowds of people, becoming more numerous with every passing day, began to be seized by similar frenzied paroxysms. Men, women, and children took part in the proceedings, crowding onto the tomb and filling the cemetery with "tears, groans, and frightful screams."[104] Some adepts would leap into the air only to fall swooning on the ground, repeating the process several times in succession—an exercise which usually left them panting and gasping for breath. The astounding gymnastics of other convulsionaries led their associates to place mattresses and cushions around Pâris' tomb as a precaution against their injuring themselves. The names of the marquis de Légal, Giroust, Maupoint, Langlois, and other "regulars" now joined that of Bescherand in the daily police reports from Saint-Médard. Initially only those who were suffering from some

98 Hérault to Fleury or Chauvelin, Sept. 10, 1731, AAE, M&D, France, MS 1270, fol. 258.

99 BA, MS 10196, *passim*, but esp. report of Sept. 13, 1731.

100 Cf. discussion of his condition in BN, NAFr., MS 3333, fols. 137-41, 151.

101 See, for example, Colbert to Caylus, Oct. 3, 1731, *Oeuvres*, III, 505.

102 Hérault to Fleury or Chauvelin, Sept. 10, 1731, AAE, M&D, France, MS 1270, fol. 258.

103 Marais, IV, 303 (Sept. 30, 1731).

104 See police report of Sept. 13, 1731 (BA, MS 10196).

disability experienced the convulsions; and at first they occurred—or at least began—only when the individual was actually touching the deacon's tomb. More and more, however, persons without any bodily infirmities were suddenly seized with agitations, and frequently they were overcome even though not on the grave site. As the "contagion" extended and grew, the tomb and the area surrounding it were some-times completely covered with shaking and writhing bodies. Indi-viduals began having convulsions of varying degrees of severity in the church, in nearby houses, even in the streets. Some continued to ex-perience such movements upon returning to their homes. Even the curious spectators were occasionally overcome with assorted spasmodic contractions.[105] Whatever the causes of these phenomena and however they were produced—whether or not the behavior was self- or group-induced, learned or involuntary, conscious or unconscious, the result of imitation, suggestion, "sympathetic contagion," or an epileptic seiz-ure, the effect of hyperventilation, sensory deprivation, overstimula-tion, or organic neuropathy, a sign of God's hand or that of the devil —the displays and activities of these new "convulsionaries" soon gave rise to a growing theological debate.[106]

Constitutionnaire detractors, already critical of the numerous incom-

---

[105] *Ibid., passim.*

[106] They also gave rise to a spate of satires. One morning in the late fall some-one posted the following notice at the entrance to the cemetery:

"Avis au Public,

"Messieurs et dames,

"La grande troupe des sauteurs et voltigeurs du Sr. Pâris, qui n'a jusques à présent cherché que le plaisir et l'édification de ceux qui luy font l'honneur de venir la voir, donnera son spectacle régulièrement soir et matin pour la com-modité du public.

"Le Sr. Bécheran le Boiteux, qui a ici l'honneur de divertir avec succès et ap-plaudissement les princes et les princesses, les seigneurs et dames de la Cour, continuera jusqu'à extinction de forces ses exercices ordinaires, et pour la satis-faction des curieux fera plusieurs fois ce nouveau saut périlleux en ne se soutenant que sur ses deux pieds et à l'aide de trois personnes seulement. . . .

"Le reste de la troupe n'oubliera rien pour mériter l'estime et la bienveillance de ceux qui honoreront son spectacle."

(*Apologie des miracles faits ou à faire au tombeau de M. de Pâris* [Brussels, 1732], p. 72; also cited in Mousset, pp. 63-64, and Noyon, p. 425.) The Jesuit playwright, Guillaume-Hyacinthe Bougeant, who was the reputed author of the above piece, also produced several highly successful plays satirizing convulsionary "theatrics," most notably, *Le Saint déniché, ou la Banqueroute des marchands de miracles, comédie* (The Hague, 1732), and *Les Quakres françois, ou les Nouvelles trem-bleurs, comédie* (Utrecht, 1732); cf. also his *La Femme docteur, ou la Théologie tombée en quenouille, comédie* (Liège, 1731).

plete, imperfect, or gradual cures which the appellants had claimed to
be miraculous, seized on the convulsions as a means of stepping up
their attacks on all of the observances at Saint-Médard.[107] They expressed outrage and alarm at the increasingly violent nature of the
manifestations at the deacon Pâris' tomb. They contended that such
violence proved that God was nowhere present at Saint-Médard. What
is more, they accused pretty women and shapely young girls of deliberately allowing themselves to become indecently exposed for long
periods, and in full public view, while they experienced their convulsions—further evidence of a malign presence at the cemetery.[108] Other
critics, while condemning these phenomena, ascribed them to purely
natural causes or dismissed them as the product of derangement, over-
active imagination, or willful fraud on the part of the convulsionary
adepts, who were out to draw attention to themselves.[109] One writer
went so far as to denounce Bescherand as a mountebank and an impostor.[110]

Forced on the defensive by these various charges, several Jansenist
apologists rushed to embrace the convulsions and to argue the fundamentally divine character of these manifestations. While acknowledging the extraordinary, almost incredible nature of the developments
at Saint-Médard and the difficulty of reaching a definitive judgment
on all the phenomena observed there, they denied that any deceit or
imposture was involved.[111] In a series of anonymous pamphlets[112] they

[107] *Dissertation physique sur les miracles de M. Pâris, dans laquelle on prouve
que les guérisons qui se font à son tombeau ne sont que les effets des causes purement naturelles, et qu'elles n'ont aucun caractère des vrais miracles* (n.d.); *Essais
de physique, où l'on démontre par les règles de la nature comment se font les
convulsions qui attaquent les malades au tombeau de M. Pâris et sur le chemin
qui y conduit* (n.d.); *Lettres au sujet des choses singulières et surprenantes qui
arrivent en la personne de M. l'abbé Bescherant à Saint-Médard* (1731).

[108] Anonymous police *mémoire*, late November 1731 (BA, MS 10196).

[109] According to the author of the *Essais de physique*, the convulsions "ne sont
que les effets d'une imagination blessée, ou qu'ils sont tous volontaires et étudiées"
(p. 6). Cf. the anonymous *Observations de médecine sur la maladie appelée Convulsion* (1732), published with *Approbation* and with the *Privilège du Roy*: "La
convulsion n'est autre chose qu'un mouvement tonique dérangé" (p. 7).

[110] *Lettres au sujet des choses singulières et surprenantes*, passim.

[111] See *Extrait d'une lettre de M. Petitpied, du 13 janvier 1732, à madame de . . .*
(n.d.). See also two letters written by the abbé d'Etemare on Jan. 25, 1732, one
to Mme. de Montagny, the other to Bescherand himself (BPR, L. P. 480, No.
60).

[112] *Dissertation, où l'on montre que des miracles opérés par degrés, ou accompagnés de douleurs, n'en sont pas moins de vrais miracles, et ont été regardés
comme tels dans l'antiquité (25 octobre 1731); Réflexions sur les miracles que
Dieu opéré au tombeau de M. de Pâris, et en particulier sur la manière étonnante*

also sought to demonstrate that the so-called *vives douleurs* and the other movements and physical sensations accompanying an increasing number of miracles were a quite normal adjunct—and even a precipitant—of certain kinds of cures. To buttress their argument several pro-convulsionary Jansenists embarked on an extensive research project in which they focused on precisely this subject. They combed through canons, doctrinal pronouncements, and theological treatises as well as numerous ecclesiastical histories and saints' lives, looking for evidence of other cures accompanied or occasioned by convulsions which the Church had accepted as miraculous. One writer claimed to have discovered at least two dozen such instances.[113] Far from unprecedented, therefore, "miraculous convulsions" were well within the orthodox Christian tradition.

Not surprisingly, such demonstrations, which left aside the question of *convulsions non-guérissantes* and ignored a number of other disputed matters, failed to convince the *constitutionnaires*. They also failed to persuade an important segment of Jansenist theologians who had likewise raised some serious objections to the goings-on at Saint-Médard, particularly to the dramatic displays of the abbé Bescherand. These Jansenists, who included the influential abbés Duguet and d'Asfeld, maintained that the actions of the convulsionaries represented a distortion (*déformation*) of the message of the Pâris cult. They regarded Bescherand's behavior and that of his cohorts not only as potentially damaging to the *anticonstitutionnaire* cause but also as insulting to the majesty and dignity of God.[114] They accused the convulsionary abbé of having "tempted God" with his theatrics; "God," they contended, then "took revenge against Bescherand by visiting him with convulsions."[115] Like the *constitutionnaires*, they denied that Bescherand had shown any improvement in his lameness. They also questioned whether any miraculous effects could ever be expected from such wild agitations as the convulsionaries were exhibiting at Saint-Médard. The growth of such anticonvulsionary sentiment among this "traditionalist" faction of Jansenists marked the beginning of what

---

et extraordinaire dont il les opère depuis six mois environ (n.d.); *Entretiens sur les miracles* (1732).

[113] Letter to an unknown correspondent, Nov. 12, 1733, BA, MS 5784, p. 88. See also *ibid.*, MS 5307, fols. 64-109, *passim*. D'Etemare and his colleagues frequently cited the example of Saint Martin of Tours, whose miracles (as reported by Gregory of Tours) were frequently "accompagnés de douleurs" (*Dissertation, où l'on montre que des miracles . . . , passim*).

[114] Dedieu, "L'agonie du jansénisme," p. 195, n. 68.

[115] See d'Etemare to Sartre, July 13, 1733, BA, MS 5784, p. 57.

was eventually to become a tense, fratricidal struggle inside the *anti-constitutionnaire* camp, a struggle which would prove significant for the future development of the Pâris cult. For the moment at least, the tone of the debate remained calm and civil; the opposing sides continued to air their views largely through the exchange of private correspondence. But that, too, would change before another full year had passed.

Despite mounting criticism from the *constitutionnaires* and growing uneasiness in certain Jansenist circles, a substantial proportion of *anti-constitutionnaires* remained as committed as ever to the Pâris cult. Likewise, the deacon's faithful adherents continued to pursue their devotions uninterrupted. Even so, the appearance of Bescherand and the other convulsionaries had introduced an element of dramatic, even "theatrical," spectacle into the observances at the deacon's tomb, thereby effecting a major change in the public devotions and producing a marked impact on the subsequent history of the cult. Amid increasing religious exaltation and growing public excitement, the scene at Saint-Médard had turned in recent months from relatively peaceful, orderly gatherings to far more disorderly, tumultuous ones.[116] Every day from well before dawn to well after dusk hundreds of people, many of them totally unconcerned about weather conditions,[117] made their way to Saint-Médard. While new "patients" arrived daily to join the ones already searching for cures, and while new convulsionaries added their agitated gestures and frenetic screaming to those of Bescherand and company, the number of curious spectators soon began to outstrip the number of convulsionaries, would-be *miraculés*, and other worshipers pressing to reach the deacon's tomb. The police frequently remarked on the noisy, jostling, tightly packed throngs which now crowded into the tiny cemetery. Long lines of people queued up daily, trying to reach the tomb itself; scores of onlookers filled the galleries which ran along the churchyard. So great were the crowds in regular attendance—*un monde infini* was the police description on December 8—that they began spilling over into the nearby alleys and streets,

---

[116] This change is reflected in two different contemporary *estampes* depicting the scenes of devotion at the shrine, one by Jean Restout (set probably in early September) and another by an unknown artist (set apparently in the late fall).

[117] In November, with the onset of cold, inclement weather, someone erected a large canvas covering above the deacon's grave to provide protection from the elements for those who continued to sprawl on top of the tomb (police reports of November 16 and 21, BA, MS 10196). A short while later, several people began assuming daily responsibility for cleaning the mud and the water from around the tomb (report of Jan. 9, 1732, *ibid.*).

disrupting activity throughout the neighborhood and rendering some sections of the *faubourg* virtually impassable.[118] The challenge to Msgr. Vintimille's authority as well as to that of the *curé* of Saint-Médard was now more manifest than ever; so, too, was the challenge to law and order. The archbishop, whose provocative intervention in July had disastrously misfired, had already begun clamoring for the crown to intervene at once. Until then uncertain on what pretext to try to put a stop to the activities at Saint-Médard, Fleury's government thought it had at last discovered the means by which it might be able to dispose of the Pâris cult without too much difficulty. The issue for the cardinal-minister had once again become one of restoring public order by police action. However, knowing as he did the political, religious, legal, and jurisdictional delicacy of the matter, he would have to proceed very cautiously. Both the strategy and the tactics he adopted were ultimately circumscribed, if not determined, by the realities of recent ecclesiastical politics.

[118] *Ibid., passim.*

CHAPTER V

The Closing of the Cemetery at Saint-Médard and the Political Aftermath

De par le roi,
Défense à Dieu,
De faire miracles,
En ce lieu.

T HESE immortal lines of graffiti penned by some anonymous wit constitute perhaps the most lasting commentary to have survived from
the history of the Pâris cult. Though most historians of the *ancien régime*
quote this memorable epigram with relish, their knowledge of the
Saint-Médard episode rarely extends beyond an awareness of the fact
that a royal ordinance shut down a Parisian cemetery in which a popular religious cult of allegedly "Jansenist" inspiration had previously
been observed. Few of them have shown any sympathetic understanding of the cult in question. Fewer still have demonstrated any familiarity with the important, indeed urgent, political, legal, institutional,
and religious considerations which lay behind the government's decision
to close the churchyard, or any comprehension of the various pressures
and the difficult problems of strategy and tactics associated with the
execution of that decision. To be sure, the exact details of the policy-
making process in this matter—as in most affairs of the *ancien régime*
—remain somewhat obscure. A substantial number and variety of documents bearing on this question have survived, however, and make it
possible not only to investigate the reasons which prompted the royal
administration under Cardinal Fleury to take that fateful course of
action, but also to examine the manner of its execution and to analyze
its dramatic political and religious consequences.

Had the authorities been confronted by a mere popular religious cult
with but a handful of adherents, the problem of suppressing it or restricting them might have been a readily soluble one. In that case the
matter might have remained a purely spiritual issue, to be dealt with
by the archbishop of Paris. But developments in 1731, both at Saint-
Médard and beyond, had already made it clear that the task of halting
the observances at M. Pâris' tomb would not be an easy one. What

had begun as a local cult to a neighborhood "saint" was now attracting many hundreds, even thousands, of persons, not only from Paris but also from other dioceses all over France. More important, the cult had been drawn into the many-faceted and turbulent debate over the bull *Unigenitus* and had gained at least the tacit support of numerous leading *anticonstitutionnaires*, both lay and clerical. For years, of course, religious disputes had been threatening the façade of stability and unity in both Church and State. In Paris, as we have seen, the tensions and strains had become especially grave, with serious challenges to the established ecclesiastical authorities having come from priests, *avocats*, and magistrates alike. The developments at Saint-Médard had only exacerbated the situation for Cardinal Fleury and Archbishop Vintimille: first, because these developments had brought large numbers of the traditionally volatile Parisian populace into the fray; and second, because the dozens of miracles already attributed to the appellant deacon Pâris had become a source of extreme embarrassment to the cardinal-minister, the archbishop, and their fellow *constitutionnaires*. Yet in point of fact it was the prolonged inaction on the part of the authorities which accounted to some degree for that state of affairs.

From the beginning, the government's own policy had been inadequate to contain the Pâris cult. In part this was a result of the sympathetic attitude which Cardinal Noailles and other Parisian ecclesiastics had displayed toward its practitioners at the outset. Though ambivalent and hesitant in most matters, the former archbishop seemed to have given the cult his wholehearted, if necessarily unofficial, support. There was little the government could do while Noailles was still alive except to persuade him to withhold formal authorization of the miracles attributed to M. Pâris. But even after his death in 1729, the royal administration and the new archiepiscopal authorities, otherwise occupied with a refractory Parlement of Paris and a no less militant group of insubordinate parish priests, took a long time to realize that in Saint-Médard they had a problem on their hands, let alone to display the kind of vigilance commensurate with that problem.[1]

The authorities did not officially break their prolonged silence concerning these goings-on until July 1731, and then only in response to

---

[1] This slowness to react, mainly the result of the more pressing problems and dangerous political circumstances in Paris, was in marked contrast to the situation which obtained contemporaneously at Reims. There, in the face of vocal appellant opposition, prompt action on the part of the ecclesiastical and civil authorities produced an effective interdiction of all observances at the tomb of the abbé Rousse (see Ch. II above).

the provocative *Dissertation sur les miracles*, published in support of the Anne Lefranc cure. By that time the cult was already attracting considerable numbers of the faithful and becoming a political and theological *cause célèbre*. As a result, when Vintimille, acting under duress, issued a decree condemning the *Dissertation sur les miracles* and the Lefranc miracle and prohibiting pilgrimages to Saint-Médard, his blast misfired and provoked widespread opposition. This first official statement on the Pâris cult not only cost the archbishop what little popular respect he had still managed to retain,[2] but also utterly failed to put a halt to the observances at the deacon's tomb or to the propaganda campaign which supported and encouraged them. Quite the contrary, for in taking an uncompromising stand on the matter, Vintimille only aroused fresh antagonisms without providing a more permanent solution. The *anticonstitutionnaire* partisans of the miracles vigorously opposed the decree, while the people flocked to Saint-Médard in greater numbers than ever. Fleury's government, strongly committed to restoring religious tranquility throughout the kingdom, thus found itself faced with a difficult dilemma. Obviously the cardinal-minister could no longer ignore the cult or leave Vintimille to his own devices in attempting to cope with it. At the same time, before taking any further steps to suppress the religious devotions, the authorities had to be careful not to make a serious political or tactical miscalculation which might exacerbate tensions still further. Given the delicate nature of contemporary ecclesiastical politics in Paris, the problem of Saint-Médard now demanded greater caution than ever.

To make matters worse, the summer of 1731, which was to see the expansion and escalation of the Saint-Médard controversy, also saw the resumption of the embittered controversies pitting Vintimille and his fellow *constitutionnaire* bishops against the magistrates and *avocats* in the Parlement of Paris. As before, the principal issue at stake concerned the court's right to hear disputed ecclesiastical cases on appeal. Once again the crown became thoroughly embroiled in the renewed debate, with Fleury's government generally defending the episcopal point of view.[3] Repeated royal commands to the Parlement to cease interfering

---

[2] "Il est triste," the *Nouvelles ecclésiastiques* declared rhetorically, but with some relish, "de voir tomber ainsi dans l'avilissement une autorité si respectable; mais à qui en est la faute?" (Sept. 25, 1731, p. 181).

[3] One can follow developments in the government's thinking about this vexing jurisdictional dispute ("sur les deux puissances") through a series of long memoranda and position papers prepared for the royal ministers. See especially AAE, M&D, France, MS 1270, fols. 128-37, 226-28, 242-45, *et passim*.

in spiritual affairs, and the *conseil d'état*'s continued evocation of *appels comme d'abus* and its suppression of the court's *arrêts* offended many of the magistrates, who saw these conciliar actions as a capricious and unjustifiable interference with their vital role of judicial review. In late July the judges responded with lengthy written remonstrances to the king. They warned of the dangerous consequences to royal authority that would arise from the "multitude of evocations and extraordinary commissions, which tend to invert the natural order of jurisdictions" and to establish a growing distinction between parlementary and royal justice. They reiterated their usual justification for parlementary involvement in religious matters, insisting that the court had no intention of intruding upon the bishops' legitimate exercise of their proper ecclesiastical authority but was concerned only to prevent the *constitutionnaire* episcopate from abusing that authority, especially in its attempts forcibly to impose the bull *Unigenitus* upon His Majesty's subjects.[4] Finally, the magistrates called upon the king to restrain the royal council from encroaching upon the sovereign court's rightful jurisdiction.

The crown, however, was not prepared to accommodate the views of the judges. To be sure, the government, in an apparent effort to soothe their ruffled feelings and to reduce episcopal-parlementary tensions, had already addressed another circular letter to all the bishops of the realm, exhorting them to refrain from characterizing the Bull as a "rule of faith" and to be satisfied with enjoining submission to it as "a dogmatic judgment of the Universal Church."[5] But this slight gesture was hardly likely to placate the *parlementaires*. When the king, in responding to their remonstrances a week later, peremptorily dismissed their appeals, the magistrates were again thoroughly outraged. To the abbé Pucelle this imperious response was further proof that

---

[4] A number of *constitutionnaire* clergy had begun to deny the sacraments to individuals who refused to accept the Bull as a rule of faith. The most spectacular of such cases involved a certain Mme. Dupleix of Orléans, whose family eventually brought an *appel comme d'abus* to the Parlement of Paris. On April 28, 1731, the court issued an *arrêt* acknowledging the abuse of ecclesiastical authority and "enjoining the bishop to see to it that no priest from his diocese require, in his administration of the sacraments, any declaration on the subject of the constitution *Unigenitus*." The bishop of Orléans refused to adhere to the order, ardently protesting the Parlement's action to the crown. On July 6 the *conseil d'état* suppressed the court's writ with a decree of its own. It was this conciliar *arrêt* that prompted the remonstrances of July 25 (Flammermont, I, 243-57; for an analysis of the Dupleix affair see *NNEE*, May 15, 1731, pp. 97-98, June 27, 1731, pp. 127-28, and Sept. 1, 1731, pp. 169-72).

[5] Circular letter of July 22, 1731, sent by Chauvelin (AAE, M&D, France, MS 1270, fols. 35-38).

"the throne was surrounded with some cardinals and several bishops who sought only to sow the seeds of discord and to set the king against his Parlement, even though it was composed of his most faithful subjects."[6] Pucelle's outspoken remarks received wide support from the other judges, who voted overwhelmingly in favor of sending the king still other remonstrances, just as "humble and respectful" as the earlier ones, but also "sharper and more urgent."[7] In mid-August the magistrates submitted their "iterative" remonstrances. Nevertheless, despite additional extended arguments against clerical excesses and in defense of "the great maxims of the kingdom, . . . the sacred rights of royal authority, . . . the tranquility of the realm, [and] the general welfare of the state," the court again failed to move the king.[8] "I am even more displeased with the second remonstrances than [I was] by the first," came the angry reproach from Louis XV, "and I am [annoyed] by the conduct of my Parlement. I forbid all deliberation on this subject, and I wish to be obeyed."[9]

At this point, with passions already inflamed, the longstanding feud between Vintimille and the *avocats* flared up anew and was injected once again into the other ongoing controversies involving crown, episcopate, and Parlement. The archbishop of Paris, indignant as ever at the widespread insubordination toward and disrespect for his authority, was still smarting from the Parlement's "unjust suppression" of his pastoral instruction of January 10, 1731, in which he had condemned the *avocats'* famous *Mémoire pour les sieurs Samson, etc.*[10] By late July, therefore, Vintimille had presented the king with a *mémoire* of his own. Drawn up in the course of long discussions with Cardinal Fleury, the *mémoire* contained yet another of the besieged archbishop's appeals for royal support to restore calm within the diocese.[11] Contending that the Parlement of Paris was continuing to usurp the jurisdiction of the French episcopate and to lend its judicial support to the

---

[6] Flammermont, I, 257.　　　　[7] *Ibid.,* p. 258.

[8] Remonstrances of August 18, 1731, *ibid.,* pp. 258-65.

[9] *Ibid.,* p. 265.

[10] See Ch. III above. The half-dozen letters sent from Vintimille to Fleury about this time (June 13-24, 1731) are very revealing: BM, MS 2357, pp. 385-87, 389-94, 398, and 400-402. Cf. Vintimille to [Chauvelin?], June 19, 1731, BA, MS 6033, fols. 144-45.

[11] *Mémoire présentée au roi par l'archevêque de Paris, au sujet de l'Arrêt du parlement, du 5 mars 1731, qui reçoit le procureur du roi appelant, comme d'abus, de son Ordonnance et instruction pastorale du 10 janvier dernier* (Paris, 1731). Cardinal Bissy, one of Fleury's principal ecclesiastical advisers throughout this period, was instrumental in revising this *mémoire* and preparing it for publication (Fleury to Vintimille, June 20, 1731, BM, MS 2357, pp. 395-96).

"Jansenist fanatics" and other "seditious enemies of Church and State," Vintimille petitioned Louis XV to reverse the sovereign court's decision of the previous March. On July 30, after belabored negotiations with Cardinal Fleury, the archbishop finally obtained a favorable *arrêt* from the *conseil d'état*. The council evoked the case from the Parlement, which had originally taken it up on an *appel comme d'abus*, reinstated Vintimille's pastoral instruction, and authorized him to distribute it throughout the diocese. Without formally quashing or reversing the Parlement's *arrêt* of March 10, the government had effectively annulled the sovereign court's original ruling.[12]

Neither Vintimille's *mémoire* to the king nor the council's *arrêt*, both dated July 30, was published immediately, since Fleury had left to Vintimille the decision as to when to issue them formally. After hesitating for some weeks, watching in vain for signs that the Parlement might be "better disposed toward peace and tranquility," the archbishop finally ordered the two pieces printed. Even as he did so, the cautious Vintimille instructed the printer not to allow the conciliar decree to be "cried in the streets," for fear of arousing the ire of the lawyers and the judges in the Parlement.[13] No amount of precautions, however, could have averted the hostile reception which the *arrêt* encountered at the Palais de Justice, particularly among the forty *avocats* who had originally signed the legal *consultation* condemned in Vintimille's January pastoral instruction. With the support of some three hundred excited colleagues, they complained vehemently that they had already explained themselves on the matter of their *mémoire* long before Vintimille first published his pastoral letter, and that the royal administration had unreservedly accepted their explanation. When they could obtain no satisfaction from the government and received no support from the *gens du roi* in their efforts to get the council's *arrêt* quashed, virtually the entire body of *avocats* resolved on a strike.[14]

[12] In addition to Vintimille's letters to Fleury (n. 10 above), see the following from the cardinal-minister to the archbishop: June 19, 1731, *ibid.*, pp. 392-93; June 20, *ibid.*, pp. 395-96; July 14, *ibid.*, p. 432; July 29, *ibid.*, pp. 452-53; July 30, *ibid.*, p. 453; and Aug. 2, *ibid.*, pp. 462-63. Cf. Barbier, II, 181-83 (August 1731). The *arrêt du conseil*, dated July 30, was published along with Vintimille's *mémoire* and may be found in AN, E2112, fols. 342-51. For a discussion, see Chauvelin to Polignac, July 31, 1731, AAE, C.P., Rome, MS 723, fols. 43-48.

[13] Vintimille to Fleury, Aug. 1, 1731, BM, MS 2357, pp. 460-62; Fleury to Vintimille, Aug. 2, *ibid.*, pp. 462-63; Vintimille to Fleury, Aug. 3, *ibid.*, pp. 463-64; Fleury to Vintimille, Aug. 5, *ibid.*, p. 465; Vintimille to Fleury, Aug. 21, *ibid.*, pp. 481-82; Vintimille to Fleury, Aug. 21, *ibid.*, p. 486; Vintimille to Fleury, Aug. 23, *ibid.*, pp. 490-91; and Fleury to Vintimille, Aug. 25, *ibid.*, pp. 491-92.

[14] Barbier, II, 183 (August 1731).

In his reference to the lawyers, Vintimille had appeared to charge them with heresy. Heretics, they declared, were unworthy of practicing law. From August 23 on, therefore, they closed their chambers; the pleading of cases was all but suspended, the course of public justice completely disrupted.

As Barbier observed, no doubt with some exaggeration, the council's *arrêt* "has raised a great stir in the city. . . . Almost everyone . . . is persuaded that the [upper] clergy wishes to assume rights and power at the expense of royal authority."[15] On August 27, while the *avocats* continued their strike, the Parlement decided to ignore the king's recent ban on remonstrances and to draw up new ones, this time centered on the *arrêt*. Three days later the crown retaliated against the *avocats*; ten lawyers received *lettres de cachet* commanding them to leave the city within twenty-four hours.[16] Their colleagues, however, encouraged by warm public and judicial support, remained steadfast in their opposition. Enthusiastic popular demonstrations—an increasingly common phenomenon during this period—took place outside the Palais de Justice. On August 31, the magistrates in the Parlement agreed to incorporate the plight of the suspended lawyers into their remonstrances, which they presented to the king on September 3.[17]

The judges, who at this time seemed about to consider Anne Lefranc's petition against Vintimille's *mandement*, reminded His Majesty that *appels comme d'abus* were incontestably within the competence of his sovereign court, and that they constituted "an invincible rampart for blocking the enterprises of the ecclesiastical power against the legitimate and immutable rights of royal authority." They insisted, moreover, that the original appeal to the Parlement in protest against Vintimille's pastoral instruction and in support of the *avocats* was quite regular and indeed necessary in order to prevent the archbishop of Paris from contravening the traditional limits of ecclesiastical authority. The king's reply, issued through his chancellor on September 6, was less belligerent in tone than the earlier ones, and much more ambiguous. The king reiterated his command that "all the disturbances on this subject must cease absolutely," but he concluded by assuring the court that he appreciated its concern with protecting his laws and preserving the public order—assurances which may have been part of the government's campaign to induce the Parlement to delay its examination of the Lefranc petition.[18]

When on September 7 First President Portail transmitted the king's

---

[15] *Ibid.*, pp. 183-84.
[17] Flammermont, I, 266-75.

[16] *Ibid.*, pp. 186-87.
[18] *Ibid.*, pp. 275-76.

ambiguous reply to the assembled company of magistrates, he had to read it twice to enable his colleagues to understand Louis' meaning. Choosing to interpret the king's concluding remarks as a vindication of their recent vigorous defense of secular authority, a majority agreed to insert the entire message into the court's registers along with a decree reaffirming "the true maxims" of royal authority and reasserting the independence of the crown from ecclesiastical intrusion.[19] This *Arrêt concernant la juridiction ecclésiastique, l'autorité du pape et le jansénisme*, which revised and updated the Declaration of 1682 (the famous "Gallican Articles"), contained the Parlement's strongly regalist views of the respective boundaries of the temporal and spiritual powers. The *arrêt* included four articles: first, "the temporal authority, established directly by God, is absolutely independent of any other . . ."; second, under no circumstances may the clerical authority fix the limits between the two powers; third, the temporal authority alone has the right to exercise the power of coercion over the king's subjects; and fourth, "ministers of the Church are accountable to the king and, in case of abuses, to his sovereign court" if, in the exercise of the jurisdiction which they hold from the king, they happen "to disturb the public order [or violate] the laws and maxims of the kingdom."[20]

Rumors about the Parlement's action were already circulating throughout the city by the time the magistrates adjourned for the day. That evening a delegation of angry *constitutionnaire* prelates, embittered by the renewed judicial efforts to circumscribe their authority, made its way to Versailles, hoping to persuade Cardinal Fleury, who had been preoccupied for nearly a week with the Lefranc case, to suppress the court's decree.[21] Since the *arrêt* was completely consonant with traditional Gallican principles, Fleury had to find some other justification for quashing it. On the following day, September 8, a writ from the *conseil d'état* declared the magistrates in violation of the council's decree of the previous March 10, which had reserved cognizance of these matters to the king alone. The council nullified the Parlement's decree as an encroachment upon the royal prerogative of lawmaking and ordered it expunged from the court's registers.[22] Finally, on September 9, the government published still another conciliar *arrêt*, this one dated September 5, which renewed an earlier injunction of silence on the vexed subject of the "two powers."[23] The council's provocative writ, copies of which were distributed and sold all over

---

[19] *Ibid.*, p. 276; Barbier, II, 193 (September 1731).
[20] Isambert, XXI, 366.   [21] Barbier, II, 194 (September 1731).
[22] Decree in Isambert, XXI, 366-67; see also Barbier, II, 194-95 (September 1731).
[23] Isambert, XXI, 365.

Paris, threatened to treat as rebels all who resumed the disputes over *Unigenitus*. The question of the Bull, the *arrêt* declared, "must be regarded on all sides as an entirely closed matter." Declaring it so, of course, did not make it so. Indeed, the appearance of the council's two well-timed decrees of September 5 and 8 would very possibly have aroused yet another series of intemperate exchanges between crown and Parlement had the magistrates not already begun their annual two-month recess.[24]

Fleury could take no more than temporary comfort in the intervention of the court's vacation at this stage. In the past several months the cardinal-minister had been faced with remonstrances that were more aggressive in tone than any previously issued by the Parlement during his ministry and confronted by the magistrates' vigorous assertion of their jurisdictional prerogatives. Where the issue of the "two powers" was concerned, the sovereign court was clearly in no mood to capitulate or even to retreat. What is more, the disturbing problem of Saint-Médard had in the meantime become still one more subject of political and judicial contention for Fleury, Vintimille, and the Parlement. On September 3, the *Grand'Chambre* had agreed to receive an *appel comme d'abus* in the Anne Lefranc case. Although the court's primary interest in the appeal was ostensibly juridical, there was a small group of vocal magistrates who had evinced a pious attachment to the memory of François de Pâris and for whom the Lefranc affair, like the entire Saint-Médard question, had become a matter of deep religious and ideological conviction, and one not to be dismissed very lightly. Prodded by this vigorous and outspoken coterie, the court stood to become increasingly and more intimately involved in the Saint-Médard controversy and appeared favorably disposed toward the participants in the Pâris cult. The nature and extent of the Parlement's subsequent involvement depended to a large degree on the official measures adopted by royal and archdiocesan authorities. The concern of these authorities was not so much that the Parlement as a body favored (that is, supported or believed in) the Pâris cult per se. Rather, the fear was that any judicial decisions the court rendered on behalf of the cult's adherents such as Mlle. Lefranc would be interpreted as a statement of judicial approval of the cult and an implicit promise of continued parlementary protec-

---

[24] Fleury was certainly not unmindful of the Parlement's approaching recess when he had the royal council publish its *arrêt* of September 5. Indeed, as in his handling of the Anne Lefranc case, much of the cardinal-minister's strategy revolved around just such considerations of timing; the government calculated many of its important policy decisions in terms of the sovereign court's calendar (cf. developments in September 1730 and September 1732).

tion for its practitioners. As a result, even though the Parlement was now in recess, and even though the *gens du roi* had managed to postpone consideration of the Lefranc appeal until at least the court's next session, Fleury and Vintimille had to be careful when they took steps against the followers of M. Pâris not to provide the magistrates with yet another pretext for launching an assault upon the ecclesiastical establishment.

Neither Fleury nor Vintimille, however, had counted on the intrusion of Rome—an intrusion which was to complicate their efforts immeasurably. For a long time, papal pressure had been mounting on the royal government to take some immediate action to halt the spreading "Jansenist-Gallican cancer." Viewed from Rome, the developments in Parisian ecclesiastical politics over the previous two years—the provocative actions of the lawyers and magistrates in the Parlement against the French episcopate, the insubordinate behavior of the refractory parish clergy, especially the *curés*, toward their archbishop, and the obstinate resistance and disrespect for authority which the faithful displayed in continuing their prohibited observances at Saint-Médard—seemed to have undermined the traditional order and hierarchy within the Gallican Church and left it in a state of virtual siege. What is more, the provocative regalist views emanating from the Palais de Justice seemed to portend an increasing secular encroachment on the integrity and inviolability of papal authority.[25]

In an effort to counter or at least deflect papal pressure for prompt action and immediate results and to satisfy the zealots in the Roman court who were not content with the bland, vague assurances of the French ambassador, Cardinal Fleury was repeatedly forced to explain his policies. Since 1730 the cardinal-minister had undertaken to correspond directly with the newly elected Pope Clement XII and with a number of the pontiff's closest advisers, including his nephew, Cardinal Corsini.[26] In one of these explanatory letters, written in October

[25] See numerous letters exchanged between Rome and Versailles, AAE, C.P., Rome, MSS 720-24, 726, 728-29, *passim*. Even the royal government had been willing to acknowledge that the *anticonstitutionnaire* party, "numerous, active, and enterprising intriguers and partisans of error," with "correspondents in foreign countries and with able pens and inexhaustible supplies of money at their disposal," appeared more formidable than ever (see Chauvelin's *mémoire* on the state of religious affairs, Aug. 21, 1731, AAE, M&D, Fonds divers [Rome], MS 61, fols. 147-55).

[26] In the election of the new pope in 1730 the French government had been actively campaigning for the elevation of a moderate candidate, one who was not "trop attaché aux maximes ultramontaines [ni] trop jaloux de les établir," and

1730, Fleury sought to justify his cautious and deliberate approach and to persuade the pope that the royal government was not only aware of the gravity of the current ecclesiastical disputes but was doing all it could to resolve them effectively.[27] "I dare to inform Your Holiness," Fleury began,

> that he does not yet know the full extent of the sickness which afflicts the kingdom and particularly the capital city. The more closely one examines it, the more one discovers its excess, and [the more] one is astonished by the number of rebels as much among ecclesiastics as among the laity, and especially among the women and the religious.

While frankly acknowledging the need "to curb the audacity" of the magistrates and the *avocats* in the Parlement, who "have become the principal support of the Jansenists," the cardinal-minister contended that "nothing is more difficult than to find the means of doing it." Furthermore, he stated:

> If one wished to punish them all at once and to use extreme measures, one would exacerbate and increase the malady instead of curing it.
> One has only to read the history books to be persuaded that violent remedies have had fatal results and have never succeeded. . . .
> I can assure Your Holiness with certainty that the zeal of the king for the faith is just what [you] could wish for, and that [the king] will not lose sight of the plan to reestablish it to its former glory. . . .
> We must therefore try not to act too precipitously and to content ourselves with taking firm, sure, but measured steps against a heresy that has already made too much progress.

Throughout the first half of 1731, as the religious problems increased and tensions mounted, the French government continued appealing to the papal authorities to remain calm and patient and exhorting them to refrain from intervening unilaterally or in too rash or provocative

---

who would not be likely to exacerbate religious tensions in France (cf. "Mémoire pour servir d'instruction à MM. les cardinaux de Rohan, Polignac, et Bissy pour le conclave . . . ," March 8, 1730, AAE, C.P., Rome, MS 718, fol. 118). In Clement XII Versailles found a pontiff rather to its liking.

[27] Letter to Clement XII, Oct. 23, 1730, *ibid.*, M&D, Fonds divers (Rome), MS 92, fols. 216-23; another copy, *ibid.*, MS 59, fols. 389-400. See also the earlier papal brief sent to the king on Sept. 11, which concerned the state of French ecclesiastical affairs; *ibid.*, fols. 383-88.

a fashion.[28] For the good of both Church and State, it was argued, Rome and Versailles must remain together in purpose and act in concert; divisions between the two courts would only give aid and comfort to their mutual enemies. Any hasty or bold action taken by Rome, it was also maintained, might further poison an already venomous atmosphere and thus make the crown's task of restoring peace and unity to the kingdom far more difficult. Fleury's administration, staunchly committed to a policy of "prudent moderation,"[29] was anxious to avoid compromising the authority of the king or precipitating another major confrontation with the Parlement of Paris over such vexed issues as "the liberties of the Gallican Church" or "the sacred rights of the crown."[30] However, the representations of Fleury, Chauvelin, and Ambassador Polignac met with little success. With Jansenist agitation continuing unabated and attracting widespread popular support, the zealous firebrands in the Holy See, encouraged by a party of equally ardent and implacable *constitutionnaires* in France (including some at the royal court), began clamoring for direct papal intervention.[31] Their vociferous demands were answered when the authorities in Rome took action against the Pâris cult.

Until late summer of 1731, the controversies "sur les deux puissances," involving the *avocats* and magistrates in the Parlement, on the one hand, and Vintimille and the rest of the *constitutionnaire* episcopate, on the other, had remained the principal concern of the Holy See

[28] Fleury to Cardinal Corsini, Aug. 5, 1730, *ibid.*, MS 59, fol. 269; Fleury to Corsini, Sept. 11, 1730, *ibid.*, fol. 316; Fleury to Corsini, May 28, 1731, *ibid.*, C.P., Rome, MS 726, fol. 328; Fleury to Corsini, July 17, 1731, *ibid.*, MS 722, fol. 368; and Fleury to Corsini, Sept. 3, 1731, *ibid.*, MS 723, fol. 200. Cf. the "Dépêches du Cardinal de Polignac à la Cour (1731)," *ibid.*, MS 728, *passim*, and the "Dépêches de la Cour au Cardinal de Polignac (1731)," *ibid.*, MS 729, *passim*.

[29] Fleury sought full submission to the Bull and compliance with his government's pronouncements on that question, but not at the expense of religious peace or public order. These last took precedence over doctrinal purity.

[30] See Chauvelin's *mémoire* of Aug. 21, 1731, AAE, M&D, Fonds divers (Rome), MS 61, fol. 149.

[31] A number of these ardent ultramontane partisans, including Cardinal Bissy and Archbishop Tencin, had begun corresponding directly with their equally intransigent counterparts in Rome. The actions of these "esprits inquiets et trop vifs" in appealing to the papal court over the king's head was causing great concern to Fleury, Chauvelin, and others in the royal administration. In addition to the letters cited above, see the "Mémoire pour servir d'instruction au Sr. Duc de Saint-Aignan," newly appointed ambassador to Rome. The duke's instructions, dated Sept. 7, 1731, contained an extended discussion of the "Intention du roi sur les disputes présentes et ses vues par rapport aux Evêques" as well as a section entitled "Personnes qui écrivent à Rome" (AAE, C.P., Rome [Supplément], MS 16, fols. 172ff.).

in its dealings with the Gallican Church. Increasingly, however, the problems of Saint-Médard had begun to loom large in Rome's thinking. According to Cardinal Polignac, a number of influential members of the Roman curia had become alarmed that Vintimille's *mandement* of the previous July "was being held in contempt," that the people of Paris "were more infatuated than ever" with the deacon Pâris, and that "the Parlement appeared ready to receive the alleged proofs" of the miracles.³² While decrying the impotence of the archbishop, the impertinence of the people and their parish priests, and the complicity of the Parlement, the pope's advisers were concerned that Versailles seemed equally unwilling or unprepared to do anything about the Pâris cult, "whether out of fear of an uprising or out of a vain hope that the falseness of the miracles would little by little make them fall on their own." So timid and irresolute an attitude, they maintained, would allow all Paris to fall victim to the partisans of error. Moreover, the miracles would receive a European-wide notoriety that might irrevocably tarnish the reputation of the Catholic Church. Finally, they contended, if no one came forward to "expose the illusion" of these miracles, then "weak Catholics everywhere would say that the [Jansenists'] appeal [against the Bull] is the way of salvation and that all the *constitutionnaire* bishops . . . are like the priests of Baal"—a "horrible consequence" which the papal authorities were not prepared to contemplate any longer.³³ By mid-August, therefore, the pope's advisers had convinced him of the need to take immediate and drastic action.

In a decree published on August 22, 1731, the Roman Inquisition, acting without any prior discussion or consultation with Cardinal Polignac, condemned one of the recently published biographies of François de Pâris to be publicly burned and declared false all the miracles attributed to the deacon's intercession.³⁴ The *Vie de M. Pâris*, observed

---

³² Polignac to Chauvelin, Oct. 4, 1731, *ibid.*, C.P., Rome, MS 724, fol. 136. In one of his earliest references to the Saint-Médard affair, Cardinal Corsini wrote of the *Dissertation sur les miracles*: "Ce sont de ces pièces sans authorité dont on ne se met point en peine, dès que des Corps entiers ne s'en mêlent. Il est cependant de la sagesse du gouvernement de s'opposer aux conséquences et aux progrès, comme V. E. le considère fort à propos . . ." (letter to Fleury, June 20, 1731, *ibid.*, MS 722, fol. 348). Cf. Fleury to Corsini, May 28, 1731, *ibid.*, MS 726, fol. 328.

³³ *Ibid.* Cf. the papal court's own defense of its actions, in Corsini to Fleury, Oct. 10, 1731, *ibid.*, fol. 155.

³⁴ The biography in question is entitled *La Vie de M. Pâris, diacre* (Brussels, 1731), with a preface attributed to Pierre Boyer and the text to either the Jansenist theologian Jacques-Joseph Duguet, or the *curé* Charpentier. The *NNEE*

the decree, was a "base, spiteful, and malicious work, . . . composed only to turn the simple faithful away from the Catholic religion and from the obedience due the Sovereign Pontiff."[35] The subject of this biography was "a rebel against the Holy See, a supporter of heretical and schismatical doctrines, a declared enemy of the constitution *Unigenitus*, in short, a persistent devotee of the Jansenist sect." Nevertheless, the inquisitors complained, "he has not only been accorded tremendous praise and honor" for his religious position, but "has also had false miracles attributed to him; what is more, he is represented in this extremely impudent work as a great model of virtue and sanctity." In proscribing the "perverse, pernicious" biography, the Holy Congregation declared the propositions and assertions contained therein to be "false, offensive to pious ears, scandalous, insulting to the authority of the Holy See, of the Church, of the bishops, and particularly of the French bishops, rash, impious, favorable to heretics, full of errors, schismatic, heretical, and full of the spirit of heresy." All who read or possessed copies of the book or who had anything to do with printing or distributing it would be liable to excommunication.

From Versailles' point of view the Inquisition's decree, promulgated just at the time when the crown was trying to reduce tensions within the Gallican Church and, in particular, to silence the Parlement of Paris, could not have come at a more inopportune moment. Archbishop Vintimille's decree condemning the *Dissertation sur les miracles* had already increased the religious ferment throughout Paris, and now the action of the Holy Congregation was deemed likely to increase it still further. "The excessive, indiscreet, and misplaced zeal exhibited in this unilateral action," an irate Chauvelin wrote the French ambassador, "will provoke a torrent of furious opposition which can serve only to undermine the authority of the king and to place him in an exceedingly awkward position."[36] Chauvelin was likewise fearful that this intemperate decree would stir up the "fanaticism of the people" and help

---

(Sept. 17, 1731, p. 179) reproduced a French transcription of the Latin decree along with some partisan commentary. Cf. also BN, NAFr., MS 3333, fol. 121; AAE, C.P., Rome, MS 727, fol. 145; and *ibid.*, MS 723, fol. 340.

[35] The Holy See regarded the *Vie* as "un ouvrage qui tend à renverser l'Eglise de fond en comble par les moyens mesmes dont Dieu s'est servi pour en faire l'établissement" (Polignac to Chauvelin, Oct. 18, 1731, *ibid.*, MS 724, fol. 196).

[36] Sept. 18, 1731, *ibid.*, MS 723, fols. 362-64. Cf. Polignac to Chauvelin, Aug. 30, 1731, *ibid.*, fol. 379; Polignac to Chauvelin, Sept. 6, 1731, *ibid.*, MS 724, fols. 21-22; and Polignac to Chauvelin, Oct. 18, 1731, *ibid.*, fol. 196. See also the "Supplément au Mémoire pour servir d'instruction au Sr. Duc de Saint-Aignan," Sept. 19, 1731, cited in G. Hanotaux (ed.), *Recueil des instructions données aux ambassadeurs et ministres de France. Rome.* 3 vols. (Paris, 1888-1913), III, 163-69.

"tie the affair of the miracles more closely than ever to the affair of the Bull, thereby rendering far more difficult the task of coping with the observances at Saint-Médard." As for the Parlement, the decree was bound to provide the magistrates with an opportunity to intrude themselves once again—legitimately and incontestably—into ecclesiastical matters from which the government had been trying to exclude them. What is more, the sovereign court, which already had the Lefranc case pending before it, would also gain yet another chance to speak out on the subject of the Pâris cult. Rome and Versailles were thus working at cross-purposes.

As Chauvelin had anticipated, attempts to introduce the decree into France did in fact bring the matter almost immediately to the Parlement's attention.[37] Although the full court was then in recess for its annual vacation, the judges sitting in the *chambre des vacations* were eager to take up the question. After a detailed examination of the decree, there was virtually unanimous sentiment against it, with a number of magistrates in favor of burning the document outright.[38] Only through the strenuous efforts of the *gens du roi*, especially Joly de Fleury, were the judges persuaded to limit their condemnation to questions of form and to set aside any discussion of the substantive issues raised in the decree.[39] On September 28, contending that such ultramontane interference was an arbitrary and intolerable violation of Gallican principles, they issued an *arrêt* ordering the decree's suppression.[40] According to the *arrêt*,

> these sorts of decrees are, properly speaking, only opinions, which can never be regarded as judgments; . . . to do so would be tantamount to elevating to a principle everything which . . . is contrary to our maxims; . . . it is necessary, therefore, to hold fast to the constant and inviolable rule which denies to such acts all authority and all force in the realm.

Although the court's denunciation derived less from a concern to protect the reputation of the deacon Pâris or the cult observed in his memory than from a desire to preserve the integrity of the Gallican

---

[37] By law and Gallican tradition no decree issued in Rome could enter the kingdom without the sovereign court's approval.

[38] Chauvelin to Polignac, Nov. 6, 1731, AAE, C.P., Rome, MS 724, fol. 203.

[39] The major problem, as Joly de Fleury saw it, was to find a way of condemning the Inquisition's decree without seeming to approve of the *Vie de M. Pâris* (BN, J.F., MS 111, fols. 216-57, but esp. 232-33).

[40] *Ibid.*, fols. 250-53; see also *ibid.*, MS 107, fols. 28-31. Cardinal Fleury even had a hand in drafting the *arrêt*, which went through several different versions (*ibid.*, MS 111, fols. 244, 247). For a discussion of the Parlement's decree, see *NNEE*, Oct. 26, 1731, pp. 201-202.

liberties and the fundamental maxims and traditions of the kingdom, the very fact that the magistrates had been willing to suppress the Inquisition's decree could not fail to give great encouragement to the followers of M. Pâris. To these people the action of the Parlement was an implicit validation of the Pâris miracles and an inspiration for restored confidence and renewed activity.[41]

The Parlement's suppression of the Inquisition's decree was followed within a week by the Paris *curés'* second petition to Vintimille requesting a canonical investigation into the Saint-Médard miracles.[42] Thus, as of early fall, the matter of the Pâris cult was much further from resolution than it had been the previous July, while the archbishop's own situation had likewise deteriorated: the Anne Lefranc appeal against Vintimille, still pending before the Parlement, threatened to embroil him in a potentially troublesome lawsuit; thousands of Parisians, with encouragement from their priests and confessors, were blatantly violating his decree and worshiping daily at François de Pâris' tomb; and dozens of allegedly miraculous cures were being attributed to the deacon's supposed influence and published without the archbishop's authorization. In addition, Vintimille was still deeply embroiled in a number of other longstanding conflicts, including one with the magistrates and *avocats* in the Parlement over his pastoral instruction of the previous January. With respect for his authority virtually at its nadir, Vintimille was also faced with incessant carping from his fellow *constitutionnaires* in Rome and in France, who were once more critical of their colleague's failure to discipline or control his insolent, intractable flock.[43] Little wonder that the archbishop, angry and frustrated, had begun complaining about the inadequate support he had been receiving from the crown and making renewed appeals to Cardinal Fleury for help.

Even before the publication of his *mandement* condemning the *Dissertation sur les miracles* and the Anne Lefranc cure, Vintimille had

[41] Chauvelin to Polignac, Sept. 18, 1731, AAE, C.P., Rome, MS 723, fol. 363. Cf. Chauvelin's remarks in his *mémoire* of August 21: "Les Parlements du royaume, loin de contenir les Peuples, leur donnent l'exemple, et leur laissent espérer des secours" (*ibid.*, M&D, Fonds divers [Rome], MS 61, fol. 149). In the same vein, cf. Marais' shrewd observations: "le peuple, qui voit le B. Pâris brûlé à Rome et le bref de Rome condamné à Paris croit que le B. est béatifié par le Parlement et y va plus que jamais. Allez-lui dire que ce n'est qu'une formalité, il n'en croira rien et les prédicateurs n'en oseront rien dire" (IV, 303 [September 30, 1731]).

[42] See Ch. III above.

[43] Vintimille interpreted the Inquisition's decree as a hostile, if oblique, judgment on his handling of the Saint-Médard situation.

written Fleury urgently requesting the royal government to intervene directly at Saint-Médard in order "to put a halt to a fanaticism which no longer knows any bounds."[44] The archbishop had been appalled that the magistrates in the Parlement, charged under their powers of *police générale* with substantial responsibility for preserving public order and decency, had done nothing to arrest such an offense against the public conscience and the laws of Church and State.[45] Indeed, he believed that the sovereign court was guilty of "displaying an excessive tolerance toward the actions of the fanatics and madmen" at Pâris' tomb.[46] Whether or not the Parlement continued to remain silent, he contended, there was enough evidence of scandal and fraud to warrant the king's issuing a formal decree authorizing M. Hérault and the other police officials in Paris to pursue "the promoters of these tumultuous assemblies and the fabricators of these counterfeit miracles" and to punish all the malefactors, both lay and clerical.[47]

But despite the importunate tone of Vintimille's pleas and despite the deep personal sympathy he felt for the archbishop's plight, Cardinal Fleury had remained reluctant to commit the authority of the crown directly in this matter. In fact, within the top echelons of the cardinal-minister's government, where discussions of the Saint-Médard problem had been going on in earnest since the beginning of the summer, opposition to direct royal interference with the Pâris cult was virtually unanimous.[48] Fears were expressed that the king's authority might become an issue in this vexed affair. Fleury himself was also worried that the monarch's involvement would represent another secular encroachment upon Vintimille's jurisdiction—a bad precedent to set, especially where the aggressively regalist Parlement of Paris was concerned.[49] Throughout July and August, therefore, Fleury had tried to avoid dealing with Vintimille's appeal, putting his friend off

[44] Vintimille to Fleury, July 15, 1731, BM, MS 2357, pp. 435-36.

[45] Vintimille to Fleury, July 13, 1731, *ibid.*, p. 430.

[46] Vintimille to Fleury, July 4, 1731, *ibid.*, pp. 423-25. Cf. letter of June 30, 1731, *ibid.*, p. 404.

[47] Vintimille to Fleury, July 13, 1731, *ibid.*, pp. 429-30; Vintimille to Fleury, July 27, 1731, *ibid.*, pp. 448-49. Cf. letter of June 30, 1731, *ibid.*, pp. 403-404. It was Vintimille's view that "depuis qu'on fabrique tous les jours de nouveaux miracles, la pluralité seule en détruit la vérité et la matière devient plus affaire de police que celle de l'Eglise" (June 24, 1731, *ibid.*, p. 402).

[48] See Fleury to Vintimille, July 30, 1731, *ibid.*, pp. 453-54, which contains a brief report of discussions held with Daguesseau, Chauvelin, Hérault, and others regarding the Pâris cult. Cf. Fleury to Vintimille, Aug. 2, 1731, *ibid.*, p. 463, and Joly de Fleury to Daguesseau, July 27, 1731, BN, J.F., MS 107, fol. 6.

[49] Fleury to Vintimille, July 1, 1731, BM, MS 2357, pp. 417-18.

with suggestions that he might at least await the impact of his *mande-ment*, which the cardinal-minister hoped might "recall many of these fanatics to their senses."[50]

Vintimille's decree had, of course, done nothing of the sort. Consequently, as summer turned into fall, and as the disturbances at Saint-Médard became more serious, other voices joined that of Vintimille in calling on the government to do something bold and dramatic to check the course of the Pâris cult. Indeed, there was no lack of advice being offered to Cardinal Fleury at this time, some of it counseling him to adopt a much harsher approach to the matter than the ever-cautious cardinal-minister was yet prepared to contemplate. The marquis d'Argenson, for example, who was just then beginning his rise into the circles of government, submitted a memorandum to the royal administration recommending that armed force be used at Saint-Médard. Writing in early September, he expressed his belief that

> the Parlement and the people of Paris are today in a situation which demands strong official action. . . . With sufficient forces one [can] overcome everything. One can command four companies of Swiss guards to seize the cemetery of Saint-Médard during the night without in any way touching the tomb of M. Pâris. It is easy to arrange this procedure and to add to it the other precautions which the *gens de guerre* may suggest in order to be confident not only of the cemetery, but [also] of the church and the entire quarter, and to prevent . . . even the least disorder.[51]

For all his own growing concern, however, Fleury still did not deem the moment opportune to risk such a drastic plan, one which seemed more likely to exacerbate than to resolve the problem. He still favored a temporizing and restrained approach—an attitude which left Vintimille feeling more than a little exasperated.

By early October, infuriated at the Parlement's recent suppression of the Inquisition's decree and unwilling to wait any longer for Fleury's dilatory administration to take some forceful action, Vintimille determined to move on his own. In a series of letters to the cardinal-minister, Vintimille proposed to issue two additional episcopal decrees

[50] Fleury to Vintimille, July 26, 1731, *ibid.*, pp. 447-48; see also Fleury to Vintimille, July 14, 1731, *ibid.*, p. 432.

[51] D'Argenson to Fleury, Sept. 4, 1731, in *Journal et mémoires du Marquis d'Argenson*, ed. E.J.B. Rathéry, 9 vols. (Paris, 1859), I, 82-83, n. 1. For a view opposing that of d'Argenson, see Joly de Fleury to Daguesseau, July 27, 1731, BN, J.F., MS 107, fol. 6. Rumors that the authorities were contemplating closing the cemetery had been circulating at least since July, especially after Vintimille published his *mandement*.

from his office, one condemning the *Vie de M. Pâris* previously censured at Rome and a second reiterating his earlier proscription of the Pâris cult and threatening with excommunication all who failed to obey.[52] Prodded by the archbishop's dramatic proposals, Cardinal Fleury summoned Hérault and his other principal civil and ecclesiastical advisers to a series of high-level strategy sessions at Versailles. Discussions were held not only to assess the advisability of Vintimille's issuing such decrees, but also to consider possible alternatives.[53] One can get some notion of the kinds of questions under debate at these meetings from examining the *Mémoire sur le culte qu'on rend au Sr. Pâris*, a long position paper which was prepared about this time by Luc Courchetet d'Esnans, legal researcher for Secretary of State Chauvelin.[54] This *mémoire* is worth looking at in some detail, for it reveals, perhaps better than any other contemporary source, the delicate problem which confronted the authorities and the nature of their thinking regarding the possible consequences of Vintimille's taking further action at this time. Courchetet's analysis also helps explain Fleury's continued hesitancy about supporting his friend's repeated calls for help.

From the outset Courchetet argued that Vintimille's proposal to forbid all observances of the "superstitious" Pâris cult and to impose the penalty of excommunication upon all who ignored the ban was too harsh and impolitic. "In the present circumstances," he contended,

> it appears that this step would be precipitous. Moreover, in the judgment of those who know the rules prescribed by the canons regarding both excommunications and the examination of new cults, it would be an imprudent action as well. It would inevitably give rise to an *appel comme d'abus*. It would stir up the people, who are greatly attached to this superstitious cult and who could [rightly] complain that we were forbidding their observances without having [previously] taken any steps to determine the cult's legitimacy.[55]

Nor, it was asserted, could Vintimille's investigation into the Anne Lefranc case still be regarded as an adequate basis for such an inter-

[52] Vintimille to Fleury, Oct. 4, 1731, BM, MS 2357, p. 516. Cf. Fleury to Daguesseau, Oct. 8, 1731, BPR, L.P. 480, No. 42 (copy).

[53] Fleury to Vintimille, Sept. 27, Oct. 2, and Oct. 5, 1731, BM, MS 2357, pp. 504, 513, and 517.

[54] AAE, M&D, France, MS 1271, fols. 60-65. Compare Courchetet's *mémoire* with similar suggestions offered by Chancellor Daguesseau at this time (BPR, L.P. 480, No. 42).

[55] AAE, M&D, France, MS 1271, fol. 60.

diction. In the first place, there were serious irregularities in the procedure which the archdiocesan authorities had followed: they had failed to call Mlle. Lefranc to testify in her own defense and had refused to hear a majority of the 120 witnesses to her cure. More important, even if the Lefranc inquiry had been properly carried out and the archbishop's findings regarded as incontestable, this single procedure was not sufficient to impose a general prohibition on the entire cult or to prove that all the other alleged Pâris miracles were similarly false.[56]

Courchetet pointed up yet other difficulties involved in attempting to take action against the religious devotions at Saint-Médard. It would be dangerous, he argued, to forbid the cult simply on the grounds that M. Pâris had been an appellant, for that pretext would serve only to provoke the very same political opposition from the *anticonstitutionnaires* which the interdiction was intended to avert. No, the supposed miracles "must be examined with exactitude, without prejudice or partisanship," so that the cult may be "proscribed on the basis of solid and numerous proofs of the falseness of the miracles." Undertaking such an objective investigation "is the only way to win back the people and remove from the Jansenists any pretext for protesting the archbishop's judgment." Only after M. Vintimille has conducted this broad and careful examination of the miracles, recognized since Trent as "one of the most essential duties of a bishop" and defined in the synodal statutes of the diocese of Paris as the exclusive responsibility of the ordinary, could his judgment on the matter be regarded as truly canonical. Nothing less could work so effectively to destroy once and for all the pretensions of the *anticonstitutionnaires* and the illusions of the people.[57]

Once M. Vintimille had brought together "a body of proper information, filled with depositions worthy of credit," Courchetet asserted, then the archbishop could proceed to prohibit further practice of the cult and even close the cemetery in which it was being observed.[58] In publishing such a ban, Vintimille could also threaten with sanctions those who willfully ignored the prohibition: excommunication in the case of disobedient faithful and suspension from their functions in the case of obdurate priests. To support these severe penalties he could also place the church of Saint-Médard under an interdict: "this interdict

---

[56] *Ibid.* "Toutes les procédures particulières sont des degrés pour arriver, ou à autoriser, ou à défendre un culte; mais il seroit sans exemple, que sur une procédure unique & irrégulière, on prononçat l'interdiction générale de quelque culte" (*ibid.*, fol. 61).

[57] *Ibid.*, fols. 60-61.   [58] *Ibid.*, fol. 62.

would be the last, and the most effective, procedure for arresting the course of the superstition."[59] Almost as if to reassure those who might have doubted the wisdom of such a plan of action, Courchetet expressed the conviction that it

> would be [not only] a sensible procedure [but] one that was safe from any *appel comme d'abus*. The archbishop would have issued a pronouncement on a matter which is unquestionably within his competence, he would have taken all the necessary steps for ascertaining the truth, [and] he would have employed spiritual penalties only with prudence and on a rather important occasion. . . .[60]

Failure to follow this procedure, he concluded, would surely result in an *appel comme d'abus* from the archbishop's sentence to the Parlement of Paris:

> in the present situation, the prohibition of this cult could have no other motive than the appeal of M. Pâris; and far from calming the people, the priests, and the Parlement by this explanation, we will see all Paris rise up against the prohibition and ensure the continuation of this cult in order to indicate their sentiments toward the Bull and toward the appeals which have been lodged against it.[61]

Despite the apparent soundness of Courchetet's arguments, he failed to persuade Vintimille or any of the other staunch *constitutionnaires* around Cardinal Fleury. They objected to undertaking a full-scale investigation into the truth or falsity of the miracles at this late stage, insisting that such an extraordinary procedure would be far too time-consuming, and that the danger posed by the "false and superstitious" Pâris cult was already much too serious to risk the delay which a complete and thorough inquest would entail. Vintimille himself argued that to embark on a series of new investigations would represent a capitulation to the *anticonstitutionnaires* and "might give rise to speculation that I am prepared to admit the authenticity of the supposed miracles which the appellants claim are proof that the truth is on their side."[62] The archbishop wished to hold fast to his original proposal.[63]

---

[59] *Ibid.*, fols. 62-63. [60] *Ibid.*, fol. 62.

[61] *Ibid.*

[62] Vintimille to Fleury, Oct. 4, 1731, BM, MS 2357, p. 515. Cf. Daguesseau to Fleury, Oct. 1, 1731, BPR, L.P. 480, No. 42.

[63] Cf. Vintimille to Fleury, Oct. 3, 1731, BM, MS 2357, p. 514; and Fleury to Daguesseau, Oct. 4, 1731, BPR, L.P. 480, No. 42.

Cardinal Fleury, hesitant as always, feared the potential difficulties and complications spelled out in Courchetet's persuasive *mémoire*. He was equally concerned that Vintimille's threat to excommunicate those who disobeyed his orders might affect upwards of 12,000 persons.[64] On the other hand, recent developments at Saint-Médard, where the abbé Bescherand and others had begun to experience almost daily convulsions, gave indications that the situation there might be getting out of hand. While still believing that an extensive archiepiscopal investigation into the alleged miracles of M. Pâris was the best means of disabusing the people of their "superstitious credulity," the cardinal-minister also understood that the problem would brook no further delay. As Fleury and most of his advisers had likewise come to realize, the best way of coping with this matter was to make more effective use of the Paris police while simultaneously reducing the public role of the archdiocesan authorities. Such a policy had at least two practical advantages to commend it to the royal government. In the first place, given the nature of recent developments in ecclesiastical politics, a "secular" or "civil" strategy might prove far less objectionable to the Parlement of Paris than the previous episcopal pronouncements and clerical procedures. What is more, reducing the role of the ecclesiastical authorities would diminish the possibility of *appels comme d'abus*, thereby depriving the cult's adherents of any legal recourse to the sovereign court, and hence restrict, if not eliminate, the magistrates' future institutional (judicial) involvement in the affair. Finally, by turning the problem over to the police, the cardinal-minister could satisfy Vintimille's longstanding complaint that the crown had failed to give him adequate support in circumstances of dire necessity. In the end, Fleury, no longer content to let events just take their course, embarked on an "experiment" which marked the first of a series of significant actions that the civil authorities were to take against the followers of M. Pâris.

Not far from Saint-Médard, in the house on the rue des Bourguignons where the deacon had once dwelled, someone had set up a little chapel which became a popular center of worship and assembly for the faithful.[65] In addition to the shrine, devotees of the cult were also attracted by a well in the back of the house which contained water re-

[64] Fleury to Vintimille, Oct. 17, 1731, BM, MS 2357, p. 526; and Fleury to Daguesseau, Oct. 8, 1731, BPR, L.P. 480, No. 42. The cardinal-minister was more than a little disturbed by Vintimille's "stubbornness," his "obstructive behavior," and his "dangerous proposals" (letter to Daguesseau, Oct. 4, 1731, BPR, L.P. 480, No. 42).

[65] See undated and unsigned "Note relative à la maison où est mort M. de Pâris," BA, MS 10200.

puted to have miraculous health-giving properties.[66] Since a cabinet-maker and several other artisans and their families still occupied most of the apartments, it proved too inconvenient to close up the entire house. But the authorities could at least bar access to the well and to Pâris' former apartment, a task which the crown entrusted to the police. Armed with a *lettre de cachet* dated October 4,[67] Hérault appointed two of his men to clear out the sanctuary and then posted one of them in front of the building in order to prevent anyone from entering who was not a resident there.[68] By Hérault's own account more than a thousand people had to be turned away in the course of the first day. But his officers carried out this operation with so little fanfare and with such unexpected ease that the police lieutenant was prompted to caution the royal administration against exaggerating the implications or even the extent of their accomplishment. "Indeed," he wrote Daguesseau, "[the people] appear so calm that if I still feel any fear it is that the success of this first effort may create the presumption that there will be a similar result from [undertaking] another, riskier operation."[69]

To the editor of the *Nouvelles ecclésiastiques* the action taken by the police was an "unheard-of precaution" and constituted "the first act of force in which the authority of the king has been employed against the word of God."[70] In this sense the closing of M. Pâris' former residence was perhaps a foreshadowing of the much more problematical and controversial enterprise undertaken early the following year at Saint-Médard. Nor was the interdiction of the deacon's apartment and well the only significant police intervention to occur at this time.

Less than a week later the police received further orders from the crown authorizing them to remove the sacristan of Saint-Médard, Sr. Martin, and the *vicaire* of that parish, Sr. Graffard, from their posts.[71]

---

[66] *Histoire des miracles et du culte de M. Pâris*, p. 102.

[67] AN, O¹ 75, p. 404.

[68] Hérault to Fleury, Oct. 4, 1731, BA, MS 10196; Hérault to Daguesseau, Oct. 5, 1731, *ibid*. See also *NNEE*, Jan. 30, 1732, p. 18. A police guard remained stationed in front of the door for over four months, frequently "doing nothing during the day except play cards with someone from the neighborhood" (*ibid.*). He was finally removed in March 1732, but only with the stipulation that the cabinet-maker, Lieutaud, would assume full responsibility for debarring the public (Maurepas to Hérault, March 7, 1732, AN, O¹ 379, p. 47; Hérault to Lieutaud, March 7, 1732, BA, MS 10196; and *NNEE*, April 4, 1732, p. 67).

[69] Letter of Oct. 5, 1731, BA, MS 10196. Cf. Fleury to Vintimille, Oct. 17, 1731, BM, MS 2357, p. 527; and Fleury to Daguesseau, Oct. 8, 1731, BPR, L.P. 480, No. 42.

[70] Jan. 30, 1731, p. 18.

[71] AN, O¹ 378, p. 294. Martin had replaced the notorious Collet Desroches,

The abbé Coëffrel had long been complaining to Vintimille about both men, and the archbishop had recently conveyed these complaints to Cardinal Fleury.[72] The sacristan, who (like his predecessor) was accused of authorizing the innumerable Masses celebrated at the church in memory of François de Pâris and of distributing relics associated with the deacon, was exiled to Reims, the diocese from which he had originally come. The *vicaire*, who was charged with "contradicting and embarrassing M. Coëffrel" and with encouraging the veneration of M. Pâris, was likewise banished from the capital. But if Fleury expected these various police actions somehow to discourage the faithful from practicing their cult, he was quite mistaken. They succeeded only in further frustrating these people without appreciably disrupting their observances at the cemetery.

In subsequent weeks and months, however, the police stepped up their harassment of the cult's practitioners and many of their *anticonstitutionnaire* allies. Throughout the fall, numerous persons were arrested "pour jansénisme" and sent to the Bastille.[73] In November the police closed down the famous Jansenist Seminary of the Thirty-Three, the party's last remaining theological establishment in Paris.[74] Hérault, in the meantime, had embarked on a semiofficial investigation into the Pâris miracles—a task that Vintimille had declined to undertake. The police lieutenant examined more than a dozen alleged cures attributed to the deacon Pâris' intercession, including several of the most celebrated ones which had reportedly occurred since the archbishop's *mandement* of July.[75] He or his representative visited the supposed

whom the police had exiled from Paris some months earlier (see BA, MS 11140, fols. 173-216).

[72] Vintimille to Fleury, Sept. 24, 1731, BM, MS 2357, p. 504; Vintimille to Fleury, Oct. 3, 1731, *ibid.*, pp. 513-14; Fleury to Vintimille, Oct. 5, 1731, *ibid.*, p. 518; and Vintimille to Fleury, Oct. 6, 1731, *ibid.*, pp. 523-24.

[73] Arrests are reported, for example, in Ravaisson, xiv, 285 and 306; *NNEE*, Jan. 24, 1732, p. 15, and March 5, 1732, p. 42; Barbier, ii, 212 (November 1731); Marais, iv, 314 (Oct. 31, 1731); Funck-Brentano, pp. 243-44; and BA, MS 11151, fols. 66-81. See also the report of the police agent Guillotte to Hérault, Oct. 29, 1731, BA, MS 10196.

[74] *NNEE*, Dec. 20, 1731, p. 248, Dec. 29, 1731, pp. 253-56, and Dec. 31, 1731, pp. 261-62. According to the *Nouvellistes*, "c'étoit la seule à Paris qui fût entièrement saine pour la théologie." In October 1730 Hérault had similarly closed down the Community of Sainte-Barbe and handed it over to the *constitutionnaires* (*ibid.*, Oct. 26, 1730, pp. 225-26).

[75] What follows is based primarily on a *mémoire* entitled "Miracles prétendus opérés par l'intercession de M. Pâris sur les dénommés cy-après" (BPR, L.P. 17, fols. 949-65). These papers form part of the manuscripts belonging to Chancellor

miraculés, talked to their neighbors, friends, and relatives, and discussed their cases with various medical experts; Hérault even had doctors of his own choosing examine some of them. Upon concluding his inquiry, Hérault reported that most of the cures had been incomplete and imperfect, involving only a temporary or partial remission of certain symptoms; a few had even been followed by serious relapses. In some instances the "facts" in the case appeared to him too equivocal to be susceptible of definitive verification or refutation. In several cases, however, he claimed to have seen clear evidence of "Jansenist maneuvers" and "pious frauds." In others he attributed the would-be cures to fertile imaginations born of excessive hopes. Where the cures seemed to be complete and permanent, Hérault ascribed them to natural causes. But there was little Hérault could do with these findings, except to forward them to Versailles, since the responsibility for formally pronouncing on the miracles still lay exclusively with Vintimille.[76] What is more, despite the nature of his conclusions and despite the police lieutenant's own intimidating presence, he was apparently unable to persuade any of these people to come forward and publicly repudiate the Pâris cult or even shake their basic conviction in the thaumaturgic powers of their saintly deacon.

For all their efforts at harassment and intimidation of persons devoted to the cult to François de Pâris, the police had still not managed to make much of an impact on the public observances going on at Saint-Médard. Moreover, police reports from the cemetery itself had been sounding a note of growing desperation. Hérault's officers stationed there seemed totally flustered by and helpless before the convulsive manifestations of M. Pâris' adherents. As early as August 4 had come the exasperated declaration that, "in truth, what is happening here is a scandal for which a remedy is urgently needed." A later report, on November 8, sounded even more desperate: "The gatherings are increasing daily and a row is inevitable if no solution is found."[77] The mere presence of the police had done little or nothing to check

---

Daguesseau; according to a note in Daguesseau's own hand, "Ce mémoire m'a été remis par M. Hérault le 14 Janvier 1732. Mes notes sont du 17 suivant."

[76] As soon as Hérault's *mémoire* was turned over to Daguesseau, the chancellor undertook to compose a series of memoranda of his own. These extraordinarily revealing documents (BPR, L.P. 480, No. 66 [copy]) contain Daguesseau's views on the problem of miracles in general and those allegedly operated at Saint-Médard in particular (cf. discussion in Armogathe, pp. 151-52). They also include an assessment of the various arguments both for and against the government's taking some form of action to halt the observances at the cemetery.

[77] Both reports are in BA, MS 10196.

the convulsions or to reduce the crowds in daily attendance. Something more than just half-measures was required to stifle these people, or so it seemed to most of the authorities concerned.

By December and early January, papal representatives in Rome and France, and even the pope himself, had begun exerting renewed pressure on Versailles to close down the cemetery.[78] The abbé Rota, the troublesome *auditeur* of the papal nuncio in Paris, had been plaguing Vintimille for many weeks, blaming the archbishop for the fact that the cemetery remained open and trying to goad him into publishing his *mandement* against the *Vie de M. Pâris, diacre*.[79] Cardinal Annibal Albani warned of "the imminent apostasy of all Paris as a result of the gatherings which assemble at Saint-Médard." Clement XII, alarmed at the "great perversity" of masses of Parisians, exhorted the king to intervene at once to remedy this dangerous situation.[80]

Ever the cautious, methodical royal minister, Cardinal Fleury was still not prepared to act too precipitously. The one thing that was already quite clear to him was that Vintimille and the other more vehement *constitutionnaire* prelates who had been clamoring for immediate action had become too much of a religious and political liability to be permitted to launch another full-scale ecclesiastical attack upon the Pâris cult. Further action on the part of the bishops, especially Vintimille, might exacerbate an already delicate situation. Indeed, developments in the late fall and early winter seemed to emphasize the possible risks associated with any further attempts to achieve an ecclesiastical solution to the "monstrous scene" at Saint-Médard.[81] Though by early December Fleury had finally negotiated a compromise with the *avocats* which ended their three-month strike,[82] the magistrates in

78 See Polignac to Chauvelin, Dec. 27, 1731, AAE, C.P., Rome, MS 725, fol. 375; Polignac to Chauvelin, Jan. 3, 1732, *ibid.*, MS 730, fol. 6; Delci to Fleury, Jan. 8, 1732, *ibid.*, M&D, Fonds divers (Rome), MS 61, fols. 447-48.

79 Vintimille to Fleury, Nov. 1, Dec. 1, 7, and 10, 1731, BM, MS 2357, pp. 540, 570, 575-76, 579. Cf. Fleury to Vintimille, Dec. 10 and 13, 1731, *ibid.*, pp. 577, 580. On Rota, see Hanotaux, III, 94-95.

80 These views are reported in Polignac's letters to Chauvelin at this time (see n. 78, above). Marais and Barbier, incidentally, both reflect a similar impatience with the government's failure to take decisive action (Marais, IV, 316 [Nov. 6, 1731], IV, 326 [Dec. 11, 1731]; Barbier, II, 224, 230-31 [December 1731-January 1732]).

81 Fleury to Vintimille, Dec. 10, 1731, BM, MS 2357, p. 577; and Vintimille to Fleury, Dec. 10, 1731, *ibid.*, p. 579.

82 Maurepas to Joly de Fleury, Dec. 1, 1731, BN, J.F., MS 100, fol. 223; *Arrêt du conseil*, Dec. 1, 1731, AN, E2113, fols. 264-65; Barbier, II, 221 (December 1731). The strike had begun the previous August, in response to the government's refusal to give the *avocats* satisfaction in their complaint against Vintimille for

the Parlement of Paris, recently returned from their annual vacation, were as stubbornly obstructive as ever.[83] Still refusing to acquiesce in the *conseil d'état*'s suppression of their Gallican decree of September 7, and determined to challenge the council's authority to silence them, the judges persisted in claiming the right as well as the duty to protect the "fundamental maxims of royal authority" against clerical encroachment. From late November to mid-January, while Fleury was busy discussing plans for dealing with the Pâris cult, several spokesmen for the Parlement continued furiously to press their case before the king and his ministers. But the magistrates' desperate efforts to regain their "traditional liberties" proved unsuccessful.[84] Even so, Cardinal Fleury could not have failed to see that the Saint-Médard affair, if carelessly or improperly handled, might prove to be a tempting issue for the magistrates to drag into their debate with the crown and the *constitutionnaire* episcopate.

Under the circumstances, Fleury was more than ever persuaded of the need for the crown to assume direct responsibility for interdicting the observances at Pâris' tomb and to give Hérault's police authority for actually closing the cemetery of Saint-Médard. Not only was there reason to expect a greater degree of public compliance with orders emanating from the king's council than there had been with those promulgated at the archiepiscopal palace,[85] but the crown's continued resort to the Paris police also gave at least the semblance of nonpartisanship, thereby eliminating the risk of offending the touchy sensibilities of the Parlement regarding alleged abuses of ecclesiastical authority. Nor could the *constitutionnaire* episcopate charge the civil

---

having insulted them. On the *procureur-général*'s role in the negotiations which brought the barristers back to their studies, see BN, J.F., MS 100, *passim*. This volume also contains a series of *mémoires* and projected *arrêts* on the same affair; cf. additional position papers in AAE, M&D, France, MS 1271, fols. 225-28, 348-49. For Vintimille's views of the *arrêt* which finally recalled the exiled *avocats*, see his letter to Fleury, Dec. 3, 1731, *ibid.*, fols. 72-74.

[83] Daguesseau to Joly de Fleury, Dec. 15, 1731, BN, J.F., MS 101, fol. 197.

[84] On the Parlement's struggles to reaffirm its authority over *la police ecclésiastique*, see the "Procès-verbaux de ce qui s'est passé au Parlement depuis et compris le 23 août 1731, jusqu'au janvier [1732] inclusivement," in *Mémoires du Président Hénault*, pp. 363-84. See also Barbier, II, 235-36 (January 1732), and Flammermont, I, 276-77.

[85] Indeed, as Chancellor Daguesseau had observed in the aftermath of the successful police operation at the deacon's former residence, "La facilité que M. Hérault a trouvée pour empêcher le concours qui se fesoit à la maison de M. Pâris montre que le nom du Roi fait plus d'impression sur le peuple que l'autorité de M. l'archevêque" (letter to Fleury, Oct. 10, 1731, BPR, L.P. 480, No. 42 [copy]).

authorities with encroaching on its preserve: the convulsions and the large crowds and disturbing spectacles they had recently created in the parish of Saint-Médard represented as great a threat to public order and morality as they did to orthodox Christian faith and therefore came legitimately under secular jurisdiction. Having thus decided to entrust the police with responsibility for shutting down the cemetery, the royal government had still to determine the most opportune moment for carrying out the action and to find a convincing justification for doing so.

The first problem was easy enough to solve. With the onset of winter it was natural to expect that fewer people would be coming to Saint-Médard. Even though Bescherand continued to make the twice-daily appearances that attracted a fairly substantial following, the police reports at this time tended to confirm this expectation.[86] It would seem that this was the moment to act, if the authorities wished to minimize popular discontent.

There still remained the second problem, that of finding a justification for the closing. To be sure, the disorder which certain people were reportedly causing at Pâris' tomb would seem to have afforded an eminently reasonable pretext for proceeding against them. The government, however, apparently decided that an investigation of the convulsionaries ought to be undertaken first. Fleury and his advisers believed that they would be able to make a far more convincing case against the practitioners of the cult if they could effectively demonstrate that, in addition to disturbing the peace, the followers of M. Pâris were practicing pious frauds at Saint-Médard. Such a demonstration, it was hoped, might forestall possible criticism of or interference with the subsequent course of action from *curés*, magistrates, or *avocats*.

The cardinal-minister's concern to avoid arousing the magistrates in the matter of the Pâris cult still had some basis in fact. Indeed, in early January, with preparations already under way for closing Saint-Médard, Fleury's plans appeared to have suffered a potentially dangerous setback. Word had begun to circulate around the Palais de Justice that certain magistrates were on the point of reviving the Anne Lefranc case, left pending since the previous September. On January 12, 1732, Chancellor Daguesseau sent a letter to Joly de Fleury expressing the cardinal-minister's concern over this troublesome news and asking the *procureur-général* "to take all possible steps to head off the affair" before it became serious.[87] The whole matter turned out to be an un-

[86] See BA, MS 10196; cf. Mousset, p. 63.
[87] BN, J.F., MS 107, fol. 91.

founded rumor.[88] It is nevertheless a measure of his uneasiness that Fleury wished to make certain that the Parlement was not about to create another disturbance. The royal government and the Paris police could now proceed, uninterrupted, to implement their solution to the Saint-Médard question.

For a long time the partisans of the Pâris cult, especially among the *curés*, had been clamoring for a canonical investigation of the miracles. On several occasions they had called on the archbishop of Paris to set up a public commission for the purpose of conducting a thorough and just hearing. However, despite the recommendations made in Courchetet's *Mémoire sur le culte qu'on rend au Sr. Pâris*, their various requests had continually fallen on deaf ears. Instead of trying to determine once and for all the nature of the allegedly miraculous cures, the ecclesiastical authorities had tried to stifle all publicity about them. Nor had Hérault's "civil inquest" into these cures been a satisfactory substitute for Vintimille's continued silence, at least insofar as the *anticonstitutionnaires* were concerned. Nevertheless, from the point of view of the authorities, the lieutenant of police had done a thoroughly creditable job of challenging the authenticity of the miracles, even if his findings had to be left unpublished. It was to Hérault, therefore, that Fleury turned once again for an investigation of the "profane and scandalous comedy" of the convulsions.[89]

In the formal charge to Hérault, Fleury commissioned the lieutenant of police to arrest a group of convulsionaries at Saint-Médard and to engage a number of notable doctors and surgeons to examine them at the Bastille. Between January 9 and January 22 the police rounded up some nine or ten persons, most of them obscure convulsionaries "de la plus vile populace."[90] The series of intensive interrogations and medical examinations of the prisoners, which took two weeks to complete,

[88] Joly de Fleury to Daguesseau, *ibid.*, fol. 94. Joly de Fleury concluded his letter by reminding the chancellor that, since August, "nous avons eu l'honneur de vous rendre compte (et à M. le Cardinal de Fleury) que la Requête nous ayant été renvoyé de la Grand'Chambre au Parquet avec un soit montré, nous avions résolu nos conclusions à rendre la Requête à la partie, ce qui fut alors approuvés" (*ibid.*).

[89] See abbé Gaillande to Fleury, Jan. 14, 1732, AAE, M&D, Ile de France, MS 1599, fols. 212-13.

[90] Funck-Brentano, pp. 244-45. Of those whose socioeconomic standing is known we have the following: *couturière, gagne-deniers, garçon boucher, apprenti bourrelier, cuisinier*, and *ouvrière en dentelles*. In other words, no convulsionary of status was arrested at this time.

began on January 11.[91] The first individual to be questioned was Pierre-Martin Gontier, arrested that very morning while returning from a visit to Saint-Médard, where he had been taken with convulsions. Gontier had been going to Pâris' tomb since August, though he had not experienced convulsions at the cemetery until November.[92] Hérault and several members of the Bastille administration, along with two doctors and two surgeons who just happened to be at the police lieutenant's *hôtel* "on personal business," served as Gontier's inquisitors. From the outset they treated him as an impostor. After conducting a long interrogation/examination, filled with hostile leading questions, the authorities managed to induce Gontier "to swear that he had willfully caused himself to have convulsions." The subject, they observed, had even "volunteered on his own to perform the same movements in their presence." They reported that he began by "first stiffening his legs and then shaking them, while contorting his body in various shapes." He repeated these convulsive agitations twice in the space of an hour and a half, during which time (not too surprisingly) "his pulse became more rapid." Then, all of a sudden, his movements ceased. The whole demonstration, his examiners concluded, was proof that Gontier "could bring on convulsions whenever he wished to do so."[93] As further confirmation of their conclusions, Hérault and the others obtained Gontier's signature on a certificate containing the medical *procès-verbal*, which the police lieutenant sent on to Fleury that same day.[94]

Satisfied that he had gotten all the information he could from so cooperative a witness, Hérault decided to release Gontier the next day. He quickly regretted that decision. No sooner was he set free than Gontier, "deeply repenting his crime," took steps to expiate it. According to a report in the *Nouvelles ecclésiatiques*, Gontier drew up a declaration in which he protested before God and man that his confessions as well as his signature had been forcibly extorted from him.

Finally, in order to render the apology as public as the crime, he made his way on the afternoon of January 14 to the little cemetery

[91] Copies of these interrogations may be found in BA, MS 11199, fols. 118-30, MS 11193, fols. 87-132, and MS 11207, fols. 235-50; BPR, L.P. 480, No. 64. This last reference is to Hérault's summaries of twelve interrogations and three declarations, documents which the lieutenant of police sent to Chancellor Daguesseau on February 9.

[92] Vintimille to Fleury, Jan. 14, 1732, BM, MS 2357, p. 599.

[93] *Procès-verbaux de plusieurs médecins et chirurgiens dressés par ordre du Roi* (Paris, 1732), pp. 1-3.

[94] *Ibid.*, p. 3. Cf. Vintimille to Fleury, Jan. 14, 1732, BM, MS 2357, p. 599.

of Saint-Médard. There, in the presence of a large throng of people from every station in society, including a considerable number of priests and *avocats* and several presidents and counselors from the Parlement of Paris, he mounted the tomb of [M. Pâris]. People stopped reciting psalms, a great silence overcame the whole place, and Gontier read the following declaration:

> In the name of the Father, etc. I declare before God and before all men that . . . I abhor, I detest and retract these lies . . . [which] the threats of M. Hérault intimidated me into telling and signing. . . . I beg God's pardon for them, and I pray the blessed François de Pâris to intercede on my behalf in order that I may obtain the remission of my sin, the grace which is necessary for the cure of my soul, and the perfection of the cure of my body, if that is the will of God. I earnestly beseech those present to be so kind as to pray to God that He pardon me for such a heinous sin and to bear witness with me by affixing [their] signatures to the present declaration.[95]

After a large number of those in attendance had signed the declaration, the assembled company escorted Gontier into a waiting carriage which spirited him off into hiding. "Ever since that memorable day," the *Nouvellistes* noted, "Gontier has been much sought after [and] at great expense, but God has kept him sheltered."[96]

Gontier's public retraction forced an embarrassed Hérault to be considerably more prudent in his subsequent examinations. On January 15, the day following Gontier's dramatic appearance at Saint-Médard, Hérault again summoned several doctors and surgeons to the Bastille for the purpose of examining and interrogating two other convulsionaries arrested that same day. The doctors alleged that these men, like Gontier, were also capable of "performing" at will, that their "convulsive" movements and agitations were not at all supernatural. Additional examinations of still other convulsionaries conducted during the following days produced much the same results. Some confessed that they had "feigned" having convulsions while at Saint-Médard, arguing that they did so only because they had learned that such convulsions were supposed to be an indispensable prerequisite to the cures for which they had gone to Pâris' tomb in the first place. Those who were

---

[95] *NNEE*, Feb. 5, 1732, p. 24. See also Vintimille to Fleury, Jan. 14, 1732, BM, MS 2357, pp. 599-600, and police report for the same date, BA, MS 10196, both of which confirm the essential details of the *Nouvellistes'* account. The police, incidentally, counted forty-seven ecclesiastics present at the cemetery on that day.

[96] *NNEE*, Feb. 5, 1732, p. 24.

prepared to make such admissions nevertheless disclaimed any fraudulent intent. They had acted not out of greed nor from a desire for personal material gain, but out of a need to be like the other convulsionaries at the cemetery, around whom the admiring faithful would regularly gather and pray for the deacon's intercession. Not all of the prisoners under interrogation, however, were so quick to admit to such "misbehavior" or "misrepresentation." A few required a second grueling interrogation before they were prepared to admit what an obviously biased Hérault wanted to hear. There were even a few who, though subjected to two such intensive grillings, continued to insist that their bodily agitations were completely "forced and involuntary."[97] But such testimony, like other evidence that was not to their liking, the authorities ultimately set aside and ignored.

Having virtually completed his examinations, a circumspect Hérault was anxious to take every precaution possible to preclude a repetition of the Gontier fiasco. On January 23 he summoned a general assembly of some two dozen doctors and surgeons to consider the five principal cases—Jean Fiet, Claude-François Tiersault, Pierre Lahir, Marie Tassiaux, and Guillaume-Antoine Maupoint—for a second time, ostensibly to review the findings of the original medical examinations, which they certified unanimously.[98] In addition to the precaution of a medical review, Hérault also decided not to release the prisoners immediately, choosing instead to exercise his discretionary authority and detaining them for periods ranging from eleven to fourteen months.[99] Finally, after consulting with Fleury, he gathered together the findings compiled in the previous two weeks and had them published, along with the carefully written medical attestations, in the *Procès-verbaux de plusieurs médecins et chirurgiens dressés par ordre du Roi.*

Hérault had done his job well. Save for his miscalculation in the Gontier affair, which was not entirely his fault, he had obtained for the government "incontrovertible proof" that fraud and deception were present at Saint-Médard.[100] On the basis of these "medical examinations," conducted in secret and at the Bastille instead of in public and at the very cemetery where the alleged crimes were being com-

[97] BPR, L.P. 480, No. 64. None of this testimony was to find its way into the official *procès-verbaux.*

[98] Hérault to [Chauvelin ?], Jan. 23, 1732, AAE, M&D, France, MS 1274, fol. 125.

[99] Funck-Brentano, pp. 244-45.

[100] "Une preuve bien autentique de la friponerie dont le parti s'est servi pour abuser de la simplicité des peuples" (Vintimille to Fleury, Jan. 23, 1732, BM, MS 2357, p. 607).

mitted, supervised and judged by Hérault and other hostile parties, and performed on only a handful of convulsionaries, thousands of participants in the Pâris cult were to be deprived of their holy sanctuary.[101] The authorities, who continued to ignore the miracles,[102] had made no attempt to undertake a full and public investigation at Saint-Médard or even to examine any of the more important and celebrated convulsionaries, such as the abbé Bescherand, the chevalier de Folard, or the marquis de Légal.[103] The findings of Hérault's "juridical investigations" thus proved to be decisive, and on January 27, 1732, Louis XV issued the famous *Ordonnance du Roi qui ordonne que la porte du petit cimetière de la paroisse Saint-Médard sera et demeurera fermé.*[104]

The drafters of the royal ordinance had taken much care not to arouse such politically sensitive groups as the Paris *curés* and the magistrates in the Parlement. The convulsions—and the lawlessness and public disorder which they had allegedly occasioned—were cited as the principal justification for the government's action. While the decree made direct reference to Vintimille's *mandement* of the previous July and to the insubordination of priests and faithful in refusing to heed its proscriptions,[105] the government studiously avoided any specific mention of the miraculous cures which had preceded the con-

---

[101] *NNEE*, Feb. 11, 1732, p. 26. The authenticity and legitimacy of Hérault's investigations were almost immediately called into question by others as well. Just before his death in March 1732, M. Chirac, one of the doctors involved in the Bastille examinations, was rumored to have issued a declaration formally and completely renouncing the statements contained in the *procès-verbaux* and declaring the lieutenant of police responsible for most of their contents (*Gazetins de la police*, March 9, 1732, BA, MS 10161).

[102] In doing so they ran the risk of further alienating the deacon Pâris' faithful adherents. A concerned Joly de Fleury had apparently discussed this very point with Hérault at the *Assemblée de Police* held on January 17: "ces démarches augmentoient de jour en jour les préjugés du public en faveur des miracles" (BN, MSS Fr., MS 11356, fol. 176).

[103] Bescherand was not arrested until February 23, when the authorities, on the urging of his uncle, the zealous *constitutionnaire* abbé of Saint-Polycarpe, sent him to Saint-Lazare (*NNEE*, Feb. 23, 1732, p. 36, and Feb. 29, 1732, p. 37). Shortly before his arrest, Bescherand had sent Vintimille an impassioned defense of the convulsionaries (copy in printed catalogue of Henri Saffroy, No. 50, November 1966, BHVP, C.P., MS 3522). Folard had been threatened with the loss of his pension and incarceration in the Bastille until his friend, the comte de Belle-Isle, intervened to save him (Godefroy, p. 159).

[104] Text in Isambert, XXI, 369.

[105] To the archbishop's great satisfaction (Vintimille to Fleury, Jan. 29, 1732, BM, MS 2357, p. 610; cf. Chauvelin to Polignac, Jan. 29, 1732, AAE, C.P., Rome, MS 730, fol. 61).

vulsions and which had still not received a proper canonical examination.[106] Drawing their evidence exclusively from Hérault's collection of medical findings and the reports of the police agents stationed at Saint-Médard, the composers of the decree denounced the convulsions as an odious and fraudulent scandal which constituted a threat to public order, both civil and religious.[107] The crowds of people, the ordinance observed, had provided "the uninterrupted occasion for licentious discourses, thievery, and libertinage." The decree was thus designed to put a stop to these large-scale assemblies as well as to the displays of convulsionary agitations. To this end the crown not only ordered the closing of the cemetery, but also prohibited all persons, "whatever their rank or quality," from gathering in nearby streets or houses. Finally, the government charged Hérault and the police with responsibility for carrying out the edict's provisions and granted the lieutenant-general wide discretionary authority to do so.[108]

The next day, January 28, Hérault communicated the decree, along with a brief covering letter, to the churchwardens of Saint-Médard, who held the keys to the churchyard and normally had charge of actually locking the gates.[109] After encountering some initial resistance from several of the principal *marguilliers*, Hérault managed to persuade them to follow his instructions.[110] Before proceeding to the execution of the ordinance, however, the lieutenant of police spent the better part of the day making various arrangements to ensure the fullest possible compliance with the king's orders.

The time had finally come to close the cemetery. At four o'clock on the morning of January 29, the cavalry patrol (*guet à cheval*), accompanied by a sizable contingent of armed guards, made its way through the *faubourg* Saint-Marceau. The men carried copies of the royal ordinance which they posted all around, but "very high, for fear that they would be ripped down. . . ."[111] Taking extraordinary pre-

---

[106] This tactical maneuver was suggested by Chancellor Daguesseau (BPR, L.P. 480, No. 66), who feared that to discuss the Saint-Médard miracles and to question their reality without having first conducted a full canonical investigation would only play into the hands of the *incrédules*.

[107] See the wily observation of Cardinal Polignac: "C'est un coup du ciel que les appellants ayent eu recours à ces contorsions, qui semblent n'avoir augmenté l'attention du public que pour vous mettre plus en état d'approfondir l'imposture" (letter to Chauvelin, Feb. 14, 1732, AAE, C.P., Rome, MS 730, fol. 241).

[108] "Lettre à Hérault pour faire fermer le petit cimetière de Saint-Médard," Jan. 27, 1732, AN, O¹ 76, fols. 32-33.

[109] Hérault to Sr. Moynerie, BA, MS 10196.

[110] Journal of De Lisle, Jan. 28, 1732, AN, U-377.

[111] Barbier, II, 242-43 (January 1732).

cautions against anticipated popular disturbances in and around the *faubourg*, the police stationed ten guards, some on horseback, others disguised in civilian clothes, at the church and cemetery and deployed three additional brigades of men—upwards of 700 to 800 was one estimate[112]—in the streets all throughout the neighborhood, where they were to remain posted around the clock for the next several days. At the same time, Hérault sent thirty additional men to help watch over François de Pâris' former residence on the rue des Bourguignons, which the authorities expected to be swarming with people once they saw they no longer had access to the deacon's tomb. The entire operation was like a well-planned, carefully coordinated military "expedition." Under these circumstances it is not too surprising that the actual execution of the ordinance proved rather easy.[113] By late morning, in addition to a considerable number of carriages parked in the nearby streets, observers noted large, but orderly crowds of people milling about outside the gates of the cemetery as well as within the church of Saint-Médard, where many of them heard Mass and said their prayers. Copies of the *procès-verbaux* from the Bastille investigations were hawked in the streets in justification of the police action. Aside from some mild expressions of disgruntlement uttered by a handful of ecclesiastics and *menu peuple*, the execution of the decree proceeded virtually without incident. Where all previous efforts, including those of Vintimille, had failed, Hérault's men seemed at last to have triumphed over the Pâris cult. As Marais perceptively observed, "Monseigneur the archbishop has won the confirmation of his decree of July 15, [while] the temporal power has gotten the upper hand . . . over the ecclesiastical power . . . M. Hérault has managed to carry out a great police action."[114]

The royal authorities did not stop, however, with the ordinance of January 27. "As God is everywhere the same," noted the editor of the *Nouvelles ecclésiastiques* sarcastically, Fleury found it necessary to suppress additional manifestations of the cult outside of Paris.[115] He

---

[112] Journal of De Lisle, Jan. 29, 1732, AN, U-377.

[113] [Hérault?] to [Chauvelin?], Jan. 29, 1732, AAE, M&D, France, MS 1274, fols. 124-25; Hérault to Fleury, Jan. 29, 1732, *ibid.*, Ile de France, MS 1599, fols. 285-86.

[114] IV, 335-36 (Jan. 31, 1732). Cf. the comments of the *greffier* De Lisle: "Que le Roy estoit le maistre il est vrai, mais qu'il mettoit la main à l'encensoir contre les droits de M. l'archevêque et des évêques, lesquels pourroient s'en plaindre comme une entreprise sur leur jurisdiction et bien d'autres choses . . ." (Jan. 29, 1732, AN, U-377).

[115] "Supplément pour 1732," p. iv. Complaints about the spreading "fanaticism of Saint-Médard" had already reached Vintimille from dioceses all over France,

sent out copies of the ordinance to the provincial intendants and governors, along with a covering letter enjoining them to prevent "the same scandal from spreading into . . . the cities and places under their jurisdiction" and authorizing them to prohibit assemblies of people from gathering to practice their observances.[116] In the interest of religious peace, Fleury also ordered these provincial officials to prohibit any unauthorized investigations of allegedly miraculous cures. In addition, several *constitutionnaire* bishops took their own measures to stop the spread of the cult, condemning the miracles and convulsions, confiscating relics, and dismissing any clergy in their dioceses who continued to encourage the worship of M. Pâris. Finally, back in Paris, Fleury had empowered Hérault and the police to arrest any convulsionaries who persisted in making public spectacles of themselves, whether at Saint-Médard or elsewhere in the city.[117]

Meanwhile, other important developments were taking place in Paris in the wake of the closing of the Saint-Médard cemetery. Vintimille, whom Fleury had successfully dissuaded from making any public pronouncements regarding the Pâris cult since his *mandement* of the previous July, took this occasion to break his long silence, at least indirectly. Disturbed by the huge throngs of people who were daily crowding into the church of Saint-Médard, in part to hear unsanctioned Masses performed in memory of François de Pâris, the archbishop issued an order on January 30 designed to eliminate all unauthorized religious ceremonies that went on there. Vintimille renewed the synodal statutes forbidding priests from other dioceses to come to Saint-Médard to celebrate Masses without his authorization and similarly banned other priests from within the diocese, but from outside the parish, who had not received the express permission of the *curé*, M. Coëffrel.[118] This decree, posted on February 4, gave Vintimille the opportunity not only to stamp out "an abuse of dangerous consequences," but also to reassert his own eroding episcopal prerogatives. In addition, the archbishop's

---

including Chartres, Bordeaux, Tarbes, Marseille, Tulle, Angers, and Beauvais (letter to Fleury, Jan. 10, 1732, BM, MS 2357, pp. 598-99).

[116] See, for example, the "Circulaire pour Mrs. les Intendants du Département de M. le Comte de Maurepas et à M. le Marquis de la Carte, Lieutenant général en Poitou," AN, O¹ 379, p. 25.

[117] Fleury to Hérault, Jan. 30, 1732, AAE, M&D, Ile de France, MS 1599, fol. 288.

[118] Copy of the order in BN, J.F., MS 107, fol. 110. Cf. Vintimille to Fleury, Jan. 29, 1732, BM, MS 2357, pp. 610-11, and Fleury to Vintimille, Jan. 30, 1732, *ibid.*, p. 611.

action indirectly signaled a change in the position of the abbé Coëffrel, who had solicited the order from Vintimille in the first place.

Only six months earlier, Coëffrel had reportedly issued a similar order, "an informal, handwritten note, without any signature and without any stamp of authority, by which it was 'forbidden on the part of the archbishop for all priests not resident in this parish to say Mass without special permission from M. Coëffrel, prior-*curé* of this church.' "[119] At that time, however, no one paid any attention to it, and the notice was soon taken down.[120] Though it has not been possible to determine what role, if any, Coëffrel played in the events leading to the closing of the cemetery adjoining his church, it was clearly to his advantage to act in concert with both the diocesan and the civil authorities. The difficulties he had faced at the outset from both his parishioners and the local clergy, as well as from the churchwardens, had persisted, principally because of his fierce opposition to the Pâris cult. However, with encouragement from Fleury and Vintimille and assistance from Hérault,[121] he had managed to dismiss several of the more troublesome priests, appointing others who shared his *constitutionnaire* views and who were thus quite willing to assist him in executing Vintimille's latest order. The new *vicaire*, M. Le Jeune, was particularly zealous in keeping out "foreign" priests who wished to say Mass. He even went so far as to bar entry to many of the faithful who had come to the church to offer their candles and devotions to M. Pâris and to interrupt others in their prayers.[122] Police *exempts* who were stationed in the church also lent their assistance to the *curé* and his *vicaire*. In the space of merely half a year, the mood of the *Nouvelles ecclésiastiques* had changed dramatically. Formerly exultant at Coëffrel's inability to win obedience, the editors were now lamenting "the present situation in this desolate church, from which they are now banishing . . . devotional exercises, after having banished good priests."[123]

The *anticonstitutionnaire* partisans of the Pâris cult did not waste any time in responding to the various actions taken by the civil and

---

[119] *NNEE*, July 14, 1731, p. 139.   [120] *Ibid.*

[121] Vintimille to Fleury, Nov. 17, 1731, BM, MS 2357, pp. 552-53. Despite the considerable support Coëffrel had been receiving from the authorities, his position within the parish remained uncertain. A large number of his parishioners continued to deny him recognition as their rightful *curé*; leading this opposition were the *marguilliers*, with whom he was still embroiled in a series of court cases. In addition, though Coëffrel had succeeded in getting rid of Sr. Martin, the sacristan who had been supporting the Pâris cult, the churchwardens had insisted on replacing him with another candidate who shared his predecessor's views, thus leaving the *curé* right back where he started.

[122] *NNEE*, Feb. 17, 1732, p. 32.   [123] *Ibid.*

ecclesiastical authorities. The *Nouvelles ecclésiastiques* launched the first attack with a tirade against the "outrageous preparations" which had preceded the closing of the cemetery. The *Nouvellistes* were shocked and dismayed that Hérault, who had long before prejudged the convulsionaries as criminals, should have been entrusted with the investigations.[124] Again and again the editor harped on the fact that the lieutenant of police, rather than the archbishop of Paris, had been placed in charge of the whole proceedings, in allegedly blatant violation of the rules prescribing a canonical investigation of such matters.[125] In its detailed analysis of the medical *procès-verbaux*, the journal displayed nothing but contempt for "the secret deliberations and questionable findings" of the doctors and surgeons.[126]

In addition to the long and vehement diatribes in the *Nouvelles ecclésiastiques*, *anticonstitutionnaire* pamphleteers and satirists published several other tirades against the events of January. In critical, sometimes scurrilous, verses, songs, portraits, and *estampes*, defenders of the Pâris cult carried their message to the streets of the city.[127] But words, even a torrent of them expressing righteous indignation and venomous anger, could not change what had happened. Still not content, however, with mere verbal or pictorial objections to a *fait accompli*, the partisans of M. Pâris tried to mount yet another counterattack. On the very day that the cemetery was closed, they reintroduced into the controversy the report of the Thomassin commission appointed by Cardinal Noailles in 1728 to investigate some of the early Pâris cures. They distributed printed copies of both the commission's findings and the first of the *requêtes* which the *curés* had presented to Vintimille, without effect, the previous August. With the *procès-verbaux* they also published a brief pamphlet, the *Réflexions sur les miracles que Dieu opère au tombeau de M. Pâris, et, en particulier, sur la manière étonnante & extraordinaire dont il les opère depuis six mois ou environ*, which reviewed most of the theological arguments previously made on behalf of the miracles. The *Nouvellistes* suggested that the public take the trouble to compare the Thomassin findings with those contained in Hérault's medical *procès-verbaux* and "judge which of these two pieces of evidence merits the greater attention from persons who love truth and [justice]."[128]

[124] *Ibid.*, Jan. 30, 1732, p. 19.

[125] *Ibid.*, Feb. 17, 1732, p. 29; see also Jan. 30, 1732, pp. 18, 20, and Feb. 5, 1732, p. 21.

[126] *Ibid.*, Feb. 5, 11, and 17, 1732, pp. 21-30.

[127] Dulaure, pp. 46-47; Manneville, p. 227. See also BN, MSS Fr., MSS 12632-33, 12674, 12701-704, 15132-33, *passim*.

[128] *NNEE*, Feb. 29, 1732, p. 40. See also the comment of Marais, IV, 340-41 (Feb. 19, 1732).

Embarrassed anew by the reappearance of these papers, and disturbed by the hints of possible police collusion in their publication and distribution,[129] the authorities could not evade the problem. On February 14, Hérault had one of his officers pay a call on the notary with whom the Thomassin papers had originally been deposited, but found everything there in order. The next day Vintimille convoked an assembly of clergy and theologians for the purpose of questioning those former archdiocesan officials who had originally been involved in the investigations of 1728. Also in attendance was the ubiquitous Hérault, "more necessary to the archbishop in such circumstances," observed the *Nouvellistes*, "than all the theologians in the world."[130] Each of the principals in the Noailles "Informations," the abbés Thomassin, Isoard, Ysabeau, and Fouquet, received a separate hearing. After their interrogations each of them agreed to sign a statement detailing his recollections of the affair, and by these independent statements they corroborated one another's accounts.[131] No one, however, seemed to have any knowledge of what had happened either to the original order which Noailles had issued to his *vicaire-général* or to the actual request which the *promoteur*, M. Isoard, had formally presented to the cardinal-archbishop. Moreover, as before, Father Fouquet would not consent to reveal the name of the person who had delivered the papers to him in the first place.[132] Vintimille remained very suspicious. Although the archbishop forwarded the several declarations on to Fleury with the recommendation that Fouquet and the others, including the *curés* who had published the Thomassin *procès-verbaux* in the first place, be punished in some fashion, no reprisals were taken against any of these people.[133] Nor for that matter was anything further done at this time to resolve the dispute. The issues surrounding the Thomassin commission's inquest were left suspended once again.

---

[129] Barbier, II, 244 (January 1732).   [130] *NNEE*, Feb. 29, 1732, p. 40.

[131] *Ibid.*; also March 5, 1732, pp. 41-42. For copies of their declarations, see BN, MSS Fr., MS 22245.

[132] Marais, IV, 343 (Feb. 22, 1732).

[133] Vintimille to Fleury, Feb. 20, 1732, BM, MS 2357, p. 627; and Fleury to Vintimille, Feb. 20, 1732, *ibid.*, p. 629. Vintimille's suspicions of Noailles' former aides were longstanding. An earlier confrontation between Thomassin and the archbishop over these same documents had taken place the previous spring, Vintimille going so far as to accuse the abbé of having secretly conducted the inquest and compiled the dossiers himself, without Noailles' knowledge or official authorization—a charge which Thomassin had vehemently denied (Vintimille to Fleury, May 19 and 22, 1731, *ibid.*, pp. 366-67, 371-72; Thomassin to Vintimille, May 22, 1731, BA, MS 10196). The appearance of the Paris *curés'* first *requête* on the miracles, published along with Thomassin's findings, led the archbishop to charge that "un esprit de parti et de cabale" was at work in the entire affair (Vintimille to Fleury, Aug. 20 and 21, 1731, BM, MS 2357, pp. 480, 483-86).

By mid-February, despite various *anticonstitutionnaire* challenges to their respective actions, Fleury and Vintimille had good reason to be exultant. The cemetery at Saint-Médard had been closed for two weeks and relative tranquility restored to the parish. Neither the *curés* nor the magistrates in the Parlement had made any move to oppose the royal ordinance. What is more, the *constitutionnaire* critics of the government were applauding these developments with great enthusiasm. The papal court was filled with "transports of joy," according to Cardinal Polignac, when news of the royal decree reached Rome.[134] The pope went so far as to call in the French ambassador for a special audience in order to offer his personal congratulations; the pontiff also conveyed his great satisfaction directly, with letters to Fleury, Vintimille, and even the king.[135]

But the authorities in France were not finished. The royal ordinance closing the cemetery of Saint-Médard and Vintimille's order restricting Masses performed at the adjacent church were only two parts of a three-pronged offensive being mounted at this time. The archbishop of Paris, his confidence, if not his actual authority, restored by the recent turn of events, sought now to deprive the cult to François de Pâris of most of its remaining claims to legitimacy. Without making a direct pronouncement on the embarrassingly well-attested miracles attributed to the deacon, Vintimille planned to "reply" to repeated *anticonstitutionnaire* demands for such a statement by publishing another *mandement*, this one censuring the *Vie de M. Pâris, diacre* and two other biographies of the Jansenist saint which had appeared at various times during the previous year and been widely circulated throughout the diocese.[136] Vintimille's decree had been in preparation since early fall, a first draft having been sent to Cardinal Fleury in mid-October.[137] Though the archbishop had agreed to most of the revisions recommended by Versailles, the publication of the decree was nevertheless subject to a series of additional revisions and further delays and postponements. By late December or early January it was decided that the *mandement*, which was originally supposed to contain a strident de-

---

[134] Polignac to Chauvelin, Feb. 28, 1732, AAE, C.P., Rome, MS 730, fols. 287-88. See also Corsini to Fleury, March 5, 1732, *ibid.*, MS 733, fol. 16. Chauvelin had conveyed the good news to Rome ("la Providence protège la bonne cause et veut faire triompher la Vérité") in a series of three letters written to Polignac in the space of two weeks: Jan. 22, 1732, *ibid.*, MS 730, fols. 51-52; Jan. 29, *ibid.*, fol. 61; and Feb. 4, *ibid.*, fols. 115-16.

[135] See Chauvelin to Polignac, March 4, 1732, *ibid.*, C.P., Rome, MS 730, fols. 255-56, and Polignac to Chauvelin, March 13, 1732, *ibid.*, MS 731, fol. 49.

[136] Vintimille to Fleury, Nov. 28, 1731, BM, MS 2357, p. 562.

[137] Vintimille to Fleury, Oct. 18, 1731, *ibid.*, p. 527.

nunciation of the Pâris miracles, would appear in conjunction with the promulgation of the king's ordinance closing the cemetery of Saint-Médard; Vintimille had determined not to speak out until and unless the crown acted first, so as to avoid a recurrence of the humiliation of the previous July.[138] Once again, however, publication was suspended, owing in large part to the representations of the *procureur-général*, whose views were held in high esteem at Versailles.[139] Joly de Fleury cautioned the cardinal-minister against allowing Vintimille to issue yet another statement on the miracles at this time, for fear that it might excite new troubles in the Parlement and create further agitation all over Paris. While acknowledging that Vintimille had good reasons for wishing to publish such a decree, the *procureur-général* was of the opinion that

> the time was never less propitious for speaking or acting on this matter. . . . We have barely recovered from the disturbances which the archbishop provoked with his pastoral instruction *sur les deux puissances* [January 1731], and now he wants to arouse new disorders. If he makes even the slightest pronouncement on the miracles he will rekindle a fire which may burn for a long time. In the debate over the limits [between episcopal and parlementary jurisdiction], . . . most of Paris looked on with indifference. . . . In the issue of the miracles, [by contrast,] the great ones and the little people, the magistrates and a very large number of *curés*, in a word, at least three-quarters of Paris . . . are persuaded of their authenticity, and I cannot repeat it too often, Your Eminence: if the archbishop acts in this way, he will not fail to compromise his authority, to make himself despised by all his flock, and, even sadder, to rend the Church from within.[140]

Cardinal Fleury, already in the midst of preparations for shutting down the Saint-Médard cemetery, appreciated Joly de Fleury's concerns and up to a point even agreed with his assessment of the political

---

[138] Vintimille to Fleury, Jan. 10, 1732, *ibid.*, pp. 597-98. Cf. Vintimille to Fleury, Dec. 12, 1731, *ibid.*, p. 579.

[139] Joly de Fleury was a close friend of Chancellor Daguesseau, his predecessor in the post of *procureur-général*, with whom he kept in frequent contact. He remained throughout most of this period an important adviser to Fleury's administration, especially to the *conseil des dépêches*, which regularly consulted him on a whole range of ecclesiastical affairs (see Michel Antoine, "Le Conseil des Dépêches sous le règne de Louis XV," *Bibliothèque de l'Ecole des Chartes*, 111 [1953], pp. 158-208, 112 [1954], pp. 126-81).

[140] Letter to Fleury, Jan. 20, 1732, BN, J.F., MS 107, fol. 99. See also Joly de Fleury to Daguesseau, Jan. 20, 1732, *ibid.*

and religious climate. But he did not share the *procureur-général*'s conclusions. "If the public is as convinced of the truth of the miracles . . . as you suggest they are," Fleury observed, "then that is all the more reason for trying to disabuse them of their illusions. . . . I know that the archbishop's authority has been too weakened for him to change the common way of thinking, but how can he continue to stand aside, silently and indifferently, watching the desolation of his people? . . . To do so would be to shirk his pastoral responsibilities. . . ."[141] Yet even as he was defending Vintimille's right to publish his decree, the cardinal-minister was having some second thoughts of his own. Indeed, only a few days later Fleury was advising Vintimille to omit from his *mandement* all mention of the miracles, arguing that such references would require a more detailed and elaborate discussion and necessitate still further delays in the decree.[142] Complying with his friend's recommendations, albeit reluctantly, the archbishop made numerous substantive changes. Finally, in late February, encouraged by the promise of royal support and protection, Vintimille was free to publish.[143]

The archbishop's long-delayed *mandement*, dated January 30, 1732, centered on a condemnation of the three biographies of François de Pâris, works written to extol the virtues of "someone who had avoided communion for many years" and who had "challenged the established religious authorities for most of his life." They contained, he asserted, propositions which were "false, scandalous, harmful to the authority of the Holy See and the Church, rash, impious, favoring the heretics, erroneous, [and] schismatic."[144] He forbade, under pain of excommunication, anyone to read or even possess the condemned works. He also renewed the earlier prohibitions contained in his decree of July 1731, declaring "illegitimate and illicit the cult rendered to M. Pâris in disregard of the general laws of the Church [and] of the aforementioned prohibitions."[145] For all of Fleury's efforts to moderate the excessive

---

[141] Jan. 21, 1732, *ibid.*, fol. 101.

[142] Vintimille to Fleury, Jan. 23, 1732, BM, MS 2357, pp. 607-608, and Fleury to Vintimille, Jan. 24, 1732, *ibid.*, p. 609.

[143] Vintimille to Fleury, Feb. 3, 1732, *ibid.*, p. 620; Vintimille to Fleury, Feb. 20, 1732, *ibid.*, pp. 626-28; Fleury to Vintimille, Feb. 20, 1732, *ibid.*, pp. 628-29; and Vintimille to Fleury, Feb. 25, 1732, *ibid.*, p. 630. Cf. Journal of De Lisle, Feb. 28, 1732, AN, U-377.

[144] *Mandement de Msgr. l'archevêque de Paris, qui condamne trois écrits, dont le premier a pour titre: "Vie de M. de Pâris, diacre," à Bruxelles chez Foppens, à l'enseigne du S.-Esprit, 1731; le second: "Vie de M. de Pâris, diacre du diocèse de Paris," en France, 1731; et le troisième: "Vie de M. Pâris, diacre," 1731; et renouvelle les défenses portées par le Mandement du 15 juillet dernier*, p. 2.

[145] *Ibid.*, pp. 13-14, 18.

remarks included in earlier drafts, the decree nevertheless contained some of Vintimille's most intemperate language. The archbishop charged the *curés* with poisoning the religious atmosphere within the diocese. He referred to these priests as "reckless pastors," who fomented insubordination and independence toward legitimate episcopal authority by encouraging the faithful to act as "credulous participants in an indecent spectacle" and as "rebellious, disobedient, and deceitful people."[146] Having expressed himself in such harsh, even venomous tones—almost as though he finally had to give vent to intense feelings that had been welling up inside for many difficult months—Vintimille agreed not to try pushing things any further. To avoid exacerbating the already considerable tensions with the *curés*, the archbishop prudently decided not to require that his *mandement* be read from the parish pulpits, contenting himself to issue it from his archdiocesan office.[147]

While Vintimille's precautions may have helped prevent a "revolt in the parishes," his decree did provoke a hostile response from other quarters. The *Nouvelles ecclésiastiques*, for example, denounced it as yet another evasion of the archbishop's episcopal responsibility to study the evidence already available to him concerning the Pâris miracles: "This latest work by M. Vintimille's theologians reduces itself to saying: 'The Bull is received by the Church; therefore it is useless to examine whether the miraculous cures operated through the intercession of M. Pâris are true or false.' "[148] Several *curés* and a number of Jansenist controversialists joined the *Nouvellistes* in denouncing Vintimille's *mandement*, as did a host of *libellistes*, wags, and versifiers.[149] By far the most important reaction, however, was that which came from the Parlement of Paris.

Except for a dozen or so judges, most of the sovereign court had not been disposed to question the government's or even Vintimille's recent actions against the observances at Saint-Médard, presumably believing that there were no legitimate political or judicial reasons to

---

[146] *Ibid.*, pp. 12-16, *et passim.*

[147] See Vintimille's earlier letter to Fleury (Nov. 28, 1731, BM, MS 2357, p. 562), in which the archbishop himself acknowledged the wisdom of such a precaution to avoid precipitating yet another confrontation with the *curés*: "bien qu'il me fut avantageux de la faire pour avoir par la une occasion de punir et de sentencier les curés discoles s'ils refusoient d'obéir. . . ."

[148] March 10, 1732, *ibid.*, p. 45.

[149] See, for example, Raunié, VI, 27: "Que l'archevêque de Paris,/ Mangeur et buveur indomptable,/ Nous fasse voir par ses écrits/ Que parfois il quitte la table." See also BN, MSS Fr., MSS 12632-33, 12674, 12701-704, 15132-33, *passim.*

warrant such a challenge. But the archbishop's latest decree, like the earlier closing of the cemetery, deeply offended a handful of magistrates who had continued enthusiastically to participate in and to champion the Pâris cult.[150] This series of actions especially angered Jérôme-Nicolas de Pâris, the deacon's brother, who was a principal spokesman for this minority contingent of magistrates. The counselor Pâris had already issued his first complaint in early February, in response to the widespread rumors that the police, seconded by the archiepiscopal authorities and by parish officials at Saint-Médard, were preparing to exhume the body of his brother. In fact, according to the *Nouvelles ecclésiastiques*, some people actually believed that this "desecration" had already been carried out, since "the little cemetery has remained day and night at the mercy of M. Hérault."[151] On February 13, despite vigorous, indignant denials from Fleury, Vintimille, and Hérault that any such action had even been contemplated,[152] Pâris submitted a formal protest to the *procureur-général* demanding that "all proceedings be stopped."[153] He also sent copies of his protest to Hérault, Vintimille, the *promoteur-général* in the archdiocese, the *procureur du roi* at the Châtelet, and the *curé* and churchwardens of Saint-

[150] Hérault to Fleury, Jan. 29, 1732, AAE, M&D, Ile de France, MS 1599, fol. 286. It is surely an indication of the government's profound concern about the Parlement's reaction in this affair that the lieutenant of police should have made a point of finding out the magistrates' views about the closing of Saint-Médard on the very day his men executed the royal decree. An anonymous *mémoire* described the pro-Pâris *parlementaires* as "des jansénistes outrés" (AAE, M&D, France, MS 1279, fol. 19).

[151] *NNEE*, March 5, 1732, pp. 42-43; see also Feb. 17, 1732, p. 31. There had apparently been a fairly longstanding fear in the parish of Saint-Médard about just such a possibility, dating back at least to August 1731. See Marais, IV, 264-65 (Aug. 6, 1731). The *greffier* De Lisle also reported numerous meetings in early February at the *archevêché* and at the Louvre involving some sixty *constitutionnaire* prelates, "pour déclarer le B. Pâris hérétique comme estant mort hors du sein de l'Eglise, . . . [et] pour parvenir ensuite à le faire exhumer" (Feb. 8 and 10, 1732, AN, U-377).

[152] See Vintimille to Fleury, Feb. 9, 1732, BM, MS 2357, pp. 623-24, and Fleury to Vintimille, Feb. 9, 1732, *ibid*., p. 625. Hérault's denial, made on Feb. 2, is cited in *NNEE*, March 5, 1732, p. 43. See also the statement of the *marguilliers* of Saint-Médard, Feb. 14, 1732, BA, MS 10196, and Le Conte to Hérault, March 26, 1732, *ibid*. Despite these various public and private disclaimers, calls were still being made for Pâris' exhumation. The Roman Cardinal Albani, for example, recommended that the authorities toss "dans la Rivière de Seine les os de ce misérable, affin d'empescher pour toujours un culte sacrilège, qui a scandalisé jusqu'à cette heure toute l'Eglise" (letter to Cardinal Bissy, March 5, 1732, AAE, M&D, Fonds divers [Rome], MS 62, fol. 31).

[153] BN, J.F., MS 107, fol. 115.

Médard.[154] By the time the question of his brother's supposed exhumation had been settled to his satisfaction, Pâris learned of the publication of Vintimille's *mandement* denouncing the three biographies of the deacon.

The archbishop's decree deeply and personally offended M. Pâris, who was determined to seek redress in the Parlement itself. On March 28, taking advantage of a moment when the sovereign court was engaged in the ceremonial reception of new officers, he presented a *requête* to the assembled chambers in the form of a complaint against Vintimille's defamation of his brother's memory.[155] Addressing himself to First President Portail, he spoke of his "bitter grief" over the public slander by which some people were endeavoring to tarnish his brother's memory. "Nature, religion, honor, and duty oblige me equally to bring a charge in this matter before the assembled company, from whom I confidently await the justice which it never refuses to any of the king's subjects."[156] The formal complaint which he left to the immediate consideration of the entire body referred also to Vintimille's earlier *mandement* against the miracles as well as to an *Avertissement* by Bishop Belsunce of Marseille, dated February 9, which likewise maligned François de Pâris by alleging that the deacon had died "outside the bosom of the Church."[157] It was Pâris' hope and expectation that his colleagues would authorize a formal hearing into these charges and that the Parlement's investigation would ultimately lead to the suppression of the two decrees in question and a judgment against Vintimille and Belsunce as arrant calumniators.[158] Such a prospect, which seemed quite likely under the circumstances, threatened to wreak havoc with official plans to eliminate the Pâris cult as a religious and political *cause célèbre*. It also threatened to embroil Vintimille once again in a major lawsuit before the hostile Parlement. What is more, it meant that for the first time since the Anne Lefranc case—still pend-

---

[154] Barbier, II, 247 (February 1732); Marais, IV, 344 (Feb. 22, 1732); *NNEE*, March 5, 1732, p. 43, and March 15, 1732, pp. 50-52. Cf. copy of an earlier letter from Pâris to Vintimille, Feb. 9, 1732, BN, MSS Fr., MS 22245, fol. 176. The complaints of M. Pâris gave rise to official concern that the followers of the deacon might attempt to preempt the authorities and exhume his body themselves. See "Ordre de Maurepas à M. Hérault de faire informer sur les faits suspects d'artifice au tombeau du Sr. Pâris," Feb. 12, 1732, BA, MS 10196, and "Lettre de marguilliers à M. Hérault promettant de veiller à ce que le corps du diacre Pâris ne soit pas enlevé," Feb. 14, 1732, *ibid.*

[155] Joly de Fleury to Fleury and to Daguesseau, March 30, 1732, BN, J.F., MS 118, fol. 30.

[156] *Ibid.*, fol. 31; cited also in *NNEE*, June 18, 1732, p. 117.

[157] BN, J.F., MS 117, fol. 226.   [158] *Ibid.*, MS 118, fol. 31.

ing after seven months—the matter of the Pâris cult was to come under the purview of the sovereign court; only this time it was a member of the Parlement itself and not just some obscure Parisian spinster who had brought suit. Given the usual mood at the Palais de Justice, the affair seemed grave indeed.[159]

As word of Pâris' *requête* spread quickly throughout the city, Vintimille was one of the first to react. Already angered at Pâris' charging him with complicity in the alleged exhumation of his brother's corpse,[160] Vintimille was even more offended by the "impudence" and "insolence" of the counselor's latest action in "characterizing my decrees as defamatory lampoons." Writing to Cardinal Fleury on March 29, he demanded immediate justice from the king, not only for the affront to his own person but also for the insult delivered to the entire French episcopate.[161] Greatly concerned to head off another dangerous confrontation between Vintimille and the Parlement, Fleury called on the *gens du roi* to try to calm their volatile colleague, M. Pâris. First President Portail, with assistance from Joly de Fleury and a number of Pâris' relatives and close friends in the court, attempted on more than one occasion to persuade him of the potentially serious consequences of his action and to prevail upon him not to pursue his complaint any further.[162] While failing to get him to withdraw his petition, they did manage to convince Pâris to withhold additional action until after the Easter recess. As he did so often, Cardinal Fleury was playing for time. But though he was able to secure temporary delays and postponements, he could not hope to keep this case suspended indefinitely.

By late April, Pâris' petition was still in the hands of the First President, and Vintimille was beside himself with anger. Insisting on the satisfaction that was "owing to a man of [his] position, character, birth, and family," the archbishop called on the king to have Pâris arrested and punished immediately for his "brazen and impudent" action. If the counselor is deemed insane, as some had suggested, then he should be confined at once, Vintimille contended.[163] Fleury's re-

---

[159] In the view of the *avocat-général*, Guillaume-François-Louis Joly de Fleury (son of the *procureur-général*), "les esprits étoient fort échauffés de part et d'autre sur ces prétendus miracles. D'ailleurs l'Archevêque de Paris étant partie dans la Requête il auroit fallu nécessairement convoqué les Paires en la Grand'-Chambre" (*ibid.*, MS 117, fol. 224).

[160] Vintimille to Fleury, Feb. 9, 1732, BM, MS 2357, pp. 623-24.

[161] *Ibid.*, p. 647.

[162] Fleury to Joly de Fleury, March 31, 1732, BN, J.F., MS 118, fol. 33; Fleury to Joly de Fleury, April 2, 1732, *ibid.*, fol. 34; Portail to Fleury, April 1, 1732, AAE, M&D, Ile de France, MS 1600, fols. 4-5; Fleury to Portail, April 2, 1732, *ibid.*, fol. 8.

[163] Vintimille to Fleury, April 19, 1732, BM, MS 2357, p. 665.

peated assurances to his friend that the king would not abandon him and that the government was doing all it could on his behalf failed to placate Vintimille.[164] In any event, developments within the Parlement rather than the archbishop's importunate pleas finally forced the cardinal-minister to take decisive action.

At the beginning of May, word reached Fleury at Compiègne that the Parlement was preparing to begin deliberations over the Pâris *requête*. The *gens du roi* informed the cardinal-minister that there was likely to be considerable support among the magistrates for their colleague's petition.[165] On May 3, fearful of the consequences of such a discussion, the king's council issued an *arrêt* which effectively evoked the case from the sovereign court's jurisdiction.[166] Designed specifically to forestall the Parlement's further consideration of the Pâris suit,[167] the conciliar decree declared that the king would thereafter reserve to himself all questions connected with the miracles and convulsions. According to the *arrêt*, which Maurepas transmitted to the *gens du roi* on May 4,[168] the king had become particularly disturbed by the attempts that were being made to turn the allegedly miraculous cures of François de Pâris to partisan advantage. The *anticonstitutionnaires*, it was claimed, had tried to forge a link between the miracles and the appellant cause, "in order to furnish weapons to those who are in revolt against the authority of the Church and to perpetuate the divisions in the kingdom regarding the bull *Unigenitus*." They had thereby contravened a series of royal declarations which commanded an end to all disputes on the subject. As a result, the king deemed it

> appropriate to continue to take cognizance of the matter, in order
> to anticipate any new situation which might disturb the tranquility

[164] Fleury to Vintimille, April 1, 1732, *ibid.*, pp. 673-74.

[165] BN, MSS Fr., MS 10232, p. 19. Cf. Hérault to Fleury, April 24, 1732, AAE, M&D, Ile de France, MS 1600, fol. 37.

[166] AN, E2120, fols. 1-4.

[167] Chauvelin to Saint-Aignan, May 12, 1732, AAE, C.P., Rome, MS 733, fols. 254-55. According to a manuscript *Journal* kept by some anonymous magistrate in the Parlement, "Cet arrêt a été donné par rapport à M. de Pâris . . . [qui] avoit fait diverses procédures depuis le 28 janvier . . . pour assurer aux cendres de [son] frère le repos qu'on ne peut dénier à celles de tout citoien irreprochable" (BN, MSS Fr., MS 10232, p. 17).

[168] Maurepas to Joly de Fleury, May 4, 1732, BN, J.F., MS 118, fol. 44. Cf. Joly de Fleury to Fleury, May 5, 1732, *ibid.*, fol. 50 (letter not sent). See also "Projet de Lettre à Mrs. les Gens du Roy," presumably sent with copies of the *arrêt*; in this letter the king's representatives were told: "vous vous y conformerez exactement et . . . ne ferez aucune démarche qui ne s'accorde parfaitement avec une résolution dont le seul objet est d'étouffer dans sa naissance tout ce qui peut estre une nouvelle matière de disputes et de trouble" (AN, O¹ 379, p. 2).

of the Church and the State. To this end, His Majesty . . . expressly prohibits . . . all his subjects, whatever their rank or status, to undertake any action or proceedings before his courts . . . concerning the aforementioned questions.

Reserving all competence to himself, the king absolutely forbade his courts to concern themselves with these matters. Henceforth the magistrates in the Parlement of Paris were to be prohibited from discussing any questions associated with Saint-Médard, including the affair raised by Jérôme-Nicolas de Pâris, or from providing judicial protection to anyone associated with the Pâris cult. The council's decree, which the colporteurs distributed to the public on May 6, but with orders not to hawk it in the streets, brought great joy to Archbishop Vintimille.[169] To the magistrates in the Parlement, however, it represented only the latest of a long series of royal actions intended to restrict the court's jurisdiction and to limit its role exclusively to secular judicial questions and functions. The issues raised with the promulgation of the *arrêt* thus went considerably beyond the matter of Pâris' *requête*. The counselor and his fellow judges were consequently eager to challenge its validity. But just as the sovereign court was preparing to launch a counterattack, the magistrates found themselves embroiled in yet another major controversy. Indeed, as it quickly became clear, a principal reason for the government's eagerness to set aside the Pâris petition was that the crown now had an even more difficult confrontation on its hands—one which had erupted in the wake of a new pastoral instruction which Vintimille had just published, this time condemning the *Nouvelles ecclésiastiques*.

Throughout this period, the *Nouvelles ecclésiastiques*, while continuing its regular weekly fare of news and commentary, had been giving especially detailed attention to the political complications associated with the closing of the cemetery at Saint-Médard and with the other official actions taken against the Pâris cult since the beginning of the year. Indeed, for almost two months the *Nouvellistes* devoted nearly every page of every issue to the affair and its aftermath, keeping their readers informed as well as agitated. The editor spared no one in his criticism, though he was particularly harsh in his attacks on Hérault and Vintimille, whom he singled out for their allegedly "villainous" activities. Police efforts to ferret out and intimidate those responsible for publishing and distributing the newspaper were no more fruitful

169 BN, MSS Fr., MS 10232, p. 16; Vintimille to Chauvelin, May 8, 1732, AAE, M&D, France, MS 1275, fols. 218-19.

than they had been before. Despite numerous arrests of individual printers and colporteurs, occasional seizures of small printing presses, and frequent confiscations of bundled copies of the paper, the enterprising, evasive editor kept his operation running without interruption. Of course, the apparently considerable police complicity in the dissemination of the journal and the willingness of sympathetic officers to wink at the journal's open violations of the law made the task of the editor, de la Roche, somewhat easier.[170] In any event, the *Nouvellistes'* continued success in disseminating their *anticonstitutionnaire* propaganda all over Paris and beyond remained a constant source of embarrassment to Hérault and the censorship authorities and left Vintimille more than a little annoyed. The archbishop was especially offended by the incessant attacks upon his recent decrees which the editor persisted in publishing, and which threatened to jeopardize the favorable results the authorities had achieved in proceeding against the practitioners of the Pâris cult. Although he had suffered a setback from the suit which Jérôme-Nicolas de Pâris had brought against him in the Parlement, Vintimille had seen his fortunes improve dramatically in recent months. His episcopal authority somewhat more secure and his own self-confidence greatly renewed, Vintimille welcomed the opportunity once more to reassert his ecclesiastical prerogatives, while at the same time denouncing the dreaded journal—an action he had already contemplated for some time.

By mid-April, Vintimille, aided by a commission of theologians,[171] had completed the draft of a *mandement*, which he sent on to Fleury. After consulting with Hérault, Chauvelin, Daguesseau, and other advisers, the cardinal-minister proposed various changes which Vintimille agreed to incorporate in a revised version of the decree.[172] By the end of the month the document was completed and Vintimille was ready to launch his direct attack on the "venomous" newspaper. He began

---

[170] *Ibid.,* MS 1274, fols. 310-11. See also Barbier, II, 244 (January 1732).

[171] Two Jesuits, Fathers Lallemand and Berruyer, appear to have been the principal drafters of the *mandement*, with Cardinal Bissy and Archbishop Languet of Sens serving as consultants (*NNEE*, June 18, 1732, p. 119; BN, MSS Fr., MS 10232, pp. 63-64; BPR, L.P. 17, fol. 971).

[172] Vintimille to Fleury, April 19, 1732, BM, MS 2357, p. 662; Hérault to [Chauvelin?], April 22, 1732, BA, MS 10171, No. 7. From the first, Daguesseau had counseled Fleury against allowing Vintimille to publish his decree, which the chancellor had reportedly found "full of abuses and capable of arousing passions all over Paris" (cited in *NNEE*, June 18, 1732, p. 117). The cardinal-minister's other advisers generally disagreed. Arguing that the decree was in fact a masterpiece of subtlety, moderation, and discretion, they managed to convince Fleury that his fears and those of his chancellor were excessive and groundless.

carefully, first recalling the Paris Parlement's own condemnation of the gazette issued early in the previous year, which he regarded as a precedent for his current denunciation.[173] In his view the journal was as much a threat to the temporal as it was to the spiritual authorities. The primary goal of the *Nouvellistes*, he contended, had been to urge various groups to revolt against the established order, which they have sought to discredit at every turn. They have resorted in their columns to all manner of cunning and seditious "artifices" in an effort to further widespread disaffection and disobedience.[174] They have strongly promoted the Pâris cult while continuing their incessant attacks on the bull *Unigenitus*. On the basis of all these "crimes," the archbishop believed he was justified in condemning the journal as "libelous, insulting to the Holy See and to the bishops, contrary to decrees received in the entire realm and by the entire Church, defending, besides, propositions which are scandalous, erroneous, favorable to schism and heresy, and even heretical." Once again brandishing the threat of excommunication, he proscribed the distribution, possession, and reading of the newspaper and of other like-minded writings. He concluded by commanding that his edict be announced from all the parish pulpits on the following Sunday, May 4.

It was Vintimille's ill-considered command to publish his *mandement* in the parishes perhaps as much as the contents of the decree itself which provoked renewed hostilities throughout the diocese. Anticipating at least some opposition to his decree, especially from the normally dissident *curés*, Vintimille had for weeks been recommending to Cardinal Fleury that the government take certain precautions to diminish the potential strength of that opposition. In particular, the archbishop deemed it absolutely essential to act promptly and secretly— perhaps through formal exile or banishment from Paris—against the abbés Isoard (*curé* of Sainte-Marine) and Rochebouet (*curé* of Saint-Germain-le-Vieux) in advance of the *mandement*'s actual publication.[175]

---

[173] The Parlement's *arrêt* was issued on Feb. 9, 1731 (BN, MSS Fr., MS 22090, (fols. 361-64). For the indictment of *avocat-général* Gilbert de Voisins and the *Nouvellistes*' reply, see *NNEE*, Feb. 24, 1731, pp. 37-39, and March 14, 1731, p. 52.

[174] *Mandement de Msgr. l'archevêque de Paris, portant condamnation de plusieurs libelles qui ont pour titre: "Nouvelles ecclésiastiques" (27 avril 1732).*

[175] Vintimille to Fleury, March 15, 1732, BM, MS 2357, p. 641; Fleury to Vintimille, March 22, 1732, *ibid.*, pp. 644-45; Vintimille to Fleury, April 19, 1732, *ibid.*, pp. 663-64; Vintimille to [Chauvelin?], April 20, 1732, BA, MS 10171, No. 21; Hérault to [Chauvelin?], April 22, 1732, *ibid.*, No. 7; and Vintimille to Fleury, April 29, 1732, BM, MS 2357, pp. 667-68. In this last letter the archbishop did have at least some "good news" to report to the cardinal-minister, namely, that the abbé Desmoulins, troublesome *curé* of Saint-Jacques-du-Haut-Pas, had just died, giving Vintimille the opportunity to replace him with a "safer" priest.

These "impudent firebrands" had long been the leaders of *anticonstitutionnaire* parochial resistance to archiepiscopal authority. Isoard, whose parish church served as a frequent meeting place for appellant priests, was also the reputed instigator of many of the concerted actions which the refractory *curés* of Paris had taken against Vintimille since the archbishop's arrival in the capital more than two and a half years earlier.[176] The *curé* of Sainte-Marine, like his colleague from Saint-Germain-le-Vieux, was also one of the staunchest and most outspoken ecclesiastical supporters of the Pâris cult.[177] But despite Vintimille's representations to Fleury seeking to obtain the suspension of these two *curés discoles* for their "pernicious excesses," the cardinal-minister remained unwilling to support any action on that score. When Vintimille's decree appeared, therefore, Isoard and Rochebouet were still firmly ensconced in their respective parishes—and ready to challenge their archbishop once more.

Even before Sunday arrived, Vintimille was confronted with widespread opposition. Having learned sometime earlier of the forthcoming *mandement*, twenty-one *curés*, led by the redoubtable Isoard and Rochebouet, were already prepared to declare their unwillingness to cooperate with the archbishop in its formal publication.[178] On Saturday, May 3, the day on which the decree was actually issued, they sent Vintimille a brief letter announcing their intention not to publish it.[179] The letter was essentially a manifesto in justification of their decision. Without attempting to defend the *Nouvelles ecclésiastiques*, the *curés* argued that they could not authorize "by their ministry writings [such as the *mandement*] which were disrespectful not only to the powers established by God, but also to truth and to charity."[180] They complained that the archbishop's decree, which was brought to them that morning by persons unknown and bearing no authentic signature, had not even been addressed to them. In addition to objecting to the unusual circumstances under which the decree reached their respective parishes,[181] the *curés* were concerned that an acceptance of "this publication might be regarded by the people . . . as an acquiescence in the

---

[176] Vintimille to Fleury, April 29, 1732, BM, MS 2357, pp. 667-68.

[177] Dedieu, "Le désarroi janséniste," pp. 559-60.

[178] The Paris *curés* had met in unauthorized assembly on April 21, during which time they presumably discussed proposals for taking concerted action against Vintimille's decree (Hérault to [Chauvelin?], April 22, 1732, BA, MS 10171, No. 7).

[179] *Lettre de MM. les curés de Paris à Mgr. l'Archevêque, au sujet de son Mandement du 27 avril 1732.*

[180] *Ibid.,* p. 1.

[181] Ordinarily the two *archiprêtres* were responsible for formally presenting the archbishop's decrees to the *curés* (BPR, L.P. 17, fol. 971).

condemnation of [past] actions which we had taken out of an attachment to the faith and to the most sacred rights of the crown and from which we shall never be able to deviate."[182] Nor were these priests satisfied with the supposedly subtle language of the decree, with its slighting references to the appellants and its suggestions that the entire Church had already received the Bull as a rule of faith. Finally, they charged that the decree contained harsh words and excessively stringent penalties that could hardly be justified, let alone imposed: it "brands as heretical unspecified propositions and . . . pronounces the penalty of excommunication merely for reading or possessing printed matter which for several years has been distributed to everyone!"[183] The *curés* were not about to renounce their past conduct, whether toward the Bull or toward the Pâris cult, especially since the miracles attributed to the saintly deacon's intercession had already served to assure them that theirs was the party of truth and righteousness.[184]

On Monday (May 5) the *curés*, having already apprised Vintimille of their reasons for refusing to publish his *mandement*, formally notified the *promoteur* of the letter they had previously sent the archbishop.[185] In succeeding days they sought to publicize their opposition to Vintimille's untimely decree and by week's end had received widespread lay support for their action even in normally "safe," *constitutionnaire* parishes. As a result, several *curés* who had agreed to promulgate the archbishop's decree were prevented from doing so when their congregations raised a great storm of protest. Despite the presence of the Paris police, deployed in various parish churches to ensure an orderly reception for Vintimille's *mandement*, many of the faithful noisily made their way to the exits, hooting, jeering, and otherwise demonstrating their displeasure with a pronouncement which, by implication at least, renewed their archbishop's previous denunciations of the cult to and miracles of François de Pâris.[186]

Efforts had been under way, in the meantime, to bring the recalcitrant parish clergy to heel. Although he himself bore a large responsibility for provoking the *curés'* hostile reply, Vintimille regarded their

---

[182] *Lettre de MM. les curés de Paris*, p. 2.

[183] *Ibid.*   [184] *Ibid.*

[185] AAE, M&D, France, MS 1275, fols. 181-83. See also Vintimille to Fleury, May 10, 1732, BM, MS 2357, pp. 682-84.

[186] BN, MSS Fr., MS 10232, pp. 38-41 (see also pp. 8-15); Vintimille to Fleury, May 11, 1732, BM, MS 2357, pp. 687-88; Barbier, II, 266-67 (May 1732); Journal of De Lisle, May 1732, AN, U-378; *Lettre écrite à un curé de Paris par les fidèles de son paroisse [Saint-Gervais] au sujet du mandement de M. l'Archevêque* (May 4, 1732); and "Lettre à M. Hérault sur le respect dû aux églises," which Maurepas sent to the lieutenant of police on May 3, 1732 (AN, O¹ 76, fol. 243).

"rebellious impudence" as wholly intolerable. In a series of indignant letters sent to Fleury and Chauvelin, the archbishop once again called upon the government to support him against these "willful, insubordinate priests," who, in expectation of support from the Parlement of Paris, had chosen "to raise the flag of schism and revolt" against their legitimate superior.[187] Redoubling his own efforts to break down the *curés'* resistance, and buoyed by promises of royal assistance,[188] Vintimille summoned an urgent meeting of his archdiocesan counselors. On May 7 the *official*, acting on an indictment drawn up by the *promoteur* with the advice and approval of Chancellor Daguesseau, issued an order enjoining these obdurate priests to publish Vintimille's decree the following Sunday or face harsh disciplinary action.[189] Only one of the twenty-one priests succumbed to these threats and withdrew his opposition.[190] The others refused to be intimidated. On the contrary, they served notice on Vintimille that they were not only prepared to challenge the *ordonnance*, but also determined to defend their actions through the judicial process of the Paris *officialité* if necessary. This awkward prospect, unforeseen when the authorities issued their injunction, threatened to plunge Vintimille and his archdiocesan officers into a long, drawn-out legal battle with the *curés*—a suit that (unlike an *appel comme d'abus*) was not susceptible of a conciliar evocation and one that the priests apparently stood a good chance of winning.[191]

This latest development placed Fleury's administration, not to mention Vintimille himself, in a rather difficult position. The archbishop was by no means willing to negotiate the issues at stake between him and the *curés*. "It must be determined," he declared, "whether I am the *vicaire* of these gentlemen or their archbishop. This entire affair comes down to a question of their submission or their disobedience."[192] Several legal consultants with whom Vintimille conferred encouraged him to reassert his authority and institute formal proceedings against the

[187] Vintimille to Fleury, May 5, 1732, BM, MS 2357, pp. 678-79; Vintimille to Chauvelin, May 6, 1732, AAE, M&D, France, MS 1275, fol. 194. See also Fleury to Vintimille, May 6, 1732, BM, MS 2357, pp. 679-80, and Vintimille to Fleury, May 8, 1732, *ibid.*, pp. 680-81.

[188] Fleury to Vintimille, May 5 and 6, 1732, *ibid.*, pp. 677 and 679-80. Cf. Chauvelin to Saint-Aignan, May 12, 1732, AAE, C.P., Rome, MS 733, fols. 254-55.

[189] BN, J.F., MS 118, fols. 40-41; *ibid.*, MS 117, fol. 224; *ibid.*, MSS Fr., MS 10232, p. 30; and Vintimille to Fleury, May 10, 1732, BM, MS 2357, p. 685. Cf. Vintimille to Chauvelin, May 13, 1732, AAE, M&D, France, MS 1275, fols. 238-39.

[190] That was M. Penet of Saint-Landry, whom Hérault had personally visited on May 10 (BN, MSS Fr., MS 10232, p. 38).

[191] *Ibid.*, pp. 33-35; BPR, L.P. 17, fol. 972.

[192] Vintimille to Fleury, May 18, 1732, BM, MS 2357, pp. 693-94.

curés at once.[193] Hesitant as always about acting on his own, the archbishop forwarded their recommendations to Chauvelin and agreed to await the government's reply before going ahead.[194] While a number of royal advisers cautioned Fleury not to interfere with the course of ecclesiastical justice nor to make any attempt to prevent the *officialité* from taking action,[195] the cardinal-minister was inclined to view the matter rather differently. "I am far from advising you to do nothing," he wrote Vintimille on May 22, "since that would be to abandon the Church and [diminish] its authority, but we must first see what develops in the affair of the Parlement." To proceed against the *curés* at this juncture, he added, would have the effect of "spreading oil on a fire; it would be better to allow tempers to cool a bit first."[196] Indeed, by this time the "affair of the Parlement" was itself reaching crisis proportions, and the authorities could not afford to get involved in another complicated legal tangle. In the end, therefore, Vintimille was persuaded not to pursue the *curés*—a decision in which the archbishop only reluctantly acquiesced.[197]

Although he had agreed to suspend all proceedings against the *curés*, Vintimille's quasi-conciliatory gesture could not undo the damage his *mandement* of April 27 had already caused. As if another confrontation with the *curés* and the Paris faithful were not enough of a problem for the authorities, the Parlement of Paris had in the meantime entered the fray. On the same day that the *curés* published their letter to Vintimille—which also happened to be the day that the king's council issued its provocative *arrêt* withdrawing the case of Jérôme-Nicolas de Pâris from the sovereign court's docket—they presented an *appel comme d'abus* to the Parlement, formally protesting the archbishop's decree. The simultaneous appearance of the conciliar *arrêt* and the priests' *appel comme d'abus* proved a fatal combination[198] and served to renew

---

[193] Vintimille to Fleury, May 11, 1732, *ibid.*, pp. 686-88. These consultants drew up a *mémoire* for Vintimille in which they laid out a fairly elaborate course of legal action to be followed in the diocesan court.

[194] Letter of May 13, 1732, AAE, M&D, France, MS 1275, fols. 238-39. Cf. Vintimille to Fleury, May 16, 1732, BM, MS 2357, pp. 690-92, and May 20, 1732, *ibid.*, pp. 697-98.

[195] See, for example, d'Argenson's "Premier mémoire sur les affaires présentes du Parlement de Paris," May 23, 1732, AAE, M&D, France, MS 1275, fol. 295.

[196] BM, MS 2357, pp. 699-700.

[197] There were also some doubts expressed by various experts in canon law, especially the bishop of Dijon, as to the regularity of the archdiocesan action in promulgating its *ordonnance* of May 7 (see two letters from bishop of Luçon to [Chauvelin?], May 21 and 22, 1732, AAE, M&D, France, MS 1275, fols. 276, 287).

[198] Ironically, one of the principal reasons behind the council's issuing its *arrêt*

the longstanding jurisdictional disputes between crown and Parlement and between Parlement and archbishop of Paris. The council's evocation and the accompanying restrictions on the court's judicial authority had already left most of the magistrates—not just the Pâris faction—in a rather belligerent mood. The *curés'* appeal thus offered them a welcome opportunity to retaliate against Fleury and Vintimille at one and the same time.[199]

The archbishop of Paris had already published one highly controversial decree since January, and only the royal council's intervention had spared him a potentially embarrassing libel suit for his efforts. From the Parlement's point of view, Vintimille's latest *mandement* contained only more of the same intemperance and vituperation he had displayed in his previous decrees and, with its unequivocal defense of the Bull, appeared to uphold ultramontane principles that were in clear violation of the tenets of the Gallican Church. In addition, the magistrates alleged that Vintimille's decree constituted an ecclesiastical intrusion into the secular sphere. In censoring the *Nouvelles ecclésiastiques*, they contended, the archbishop had gone beyond his proper jurisdiction into a "matter of pure police," that is, a matter of public order, one to which the court had addressed itself in an *arrêt* of the previous year. What is more, by commanding the *curés* to publish a decree which he knew clearly they could not support, the archbishop had deliberately provoked them into another public confrontation, needlessly arousing dissension and disorder throughout the capital. By hurling threats of excommunication at those who failed to heed his strictures and by authorizing confessors to withhold absolution from anyone who admitted to having violated his order, he had caused widespread confusion and fears among the Paris faithful. Finally, by speaking of the bull *Unigenitus* as having been received as an apostolic judgment throughout the kingdom, he had disseminated false information and purposely chosen to ignore the considerable body of clerical and judicial opinion still in opposition to the papal decree. The only effective remedy for such offenses, the magistrates concluded, was an *appel comme d'abus*, which the *curés* were perfectly justified in bringing to the court's con-

---

at this juncture was to prevent the Parlement from dealing with two such potentially explosive issues at the same time (see Chauvelin to Saint-Aignan, May 12, 1732, AAE, C.P., Rome, MS 733, fols. 254-55). Of course, as things turned out, the decree had precisely the opposite of its intended effect.

[199] On the struggles involving the Parlement and the royal government between May and December, see, in addition to the documents cited below, "Journal de ce qui s'est passé au Parlement depuis le 1er janvier [*sic*] jusqu'an 11 décembre suivant," in *Mémoires du Président Hénault*, pp. 384-433; see also *NNEE*, *passim*.

sideration.[200] Another serious jurisdictional/constitutional crisis was thus at hand. The rumblings from the Palais de Justice now gave way to full-scale opposition, next to which the Parlement's previous disputes with Cardinal Fleury's government would pale.

Despite the delicate nature of the situation, Fleury determined to take firm, resolute action against the sovereign court. In the conciliar *arrêt* of May 3, the crown had already announced that all matters concerned with "illegal" or "subversive" publications would be strictly reserved to the royal council. Two days later the administration ordered the Parlement not to issue any judgments on the *curés'* appeal without the king's instructions.[201] But the magistrates were prepared not only to disregard this latest injunction but also to ignore the earlier conciliar *arrêt*. The counselor Pâris, who had been willing to modify, if not entirely abandon, his libel suit against Vintimille, was deeply offended at the royal council's decree, which appeared to have been directed expressly at him. Although the king had commanded the court not to act on his *requête*, Pâris resolved to continue the fight at the next meeting of the assembled chambers, already scheduled for Friday, May 9. But that meeting, at which the magistrates were also expected to consider the complaints contained in the *curés'* appeal, never took place. Having learned of the agenda for the court's session of May 9, the government decided to force a postponement for at least the weekend by ordering the *gens du roi*, two presidents, and the chancellor to meet at Compiègne on that day with the king and his ministers.[202] The discussions with the crown lasted for two days, Fleury and Daguesseau informing the delegation that His Majesty had prohibited the court from taking further cognizance of any and all questions related to the bull *Unigenitus*.[203] The cardinal-minister also commanded them to offer no further remonstrances nor even to deliberate upon this newest prohibition.

The royal order of silence, which the parlementary delegation communicated to the full court on May 12, was designed, of course, to forestall any action the magistrates may have contemplated on either Jérôme-Nicolas de Pâris' petition or the *curés'* appeal. Once again, however, the judges refused to obey and even forbade the *greffier* to

---

[200] BN, J.F., MS 117, fols. 225-26.

[201] *Ibid.*, fol. 224; Maurepas to Joly de Fleury, May 4, 1732, *ibid.*, MS 118, fol. 42.

[202] *Ibid.*, MS 117, fol. 225; *ibid.*, MSS Fr., MS 10232, p. 26.

[203] BN, J.F., MS 117, fol. 226; BPR, L.P. 17, fol. 971. The government actually renewed the earlier orders of silence issued in September 1731.

inscribe the king's order in his registers.[204] With a bitterly defiant abbé Pucelle voicing the most strenuous objections, the magistrates sought to defend their own prerogatives as well as the "fundamental laws of the realm and the very institution of justice. On May 14 Pucelle was arrested along with the counselor Titon and banished indefinitely. The government's rather arbitrary handling of the whole affair merely increased the tension and forced the Parlement to employ new tactics. Affronted by the arrest of their two colleagues, the magistrates resolved on a judicial strike, to continue so long as the royal prohibition remained in effect and until Pucelle and Titon were permitted to return from exile.[205]

Initiated on May 16 and upheld even by the normally compliant *Grand'Chambre*, the strike ended within two weeks, when the king commanded the members of the court to resume their functions. However, while they obeyed the royal order, the magistrates also insisted on their right to judge the legality of Vintimille's *mandement*, which they again denounced as a manifest abuse of ecclesiastical authority. As a result, more trouble broke out immediately and continued to grow in the ensuing weeks.[206] In early June, when the *gens du roi* declined to receive the *curés* as *appelants comme d'abus*,[207] the magistrates named one of their company to assume the functions of the *procureur-général* and issue an *arrêt* admitting the priests' appeal. On June 13 the Parlement issued another *arrêt* banning Vintimille's decree, and on the same day had the latter *arrêt* printed and distributed in public.[208] On the chancellor's recommendation, the government replied to the court's insubordination by ordering the arrest of President Ogier and counselors Robert, de Vrévin, and Davy de La Fautrière.[209] In addition, the king's council issued an *arrêt* of its own, annulling the Parlement's decree of June 13 and forbidding the judges to propose anything which was contrary to His Majesty's orders, "on penalty of confiscation of their offices."[210]

---

[204] The magistrates contended, among other things, that the king could not issue such an order through a mere parlementary delegation that had been only informally deputed to represent the sovereign court before the monarch (BPR, L.P. 17, fol. 971).

[205] For details (down to the events of July 10, 1732) see BN, MSS Fr., MS 10232, pp. 25-32, 41-45, 47-62, 64-225.

[206] Villars, v, 342-43.

[207] For their legal objections see BN, J.F., MS 117, fols. 235-36.

[208] BN, MSS Fr., MS 22091, fols. 20-21.

[209] The *lettres de cachet* were dated June 15, 1732 (AN, O¹ 76, p. 340).

[210] The *arrêt* was dated June 16, 1732 (AN, E2120, fols. 64-65).

With both sides resorting to ever more extreme measures, the deteriorating relations between government and Parlement finally culminated in a collective resignation on June 20 of virtually the entire court, except for the members of the *Grand'Chambre*.[211] The administration of justice came almost to a halt. It was quite a remarkable event, considering the small minority of militant *anticonstitutionnaires* within the entire company.[212] By now, of course, the issues at stake clearly transcended the question of the bull *Unigenitus*. Such was the judges' resentment of their arbitrary and dishonorable treatment from Fleury's government that the proposal of a mass resignation was able to carry a majority of counselors, radical and moderate alike, from among the ordinarily fragmented judicial chambers. The growth of solidarity in parlementary ranks and the building of a united front against objectionable royal policies constituted a major setback for the administration in its efforts to overcome the court's intransigence.

But this mass resignation, this act of ultimate defiance of the royal will, did not force Fleury to capitulate; nor did it dispose him to make any important concessions. On the contrary, for in the view of the cardinal-minister and his advisers, more than just the honor and reputation of the crown were now at stake. Mere magistrates with grand visions of their legitimate prerogatives had called into question the very nature and credibility of royal authority.[213] Fleury would not—indeed, he could not—retreat, for to do so would have been to allow the Parlement's "rebellious insubordination" to get completely out of hand. Two very difficult weeks went by before the judges themselves, under vigorous pressure from the government, finally yielded.[214] On July 6 the entire company reluctantly withdrew its resignations and returned to its functions. But the magistrates were far from ready to submit. No

---

[211] Villars, v, 345-46.

[212] The occasion was described by Barbier, with more than a little exaggeration, as "le plus grand événement que l'on ait vu depuis la monarchie" (II, 295 [June 1732]).

[213] The marquis d'Argenson, long an advocate of forceful, rigorous measures to bring the recalcitrant *curés* and magistrates to heel, produced a substantial number of legal memoranda and position papers for the administration throughout this period. See, in particular, "Mémoires sur les affaires du Parlement" (AAE, M&D, France, MS 1276, fols. 86-91) and "Projet pour la suppression des charges de ceux qui ont donné leur démission" (*ibid.*, fols. 94-95); both of these proposals were offered in late June. For additional such projects and *mémoires* drawn up in the midst of this crisis, some by d'Argenson, others by Courchetet, still others from unknown sources, see *ibid.*, MS 1275, fols. 292-99, 312-15, 330-39, 354-57; *ibid.*, MS 1276, fols. 6-12, 14, 80-84, 92-93; and *ibid.*, MS 1279, fols. 7-15, 25-28, 32-64, 157-63, 183-90. See also d'Argenson's *Journal et mémoires*, I, 115-24, 130-38.

[214] Villars, v, 349.

sooner had they resumed their duties than they became embroiled in still another battle.

Weeks of protracted discussions with the crown over the government's allegedly arbitrary attempts to restrict their jurisdiction proved wholly fruitless. On August 4, therefore, the magistrates presented illegal remonstrances to the king.[215] They vigorously reasserted their opposition to clerical intrusions into the temporal sphere and their absolute right to receive *appels comme d'abus*. They also reiterated their claims to autonomy in the execution of the law. Finally, they demanded the immediate return of their exiled colleagues. Two weeks later, on August 18, the king responded with a lengthy declaration which he ordered the Parlement to register without discussion.[216] The declaration stated that the *Grand'Chambre*—the most conservative and malleable members of the court—should thenceforth have exclusive competence over matters connected with the "fundamental maxims of the realm," including issues of Church-State relations, and have the right to control the plenary sessions of the Parlement, at which political affairs were debated. It severely restricted the court's receipt of *appels comme d'abus* to cases initiated directly by the First President or the other *gens du roi* and prohibited all judicial strikes. It defined the character of remonstrances and limited them "to matters which are within the province of the Parlement."[217] It was, in short, a strong rebuke to the pretensions of the sovereign court to broader jurisdictional competence.[218]

The magistrates, however, concerned that the crown was attempting to ride roughshod over their powers and privileges, would have none of this browbeating. In direct defiance of royal authority, they refused to register the declaration and once again went on strike. On Fleury's advice the king held a *lit de justice* at Versailles on September 3, for the purpose of imposing registration.[219] Even so, the very next day an obstinate Parlement, assembled amid an enthusiastic throng of Parisian well-wishers,[220] announced its refusal to recognize the declaration as legal and binding and its unwillingness to resume its judicial functions.[221] The government was no longer in a mood for temporizing. On

---

[215] Flammermont, I, 277-86.   [216] Isambert, XXI, 374-78.

[217] *Ibid.*, p. 374.

[218] See analysis of Barbier, II, 329 (August 1732).

[219] Flammermont, I, 288-97.

[220] According to d'Argenson, "les zélés Jansénistes étoient répandus et souffloient partout" (letter to [Chauvelin?], Sept. 5, 1732, AAE, M&D, France, MS 1277, fol. 31; see also d'Argenson to [Chauvelin?], Sept. 6, 1732, *ibid.*, fols. 33-35).

[221] Flammermont, I, 298; Barbier, II, 345-56 (September 1732).

September 7 the royal council had 139 presidents and counselors from the chambers of *enquêtes* and *requêtes* exiled to various provincial towns and to other more isolated sections of the kingdom.[222]

These harsh measures resolved nothing and created some severe problems. To be sure, the *Grand'Chambre*, none of whose members was banished, constituted itself a makeshift *chambre des vacations* and obediently registered the royal declaration of August 18. But while Fleury was punishing the rest of the sovereign court, the administration of justice was once again seriously disrupted.[223] During this state of emergency intermittent negotiations were carried on between the government and a number of the magistrates, with Joly de Fleury serving as mediator.[224] Discussions aimed at resolving the crisis were long and involved: at stake were the authority and prestige of the king and the Parlement—not to mention the archbishop of Paris.

Though by mid-November Fleury had agreed to revoke the *lettres de cachet*, it took another few weeks before the two sides could reach a complete accord. Most of the magistrates were back at the Palais de Justice by the first week in December, the judges getting a boisterous reception from the Parisian crowds lining the nearby streets.[225] On December 5, in a formal ceremony at Versailles, the First President assured the king that: "We recognize the entire extent of your absolute and sovereign power; we respect it, and we shall always be ready to set the example for your subjects; we know that you are our master, that it is for you to command and for us to obey. . . ."[226] In exchange for the Parlement's demonstration of obedience, Louis XV permitted all the exiled judges to return to their functions. Replying through his chancellor, the king announced to the parlementary delegation that despite his earlier displeasure with the court, he was willing "to let

[222] AN, O¹ 76, pp. 476-78. Cf. Villars, v, 358-60.

[223] Barbier, II, 358, 360 (October-November 1732).

[224] BN, J.F., MS 117, fols. 117-18. D'Argenson, in the meantime, kept urging the crown to take much harsher measures against the Parlement. In a "Mémoire sur les mesures qui paroissent les meilleures à prendre à l'égard du Parlement de Paris à la Saint-Martin prochaine," dated Sept. 22, 1732, the marquis contended that there was "une forte opinion que le gouvernement étoit extrêmement doux, ou au moins lent à punir"; he also argued that in the sovereign court there reigned "un jansénisme déguisé et un fanatisme violens contre un prétendu danger d'ultramontanisme qui n'existoit point" (AAE, M&D, France, MS 1277, fols. 78-87).

[225] Barbier, II, 366 (December 1732). For a sample of the large number of verses and songs composed in honor of the Parlement, see Raunié, VI, 8-10, 14-19, 27, *et passim*.

[226] Barbier, II, 370 (December 1732). A long excerpt from the *procès-verbal* of the meeting between the king and the parlementary delegations is in Flammermont, I, 298-302.

himself be moved by assurances . . . of respect and submission." He expressed the hope that the magistrates' future conduct would be more pleasing to him. Finally, as a "sign of his confidence and his benevolence," he agreed to suspend the obnoxious declaration of August 18 without actually revoking it or withdrawing it from the Parlement's registers.[227] At last the battle was over.

Historians have long debated whether Fleury or the Parlement was the real victor in this particular phase of their long struggle. Contemporaries were themselves unable to agree in their evaluation of the outcome. "The Jansenists are exultant," observed Barbier,

> and all the young counselors [in the Parlement of Paris] . . . are very proud of having forced the minister [Fleury] to yield. For his part the minister estimates that he has preserved the authority of the king by not actually withdrawing the declaration of last August 18 but only suspending it. . . . The bishops are declaring themselves vanquished, but they do not despair of wreaking their revenge on the Parlement. And the sensible people [*gens sensés*] see the matter as [nothing but] a patchwork compromise, since the heart of the quarrel, which is Jansenism, still remains.[228]

The *gens sensés*, among whom Barbier of course numbered himself, were undoubtedly correct. The accommodation had left essentially unresolved all the fundamental questions—political, juridical, ecclesiastical, and constitutional—surrounding "Jansenism" and the bull *Unigenitus*; they had been papered over in a compromise settlement. Nevertheless, it would be some time before the magistrates, many of whom had spent several very inconvenient and highly unpleasant months in the provinces, were to offer the same vigorous and spirited opposition to government policies that they had displayed in 1732. In that sense one might say that Fleury was the victor. On the other hand, as one historian recently concluded, "the suspension of a declaration which had been registered with all the solemnity of a *lit de justice* represented . . . a setback for the cardinal in his quarrel with the Parlement; it was also damaging to the prestige of the law and to the king's authority."[229] Indeed, in forcing the suspension of the declaration, the magistrates could feel satisfied at having successfully challenged, or at least frustrated, the government's religious policy and at having managed to reassert their claims to broad jurisdictional compe-

[227] Barbier, II, 371 (December 1732); BN, J.F., MS 117, fols. 42-43.
[228] II, 372-73 (December 1732).
[229] J. H. Shennan, *The Parlement of Paris* (Ithaca, 1968), p. 306.

tence in ecclesiastical affairs. Nor was that all. Vintimille's decree officially condemning the *Nouvelles ecclésiastiques*, which months earlier had helped spark this long and drawn-out controversy, remained unenforced—not to say unenforceable—and the archbishop's authority vis-à-vis both the Parlement and his own parish clergy seemed more compromised than ever. Throughout months of almost incessant conflict—now finally subsiding—between Vintimille and the *anticonstitutionnaire* clergy, not a single recalcitrant *curé* had suffered so much as a temporary suspension.[230] And the forbidden *Nouvelles ecclésiastiques*, which had managed to fill its pages all through the summer with verbatim reports of the debates taking place in the Parlement, continued as before to publish without interruption, attracting by now even wider and more favorable attention that it had earlier.

A year which had apparently begun so auspiciously for Archbishop Vintimille, with the various initiatives taken at Saint-Médard, had ended in near disaster. Indeed, as Cardinal Fleury himself was forced to admit, his friend had come out of the crisis of 1732 with the "deepest wounds."[231] In the meantime, while all the wrangling was taking place among crown, Parlement, archbishop, and *curés*, the followers of François de Pâris, observing the struggles with great interest, had been forced to make a major readjustment in the nature of their religious devotions. In the aftermath of the closing of the Saint-Médard cemetery, the convulsionaries, deprived of their blessed shrine at Pâris' tomb, had turned to ever more unusual clandestine practices. For all the outward calm and composure most of them had displayed when the police executed the royal ordinance of January 27, M. Pâris' dedicated adherents had in no way renounced or foresworn their attachment to the saintly deacon's cult. In this respect, too, Vintimille had seemingly expended his energies in vain.

[230] Journal of De Lisle, Sept. 27, 1732, AN, U-378. The *greffier* suggested that "l'on craignoit la révolte dans plusieurs paroisses qui aimoient fort leurs curez."

[231] Fleury to Vintimille, Dec. 20, 1732, BM, MS 2357, p. 821. Cf. the cardinal-minister's very revealing private assessment of Vintimille and of the archbishop's problems in administering his archdiocese (letter to Cardinal Corradini, April 13, 1733, AAE, M&D, Fonds divers [Rome], MS 74, fols. 27-29).

CHAPTER VI

Beyond Saint-Médard:
The Emergence of the Convulsionary Movement*

INSOFAR as Cardinal Fleury's government had intended the closing of the cemetery at Saint-Médard to be accomplished without exacerbating the perennial tensions of ecclesiastical politics, the carefully calculated maneuver had largely been a success. In all the prolonged and involved struggles of 1732, many issues had been heatedly debated, but the question of the royal ordinance of January 27 had never been very seriously joined.[1] To the extent, however, that the cardinal-minister had promulgated the edict with a view toward putting an end to the cult to M. Pâris, the strategy quickly proved a dismal failure. Indeed, the government's action had served as a principal catalyst in the transformation of the cult observances into a quasi-millenarian religious protest movement.

The royal decree, executed by the Paris police on January 29, made an immediate and powerful impact upon the crowds that had been attending the cemetery and worshiping at the tomb of François de Pâris. A report in the *Nouvelles ecclésiastiques* described the pathetic scene among the shocked and troubled people at Saint-Médard. They gathered around the little parish church, consternation and despair visible on nearly every face. Some were moaning or sobbing, others stood in stunned, disbelieving silence. This pitiful, moving spectacle seems even to have touched the large contingent of police officers charged with watching over the area as a precaution against potential

---

* An earlier version of this chapter was first published as "Religious Enthusiasm in Early Eighteenth-Century Paris: The Convulsionaries of Saint-Médard" (*Catholic Historical Review*, 61 [1975], 353-85). The author gratefully acknowledges permission for its use.

[1] For this reason some high government officials saw fit to congratulate themselves—a bit prematurely as matters turned out—on their handling of the "affaire de Saint-Médard." "On a laissé les prétendus miracles devenir tout à fait ridicules," wrote d'Argenson to Chauvelin, "et alors l'authorité a opéré avec applaudissements" (Sept. 6, 1732, AAE, M&D, France, MS 1277, fol. 34). Cf. Fleury to Clement XII, March 24, 1732, AAE, C.P., Rome, MS 733, fols. 12-13.

disturbances—although pity never deterred these guards from effectively carrying out their duty.[2] Indeed, the intimidating presence of
the police no doubt served to deter large numbers, priests and worshipers alike, from publicly venting their true feelings of hostility and
frustration. Submission and patience rather than tumultuous uproar
thus constituted the predominant outward reaction among the faithful.[3]

Nevertheless, to the devoted followers of M. Pâris the closing of the
cemetery merely capped a long series of unjust and repressive measures
which the civil and ecclesiastical authorities had been directing against
them. Even before the royal ordinance, the adherents of the Pâris cult
had endured much adversity and harassment from hostile officials
anxious to stifle their spiritual aspirations and to disrupt their religious
observances.[4] In denying them access to their sacred shrine, however,
the government struck these pious souls an especially severe personal
blow that seemed to threaten their cult's very existence. For most of
these people, therefore, the period after January 1732 was a time of
profound psychological crisis, a period of great uncertainty and major
readjustment. Punished and reviled for their extraordinary love of and
devotion to François de Pâris, regarded as criminals by the State,
effectively isolated within the Church, and forcibly dispossessed of a
major source of spiritual sustenance, the participants in the Pâris cult
found themselves in a difficult situation.[5] The action of the police, so
dramatic and unexpected, not only left the deacon's anxious followers
in a precarious and virtually defenseless position, but also enhanced
their consciousness of persecution and their awareness of their own
impotence. Under these stressful circumstances a major transformation
took place in the fundamental emphasis, character, and purpose of their
religious devotions. Longing for collective deliverance from their
present misfortunes, for an effective release of their undischarged
frustrations, and for a reassuring message of future hope and consola-

[2] *NNEE*, Feb. 17, 1732, pp. 31-32; Hérault to Fleury, Jan. 29, 1732, AAE, M&D,
Ile de France, MS 1599, fols. 285-86; [Hérault?] to [Chauvelin?], Jan. 29, 1732,
AAE, M&D, France, MS 1274, fols. 124-25; Journal of De Lisle, Jan. 29, 1732, AN,
U-377; Barbier, II, 242-43 (January 1732); Marais, IV, 335-36 (Jan. 31, 1732).

[3] Hérault to Fleury, Jan. 29, 1732, AAE, M&D, Ile de France, MS 1599, fol.
285; *NNEE*, Feb. 17, 1732, p. 32.

[4] For direct testimony as to the psychological impact of official repression, see
BHVP, C.P. 3509, p. 1.

[5] Cf. Denton Morrison, "Some Notes Toward Theory on Relative Deprivation,
Social Movements, and Social Change," *American Behavioral Scientist*, 14 (1971),
pp. 675-90; Anthony F. C. Wallace, "Revitalization Movements," *American Anthropologist*, 58 (1956), pp. 264-81; and Michael Barkun, *Disaster and the Millennium* (New Haven, 1974), esp. pp. 34-41.

tion, many of these people turned eagerly to the quasi-millenarian eschatology that was introduced into convulsionary circles at this time by a group of Jansenist priests and theologians.[6]

Over the centuries, in the wake of innumerable social and religious crises, apocalyptic lore had been analyzed, reinterpreted, and vulgarized, often by anonymous and wholly obscure individuals. Though long since ruled out of official doctrine, the eschatological perspective and its apocalyptic and millenarian forms had remained a vital and highly adaptable element of the Christian tradition, persistently retaining its place in what one writer has described as "the obscure underworld of popular religion."[7] Emotionally charged eschatological fantasies about the Last Days, derived in particular from the Book of Revelation as well as from Daniel and other Old Testament prophets, had repeatedly attracted the oppressed and the unprivileged, the frustrated and the discontented—individuals and groups faced with crises in their religious or secular experience and overcome by a sense of disorientation and dislocation. These mystifying apocalyptic visions, full of fantastic, sometimes savage, imagery, often provided a vehicle whereby such people could articulate their grievances and project their

[6] Although it is difficult to determine the precise makeup of this influential group of appellants, they would seem to have come from among the same circle of ecclesiastics who had already done so much to prepare the followers of François de Pâris to interpret the miracles as validation for the *anticonstitutionnaire* cause and had been largely responsible for overseeing the "organisation merveilleux" at the church and in the cemetery of Saint-Médard. See *NNEE*, Aug. 10, 1731, p. 159; *Histoire des miracles et du culte de M. Pâris. Avec les persécutions suscités à sa mémoire et aux malades qui ont eu recours à lui. Pour servir de suite à la Vie de ce saint diacre* (1734), pp. iv-v; *Réflexions sur les miracles que Dieu opère au tombeau de M. Pâris* (n.d.), p. 33; and Jean-Baptiste-Raymond de Pavie de Fourquevaux and Louis Troya d'Assigny, *Catéchisme historique et dogmatique sur les contestations qui divisent maintenant l'Eglise*, 5 vols. (Nancy, 1750-68), IV, 372.

[7] *The Pursuit of the Millennium*, 3rd ed. (New York, 1970), p. 30. In addition to this work by Cohn, there is a large and growing body of literature on apocalyptic and millenarian movements, of which I have found the following particularly useful: Sylvia Thrupp (ed.), *Millennial Dreams in Action* (New York, 1970); Peter Worsley, *The Trumpet Shall Sound*, 2nd ed. (New York, 1968); Henri Desroche, *Dieux d'hommes: Dictionnaire des Messianismes et Millénarismes de l'ère chrétienne* (Paris-The Hague, 1969); Eric Hobsbawm, *Primitive Rebels* (Manchester, 1959); Bryan R. Wilson, "Millennialism in Comparative Perspective," *Comparative Studies in Society and History*, 6 (1963), pp. 93-114; Yonina Talmon, "Pursuit of the Millennium: The Relation Between Religious and Social Change," *European Journal of Sociology*, 3 (1962), pp. 125-48; *idem*, "Millenarian Movements," *ibid.*, 7 (1966), pp. 159-200. See also the recent work of Michael Barkun, cited in n. 5 above.

aspirations. Even while pointing to goals that were generally quite illusory, the richly extravagant scenarios not only offered believers a concrete and meaningful explanation of events, but also held out the hope of ultimate deliverance from current adversity in a new age, one in which God would display His mercy to the persecuted and His vengeful justice to their more powerful enemies. Indeed, it was primarily in and through elements of this apocalyptic tradition—as presented in a modified eighteenth-century Jansenist[8] version—that the convulsionaries would find their greatest inspiration, justification, and consolation.

For over two decades a number of prominent *anticonstitutionnaires*, initially aroused by the arbitrary destruction of Port-Royal and despairing of the fate of Christianity, had been employing the traditional method of "figurative" exegesis of Scripture in use since the days of St. Paul.[9] In developing these exegetical techniques and applying them specifically to the controversy surrounding the bull *Unigenitus*, these theologians followed in particular the influential and prolific Jean-Baptiste Le Sesne des Ménilles, abbé d'Etemare,[10] lecturer at the famous Oratorian seminary of Saint-Magloire in Paris, whose numerous disciples included theologians, bishops, and lower clergy, among them François de Pâris himself.[11] These "figurists" were especially interested

[8] One can begin to appreciate the changes in character and emphasis which the Jansenist movement had undergone by the eighteenth century if one recalls the basic hostility to chiliasm that had earlier been associated with Port-Royal. For a brief analysis of this question, see Alfred-Félix Vaucher, *Une célébrité oubliée: le P. Manuel de Lacunza y Diaz (1731-1801)* (Collonges-sous-Salève, 1941), pp. 163-64, n. 350.

[9] See, in particular, *Les [3] Gémissements d'une âme vivement touchée de la destruction du saint monastère de Port-Royal-des-Champs* (1710-13). There was also a *4ᵉ Gémissement d'une âme vivement touchée de la constitution [Unigenitus]* . . . (1714), which was in the same figurist vein as the three previous ones. All four tracts were written by the abbés d'Etemare and Boyer. Cf. also *NNEE*, March 26, 1729, p. 44; BA, MS 5307, *passim* ("Lettres adressées à l'abbé François de Joubert").

[10] On d'Etemare see obituary in *NNEE*, Feb. 13 and 27, 1771, pp. 25-33. Cf. Bruno Neveu, "Etemare," *Dictionnaire de biographie française*, XIII, cols. 185-86. This long-lived Jansenist (1682-1770) left an enormous correspondence, most of which is now in Utrecht, AFA; see also BA, MS 5784, which contains copies of many of d'Etemare's letters on the Saint-Médard episode.

[11] *NNEE*, April 8, 1735, p. 51. There is a need for a careful and thorough study of Jansenist "figurism." The available secondary literature, inadequate and often rather superficial and misleading, includes: E. Mangenot, "Figurisme," *DTC*, V², cols. 2,229-304; Roger Mercier, *La réhabilitation de la nature humaine (1700-1750)* (Villemonble, 1960), p. 283; Dedieu, "L'agonie du jansénisme," pp. 199-200,

in the eschatological aspects of Scripture and in the application of various millenarian predictions to the contemporary state of the Church.[12] Meeting in small study-groups at Saint-Magloire and elsewhere, they attempted through careful examination of and meditation upon the sacred texts to penetrate beyond the most obscure and enigmatic passages, to discover biblical prefigurations of religious events down to the present and into the future, and to reveal the meaning or purpose behind the ordeals of persecution to which they and their coreligionists were being subjected. Though their work was scarcely original,[13] these learned divines claimed to discern striking parallels between cataclysmic situations described or announced in Scripture and those which had befallen the Church in early eighteenth-century France. They argued, in particular, that the destruction of Port-Royal, the promulgation of the bull *Unigenitus*, and the series of royal and ecclesiastical pronouncements issued in support of it were evident portents of the universal apostasy at the end of time which had been proclaimed by the Old Testament prophets and predicted by St. Paul. While denouncing the "present evils" and decrying the "corruption

---

et passim; and Préclin and Jarry, *Les luttes politiques et doctrinales*, I, 250-51. More reliable, but still not very satisfactory are Desroche, pp. 14, 110, 115, 117-18, 134, 155, 168, 186; and Vaucher, *passim*. The best place to begin an examination of this subject is the Bibliothèque municipale de Troyes, which contains probably the single most complete collection of figurist tracts. This extraordinary collection includes some short pieces, but the majority consists of book-length manuscripts; many represent "conférences faites à Saint-Etienne-du-Mont" in Paris. The *cotes* of the relevant MSS are as follows: 771, 939-40, 945, 1009-15, 1017-19, 1050, 1052-53, 1055-56, 1058-62, 1065, 1073, 1104, 1122, 1190-91, 1198, 1277, 1281, 1338, 1567, 1577, 1585, 1587-88, 1642-45, 1650, 1653, 1658, 1660, 1663, 1665, 1670, 1672, 1674-78, 1793, 1798, 1803-1804, 1809-10, 1818-19, 1821-23, 1825, 1827, 1833, 2079, 2094, 2097-98, 2100, 2106, 2114, 2116, 2119-20, 2125, 2129-30, 2150, 2163, 2174, 2178. Perhaps the best exposition of the figurist position is Fourquevaux, *L'introduction abrégée à l'intelligence des prophéties de l'Ecriture, par l'usage qu'en fait saint Paul dans l'Epître aux Romains* (1731); cf. also *idem, Catéchisme historique*, II, 291-301, for a brief survey of the subject.

[12] *Parallèle de la vie du sauveur au temps présent* (BPR, L.P. 481, No. 6); [d'Etemare], *Essai d'un parallèle du temps de Jésus-Christ et des nôtres* . . . (n.d.); [François Joubert], *Parallèle abrégé de l'histoire du peuple d'Israël et de l'histoire de l'Eglise* (1723); [abbé Gudver], *Jésus-Christ sous l'anathème et l'excommunication* (Amsterdam, 1731; numerous subsequent editions).

[13] Any study of figurism would need to take cognizance of the similarities (and differences) between the doctrines of this "school" and the teachings of medieval Joachites and Renaissance cabalists. See, for example, William J. Bouwsma, *Concordia Mundi: The Career and Thought of Guillaume Postel, 1510-1581* (Cambridge, Mass., 1957), pp. 39-40, *et passim*; and Joseph L. Blau, *The Christian Interpretation of the Cabala in the Renaissance* (New York, 1944), esp. pp. 2-6.

and degeneration of the Church," they also became increasingly pre-occupied with reviving the ancient theme of the return of the prophet Elias, or Elijah, the eschatological precursor whose mysterious advent was traditionally interpreted as a prelude to the conversion of the Jews to the Christian faith and their restoration to their homeland, as a herald of the coming of Jesus Christ and the incarnation of the Holy Spirit, and as an announcement of the imminence of the Last Days— all events which must precede the spiritual regeneration of the world.[14] In short, their work combined a sense of both apprehension and hope; their despondency over contemporary spiritual corruption was tem-pered by consoling predictions of eventual delivery at an indefinite future date.

Although these "figurist" ideas and theological musings had already been circulating in *anticonstitutionnaire* circles for some twenty years, they had until recently reached no more than a limited audience. Be-fore the mid-1720s only a few of the major exegetical works had been published, the others remaining in manuscript form.[15] But even after a steady stream of important treatises had begun to appear in print, the figurist viewpoint had remained confined to a fairly narrow group of theologians and clergy.[16] In the early 1730s, however, a handful of *anticonstitutionnaire* writers, with the support of a small group of appellant priests who had long been active participants in the Pâris cult, began a concerted effort to adapt the figurist writings to a less

[14] D'Etemare's principal figurist works on these subjects are listed in the bibli-ography. Among the numerous treatises published during this period on the coming of Elijah, perhaps the most important was that of Alexis Desessarts, *De l'avène-ment d'Elie*, 2 vols. (1734-35). On the conversion of the Jews, cf. "XIV vérités sur la conversion des juifs," in Jacques-Joseph Duguet, *Règles pour l'intelligence des Ecritures saintes* (1716); and the anonymous *La tradition des Saints Pères sur la conversion des juifs* (1724).

[15] Two other leading Jansenists who, along with d'Etemare, made a major con-tribution to the early development of figurist exegesis were the Oratorian Father Duguet, friend and confidant of Arnauld and Nicole, and his disciple and col-league, Jacques-Vincent Bidal d'Asfeld. At the parish churches of Saint-Roch and Saint-Etienne-du-Mont between 1710 and 1721 these two men conducted numerous *conférences ecclésiastiques* in which they offered doctrinal instruction on the "rules for understanding Holy Scripture" (see Sainte-Beuve, III, 510-12). These *figuristes mitigés* were not prepared to push their allegorical interpretations of Scripture as far as d'Etemare and his disciples and eventually were to split with the latter over the question of the convulsionaries. Most of Duguet's works were published posthumously (i.e., after 1733); d'Etemare's *Explication de l'Apoca-lypse*, written in collaboration with two fellow Jansenists, Paul Mérault and Nicolas Le Gros, was not even published until 1866.

[16] Dedieu, "Le désarroi janséniste," p. 579. See also Fourquevaux, *Catéchisme historique*, II, 291-301.

learned public.[17] Together they hoped to make the chaotic sequences, esoteric prophecies, and cryptic symbolism contained in the apocalyptic writings more accessible to the faithful adherents of M. Pâris and to give the activities of his followers a more explicitly pro-Jansenist theological impetus. By the spring of 1732, without necessarily committing themselves fully to a millenarian ideology or assimilating the entire figurist package, the convulsionaries afforded these priests and theologians a receptive audience.[18]

Eventually exploited in justification of the convulsionaries' own prophetic visions and ecstatic religious experiences, the controversial eschatological views of the figurists also formed the basis of the movement's newly found conception of its vital mission: to prepare for the creation, and assist in the establishment, of a new dispensation and to effect thereby nothing less than a total religious renewal of the Church. In this time of patent injustice, moral corruption, and spiritual bankruptcy, the convulsionaries began to believe that they had been specifically chosen by God to combat the malevolent forces in the ecclesiastical establishment and entrusted with the responsibility of somehow purging the Church and restoring it to the pure faith and simple virtue of the apostolic age. They came to feel that they had received a divine call to be the messengers of redemption, and that their appointment to such an awesome task had clear antecedents and precedents which could be traced back to the very sources of Christianity. The holy document of the primitive church itself seemed unambiguously to define their redemptive mission.[19] Like the first Christians and the early martyrs, fellow defenders of the true faith with whom they increasingly identified themselves, the convulsionaries determined to carry on the struggle in the face of persecution and to continue practicing their devotions, even if these efforts required their own ultimate martyrdom.[20] Although they never managed to produce any formal

---

[17] *NNEE*, Nov. 25, 1731, p. 227. Fourquevaux's *Introduction abrégée* was designed to bring together the figurist ideas in a clear, organized format, "à la portée des simples fidèles."

[18] Cf. the analysis of "the disaster origins of millenarian movements" in Barkun, Ch. 2, but esp. pp. 55-57.

[19] Though not cited by them specifically, I Cor. 1:26-29 and 12:27-28, along with other similar biblical passages, must have been very familiar to the convulsionaries and no doubt provided them with descriptions of early evangelical communities which closely resembled their own.

[20] A knowledge of the ordeals suffered by many of their brethren, past and present, continued to be transmitted through pious biographies, necrologies, and pamphlets as well as by oral tradition and provided the convulsionaries with their own equivalent of a martyrology. See, for example, Pierre Barral, *Appellans célèbres* (1753); René Cerveau, *Nécrologe des plus célèbres défenseurs et con-*

or well-coordinated program for achieving these goals, the convulsionaries' growing sense of collective mission gave their movement a more
definite focus and direction than it had ever had before January 1732.
At the same time, such beliefs did much to shape the self-conscious
group identity which developed within the movement in subsequent
months and years.

Far from stifling the convulsionaries' dedication to the memory of
François de Pâris or putting an end to their observances in his honor,
the closing of the cemetery at Saint-Médard thus served only to deepen
their commitment. What is more, by forcing the convulsionaries to
disperse, the royal ordinance had the unanticipated effect of further
spreading the cult and rousing its adherents to even greater heights
of religious enthusiasm. In the months which followed the interdiction
of the cemetery, alternative holy sites proliferated; the presence of relics from M. Pâris, including dirt from his tomb and water from a well
which had once belonged to him, inspired religious services which
were often far more spectacular and controversial than those that had
been witnessed at the deacon's grave. Largely in an effort to escape
police surveillance, the convulsionaries—like the first Christians, intense and insecure—formed themselves into small bands and began to
hold clandestine meetings at private homes and religious houses[21]
throughout the city. Joining together for mutual comfort and support,
they patterned these embattled conventicles after the model of the
apostolic church, and, in conscious emulation of their sacred forebears,
turned these places into "domestic churches, places of worship and
prayer, and, so to speak, stations of the little cemetery of Saint-Médard."[22] Scattered about though they were, each of the convulsionary
groups maintained some kind of contact, usually informal, with the
others. The city of Paris, an anonymous writer declared, had been
turned into one large temple.[23]
While the convulsionaries refrained from any concerted campaign
of evangelism to recruit converts to their cause, they quite openly

---

fesseurs de la Vérité du 18ᵉ siècle, 2 vols. (1760); and the numerous obituaries
published in the *Nouvelles ecclésiastiques* throughout this period.

[21] The cult flourished in several monastic settings in Paris, particularly in female
orders and congregations, including the convent of Sainte-Agathe, the Sisters of
the Visitation, the Ursulines, and the Sisters of Sainte-Marthe.

[22] *Pensées sur les prodiges de nos jours*, p. 9. Similar references to such "petites
églises domestiques" are found in Frère Hilaire (chevalier de Blaru, convulsionary)
to Soanen, Nov. 28, 1733, AFA, P.R. 6439.

[23] *Entretiens sur les miracles*, p. 12.

welcomed new "members," fellow *amis* (and *amies*) *de la Vérité*, to join in their observances and to share in the experience of spiritual renewal.[24] Despite a sectarian sense that they constituted a divinely chosen elect, a gathered remnant charged with special responsibilities, the convulsionaries do not seem to have believed that they were to remain limited in size by divine command. They never asserted an absolute exclusiveness, and precluded no one from becoming a full-fledged participant in their devotions. Most new adherents, attracted primarily by word of mouth or through face-to-face contact, were specifically "sponsored" or invited by someone—a relative, friend, or neighbor—already active in the group and were thus accepted without any prerequisites of entry. However, as a precaution against the infiltration of police spies or of other undesirable intruders, anyone who sought to gain admittance on his own was frequently required to know a certain secret signal.[25] Even so, there was no covenant or oath of membership to which the individual had to adhere in order to "join" the movement, no rites of initiation, no strict doctrinal or behavioral standards of admission to the fellowship, no process of "socializing" newcomers. There were, moreover, no tests of good faith, no sanctions against those who contravened the movement's fundamental precepts, no specific grounds for or means of expulsion. On the other hand, considering the risks incurred in belonging to such a proscribed group, continued membership and active participation presumably indicated a fairly intense commitment and attachment to the fellowship itself.

It would be of great interest to know in some detail what sorts of people were drawn to these convulsionary conventicles. Unfortunately, however, the evidence available does not permit one to gain a very clear or precise picture of the social composition of the movement or to draw an adequate psychological profile of the sect's adherents. Despite a wealth of surviving materials bearing on convulsionary beliefs and activities, the documents do not yield much specific data on such critical questions as the provenience of members, recruitment patterns, intensity of commitment, and turnover of participants.[26] Nevertheless,

---

[24] Testimony of Femme La Coste (convulsionary), AN, X-1b 9690.

[25] According to the testimony of Claude Chambon (*ibid.*), "il falloit avoir à la main un papier roullé"; cf. BA, MS 11218, fol. 34; and Barbier, II, 385, February 1733.

[26] The abundant police records, potentially the most promising, are notably disappointing in this regard. Despite the hundreds of arrests and scores of intensive interrogations, neither police nor parlementary inquisitors were able to elicit much detailed information of this sort from their convulsionary captives, most of whom remained tight-lipped and uncooperative. Biographical data which might disclose

some general patterns in the nature of the sect's membership do emerge from the sources, uneven though these are. As was the case at Saint-Médard before the closing of the cemetery, a very mixed company, persons of every age, condition, and temperament, was attracted to the convulsionary meetings.[27] To be sure, the great majority continued to come from the obscure and relatively uneducated laboring poor, individuals who had at best a fairly marginal relationship to established sources of power. But these were not, by and large, the most deprived or the most vulnerable segment of this chronically disadvantaged population. The miserable, rootless dregs of society, the wretched, unassimilated provincials and outcasts who constituted the principal recruiting ground for many other medieval and early modern millenarian movements, do not seem to have flocked to the convulsionary *séances* in any significant numbers. On the contrary, the *menu peuple* who joined the convulsionary movement comprised a relatively settled population. While leading lives of varying degrees of precariousness, most of them were apparently long-time residents of Paris, with fixed abodes and fairly regular, if not always adequately compensated, employment: tanners, stocking-weavers, cabinet-makers, locksmiths, cloth-workers, laundresses, and domestics, to cite just a few of the most common occupations.

Although the *menu peuple* constituted a clear majority of the movement's adherents, most of the other status and social groups of *ancien-régime* France were likewise represented at these conventicles. At one time or another during the early 1730s the convulsionaries could count among their number regular and secular clergy, nobles of the robe and sword, merchants and financiers, cultivated men of letters and royal functionaries, lawyers and notaries—high-status, solidly respectable persons of education and influence. The membership, of course, was in a constant state of flux, but many of these "notables" remained active, committed participants in the sect's affairs throughout this period, providing much of the patronage and protection which helped to sustain the movement even in the worst of times.[28]

---

the actual reasons for commitment to (or withdrawal from) the convulsionary cause are likewise very scant. The fact that most parish records for *ancien-régime* Paris have not survived only compounds these problems.

[27] *Recherche de la Vérité, ou Lettres sur l'oeuvre des convulsions* (1733), p. 8; *Lettre d'un ecclésiastique de province à un de ses amis, où il lui donne une idée abrégée de l'oeuvre des convulsions* (1733), pp. 16-17.

[28] Some of these people offered their homes both as sanctuaries from the police and as places of worship. Others used their influence to intercede with the police on behalf of convulsionaries who had already been arrested. They also provided substantial material assistance to those in need.

Social diversity notwithstanding, status within the various conventicles derived exclusively from the individual's contribution to the group itself—without reference to wealth or to the noble and honorific ranks, titles, and privileges which obtained in the society at large. Theirs was fundamentally a community of religious equals, each member having the same "quality" as every other and all activities taking place in a relatively open and democratic atmosphere. On entering into the movement, everyone adopted a pseudonym, *Soeur* "X" or *Frère* "Y," not only to preserve anonymity and thereby perhaps escape detection by the police—which was naturally essential for the continued survival of the movement—but also to sustain the sect's fraternal and egalitarian spirit and the mystique of an in-group.[29] Some of the names were borrowed from Scripture, others drawn from the hallowed tradition of Port-Royal. Still other names derived from distinctive physical traits of the individual or from important personal reminiscences or events in his life.[30] Whatever the source of their names, many of these people, previously complete strangers, continued to know and to address one another only by such appellations, even after long and close personal contact in convulsionary circles. Any role differences or distinctions among the brethren were founded ostensibly on a differentiation of the divine gifts (*dons charismatiques*) bestowed by God upon the individual convulsionary and of the particular services, material or spiritual, which each member performed for the collective body.[31] As with many other such movements the convulsionaries also elevated the religious standing of women, opening to them all the

[29] It is not clear whether any religious ceremony—some kind of second or "rebaptism"—accompanied the adoption of these new names, but in any event this act apparently marked the individual's admission into the fellowship and served to symbolize the beginning of his personal renewal and "resurrection" and his dedication to the convulsionary mission.

[30] Some examples: Soeur La Croix (Marie Gault or Got) was so named because she was born on Good Friday; Soeur Roch (Suzanne Cellier) received her name because she had her first convulsions on the Feast of St. Roch; "La Soeur au Petit Pain" (Dame Roger) was so called because "elle fait des petits pains, dans lesquels elle met des reliques de M. de Pâris et autres, et qu'elle distribue à toutes les convulsionnaires . . . pour guérir les malades" (testimony of Soeur Virginie, AN, X-1b 9690). Of course, their use of pseudonyms could give rise to a great deal of confusion, especially for the historian, since some names were adopted by more than one person, while some people—mostly as an added precaution against identification or capture by the police—went by more than one appellation.

[31] See BN, NAFr., MS 4262, fol. 82, *et passim*. Held in especially high regard were the so-called *quatre grands frères*: "Ce nom leur a été donné parce qu'ils ont prononcé les plus beaux discours et ont annoncé les plus grands événements et non parce qu'ils occupoient un rang [supérieur]" (*ibid.*, fol. 83).

important service and ritual roles and welcoming them as full and active participants on a basis of complete spiritual equality.[32] In short, in the convulsionary community, unlike either the Gallican Church or the French state, neither social nor legal status—not even gender—counted for very much. From the highest noble to the lowliest and most humble of the laboring poor, all were *frères* and *soeurs*, leveled to a common condition and equally members of the *justes*.

The *séance* gatherings were not intended as an all-consuming activity or designed to provide a stable, all-inclusive environment for their members; the loyalties and commitments generated among the brethren were not total ones. The communal solidarity of these people did not demand that the participants remain together when they were not holding worship services (though there might be a good deal of other contact among adherents during the rest of the week), nor was it built upon a complete rejection of the world outside. Despite an undercurrent of frustration and dissatisfaction with the established secular order and certain of its dominant values, the convulsionaries had no particular obsession about withdrawing or segregating themselves from an "unredeemed" society at large. In addition, though some convulsionaries appear to have been less than assiduous in the fulfillment of their prescribed religious duties and though others may have ceased to attend church altogether, such behavior was not always intended as a sign of disrespect. One woman was reported to have stopped attending Mass simply because she was overcome by violent convulsions whenever she did so.[33] With few exceptions,[34] most of the brethren continued to pursue their normal, mundane activities—including regu-

---

[32] The opportunities afforded women in "peripheral" religious movements of this sort have frequently been remarked. See, in particular, Knox, *Enthusiasm*, p. 20; Keith Thomas, "Women and the Civil War Sects," in Trevor Aston (ed.), *Crisis in Europe, 1560-1660* (New York, 1965), pp. 317-40; and Natalie Z. Davis, "City Women and Religious Change," in *Society and Culture in Early Modern France* (Stanford, 1975), esp. pp. 66-67. Cf. also I. M. Lewis, *Ecstatic Religion: An Anthropological Study of Spirit Possession and Shamanism* (Harmondsworth, 1971), esp. Ch. 3.

[33] BA, MS 11285, fol. 121.

[34] While the majority saw nothing incompatible about remaining in their usual jobs, others believed that they had been called by God to devote themselves full time to the *oeuvre*. Some were simply unable to continue their normal way of life because of the persistent convulsions they continued to experience for months —and in certain cases for years—at a time; these people were forced to rely on others for financial support. See the testimony of Frère Noel (J.-B. Lamain), AN, X-1b 9690 and that of Jacques Spayement, *ibid.*; see also the cases of Frère Didier (M. Fontaine), Frère Simon (M. Auffroi), and Frère Louis (Louis Sabinet), BN, NAFr., MS 4262, fols. 90, 92, 99, and 122-23.

lar church attendance—gathering together as a community only to participate in their religious observances.

The convulsionary movement thus comprised an ill-defined, poly-cephalous network of small, semiautonomous local cells, without a specific, unified leadership or channel of authority and command, but with a large and diverse body of ardent believers. In the absence of any formal, centralized structure or clearly articulated organization, it was the immediate personal ties and interactions among the adherents within each group as well as their intimately shared religious experiences and common liturgical rituals which seem to have been major sources of the movement's initial cohesion. Typically,[35] the convulsionary meetings brought together anywhere from a handful to two dozen or so devotees,[36] some of whom in preparation for these sessions and in imitation of François de Pâris had already undergone extended periods of austere penitence, including intense mortifications, prolonged sleep deprivation, and excessive fasting—self-imposed physical punishments which no doubt help to account for some of the ecstatic experiences which subsequently dominated the sect's activities.[37] These small bands of convulsionaries would ordinarily gather together at the same place several times a week and at a fixed time of the day, usually in the evenings; generally the sessions lasted several hours, but

[35] What follows is a composite based on manuscript sources and on several published convulsionist tracts, nearly all of them anonymous. Among the most useful manuscript materials are the sworn depositions of the following: Michel Meignan (AN, X-1b 9692), Louis-Alexandre Doutreleau (*ibid.*), Claude Chambon (*ibid.*), Edme Pierre Le Plaideur Sigy (*ibid.*), and Femme La Coste (X-1b 9690). In addition to the pamphlets already cited above, the most useful include: *Réflexions sur l'Ordonnance du roi du 17 février 1733* (1733); [Julien-René-Benjamin de Gennes], *Coup d'oeil, en forme de lettre, sur les convulsions* (1733); [Poncet Desessarts], *Lettres de M.* à un de ses amis, sur l'oeuvre des convulsions* (1734); [abbé d'Etemare], *Lettre d'un ecclésiastique à un évêque* (n.d.); [Nicolas Le Gros], *Lettre . . . à un de ses amis, au sujet de l'oeuvre des convulsions* (1734); Louis-Basile Carré de Montgeron, *La vérité des miracles opérés à l'intercession de M. de Pâris et autres appelants . . .* (1737), and his *Continuation des démonstrations des miracles . . .* (1741); and *Défense de l'autorité et des décisions des merveilles que Dieu ne cesse point de faire en France depuis un grand nombre d'années*, 2 vols. (1752).

[36] They tried to keep their numbers within each group fairly small and to practice their ceremonies as quietly and as unobtrusively as possible in order to avoid arousing the suspicions of unfriendly neighbors or those of the police (M. Le Grand to Bishop Soanen, Oct. 6, 1736, AFA, P.R. 6685).

[37] It was widely believed that subjecting oneself to the same sorts of bodily deprivations as M. Pâris had endured was a necessary prerequisite for obtaining the deacon's intercession.

they could go on for one or two full days.[38] Since there were no initiation rites and no one was required to pledge exclusive allegiance to any particular group, individuals could (and did) feel free to attend several different conventicles in a given week. Thus, while each conventicle had a core group in more or less regular attendance, there was much overlapping of membership between and among conventicles, and the composition of any one congregation might vary from session to session. In this way the various convulsionary groups were able to maintain their cohesion and ideological unity across the loose and informal network which tied them all together.

These private services were conceived of as a direct extension of the religious ceremonies conducted at François de Pâris' sacred tomb. The fact that each conventicle—and sometimes every member in the conventicle—possessed some relic associated with M. Pâris guaranteed the deacon's spiritual presence in their midst at all times.[39] The group "renewed itself" with each meeting, which took place in an atmosphere of intense devotion and collective exaltation. In order to preserve a constant sense of anticipation and spontaneity among the congregation and to allow the power of the Holy Spirit to work its full effect upon the assembly, an effort was made to avoid imposing any prescribed set of rites and practices in the observances. A high degree of informality and spontaneous lay participation thus came to mark these services; each individual became in some way an actor in the religious drama, rather than a passive observer. At the same time, however, though no one was actually delegated responsibility for managing or structuring the group's activities, priests and other ecclesiastics present frequently tended to assume various leadership functions, opening and sometimes conducting the ceremonies, offering uplifting words of encouragement and exhortation to the faithful, and in general ensuring that the services did not proceed in a wholly random or chaotic manner.[40] It was largely as a result of such priestly guidance and supervision that certain patterns of procedure (with occasional variations in sequence) seem to have developed at these meetings.

The session usually began with a period of common prayers and

[38] See, for example, BN, MSS Fr., MS 22326, pp. 457-89.

[39] Some especially prized relics were shared in common among the various conventicles. Father Pierre Boyer, who possessed the *ceinture* of M. Pâris, brought it around to the different *séances* he attended and put it on anyone who wished to wear it (testimony of Femme La Coste, AN, X-1b 9690).

[40] The very presence of substantial numbers of priests in their midst no doubt served as an implicit legitimation of the movement for many of the participants, who might otherwise have been more hesitant about joining.

meditation and the invocation of the Holy Spirit through the intercession of François de Pâris. Someone would read and interpret a passage from Scripture, whereupon the assembled company joined in a recitation of psalms. Other acts of worship were similarly performed in common and served to reaffirm the unity of the members and the communal purpose of the group. The brethren regaled each other with stories of miraculous cures they had heard about or personally experienced during the week. They also joined together to request cures for fellow sectaries as yet not so fortunate. Thus was built up the feeling of solidarity and pious fellowship that served to reinforce their faith in and attachment to M. Pâris.[41]

These people had not come together in secret, however, simply for the purpose of holding prayer meetings and pietistic devotions or exchanging marvelous tales, no matter how uplifting these may have been. Indeed, various other activities, many of them quite remarkable and strange, some seeming to defy rational explanation or scientific understanding, went on at these group sessions and help to account for the subsequent uproar which greeted the *oeuvre des convulsions*.[42] At some point during the *séance*, while the assembled company redoubled their prayers and collectively reached extreme heights of religious enthusiasm, at least one of their number would suddenly lapse into uncontrolled motor activity of varying duration and degrees of intensity. Emotionally overwrought and overcome by the mounting fervor and group tension, many of these adepts would be seized with violent movements and astounding agitations of the body, often far more elaborate than the spasms and convulsions which had previously been observed at Saint-Médard. They thrashed about on the floor in a state of frenzy, screaming, roaring, trembling, and twitching. Some adopted strange postures and expressions, their bodies and features often twisted into grotesquely contorted shapes. The excitement and the disordered movements, which might last for several hours, usually proved highly contagious, with certain convulsionaries apparently

[41] *Lettre d'un ecclésiastique de province*, p. 17; BHVP, N.A. 125, 1, 369.

[42] BN, NAFr., MS 4262, fol. 82, *et passim*. The brethren used both *oeuvre* and *oeuvre des convulsions* to describe the diverse activities in which they engaged after the closing of the Saint-Médard cemetery. The terms are discussed in several works, most notably the anonymous *Mémoire sur le terme d'Oeuvre des convulsions* (n.d.). On the tremendous variety of phenomena associated with the *oeuvre*, see the *Lettre d'un ecclésiastique de province*, p. 18. For recent accounts of the more lurid and sensational aspects of the convulsionary movement, see Knox, pp. 372-88; and Eric Dingwall, *Some Human Oddities: Studies in the Queer, the Uncanny and the Fanatical* (New York, 1962), Ch. 4.

serving as a catalyst for the onset of various bodily agitations in others gathered about the room.[43] As intense waves of emotion swept over the group, individuals of a "hysterical nature" and those who were most suggestible were probably among the first to begin experiencing these seizures.[44] The ability to have convulsions—a behavior which, depending on cultural environment, conditioning factors, and expectations, apparently can be systematically induced, transmitted, or taught[45] —became itself a prestigious status symbol, a sign of truly belonging, as well as a manifestation of the divine presence; and no doubt, it earned for at least some of these previously obscure, neglected indi-

[43] Testimony of Denise Regnier, AN, X-1b 9690.

[44] From among the large body of medical and psychological literature on the concept of "hysteria," I have found the following particularly useful: George L. Engel, "Conversion Symptoms," in Cyril M. MacBryde and Robert S. Blacklow (eds.), *Signs and Symptoms: Applied Pathologic Physiology and Clinical Interpretation*, 5th ed. (Philadelphia, 1970), pp. 650-68; Henri Ey, "Introduction à l'étude actuelle de l'hystérie (Historique et analyse du concepte)," *La revue du praticien*, 14 (1964), pp. 1,416-31; John C. Nemiah, "Hysterical Neurosis, Conversion Type," in *Comprehensive Textbook of Psychiatry*, ed. Alfred M. Freedman, Harold I. Kaplan, and Benjamin J. Sadock, 2nd ed., 2 vols. (Baltimore, 1975), I, 1,208-20; Paul Chodoff, "The Diagnosis of Hysteria: An Overview," *American Journal of Psychiatry*, 131 (1974), pp. 1,073-78. Cf. also Alan R. G. Owen, *Hysteria, Hypnosis, and Healing: The Work of J.-M. Charcot* (New York, 1971), esp. pp. 55-123. Of course, the diagnosis of "hysterical" seizures is problematical at best, even with live patients, and speculation about the medical or psychological nature of these manifestations among the convulsionaries is thus extremely difficult.

[45] This type of behavior and the altered mental states associated with it are still not very well understood. As one writer has pointed out, this "relatively uncharted realm of mental activity . . . [has] been neither systematically explored nor adequately conceptualized" (Arnold M. Ludwig, "Altered States of Consciousness," in *Trance and Possession States*, ed. Raymond Prince [Montreal, 1968], p. 69). According to some researchers, complex biochemical and neurophysiological mechanisms are apparently involved in the various forms of behavior ordinarily grouped under the term, "hyperarousal dissociation." See, for example, I. C. Stoddard, "The Effects of Voluntarily Controlled Alveolar Hyperventilation on CO_2 Excretion," *Quarterly Journal of Experimental Physiology*, 52 (1967), pp. 369-81. On the cultural and social mechanisms which may also be at work here, see Felicitas Goodman, *Speaking in Tongues: A Cross-Cultural Study of Glossolalia* (Chicago, 1972); idem, Jeannette Henney, and Esther Pressel, *Trance, Healing, and Hallucination: Three Field Studies in Religious Experience* (New York, 1974); Erika Bourguignon (ed.), *Religion, Altered States of Consciousness, and Social Change* (Columbus, 1973); idem, "The Self, the Behavioral Environment, and the Theory of Spirit Possession," in Melford E. Spiro, ed., *Context and Meaning in Cultural Anthropology* (New York, 1965), pp. 39-60; and Alfred Métraux, "Dramatic Elements in Ritual Possession," *Diogenes*, no. 11 (1955), pp. 18-36. Finally, cf. Carroll Smith-Rosenberg, "The Hysterical Woman: Sex Roles and Role Conflict in 19th-Century America," *Social Research*, 39 (1972), pp. 652-78.

viduals, now the focus of the group's attention, a degree of esteem and a measure of fame that few would otherwise have ever known.[46] Under such circumstances the *séances* must have encouraged the onset of renewed episodes and presumably attracted a fair proportion of persons already suffering from a variety of psychomotor disturbances and chronic nervous disorders, especially epileptics—a situation which probably helped to swell the numbers of actual convulsionaries within the movement. In fact, after the first year or so following the closing of the cemetery, several hundred people, a large majority of them women, were reportedly overcome with these seizures.[47]

Many of those who exhibited this unusual kinetic behavior professed to be in excruciating pain during the experience and demanded relief. Their suffering, it was discovered, could be alleviated only by the application of what came to be called *secours*.[48] The term *secours*, which incorporated the meaning of both assistance and relief (succor), referred to a series of diverse procedures administered to the convulsionaries by fellow participants in the cult known as *secouristes* (or *valets de chambre*), who assumed the responsibilities of surveillance and assistance once the adepts were seized by these convulsive move-

[46] At the same time, each assembly came to acquire a certain notoriety and reputation, depending on the different aspects of the *oeuvre* featured there and the variety of *dons charismatiques* or special skills displayed by its "stars."

[47] It is very difficult, if not impossible, to determine with any degree of assurance the number of people who actually experienced these convulsions, especially since both proponents and opponents of the movement—none of whom could have possibly attended all of the *séances*—had their reasons for exaggerating the numbers. In addition, not only was sectarian participation generally a well-kept secret, but "membership" was constantly changing, with frequent comings and goings occurring in the various conventicles all over Paris (*Recherche de la Vérité*, p. 8). Between August 1731 and late December 1732, according to one insider's report, some 270 people had been overcome with convulsions in Paris alone, of whom about 200 were women (unsigned letter of Dec. 27, 1732, BA, MS 5784, fols. 16-17). As of early 1733 the most reliable estimates for Paris place the figure as low as 400 (*Lettre d'un ecclésiastique de province*, p. 7) and as high as 600-700 (*Recherche de la Vérité*, p. 8) and note that up to three-fourths of the adepts were women. See also AN, U-379, January-February 1733, in which the *greffier* De Lisle, an ardent convulsionist, reports two different figures, 600 and 800 respectively. Trustworthy calculations of the total number of participants in the *oeuvre*—whether actually subject to convulsions or simply witnesses—are even harder to come by. Estimates given by sympathetic observers range from several thousand (*Lettre d'un ecclésiastique de province*, p. 16) up to 20,000 ([Poncet Desessarts], *XII* Lettre de M.*** à un de ses amis, au sujet de la Consultation contre les convulsions* [1735], p. 32), the latter figure applying to a slightly later period.

[48] Cf. André Rétif, "Histoire étrange du mot 'Secouriste,'" *Vie et langage*, No. 217 (April 1970), pp. 223-27.

ments.[49] The *secours* themselves were of two types. In the so-called *petits secours*, some pressure was applied to, or moderate blows struck upon, various parts of the body. The controversial *grands secours*, also known as *secours meurtriers*, involved much more violent forms of bodily punishment. An almost unimaginable variety of physical "tortures" was available on demand, ranging from severe beatings that were dealt with very heavy and fearsome objects, to knives, pins, and even sharply pointed swords that were forcibly pressed against the body.[50] Occasionally the convulsionary called for a board to be placed on top of his body and had as many as a dozen people stand or jump up and down on it for long periods of time. Others allowed themselves to be dragged and pushed along the floor, face down, for hours on end. Still others demanded to be choked or even crucified, all the while praying for the patience, the will, and the strength to endure.[51] Whatever the means employed, the results, according to most sympathetic observers, were generally the same. Those subjected to this treatment,

[49] *Entretiens sur les miracles*, pp. 129, 131. The author of the *Lettre d'un ecclésiastique de province* claims that there were at least 3,000 or 4,000 such *valets de chambre* in Paris as of early 1733 (p. 16). In the case of women, the task of the *secouristes* included making sure that the convulsionaries did not become immodestly exposed when they were thrashing about—a task some of them had previously performed at Pâris' tomb. Despite the defamatory strictures of their critics, most of the brethren, it should be noted, were very much concerned with abiding by stringent standards of decency and propriety. See Jeanne-Marthe Le Grand to Bishop Soanen, Oct. 6, 1736, AFA, P.R. 6685.

[50] More nonsense has been written on this aspect of the *oeuvre des convulsions* than on any other. Much of it can be traced to hostile *constitutionnaire* writers who pointed to the *secours meurtriers* as symbolizing the fundamentally fanatical and degenerate character of the entire convulsionary movement. See, for example, Mme. Duguet-Mol, *Journal historique des convulsions du temps* (1733) and Louis-Bernard La Taste, *Lettres théologiques aux écrivains défenseurs des convulsions et autres prétendus miracles du temps* (1733-40). The *secours* were also at the heart of the split which developed among the *anticonstitutionnaires* over the issue of the convulsionaries; hence a lot of distortion, exaggeration, and misstatement of facts came from appellant pens as well. It is not surprising, on the other hand, that the devices employed in the *secours* should have given rise to the kinds of views represented here. In a police raid conducted in the 1740s, for example, the authorities found "les ustansiles [*sic*] de la convulsionnaire qui consistent en un marteau de forges pesant 15-20 L[ivres], 5 pelles à feu, une grosse corde, . . . des lisières, et une planche de chêne, et un habit qu'elle met exprès pour souffrir les opérations de la convulsion et les secours" (BA, MS 11525, fol. 115).

[51] Firsthand personal experiences of the *secours* are reported by Marguerite Turpin (AN, X-1b 9690) and Jeanne-Marthe Le Grand (*ibid.*, and letter to Bishop Soanen, Oct. 6, 1736, AFA, P.R. 6685). See also the testimony of Claude Chambon (AN, X-1b 9692).

many of whom had fallen into a trance-like, semiconscious state of intense ecstasy, seem to have felt little or no pain; some even found the experience highly pleasurable.[52] What is more, they reportedly showed no signs of injury, not the slightest trace of wounds or bruises. Even persons in a relatively delicate physical condition allegedly came out unscathed, obtaining in the process the "relief" which they had been seeking.

This apparent invulnerability, as well as the accompanying sense of relief, seems to have depended in large measure on the proper management and regulation of the *secours*.[53] It was necessary that the type used and the exact location and duration of its application conform to the particular requirements of the individual convulsionary. In addition, it was important that they be administered by degrees and with great care. The successful administration of the *secours* thus depended on the existence of a close, trusting relationship between the convulsionary and his or her *secouristes*. At intervals throughout the session the convulsionary signaled his special needs with various gestures, body movements, and vaguely expressed instructions. The *secouristes*, for their part, were responsible for recognizing and interpreting these signals and adjusting the intensity, pressure, and extent of their "assistance" accordingly, so as to ensure that the *secours* would fulfill their purpose of providing relief. It was not uncommon for convulsionaries, on receiving these various blows, beatings, and thrashings, to exclaim rapturously, "that is going well! that feels good!"[54] As a result, therefore, even in the face of the treatments ominously dubbed *meurtriers*, the recipients submitted "with a confidence full of joy."[55] Indeed, despite their frightful appearance, the *secours meurtriers* apparently gave those who experienced them not only instant relief from

[52] See the somewhat dated, though still useful, medical discussion in Paul Richer, *Etudes cliniques sur l'hystéroépilepsie ou grande hystérie* (Paris, 1881), p. 694; and J.-M. Charcot, *Lectures on the Diseases of the Nervous System*, 2 vols. (London, 1877), 1, 249. Both Richer and Charcot (the former's mentor and colleague) along with other leading French neurologists at the end of the nineteenth century demonstrated an unusually keen interest in the various "hysterical" phenomena associated with the entire convulsionary episode. Cf. Charcot's own article, "La foi qui guérit," *Revue hebdomadaire*, 7 (1892), pp. 112-32, which deals in large part with this very subject.

[53] *Lettre d'un ecclésiastique de province*, p. 24; testimony of Marguerite Turpin, AN, X-1b 9690.

[54] *Lettre d'un ecclésiastique de province*, p. 16. See also the testimony of Marguerite Turpin, AN, X-1b 9690, and that of Claude Chambon, AN, X-1b 9692.

[55] *Recherche de la Vérité*, p. 8. The ability stoically to endure the intense pain some of them actually experienced may have also served to show the strength of their commitment to the *oeuvre*.

the pains they had been feeling but also a tremendous sense of interior consolation. One adept reportedly found the spiritual consolation so rewarding that she confessed a willingness to endure the *secours* for the rest of her life in exchange for "the small moment of joy which God pour[ed] into her heart at the end of each torture."[56] Equally striking, when the administration of the *secours* was all over—sometimes after several hours—the convulsionary was usually quite calm and refreshed.[57]

These mysterious goings-on aroused widespread curiosity and alarm about possibly immoral practices and promiscuous behavior. Indeed, some critics of the convulsionaries, scandalized by rumors of licentiousness and debauchery, denounced the assemblies as little more than unrestrained orgies, an allegation for which there is no proof.[58] At the same time, however, there is no doubt that the *secours* did have erotic and sado-masochistic overtones. When, for example, women occasionally called on their male *secouristes* to press and to pull their breasts or to pierce their bodies with swords and pins, the sexual symbolism is unmistakable. It seems likely, too, that certain of these convulsionaries allowed themselves to be subjected to various tortures as a substitute for actual sexual experience, achieving excitement, arousal, and tremendous gratification—if only at the level of unconscious fantasies.[59] For others the pain and suffering of the *secours* may have served

---

[56] *Lettre d'un ecclésiastique de province*, p. 16.

[57] *Ibid.*, p. 9. On this point see also the testimony of Jeanne-Marthe Le Grand, Marguerite Turpin, and Denise Regnier (AN, X-1b 9690). While some adepts had remained clearly in touch with their environment throughout and remembered what they had undergone, others had little or no recall of their experiences. As for their *secouristes*, they often came out of the *séances* thoroughly exhausted, a few reportedly collapsing from fatigue when the sessions were over.

[58] Cf. Kaplow, *The Names of Kings*, pp. 124-25.

[59] For a nineteenth-century view of this supposed concern of the convulsionaries to satisfy "des instincts lubriques," see Richer, p. 694. More useful, though not directly related, is George L. Engel, "'Psychogenic' Pain and the Pain-Prone Patient," *American Journal of Medicine*, 26 (1959), pp. 899-918. It has been intriguingly suggested that "the austerities and moral rigorism . . . which are so central to Jansenist belief and practice and so much a part of Jansenist penitential tradition placed intolerable repressive burdens on the faithful [and that] in the *séances* [the convulsionaries] were able to seek relief from them and to do so moreover in a trance-like, possessed, hence, unconscious state, which concealed from them the full impact of the contradiction between their professed beliefs, their ordinary sexual practices, and their exact reversal in the sanctioned [and less inhibited] environment of their rituals" (Harvey Mitchell, "Commentary," Session on Popular Religion in the *Ancien Régime* [Annual meeting of the Society for French Historical Studies, Madison, April 1975]). Cf. Emmanuel Le Roy Ladurie, *Les paysans de Languedoc*, 2 vols. (Paris, 1966), I, 644; and Engel, "Conversion Symptoms,"

as a vehicle for expiating personal guilt,[60] for still others as a symbolic means of acting out pent-up aggressions, a nonverbal outlet for discharging repressed hostilities.[61]

Whatever their clinical nature or their latent sexual content, about which one can only speculate, these physical manifestations served to evoke the movement's aspirations as well as to reaffirm its collective existence and emotional power. According to the figurist exegetes, who continued to provide the votaries with ideological justification of and legitimation for their behavior, the wildly convulsive agitations and the so-called *secours meurtriers* were all forms of religious witness, fraught with symbolism related to the convulsionaries' mission of redemption and designed to instruct and to warn both the participants in the *oeuvre* and their "malevolent" enemies. These "supernatural" manifestations were said to be, in part, a living representation of the current spiritual turmoil within the Church that began with the promulgation of the bull *Unigenitus* and culminated in the closing of the cemetery at Saint-Médard: the convulsionaries represented the righteous defenders of the Truth, whereas the *secouristes*, the agents of violence and corruption, were their evil tormenters and oppressors.[62] In addition, while holding up a "mirror" to the sins and crimes committed against God and the faithful in the present, the *secours* were supposedly symbolic of the long and painful persecutions that had preceded God's deliverance of His people in the days of the first Christians. Finally, and perhaps most important, the symbolic bloodletting of the *secours* purportedly gave the convulsionaries the feeling that they were figuratively sacrificing

---

p. 658. The apparent association of erotic and religious elements is a not uncommon phenomenon in the history of Christianity; the case of tarantism is perhaps the most notable (see Lewis, esp. pp. 89-92).

[60] Such chronically guilt-ridden "moral masochists" were especially numerous in the earlier history of Jansenism, though François de Pâris was himself an excellent example of this personality type. The literature on the psychology of pain and on the role of suffering as a psychic means of achieving expiation and forgiveness is of course very extensive. Here again the articles by Engel, "Conversion Symptoms" and " 'Psychogenic' Pain," both *passim*, are especially helpful.

[61] The abreactive or cathartic function of ecstatic behavior has frequently been remarked. On the various therapeutic effects thought to be associated with such ritualized emotionalism, see George Rosen, "Psychopathology in the Social Process: A Study of the Persecution of Witches in Europe as a Contribution to the Understanding of Mass Delusions and Psychic Epidemics," *Journal of Health and Human Behavior*, 1 (1960), p. 210; *idem, Madness in Society: Chapters in the Historical Sociology of Mental Illness* (Chicago, 1968), pp. 195-225; and Lewis, esp. Ch. 7. Cf. also Barkun's discussion of the sources and functions of ecstatic behavior in *Disaster and the Millennium*, Ch. 5, *passim*.

[62] Unattributed letter of Nov. 4, 1732, BA, MS 5784, fols. 298-99.

themselves to assuage God's anger. Before God would renew the Church, it was maintained, His wrath had first to be appeased.[63] He would accomplish His promises of assistance and consolation only "to the extent that He is moved by the laments of the dove."[64] Arousing and physically embodying such laments was thus a primary task of the convulsionaries, who resolutely offered themselves in Christ-like fashion—"victims" by and through whom the Church was to be renewed.[65] From their role as figurative victims of sacrificial propitiation and the chosen instruments of divine justice and renewal, they derived "the force and the courage necessary to sustain all the trials to which they [might] be exposed."[66] Like their immediate inspiration, François de Pâris, and like many of the early Christian martyrs as well, the convulsionaries believed that they would "triumph with Jesus Christ only through suffering."[67]

The apocalyptic tradition provided an additional sanction for the convulsionaries' extravagant behavior and for the apparent violence of some of their rituals. According to several figurist theologians associated with the *oeuvre*, the convulsionaries were the spiritual precursors of the prophet Elijah, who at some unspecified time was to return mysteriously to earth as one of the chief witnesses against Antichrist and as a herald of the new age.[68] As a minister of divine justice and an agent of religious renewal, Elijah was expected to place himself at the head of the convulsionary brethren, to liberate the persecuted, to ensure the triumph of the true faith, and eventually to reestablish peace and righteousness throughout the Christian community.[69] In the course of his dramatic earthly career, this formidable prophet and preacher of repentance would also accomplish the reprobation of the

---

[63] *Entretiens sur les miracles*, pp. 144-45.

[64] *Ibid.*, p. 145.

[65] "C'est par l'oeuvre des Convulsions qu'il [Dieu] se prépare des victimes, qu'il les annonce, et qu'il commence à les former . . . et ils le prient avec instance de hâter le temps de la persécution, afin de voir ensuite celui de sa miséricorde" (*ibid.*). Cf. BHVP, N.A. 125, I, 3.

[66] *Entretiens sur les miracles*, p. 158.

[67] *Réflexions sur l'ordonnance du roi, en date du 27 Janvier 1732*, p. 88.

[68] The principal Old Testament references to the prophet Elijah are I Kings 17 through II Kings 2, *passim*, and Malachi 4:4-6; passages in the New Testament include Matthew 11:14, 17:10-12; Mark 9:11-13; and Luke 1:17.

[69] "Prière à Dieu le Fils par le Saint Diacre," in *Supplément des Nouvelles ecclésiastiques*, April 8, 1735, p. 51; *Entretiens sur les miracles*, p. 149. According to one prominent writer, God had exclusively designated the convulsionaries "à le reconnoître et de les engager à se préparer à ce grand événement par la pénitence et la prière" (Montgeron, II: "Idée de l'état des convulsions," p. 5).

Gentiles and the conversion of the Jews as signs of the coming new epoch.[70] But before his arrival "to restore all things," it was necessary that all crimes first be honorably expiated and that there be a flowing of blood, symbolic or real, representing the blood of Jesus Christ, to mark the beginning of the Last Days. From this point of view the convulsionaries' ritual measures of symbolic self-sacrifice—of suffering inflicted and suffering endured—were a means of preparing the way for Elijah's awaited return and of thereby hastening the moment of decision and change. In this sense, too, the *secours*, while symbolizing the evils and corruption that had already overtaken the Church, were also supposed to represent the additional ordeals (*épreuves*) which the Church would endure in some unspecified future—a period of terrible catastrophe and confusion which must precede, accompany, and follow the advent of Elijah, who would himself be subjected to persecution for assisting the convulsionaries to resist the "tortures" of the established authorities.[71]

These elaborate figurist interpretations of the *secours*, developed in numerous tracts by various convulsionist spokesmen, provided the convulsionaries with a convenient theological justification for (and rationalization of) their actions and rituals. The *secours*, like the convulsive movements, were simply the physical manifestations God had chosen to prepare the followers of M. Pâris both to receive and to announce the most sacred truths. God had rendered some of the convulsionaries invulnerable—just as He had cured others—in order to demonstrate their conspicuous worthiness and to show that He favored their cause. As far as they were concerned, divine intervention enabled them to endure what would otherwise have been quite impossible and thus furnished them with clear, irrefutable proof of their divine election and convincing evidence that God's influence and protection

[70] *NNEE*, Nov. 25, 1731, p. 227. According to Arthur Hertzberg, the conversion of the Jews was seen as "a central task of Christianity" and "the indispensable tool for the Church's restoration and regeneration . . . , a necessary preamble to Christian eschatology" (*The French Enlightenment and the Jews* [New York, 1968], p. 259). However, though there are numerous references to the Jews in contemporary Jansenist works of propaganda and biblical exegesis, interest in this subject remained confined to a handful of controversialists and exegetes and never became a central Jansenist or convulsionary preoccupation. The abbé Duguet is the only major theologian to have placed this theme at the heart of his eschatological interpretation of contemporary events. Cf. the summary in *Entretiens sur les miracles*, esp. pp. 151-58.

[71] BHVP, N.A. 125, I, 26; Frère Hilaire to Bishop Soanen, Nov. 28, 1733, AFA, P.R. 6439; *Entretiens sur les miracles*, pp. 150-51; Montgeron, "Dissertation sur l'autorité des miracles," II, 50.

graced the entire movement.[72] In practicing their religious observances (the *oeuvre*), therefore, they were fulfilling a holy responsibility and performing the work of God, the *ouvrage de Dieu* or *opus Dei*. Such an interpretation, moreover, allowed the convulsionaries to "prove" that they were neither fanatical nor insane. Their various activities were simply the outpourings of the Holy Spirit, demonstrably orthodox and rooted in traditional religious conviction; what might have appeared as fanaticism, indecency, cruelty, or madness in the *oeuvre* was designed as a deliberate veil of obscurity to hide the divine message from the enemies of Truth.[73]

The convulsionaries utilized other methods or forms of bearing witness to the divine presence and of representing what they held to be the divine message, though none of these was quite so spectacular, or in such great need of "decoding," as the *secours meurtriers*. Each of these phenomena represented a different degree and kind of supernatural inspiration. Large numbers of miraculous cures, for example, continued to occur at these *séances*, many of them accompanied by convulsions.[74] Though most such cures were still attributed to the direct intercession of François de Pâris, whose relics were as usual touched to the afflicted person's body, others were "performed" by individual brethren to whom M. Pâris' thaumaturgic powers were said to have been communicated. In addition to the cures, some convulsionary conventicles apparently witnessed a variety of other, far more exceptional paranormal manifestations. Certain convulsionaries reportedly displayed extraordinarily acute faculties of penetration and insight, including gifts of apparent clairvoyance and an ability to "discern hidden things." There were a few cases of convulsionary adepts who claimed to possess an olfactory sense so highly developed that they were able to distinguish merely by smell between genuine and false relics and between true believers and clever impostors, each of whom (or which) supposedly had a characteristic and easily detectable odor. Others claimed an ability to read with their eyes closed and bandaged, "utilizing their sense of smell to discern the letters."[75] Such prodigious

[72] Testimony of Denise Regnier, AN, X-1b 9690; cf. *Entretiens sur les miracles*, p. 158.

[73] BHVP, C.P. 3509, pp. 2, 5. Their enemies would denounce this argument as pure casuistry, as an attempt to cover up obviously degrading and insane practices.

[74] For a figurist interpretation of the Pâris miracles, see BA, MS 5307, fols. 64-67, but also fols. 68-109, *passim*.

[75] *Coup d'oeil, en forme de lettre, sur les convulsions*, p. 9; cf. BHVP, C.P. 3509, pp. 41-42.

feats were obviously limited to a very few. Much more common were the diverse types of "figurative representations" in which the adepts, again allegedly under divine inspiration, claimed to be acting out important episodes in the history of the Church. Some convulsionaries made various involuntary gestures and movements which were interpreted as representing important events in the life of Jesus Christ, particularly His sufferings, crucifixion, and final Ascension.[76] Acting as "instrumentations of the Spirit," others "recreated" the conversion of St. Paul or "depicted" some act of François de Pâris.[77] These so-called *tableaux vivants* served an essentially didactic function and were among the most innocuous and least controversial aspects of the entire *oeuvre*.[78]

Far more controversial and in greater need of interpretation were the blasphemous utterances and the acts of (apparent) profanation committed by a number of convulsionaries. One semiconscious woman, for example, reportedly threw a bible on the ground and stamped upon it; when she came out of her "convulsive state," she begged God for forgiveness. Such strange behavior was easily explained as yet another divinely inspired "figurative representation." God had chosen this symbolic act as a means of dramatizing the "horrible profanations"

[76] Frère Hilaire, for example, occasionally fell into a protracted stupor, a so-called *état de mort*, in which he supposedly "represented the Passion and death of Our Savior." On Jan. 31, 1733, the convulsionary experienced such an *état de mort*, with a virtual physical collapse and suspension of senses, which lasted 21 consecutive hours (BN, NAFr., MS 4262, fol. 79). Several years later Jeanne-Marthe Le Grand reported a similar *aliénation des sens* which continued for almost three full days (letter to Soanen, Oct. 6, 1736, AFA, P.R. 6685). Cf. Montgeron, "Idée de l'état des convulsions," II, 48, 86.

[77] *Lettre d'un ecclésiastique de province*, p. 11. For a more elaborate and detailed description of the various kinds of figurative representations, see *ibid.*, pp. 10-11. See also *Recherche de la Vérité*, p. 9.

[78] Nevertheless, some of these "figurative representations" actually did arouse a great deal of criticism. Certain female convulsionaries, for example, were charged with performing baptisms, saying Mass, and performing other priestly functions during the *séances*. Cf. Colbert to [d'Etemare?], May 8, 1733, BA, MS 5784, p. 53; *Observations sur l'origine et le progrès des convulsions qui ont commencé au cimetière de Saint-Médard, où l'on montre qu'elles sont des effets naturels, et que rien n'oblige de les regarder comme divines* (1732), pp. 24-25. In fact, however, as one convulsionist defender pointed out, "il s'agit d'une simple imitation des gestes d'un Prêtre qui célèbre, sans pain ni vin, sans vases sacrés, sans ornemens sacerdotaux, sans même aucune représentation d'autel . . . Dire la messe lorsqu'on n'est pas prêtre est un attentat que les lois punissent par le feu. Pourquoi donc affecter d'exprimer par le nom d'une profanation horrible, une action qui en est si prodigieusement différente?" (*Exposé de la manière de penser de M. l'abbé [d'Etemare] touchant l'événement des convulsions* [1735], p. 8).

to which the wicked *constitutionnaires*, through the bull *Unigenitus*, had subjected Holy Scripture.[79]

However controversial or instructive their diverse "performances" sometimes were, these physical manifestations of the *oeuvre* were by no means the only way in which God was believed to have made His presence felt among the brethren. Indeed, perhaps the most noteworthy feature of their sessions—and, with the *secours*, the most widely debated—was the different kinds of speech which many of the convulsionaries pronounced at various points in the *séance*. Suddenly "overcome by the spirit," often in the very midst of a convulsive seizure or even during the administration of the *secours*,[80] the inspired one gave out with a variety of vocal utterances. Some of this "speech," serving perhaps as forms of prayer, consisted of little more than unintelligible mutterings and a steady stream of incomprehensible exclamations. In other cases it involved equally incoherent screaming and roaring, howling and yelling.[81] Still other convulsionaries spent these periods of "inspiration" making utterly obscure pronouncements that were without any particular logic, sequence, or theme. The phenomenon of glossolalia, or speaking in tongues, in a strange, new "language" of words, syllables, and sounds they had never learned and did not comprehend, was also quite common and gave many convulsionaries both a feeling that the Holy Spirit was present within them and a sense of direct communication with God—experiences which served in a way to validate their commitment to the *oeuvre*.[82]

Along with these relatively inarticulate and virtually impenetrable outpourings, there was a large number of far more elaborate speeches given during the *séances*. These discourses, some of which went on almost uninterrupted for several hours, were supposedly delivered spontaneously, without any preparation or conscious effort on the part of the speaker, who frequently felt himself divorced from ordinary reality, as "in a kind of ecstasy, stupor, or dream."[83] In the highly charged atmosphere which characterized the assemblies held all over Paris, some 300 persons were said to have been blessed with this particular divine gift within the first year and a half after the closing of the cemetery at Saint-Médard.[84] The presence in each conventicle of a scribe charged with the responsibility of keeping a journal of whatever

[79] *Entretiens sur les miracles*, p. 156.
[80] Frère Hilaire, Jan. 31, 1733, BN, NAFr., MS 4262, fols. 79-80.
[81] One female convulsionary, known for her "barking," was dubbed *l'aboyeuse*.
[82] Cf. the "gifts of the Spirit" described in Acts 2:4 and 1 Cor. 14:2.
[83] *Recherche de la Vérité*, p. 7.
[84] D'Etemare to Pierre Sartre, July 18, 1733, BA, MS 5784 fol. 26.

activities went on at the session, and particularly of recording the discourses, has meant that many hundreds, perhaps thousands, of these documents have survived.[85] Although certain *frères* and *soeurs* at times spoke too quickly for the scribe to keep pace with them and occasionally allowed their voices to trail off in a whisper or to be drowned out by their own or others' convulsive movements, the "secretary," using a barely legible scrawl and various shorthand notations, apparently managed to take down most of the speeches substantially "as dictated," and sometimes was even able to provide surprisingly rich and detailed accounts of the accompanying changes occurring in the speaker's bodily movements, gestures, facial expressions, or general mood and demeanor.[86] Once the session was over, the copyist, usually working from rough and uncorrected notes, would often transcribe the discourse in a fine secretarial hand and make a few interpolations and editorial additions, sometimes providing brief theological explanations or supplying appropriate biblical references.[87] Speakers who could recall with any precision what they had said might assist the scribe in filling out lacunae, correcting errors, or interpreting incomprehensible passages.[88] Discourses of exceptional quality[89] were subsequently copied and recopied, exchanged among the different con-

[85] Major collections in Paris may be found at the AN, the BHVP, the BN, and the BPR as well as at the Archives Historiques de l'Archevêché de Paris and the Bibliothèque de la Société de l'Histoire du Protestantisme Français.

[86] On the importance of scribes, see the testimony of Claude Chambon (AN, X-1b 9692) and that of M. Prévost, Soeur de la Confession (*ibid.*, X-1b 9691). On the problems confronting these scribes, see the testimony of Femme La Coste (*ibid.*, X-1b 9690) and the comments made by one such copyist after a *séance* held in June 1733 (BA, MS 10204).

[87] One of the principal convulsionist scribes for many years was the noted Jansenist *avocat*, Louis-Adrien Le Paige. Surprisingly neglected by most historians, this curious and important individual, whose life (1712-1802) spanned the entire eighteenth century and who was intimately, if unobtrusively, involved in the affairs of the Paris Parlement—especially during the midcentury campaign against the Jesuits—definitely merits a full-length study. The extraordinary *Collection Le Paige* at the BPR, consisting of hundreds of huge bound volumes of manuscript and printed documents dealing with the religious controversies of his day, would be the natural starting point. Cf. also Van Kley, *passim*, and J.M.J. Rogister's article in *English Historical Review*, 92 (1977), pp. 522-39.

[88] Montgeron, "Idée de l'état des convulsions," II, 48, 80, 86.

[89] Included in this category were the discourses of the so-called *quatre grands frères*—Hilaire, Noël, Etienne, and Pierre—and those of a handful of women, Soeur Colombe and Soeur La Croix Gault (or Got) among them. According to a fellow convulsionary, Soeur La Croix was regarded "comme une sainte, comme un oracle, qu'elle savoit tout . . ." (Testimony of La Virginie, AN, X-1b 9690).

venticles, passed on from one *frère* or *soeur* to another, and eventually circulated—separately or in bound collections and "anthologies"—within convulsionary circles all over France.[90] They were carefully preserved, both by individual brethren and by the various conventicles, and treated as highly treasured possessions. Indeed, they served as major sources of edification and inspiration for all those in the *oeuvre* and were frequently read, discussed, or commented upon during the *séances*.[91]

Reflecting the diversity of backgrounds, abilities, and preoccupations which characterized the membership in the *oeuvre*, these discourses (or "colloquies with God") were tremendously varied in quality, style, and major themes. Though little is known about the specific personalities of the individual speakers, it would appear that a majority were persons of limited intelligence, with little or no formal education or religious training; some were even quite young children. Not surprisingly, many of these people were limited in their vocalizations to monotonous evocations of simplistic or banal biblical images and symbols, their discourses consisting of little more than the recitation or paraphrase of certain scriptural passages that had frequently been discussed among the brethren.[92] They also tended to repeat a large number of memorized formulae, clichés, and set phrases and to mouth a variety of *anticonstitutionnaire* slogans. At the same time, there were convulsionaries from reportedly the same milieux who somehow demonstrated in their discourses a level of knowledge and a degree of sophistication and understanding which seemed to go far beyond their ordinary capacity and to surpass anything they had displayed in their "natural state." Admiring observers frequently marveled at their command of the language, the richness of imagery, the great eloquence and forcefulness of tone. These same *frères* and *soeurs* also displayed a remarkably penetrating familiarity with Scripture, often providing extended explications of particular biblical texts. Others even demonstrated an ability to expound at great length and with apparent erudition on some of the most abstruse questions of theology and mysteries of the faith.[93]

Though they have until recently remained virtually unexplored,[94]

---

[90] BHVP, C.P. 3509, p. 36; cf. BA, MS 11439, fols. 154-55, and *ibid.*, MS 11377, fols. 185, 209. I have located substantial collections of discourses in more than a dozen libraries outside of Paris.

[91] Testimony of La Virginie, AN, X-1b 9690.

[92] Testimony of Frère Paul le Petit (Paul-François Langlade), AN, X-1b 9691.

[93] BHVP, N.A. 125, I, 24; Montgeron, "Idée de l'état des convulsions," II, 17-18; BN, NAFr., MS 4262, fols. 123-24, 130-31 (observations of Le Paige).

[94] Aside from the work of the present author, the only other attempt to deal

the discourses are among the most revealing and instructive sources available for entering into the convulsionaries' mental universe.[95] These discourses were a verbal analogue and an oral confirmation of the physical exhibitions of convulsions and *secours*, with many of the same themes of official persecution and spiritual renewal recurring in the "language" of both. But whereas the various physical manifestations of the *oeuvre* supposedly gave bodily expression to certain of the movement's fundamental principles and may have provided the convulsionaries with a means of symbolically venting and articulating their pent-up frustrations, the discourses, pronounced aloud in the very midst of the *séances*, served as a more direct vehicle for enunciating convulsionary attitudes and for defining the hopes and fears of the brethren themselves. Without necessarily regarding themselves as actual prophets, the convulsionaries did believe that God was speaking directly through them, and that they were acting as His inspired "instruments," conveying the divine will and transmitting the Lord's message to the assembled faithful.[96] Although some speakers were primarily preoccupied with the defense of "true" doctrine and piety and the refu-

---

with the discourses is a *mémoire de maîtrise* by a student of Jean Delumeau, named Roxanne Kural, who has analyzed two large volumes of discourses (MSS 196 and 197) in the collection of the Bibliothèque de la Société de l'Histoire du Protestantisme Français. The title of her work is: *Contribution à l'histoire des mentalités de l'Occident pré-industriel: Etude de deux manuscrits de convulsionnaires jansénistes du milieu du XVIIIe siècle* (University of Paris, 1970-71). Notwithstanding these preliminary efforts, this vast body of source materials, which extends throughout the century and even beyond the Revolution, definitely merits further serious study and close textual analysis—of thematic content as well as of linguistic structure, grammar, syntax, and vocabulary. Cf. the passing comments of Delumeau, *Le Catholicisme entre Luther et Voltaire* (Paris, 1971), p. 226 (offered in a somewhat broader context); and Dominique Julia, "Problèmes d'historiographie," p. 87. It would also be interesting to compare these discourses with sermons and other religious literature of the eighteenth century and with millenarian documents from other periods and places. Of course, to reach a much fuller and more sophisticated understanding of convulsionary discourses and to decode the signs and symbols embedded in convulsionary rituals would require the skills of an experienced linguist, semioticist, or ethnographer.

[95] Such a view of the significance of the discourses was also shared by the convulsionaries. According to Soeur Colombe (AN, X-1b 9690), "ils contiennent l'explication de l'oeuvre"; while the editor of a published collection of these discourses (*Recueil de discours de plusieurs convulsionnaires* [1734], "Avertissement") noted that, "On y trouvera de quoi d'instruire d'une manière très solide et très juste sur l'oeuvre des Convulsions . . . , ce qui est bien plus capable de donner une juste idée des Convulsions que tous les Ouvrages qu'on a tant multiplié inutilement sur cette matière."

[96] BN, NAFr., MS 4262, fol. 96; testimony of Soeur Colombe, AN X-1b 9690.

tation of the "false,"[97] for the most part their utterances purported to fulfill a much more dramatic and immediate purpose. In particular, they served to provide the brethren with signs of the impending calamities that were to be visited upon Christendom and to offer vital instructions to enable them to prepare for the events to come.[98] Evoking a mood of eschatological tension, the speakers broadly foretold developments of a terrible, destructive nature. At the same time, by holding out the promise of ultimate deliverance—membership in the *oeuvre* was commonly compared to the ark of Noah riding out the cataclysmic Flood, a favorite convulsionary metaphor—they also exhorted all those present to place their trust "in God and in the force of His grace."[99]

A powerful consciousness of their persecution and an exaggerated sense of putative martyrdom called forth feelings of terror, pride, and hope, all of which found expression in these speeches. Throughout the discourses, frequent and impassioned invocations addressed to Elijah were accompanied by equally fervent apostrophes to God and to François de Pâris, as the convulsionaries appealed for divine protection for the righteous brethren and simultaneous punishment for their corrupt and perfidious persecutors.[100] Speaking with great force and conviction, they decried the evils which had befallen the Church and denounced the apostasy of the Gentiles. They announced, sometimes with the most violent and frightening imagery, the eventual doom that awaited all who rejected or oppressed the "Truth." Although they seemed quite certain that a "new order" would somehow come about through divine intervention, they provided no detailed eschatological

[97] The locksmith Louis Sabinet, for example, explored at some length various questions of dogma and Christian morality (BA, NAFr., MS 4262, fol. 131). Many of these speakers delivered long harangues against the Jesuits and their Molinist theology, whether they understood these doctrines or not. In particular, they charged the Jesuits with responsibility for the hypocrisy and duplicity, the worldliness and corruption which had allegedly overtaken the Church.

[98] *Entretiens sur les miracles*, p. 158; cf. Simart to Soanen, July 19, 1733, AFA, P.R. 6863.

[99] Although the two-sided, "paradoxical" nature of God appears throughout these discourses with striking force and frequency, it is the menacing vision of the wrathful, vengeful God of justice which prevails over the more directly consoling image of the loving, compassionate God of mercy. See *Entretiens sur les miracles*, p. 163; Frère Simart to Soanen, July 19, 1733, AFA, P.R. 6863; and Frère Hilaire to Soanen, Nov. 29, 1733, AFA, P.R. 6439. On the metaphor of Noah's ark, which appears most prominently in the celebrated and widely circulated discourses of Frère Hilaire, see the brief excerpt and discussion in BN, NAFr., MS 4262, fols. 80-81.

[100] The convulsionaries' evil oppressors were likened to the faithless hordes who perished in the Flood (BN, NAFr., MS 4262, fols. 80-81).

program, no clearly articulated picture of the actual process of transformation and redemption with which they and their fellow brethren presumed themselves to be involved. Their sweeping forecasts of impending change and their repeated auguries of a future millenarian dispensation were, like convulsionary apocalyptic expectations in general, without any specific temporal or spatial dimensions and contained little more than vague indications that these speakers believed the course of history had reached (or would soon reach) something of a turning point. Nevertheless, despite their fundamental vagueness and lack of clear focus, these heavily oracular pronouncements stirred the imaginations of their listeners and served as a powerful reminder to all the convulsionaries of the central role they had to play in the eschatological drama that was gradually unfolding around them. The discourses were also viewed as yet one more piece of evidence of the convulsionaries' contact with higher powers and of their direct access to recondite sources of knowledge and authority.[101] Alternately prayerful and hortatory, consoling and accusatory, these dramatically impassioned speeches and vehement harangues appear to have made a great impression not only upon those *frères* and *soeurs* present during their delivery, but also upon those fortunate enough to possess copies of their own.[102]

Except for a final brief period of common prayers, the termination of the discourses along with the cessation of the *secours* generally marked the conclusion of the congregation's devotional exercises. Once tentative plans were made for their next communal assembly, the brethren left, having experienced a profound emotional catharsis. Indeed, for most convulsionaries the rewards of membership and active participation in this select fellowship were apparently quite considerable. Here was a secure and supportive environment, a milieu in which

---

[101] The convulsionaries held a similar view regarding the variety of strange dreams and heady visions related at (or even experienced during) the *séances*. See, for example, the testimony of Claude Yvon, a *maître perruquier*, who reported having "des visions pendant lesquelles [son père] voit des soleils, des étoiles, des diamants, des tabernacles, des suspensions et autres choses" (AN, X-1b 9690).

[102] Testimony of Marguerite Turpin, Femme La Coste, Soeur Colombe, and others (AN, X-1b 9690, 9692). Faced with charges that false statements were sometimes mixed up with the true, that most predictions never came to pass, or that occasionally certain speakers expressed things that were frivolous, puerile, indecent, or misleading, spokesmen for the convulsionaries sought to explain these away as assaults of the devil, whose influence God had allowed to intrude as a means of testing the brethren's faith (see d'Etemare to unknown correspondent, Nov. 4, 1732, BA, MS 5784, fols. 298ff.; and BHVP, C.P. 3509, p. 5).

they were able to overcome, even if only temporarily, the status inferiority and sense of impotence many of them must have endured on the outside. The elaborate religious ritual and ceremonial conducted at the *séances* also served as a liberating experience, affording these adepts a sanctioned, indeed sanctified, vehicle for venting their feelings of frustration and hostility toward the established authorities and providing them a rare opportunity to protest, however indirectly or obliquely, the religious condition of Catholic France. Continually reassured of the Lord's acceptance and protection, they apparently felt a highly satisfying sense of personal exaltation and renewed spiritual vitality. Many convulsionaries reported a feeling of deep inner well-being, of intense warmth and joy, of divinely communicated "power," as a result of their direct encounter with God during these religious services. Although a mere collection of words can hardly begin to convey the full impact of these extraordinary psychodramas which were daily being reenacted all over Paris, it is clear that these votaries were able to attain through the sacred theater of the *oeuvre* a degree of emotional gratification and a kind of spiritual energy that had been previously available nowhere else—not even at Saint-Médard. Those who had been favored with special gifts were able to rise above the monotony and anonymity of their workaday lives and achieve some measure of glory and excitement, individuality and recognition. But even for those not so blessed the feelings of religious solidarity, born of an enthusiastic commitment to a common purpose, were a source of great strength and endowed their lives with new significance and an enhanced dignity and self-esteem.[103]

Such was the status of the convulsionaries as of the early days of 1733. The royal declaration of January 1732, promulgated a year before, had been the catalyst that helped transform the observances at the deacon Pâris' tomb into a full-fledged religious movement, with a set of shared rituals and doctrines, a wide variety of charismatic mani-

---

[103] Though rarely stated quite so explicitly, such sentiments about the psychological benefits of membership in the *oeuvre* seem to underlie the testimony obtained from those convulsionaries willing to talk about their experiences (AN, X-1b 9690, 9692, *passim*); they are also implicit in the observations which many of the sect's defenders offered in both their published tracts and their manuscript correspondence (e.g., BN, NAFr., MS 4262, fol. 120). Cf. Lewis, esp. Ch. 7, *passim*; Jerome Frank, *Persuasion and Healing: A Comparative Study of Psychotherapy* (Baltimore, 1973), pp. 79-85; and Leon Salzman, "The Psychology of Religious and Ideological Conversion," *Psychiatry*, 16 (1953), pp. 177-87. Cf. also Victor Turner's analysis of "liminality and communitas," in *The Ritual Process: Structure and Anti-Structure* (Chicago, 1969), esp. Chs. 3-5, *passim*.

festations, and thousands of intensely dedicated adherents. Indeed, the attachment to the *oeuvre* of those who had remained devoted to François de Pâris was now more intense than ever. The official measures, both civil and ecclesiastical, that had been adopted in an effort to interdict the Pâris cult and to deprive its votaries of their sanctuary had thus failed completely to achieve their purpose.[104] Throughout the previous year, however, while the convulsionary movement was in the process of taking shape and while publicity about its adepts' activities was beginning to spread, expressions of hostility toward the brethren had come to be heard with increasing frequency and intensity. Where the subject of the convulsionaries was concerned, impartiality and indifference were no longer possible. To be sure, the convulsionaries neither envisioned nor advocated any fundamental innovation in or active disruption of the established social order. Despite the openly aggressive, even menacing tone of much of their rhetoric, despite the apparently strong sense of urgency of redemption, these religious enthusiasts were not especially militant or radically change-oriented. There is, in fact, a striking absence of explicit social or political preoccupation amid the welter of millenarian themes taken up in their *séances*. Nevertheless, even though the convulsionaries had staked out an essentially passive and ritual role for themselves, their unorthodox beliefs and unconventional behavior were perceived as a dangerous challenge to the Church's authority as well as a threat to existing forms of social control, arousing widespread fears and suspicions in *constitutionnaire* and *anticonstitutionnaire* circles alike. The hostile attacks against these supposedly "debased Jansenists" began appearing from all sides and were to have serious consequences for the subsequent development, and even the survival, of the new movement.

[104] See President Bouhier's prescient observations to the *avocat* Marais: "Le fanatisme de Saint-Médard durera tant qu'on voudra s'y opposer. Je m'imagine qu'on court aux miracles défendus comme aux livres de contrebande" (April 1, 1732, BN, MSS Fr., MS 25541, fol. 17).

CHAPTER VII

Mounting Persecution, Growing Divisions

T HE year 1732 had been a time of serious challenges to established authority in both Church and State. In Paris the stormy confrontations which resumed in early spring between the *curés* and their archbishop, on the one hand, and the Parlement and the Fleury administration, on the other, had by late summer reached crisis proportions. By December, however, though the issues so hotly debated in the course of the year still remained fundamentally unresolved, tempers on all sides had apparently cooled—at least temporarily. Developments in the Saint-Médard affair, in the meantime, had produced quite a different result. The attempted interdiction of the Pâris cult had been a total failure, the devotions to the deacon's memory having become by early 1733 more intense and animated than ever. The persistent and vigorous growth of the convulsionary movement as well as the unconventional activities and the ominous, albeit vague, prophecies of its adherents represented perhaps the most vexing problem confronting the civil and ecclesiastical authorities at this time. But with the other religious disputes set aside for the moment, the royal government was now somewhat freer to turn its attention to the convulsionary issue. In proceeding against the convulsionaries, the crown was to find welcome, if unanticipated, support even from the *anticonstitutionnaire* camp, where disenchantment with the *oeuvre* was becoming rife. At the same time, in mounting its anticonvulsionary campaign, the government was to be the midwife once again to a major series of changes within the beleaguered movement.

For some months already the pressure had been mounting on Cardinal Fleury's administration to take some action to stifle the convulsionary "contagion." Sensationalist writers as well as vulgar scoffers and gossipmongers had been disseminating luridly detailed accounts of the alleged goings-on within the different conventicles—accounts which helped feed the fires of anticonvulsionary opposition. Some fairly mild critics of the *oeuvre* sought to explain away the whole thing by charging fraud and imposture.[1] Others, including the Jansenist physician Philippe

---

[1] See, for example, *Entretiens sur les miracles des derniers temps, ou Les Let-*

Hecquet, ascribed these phenomena to various natural causes—"hysteria," "erotic vapors," "melancholia," "derangement," "imagination," and the like—which they claimed belonged within the exclusive province of the medical profession.[2] Most critics, however, were much harsher in their attacks. *Constitutionnaire* theologians, in particular, contended that the subject of the convulsionaries came primarily within their area of competence and insisted on treating the *oeuvre* as a problem of doctrinal deviation.[3] Fundamentally distrustful of religious nonconformity and spiritual novelties of any sort, these writers went so far as to attribute the actions of the convulsionaries to "diabolic intervention." They regarded the symptoms of religious ecstasy which went on in the convulsionary *séances* as obvious evidence of demoniacal possession or at least of the entrance of evil spirits into the *oeuvre*. The bodily contortions, the wild, hysterical fits, the glossolalia, the blasphemous utterances, the sacrilegious acts of profanation, and, above all, the *secours meurtriers*—forms of behavior which the convulsionists had interpreted as "figurative representations" and manifestations of the divine presence—were for these censorious observers of the movement undeniable indications that satanic forces were actually at work. As one writer has remarked, neither side could differentiate "between celestial and infernal influence except on *a priori* principles, which were precisely those in dispute."[4] Nevertheless, to the Jesuits and other influential *constitutionnaire* theologians, such behavior as the convulsionaries exhibited could no longer be countenanced, for to do so, it was argued, might cause irreparable damage to the faith.

Along with the complaints and denunciations of the theologians

---

tres de M. le chevalier*** (1732), and *Observations sur l'origine et le progrès des convulsions qui ont commencé au cimetière de Saint-Médard, où l'on montre qu'elles sont des effets naturels, et que rien n'oblige de les regarder comme divines* (1733).

[2] [Ph. Hecquet], *Le Naturalisme des convulsions dans les maladies de l'épidémie convulsionnaire* (1733). For a contrasting medical view: *Lettre à un confesseur, touchant le devoir des médecins et chirurgiens au sujet des miracles et des convulsions* (1733). In reply: Hecquet's *Réponse à la "Lettre à un confesseur . . ."* (1733), and his *Le Naturalisme des convulsions démontré par la physique, par l'histoire naturelle et par les événemens de cette oeuvre, et démontrant l'impossibilité du divin qu'on lui attribue dans une lettre sur les secours meurtriers* (1733). On Hecquet, see Temkin, p. 213. For general surveys of early modern medical views of epilepsy and hysteria see *ibid.*, and Ilza Veith, *Hysteria: The History of a Disease* (Chicago, 1965).

[3] Louis-Bernard La Taste, *Première lettre théologique aux écrivains défenseurs des convulsions du temps* (1733).

[4] Knox, p. 386.

came appeals from various *constitutionnaire* prelates, concerned to halt the convulsionary movement before it "captured" their dioceses. As the observances of the *oeuvre* continued to expand far beyond Paris and to penetrate into every corner of the kingdom,[5] such episcopal alarm, echoing the fears which Archbishop Vintimille had been voicing for many months, became increasingly widespread. The archbishop of Rouen, who was one of Cardinal Fleury's closest advisers, spoke for many of his ecclesiastical colleagues when he declaimed indignantly against the "fanaticism" of the convulsionaries and the "scandalous disorder" they had occasioned, and when he expressed his fears that the *menu peuple* in his diocese "ran the risk of being seduced," like those in Paris, unless the administration took steps to arrest this "epidemic contagion" at once.[6] The papal court evinced similar concern.[7] Indeed, *constitutionnaire* opinion was virtually unanimous in demanding that more rigorous action be taken by the civil authorities, especially in the capital.

Not surprisingly, the growing appeals for immediate government intervention to extirpate the convulsionary movement received a most sympathetic hearing at Versailles, where the matter had been under discussion for some weeks. In the meantime, serious developments on the international front had given a new urgency to Cardinal Fleury's quest for a solution to the convulsionary problem. An opportunity had

[5] Sympathetic ecclesiastics bore major responsibility for the diffusion of the convulsionary movement (see complaints of the bishop of Chartres to Fleury, May 27, 1736, BA, MS 11285, fol. 173). References to convulsionary activities outside of Paris may be found in *NNEE* and *Supplément des Nouvelles ecclésiastiques*, both *passim*. See also the following: Bachelier, pp. 191-96; Paul Ardoin, *La bulle Unigenitus dans les diocèses d'Aix, Arles, Marseille, Fréjus, Toulon*, 2 vols. (Marseille, 1936), II, 72-93; Durand, pp. 326-29; G. Arnaud d'Agnel, "Les convulsionnaires de Pignans," *Annales du Midi*, 19 (1907), pp. 206-20; Joseph Dedieu, "Un nouveau Port-Royal au diocèse d'Auxerre," *Le Correspondant*, 101 (September 1929), pp. 641-61; Jean Meyer, *La noblesse bretonne au 18ᵉ siècle*, 2 vols. (Paris, 1966), II, 990-92; P. Gagnol, *Le jansénisme convulsionnaire et l'affaire de la Planchette* (Paris, 1911); Emile Appolis, "Une controverse autour d'un 'miracle' janséniste," *Monspeliensis Hippocrates*, 44 (1969), pp. 20-28; *idem*, "Les 'miracles' jansénistes dans le Bas-Languedoc (1732-45)," *Annales du Midi*, 67 (1955), pp. 269-79; Marguerite Rebouillat, "Les convulsionnaires dans le Forez," *Actes du 98ᵉ Congrès national des Sociétés savantes. Section d'histoire moderne et contemporaine* (St.-Etienne, 1973), 2 vols. (Paris, 1975), II, 105-13. In some of these areas the *oeuvre* was just beginning to penetrate in 1733, with some anonymous convulsionist writers embarking on a public campaign to establish close contacts between Paris and the provinces (see, e.g., *Lettre d'un ecclésiastique de province à un de ses amis*, esp. pp. 3-4).

[6] Letter to Chauvelin, Feb. 8, 1733, AAE, M&D, France, MS 1282, fols. 145-46.

[7] Cf. *ibid.*, MS 1283, fols. 105-107, 196-211, *et passim*.

arisen to take advantage of the unstable situation in Poland, where Augustus II, Elector of Saxony and elective King of Poland, died on February 1, 1733. Though the War of the Polish Succession was not to break out until the following October, Augustus' death immediately occasioned a significant realignment in European diplomatic relations.[8] Pressed by the war party under Chauvelin, who had long been clamoring for a confrontation with Great Britain or Austria, Fleury was eventually prevailed upon to support the pretensions of Louis XV's dispossessed father-in-law, Stanislaus Leczinski. But large-scale French involvement in a foreign war would entail a considerable expenditure of the government's limited time and energy. If the cardinal-minister intended to devote the attention necessary for the wrangling and maneuvers of foreign affairs, it was imperative that matters at home be settled. In Paris, at least, the ability of the authorities to restore domestic peace depended in large measure on their ability to dispose of the convulsionaries. To be sure, the unusual nature of their *séance* activities and the potentially "epidemic" proportions of the convulsionary "contagion" were already enough to justify an attempt by the royal administration to bring the sect's adherents firmly to heel. With the possibility of war growing daily more likely, the government now had additional reason to step up the offensive against the movement. The time had come, therefore, to intensify the intervention of the Paris police.

For all of Cardinal Fleury's continued confidence in his lieutenant-general of police, the men under Hérault's command had not acquitted themselves very well thus far in the official campaign to stifle the Pâris cult and the convulsionary movement. Notwithstanding frequent complaints from the convulsionaries regarding wholesale arrests and extremely severe persecution, the alleged police repression following the closing of the cemetery at Saint-Médard had in fact been fairly restrained. That there had been considerable harassment and intimidation was, of course, undeniable.[9] The convulsionaries were, after all, disturbers of the religious and civil peace. The acts of repression, however, had hardly occurred on the exaggerated scale reported by adherents of the sect. In all of 1732, for example, only twenty prisoners were sent to the Bastille "sous prétexte de convulsions."[10] To be sure,

[8] Arthur M. Wilson, *French Foreign Policy During the Administration of Cardinal Fleury, 1726-1743* (Cambridge, Mass., 1936), p. 239.

[9] Cf. Louis Sabinet's descriptions of his interrogations in prison (BN, NAFr., MS 4262, fols. 126-28).

[10] Funck-Brentano, pp. 244-48; *Le Calendrier ecclésiastique. Avec le nécrologe*

there were numerous additional "gens du parti" arrested on various other charges who were nevertheless active participants in the *oeuvre*.[11] Occasionally there were also embarrassing moments of overzealousness on the part of the police. One officer, in his eagerness to catch likely suspects, arrested a certain Mlle. Lelièvre "for having feigned convulsions." Hérault was forced to release her two days later after discovering that the woman was an epileptic who had had the misfortune of being taken with a seizure in the street.[12] It is also true that Hérault, with his great emphasis on espionage and order, made considerable use of a vast network of spies, whom he and his inspectors deployed in a number of vital locations. For example, the Jesuit confessor in the Bastille, Father Couvrigny, kept Hérault constantly informed of what went on inside the prison, where despite their incarceration many of the convulsionaries continued to practice the *oeuvre* in their cells and even maintained regular contact with some of their brethren on the outside.[13] Couvrigny's reports, however, were of limited utility. The prisoners' reluctance to give confession before a Jesuit priest or to have anything else to do with him made his task an almost impossible one. He thus met with little success in his various attempts at discovering for Hérault the whereabouts of certain convulsionaries whom the police lieutenant had been unable to locate. Equally fruitless were the confessor's numerous efforts to get the prisoners to admit that their convulsions were fake, to repent of their alleged misdeeds, and to promise never to return to the *séances* once they were released.[14] Indeed, so strongly and enthusiastically did the *embastillés* convulsionaries cling

---

des personnes qui depuis un siècle se sont les plus distinguées par leur piété, leur attachement à Port-Royal et leur amour pour les vérités combattues . . . (1735), p. 105.

11 See Funck-Brentano, *passim*. The following are some of the categories employed by the police: *Jansénisme*, *Imprimerie clandestine*, *Colportage*, and *Graveurs prohibés*. How many individuals were sent to other Paris prisons cannot be determined with much precision, since most of the records for these houses of detention have been irretrievably lost as a result of various disasters, natural and man-made ("Incendie des archives de la Préfecture de police," *Bibliothèque de l'Ecole des Chartes*, 32 [1871], pp. 225-26).

12 BA, MS 11195, fols. 40-53. Cf. Dubut to Hérault, Feb. 4, 1732, and Barrangue to Hérault, Feb. 6, 1732 (Ravaisson, xiv, 296). Some individuals also had the misfortune of being arrested on the basis of mistaken identity or deliberately false accusations (see, e.g., BA, MS 11193, fols. 87-132).

13 But cf. Hérault to M. de Longpré, Oct. 29, 1732, BA, MS 12487, fol. 222.

14 See three letters from Couvrigny to Hérault, BA, MS 11097, fols. 106-11. The length of a prisoner's confinement "was rarely fixed by the Lieutenant of Police and depended instead on a prisoner's conduct after entering the [Bastille]" (Williams, p. 377).

to their faith that complaints began to be heard from the Bastille administrators that the "infectious contagion" was spreading among the other prisoners.[15]

Outside the Bastille the police and their numerous spies met with only slightly greater success. Anonymous informers, including some parish clergy,[16] continued to busy themselves with watching out for possible disturbances. Hérault occasionally sent one of his own officers to nose about and observe the behavior and activities of suspected members of the sect. In his continuing efforts to preserve law and order, the lieutenant of police charged these various informers as well as the commissioners and inspectors serving in each *quartier* not only with the constant surveillance of local activities but also with the preparation of frequent reports on what they observed.[17] From time to time some unfriendly, if not downright hostile, neighbor would take upon himself the duty of notifying the police of a clandestine assembly going on nearby.[18]

Despite some very close surveillance and pursuit of individuals as well as occasional mass arrests, the overall police response remained rather sporadic and ineffectual. Of course, as Hérault himself conceded, the problem of the convulsionaries was not one readily susceptible of a police solution. "Nothing was more likely to win them support," he observed, "than the resort to force, and nothing more likely to cause them to fall than silence." Passionately held beliefs, such as those espoused by the convulsionaries, could not easily be uprooted by force or mere executive fiat.[19] But the problem went further than that. For one thing, there was evidence of widespread laxness and ineptitude

[15] Le Camus to Hérault, March 5, 1734, BA, MS 11253, fol. 69.

[16] Cf. J. Bruté (*vicaire* of Saint-Laurent) to Hérault, March 1734, *ibid.*, fols. 37-38.

[17] Ravaisson, XIV, 474, n. 1. The considerable sum of money spent on intelligence in this period provides some indication of the seriousness with which the government regarded the convulsionary problem. According to the most recent student of this subject, "it appears that there may have been more police spies at work in Paris during the 1730s under Hérault than at any other time during the century" (Williams, p. 371; see also p. 170, n. 141).

[18] Coëffrel to Fleury, Dec. 8, 1733, BA, MS 10197, fol. 290. Many of these informers were quite insistent about preserving their anonymity (Ravaisson, XIV, 297, 307). Despite their timidity and hesitations, they continued to inform on the convulsionaries throughout this period. On the matter of offended neighbors' officiousness and hostility, see Williams, pp. 24-25.

[19] *Assemblée de Police* (discussions between Hérault and Joly de Fleury), Jan. 22, 1733, BN, MSS Fr., MS 11356, fol. 198 (Art. 334). On the nature and importance of the *Assemblée de Police* in coordinating and charting policy affecting the city of Paris, see Williams, pp. 286-301.

on the part of numerous police officers.[20] Even more serious, there were many convulsionary sympathizers—including "double agents" and "spies" for the brethren—within the police force itself.[21] A substantial body of *gardes françaises* was even reported to be among the actual devotees of the Pâris cult.[22]

For a variety of reasons, therefore, none of the ordinary means of vigilance employed by the authorities to combat the convulsionaries—neither occasional police intimidation and surveillance nor the decrees, ordinances, or pastoral letters raining down from both the secular and the ecclesiastical powers, not even incarceration in the Bastille and other Paris prisons—had arrested the course or diminished the impact of the convulsionary "contagion." The followers of the deacon Pâris continued to meet in their clandestine conventicles, observing practices and subscribing to beliefs that were substantially more unorthodox than any of those which had antedated the closing of Saint-Médard. Nevertheless, despite the failure of the police to eliminate the cult to M. Pâris or the convulsionary movement, Cardinal Fleury, bending before the pressure of his fellow *constitutionnaires* and faced with an impending international crisis, decided to promulgate yet another ordinance, this one more severe than the first, to stifle convulsionary activities. Politically at least, the time seemed propitious, for none of the influential groups that might possibly have objected to such an ordinance appeared likely to interfere at this point. The magistrates in the Parlement of Paris and the dissident *curés* in the diocese had all but exhausted themselves in their recent confrontations with the cardinal-minister and Archbishop Vintimille. What is more, occupied with other matters, they had begun to show less interest in or sympathy for the fortunes of the convulsionaries, particularly as the behavior of these religious enthusiasts had become increasingly more bizarre. From the perspective of ecclesiastical politics, therefore, Fleury could feel rather confident in proceeding with the publication of a second ordinance against the cult to M. Pâris—this time without recourse to any of the elaborate precautions and careful preparations which had of necessity preceded the first one.

On February 17, 1733, the royal council issued a decree prohibiting any and all convulsionary activities, no matter whether they occurred in public or in private.[23] The decree was promulgated as an explicit

---

[20] Cf. complaints of Labbé, *commissaire* for the *faubourg* Saint-Antoine (Ravaisson, XIV, 328-29), and Hérault's earlier reprimand of the entire body of *commissaires du Châtelet* (cited in *NNEE*, Dec. 20, 1731, pp. 246, 248).

[21] See, e.g., BA, MS 11218, fol. 34.

[22] Journal of De Lisle, December 1732, AN, U-379.

[23] Isambert, XXI, 378-79.

reaffirmation and extension of the earlier order which had closed the cemetery of Saint-Médard. According to the new decree, the convulsionaries were either mentally deranged or impostors. Whichever they were, their "fanatical rites" constituted a danger to the faith and, more important, were in violation of the laws in respect of public order and decency. The terms used to indict the convulsionaries—"seducers and disturbers of public tranquility"—demonstrated more than ever that the government was pursuing them primarily as civil criminals rather than as religious heretics, though the distinction was not always made in practice.[24] Despite the fact that the new law contained no specific instructions for its enforcement, there was no mistaking its tone: Fleury was announcing an unequivocal message of all-out repression.

The decree, as expected, brought the royal government enthusiastic congratulations from *constitutionnaires* all over France and even a rather warm response from Rome.[25] Among the *anticonstitutionnaires* the response was mixed, a situation which must have pleased Cardinal Fleury. Unlike the first royal ordinance, which had aroused almost universal criticism from the Jansenist camp, this one provoked a significant division of opinion. As Fleury had no doubt anticipated, the Parlement of Paris greeted the new ordinance with virtual silence. Individual magistrates may have voiced their personal displeasure, but the court as a body was unmoved. The Parisian *curés* likewise remained relatively quiet. However, the reticence of the Parlement and the *curés* did not prevent others from voicing strong opinions on the matter. One of the earliest responses came, as usual, from the *Nouvelles ecclésiastiques*, ever vigilant to defend the cause of *la Vérité* oppressed. In the previous year the journal had given over a substantial number of its weekly issues to the closing of Saint-Médard and its aftermath as well as to the related conflict between the royal government and the Parlement of Paris. In the meantime, the editor and his colleagues had been closely observing the developments in the *oeuvre des convulsions*, while cautiously reserving judgment on the unusual character of the *séances*. The *Nouvellistes*, however, found the charges contained in the February decree to be highly objectionable and thus finally broke their prolonged near-silence. In a sharp rebuke to the authorities, the editor charged that the convulsionaries had been condemned on

[24] *Ibid.* In a letter to the French ambassador at Rome, the duc de Saint-Aignan, Chauvelin stated that, "Quoique le bien de la Religion en ait esté le premier mobile, celui de la bonne police y a eu part" (April 14, 1733, AAE, C.P., Rome, MS 740, fol. 139).

[25] Saint-Aignan to Chauvelin, April 30, 1733, *ibid.*, MS 730, fol. 328.

insufficient grounds and without a full or proper hearing.[26] Not only was there no proof to substantiate the various allegations contained in the ordinance, he argued, but the description of the convulsionaries as impostors, religious fanatics, and disturbers of the peace was utterly meaningless, indeed preposterous, since the same groundless accusations had also been lodged against the followers of Jesus Christ.[27] By way of a conclusion, the editor once again raised the important question of juridical competence. It was a blatant irregularity, he asserted, for the royal council to pass judgment on what was clearly a religious matter, a subject with which it was not competent to deal in the first instance:

The temporal power cannot prejudge what concerns Faith and Dogma. Its *gloire* consists in supporting with its authority the canonical decisions of an ecclesiastical Tribunal. Has there as yet been any such tribunal before which one may say the convulsionaries have been legitimately called, heard, and judged? Would to God that there had been in the King's Council, instead of a Cardinal from the Roman Church, a GAMALIEL, who, well aware that sincere respect must be founded upon the truth, might have spoken nobly to the Prince:

". . . keep away from these men, and let them alone; for if this plan or this undertaking be of men, it will fail; but if it is of God, you will not be able to overthrow them. You might even be found opposing God!"[28]

Although the editor was speaking here for many of his fellow *anticonstitutionnaires*,[29] it quickly became clear that the views of the *Nouvelles ecclésiastiques* were not entirely representative of overall appellant opinion, at least insofar as the subject of the convulsionaries was concerned. Indeed, even as the editor of the journal was voicing his strenuous objections to the latest royal decree, a substantial body of Jansenist theologians had begun publishing tracts which conveyed a rather different attitude toward the whole question. Far from looking askance at the government's action, this group actually welcomed it. Disenchanted with the activities and the spiritual claims of the convulsionaries, these *anticonstitutionnaires* had already resolved on the urgency of dissociating themselves from those of their erstwhile com-

---

[26] *NNEE*, March 12, 1733, p. 52.   [27] *Ibid.*

[28] *Ibid.* Translation of biblical passage (Acts 5:38-39) from Revised Standard Version.

[29] Cf. *Entretiens sur les miracles*, pp. 138-39.

rades who still wished to support and encourage the followers of M. Pâris. A fierce and heated debate over the convulsionaries had in fact been going on for most of 1732 between rival Jansenist factions.

From the very beginning, the *anticonstitutionnaire* "party" had comprised a makeshift coalition of diverse interests—(Jansenist) theologians and priests, bishops and *curés*, clergy and laity, magistrates and lawyers—with the potential for serious divisions along theological, ecclesiastical, or political lines. Among the theologians, who were the most prolific spokesmen for the appellant position, the differences of opinion had always been especially pronounced. Large numbers had fallen away for a variety of reasons since the original appeal in 1717. But as late as 1727-1728 those who remained attached to the appellant cause could still be more or less united in their opposition to the "rigged" Council of Embrun and its deposition of Bishop Soanen. By the late 1720s and early 1730s, however, while Fleury was cutting still further into their numbers and had barred all appellants from the Sorbonne, the appearance of various doctrinal divisions and the emergence of bitter personal feuds seriously split the much-weakened forces of *anticonstitutionnaire* doctors.[30] Not the least significant issue creating this internecine strife and dislocation was the popular cult to François de Pâris.

The appellants, as we have seen, had never been completely united in their support of the miracles and other events taking place at Saint-Médard. Indeed, some of the most illustrious members of the party had been opposed from the first to the tactical "marriage of convenience" informally concluded in early 1731 between the *anticonstitutionnaire* cause and the Pâris cult, a fact which accounts in part for the slowness of the appellants to adopt the cult and exploit it to their advantage. That there was considerable reluctance is hardly surprising. Nor was the opposition motivated exclusively, or even primarily, by theological considerations. It involved a fundamental divergence in perspective and point of view. Many of the appellants, particularly the older ones, rigorous Jansenists weaned on theological debate, remained social and political traditionalists, quite cautious and conservative in their outlook.[31] Prudence, moderation, respectability,

---

[30] *Lettre d'un ecclésiastique à un évêque*, pp. 1-4. One can follow the course of the dispute in the *Nouvelles ecclésiastiques* and in the pamphlets collected in BPR, L.P. 483, as well as in d'Etemare's correspondence, BA, MS 5784. Though not always reliable, see also Dedieu, "L'agonie du jansénisme."

[31] On the conservative nature of Jansenist political and social thought, see James, *Nicole*, pp. 138-46; Taveneaux, *Jansénisme et politique* (Paris, 1965), pp. 90-91; *idem*, "Jansénisme et vie sociale en France au 17ᵉ siècle," *Revue d'his-

and propriety were their watchwords. A strong sense of ecclesiastical rank and order, hierarchy and subordination—of laity to clergy, priests to bishops—pervaded their writings. They repudiated the Richerist ecclesiology which many *anticonstitutionnaire* priests had been espousing and disavowed the liturgical innovations on behalf of the laity which certain of their colleagues had attempted to introduce into church ceremonies in Paris and elsewhere.[32] Considering themselves the king's most faithful subjects, they shuddered as much at the thought of ecclesiastical or spiritual novelties as they did at the prospect of civil disorder and disruption. Like their *constitutionnaire* enemies, with whom in this respect they shared a great deal, they had a considerable attachment to the status quo. Finally, a strongly aristocratic or snobbishly elitist strain in their social outlook disinclined them from uniting with the *menu peuple*, and also left them rather prone to embarrassment by the activities of Saint-Médard, located as it was in the heart of a lower-class district in the *faubourg* Saint-Marceau.

Even before 1732 this group of anti-"illuminist" appellants, possessed of an almost constitutional aversion to religious enthusiasm of any sort, had become disturbed by the strange manifestations at Pâris' tomb.[33] But the activities of the abbé Bescherand and the others at Saint-Médard were nothing in comparison with the behavior of the convulsionaries after the cemetery was closed down. As a consequence, there was a noticeable increase in the number of appellants opposed to the Pâris cult and especially to the "pentecostal ecstasies" associated with the *oeuvre des convulsions*. They were deeply disturbed by the violence of the phenomena and positively scandalized by the lengths to which these people seemed prepared to go in their quest for a meaningful religious experience. The apparent cruelties of the *secours meurtriers* they found particularly objectionable. These critics claimed to see in the *oeuvre* unmistakable signs of *illuminisme*, of visionary fanaticism not unlike that of the Camisards in the Cévennes.[34] Fearing

---

toire de l'Eglise de France, 54 (1968), pp. 27-46; and J.A.G. Tans, "Les idées politiques des jansénistes," *Neophilologus*, 40 (1956), pp. 1-18.

[32] See Dedieu's review of Préclin, *Les jansénistes*, in *Revue d'histoire de l'Eglise de France*, 16 (1930), pp. 68-75.

[33] Cf. the general comments of Taveneaux, *La vie quotidienne*, pp. 199-200.

[34] Allegations of a direct relationship between the extravagant behavior of the Camisards and that of the convulsionaries were not uncommon in this period. See, e.g., Bishop Souillac of Lodève to Fleury, Oct. 1, 1734, cited in Appolis, "Les 'miracles' jansénistes," p. 277; archbishop of Rouen to Chauvelin, Feb. 8, 1732, AAE, M&D, France, MS 1282, fol. 146; and *Supplément des Nouvelles ecclésiastiques*, Dec. 8, 1734, p. 152. The view of Jansenism as a conspiracy of

the charges of guilt by association that were the immediate—and expected—response of their *constitutionnaire* opponents, they hoped by
a disavowal to preserve their own integrity. They also thought thereby
to prevent the extravagant behavior of the convulsionaries from compromising, if it did not utterly destroy, the interests and dignity of the
appellant cause. Consequently, they began publishing a series of tracts
and pamphlets designed to repudiate the *oeuvre*, not only as demeaning
the majesty of God, the holiness of His worship, and the honor of
His church, but also as violating the purity of morals and contravening
the basic standards of public decency.[35]

However, these Jansenists had still other, similarly compelling, reasons for their concerted opposition. It was bad enough, they insisted,
that the cause to which they had been devoted for so long had given
itself over to a popular cult and made an issue of questionable supernatural phenomena occurring among people unworthy of receiving
divine gifts. But now some of their fellow theologians, following the
"democratic" lead of certain Paris priests, were conferring upon the
convulsionary laity a substantial role within the Church polity. The
convulsionaries, "cette vile canaille sortie de la poussière," as one of
their principal Jansenist detractors scornfully referred to them,[36] had
no business meddling in high politics, whether religious or secular.
Nor had the other appellants any right to delegate to these people so
important a responsibility. This active entrance of the *menu peuple*
into the debates of contemporary ecclesiastical politics appeared all the
more threatening because it raised the ominous possibility that the
Jansenist theologians might be forced to relinquish direction of *their*
cause to a pro-convulsionary wing that appeared to be much less concerned with the vital doctrinal issues surrounding the Bull. For them
this was perhaps the most disquieting prospect of all; it was a case of
allowing the tail to wag the dog, popular judgments seemingly replacing those of the theologians.

While the cult to M. Pâris had derived much of its initial unity,
direction, and force from its association with the *anticonstitutionnaire*
cause, the appellants were not able to exercise very much control in ori-

---

"crypto-Calvinists" or of "Calvinists who said Mass" was a longstanding one
in Jesuit and other hostile circles.

[35] These works are surveyed in Dedieu, "L'agonie du jansénisme," pp. 184-86,
et passim.

[36] Words attributed to the abbé d'Asfeld, BA, MS 5784, fol. 23. According to
another version of these remarks, d'Asfeld described the convulsionaries as "une
vile canaille qu'il falloit faire rentrer dans la poussière d'où ils étoient sorti,"
BHVP, N.A. 125, I, 265.

enting the convulsionary movement specifically or exclusively around the Bull. Although it is true that numerous appellants did play a guiding role in the *oeuvre*, the convulsionaries as a body had never perceived the defense of the appeal as their principal *raison d'être*. What is more, whereas many of the *anticonstitutionnaires* might have been satisfied to put away some of their differences with the *constitutionnaires* if only the pope would have "explained" the condemned propositions in *Unigenitus*, no such acquiescence or accommodation was likely from the followers of M. Pâris. As they conceived the issues at stake, the pope could have even withdrawn the Bull without greatly affecting their activities. For them the problem was not really one of defending the theological or ecclesiastical positions which *Unigenitus* was threatening to destroy; they were not intimately involved with the doctrinal questions over which old or former *Sorbonnéens* had engaged in interminable disputations. Their interest was concentrated on the eventual return of the prophet Elijah, who would open an era of renewed piety, spirituality, and universal brotherhood. The anticonvulsionary Jansenists thus had still another reason for abandoning and disavowing these people, whose subordination of doctrine to enthusiastic religious experience they regarded as an unpardonable deviation. The efforts made to prepare apologetic and polemical tracts on behalf of the Pâris cult, they maintained, were needlessly threatening to redirect vital energy and attention away from the more important doctrinal and constitutional questions related to the Bull. By mid-1732 they had launched an active campaign to discredit the convulsionaries and their supporters.

The case of the abbé Bidal d'Asfeld is both interesting and instructive. Among the important Jansenist theologians of the period, a former spiritual adviser to the deacon Pâris, and the author of numerous "figurist" treatises, d'Asfeld had actually been one of the first and most ardent supporters of the Saint-Médard miracles. He had written to his colleagues almost rapturously, encouraging them to "draw near to these people [at Pâris' tomb] in order to hear the voice [of God]."[37] But d'Asfeld was also one of the first of these notable theologians to detach himself from the convulsionaries and became one of their most vocal detractors, ostensibly because he feared that many of them were mad and also because he considered their behavior to be indecent, hysterical, and "contrary to reason." He argued, further, that such "delirious persons" should not be allowed to "instruct the people in place of the

[37] Cited in Dedieu, "L'agonie du jansénisme," p. 184, n. 46. Cf. BHVP, N.A. 125, I, 265.

theologians. To give free reign to such preachers would degrade the dignity and authority of the ministry."[38]

Further evidence of the discord among the appellants came from the conservative abbé Duguet,[39] who in 1732 broke publicly with the *Nouvelles ecclésiastiques* over the issue of the convulsionaries.[40] Having been embarrassed by his close association, thirty years earlier, with the famous Soeur Rose—the self-styled prophet, miracle worker, and visionary, who turned out to be a fraud—Duguet was determined not to be "deceived and duped a second time."[41] With the encouragement of his imperious niece, the vitriolic Mme. Duguet-Mol, who dominated her uncle throughout his last years and worked actively to render the split with the *Nouvellistes* permanent,[42] Duguet categorically repudiated the *oeuvre* and all of its Jansenist defenders. Appalled by a series of articles in the *Nouvelles ecclésiastiques* which had celebrated the divine character of the convulsionary displays, he severely re-

[38] Cited in Dedieu, "L'agonie du jansénisme," pp. 186-87, n. 53.

[39] See Sainte-Beuve's characterization of Duguet (III, 528-29).

[40] On Duguet's relationship with other appellants during this period, see Paul Chételat, *Etude sur Duguet* (Paris, 1879), pp. 52-57, and *NNEE*, Nov. 23, 1733, pp. 234-35. See also Boursier to Fouquet, Nov. 16, 1732, AFA, P.R. 5988, and Foucquet to Soanen, July 13, 1734, *ibid.*, P.R. 6568.

[41] Cited in Chételat, pp. 62-63; cf. Sainte-Beuve, III, 512-14. On Soeur Rose see BN, MSS Fr., MSS 18832, 19855, and 20973.

[42] This "Enragée de Troyes," as Bishop Caylus of Auxerre later referred to her, was a furious and indefatigable controversialist, who claimed to be acting out of loyalty to her uncle, defamed by "des amis [appellants] remplis de noirceur." More to the point, however, she was acting as a secret spy for Hérault against both the *anticonstitutionnaires* and the convulsionaries. In this capacity, she was the most active agent in fomenting disunity and in helping to detach many Jansenists from the convulsionary camp. Her *Journal historique des convulsions du temps* (1733), the most famous of the pamphlets she wrote maligning the cause of M. Pâris, contained a mass of baseless charges. In an attempt to explain away the convulsionaries with a conspiratorial thesis, she invented a *Sénat*, guided by *Présidens*, who supposedly led the whole "show" and issued all the statements contained in various convulsionist pamphlets; this handful of people had formed a "plot" to undermine the authority of both Church and State. Her descriptions and analysis of the activities of the sect, whether in or out of the *séances*, not only convinced the majority of her *anticonstitutionnaire* contemporaries, but have also survived in the pages of virtually every single historical work on this episode. For more information on Mme. Duguet-Mol, from one who has accepted her version of the convulsionary story, see Dedieu, "L'agonie du jansénisme," pp. 194-95, n. 66. For her correspondence with Hérault, see BA, MS 11223, fols. 100-330. For a contemporary *anticonstitutionnaire* assessment of her troublesome character and divisive activities, see an undated, unsigned letter (by d'Etemare?), AFA, P.R. 2597.

proached the journal's editor for his "imprudence, temerity, and false zeal" and charged him with "abandoning religion to the doubts of the impious."[43] On several other occasions he expressed his resentment at the distorted use to which certain convulsionists had put his "figurist" writings and raised objections to their "translation" for and introduction into convulsionary circles.[44] It is easy to imagine the great pleasure that these reflections and those of d'Asfeld must have given the *constitutionnaires*.

In subsequent months, while a growing faction of Jansenist theologians was rallying to the side of d'Asfeld and Duguet, another group took up the convulsionary cause with even greater enthusiasm than before, thus guaranteeing that the much-deplored split would not be easily healed. Those who remained dedicated supporters of the Pâris cult agreed with the editor of the *Nouvelles ecclésiastiques* that the convulsionaries had done nothing to detract from or offset the miracles, and, more important, that their activities had in no way prejudiced the *anticonstitutionnaire* position. Quite the contrary, contended these convulsionists, the *séances* were making such an extraordinary impact upon popular piety that they had had a very salutary effect on the Jansenist cause itself.

The rebuttal to the Duguet-d'Asfeld criticism was contained in a number of vigorous and eloquent statements. In a letter written in December 1732, the abbé d'Etemare, an eyewitness to and participant in convulsionary activities (unlike most of the movement's detractors), claimed to describe the situation that had obtained in Paris as a direct result of the *oeuvre*. According to him, the *oeuvre*—especially the miracles and the discourses—had deeply touched thousands of persons with no previous knowledge of or interest in the cause of the appeal and had convinced them of the righteousness of the appellant position.[45] If the critics were concerned that the appeal was still not the central or exclusive convulsionary preoccupation, d'Etemare observed, they had only themselves to blame, for they had neglected to provide the faithful with the kind of solid, effective instruction—clear, methodical, and at their level of understanding—which might have awakened popular interest more quickly and more profoundly. As for those who have complained about alleged "abuses" in the midst of the *oeuvre*, "where

[43] *Lettre de M. l'abbé Du Guet à un professeur d'un Collège de l'Oratoire* (n.d.).
[44] See Chételat, pp. 54-57. Cf. "Prière d'un convulsionnaire pour M. l'abbé Du Guet encore vivant pour lors" (*ibid.*, pp. 68-69).
[45] Cited in the anonymous *Défense de l'autorité et des décisions des merveilles que Dieu ne cesse point de faire en France depuis un grand nombre d'années* (1752), p. 332.

were they when the convulsions first began, when they might have proposed the various rules to which they expected the convulsionaries to conform?" In fact, "they had scornfully dismissed the convulsionaries and declined to inform themselves any further about the movement's activities or about the public's attitude toward the *oeuvre*."[46] And yet, d'Etemare asserted, "had there not been any convulsions, all of these simple faithful would still be just as ignorant and indifferent as they had been in 1730."[47]

Another outspoken defender of the convulsionaries, the theologian Poncet Desessarts, echoed d'Etemare's sentiments in a letter sent to a colleague at the end of January 1733:

> I have found in Paris a renewal of piety which is growing stronger and increases daily by means of the convulsions. I have no difficulty believing what M. d'Etemare has told me, [namely,] that there are at present 10,000 souls who have had no other instruction than that which they have received from the convulsionaries and from those who congregate around them. The convulsionaries are accomplishing what we (the theologians) failed to do. They are announcing the Gospel to the poor and the common people.[48]

Another convulsionist pamphleteer, the anonymous author of the *Entretiens sur les miracles*, emphasized the point that the convulsionaries were directly linked with François de Pâris, their inspiration and immediate precursor. Those who still accepted the miracles while rejecting the convulsions, he argued, had lost sight of this crucial connection and failed to understand that the mission of the convulsionaries, like that of M. Pâris himself, was "to obtain the abolition of the Bull, the triumph of the Truth, and the renewal of the Church."[49]

It was the general belief of these apologists, then, that before the appearance of the convulsionaries few people had even been aware of the evils of the Church; fewer still had grieved at this terrible state of affairs and been concerned enough to wish a remedy. The *oeuvre* had served as a "brief catechism"[50] through which God had made even the most unenlightened people sensitive to these evils and dramatically announced the forthcoming renewal and regeneration of the faith.[51]

[46] D'Etemare to Pierre Sartre, July 13, 1733, BA, MS 5784, p. 62.
[47] *Ibid.*
[48] Letter to Nicolas Le Gros, cited in *Défense de l'autorité et des décisions des merveilles*, p. 332.
[49] *Entretiens sur les miracles*, p. 146; see also p. 141.
[50] *Coup d'oeil en forme de lettre sur les convulsions* (1733), p. 32.
[51] *Entretiens sur les miracles*, p. 116.

Indeed, the miraculous spectacle was more effective in reaching the *menu peuple* than the best sermons or books of piety. The *oeuvre* had made them familiar with and—more important—attentive to matters with which they would otherwise have had no contact, matters which had formerly been the exclusive concern of theologians. The people had come to understand that a large number of the propositions condemned in the Bull were at the very heart of the true faith. They had also come to recognize "the rarity of good guides, and the advantage of choosing them among the appellants."[52] Such popular involvement in the *Unigenitus* controversy, these pro-convulsionary Jansenists concluded, should surely be welcomed, since such obvious residual benefits had accrued to the *anticonstitutionnaire* cause as a result of it. Their conclusions, however, were markedly at variance with the position of the Duguet-d'Asfeld faction, whom they regarded as completely misguided and utterly misinformed. The possibility of reaching a compromise seemed bleak indeed.

Despite the apparent deadlock, attempts had been made to effect a reconciliation between the rival groups. Representatives of the opposing sides had already been meeting together "to examine the nature and implications of the sect's activities and to discuss the rules which should apply in judging them."[53] The secret conferences, which brought together at least a dozen Jansenist theologians, began in November 1732 and continued, with several interruptions, until January 1733.[54] As early as December, sentiment was virtually unanimous for condemning any immodesty, indecency, or violence in the *secours* rendered at the *séances*.[55] However, the matter of the *secours meurtriers* was almost the only question on which the conferees could reach substantial agreement. Although in accord that the "astonishing manifestations seen in the convulsions were beyond the ordinary course of nature," they were unable to agree on the relationship between the miracles and the convulsions.[56] Nor could they agree on whether God or the devil was the primary cause of these unusual phenomena.

Even after further discussing these manifestations in the light of principles drawn from Scripture and tradition, and after reading various dissertations on the subject, the theologians remained split into two

---

[52] *Coup d'oeil*, p. 32.

[53] *Lettre d'un ecclésiastique à un évêque* (n.d.), p. 10.

[54] According to the notes of one participant, "Ce fut pendant la 2ᵉ conférence qu'arriva le miracle de la petite Aubigan," which caused a major interruption, since there were several theologians "qui pour en être témoin se transportèrent chez M. le curé de Saint-Germain-le-Vieux." Several even withdrew entirely ("Observations sur différens sujets relatifs à nos disputes," BPR, L.P. 490, No. 59).

[55] *Lettre d'un ecclésiastique à un évêque*, p. 10.   [56] *Ibid.*

factions. Finally, on January 29, 1733, their numbers now reduced to seven, they announced their conclusions. Two conferees[57] were agreed on attributing "all that is seen in the convulsions to an evil principle, that is to say, to sickness, imposture, or the devil."[58] Four others,[59] subsequently known as *discernants*, concluded that "it was necessary to make distinctions (*discerner*), that there were some effects which could not be attributed to God, while there were others which appeared certainly to come from Him. . . ."[60] A seventh theologian,[61] uncertain what to make of the whole question, decided at this time to abstain, though he would eventually range himself on the side of the anticonvulsionaries.

The conferences had clearly settled nothing.[62] Even though the abbés d'Etemare and d'Asfeld subsequently held a number of private meetings in a final effort to reach some kind of accommodation, their secret discussions proved similarly fruitless. The break was irreconcilable— and irrevocable. Indeed, in the course of defining their arguments much more sharply, the theologians had also hardened the lines of division. In the months that followed, the discord among the appellants was vented in public through innumerable letters, pamphlets, and broadsides, most of them issued anonymously. The theologians were engaged in an emotion-charged, but tiresomely sterile and repetitious debate. Even worse than the obscurantist and petty theologizing was the excessive vituperation: it was a virulent campaign, filled with personal attacks, outrageous accusations, and recriminations, that brought discredit upon all concerned and no doubt filled their *constitutionnaire* enemies with glee. Still other doctrinal controversies raging among the appellants, involving vexed dogmatic questions left over from the seventeenth century, served to exacerbate the conflict raging over the convulsionaries and to dissolve further the ties that once bound. The disputes ultimately were to have dramatic consequences for the convulsionary movement itself.

In the meantime, while the theologians continued their debates, the authorities, buoyed by the breach in the Jansenist ranks, were already

[57] The abbés d'Asfeld and De Lan.

[58] [D'Etemare], *Exposé de la manière de penser de M. l'abbé de*** touchant l'événement des convulsions* (1735), p. 18.

[59] D'Etemare, Boursier, Maillard, and Gourlin or Coudrette.

[60] [D'Etemare], *Exposé de la manière de penser*, p. 18. Both positions involved a determination as to whether the convulsions, discourses, etc. represented a single *oeuvre* and whether God could be involved in phenomena which had apparently "nondivine" features.

[61] Besoigne.   [62] See BA, MS 5784, *passim*.

acting to execute the provisions of the second royal ordinance against the convulsionaries, which had called for an end to their *séances*. Perhaps inspired by the decree or goaded by the dressing-down many of them had received from the lieutenant of police, Hérault's men made a series of quite spectacular mass arrests. The most noteworthy occurred at the home of a certain M. Chrétien, *marchand de dorure* on the rue Saint-Honoré.[63] Defying the law against clandestine assemblies, Chrétien, whose house had a convenient and well-disguised rear entrance, had dared to receive convulsionaries and spectators in meetings held at night.[64] By mid-March, however, a spy had tipped off the police about these assemblies.[65] They arrested Chrétien along with ten other persons, including several priests and the well-known convulsionary, Denise Regné ("la Nicette"), and sent them all to the Bastille.[66] Additional arrests followed in succeeding weeks, as the police bent to their task of pursuing the convulsionaries with renewed zeal.[67]

Hérault's officers were not the only Paris authorities to harass the convulsionaries during this period. The nasty-minded *curé* of Saint-Médard, Coëffrel, and his equally mean-spirited *vicaire*, Le Jeune, had been doing their best for over a year to disrupt all observances of the *oeuvre* at their parish church. There was a great deal for them to disrupt. Though the police stationed around the parish had managed to restore a degree of peace and tranquility to Saint-Médard following the closing of the cemetery, their ominous presence had failed to intimidate most devotees of François de Pâris into staying away from the church.[68] Undeterred, substantial numbers had continued their regular, daily appearances there, offering redoubled prayers to God and to the saintly deacon. As before, some of them went in order to recount to their coreligionists tales of miraculous cures which they had recently experienced. Still others even had convulsions while there.[69] Despite prohibitions against the sale of candles to be burned

[63] BA, MS 11218, fols. 1-221. See also Barbier, II, 390 (March 1733), and *NNEE*, April 4, 1733, pp. 62-64.

[64] Barbier, II, 390.

[65] According to a note which the police added to the dossier, "On trouve dans cette liasse [fols. 12-17, 22, 34, 41-42] des lettres et avis du Sr. Du Portail au ministre contre Chrétien. Le Sr. Du Portail avoit été l'ami de Chrétien et s'étant brouillé avec lui, il découvrit tout au ministre et lui servoit d'espion contre les convulsionnaires" (BA, MS 11218, fol. 11). Cf. Ravaisson, XIV, 330-31, 333.

[66] The police also confiscated a daily journal of convulsionary *séances* which covered assemblies for the previous week and a half (BA, MS 11218, fols. 124-45).

[67] See BA, MSS 11219, 11229, and 11237.

[68] See the daily police reports for this period, BA, MSS 10196-97.

[69] Police report of Feb. 19, 1732, BA, MS 10196; Coëffrel to Hérault, May 2,

in honor of M. Pâris or of *estampes* bearing the revered deacon's portrait, vendors of these and similar articles went on publicly, albeit cautiously, plying their trade to a large and enthusiastic clientele.[70] Others made available—whether for purchase or distributed free—various relics and sacred objects associated with M. Pâris, in addition to miracle-working dirt from his grave and water from the well attached to his house on the rue des Bourguignons.[71] At the same time, with the active support and complicity of sympathetic parish officials, especially the sacristan and the churchwardens—with whom Coëffrel had been engaged in a longstanding legal dispute—a few priests from outside the parish defied Vintimille's ban of January 1732 and continued to offer regular Masses in honor of François de Pâris.[72] In addition, the faithful testified to their own undiminished zeal and their tenacious dedication to Pâris' memory by continuing to post their placards, scrawled prayers, and devotional petitions on the inside walls of the church.[73] Notwithstanding the ubiquitous presence of the police, the degree and extent of public devotions at Saint-Médard thus appeared to be almost as great as ever. Early in the morning of May 1, 1732, for example, the fifth anniversary of the saintly deacon's death, the church was filled with "an astonishing crowd of people," including a large proportion of ecclesiastics and *gens de considération*.[74] Such a scene was to mark every May 1 at Saint-Médard for the next two dec-

---

1733, *ibid.*, MS 10197, fol. 263; Jeanne-Marthe Le Grand (convulsionary) to Bishop Soanen, Oct. 6, 1736, AFA, P.R. 6685. Since the incidence of such convulsions was in contravention of the royal ordinance of Jan. 27, 1732, it was common for their fellow brethren to carry away persons so overcome or to lead them off to nearby homes (cf. Journal of De Lisle, Feb. 5, 1732, AN, U-377).

[70] Le Jeune to Fleury, Feb. 6, 1733, BA, MS 10197, fol. 223; Coëffrel to Hérault, May 2, 1733, *ibid.*, fols. 262-63; Le Jeune to Fleury, June 12, 1733, *ibid.*, fols. 265-66; Dubut (police officer) to Hérault, July 11, 1733, *ibid.*, fol. 269.

[71] Le Jeune to Fleury, April 2, 1732, BA, MS 10196; Jacques Charles Pisot (Frère Jacques, convulsionary), testimony before Parlement of Paris, AN, X-1b 9691.

[72] Augustin Husse, the sacristan who authorized these Masses, was eventually dismissed by Coëffrel—an action which precipitated yet another confrontation between the *curé* and the pro-Pâris *marguilliers* (cf. the petition of the latter to Hérault, protesting Husse's dismissal, Oct. 20, 1732, BA, MS 10196).

[73] Journal of De Lisle, February 1732, AN, U-377; Coëffrel to Hérault, May 17, 1732, BA, MS 10196; Coëffrel to Fleury, Sept. 3, [1732], *ibid.*, MS 10202; Coëffrel to Fleury, Oct. 2, [1732], *ibid.*, MS 10200.

[74] Barbier, II, 261-62 (May 1732); Journal of De Lisle, May 1732, AN, U-378. See also Coëffrel to Fleury, May 30, 1732, AAE, M&D, Ile de France, MS 1600, fols. 107-108, and Coëffrel to Hérault, May 2, 1733, BA, MS 10197, fols. 262-63.

ades, until in the 1750s alarmed authorities finally began locking the church doors.[75]

Even more audacious than the worshipers at the church were the groups of people who occasionally inveigled their way into the cemetery itself. Some of them seem to have obtained access by bribing an indifferent police *exempt* or a church official.[76] More frequent still were those who entered on the pretext of participating in legitimate burial services which the king's ordinance of January 27 had specifically excluded from his proscription. There was little that could be done about the bribes. As for the interments, they were definitively proscribed by another royal order, this one dated December 3, 1732, and addressed to Father Coëffrel, who had solicited the decree and was given responsibility for its execution.[77]

For his part, Coëffrel, with assistance from his loyal *vicaire* and the support and encouragement of Fleury, Vintimille, and Hérault, had busied himself since January 1732 in a rather heavy-handed campaign to halt, or at least impede, the unauthorized devotional activities at Saint-Médard. In sermons and during religious instruction the zealous *curé* and his *constitutionnaire* subordinates frequently denounced François de Pâris as a damned heretic, unworthy of the respect, let alone the reverence, of anyone.[78] They even threatened to withhold the sacraments from those parishioners who persisted in their devotion to the deacon.[79] Not satisfied with defaming Pâris' character and threatening various sanctions for continued participation in the cult, Coëffrel and Le Jeune sometimes went around the church defacing or tearing down placards and knocking over or extinguishing candles lit in the deacon's memory—actions which resulted in several tense confronta-

[75] The same large crowds also appeared annually on October 4, the Feast of Saint Francis of Assisi (M. Pâris' patron saint). The police reports for these years indicate that the church was sometimes locked even on the days immediately succeeding and following May 1 and October 4 (BA, MSS 10200-202, *passim*).

[76] Mousset, p. 76.

[77] Archives de département de la Seine et de la ville de Paris, D. 4G¹.

[78] Joly de Fleury to [Fleury?], May 7, 1733, AAE, M&D, France, MS 1283, fol. 25; cf. police report of Nov. 2, 1732, BA, MS 10196.

[79] In April 1733, in a case which eventually reached the Parlement of Paris and resulted in the sovereign court's issuing a major remonstrance on the subject, Coëffrel actually denied the sacraments to a certain Jeanne Tavignot, a parishioner who had professed a profound reverence for François de Pâris and an opposition to the bull *Unigenitus* (see declaration of Coëffrel, April 15, 1733, BA, MS 10197, fol. 238; Vintimille to Fleury, April 15, 1733, BM, MS 2358, pp. 104-105; Fleury to Vintimille, April 18, *ibid.*, p. 106; and Vintimille to Fleury, April 25, *ibid.*, pp. 106-108; the Parlement's remonstrance, dated May 15, is in Flammermont, I, 303-13).

tions with the faithful. Le Jeune, in particular, became embroiled in a series of vehement, vituperative exchanges which on more than one occasion led to threats of physical assault against the *vicaire*.[80] Though he was subsequently to devise still other methods of interfering with the cult—closing the church in the afternoons, spreading oil and mud in the areas of the church where the convulsionary faithful knelt to pray to M. Pâris, and the like—by the spring of 1733 Coëffrel's various obstructive acts and intemperate pronouncements had made him an object of public hatred. Nor had the royal appointment of a *suisse*, designed to ensure that his parishioners treated him with "the proper respect and deference,"[81] in any way affected the contempt and low esteem in which they now held him and the rest of his clergy. It is hardly surprising, therefore, that the efforts of the *curé* and his *vicaire*, even those taken in concert with the police, should have failed to halt the public observances of the *oeuvre* at Saint-Médard.

But it was the *private* devotions of the convulsionary devotees of François de Pâris which remained the major source of concern to the civil and ecclesiastical authorities. Since the convulsionaries still continued to ignore the decree of February 1733 and persisted in spreading their "dangerous fanaticism" and "spirit of imposture and seduction" throughout Paris and beyond, it was decided to take further steps to implement the royal ordinance. In early April the king's council issued an *arrêt* which placed Hérault at the head of a specially appointed tribunal of twelve *maîtres des requêtes* that was established at the Arsenal and charged with exclusive jurisdiction over those convulsionaries—beginning with the people arrested at Chrétien's house in mid-March—who were found in contravention of the law.[82] However, the establishment of this extraordinary commission of justice aroused considerable apprehension and hostility at the Palais de Justice. The Parlement of Paris, having been previously deprived of jurisdiction in the entire affair, regarded the new tribunal as a blatant violation of its own judicial duties and prerogatives. Portraying themselves once again as "enemies of arbitrary government" and "upholders and interpreters of fundamental law," the magistrates charged the administration with attempting to reinstitute a "tyrannical inquisition" in the very heart of the capital. After weeks of discussion and negotiation in Paris and at Versailles, the representations of the First President and of other in-

[80] Police reports for October 1732, BA, MS 10196, *passim*; Le Jeune to Fleury, Feb. 6, 1733, *ibid.*, MS 10197, fol. 223; Coëffrel to Hérault, May 2, 1733, *ibid.*, fols. 262-63; Le Jeune to Fleury, June 12, 1733, *ibid.*, fols. 265-66.

[81] AN, O[1] 76, April 11, 1732, fols. 197, 249.

[82] Copy of *arrêt* in BA, MS 11218, fol. 48.

fluential magistrates in the sovereign court apparently succeeded in persuading the king's ministers of the wisdom of abolishing the newly appointed commission.[83] Nothing further was heard of its activities after mid-April. Once more the threat of a potentially serious jurisdictional squabble involving the Parlement had prevented Fleury's administration from proceeding against the convulsionaries as the government wished. To a public grown more and more accustomed to viewing the court as the defender of those subjected to ecclesiastical repression, the magistrates had once again seemed to show themselves as the protectors of the convulsionaries—a perception of which the convulsionaries themselves were only later to be disabused.

In any event, this latest, unexpected setback could not have failed to dampen Fleury's spirits. Originally elated at the news of the successful raid at the Chrétien home only a month earlier[84] and hopeful of being able to pursue the convulsionaries more effectively through the now-defunct "14e Bureau des Commissions extraordinaires,"[85] the cardinal-minister had grown dejected by the end of April. His reaction to the convulsionaries had always betrayed a strong element of fear: fear of the unknown and unseen force that apparently lurked behind their activities; fear of their potential for disrupting and even undermining the established order. But it was in a note sent to Hérault at this time that Fleury gave the first definite indication that he had finally begun to understand the awesomely strong-willed character of these people and to become aware—as his police-lieutenant already was—that perhaps they could not be handled by a simple resort to force. Referring to Hérault's recent interrogation of convulsionary prisoners, Fleury observed:

> There is little likelihood that you will extract any information from the prisoners, for there is something supernatural in the invincible obstinacy of all these sorts of persons; even the very scum of the people are unwilling to give the slightest confession or bit of information. I am at a loss to say where we will put all

[83] *Nouvelles publiques*, April 6, 7, and 13, 1733, *ibid.*, MS 10163, fols. 154, 164-65. These *Nouvelles publiques*, which consist of the gossip and rumor discussed in cafés, gardens, and other public gathering places around Paris, were compiled by various police spies. Since most of the official documents bearing on this matter seem to have disappeared, and since the commission received only passing notice in contemporary memoirs and journals (cf. Barbier, II, 390 [March 1733], and *NNEE*, May 3, 1733, p. 85), I have been forced to make greater use of these not always reliable sources than one would ordinarily choose to do.

[84] Fleury to Hérault, March 20, 1733, in Ravaisson, XIV, 334.

[85] *NNEE*, May 3, 1733, p. 85.

these prisoners afterward, since we cannot dream of ever setting them free.[86]

Fleury's reaction, especially as revealed in the very last part of his statement, was surely somewhat extreme and was, in fact, belied by the government's action of releasing most of the arrested convulsionaries within a few weeks or months of their capture. But there was increasingly good reason for Fleury to be speaking now in this way.

Despite the mounting opposition to their *séances* from appellants and *constitutionnaires* alike and despite the stepped-up activities of the police, most of the convulsionaries had remained undaunted. Cut adrift by a growing number of their former supporters-turned-defectors and increasingly isolated by official actions and pronouncements, they were still managing to survive as a more or less autonomous movement. To be sure, some of the more fainthearted and disillusioned dropped out as a result of police intimidation. But the others, though they were now under more watchful surveillance than ever, being frequently followed[87] and searched, nevertheless persisted in practicing their observances. The greater the persecution and threatened reprisals, the more tenaciously they clung to their beliefs and their assemblies, and the more convinced they were of the righteousness of their position. The February decree was proof, according to one convulsionist, of "a growing blindness and callousness" on the part of those who have "declared war against the *oeuvre*. The more strongly they commit themselves against the convulsionaries," he averred, "the more strongly will they convince me that the cause [of the *oeuvre*] is linked to that of Truth and Justice."[88] The decree served to confirm the movement's adherents even further in their identification with the first Christians. Those who were arrested reveled in their sufferings and martyrdom.[89]

[86] Letter of April 23, 1733, in Ravaisson, XIV, 340-41.

[87] A royal order of April 30, 1733, had even authorized the police to follow the counselor Titon, an active participant in the convulsionary *séances*, and to report his comings and goings to Hérault (AN, O¹ 77, p. 50). The surveillance of a parlementary magistrate caused quite a stir in the Palais de Justice, and Titon's own complaints finally brought the matter to an end (Joly de Fleury to [Chauvelin?], May 1733, AAE, M&D, France, MS 1283, fols. 9-10, 13-14; cf. Barbier, II, 402-404 [May 1733]).

[88] *Réflexions sur l'Ordonnance du roi du 17 février 1733* (n.d.), p. 4.

[89] "La Nicette," for example, was alleged to have compiled a diary relating her experiences during her incarceration, first at the Bastille and later in Vincennes to which she was transferred. This diary itself must surely have been a miracle, since Mlle. Regné was illiterate! See the anonymous *Anecdotes aussi sûres que curieuses touchant la conduite tyrannique et barbare qu'on a exercée sur Denyse Regné à la Bastille* (1760).

They were, in turn, glorified by their coreligionists, for they had become "truly and more really victims," no longer merely "partial or figurative victims."[90] The government's second major intervention thus seemed to be as ineffectual as the first. What is more, amid the incessant persecution, a small, but significant, number of convulsionaries had begun to exhibit a growing conviction that the arrival of the millennium was indeed imminent and to become increasingly preoccupied with eschatological fantasies and apocalyptic calculations about the appearance of the prophet Elijah within their very midst.

At first, much of this apocalyptic speculation was centered on the notion that the Parlement of Paris would play a central role in the unfolding drama. Such a view had initially emerged in the course of 1732. Throughout that year the convulsionaries had become intensely interested in the events going on outside their *séances*, especially those associated with contemporary ecclesiastical politics. The renewed struggles between crown and Parlement seem to have particularly attracted their attention, the convulsionaries enthusiastically supporting the cause of the magistrates, their apparent allies and protectors, against Fleury, their common persecutor. Convulsionary discourses even contained occasional references to the political events of the day, along with approving remarks about the judges in the sovereign court.

It is easy to see how such a perception of the Parlement might have developed. For one thing, the court's various judicial actions since 1731 —its defense on numerous occasions of the Paris *curés*, many of whom had been active sponsors of the Pâris cult; its suppression of the Roman Inquisition's decree condemning a biography of François de Pâris; its frequent challenges to decrees and pastoral instructions issued by Archbishop Vintimille, several of which had been designed to stifle the observances in Pâris' memory; and its willingness to hear Anne Lefranc's appeal against the archbishop's *mandement* of July 1731—all suggested quite strongly that the Parlement's sympathies, at least on important juridical questions, lay with the followers of M. Pâris. For another, the presence in the sovereign court of a handful of ardent supporters of the cult, including the saintly deacon's brother, was evidence of a certain degree of spiritual affinity and sympathy of mind between court and cult. Of course, as with so much else in the convulsionary movement, the *anticonstitutionnaires*, among them various magistrates in the Parlement itself, bore a principal responsibility for fostering this growing identification of the judges as active champions of the *oeuvre*. In an attempt to arouse general support for their position

[90] *Entretiens sur les miracles*, p. 148.

against the crown, these magistrates had allowed most of the court's major resolutions and remonstrances in 1732 to be printed and distributed to the public, illegal though this self-serving action was.[91] Leaks of privileged information were so detailed, comprehensive, and frequent that the *Nouvelles ecclésiastiques* was able to keep its readers very reliably informed of the actual debates going on within the Palais de Justice during the whole busy spring and summer. For many weeks entire issues of the journal contained no other news, while the editor, adding his own approving commentary, "embarked on something approaching the mass canonization of the *parlementaires*."[92] By mid-year the magistrates stood before the public as the unflinching champions of religious liberties and defenders of individual conscience against a repressive government and Church hierarchy.

Actual public agitation on behalf of the Parlement began in late spring. The magistrates' protest and walkout in June inspired an enthusiastic crowd stationed at the Palais de Justice, convulsionaries and convulsionists no doubt among them, to cast the judges in the role of tribunes: "Voilà de vrais Romains et les pères de la Patrie!" they were said to have exclaimed.[93] During the summer, even before the exile of the chambers of *enquêtes* and *requêtes*, *estampes* were hawked in the streets of Paris which depicted a group of Jesuits clutching the royal crown in their hands, while another group was dragging the corpse of the Parlement of Paris along the ground.[94] Most sentiment of this type continued as before to find expression in broadsides and popular verses, which circulated far and wide. In addition, numerous *anticonstitutionnaire* pamphleteers, several of them active defenders of the *oeuvre des convulsions*,[95] waxed eloquent in extolling the Parlement's virtues while decrying the actions of Fleury and his administration. The anonymous author of the *Refléxions sur l'Ordonnance du Roi, en date du 27 janvier 1732*, for example, lauded the magistrates' "generous resistance" and claimed that the Parlement, like the convulsionaries, had been made the victim of an evil *constitutionnaire* conspiracy.[96] By

[91] "The crown repeatedly but in vain rebuked the courts for these breaches of their members' oath of secrecy, for a magistrate in a sovereign company remained in theory one of the king's confidential counselors" (Franklin L. Ford, *Robe and Sword: The Regrouping of the French Aristocracy after Louis XIV* [Cambridge, Mass., 1953], p. 101). See also Shennan, "Parlement of Paris under Fleury," pp. 530, 540-41.

[92] Ford, p. 100.   [93] Barbier, ii, 295 (June 1732).

[94] *Ibid.*, p. 361 (November 1732).

[95] *Entretiens sur les miracles*, pp. 20-22.

[96] P. 86. Similar views were reported in the police *gazetins* (BA, MS 10163, *passim*). Cf. also the observations of the marquis d'Argenson (letters to Chauvelin,

the time the magistrates had returned from exile in December, popular adulation was at its height, the abbé Pucelle, heroic leader of the parlementary opposition, drawing the loudest and most ardent cheers from the large throng lining the streets surrounding the court.[97]

Convulsionary enthusiasm for the parlementary cause was echoed even more eloquently within the conventicles themselves. Perhaps the most important evidence of this attitude comes from a memorable and widely circulated discourse attributed to Marie-Anne Gault (or Got), a laundress better known as Soeur La Croix. In the midst of a speech decrying the lamentable condition of the Church and condemning the Jesuitical conspiracy which had captured the State, the convulsionary noticed the arrival of a magistrate recently returned from exile. Immediately she "fell into an ecstatic rapture." Through the magistrate, identified as the counselor Titon, long an assiduous participant in observances of the *oeuvre*, Soeur La Croix addressed an exhortation to and an apotheosis of the entire sovereign court:

> Generous Magistrates! . . . you have been the strength and the salvation of the Holy Nation; you have been the Fathers of the People, and the protectors of the Throne. Those who rendered justice in Israel were only the symbol of what you have done to maintain our holy Laws. Guided by passionate zeal, you have sacrificed yourselves to the interests of the Faith, the Prince, and the State; and presenting yourselves at the head of the Army you have received the blows intended to strike down the Pastors of Israel [the *curés*]. . . . There still remain some enemies to withstand. Gather your strength to leave Egypt; God Himself, for Whom you have taken up arms, will open a pathway for you across the waters: the Pharaohs and their Magicians will pursue you, but you will depart victorious, and the water, falling back in place, will drown your enemies.[98]

This passage is filled with a considerable amount of obviously significant millenarian metaphors, most of them bearing directly upon

Sept. 5 and 6, 1732, AAE, M&D, France, MS 1277, fols. 31, 33-35), and the anonymous government *mémoire*, "Considérations politiques sur l'état présent des anti-constitutionnaires" (*ibid.*, MS 1283, esp. fols. 196-97).

[97] Barbier, II, 366 (December 1732). Cf. [Nicolas Jouin], *Les très-humbles Remercîments des habitants de Sarcelles au roi, au sujet du retour du parlement de Paris* (1732).

[98] BN, NAFr., MS 4091, pp. 165ff.; another copy, *ibid.*, MS 4094, p. 8. A printed version of the discourse may be found in *Nouvelles observations sur les convulsions, à l'occasion d'une lettre écrite au mois de janvier en faveur des convulsions* (1733), pp. 24-25.

the contemporary ecclesiastical/political situation—a situation which seemed to encourage millenarian excitement. In her evocation of the biblical epoch of the "Judges," heroic champions, vindicators, and deliverers of the oppressed, Soeur La Croix sought to identify the plight of the convulsionaries with the tribulations of the children of Israel and to depict the magistrates in the Parlement as the principal source of protection and justice for the embattled defenders of the true faith, lay and clerical. The affirmation that the magistrates were the "strength and salvation" of the nation was at the same time an implicit recognition that the crown had abandoned its responsibility for spiritual leadership. The monarchy, captured and corrupted, had become an "Egypt," a damned and condemned land, governed by "pharaohs" and their "magicians," supposedly representing "that wicked group of ultramontane advisers and ministers who were exercising a tyranny in the king's name."[99] Having rejected the "holy nation," the party of Truth, the crown must also be rejected in its turn. With the true throne thus left vacant, it had been left to the Parlement to lead the "holy nation," constituted by the convulsionaries, victoriously out of Egypt. It is hardly surprising, given such views, that the return of the magistrates from exile should have been greeted with unbounded enthusiasm in convulsionary circles.[100]

The restoration of the magistrates to their judicial benches had also been marked by the appearance of an extraordinary document, the *Calendrier mystérieux pour l'année 1733 exactement supputé sur l'Apocalypse de Jean l'Evangéliste (XIII, 5-18) et sur la Prophétie d'Isaïe (I, 26)*.[101] In this brief, but highly significant piece of figurist exegesis the anonymous author offered both a devastating indictment of the established order and a message of hope and consolation to his fellow convulsionary brethren. Drawing first on the apocalyptic symbolism in the Book of Revelation, the author claimed to be announcing the end of all the persecutions which the Church of France had suffered and endured for a long time. " 'And the beast was given a mouth uttering haughty and blasphemous words, and it was allowed to exercise authority for forty-two months' (Rev. 13:5), which makes three and a half years." According to the author's reckoning, "This *Beast* is the *Constitution* [*Unigenitus*]. The period of three and a half years began with the Declaration of March 1730 and will end in September 1733." As for the name of the Beast or the number of its name, which

99 Cf. *Entretiens sur les miracles*, p. 25. See also a later discourse delivered by Soeur Françoise, BHVP, N.A. 136, p. 376.

100 Marais, IV, 447 (December 6, 1732), and Barbier, II, 366-67 (December 1732).

101 BN, MSS Fr., MS 13812, fols. 50-53.

is figured as 666 (Rev. 13:17-18), the author's calculations designate Louis XV as the malign, frightful Antichrist himself: LUDOVICUS, in Roman numerals, equals the Number of the Beast. In verification of this designation the author also calculated the king's "full name": LUDOVICUS DECIMUS QUINTUS FRANCIAE ET NAVARRE REX, which totaled 1733!

But if the Beast of the Apocalypse was in the convulsionaries' midst, so, too, were their prospective deliverers, as the *Calendrier mystérieux* proceeded to demonstrate. It so happened that the Parlement's return to the Palais de Justice on December 1—the only time in memory the court had opened its winter term on that late date—coincided with the reading at Advent of passages from the prophet Isaiah.[102] The text for that particular day included the following verse: "And I will restore your judges as at the first, and your counselors as at the beginning. Afterward you shall be called the city of righteousness, the faithful city" (Is. 1:26). To a people predisposed to finding symbolism even in mundane events, this was more than just a happy coincidence. The author of the *Calendrier mystérieux* even chose to offer his own rendition of the passage in question: "I will restore your judges as at the first, and your counselors *with their former prerogatives.*" Finally, the author, depicting the magistrates once again as the true saviors of the Church, returned to the actual text of Isaiah: "Zion shall be redeemed by justice," the prophet announced, "and those in her who repent, by righteousness. But rebels and sinners shall be destroyed together, and those who forsake the Lord shall be consumed" (Is. 1:27-28).

It is not known from what convulsionary circles the "mysterious calendar" had come or whose views it represented. What is certain, however, is that a vocal segment of the convulsionary movement had begun to interest itself very seriously in apocalyptic calculations of the Last Days and to cast the Parlement in a major role in the forthcoming eschatological drama. Not only were manuscript copies of the *Calendrier mystérieux* in circulation throughout Paris by the middle of 1733, but a printed version of the work was to appear soon thereafter.[103] About the same time, some anonymous convulsionists reissued the *Conjectures des derniers tems*, composed in 1452 by Cardinal Nicholas of Cusa.[104] In this work, first translated into French in the

---

[102] Barbier, II, 366-67 (December 1732).

[103] Copy found in AN, X-1b 9693.

[104] BA, MS 6882. Cf. Dominique de Colonia and Louis Patouillet, *Dictionnaire des livres jansénistes, ou qui favorisent le jansénisme*, 4 vols. (Antwerp, 1752), I, 308-309.

mid-sixteenth century, the German philosopher-theologian had warned that Jesus Christ would one day suffer in His "mystical body" what He had previously suffered in His "natural body" at the time of His crucifixion; that the successors of Peter would renounce Him; that the episcopal successors of the Apostles would all abandon Him; that the preachers of the truth would become silent; and that the Church itself would seem to have perished. What is more, Cusa had also predicted with some assurance that this series of events would come to pass between 1700 and 1734, and that "once Antichrist had been vanquished, the Resurrection of the Church would be absolutely glorious."[105]

Like the *Calendrier mystérieux*, Cusa's *Conjectures* circulated in both manuscript and printed editions and must have reached a substantial body of convulsionaries and convulsionists. Few partisans of the *oeuvre*, however, were prepared to take these prophecies literally,[106] particularly when no one in the Parlement came forward to lead the convulsionaries "out of Egypt" or anywhere else for that matter. Nevertheless, although the court had failed to play its appointed role in the convulsionaries' "pursuit of the millennium," no doubt bringing some disappointment to many of the brethren, that fact did not deter everyone. Indeed, in spite of this disappointment, or perhaps because of it, a more militantly activist offshoot of the convulsionary movement emerged at this time, its adherents dominated by a sense of deepening crisis and convinced that some effort must be made at once to hasten the arrival of the prophet Elijah and to prepare for the radical transformation of the status quo that would soon be at hand. The appearance of this sect was to mark the beginning of a growing split within the convulsionary movement itself, a split which had begun to develop, at first only vaguely and imperceptibly, in the course of 1733 and which would ultimately accomplish for the authorities what neither edicts nor arrests had been able to do.

The new sect developed around the abbé Pierre Vaillant, a gentle and deeply pious priest originally from the diocese of Troyes, who had for years been a convinced adept of the figurists. A former aide to Bishop Colbert of Montpellier and later secretary to the editor of the *Nouvelles ecclésiastiques*, Vaillant, widely respected for his piety and dedication to the appellant cause, had already endured nearly three years' imprisonment in the Bastille for having distributed the *anticon-*

---

[105] *Conjectures*, pp. 17, 21.
[106] Cf. *NNEE*, Nov. 15, 1731, pp. 217-18, and *Entretiens sur les miracles*, pp. 58-59.

stitutionnaires' clandestine gazette.[107] He had been released in April 1731 with an order banishing him from the realm. Ignoring the order, he had remained the whole time in the vicinity of Paris, where he became an assiduous devotee of the observances at Saint-Médard and then an equally zealous participant in convulsionary *séances*. In the meantime, as we have seen, while convulsionary misfortunes had been on the increase, various figurists, including the anonymous author of the *Calendrier mystérieux*, had been predicting that the so-called War of the Beast of the Apocalypse against the Saints would come to an end in September 1733, presumably with the return of the prophet Elijah. That fateful date happened to coincide with the seventeenth centenary of the death of Jesus Christ. Inflamed by messianic hopes and convinced of the special urgency of their mission, a small number of convulsionaries who took the prediction literally believed that the time of Elijah's return to renew the Church was known quite precisely. It was while they were making preparations to meet Elijah that the abbé Vaillant (now also known as Frère Victoire) began asserting his claim to be the prophet's true reincarnation, insisting that he had been sent on a divine mission to recall the Jews to Jesus Christ.[108]

Apparently, however, chiliastic expectations were not sufficiently widespread nor Vaillant's claims sufficiently credible for him to attract very many adherents. While most of his fellow brethren declined to receive him as the prophet he claimed to be, many of the leading Jansenist supporters of the *oeuvre* expressed skepticism, if not downright hostility, at his pretensions.[109] The abbé d'Etemare, principal

---

[107] The Bibliothèque de l'Arsenal has three huge cartons on Vaillant. The first (MS 11032) is entitled "Pièces relatives à la détention de l'abbé Vaillant (1728-61)." The other two (MSS 11033-34) include "Ecrits de l'abbé Vaillant" as well as miscellaneous *opuscules jansénistes*. Most of what follows is based on materials contained in these three cartons.

[108] See BA, MSS 11033-34, especially Vaillant's own "Extrait des Divines Ecritures sur l'enlèvement et le retour du prophète Elie" (MS 11034) and assorted commentaries on the Old Testament prophets (MS 11033, *passim*). According to an undated note by the police officer Duval, "Dans le tems de sa première détention à la Bastille . . . il [Vaillant] a dit souvent devant les officiers du Château que le Messie alloit bientôt descendre sur la terre pour juger les Gentils, convertir les juifs, et les remettre en place; que le prophète Elie étoit dans Paris, qu'il lui avoit parlé, que cette conversation avoit opéré sa conversion, ayant eu des moeurs irréguliers dans sa jeunesse avec le sexe, et il a prêché souvent les officiers en invoquant pour eux le prophète Elie son bon ami" (BA, MS 11032). By the time of his release, Vaillant seems to have identified himself with Elijah. Cf. also his letters, BPR, L.P. 486, Nos. 41-43.

[109] The Vaillantistes went so far as to send a special deputy, Frère Amboise, to see Bishops Colbert and Soanen in a fruitless effort to win them over (BA, MS 5784, p. 158).

convulsionary figurist of the period, likened Vaillant to Don Quixote and, employing such terms as *folie, séduction, illusion, imposture,* and *fanatisme* to describe his state of mind, dismissed him as a "false messiah."[110] Nevertheless, despite the widespread opposition, Vaillant was certain that he was involved in a providential conjunction of circumstances for propagating his message—a conviction that was shared by a small, but dedicated band of followers. Although September 1733 somehow went by uneventfully, this apparent setback to their expectations does not seem to have adversely affected the prophet or his adherents.[111] In March 1734, accompanied by some thirty ecclesiastics,[112] and a number of others who made up the sect known as Vaillantistes or Elyséens, Vaillant made his way to Metz, hoping to win over to his cause a substantial number of the Jews resident in that town. He preached in the synagogue about the imminent millennium (no longer dated so precisely as before) and announced to the Jews that he had been sent—the reincarnation of Elijah—to convert them to Christianity. The Jews, however, would have nothing to do with his brand of evangelism and greeted his overtures with uncompromising hostility. Returning from Metz to Paris in May, he was arrested and again thrown into the Bastille "pour jansénisme."[113]

After his arrest, Vaillant penned several different statements disclaiming any prophetic talents.[114] Yet despite Vaillant's capture and apparent renunciation of all spiritual pretensions, his troublesome sectaries, believing that the government had extorted the abbé's disavowal, continued to regard him as the prophet he had originally claimed to be and agitated for his release. Occasionally they marched in a procession around the Bastille, offering prayers on behalf of their imprisoned leader and threatening destruction upon the French Babylon if Vaillant remained confined. A handful of his disciples maintained a regular vigil at the site, reportedly in expectation of his miraculous deliverance

---

[110] *Ibid.* See also the "Consultation et Réponse sur le Système des Vaillantistes," Oct. 27 and Nov. 8, 1734, AFA, P.R. 5961.

[111] Cf. the classic study of Leon Festinger, Henry W. Riecken, and Stanley Schachter, *When Prophecy Fails* (Minneapolis, 1956).

[112] These included several *curés* who had reportedly abandoned their benefices to join him (see anonymous *mémoire,* October 1734, BA, MS 11032).

[113] *Ibid.*

[114] "Décidément, Monsieur," he wrote Hérault, "je ne suis pas le prophète Elie; Dieu me l'a fait voir dans une circonstance toute récente. Le tourbillon n'étoit pas pour moi. Après avoir rempli les fonctions de ce prophète avec quelque éclat, je me vois forcé par la vérité d'avouer que je ne le représente plus et que je n'ai aucune mission pour l'annoncer, ni pour agir ou parler en son nom" (*ibid.*). Vaillant actually issued several different statements of this sort; they may all be found in this same carton.

from the hands of his captors—in the style of St. Peter—or perhaps with the intention of assisting him in an escape patterned after that of St. Paul.[115] To a government obsessed with preserving law and order, such a state of affairs seemed potentially dangerous. When Hérault wrote Fleury a few years later, the police lieutenant offered his recommendation for handling M. Vaillant:

> I think . . . that it [will] be necessary to keep him always locked up. He is so weak of mind that his disciples . . . have only to show him the slightest respect or veneration, and he will again believe himself more than ever to be the prophet Elijah and, as a result, act like a preacher.[116]

In fact, despite many long petitions that Vaillant himself was to submit to Hérault and his successor, Marville, requesting to be set free, it became official policy not to release the would-be prophet under any circumstances. As a consequence, Vaillant was to languish in prison until his death in 1761.[117]

For all the embarrassment Vaillant's "extravagant delusions" brought to the majority of convulsionaries, the behavior of the abbé and his followers was but a minor annoyance when compared to the troubles which a second dissident sect, also emerging at this time, visited upon the movement. The emergence of this second unwelcome offshoot of the original movement—a radical sect known as the Augustinistes— was not only to deprive the convulsionaries of all semblance of orthodoxy or legitimacy in the eyes of the authorities, but was also to ensure that the *oeuvre* would lose most of its remaining credit and support in parlementary and Jansenist circles as well. What is more, the appearance of these Augustinistes was to provoke so much internal dissension within convulsionary ranks that it seemed to threaten the very integrity and survival of the movement.

[115] Acts 5:17-26 and II Cor. 11:32-33. See discussions between Hérault and Joly de Fleury, Dec. 2, 1734, BN, MSS Fr., MS 11356, fol. 255, and police memorandum of October 1736, BA, MS 11032.

[116] *Ibid.* Reprinted in Ravaisson, XIV, 384.

[117] Two decades later the government was still afraid of Vaillant. In 1756, sixty-eight years old and quite ill, he requested and was granted a transfer from the Bastille to Vincennes, in order to have "more air" for his health. He died in Vincennes of a stroke on Feb. 20, 1761, after twenty-seven years of imprisonment. It was proposed, nevertheless, that he be buried "avec toutes les précaution nécessaires pour le secret . . . pour empêcher qu'il ne vienne par dévotion"; he was even given another name, the "comte d'Ipsum, étranger," before he was laid to rest (Guyonnet to Sartine and Sartine to Saint-Florentin, Feb. 19, 1761, BA, MS 11032; reprinted in Ravaisson, XIV, 396-97).

Vaillant was not the only visionary and self-proclaimed prophet to appear on the scene during this period.[118] In 1733, some months after the royal ordinance proscribing convulsionary activities and after the first public "betrayal" of the *oeuvre* by numerous Jansenist theologians, there appeared another would-be prophet, Jean-Robert Cosse, or Causse, who had recently adopted the name Frère Augustin. Originally from Montpellier, where his father was a bookseller, Causse had come to Paris some years earlier, a very humble, gentle, and pious young man, well informed on the ecclesiastical issues of the day, with a strong commitment to the *anticonstitutionnaire* cause, and with the express intention of pursuing a sacerdotal career. To that end he spent considerable time as a student at the Jansenist *collège* of Sainte-Barbe and at the religious community of Saint-Hilaire and served a period as sacristan at the petits Cordeliers. But he never did receive orders.[119] In the meantime, he had become fairly active, along with his sister, Jeanne, in certain convulsionary circles. Though he himself had not initially experienced any convulsive agitations, he quickly became celebrated among some of his fellow brethren both for the austerities he practiced and for the uplifting words he preached "with inspired eloquence" in their midst.[120] An edifying figure, highly ascetic in his pursuit of perfection and his quest for godliness, Causse subjected himself to long periods of bodily and spiritual abnegation. As he detached himself more and more from life's daily concerns and devoted all his energies to these spiritual exercises, he reportedly began to exhibit increasingly extravagant behavior.[121] Friends and acquaintances who had known him from his school days were later to recall that Causse had already displayed certain mystical tendencies and an abiding obsession with eschatological fantasies. It was in the convulsionary milieu, however, that his stability seems to have become especially precarious. In late May or early June 1733, following a forty-day fast, Causse experienced his first convulsions—an event which transformed his life and that of the persons around him.[122]

Causse, now Frère Augustin, began at this point to make excessive

[118] In addition to Frère Augustin, discussed below, the next several years saw the abbé Alexandre D'Arnaut, a former Oratorian, claim to be "Frère Amboise ou prophète Enoch, compagnon d'Elie" (BA, MS 11271, fol. 176), and Françoise Marie Durié dite Noël claim to be the wife of the prophet Elijah (BA, MS 11531, fol. 204; MS 11540, fols. 209-413).

[119] Testimony of Jeanne Causse, AN, X-1b 9690. Cf. BHVP, C.P. 3509, p. 36.

[120] *Ibid.,* pp. 56-58.

[121] Testimony of Antoine Le Gras, Armand Victor Guichon, and Henri de Roquette, AN, X-1b 9692.

[122] BHVP, C.P. 3509, pp. 16-17, 36.

claims for himself.[123] Whereas Pierre Vaillant had claimed to be Elijah in person, Frère Augustin, acting independently of the abbé from Troyes, now cast himself in the role of Elijah's divinely appointed representative and reportedly announced that he was the servant of the servants of God and the fourth person of the Trinity [sic].[124] To support his claim that he was the chosen precursor of Elijah's coming, he wore over his soutane a cloak supposedly inherited from the prophet himself. But Frère Augustin went much further. Invoking the direct blessings of the divinity, Augustin, a man like any other when in his "natural state," asserted that while *en convulsion*—in his case, a state of mind apparently bordering on ecstasy rather than a state of actual physical agitation—he was freed from the traditional norms of the "common order" and was above all rules or laws, including those laid down in the Bible. Believing himself to be subject to no moral or legal restraints in his own behavior or in his relations with outsiders, he held that he could commit all sorts of crimes, forbidden acts, or mortal sins without any feelings of guilt or taint of sin. God had suspended the laws for him just as He had done for Abraham, Hosea, and Moses, so that in his state of exaltation Augustin, unlike the unredeemed humanity at large, was beyond good and evil.[125] Nor was that all. Like some of his fellow convulsionaries, but with a degree of self-glorification that went well beyond the others, Frère Augustin saw himself as an expiatory "victim" who had been singled out for persecution and was about to be sacrificed.[126] Indeed, Augustin frequently compared himself to Jesus Christ and claimed that he would be treated like the Son of God, scorned and maligned by the "iniquitous Gentiles" and forced to shed his blood for the salvation of his brothers. According to a police report drawn up some years later, the prophet apparently believed that he was going to be "put to death, because others regard him as a heretic, a seducer, [and] a blasphemer, but that

---

[123] In addition to the sources listed above, see also BA, MSS 11462, 11606, and 11630, all *passim*, for details on Augustin's career.

[124] But according to one Augustiniste, the prophet never made any such claims (see explanation in BHVP, C.P. 3509, pp. 102-103). According to another disciple, however, from time to time "Dieu lui a fait faire différens personnages, ceux de Jean Baptiste, d'Elie, et de Jésus Christ" (*ibid.*, pp. 17-18).

[125] These views were attributed to him by Father Pierre Gourlin, priest from Saint-Séverin in Paris, who had attended one *séance* in the summer of 1733 where Augustin was present (AN, X-1b 9692). Another eyewitness, the abbé de Roquette, insisted Frère Augustin had gone so far as to assert that his "words are worth more than Scripture" (*ibid.*). Cf. also the anonymous Augustiniste tract, *L'idée de la parfaite sainteté* (excerpts and discussion in BHVP, C.P. 3509, pp. 28-30).

[126] *Ibid.*, pp. 33, 102-103.

he [would] return to life victorious and glorious." He also reportedly insisted that he "embodied all the convulsionaries" and asserted that he was an inspired vehicle of final truth, that while *en convulsion* "it was God who spoke through his mouth."[127] Sometimes, dressed in an ecclesiastical habit, he would lie on an altar, assume the position of the lamb of God (Jesus Christ), and demand adoration.[128]

This self-styled preacher of eternal truth, herald of the messianic age, and "savior of the world" became an increasingly mysterious and shadowy figure, making only infrequent (and previously unannounced) appearances at a select number of convulsionary *séances* in and around Paris and especially at certain conventicles held in the Chevreuse valley near the ruins of Port-Royal-des-Champs. There he often assumed the figurative role of a priest and performed—symbolically— the sacraments of baptism and ordination upon his followers, whereby he welcomed them into the sect. On occasion he would also preach to the assembled brethren at some length about the conversion of the Jews and the reprobation of the Gentiles and endeavor to explain the meaning of the *oeuvre* and to indicate its scriptural basis.[129] More noteworthy, perhaps, was the fact that each of these sudden and unexpected appearances was usually marked by some spectacular or extraordinary occurrence, as the prophet apparently sought to demonstrate the reality of his charismatic gifts.[130] On one occasion Frère Augustin, "filled with the spirit of God" and hence "raised above the status of a vile creature," caused an arm of the convulsionary Soeur Virginie to become paralyzed simply by the power of his voice. He followed up this prodigious feat by rendering various parts of Virginie's body totally insensitive to pain. Another time he "touched" a nine-year-old girl and reportedly caused her to become temporarily blind, mute, deaf, and paralyzed; a short while later he restored the child to her original condition. Nor were these the only prodigies attributed to the prophet. Legends circulating in Augustiniste circles even had him restoring the dead to life.

Though Frère Augustin, like Pierre Vaillant, was able to attract only a small number of adherents—some fairly reliable sources say as few

[127] Dubut to Marville, Sept. 3, 1740, in Ravaisson, xv, 60-61. Cf. BHVP, C.P. 3509, pp. 17, 79, 114-15, 165.

[128] *Ibid.*, p. 14. According to the testimony of Father Boyer, Augustin had even announced that, "Il avoit les stigmates dans les mains et aux lèvres, mais tout étoit invisible" (AN, X-1b 9692).

[129] BHVP, C.P. 3509, p. 58.

[130] *Ibid.*, p. 16. See also "Relation de ce qui s'est passé dans une maison où Frère Augustin est resté quelques jours et de ce qui s'en est ensuivi, depuis le 18 jusqu'au 25 juin 1733" (BN, NAFr., MS 10967, fols. 1-94).

as forty[131]—they did manage to give notoriety to his sect. His disciples, attracted both by his message and by his dramatic activities, included a handful of priests distinguished for their piety and several persons of some wealth and social standing. But for the most part they comprised an especially anxious, disoriented, and insecure group of laboring-class convulsionaries, desperately in search of more immediate eschatological gratification and prepared to split from the parent movement in an effort to satisfy their needs. Their commitment to the *oeuvre* was in fact more complete and all-embracing than that of their "orthodox" predecessors and their chiliasm somewhat more radical. Craving religious certainty, they hoped Frère Augustin would prove a genuine prophet who might lead them to the new dispensation. This small company of ardent sectaries accepted his assertion that he was an infallible oracle and a man without sin, that whenever he spoke or acted *en convulsion* it was God who made him speak and act.[132] One of his votaries reported that she and others had signed "a kind of declaration of their sentiments toward Frère Augustin," which they regarded as a means of bearing witness before God.[133] What is more, they allegedly began to believe in their own collective exaltation and emancipation. Like Augustin himself, his followers held that the authority of God annulled the law's hold over them and that they, too, were free to commit or display all sorts of apparently indecent, immodest, and sacrilegious acts or norm-violating forms of behavior, so long as they did so while *en convulsion*—and thus acted in a symbolic or figurative manner. Before Elijah came, the prophet had reportedly convinced the Augustinistes, all crimes must first reach their height and must symbolically be expiated by the zeal of the brethren.

While it is virtually impossible to determine what, if any, "crimes" the Augustinistes actually committed in order to represent the so-called "crimes of the Gentiles," rumors of their extravagant behavior, including clearly exaggerated reports of obscene rites, promiscuous orgies, and sacrilegious parodies of Catholic ceremonies, were circulating all over Paris by 1734. Frère Augustin was alleged to have encouraged his disciples to subscribe to a creed of total emancipation and to practice a "mystical marriage," by which they could supposedly indulge in the most wildly impulsive sexual behavior with

---

[131] Testimony of P. C. Cossart, AN, X-1b 9692. One Augustiniste gives a figure of 100, adding that Frère Augustin was not out to attract proselytes and deliberately sought to cultivate the image of a small, persecuted minority (BHVP, C.P. 3509, pp. 11, 58).

[132] *Ibid.*, p. 165.

[133] Testimony of Marguerite Roussel, AN, X-1b 9690.

total impunity. Together, inspired by a messianic conviction of the need to purify, they were said to have deliberately committed abominable offenses in order to hasten divine vengeance and "restore all things." Augustin's own behavior no doubt helped foster such rumors. The prophet was often accompanied by a woman known as Soeur Alexis or "La Restan," herself a convulsionary of considerable reputation, for whom Augustin claimed the same freedom from the requirements of the moral law.[134] Indeed, on at least one occasion they were charged with fornicating together while their fellow Augustinistes knelt near their bed—curtains drawn around the two partners—and prayed that out of this "spiritual marriage" would spring forth a son who would be "l'aîné de Jésus-Christ."[135]

Other unusual activities also drew attention to the members of the sect. They organized various nocturnal processions through the streets of Paris, beginning in the *faubourg* Saint-Jacques and ending either at the cathedral of Notre-Dame or near the Place de Grève, where the troop of convulsionaries, ropes about their necks and tapers in their hands, held a variety of unorthodox religious ceremonies. The ritual practices performed at these assemblies were all supposedly designed to hasten the "final days" as well as to fortify the brethren against the coming persecutions. The Augustinistes also made a number of such "processions of expiation" to Port-Royal-des-Champs, hallowed ground which in the 1730s had been a much-frequented pilgrimage site for convulsionaries and others. There, legend has it, on at least one occasion, "they slew an animal, after which they marked with its blood all the houses—as far as Versailles—which would be spared by the Destroying Angel at the coming of Elijah."[136]

Though it was (and is) hard to determine the exact nature of Augustiniste practices or to distinguish fact from legend and reality from fantasy, the wild claims made by the prophet and his followers were enough to arouse great alarm among the authorities. The apparent moral antinomianism and religious anarchism of the Augustinistes represented a threat to the relatively static, custom-bound society of *ancien-régime* France. Their occasionally indecorous spontaneity, their free and uninhibited expressions of religious emotionalism were beyond the under-

[134] On La Restan, who was also said to be a "chosen victim," see BHVP, C.P. 3509, pp. 19-21.

[135] Many of these charges were raised in the course of the interrogations conducted by the Parlement of Paris beginning in 1735 (AN, X-1b 9690, 9692, *passim*).

[136] Simon-Henri Dubuisson, *Mémoires secrets du 18ᵉ siècle: Lettres du commissaire Dubuisson au Marquis de Caumont, 1735-41*, ed. A. Rouxel (Paris, 1882), p. 6.

standing or sympathy of most contemporaries, who indiscriminately hurled charges of moral depravity, unbridled sexuality, and arrant hedonism at these "scandalous libertines." Whether possessed by the devil or suffering from some form of mental illness—the two alternative diagnoses of most hostile critics anxious to discredit the sect—the prophet and his band of disciples seemed to their detractors to be deliberately flaunting and attempting to subvert all traditional religious and ethical standards and social norms.[137]

While the strange, nonconformist behavior of the Augustinistes presented some obvious problems for the civil and ecclesiastical authorities, they were perhaps regarded with even greater horror by the "orthodox" convulsionaries. The Augustinistes, like the Vaillantistes before them, had attempted to insinuate their way into the heart of convulsionary activity in Paris, not to undermine that activity but rather to find converts to their cause and *oeuvre*. However, most of the "orthodox" brethren, initially cool to or disapproving of these proselytizing efforts, expressed great shock and horror at the allegedly depraved behavior and the supposedly blasphemous discourses attributed to these "fanatics" and "half-mad visionaries."[138] Whereas Frère Augustin and his followers were reportedly prepared to go to extravagant lengths to engage in activities which would have brought damnation to the ordinary worldling, the original followers of François de Pâris had for the most part consciously eschewed indecent, promiscuous, or unseemly public behavior of any sort, emphasizing in their *oeuvre* the virtuous purity and innocent simplicity of the apostolic life. These "orthodox" convulsionaries, along with their convulsionist spokesmen, considered the conduct attributed to the "fanatics," especially their apparent sacrileges and profanations, as utterly abominable and dangerously subversive of all religious morality. They believed, furthermore, that Frère Augustin and his band were perverting the message of M. Pâris and of the miracles and convulsions, posing as false prophets and performing works of the devil in their "synagogue of Satan."[139] They argued that the *oeuvre* of Frère Augustin, though it had emerged from the cult to M. Pâris, was no more part of the Pâris *oeuvre* than is a heresy which has emerged from the Church. Augustin, they contended, had no business placing himself above all rules and claiming

[137] Cf. discussion in Norman Cohn, *Europe's Inner Demons* (London, 1975), esp. pp. 259-61.

[138] Soeur La Croix Got sought to avoid any further contact with one convulsionary (Soeur La Croix Fontaine) on learning that the latter was an Augustiniste (testimony of September-October 1736, AN, X-1b 9690).

[139] *Pensées sur les prodiges de nos jours*, pp. 9-10. Cf. Cohn, *Demons*, pp. 260-61.

absolute independence from all authorities. They went on to charge that most of those whom this "impostor" had attracted and seduced (sometimes literally) were persons apparently unconcerned "to follow the precepts which the Apostles believed necessary even in their time," and were interested only in leading dissipated lives. The "orthodox" denounced Augustin and his followers, therefore, as "errant convulsionaries" who had "surrendered to a spirit of error and illusion."[140]

Public denunciations of Frère Augustin which issued from the Jansenist camp, especially from the convulsionists, grew more frequent and caustic by midsummer 1734. Greatly embarrassed by the pronouncements and pious excesses attributed to the Augustinistes, these convulsionists had found themselves on the defensive, trapped in a situation not unlike the one in which the anticonvulsionary appellants had earlier been caught. For his part, an angry Frère Augustin, whom the initiated now referred to as Frère Jean or Frère Robert, responded in kind. In a series of vituperative letters and manifestoes circulated in manuscript, Augustin unequivocally denied all charges of blasphemy and sacrilege leveled against him and denounced his severest Jansenist detractors as vicious traitors.[141] In betraying the Augustinistes and trying to stifle their *oeuvre*, he charged, the Jansenist doctors, particularly the convulsionists, had capitulated to their putative Jesuit enemies. The embittered "prophet" likened their concerted attacks on him and his followers to the actions of King Herod, the procurator Pilate, and the high priest Caiaphus—the persons most responsible for the crucifixion of Jesus Christ. Adopting the "figure of Christ," Augustin warned his brethren not only to "beware of the children of Antichrist" (the Jesuits), but also "to watch out for the ravishing wolves dressed in sheep's clothing" (the Jansenists), who were in their very midst. He went on to announce in menacing tones that he would thereafter assume responsibility for destroying these unworthy doctors, Jansenist and Jesuit alike.

Augustin's verbal threats, which were accompanied by a detailed and uncompromising reiteration of Augustiniste doctrine, served to arouse even greater hostility on the part of the convulsionists whom he had so scathingly attacked. For almost two years the *Nouvelles*

---

[140] *Pensées sur les prodiges de nos jours*, pp. 9-10, 18. One Augustiniste claimed to have actually been "excommunicated" by his erstwhile brethren for having transferred his loyalties to Frère Augustin (BHVP, C.P. 3509, p. 14).

[141] Testimony of Pierre Boyer and Antoine Le Gras, AN, X-1b 9692; BN, MSS Fr., MS 8989, fols. 82-106. Copies of Augustin's various diatribes may be found in AN, X-1b 9691. Cf. the views of an anonymous Augustiniste disciple (BHVP, C.P. 3509, pp. 1-2, 15, 18-20, 23-24, 56-58, 60-61).

ecclésiastiques had attempted to disregard the Augustinistes, in the (vain) hope that their sect might quickly die out. But the editor deemed it necessary toward the end of 1734 to issue an unequivocal repudiation of these people. Their behavior and claims, the journal charged, "prove only too well what power the devil has today to deceive men, [and,] as a consequence, how much more necessary it is than ever to walk with great circumspection between the two dangers of human wisdom and fanaticism."[142] The abbé Fourquevaux unequivocally condemned Augustin's "monstrous system."[143] Bishop Colbert voiced a similarly vehement denunciation, as did the deposed Bishop Soanen from his exile retreat in Chaise-Dieu.[144] Perhaps the most prescient remarks, however, were those which came from the anonymous author of the *Pensées sur les prodiges de nos jours*. While agreeing with his convulsionist colleagues in their attacks upon the "fanatics," he was also concerned about the dangerous consequences which seemed likely to arise out of these latest developments. "Further divisions will appear," he warned; "there will be more suppression, and this river born at Saint-Médard, which grew so strong, will become little more than a rivulet which we will be barely able to detect."[145] But the warning was too late; the prediction was beginning to come true.

It hardly mattered that the *vrais convulsionnaires* and their apologists had scornfully dissociated themselves from the Augustinistes and put them down to the agency of the devil. The appearance of these "fanatics," however unequivocally they had been repudiated and however small their numbers, had already changed the complexion of the *affaire convulsionnaire*. Both the civil and ecclesiastical authorities had found their pretext for discrediting the entire convulsionary movement. The statements and actions widely attributed to Frère Augustin and his equally alienated adherents confirmed the worst suspicions harbored by the anticonvulsionaries and established that the movement had reached the heights of undisguised immorality, indecency, and impiety to which it had presumably been destined from the outset. Though there was no evidence to indicate any direct connection between Vaillant and Augustin, an immediate attempt was made to link them together and, even more important, to associate their sects—especially the fearsome Augustinistes—directly with the original convulsionaries of Saint-Médard.

[142] *NNEE*, Oct. 6, 1734, p. 172. It is worth noting that this reference, the *Nouvellistes'* first mention of the "fanatics," was relegated to a postscript attached at the end of the issue.

[143] Letter to the abbé d'Etemare, Nov. 23, 1734, BA, MS 5784, fol. 92.

[144] *NNEE*, Nov. 15, 1734, p. 197. Cf. Soanen to Colbert, Nov. 2, 1735, BA, MS 5784, fol. 124.

[145] P. 10. This "anonymous author" was probably Pierre Boyer.

All essential distinctions were quite conveniently confused and blurred. Lurid publicity and sensational "revelations"—more fantastic and titillating than ever—about the apparently sinister behavior of all convulsionaries were helpful in creating an atmosphere of mounting hostility in parlementary and Jansenist circles and in justifying the growing suspicion of the entire movement. No matter how tenuous the evidence, it now seemed possible for the various enemies of the *oeuvre* to portray all convulsionary activities as a simple erotic delirium—a kind of Sade boudoir romp half a century before the illustrious master.

Additional circumstantial evidence for establishing the link between "fanatical" and "orthodox" convulsionaries and for demonstrating the subversive character of the movement became available during the summer of 1734, with the appearance of a *Recueil de discours de plusieurs convulsionnaires*, followed in early December by a supplementary collection, the *Suite des discours*. These printed anthologies of discourses, several of which were of Augustiniste inspiration, raised quite a scandal. While the great majority of these "speeches," delivered under allegedly divine inspiration, dealt primarily with spiritual and ecclesiastical questions and included comments critical of the Jesuits, Cardinal Fleury, and other *constitutionnaire* persecutors of the *oeuvre*, several of them went so far as to encompass fairly direct attacks on the king himself. One convulsionary beseeched the monarch not to persecute "his most loyal subjects":

> Prince, we wish to strengthen your crown by supporting your rights, and you take for disturbers of public order those who are the most zealous for the interests and the peace, for the honor and the glory of their king and their native land! You knock down, you torment, and you crush those who have the greatest affection for you; you reject your most faithful subjects; you hold them of no account.[146]

Another convulsionary appealed to God "to rescue us from the injustice and the violence of those [kings] whom You Yourself have placed in power over us, [and from] the unjust severity of their evil judgments, [to which] You continually expose us." References to an "impious prince," a "Pharaoh of hardened heart," and the like run through at least half a dozen of these discourses. The king is charged with ignoring "the cries of the innocent," in the words of yet another convulsionary, who announces that "the Lord will rise up and visit His judgment upon him." It is not surprising that such statements against the king, appearing in print little more than a year after the appearance

---

[146] Cited by Mousset, pp. 127-28.

of the *Calendrier mystérieux*, which had likened Louis XV to the dreaded Beast of the Apocalypse, should have aroused still new alarms within the royal government.

Nevertheless, for all the evidence of (apparent) subversion and fanaticism which had been uncovered in the convulsionary movement, Cardinal Fleury still could not be certain that the magistrates in the Parlement of Paris were prepared to take judicial action against the practitioners of the *oeuvre*. On August 30, 1734, the police raided an assembly of convulsionaries gathered at the home of a M. Mozart. They arrested fourteen or fifteen persons and confiscated innumerable pamphlets against the Bull, along with portraits and relics of M. Pâris and some dirt said to have come from his grave.[147] The news of this mass arrest naturally pleased Fleury, who sent a message of congratulations to Hérault. But a sense of triumph was notably absent from the letter, as the cardinal-minister revealed his abiding concern about the attitude of the Parlement toward the convulsionaries. "You have made a good catch," Fleury commended the police lieutenant,

> and it would be desirable if there remained nothing more to do; but the fanaticism is growing instead of diminishing, and it is to be feared that it will increase still more. If the convulsions were common among the *constitutionnaires*, there would already have been fifty *arrêts* from the Parlement to punish them; but they are treated as sacred in the case of the Jansenists.[148]

As Fleury's note clearly implied, the Parlement still could not be counted on, as late as the summer of 1734, to proceed against all the followers of M. Pâris. Nevertheless, the cardinal-minister could at least feel some satisfaction that the royal council's decree of May 1732 had succeeded in keeping the court fairly silent on the whole Pâris question for quite some time. How much more satisfying, indeed momentous, for Fleury if he could somehow obtain from the most prestigious court in the realm a complete and unequivocal repudiation of all the convulsionaries!

In fact, there was little that the cardinal-minister himself could do to change the attitude of the Parlement of Paris. Yet by the end of the year, Fleury, engaged in a foreign war over the Polish succession, was beginning to see one of his major domestic problems being resolved without his government's having had to take any further dramatic action on its own. By the end of 1734 the sovereign court had become

---

[147] BA, MS 11257, fols. 76-133.
[148] Aug. 30, 1734, in Ravaisson, XIV, 373.

concerned about the spread of the execrable doctrines and extravagant behavior of the new "Free Spirits."[149] The blatant attacks on the king which were published in the *Recueil de discours* demonstrated a degree of disrespect for monarchial authority which the magistrates obviously could not tolerate. Just as the disturbances of public order attendant upon the activities of the abbé Bescherand and others had provided Fleury with the opportunity to close Saint-Médard without much parlementary objection, this time the uproar created by the "fanatics" afforded the means—or the pretext[150]—for drawing the magistrates back into the dispute, this time presumably on the side of the government. It was thus Fleury's tremendous good fortune that the arrival on the Paris scene of the two self-styled prophets, Vaillant and especially Causse, both of them liberated of clerical control, had opened the way for a judicial proceeding against the convulsionaries and an open break between the Parlement of Paris and the convulsionary movement. The efforts of these two prophets, independently working to canalize some of the apocalyptic enthusiasm conspicuous among the devotees of the *oeuvre*, succeeded only in exacerbating the fissiparous tendencies already inherent in convulsionism and in drawing down upon all convulsionaries the scornful wrath of most "rational" and "respectable" Frenchmen. They also gave Cardinal Fleury the opportunity to exploit the serious and mounting ideological cleavages within the *anticonstitutionnaire* party. The emergence of the Augustinistes, depicted as sensual voluptuaries and apologists of lawlessness and moral turpitude, was thus to provide the common stick which the authorities, the *constitutionnaires*, the Parlement, and a great majority of Jansenist theologians could use in attempting to discredit and ultimately beat down the convulsionaries.

[149] On the "Free Spirits" of the medieval period, see Robert E. Lerner's excellent study, *The Heresy of the Free Spirit in the Later Middle Ages* (Berkeley, 1972).

[150] As the abbé de la Rue observed at this time: "On assure que Mr. le lieutenant de police est suffisamment informé de toutes ces horreurs, mais qu'il a un ordre secret de la cour de les laisser aller aux derniers excès, parce que toutes ces extravagances contribuent plus que les meilleurs écrits à ruiner le parti Jansénien dans l'esprit de quantité de gens de bonne foi et d'honneur qui s'en détachent de jour en jour et reviennent au giron de l'Eglise catholique et romaine" (letter to d'Inguimbert, November 1734, in Th. Bérengier (ed.), *Une correspondance littéraire au 18e siècle entre Dom de la Rue, Bénédictin de la Congrégation de St.-Maur, et Mgr. d'Inguimbert, évêque de Carpentras* [Avignon-Paris, 1888], p. 36).

CHAPTER VIII

Parlementary and Jansenist Repudiations

A dramatic and irreversible turn in the political fortunes of the convulsionary movement and the Pâris cult occurred in 1735, when expressions of parlementary and Jansenist disenchantment with convulsionary activity grew more vocal than ever. The year began with a judicial investigation of the dissident sect of Augustinistes. Authorized by the royal government and conducted under the auspices of the *Grand'Chambre* of the Paris Parlement, this investigation had far-reaching consequences for all the convulsionaries, "orthodox" and "fanatical" alike. The opening of the Parlement's inquest was followed almost immediately by the publication, under somewhat unusual circumstances, of the highly controversial *Consultation des Trente*. This document, in which thirty leading Jansenist theologians and *curés* unequivocally condemned the convulsionaries and their *oeuvre*, brought the already intense polemical debate over the convulsions to a new peak. Although the issue of the convulsionary movement would remain for several years a vital subject for heated dispute, and although the clandestine practice of the *oeuvre* would persist well beyond the 1730s, the combination of parlementary and Jansenist repudiations marked the beginning of a dramatic change in the political fortunes of the movement.

The entire series of developments, though ultimately crowned with success for the established authorities, did not begin very auspiciously for them. Despite the stepped-up police repression in the months following the second royal decree against the convulsionaries, the observances of the *oeuvre* had continued to flourish and even to take a more radical turn, prompting renewed charges from some quarters that large-scale complicity on the part of the police lay at the source of all these disorders.[1] While these allegations were no doubt exaggerated, it is nevertheless clear that the efforts of Hérault and his men —including scores of arrests and intensive surveillance—were inadequate to contain, much less to halt, convulsionary activities. Nor were

[1] Barbier, II, 528 (December 1734).

the police entirely to blame for failing to produce the hoped-for results. As Cardinal Fleury had himself come to realize, no satisfactory
method had yet been found for dealing with these people or for quell-
ing their disturbances.[2] What is more, the movement's adherents were
simply too tenacious in their beliefs and too dedicated to their cause
to be easily intimidated by police measures or governmental and episcopal decrees.[3] And yet, if the authorities could not put a halt to
convulsionary activities, prospects appeared much more promising for
reducing, and even eliminating, the movement's remaining importance
as an issue of religious politics. For even as the convulsionaries persisted in their unusual observances, the government had hopes of
winning over the Jansenist theologians and the magistrates in the Parlement of Paris to its side and thereby completely neutralizing the Pâris
cult as a political-ecclesiastical problem. Fleury thus expended considerable energy throughout this period attempting to break what
links remained between the convulsionary cause, on the one hand,
and the opposition to the bull Unigenitus, on the other.

It was Fleury's good fortune that the domestic political and constitutional scene was relatively quiet in these years, at least as far as
dealings between crown and Parlement were concerned. Even though
the magistrates were far from inactive on religious and other matters,[4]
parlementary politics became much less dramatic and disruptive than
they had been in 1732. For one thing, the long and bitter disputes of
that stormy year had left both sides more than a little exhausted. For
another, the foreign crisis over the Polish succession had made the
establishment and maintenance of domestic peace more urgent than
ever and had also begun to divert much of the attention of high politics from the theater of religious and constitutional confrontation.[5]

[2] "Le secret est si profond dans cette maudite secte," the cardinal-minister later
observed to Vintimille, "qu'il est bien difficile d'y rien pénétrer" (Aug. 17, 1735,
BM, MS 2358, p. 582). Cf. Villars, Mémoires, V, 397, 402.

[3] According to Barbier, "Si l'on se contente de punir ces gens-ci secrètement et
dans la Bastille, le peuple . . . criera à l'injustice. On dira que ce sont des martyrs
et que par des suppositions on a sacrifié des personnages saints" (II, 526 [December
1734]).

[4] See, for example, the Parlement's remonstrances of May 15, 1733, in Flammermont, I, 303-13, and Mention, II, 76-87. For a discussion see also G. Hardy, pp.
293-95.

[5] In a "Mémoire pour le Conseil du Roy," dated April 28, 1733, Chauvelin
wrote: "L'on sent que la guerre en soy est un grand engagement, mais si elle est
convenable, . . . elle est utile pour faire diversion à l'esprit de liberté que s'établit
dans une nation dont il faut que la vivacité soit occupée d'un côté ou d'autre
. . ." (AAE, M&D, France, MS 503, fols. 124-25, cited in Wilson, p. 238, n. 71).
In a similar vein, Chauvelin reportedly also observed: "Une petite bataille gagnée

Consequently by October 1733, when war was declared, relations between Fleury and the magistrates had become, if not exactly cordial, at least considerably less strained.

The same could not be said of relations between the Parlement and the zealous *constitutionnaire* bishops with whom the magistrates had been doing battle for quite some time. Indeed, convulsionaries apart, these inflexible prelates, still encouraged by a clique of uncompromising bishops and cardinals at Rome and supported by a large number of equally intransigent parish clergy all over France, now represented the major threat to the religious pacification of the kingdom. In this matter —at least for the time being—the mutual interests of sovereign court and royal government very nearly coincided. The Parlement, as usual, resented what it regarded as the bishops' extreme ecclesiastical and political pretensions, especially their continued insistence that the bull *Unigenitus* was a "rule of faith" and their increasing refusal of the sacraments to persons who did not acknowledge it as such.[6] At the same time, Fleury feared that to allow these bishops to continue asserting their excessive claims of independent and unlimited spiritual authority would afford the magistrates some new pretext for resuming their own protests and interventions, further embittering relations between Parlement and episcopate and thereby destroying the government's campaign to impose silence on all parties to the controversy. Fleury and the judges thus found they could temporarily make common cause.

Between 1733 and 1735 the royal administration expended considerable energy in an attempt to restrain the "indiscreet zeal" of certain *constitutionnaire* bishops.[7] The notoriously outspoken Bishop La Fare

---

ou une ville prise rendra le roi et le ministre absolu dans l'intérieur" (AAE, M&D, Rome, MS 75, fol. 91, cited in Sareil, p. 245). So little of importance was happening at the Palais de Justice that Barbier was prompted to remark: "Ce Parlement-ci n'a été que trop tranquille sur les affaires du temps. Cela forme une stérilité de nouvelles et d'événements, et les bruits de guerre ont furieusement étouffé les affaires de la constitution" (II, 422 [September 1733]).

[6] See the remonstrances of May 15, 1733, cited in n. 4 above, which dealt in large part with the case of a denial of sacraments at the parish of Saint-Médard in Paris, where a certain Dlle. Tavignot had refused to renounce her adherence to the Pâris cult or to declare her acceptance of the Bull as a "rule of faith." On this case see also Fleury to Vintimille, April 18, 1733, BM, MS 2358, p. 106, and Vintimille to Fleury, April 25, 1733, *ibid.*, pp. 106-108. On the whole matter of the withholding of sacraments in this period, see Philippe Godard, *La querelle des refus de sacrements (1730-65)* (Paris, 1937).

[7] A *mémoire* dealing with this problem was drawn up in mid-1733 (AAE, M&D, France, MS 1283, fols. 157-59).

of Laon, who had first come under royal censure for his uncompromising decrees and pastoral letters as early as September 1731, and Bishop Lafiteau of Sisteron, his somewhat less truculent colleague, were two of the prelates whom Fleury singled out for disciplinary action during this period.[8] Several of their anti-Jansenist, antiparlementary writings, published without permission, were suppressed as offenses against the royal declaration of silence.[9] But the cardinal-minister did not confine his rigorous attentions to individual bishops. An Extraordinary Assembly of the Clergy, called in 1734 to vote a subsidy for the war effort, was not even permitted to treat religious questions, except incidentally. In a similar way the government was careful to control the agenda of the regular Assembly of 1735 right from its convocation, in order to guarantee that "dangerous subjects" would not be considered and to prevent the more extremist bishops within the Gallican Church from issuing the kinds of provocative pronouncements that had come out of the Assembly of 1730.[10] Finally, a "Mémoire sur l'Assemblée prochaine," which the *conseil ecclésiastique* at Versailles drafted in February 1735, cautioned against any references to the Bull, to the "contemporary fanaticism" of the convulsionaries, or to "the wounds which the ecclesiastical jurisdiction [had] received from nearly all the parlements."[11]

At the same time, Fleury could not entirely restrain the magistrates from issuing *arrêts* of their own.[12] Indeed, the cardinal-minister was willing to tolerate these writs, without resorting to conciliar evocations, so long as the Parlement did not attempt to interfere with royal

---

[8] On La Fare's difficulties with crown and Parlement, see *ibid.*, MS 1284, fols. 277-84; BN, J.F., MS 99, fols. 1-251; BA, MS 6033, fols. 120-42. His own voluminous papers are in BN, MSS Fr., MSS 23441-58.

[9] G. Hardy, pp. 299-300. On Oct. 22, 1733, the *conseil d'état* suppressed two of La Fare's decrees (BA, MS 10327; cf. discussion in *NNEE*, Dec. 11, 1733, p. 248). Not surprisingly, the *constitutionnaires* raised very strenuous objections to Fleury's heavy-handed suppression of their writings. Nine of the prelates, including La Fare, went so far as to issue *Lettres de plusieurs Archevêques et Evêques au Roi* in protest against the cardinal-minister's policy; their appeal was promptly quashed by yet another *arrêt*, dated Aug. 14, 1734 (*NNEE*, Sept. 26, 1734, pp. 167-68). See also *ibid.*, June 29, 1733, p. 131, for a discussion of other *constitutionnaire* reactions in the affair. For an analysis of Fleury's relationship with these difficult bishops, especially Tencin, see Sareil, pp. 243-48.

[10] G. Hardy, pp. 301-306; J. Bourlon, *Les Assemblées du clergé et le jansénisme* (Paris, 1909), pp. 225-29.

[11] AAE, M&D, France, MS 1296, fols. 85-92, 195-99; cf. fols. 219-23.

[12] Especially in the case of Msgr. La Fare, who was the object of almost a dozen such *arrêts* in the space of only a few years.

arrêts[13] and limited itself to a simple suppression of the episcopal decrees. Fleury certainly did not intend to suggest that the magistrates were thereafter free to attack the *constitutionnaire* bishops with impunity or that they could expect the government to countenance any attempt to renew their vocal opposition to the Bull. Indeed, as one historian has remarked, "each time that [the judges] sought to prevent the Bull [from] being given unqualified recognition—as in April 1733 when Pucelle denounced two volumes in which *Unigenitus* was described as a rule of faith . . . —Fleury produced a council decree forbidding the court to concern itself with the subject."[14] According to the observant Barbier, Fleury was in a somewhat difficult situation: "It would be equally dangerous to give the upper hand absolutely to the Parlement, which might abuse its authority, as [to give it] to the clergy, whose ambition is to be feared."[15]

While Fleury could not hope to find any easy or permanent solution to this perennial problem, which lay at the very heart of *ancien-régime* religious politics, recent developments in the convulsionary movement indicated that his chances of resolving this other vexing problem appeared much brighter than ever. By late 1734, having managed to preserve a delicately balanced truce with the Paris Parlement, he had reason to believe that a less belligerent sovereign court might now be willing to lend him direct assistance against the convulsionaries. To be sure, despite the growing charges of fanaticism being hurled at certain convulsionary circles, a handful of outspoken magistrates continued to feel a genuine sympathy for the followers of François de Pâris and were therefore reluctant to do the cardinal-minister's bidding, to accept a responsibility which, they believed, amounted to betrayal. In the meantime, however, a majority of their colleagues had become rather alarmed, even scandalized, by the alleged disorderliness, immorality, and impiety of the Augustinistes—behavioral transgressions which offended the judges' sense of propriety and decency. In their capacity as traditional guardians of a vaguely defined *police générale du royaume*, the magistrates had responsibility for the protection and preservation of public order and the enforcement of civil

13 "En sorte que les ouvrages molinistes et approbatifs de la Constitution sont condamnés par le Parlement, et ceux du parti janséniste sont condamnés par le Conseil" (Barbier, II, 400-401 [April 1733]). In addition, the court had begun to suppress a series of radical *anticonstitutionnaire* and "Richerist" works as well.

14 J. H. Shennan, "The Political Role of the Parlement of Paris under Cardinal Fleury," *English Historical Review*, 81 (1966), p. 538.

15 II, 401 (April 1733).

law.[16] Though the court had increasingly come to share with the lieutenant-general of police many of the wide-ranging administrative functions which were included under the vaguely defined "police power," the judges nevertheless continued to exercise a significant role of surveillance and law enforcement—activities that remained inseparable from the Parlement's judicial functions. It was to their duties as judicial policemen of the *ancien régime* and as guardians of an orderly society (*un état policé*) that Fleury ultimately appealed in an effort to overcome their dogged suspicion of the cardinal-minister's administration and in an attempt to obtain from them a public repudiation of the entire convulsionary movement. As Barbier perceptively observed, such a condemnation from the Parlement was expected to "inspire more respect from the people than had the royal *lettres de cachet*, which are always regarded as [a form of] harassment and persecution."[17] In December 1734, therefore, Fleury sent a royal order restoring the court's cognizance of the affair.[18] In effect, the king was returning to the magistrates the very jurisdiction of which he had deprived them in May 1732.[19]

[16] The royal government had repeatedly reproached the Parlement for its failure to intervene against the devotees of the Pâris cult. See the anonymous *mémoire* composed in justification of the conciliar *arrêt* of May 3, 1732, which evoked the entire affair to the king: ". . . Rien ne méritoit davantage l'attention d'une cour qui a la police supérieure que les désordres arrivés dans l'Eglise de S.-Médard. Le culte public qu'un peuple aveugle rendoit aux cendres d'un particulier, les faux miracles, les fourberies, les spectacles honteux, que l'esprit de fanatisme et de vertige a donnés dans cette capitale. En toute autre occasion le parlement se seroit fait un devoir d'arrester le cour de ces désordres; mais ils avoient une liaison trop étroite avec les nouveautés. Ils n'avoient été suscités que pour faire acroires que le ciel mesme se déclaroit en faveur des erreurs du tems. C'est le motif de l'inaction du parlement, c'est ce qui l'engage à tolérer que des Magistrats mesmes de sa compagnie donent dans une illusion aussi grossière, dans une association déshonorante pour la magistrature et dangereuse pour l'état . . ." (AAE, M&D, France, MS 1298, fol. 86). Cf. also comments of an anonymous police informant, made sometime in 1733 (BA, MS 10170, fol. 228); the remarks of the archbishop of Rouen to Chauvelin, Feb. 8, 1733 (AAE, M&D, France, MS 1282, fols. 145-46); and the anonymous government *mémoire*, "Considérations politiques sur l'état présent des anticonstitutionnaires," June 1733 (*ibid.*, MS 1283, esp. fols. 196-97).

[17] III, 2 (January 1735).

[18] *Ibid.*, II, 525 (December 1734). On the favorable reception which greeted this news in Rome, see the Duke de Saint-Aignan to Chauvelin, Feb. 26, 1735, AAE, M&D, Fonds divers (Rome), MS 64, fol. 251.

[19] Barbier commented wryly that Hérault, "qui en avoit la commission, a cherché à s'en débarrasser. Il n'y a pas de sûreté à juger des fous" (II, 525 [December 1734]). Cf. remarks in a similar vein in the Journal of De Lisle, December 1734 and January 1735, AN, U-383.

The order which the cardinal-minister communicated to the Parlement restoring the court's judicial competence in the convulsionary affair had actually been solicited by the *gens du roi*, particularly Joly de Fleury. The *procureur-général* had grown increasingly alarmed in recent weeks over reports that had been circulating about various Augustiniste activities in and around Paris and over the seemingly subversive contents of the just-published *Recueil de discours*. The subject of the Augustinistes' extravagant behavior had actually been a major topic of discussion at an early December meeting of the *Assemblée de Police*, at which Hérault, Joly de Fleury, and the First President of the Parlement were the principal officials involved. Five members of the "sect" had already been arrested and in their interrogations had supposedly confirmed most of the charges alleged against Frère Augustin and his disciples. All three officials had agreed, therefore, on the urgent necessity to take coordinated action to halt these "dangerous fanatics," who posed a serious threat "both to the faith and to civil society."[20] Just as the discussions began as to precisely how the sovereign court would take up the matter,[21] the abbé Pierre Boyer came forward with a formal complaint against Frère Augustin which he presented to the *procureur-général* in late December or early January.

Father Boyer, author of one of the principal biographies of François de Pâris and long active in convulsionary circles, had first met Frère Augustin (then known as Robert Causse) by chance at a *séance* held somewhere in Paris in June 1733 and was initially impressed by the fervent piety and strong commitment to the *oeuvre* which Augustin demonstrated on that occasion.[22] In subsequent encounters, however, as Augustin began to make increasingly extravagant claims for himself, Boyer came to suspect "some mental derangement caused by excessive

[20] Hérault and Joly de Fleury were in full agreement on this matter: ". . . il seroit plus avantageux pour faire connoître au public la réalité et le danger d'un pareil phanatisme que le procez leur fut fait par l'autorité du Parlement, qui pouroit punir avec sévérité ceux qu'on trouveroit de mauvaise foy, ou avoir réellement commis des crimes, et mettre dans des communautés ceux qui se trouverroient dans la bonne foi qu'on pourroit regarder comme des insensez qu'il falloit instruire et qu'on pourroit peut estre espérer de faire revenir de leurs préventions, sur quoy on a dit qu'il falloit y penser sérieusement d'autant plus qu'il avoit paru depuis peu un Imprimé énorme contenant plusieurs discours de convulsionnaires remplis de ces mauvais principes . . ." (meeting of Dec. 2, 1734, BN, MSS Fr., MS 11356, fol. 256).

[21] The police authorities had already been making plans to round up known or suspected Augustinistes for interrogations (*Mémoire* of Dec. 6, 1734, BA, MS 11375, fols. 67-68; see also letter of De la Rue to d'Inguimbert, Dec. 20, 1734, *Correspondance*, pp. 46-47).

[22] Testimony of Boyer, AN, X-1b 9692.

fasting" and sought to dissociate himself from the would-be prophet. By the time of their fourth meeting, Boyer was convinced that "the mind of Frère Augustin was entirely deranged," a conviction which the convulsionary's continued bizarre behavior served only to confirm. Augustin, in the meantime, had begun to claim that Father Boyer was personally responsible for raising him to his "superior state," since Boyer had allegedly offered this "humble penitent" formal absolution and pronounced a benediction upon the prophet immediately prior to Augustin's first pilgrimage to Port-Royal during the summer of 1733. Boyer, who denied ever having performed any such acts, not only refused to acknowledge Augustin's supposed spiritual exaltation, but also began to denounce Augustin to fellow Jansenists and convulsionaries.

As antagonism between the two men continued to grow, Frère Augustin, still hopeful of persuading Boyer to his point of view, sought on several occasions to secure a personal interview with the Oratorian priest. When Boyer repeatedly refused, Augustin and his disciples began a campaign of relentless harassment. In a series of letters written in late September 1734,[23] the prophet claimed that Boyer had libeled him by deliberately spreading false and malicious charges about his beliefs and activities, and he threatened to denounce his critic in public as a vicious calumniator if Boyer persisted in his refusal to speak with him or to retract the abusive remarks uttered "against my innocence." While declining once again to see Frère Augustin, Boyer promised several of the convulsionary's deputies that he would prepare a detailed response to these letters, laying out all of his complaints against the Augustinistes and their leader. But Boyer never did so.[24] Instead, he continued with his public denunciations of these "fanatics" and was soon joined by several prominent Jansenist theologians and convulsionists, including the abbés Isoard and Rochebouet, *curés* of Sainte-Marine and Saint-Germain-le-Vieux.[25] Feeling betrayed, the Augustinistes retaliated. In early December one of the prophet's disciples,

[23] Frère Augustin to Boyer, Sept. 24, 1734, BN, MSS Fr., MS 8989, fol. 82, and Augustin to Boyer, Sept. 29, 1734, *ibid.*, fols. 82-106. The second is a long, rambling letter, written in figurist language and allegedly composed "en convulsionant." On Boyer's views of this letter, see his testimony, cited above. Cf. the abbé d'Etemare's comments: "il y a les maximes les plus horribles . . . c'est un écrit qui est fou, mais schismatique dans sa folie. . . . Cet écrit est diabolique" (BA, MS 5784, p. 192).

[24] BN, MSS Fr., MS 8989, fol. 82.

[25] See testimony of Antoine Le Gras and Michel Colas, AN, X-1b 9692; Vintimille to Fleury, Oct. 18, 1734, BM, MS 2358, p. 420, and Fleury to Vintimille, Oct. 19, 1734, *ibid.*, p. 421.

a certain Frère Athanase, addressed a letter in the form of a manifesto to their various detractors, a bitter diatribe in which he referred to these priests as "adulterers, fornicators, homicides, and blasphemers." Athanase attacked the "Jansenist doctors" for having "abandoned the truth . . . and for having condemned the just and the innocent for crimes of which [they themselves] were guilty." He went on to announce in menacing tones that the prophet and his adherents were preparing "to destroy these prideful, unworthy doctors" in order to make way for the new dispensation. "The spirit of Jesus Christ," he proclaimed, "will triumph over that of Satan."[26] Figurative or not, the language employed in this letter and the violent invectives uttered throughout left Boyer and his colleagues more than a little concerned. It was this threatening manifesto, in fact, which ultimately persuaded Boyer to make his formal appeal to the *procureur-général*.

In presenting his petition to Joly de Fleury, Boyer was hopeful that the *procureur-général* would bring the case before the Parlement for an immediate court hearing and investigation. Joly de Fleury was not only the king's chief representative in the sovereign court, charged with upholding the royal interest in legal actions, but also bore responsibility, as principal "police officer" in the Parlement, for overseeing the maintenance of public order. In this latter capacity he frequently acted as a kind of public prosecutor, empowered with bringing alleged malefactors to justice by instigating a judicial action. When he agreed to introduce the Augustiniste case to the Parlement on appeal from Pierre Boyer, a private citizen seeking legal redress, Joly de Fleury was in fact agreeing to "promote a public action on the king's behalf" and thus became, as it were, "the sole plaintiff."[27] On January 18, 1735, therefore, the *procureur-général* presented the *Grand'Chambre* with a request in the form of a complaint against "the fanaticism of those who, under the pretext of supposed convulsions, teach a very pernicious doctrine."[28] The complaint, based on Father Boyer's original petition, was directed specifically and exclusively against the Augustinistes, for the only persons named were Robert Causse (Frère Augustin), La Restan, his "mistress," and Louis

---

[26] The manifesto was addressed to "Messieurs d'Asfeld, Boyer, Rochebois [*sic*] curé de St. Germain le Vieux, M. le Curé de Ste.-Marine, et tous les autres partisans de l'Assemblée opposée à l'Oeuvre Sainte de Mon Sauveur J.-C." (AN, X-1b 9690). Cf. testimony of P. C. Cossart and Antoine Le Gras, AN, X-1b 9692. For a less caustic, but equally pointed attack on the Jansenist doctors, see BHVP, C.P. 3509, pp. 1-2, 15-16.

[27] Shennan, *Parlement of Paris*, p. 67.

[28] AN, X-1b 9692. Cf. *NNEE*, March 14, 1735, p. 40, and Barbier, III, 1 (January 1735).

Hochède (Frère Athanase), who were said to be the three leading members of the sect. The *requête* also included a complaint against the published *Recueil de discours*.[29]

That same day, in response to Joly de Fleury's action, the *Grand'-Chambre* handed down a formal indictment of the Augustinistes, which began by acknowledging the need for action against these fanatics in the name of "security, tranquility, and public decency."[30] The indictment went on to decry the "excesses," "indecencies," and "crimes," both religious and civil, of the sect's adherents and to attack their pretensions to divine inspiration and their claims that the destruction of the Church was imminent. The indictment also charged the Augustinistes with deceiving the credulous into donating considerable sums of money to sustain their cause. It further accused them of fomenting insubordination toward all authority by the publication of the *Recueil de discours*. The pronouncement ended with a ringing denunciation of the sect[31] and authorized a full-scale investigation into their "scandalous crimes" to be undertaken as soon as possible.

In support of the various charges contained in the indictment, the *Grand'Chambre* submitted as evidence a copy of the *Recueil de discours* and copies of the several threatening letters which Frères Augustin and Athanase had sent to Father Boyer and to other prominent Jansenist clerics and theologians.[32] The court also issued a writ authorizing the gathering of information and naming M. de Vienne, counselor in the *Grand'Chambre*, as examining judge and *rapporteur*, with responsibility for receiving the testimony and depositions of the witnesses to be called before him in the inquest, for compiling and evaluating the evidence as it accumulated, and for making periodic reports to the court on the progress of his investigations. However, a fellow counselor, M. Sévert, almost immediately replaced Vienne as head of the fact-finding commission, when family illness forced the latter to resign his appointment.

[29] See Ch. VII above. The case of Père Boyer vs. Frère Augustin was ostensibly a *civil* one, since it involved a quarrel between individuals; in some sense, however, it was also a *criminal* case, one to which the State was a party.

[30] AN, X-1b 9692.

[31] "Que ces excès si scandaleux, et des principes si erronées, que l'imposture, les prestiges ou le fanatisme produisent et entretiennent et qui tendent à la subversion des moeurs, à troubler l'ordre de la société civile, à se porter enfin aux excès les plus énormes sur le faux prétexte de la religion, exigeant que la Cour y pourvoye par son autorité. Qu'elle trouve des preuves trop sensibles de ces excès dans l'imprimé que dans tout ce qu'il contient et dans les lacunes qui se trouvent remplies à la main ne respire qu'une Révolte contre toute Autorité" (*ibid.*).

[32] *Arrêt du Parlement*, Jan. 18, 1735, *ibid.*

The judicial investigations began ostensibly as an examination into the activities and conduct of the Augustiniste sect. But the police authorities under Hérault were unable to locate the three principals named in the Parlement's indictment, the very persons whose alleged crimes were expected to be the focus of the *procès*. Almost from the outset, therefore, Sévert undertook to broaden the nature and scope of the inquest. As early as January 19 the counselor started taking depositions from a steady stream of witnesses, many of whom were without any known affiliation, past or present, with the Augustinistes.[33] Nor were the interrogations confined to discovering material only on Frère Augustin and his followers. Indeed, even though the *Grand'Chambre*'s original authorization had seemingly circumscribed his jurisdictional competence to an investigation of these "fanatics," and even though the discovery of Augustin's whereabouts and the trial of the prophet and his two closest disciples remained the overriding concern of his inquest, Sévert soon extended his commission, gradually transforming his hearings into a general examination of virtually the entire convulsionary movement. Yet in apparently exceeding his initial commission, thus presumably changing the Parlement's original intent, Sévert acted always with the full knowledge and the explicit backing of the *procureur-général* and his fellow counselors in the *Grand'Chambre*.

In general, Sévert received considerable cooperation from the Parlement in the conduct of his hearings. A series of court orders issued during the course of the *procès* spelled out certain procedural details for the inquest and redefined the areas of investigation, thereby serving to enhance the *rapporteur*'s already broad discretionary authority.[34] The *Grand'Chambre* empowered him to subpoena, arrest, and interrogate not only those who were accused of associating with Frère Augustin and might have possessed information as to his whereabouts, but also those who had only been witnesses to or participants in the more "orthodox" convulsionary *séances*. In practice this meant that all present or former convulsionaries who could be identified and apprehended were liable to receive a summons to appear before the Sévert commission. As a precaution against their fleeing and to ensure their availability for questioning, the *rapporteur* was authorized to detain them

---

[33] See *procès-verbaux, ibid.*, and X-1b 9690-91.

[34] Numerous *arrêts du Parlement*, issued primarily in response to requests from Joly de Fleury, may be found in AN, X-1b 9690-91. It was the responsibility of the *procureur-général* periodically to review the dossiers of all the accused, to oversee the *procès* through its different stages, and to determine whether the cases should be continued. On Sévert's activities and responsibilities, see AAE, M&D, France, MS 1296, fol. 239; and Journal of De Lisle, April 2, 1735, and Aug. 8, 1735, AN, U-384.

indefinitely. Sévert was in fact prepared to keep them incarcerated for as long as he deemed their testimony necessary to the progress of his case or until he was satisfied that they had fully confessed to and repented of their own alleged misdeeds. Distinctions between "witnesses" and the "accused" thus tended to become increasingly blurred. As for the interrogations themselves, these were not held in any single or fixed location. Sévert was given authority to shift his hearings from one prison to another, even to the Hôpital-Général, for the purpose of taking testimony. At his convenience he was also allowed to transfer prisoners from one place of detention to another, and to confront them at times with other suspects or with their various accusers. Finally, he was empowered to continue his peripatetic investigations during periods of the Parlement's vacations, even though the court itself was not in regular session. In addition to the wide latitude the Parlement granted to him throughout these hearings,[35] Sévert also had Hérault's police and the court's own *huissiers* and sergeants placed at his disposal. Under Sévert's direction these various law officers carried out orders for the arrest of numerous suspected persons and others wanted as prospective witnesses. They also took charge of seizing and sealing the enormous quantities of papers and other effects occasionally discovered at the time of the arrests. These confiscated documents were eventually utilized in subsequent interrogations.[36]

Armed with extensive investigative authority, Sévert embarked on his appointed task with great enthusiasm. As was the customary practice in the inquisitorial procedure appropriate to such investigations, Sévert conducted his interrogations in private, hearing the various witnesses and accused separately and in absolute secrecy, with only a *greffier* present to make verbatim transcripts of the proceedings. Throughout the inquest the magistrate saw his principal task to be that of digging out evidence and penetrating the veil of secrecy and obscurity surrounding the convulsionaries. His questions were consequently directed toward that end.[37] In the first place, Sévert sought to find out all he could about the nature and extent of the involvement in the *oeuvre* of each of the individual convulsionaries called to testify

[35] On occasion Sévert himself specifically requested and received additional authority from the court on a wide variety of matters, especially concerning the disposition of individual cases (see *ibid.*, Sept. 4, 1735, AN, U-386).

[36] The *procès-verbaux*, containing complete descriptions of these seized materials, were deposited along with the materials themselves in the office of the *greffier en chef*. Many of these papers may be found in AN, X-1b 9692-93.

[37] What follows is based on scores of interrogations, some of them running to over one hundred folio pages, found *ibid.*, X-1b 9690-92.

before him. What had they witnessed in their respective conventicles? What had been their own contributions to the *séances*? Had they ever seen or experienced convulsions, heard or given out with discourses? Had they undergone *secours* or perhaps served as *secouristes* themselves? What exactly had these various activities entailed? Another set of questions was designed to elicit information about other convulsionaries as well. Sévert was especially concerned to establish the relationships between and among the brethren and to determine the identities of as many *frères* and *soeurs* as possible, both their real names and their *noms de convulsion*. He was also interested in knowing where they met, when, how often, and so on. Much of this aspect of the interrogations centered on Frère Augustin himself, as Sévert attempted desperately to learn more about the prophet, his background, his beliefs and practices, his particular activities in the *oeuvre*, and, above all, this elusive figure's present whereabouts. There were also numerous questions dealing with various convulsionary documents, printed and manuscript, which had been accumulating since the opening of the *procès*; these included the *Recueil de discours*, the letters attacking Boyer and other Jansenists, and the *Calendrier mystérieux*. Sévert interrogated everyone very closely regarding the origin, authorship, and interpretation of these "subversive" writings. As new documents were seized, they provided new evidence for follow-up interrogations. Finally, the tenacious counselor posed a wide range of hostile leading questions, many of them framed in terms of the unfavorable rumors and hearsay evidence which had been circulating throughout Paris since the onset of the convulsions at Saint-Médard, and all of them designed to elicit incriminating evidence or admissions from the mouths of the accused themselves. These were thorough interrogations. Indeed, in the case of certain convulsionaries whom Sévert had to recall repeatedly for additional testimony, the questioning sometimes went on for days, even weeks, on end. But despite his exhaustive efforts to penetrate convulsionary secrets and thereby break up the sect, he did not always meet with success.

Many of the convulsionaries whom Sévert called to testify, especially those who had been closely associated with Frère Augustin, were extremely hostile toward the *rapporteur* and adamantly refused to cooperate in any way with his investigation. Some absolutely refused even to take the oath demanded of all witnesses at the commencement of each day's interrogations or to sign the *procès-verbaux* at the end. Though subjected to long and intense examinations, most of these recalcitrant witnesses declined to answer any specific questions about themselves or their fellow brethren, insisting that to do so would constitute an act of complicity with the movement's persecutors and a betrayal of the *oeuvre*.[38] Others deliberately lied or provided only vague, evasive replies to their inquisitor's questions; still others conveniently forgot or were unable to recall certain facts. On occasion Sévert was successful in browbeating a reluctant subject into revealing detailed secrets about his own activities and those of fellow convulsionaries.[39] Many convulsionaries, however, persisted in their silence even under continual threats and intimidations. Jeanne Causse, for example, who was Frère Augustin's convulsionary sister (also known as Soeur Félicité, Soeur Robert, or Soeur Noir), declined to answer some three hundred questions asked of her over the course of several gruelling interrogations.[40] She explained repeatedly that she was not prepared to recognize Sévert's authority to examine her and insisted that she would testify only before the entire court or in front of the king himself if necessary. For days, in fact, the only comments Soeur Félicité would utter before the *rapporteur* and his *greffier* were denunciations of the "injustice and cruelty" of the whole "illegitimate procedure." Her long silences were punctuated only by occasional torrents of epithets hurled at the two men: *deux misérables impies, empoisonneurs, impudiques, faussaires, calomniateurs, médisants, bourreaux,* all of which were faithfully inscribed in the records.[41]

While Mlle. Causse and others were heaping verbal abuse upon M. Sévert, a number of staunchly dedicated Augustinistes actually experienced convulsions in his presence, thereby giving physical expression to their revulsion at the counselor's inquest. In the very course of the interrogations these convulsionaries began to thrash about uncontrollably, their bodily writhings accompanied by screams, cries, tears, and groans; at times they even gave out with long, impressive discourses decrying the malevolence of their tormentors in both Church and

[38] See, in particular, the testimony of Etienne Boileau, Nicolas Simart, and Joseph Orry (*ibid.,* X-1b 9690). The abbé Orry, *curé* of la Chapelle-Milon (near Port-Royal-des-Champs), was accused of having harbored Frère Augustin several months earlier, when the prophet had sought refuge from the Paris police, and of permitting Augustin to administer the sacrament of baptism. Orry denied these charges and also refused to answer many of the other questions put to him, invoking "clerical privileges" and complaining that the court was involving completely innocent, pious Christians in its criminal investigations.

[39] Boileau was one whom Sévert successfully intimidated in this way (*ibid.*).

[40] Mlle. Causse's interrogation ran to some seven hundred questions in all and covered well over one hundred pages—despite the hundreds of silent "replies" (*ibid.*).

[41] She reserved some of her most derogatory remarks for Sévert alone, calling him "le plus grand des misérables qui mérite de pourrir dans une basse fosse," and "un corrompu, un insensé, indigne de connoître l'oeuvre de Dieu" (*ibid.*).

State.[42] Though Sévert was aghast at such unexpected and bewildering displays, the onset of which usually forced a temporary suspension of the interrogations, these manifestations nevertheless left him only more determined than ever to put a halt to the "fanaticism" he had been commissioned to investigate.

Of course not all of the witnesses were so hostile or uncooperative. Some individuals, including a handful of the accused, were actually quite open and forthcoming in their depositions, giving long and detailed answers to the questions posed and providing valuable firsthand information about the movement—information available nowhere else. They also displayed a keen awareness of the major issues, spiritual and ecclesiastical, at stake in the *Unigenitus* controversy. Even so, there were few Augustinistes among these convulsionaries who were willing to reveal all they knew. In addition, many of the "orthodox" convulsionaries who were prepared to cooperate with Sévert were unlearned adepts with little or no comprehension of what they had seen or experienced and thus unable to interpret what had gone on. Some were unclear about the nature and meaning of convulsionary "doctrine," leaving many points vague and confused, particularly regarding the Augustinistes, about whom these witnesses were generally uninformed. Unfortunately for Sévert, in fact, the individuals who might have been able to provide him with the most accurate information concerning Frère Augustin and company were the ones who remained the most tenaciously tight-lipped of all.

This failure to obtain substantial concrete evidence regarding the Augustinistes was only one of a number of disappointments for Sévert during the first year of his investigation. The counselor's interrogations had increasingly centered on a series of questions concerning the convulsionaries' allegedly rebellious and subversive activities and utterances. He made repeated inquiries into their supposedly scandalous behavior and disturbances of the public order and questioned them about *menaces* against the king and the civil and ecclesiastical authorities. But if Sévert expected to extort dramatic confessions from these people, he was greatly mistaken. Not surprisingly, nearly all of the witnesses denied any imputation of bad conduct, any wrongdoing, and insisted that they and their fellow adepts adhered strictly to the "holy laws of religion, morality, and justice."[43] Furthermore, while refusing to "repent" of any alleged crimes or misdeeds, all of them believed

---

[42] Marguerite Roussel (on Oct. 21, 1735) and Soeur La Croix Fontaine-Maillet (on Sept. 17, 24, and 27, 1735) experienced convulsions during their interrogations (*ibid.*).

[43] *NNEE*, March 14, 1735, p. 40.

wholeheartedly—and with apparent sincerity—that they spoke in the name of God and that the *oeuvre* was essentially divine.[44]

As for their attitudes toward the king and his ministers, their testimony did not indicate any fundamentally destructive or revolutionary intent. Virtually all of those called to testify either disclaimed any knowledge of the infamously antiroyalist *Calendrier mystérieux* or repudiated its identification of Louis XV with the Antichrist.[45] To be sure, several of the respondents, mainly the Augustinistes, did have somewhat unfavorable comments to make about the king. Claude Yvon, for example, believed that the discourses of the convulsionaries were all inspired by God, even those which included statements critical of the monarch. The convulsionary known as Soeur Colombe asserted that "she respects the physical person of the king, which is sacred, and that she respects his ministers, but that she cannot and must not respect their crimes." She also expressed the fear that deceitful advisers were misleading the king into "protecting the faithless persecutors of the Truth."[46] Françoise de Livry contended, somewhat more circumspectly, that "the convulsionaries say what God makes them say, even in their attacks on the king, but [once they are] out of this state [of divine inspiration] they are very obedient to the monarch and to their superiors." Although one priest did indeed speak of the convulsionary assemblies as places where "new Ravaillacs were in the process of being formed,"[47] for the most part these *frères* and *soeurs* were quite respectful toward the king and regarded themselves as the monarch's dutiful subjects.[48] They reserved their harshest remarks for the king's ministers, especially Cardinal Fleury, and for the other authorities in both Church and State, including the pope, the Jesuits, Archbishop Vintimille, and police-lieutenant Hérault, all of whom they accused of "gross impiety," "thoughtless sacrilege," and "ungodly blasphemy."[49]

While there was nothing particularly fanatical or subversive about either the actions or the pronouncements of the overwhelming majority of the people called before him, Sévert persisted in his tenacious, indiscriminate, and almost vindictive pursuit of the convulsionaries and

---

[44] *Ibid.*

[45] What follows is based on material in AN, X-1b 9690, *passim.*

[46] She went on to add that, "C'est Dieu qui lui a fait . . . dire que le Roi est un Achab et un Roi de Boue dans la maison duquel il se commet toutes sortes d'abominations" (*ibid.*).

[47] Testimony of Louis Alexandre Doutreleau, *ibid.,* X-1b 9692.

[48] Cf. earlier comments of Louis Sabinet (Frère Louis), BN, NAFr., MS 4262, fol. 128.

[49] Testimony of Claude Chambon, AN, X-1b 9692, and Marguerite Roussel, *ibid.,* X-1b 9690.

their sympathizers. Most of those subjected to Sévert's inquisitorial proceedings were poor, virtually defenseless adherents of the movement, forced to languish in prison for months on end, some without even being charged, others under charges that appear to have been without foundation and that were never satisfactorily substantiated. In the midst of these investigations, however, three such victims of Sévert's rigorous prosecution—the celebrated convulsionaries Charlotte de la Porte, Denise Regné, and Marguerite-Catherine Turpin—attempted to take countermeasures to offset the counselor's severe actions. Sévert had accused all three women of imposture in their convulsions and sent them to the *maison de force* of the Salpêtrière.[50] Protesting these accusations and Sévert's harsh treatment of them, they managed to find several influential and articulate defenders to intercede on their behalf. As a result, their protests soon obtained considerable notoriety and subsequently became the subject of some widely publicized litigation.

In July 1735 the *procureur-général* received petitions on behalf of the three women in which serious questions were raised about the alleged "facts" that had formed the basis of Sévert's charges against them.[51] The fifty-four-year-old Mlle. de la Porte, who presented her own *requête*, denied any knowledge of or connection with Frère Augustin and his sect and begged the court's permission to call additional witnesses to refute the accusations of imposture. She offered as "incontestable evidence" the medical reports of the two doctors who had treated her and who were acquainted with her condition both before and after the convulsions. She even declared her willingness to undergo yet another medical examination for the purpose of demonstrating her present physical state. Her case also received additional, unexpected support from other quarters, when several persons came forward with unsolicited depositions attesting that Mlle. de la Porte had cured their children by sucking out gangrenous sores.[52] What is more, the accused found a powerful defender in Mme. Joly de Fleury herself, wife of the *procureur-général*, who attested to Charlotte's having suffered from several congenital disorders of the spine and foot—disorders apparently cured through the intercession of François de Pâris and in the midst of violent convulsions.[53] Finally, submitted along with her *requête* was a *consultation* drawn up by twelve of the leading

[50] *NNEE*, Oct. 29, 1735, p. 169.   [51] *Ibid.*

[52] For these fantastic, though bizarre, abilities as a "miracle worker," she earned the nickname, "La Suceuse."

[53] Louis Boucher, *La Salpêtrière, son histoire, de 1651 à 1790, ses origines et son fonctionnement au 18ᵉ siècle* (Paris, 1883), pp. 50, 122-24.

avocats in the Parlement, dated May 26, 1735, which provided a legal justification for her plea to the court.[54]

The *requêtes* in the cases of Denise Regné and Marguerite Turpin essentially followed the same pattern, with the petitioners again challenging Sévert's charges of imposture as false and baseless and offering to provide the court with the names of witnesses who could corroborate the defendants' versions of the facts. The three petitions, along with the supporting legal briefs, were delivered into the hands of Joly de Fleury for further consideration.[55]

After some delay the *procureur-général* finally passed the *requêtes* on to M. Sévert, advising him that "the king did not mind if [these] petitions were joined to the trial" so that the court, in judging them, might state what the law was and how it applied to the three cases.[56] Some convulsionist sympathizers within the Parlement anticipated that the court, forced to rule on the validity of the miracles, would actually pronounce in their favor. Less than a month after receiving the petitions from Joly de Fleury, however, Sévert delivered his own report to the *Grand'Chambre* in which he was unequivocal in his denunciation of their contents. Concentrating his attention on the case of Charlotte de la Porte, he recommended that her request be dismissed out of hand on the grounds that "the captious petition tended to enter into the proofs of miracles . . . and that there would be nothing so dangerous as to subject such facts to judicial proof."[57] After a prolonged and heated debate, the prevailing opinion among the judges favored declaring the request "inadmissible for the present." Speaking for the majority, President Maupeou observed that "Charlotte de la Porte should have been content with proving the reality of her convulsions by the bodily changes which she experienced, without claiming, as she has done, that these changes were miracles, . . . [for] the Parlement [does] not have the right to verify miracles. . . ."[58] Such matters he deemed beyond the court's legal competence, belonging rather to those with theological or medical expertise. Maupeou's speech eventually formed the basis of the *Grand'Chambre*'s *arrêt*. As for the other two *requêtes*, Sévert suggested that, owing to a lack of time for further deliberation,[59] they be included in the same *arrêt*. The other magistrates concurred.

---

[54] The *Requête présentée au Parlement par Charlotte de la Porte* was published with a baptismal certificate and medical reports as well as the *consultation*.

[55] *NNEE*, Nov. 5, 1735, pp. 173-74.   [56] *Ibid.*, p. 174.

[57] *Ibid.*   [58] *Ibid.*, p. 175.

[59] The court was about to recess for its annual vacation.

What became of the women is uncertain,[60] although in the months that followed, their cases continued to receive widespread attention in contemporary pamphlet literature.[61] But the efforts of convulsionists, *avocats*, and other sympathizers who had rallied to support the three convulsionaries and their other jailed compatriots were all in vain. Their only hope had lain in the Parlement's reversal of Sévert's action, but the *Grand'Chambre*, with its three "non-admissibles pour le présent," had refused even to deal with the matter.

The court's action (or inaction) in these three cases demonstrated quite clearly that the judges had made a virtually complete *volte-face* where the convulsionaries were concerned. In the one major judicial test of Sévert's handling of the *procès*, his fellow magistrates had declined to intervene. In the meantime, while the barrage of tracts both for and against the three convulsionaries continued to hail down on the streets of Paris, an opportunity had presented itself for rounding up a substantial number of the Augustinistes who still remained at large. In early January 1736 the police received an anonymous tip that a band of Frère Augustin's disciples was planning to go on a holy pilgrimage to Port-Royal-des-Champs in the very near future. Such processions to the hallowed ruins of the Jansenist monastery had of course been quite common throughout this period. Various convulsionary groups, sometimes up to fifty or sixty people at a time, regularly made their way to the site, many of them on foot.[62] Some brethren actually conducted regular *séances* among the ruins, reciting prayers, singing psalms, and even experiencing convulsions, applying *secours*, and pronouncing discourses. In the case of the Augustinistes these processions tended to be nocturnal affairs and were usually undertaken as an act of penance. Thus, on the night of January 12, twenty-six members of the sect embarked on such a ceremonial procession. For many of those involved this was to be their last pilgrimage for a long time. Anticipating the procession as a result of their informant's tip, the authorities had sent out a contingent of police officials on the tenth. Led by the *exempt* Dubut, the police were already waiting for the Augustinistes on their arrival and arrested every last one of them.[63]

[60] A letter from Soanen dated April 13, 1737 (AFA, P.R. 7023, pp. 1,024-25) suggests that they were still in prison as late as the spring of 1737.

[61] Among the half-dozen or so pamphlets produced on both sides of the question, the most important were: *Réflexions sur la requeste de la nommée Charlotte* (anti); *Lettre à l'auteur . . . au sujet de ses réflexions* (pro); *Réflexions sur la requeste de Denize . . . & nouvelles remarques sur celle de Charlotte* (pro); and *Le Naturalisme des 4 Requestes* (anti). Cf. *NNEE*, Nov. 12, 1735, pp. 177-78.

[62] *Pensées sur les prodiges de nos jours*, p. 9; Ravaisson, XIV, 337, 341, 344-49.

[63] Testimony of Etienne Jules Durand, Antoine Culsac, Jean Perrault, and

The newly captured convulsionaries, who included most of the leading adherents of Frère Augustin,[64] though once again not the prophet himself, now joined the others already being detained in various Paris prisons and were themselves immediately subjected to a series of long and intensive interrogations. Indeed, for the next few months Sévert was to concentrate most of his attention on these recent captives in an effort to obtain some fresh information regarding the Augustiniste sect.[65] But Sévert's best efforts again proved as fruitless as his earlier ones had been; like their colleagues who had preceded them, the majority of these people adamantly refused to cooperate with his investigation. After a while, however, the long months of incarceration in close, overcrowded quarters (especially at the Conciergerie) and the repeated interrogations began to take their toll. In the confrontation hearings conducted between witnesses and accused, Sévert attempted with some success to drive a wedge between "orthodox" and Augustiniste convulsionaries. Dissension among the prison population was in fact mounting, as rival groups of convulsionaries bitterly charged one another with "harboring a nest of vipers." Pressured by relatives and various spiritual advisers, including the prison confessor, disillusioned and scandalized by the illicit goings-on among some of their erstwhile brethren imprisoned with them,[66] and anxious to secure their release in exchange for cooperating with the authorities, several former diehards agreed to repudiate Frère Augustin and his entire band of votaries and to reveal all that they knew of the sect's activities. Nevertheless, despite the numerous disavowals Sévert managed to obtain in this manner, and despite the bulging dossiers he succeeded in compiling as a result, the counselor still had no luck in tracking down the individuals who were the original objects of his whole investigation.

Etienne Bazin, AN, X-1b 9692. See also the *arrêts du Parlement* of Jan. 24, 1736 and March 12, 1736, *ibid.*; and BA, MS 11314, fols. 322-27.

[64] Perhaps the most notable was the venerable octogenarian, abbé Mathieu de Barneville, originally from Dublin, who had become an ardent convulsionary in 1731. For an assessment of his "saintly piety," see BHVP, C.P. 3509, pp. 87-89; for a copy of his *profession de foi*, sent to the Parlement of Paris on Dec. 18, 1736, see AFA, P.R. 4665. Cf. Ruth Clark, *Strangers and Sojourners at Port-Royal* (Cambridge, Eng., 1932), pp. 251-52.

[65] AN, X-1b 9691, *passim*.

[66] *Ibid., passim.* Cf. BHVP, C.P. 3509, p. 74 (letter dated July 12, 1735). Jeanne Gymatte had actually become pregnant as a result of her "spiritual marriage" to a fellow convulsionary (testimony of Jean-Baptiste de Lamain, Claude Yvon, and others, AN, X-1b 9691). The "immoral" activities of Frère Polle and Soeur Fontaine were also condemned by several fellow prisoners (see, for example, testimony of Marie-Catherine De Fer, *ibid.*).

Frustrated, but undaunted, Sévert doggedly persisted in his hearings, which dragged on indefinitely without attracting very much publicity or troublesome interference from any quarter. He continued for many years to find and detain large numbers of people—witnesses and accused—at the Conciergerie, where some were repeatedly overcome with convulsive seizures while pursuing their religious devotions. But the principal Augustinistes, the prophet and his companion, La Restan, had gone into hiding and with the help of their loyal followers managed to escape entirely the "preliminary inquest" initially undertaken to bring them to justice.[67] Although the Parlement never did promulgate or execute a final judgment in the case,[68] that fact was but small consolation to the various practitioners of the *oeuvre*, for the court's action in authorizing the Sévert *procès* in the first place had already done great damage to the convulsionary cause. Despite an earlier reluctance to join forces with Church and State against the convulsionaries, the magistrates, apparently convinced that the "enthusiasts" constituted a clear and present danger to public order, were now making common cause with Fleury and the *constitutionnaires* and had all but abandoned the entire convulsionary movement—"fanatics" and "orthodox" alike—to its enemies.

The Parlement's virtually complete repudiation of the followers of M. Pâris had not been entirely unexpected in some convulsionary circles. As early as April 1733, Frère Pierre, one of the most celebrated participants in the *oeuvre*, had obliquely warned his fellow brethren of the possibility of a future betrayal. In a famous discourse known as "Les trois fosses," Pierre observed: "Even if the majority [of magistrates] have until now declared themselves for us, do not count forever on human support. Place all your hopes in God and in the cross of His son."[69] Expected or not, the trial launched by the Parlement con-

---

[67] BHVP, C.P. 3509, p. 27. According to an anonymous reference (dated May 1813) in a manuscript at the Bibliothèque de l'Arsenal, "Le Frère Augustin a, dit-on, réformé son système et depuis a été si touché des grands maux de ce système qui lui a été attribué qu'il s'est condamné à la pénitence la plus austère et à la retraite la plus profonde où il a versé un torrent de larmes pour expier le scandale auquel il pouvoit avoir donné lieu et enfin est mort à Montmorency près Paris en union persévérante pendant peut être plus de 40 ans au culte extérieur de l'Eglise et muni des derniers sacremens à la mort vers 1787" (MS 6890, fols. 196-97).

[68] The sovereign court's pursuit of the convulsionaries was to continue at least into the 1760s (see BN, J.F., MS 313, fols. 220-22, and MS 451, fols. 196-99). Marguerite-Françoise de Livry (Soeur Françoise), arrested in the mid-1730s, was still in prison as of 1765.

[69] Bibliothèque de la Société de l'Histoire du Protestantisme Français, MS 196,

stituted a severe setback for the movement.[70] Nor was the court's active pursuit of the convulsionaries the only serious blow dealt them in this critical period.

Another major controversy had, in the meantime, been reaching a climax. Since the failure of their conferences in 1732-1733, the two dissident camps of Jansenist theologians had been engaged in a fratricidal polemical debate over the convulsionaries. Repeated attempts by individual ecclesiastics[71] and even the *Nouvelles ecclésiastiques* to mediate the dispute failed to restrain or reunite the factions. Although the *Nouvellistes* appealed in irenic tones for a lowering of voices,[72] the journal, itself an interested party in the affair, was no longer the instrument for healing such internecine discord. What is more, with the appearance of the Vaillantistes and especially the Augustinistes, such pleas for harmony were quickly lost amid the din of an escalating controversy. From both sides came an almost inexhaustible flood of writings, pamphlets, vicious lampoons, and so-called *dissertations raisonnées*. Spinning out very complicated and long-winded arguments, each side claimed to have crushed the other with "irrefutable" demonstrations and "incontrovertible" proofs. As before, it was a fiercely ani-

---

p. 59 (April 18). This discourse is one of Frère Pierre's most famous, with copies appearing in many collections compiled during this period.

[70] It also led to a marked change in the convulsionaries' attitude toward the court. As a consequence of having abdicated their role as protectors of the sect, the magistrates began to lose that special place as heroes they had held among the convulsionaries since 1731-1732. Once it was recognized that most of them had taken their stand largely out of political expediency and were prepared to dissociate themselves from the movement when they found it to be too much of a liability, the convulsionaries no longer regarded their erstwhile benefactors as "pères de la patrie" or "généreux magistrats . . . , la force et le salut de la Nation sainte" (see discourse of Soeur La Croix Got, Ch. VII, p. 302). By 1756 the celebrated Soeur Holda was bitterly denouncing the magistrates as "des serviteurs inutiles en sa présence, sans foi et sans amour, sans lumière ni intelligence. Ils sont amateurs d'eux-mêmes et non de la vérité qui devroit faire toute seule les chartes délices de leur âme" (*Recueil des prédiction* [1792], I, 168; see also pp. 45-47).

[71] On the efforts of Bishop Caylus of Auxerre, see BA, MS 11304, fols. 111-12. Bishop Colbert was also working hard to restore peace and civility to the appellant camp. Cf. his letter "au Confrère le Roi de l'Oratoire," Dec. 28, 1734, *Oeuvres*, III, 706-707, as well as earlier ones to the abbé Petitpied (April 9, 1734, *ibid.*, pp. 655-56) and to Bishop Caylus (April 9, *ibid.*, p. 656). "Faut-il, dès qu'il y aura quelque partage de sentimens entre les amis de la vérité, le dénoncer au public?" Colbert wrote Petitpied. "Nous devons agir de concert, et tenter, ce me semble, toutes les voies de conciliation, avant que d'en venir à un éclat, si l'on trouve que le sujet le mérite" (*ibid.*, p. 655).

[72] See, for example, Aug. 22, 1733, p. 172.

mated, but rather sterile, exchange of theological apologetics and polemics, accusations and recriminations. In this combative atmosphere the effort to clarify the obscurities produced only further obfuscation.[73]

Fleury sought to exploit the opportunity which these divisions provided him.[74] In violation of the government's own longstanding prohibitions against the publication or distribution of any provocative writings on ecclesiastical subjects, the royal administration itself began to authorize Jansenist works which explicitly condemned the convulsionaries.[75] As early as 1733 the crown initiated the practice of granting *permissions tacites* to such works and allowing them to be publicly distributed, with police protection, even though they all contained propositions strongly favorable to the appeal and some had arguments in support of the miracles of François de Pâris.[76] That was a small price to pay for the desired condemnations, and Fleury was willing to pay it. Jansenist supporters of the convulsionaries repeatedly decried this complicity.[77] But the cooperation of certain *anticonstitutionnaires* contin-

---

[73] One of the most bitter series of exchanges included the following: *Essai d'un plan sur l'oeuvre des convulsions* (n.d.); [De Lan], *Réponse à l'écrit intitulé: "Plan général de l'oeuvre des convulsions"* (1733); *Plan général de l'oeuvre des convulsions, avec des Réflexions d'un laïc en réfutation de la Réponse que M. l'abbé de L[an] a faite à ce Plan* (1733); [De Lan], *Dissertation théologique contre les convulsions, adressée au laïc auteur des Réflexions sur la Réponse au Plan général* (1733); *Remarques sur la "Dissertation théologique contre les convulsions"* (n.d.). Summaries and analyses of these and other such works were given in the *Nouvelles ecclésiastiques* throughout this period, *passim*.

[74] See, for example, abbé Favier (Congrégation de Sainte-Geneviève) to [Fleury?], June 2, 1733, BA, MS 10008, fol. 171.

[75] All along, of course, the government had been subsidizing and/or sponsoring *constitutionnaire* publications as well (see Paul Denis, "Le Cardinal de Fleury, Dom Alaydon et Dom Thuillier," *Revue bénédictine*, 26 [1909], pp. 325-70). The notorious Benedictine theologian, Louis-Bernard La Taste, composed many, if not most, of his long polemical tracts against the Pâris miracles and convulsionaries after official consultation and approval (see Le Rouge to [Hérault?], May 22, 1733; Rouïlle to Hérault, May 26, 1733; and Rouïlle to Hérault, June 2, 1733, BA, MS 10297). Cardinal Fleury personally praised La Taste for his efforts (see letters of Aug. 3 and 9, 1733, BN, MSS Fr., MS 19667, fols. 160-61). On La Taste, see Jean-Baptiste Vanel, *Les Bénédictins de Saint-Germain-des-Près et les savants lyonnais d'après leur correspondance inédite* (Paris-Lyon, 1894), pp. 262-84. Manuscript collections of his writings and correspondence are in BN, MSS Fr., MSS 19667-68, 15802-804, 17714-15.

[76] *NNEE*, Aug. 22, 1733, p. 172. The abbé De Lan's *Réponse à l'écrit intitulé: "Plan général de l'oeuvre des convulsions"* was published "avec permission tacite et vendue publiquement."

[77] The *Nouvellistes* led the way in making this complaint: Aug. 22, 1733, p. 172; Sept. 5, 1733, p. 179; Oct. 3, 1733, p. 199; Oct. 6, 1734, p. 171. As the anony-

ued, culminating in the government-sponsored *Consultation des Trente sur les Convulsions*, which appeared, perhaps not coincidentally, shortly before the royal government restored the Parlement's competence in the convulsionary affair and permitted the court to begin its long *procès* under counselor Sévert.

The outspoken and uncompromising *Consultation*, apparently undertaken with the full knowledge and encouragement of the authorities, was thus only the most celebrated and successful of a series of anticonvulsionary appellant tracts to which Cardinal Fleury granted special treatment. It climaxed his search for an unequivocal theological statement from the *anticonstitutionnaire* camp condemning the convulsionary movement. In September 1734, in fact, the cardinal-minister's government had even permitted the well-known Jansenist theologian, the abbé Nicolas Petitpied, to return to Paris from exile in Holland mainly on condition that he would help compose such a document or in some other way assist in mobilizing his fellow Jansenists into taking a firm stand against the *oeuvre*.[78] Petitpied expressed a willingness to abide by such a stipulation, though without renouncing his determined opposition to the bull *Unigenitus*.[79] The veteran and highly talented controversialist was an excellent choice for the project, since his considerable stature in most Jansenist circles was expected to lend any such pronouncement a certain measure of prestige and authority.[80] Petitpied, for his part, was only a relatively recent convert to the anticonvulsionary camp. Living in Utrecht since 1729 and forced to rely on the information received from some convulsionist friends in Paris, he had originally been prepared to believe that the *oeuvre* was divinely in-

---

mous author of the *Pensées sur les prodiges de nos jours* also observed, "Déclarez-vous contre les Convulsionnaires, vous aurez aujourd'hui la paix de ce monde, du moins le monde fait trève avec vous" (p. 12).

[78] Barbier, III, 6 (February 1735). The *NNEE* had earlier reported, without any comment, that "le célèbre M. Petitpied, Docteur de Sorbonne, étoit arrivé d'Hollande, avec permission de la Cour de demeurer à Paris" (Oct. 6, 1734, p. 171). According to the abbé Rochebouet, *curé* of Saint-Germain-le-Vieux, Petitpied had returned "pour être le pacificateur et pour tomber sur les convulsions . . ." (letter to Bishop Colbert, Jan. 20, 1735, AFA, P.R. 5547).

[79] Vintimille to Fleury, Sept. 5, 1734, BM, MS 2358, p. 409; Fleury to Vintimille, Sept. 6, *ibid.*, p. 410; Vintimille to Fleury, Sept. 11, *ibid.*, p. 414; Vintimille to Fleury, Oct. 18, *ibid.*, pp. 419-20; and Fleury to Vintimille, Oct. 19, *ibid.*, p. 421.

[80] On the other hand, Petitpied had recently fallen out with many of his colleagues—d'Etemare, Le Gros, Boursier, Jean-Baptiste Desessarts, and the editor of the *Nouvelles ecclésiastiques*—over a number of other theological issues (see *NNEE, passim*; BA, MS 5784, passim; and also BPR, L.P. 445-47, 452-54, which contain scores of tracts and treatises composed during this period).

spired. He had even declared himself quite strongly in favor of its earliest manifestations. By late 1732, however, having been more fully apprised of the actual character of the movement's activities by others much less sympathetic with the convulsionary cause,[81] he began to change his mind. "I am disturbed," he confessed, "that I went so far [in praising the *oeuvre*]. . . . I did not know enough about the convulsions then."[82] By July 1733, the change of opinion was even more complete, as Petitpied found it impossible to defend or countenance the convulsionary movement any longer: "I can only regard the convulsions as a sickness," he wrote, because they are "accompanied by puerile, indecent, [and] extravagant actions, [and] by false predictions which should have opened the eyes of those who had until then viewed this *oeuvre* as divine."[83] Such sentiments, repeated in conversations Petitpied had with Fleury and Vintimille in October 1734, coincided with the position of the civil and ecclesiastical authorities and were soon to be embodied in the *Consultation*.[84]

A thirty-page manuscript was completed by early January 1735. The sponsors of the project, including the abbés Petitpied and d'Asfeld, circulated several copies throughout Paris, soliciting signatures to the tract from some one hundred Jansenist theologians of their acquaintance. Only thirty of their colleagues, all of them former Sorbonne theologians who had been chased from the Faculty during the purge of 1729, joined in signing the *Consultation*.[85] Some of them were no doubt eager to register their convictions in order to ingratiate themselves with the authorities and perhaps thereby obtain permission to resume their positions at the Sorbonne.[86] Self-serving considerations

---

[81] Since 1732, one of the most important figures working to detach Petitpied and other appellants from the convulsionary camp was the indomitable Mme. Duguet-Mol, niece of the *anticonstitutionnaire* abbé Duguet.

[82] Cited in Durand, pp. 341-42.

[83] *Ibid.*, p. 342. On the development of Petitpied's thought on the convulsionaries, see BN, MSS Fr., MS 20115, fols. 20ff.; see also his correspondence, *ibid.*, MS 24876-77, *passim*.

[84] Vintimille to Fleury, Oct. 18, 1734, BM, MS 2358, pp. 419-20, and Fleury to Vintimille, Oct. 19, 1734, *ibid.*, p. 421. Most of the actual writing appears to have been done by the abbé Fouillou; the abbés d'Asfeld and Nivelle were also involved in its preparation (Dedieu "L'agonie du jansénisme," p. 200, n. 75).

[85] Barbier, III, 6 (February 1735); cf. d'Etemare to Soanen, Feb. 25, 1735, BA, MS 5784, fol. 109. For some reason, perhaps to hide his direct engagement in the project, Petitpied's name was not among the four who signed the original manuscript version, nor, for that matter, were the names of the others who helped draw up the *Consultation* (NNEE, March 28, 1735, p. 50).

[86] Abbé Boullenois to Soanen, Jan. 13, 1735, AFA, P.R. 6453. The *curés* of Sainte-Marine and Saint-Germain-le-Vieux, themselves former Sorbonnéens, made a major effort to dissuade their fellow ecclesiastics from adhering to the *Con-*

aside, all of the signatories, including five *anticonstitutionnaire* Paris *curés*, claimed that they had been scandalized by the "undisguised indecency, immorality, and impiety" of the convulsionaries, especially the "fanatical" Augustinistes, and were eager "to repudiate all connection with [the convulsionary movement] both for themselves and for the appellant cause."[87] In any event, within a month their tract had passed through the department of the royal censor, M. Targny, and was granted an official *permission tacite* for publication.[88]

In the very first page of the *Consultation* the authors announced that they had undertaken the work to resolve the doubts of some anonymous person who had been following the activities of the convulsionaries with some perplexity and wanted to understand whether or not the *oeuvre* was of divine inspiration. According to the *consultants*, this unnamed individual had become confused by the seemingly discordant and incompatible character of certain features of the *oeuvre*.[89] To assist him in making up his mind about the convulsionaries, the writers addressed themselves to a series of twelve closely related "questions." The first question dealt with the allegedly divine origin of the sect's activities.[90] The seven questions which followed were concerned with specific features of the *oeuvre*: the predictions, the *secours*, the discourses, and the figurative representations. Question nine raised the problem of "the immodesties and the criminal appearances of some convulsionary operations," the *consultants* asking whether or not these might be excused because of their allegedly symbolic or "figurative" nature.[91] The tenth question dealt with the issue of the alleged supernatural cures which had occasionally occurred in the midst of convulsive seizures. Do such cures, they asked, prove the divine quality of the *oeuvre*? Question eleven demanded if the *oeuvre*, demonstrably tainted with certain "nondivine" elements, could still be regarded as somehow "semi-divine," that is, "un état mêlé."[92] In the twelfth and last question, which involved a direct reference to those Jansenists who had criticized the *consultants* for passing judgment on the *oeuvre* too precipitously,[93] they dealt with the significant proposi-

---

sultation (Rochebouet to Colbert, Jan. 20, 1735, *ibid.*, P.R. 5547; BA, MS 5784, fol. 190).

[87] "Petite relation de la Consultation contre les Convulsions, et quelques anecdotes sur le même sujet," BA, MS 5784, p. 372.

[88] *Ibid.*   [89] *Consultation*, pp. 3, 5-6.

[90] *Ibid.*, p. 6.   [91] *Ibid.*

[92] *Ibid.*, p. 7.

[93] *Plan de diverses questions sur un bruit répandu dans le public, qu'actuellement on fait signer une consultation sur les convulsions* (1735), *passim*.

tion, "whether one must wait for God to declare Himself further, and whether [therefore] one must still suspend one's judgment."[94]

The *consultants* based their responses to their own contrived questions on two fundamental premises enunciated in the next section of the pamphlet. In the first place, they contended that the various activities of the convulsionaries, and hence the different parts of the *oeuvre*, had to be seen in their totality and regarded as a single, unique whole.[95] Second, in rejecting the *discernant* distinction between the so-called divine and nondivine elements, they also rejected, at least by implication, the differentiation between "orthodox" and "fanatical" convulsionaries.[96] For them, consequently, the entire convulsionary movement had to stand or fall as an entity.

From these basic premises the remainder of the *Consultation* followed logically and predictably. The authors rejected out of hand the claim that the *oeuvre* was in any way prophetic, figurative, or divine. They attributed the diverse convulsionary manifestations variously to physical disorder, mental derangement, diabolic possession, or, alternatively, a combination of these causes. Their concluding remarks, embodied in the reply to the twelfth and final question, were especially noteworthy. Both in language and tone they represented conclusions that had already been reached by the authorities themselves:

> After what we have just said in response to the preceding questions, it is evident that there is no longer any [purpose] in waiting to judge the convulsionaries. When one reflects seriously on the matter, one cannot remain in doubt. Everything cries out against [them]. The majesty of God, the sanctity of His worship, the honor of the Church, the purity of morals, public decency [and] order, the maintenance of rules demand that all who are interested in the welfare of the faith must cooperate, with as much zeal as is in them, to put an end to a scandal which has lasted far too long and to an illusion which can only have baneful consequences.
>
> But before finishing, we cannot hold back the righteous indignation which certain outrageous writings, breathing nothing but revolt, must cause to all the king's faithful subjects, who respect in the sacred person of His Majesty the Lord's Anointed, and to all good citizens who love the country and the state. . . . It is the dangerous excess to which . . . the fanaticism of the convulsionaries leads. . . . This current spectacle, authorized by a mis-

[94] *Consultation*, p. 7.   [95] *Ibid.*   [96] *Ibid.*, p. 8.

placed admiration, deserves to be fully scorned. May it forever sink into oblivion![97]

The *consultants* also expressed the hope that the moral revulsion which the Augustinistes had occasioned would induce those *anticonstitutionnaires* still sympathetic to the *oeuvre* to join them in their total repudiation of the convulsionaries.[98]

The *Consultation*, published in early February and widely distributed throughout Paris and even in the provinces, provoked a tremendous reaction from the convulsionists, appalled by what they could only regard as the most serious act of betrayal yet perpetrated by their erstwhile friends and colleagues.[99] The *Nouvelles ecclésiastiques* led the protest, giving over its entire issue of March 28, 1735—expanded to six pages—to an analysis of the *Consultation*.[100] Critics of the tract argued that most of those involved with its composition had made their doctrinal judgments on the basis of hearsay evidence without ever having witnessed the *oeuvre* at first hand. They also noted that the *consultants*, hesitant about compromising in any way their zealous stand against the convulsionaries, had studiously avoided all mention of the miraculous cures of François de Pâris, conveniently ignoring the fact that both the miracles and the convulsions had originally occurred together at Pâris' tomb in Saint-Médard.[101] The convulsionists further argued that the *Consultation* was not representative of *anticonstitutionnaire* thinking on the matter, since it had been drawn up by a mere handful of theologians, signed by a total of thirty, and published without any "consultation" with Bishops Colbert and Soanen or, for that matter, the similarly *discernant* editor of the *Nouvelles ecclésiastiques*.[102] It was the view of these *discernant* critics that the *oeuvre* of the convulsionaries came from God, but that He also permitted the occasional intrusion of "obscure" elements whose meaning it was difficult to interpret and even of a "foreign hand" (the devil), which He employed "to serve His own inscrutable designs."[103] In addition, the *discernants* insisted that the various parts of the *oeuvre* were independent of each other, so that any "effects unworthy of God" which were found in the midst of the convulsions could not taint the other,

---

[97] *Ibid.*, p. 29.   [98] *Ibid.*

[99] See remarks in BHVP, N.A. 125, I, 265.   [100] Pp. 45-50.

[101] *Plan de diverses questions*, p. 15. Cf. criticisms made in abbé Rochebouet to Colbert, Jan. 20, 1735, AFA, P.R. 5547.

[102] Colbert to Caylus, Feb. 25, 1735, *Oeuvres de Colbert*, III, 723-24; d'Etemare to [Roussel?], July 17, 1736, BA, MS 5784, fol. 160.

[103] *Pensées sur les prodiges de nos jours*, p. 13.

indisputably divine elements.[104] At the same time, they conceded that the *oeuvre* by itself constituted neither a rule of faith nor a rule of conduct, but was subject to established rules and laws, and that convulsionaries who violated them were to be recalled to their duties.[105] On these grounds the *discernants* had from the first unequivocally repudiated the view held by the Augustinistes that everything in the *oeuvre*, whatever its character, was equally admirable and wholly divine: what was objectively criminal, immoral, or sacrilegious, they countered, could not possibly be sanctioned by God. On these same grounds, however, they also denounced the *consultants'* identification of a part for the whole. Both the "fanatics" and the *consultants*, they maintained, had failed to "discern" this crucial distinction.[106]

But the critics of the *Consultation* were much more deeply disturbed by the potentially grave political consequences of the tract. Some expressed a general concern that the work might give rise to yet another Formulary-like "test act," whereby *constitutionnaire* bishops could demand adherence to the *Consultation* as a condition of retaining or receiving an ecclesiastical appointment. They were also afraid that the government might single out for persecution those prominent appellant theologians who had refused to sign the manifesto.[107] Others were particularly fearful that the *Consultation* might be more damaging to the convulsionary cause than the earlier Jansenist defections had been, especially because of the timing of its publication. They insisted that the *consultants*, with their public denunciation of the *oeuvre* and their failure to defend the miracles and the appeal, had played into the hands of inveterate enemies, such as Archbishop Languet and Dom La Taste, at a time when these notorious *constitutionnaires* "wish[ed] to profit from the [convulsionaries'] weakness in order to crush them."[108]

Indeed, just as the *discernants* predicted, the *Consultation* did bring considerable aid and comfort to the *constitutionnaires*. Enemies of the convulsionaries, they also relished the divisions that were tearing the Jansenists apart and quickly rushed to embrace the *Consultation* and exploit its conclusions for their own ends. A triumphant Archbishop Languet led the way as usual. On February 25, with almost malignant

---

[104] *Ibid.*, p. 16.   [105] *Ibid.*

[106] "Les magistrats [du Parlement de Paris] savent mieux faire le discernement que les Docteurs," wrote the *curé* Rochebouet to Colbert (Jan. 20, 1735, AFA, P.R. 5547). As the Parlement's *procès* continued, however, the court, too, would eventually obscure the distinction.

[107] Boullenois to Soanen, Jan. 13, 1735, *ibid.*, P.R. 6453.

[108] *Plan de diverses questions*, p. 2; see also *NNEE*, March 28, 1735, p. 45, and Journal of De Lisle, February 1735, AN, U-383.

and unhallowed satisfaction, he published his *Remarques sur la "Consultation des XXX" et sur les Écrits composés pour la combattre*. In this work, which even the royal government criticized for its excessively intemperate language and its harsh, insulting tone, Languet used the *Consultation* as a stick to beat all the Jansenists, including, ironically, "Messieurs les Consultants"![109] The *Supplément des Nouvelles ecclésiastiques*, a journal founded in 1734 by the Jesuit Father Louis Patouillet and others to combat their rivals' own clandestine gazette,[110] also sought to capitalize on the *Consultation* and the discomfiture it caused the appellant defenders of the *oeuvre*. Finally, the Benedictine La Taste continued to devote all his considerable energies, erudition, and polemical resources to demonstrating—what the *consultants* left equivocal—that the convulsionaries were all "dupes of Satan's cunning."[111]

Nor was the *constitutionnaires'* propaganda victory the only significant consequence of the *consultants'* unfortunate timing. The *Consultation* also had an important effect on the *procès* of the Augustinistes going on concurrently in the Parlement of Paris. Some convulsionists insisted that the manifesto was responsible for encouraging the magistrates to proceed with much greater vigor against the entire convulsionary movement.[112] Indeed, the terms used to describe the activities of the various convulsionaries were said to have given support—unwitting or not—to those opponents of the *oeuvre* who had been claiming all along that the sect constituted a factious group of Jansenist

[109] *NNEE*, March 28, 1735, p. 46. Reproaching Languet for his imprudent lack of moderation and charity, an anonymous government *Mémoire sur l'écrit de M. [Languet], "Remarques sur la 'Consultation des XXX' "* (July 1735) observed: "Il me semble que quand des hommes habiles se sont égarés et qu'ils font un pas vers la vérité, il ne faut pas leur faire des reproches sur le passé, mais louer le commencement de leur retour, donner des éloges aux bonnes qualités et faire des voeux afin qu'ils soient tout à fait éclairés et qu'on puisse faire usage de leurs talents" (AAE, M&D, France, MS 1297, fols. 126-27; cf. Daguesseau's similar observations, *ibid.*, fol. 139).

[110] The *Supplément des Nouvelles ecclésiastiques*, published only from 1734 to 1748, issued a manifesto at the head of its first number (Jan. 25, 1734) which is reprinted in Eugène Hatin, *Histoire politique et littéraire de la presse en France*, 4 vols. (Paris, 1859), III, 442-43. To my knowledge there are no copies of the *Supplément* anywhere in the United States, except a microfilm at the University of Chicago and one in my possession. I am planning a study of the short-lived newspaper, about which little has been written.

[111] *Lettres théologiques aux écrivains défenseurs des convulsions et autres prétendus miracles du temps* (1733-40), II, 703.

[112] BA, MS 11304, fol. 117. This was also the view of the counselor Carré de Montgeron (letter to Colbert, July 19, 1735, AFA, P.R. 4935).

subversives plotting to undermine the established order. The allegation of a plot, never disavowed by the authors of the *Consultation*, received widespread publicity in some of the works written during 1735 in support of their tract. What is more, a great effort was reportedly undertaken to make certain that word of such charges reached the Parlement, particularly those magistrates who were most directly involved in the investigation of the convulsionaries.[113] Would all those convulsionaries have been ordered arrested by the counselor Sévert, the *Nouvellistes* asked plaintively, and would the Parlement have acquiesced in their arrests, if this idea of a plot, which the *Consultation*'s conclusions had supported, had not begun to disturb the court?[114] There was also the further problem that at least some of the *consultants* had begun actively to encourage the *Grand'Chambre*'s pursuit of certain convulsionaries. For example, although published anonymously, the vitriolic *Réflexions sur la requête de Charlotte*, an attack both on the petition which Mlle. de la Porte presented to the Parlement in May 1735 and on the convulsionary herself, was known to have come from *consultant* circles.[115]

While contributing to the growing antipathy toward and persecution of the convulsionaries, the *Consultation* did not put an end to the controversy surrounding the *oeuvre*, much less to the convulsionary movement itself. If anything, in fact, it provoked yet another fierce polemical debate among the Jansenists, a debate that would continue to rage in full public view for several more years.[116] The balance of forces, however, had tipped overwhelmingly to the side of the convulsionaries'

[113] *NNEE*, Jan. 7, 1736, p. 3. According to another writer, "des Magistrats qui supposeront que ces Messieurs auront tout pesé au poids du Sanctuaire, prendront à la lettre toutes leurs paroles; ils croiront ne pouvoir mieux faire que de n'en rien rabattre: fondés sur une telle autorité, ils regarderont le nom des Convulsionnaires, comme un nom qui porte avec soi sa tache & son soupçon" (*Exposé de la manière de penser de M. l'abbé [d'Etemare] touchant l'événement des convulsions . . .* , p. 7).

[114] *NNEE*, Jan. 7, 1736, p. 3.

[115] See *ibid.*, Nov. 12, 1735, pp. 177-78, and Jan. 14, 1736, p. 5. Cf. Montgeron to Colbert, Oct. 14, 1735. AFA, P.R. 4935.

[116] The controversy centered on a series of works by the *antidiscernant* Jansenists, especially *Le Système du Mélange dans l'oeuvre des convulsions, confondus par ses ressemblances avec le système des augustinistes, et par les erreurs et les défauts qu'il renferme* (1735), and *Le Système des Discernants dans l'oeuvre des convulsions, confondu par la doctrine des saints Pères* (1735), which denied the distinctions which the opponents of the *Consultation* had sought to make between "divine" and "nondivine" elements of the *oeuvre*. Cf. comments on the dispute in *NNEE, passim*, and in [Soanen] to Joubert, Jan. 20, 1736, BA, MS 5307, fol. 96.

enemies. Already by late 1735 the combination of defections and re-pudiations, embodied in the Parlement's *procès* and the Jansenists' *Consultation*, left the convulsionary cause harassed from all sides and looking bleak indeed. Though the movement would remain a lively subject of theological debate for some time to come, it was no longer to pose the same threat to the authorities that it had appeared to rep-resent in the past. The authorities, however, could hardly claim credit for these developments, though they did manage to take advantage of them. For all the efforts of Fleury, Vintimille, and Hérault to maneuver the convulsionaries into quiescence, the official repressive policies for-mulated by the king's council at Versailles and developed at the archi-episcopal palace and the Châtelet in Paris had made little impact on convulsionary beliefs or practices—except to strengthen the tenacity and increase the commitment of the movement's adherents. Indeed, the history of the early 1730s suggests that the power to quash such a movement through a policy of repression was not really there, and that even the king's authority was insufficient to do it so long as literate opinion could identify with the followers of François de Pâris. It was the knowledge and rumor, broadly disseminated, of "bizarre" con-vulsionary activities which ultimately turned most "educated" groups —including many *anticonstitutionnaire* judges, lawyers, priests, and theologians who had until then supported the movement's spiritual aspirations—against the *oeuvre* and permitted Cardinal Fleury to ac-complish what he did. In short, in the eyes of the *gens raisonnables* the convulsionaries had discredited themselves. The more extravagant and "enthusiastic" their behavior seemed to be, the more "radical" and millenarian the views they were believed to espouse, the less at-tractive and worthy of support they appeared to those who described all this as "bizarre."[117]

As an issue of religious politics the problem of the convulsionaries had thus been virtually set aside. Even so, the equally vital issue of the Pâris miracles, of miracles authenticated by "sane," "rational" men, still remained far from resolved. The controversy over that vexed question—a controversy into which such luminaries as Voltaire, Hume, and John Wesley would eventually intrude themselves—would not reach its climax for some time to come.

[117] Cf. analysis of Cardinal Fleury (letter to Cardinal Corradini, Aug. 5, 1737, AAE, C.P., Rome, MS 764, esp. fols. 164-65).

CHAPTER IX

Miracles and Religious Politics: A Last Reprise

For several years the turmoil surrounding the convulsionaries had overshadowed the separate, though related, issue of the Pâris miracles, which had nevertheless remained a subject of lively contention in its own right during this period. Although the advent of the convulsionaries, and especially of the Augustinistes, had occasioned widespread *anticonstitutionnaire* defections from the *oeuvre*, the lines of debate over the miracles were still drawn essentially between proponents and opponents of the bull *Unigenitus*. This renewed controversy, which had been raging since early 1733, was to continue for more than four years and would once again draw all the contending forces of eighteenth-century ecclesiastical politics back into the fray. Though the *constitutionnaires* were ultimately successful in dealing with the political and ecclesiastical aspects of this problem, as they were in the matter of the convulsionaries, their "victory" would not be untainted nor would it come without great effort. What is more, it was to be an achievement which would not give the authorities complete satisfaction, since the popular cult which they had been seeking to stifle for almost a decade would survive the struggles of the 1730s and remain a vital spiritual, if no longer a significant political, phenomenon well after Fleury, Vintimille, and the others had passed from the scene.

The latest "querelle sur les miracles" began as a dispute among bishops, but also directly involved the royal government. As before, the prolific and indefatigable Colbert, dubbed the "apologist of the miracles," bore the major responsibility for rekindling the debate. On February 1, 1733, some two weeks prior to the appearance of the second royal ordinance against the convulsions, he issued a celebrated *Instruction pastorale* on the Pâris miracles.[1] The first formal episcopal letter on behalf of the miracles of and cult to François de Pâris, the instruction constituted at the same time a deliberate—and inevitably

---

[1] *Instruction pastorale de monseigneur l'évêque de Montpellier adressée au clergé et aux fidèles de son diocèse, au sujet des miracles que Dieu fait en faveur des appelants de la bulle "Unigenitus,"* in *Oeuvres,* II, 13-50.

provocative—defense of the appellant cause. It was, in short, a compendium and summary of the various theological and political arguments made to that point by *anticonstitutionnaire* supporters of the Pâris cult. The *Nouvelles ecclésiastiques*, as expected, heaped praise upon the author, as did other leading appellants.[2] The *avocat* Barbier even spoke of the work in glowing terms.[3] The government, however, took a rather different view.

As usual the crown was concerned that the pastoral instruction might weaken royal and ecclesiastical authority and disturb the civil and religious order. On April 25, 1733, therefore, a decree of the *conseil d'état* suppressed the work.[4] According to the royal *arrêt*, Colbert's letter had been issued without privilege and without the name of the printer—a blatant violation of the censorship laws. The instruction was said to depict the Church as being "threatened with imminent destruction and with a revolution that will cause the succession of a new Church, composed of those who resist the present one." "The prophetic tone of the work," the council contended, "may spread groundless fears and false impressions in the minds of the people, inspire them with aversion or scorn for the Pope and for the Bishops, and diminish or weaken in their hearts respect for the faith itself."[5] The *arrêt* contained not a word about the miracles, the very subject of the condemned instruction, the royal council presumably regarding such theological pronouncements as outside its jurisdiction or competence.[6]

Although the council's silence on the question of the miracles was understandable, to the numerous *constitutionnaire* bishops and theologians residing in Paris and at Versailles the royal *arrêt* had not gone far enough. For a long time many of them had been clamoring for Fleury's government to take stronger, more direct action against their Jansenist colleague from Montpellier. The idea of bringing Colbert before a provincial council like the one at Embrun which had deposed Jean Soanen from his see at Senez had been under discussion for more than a decade and had received considerable support in Rome.[7] For

[2] *NNEE*, June 22, 1733, p. 125. See also Jérôme-Nicolas de Pâris to Colbert, May 29, 1733, AFA, P.R. 5455.

[3] II, 400 (April 1733). [4] BN, MSS Fr., MS 22091, fols. 90-91.
[5] *Ibid.*

[6] On the difficult question and delicate nature of royal/civil competence in such matters, see Daguesseau to Chauvelin, Oct. 29, 1733, AAE, M&D, France, MS 1284, fols. 124-25. See also Languet to [Chauvelin?], Aug. 6, 1734, *ibid.*, MS 1289, fol. 334.

[7] The 1730 sessions of the Assembly of the Clergy had taken up the subject in especially great earnest (see Vintimille to Fleury, Aug. 29, 1730, BM, MS 2357, pp. 233-35). See also Marcel Laurent, "Deux évêques contre la bulle Uni-

various reasons, however, such a council, proposed for Narbonne, was never actually called—a fact which had brought great frustration to Colbert's host of enemies. In the spring of 1733 a group of these *constitutionnaire* prelates held a series of conferences at which they considered a number of alternative proposals.[8] Supported by Cardinals Bissy and Rohan, they recommended the convocation of a national council as the sole means of resolving the conflicts then convulsing the Gallican Church, including the problem of Colbert and the question of the miracles. In prolonged discussions among the royal ministers and in correspondence exchanged between Rome and Versailles there was considerable division of opinion as to the prudence of such an enterprise.[9] Although plans for an assembly were actually drawn up and approval obtained from Rome, it was finally decided that the "dangers and inconveniences" anticipated from a meeting of that sort would only exacerbate the religious crisis. What is more, the growing emergency associated with the Polish succession question was beginning to occupy more and more of the government's attention, convincing Cardinal Fleury of the wisdom of abandoning the proposed assembly at this time.[10]

In the meantime, however, a few of the more zealous *constitutionnaire* bishops had grown very impatient. Having already warmed to the challenge of Colbert's latest pastoral instruction, these contentious prelates resolved on issuing their own replies, authorized or not. Despite various royal decrees commanding silence, Archbishop Tencin of Embrun opened the attack with a series of replies to Colbert. A brief pastoral letter and ordinance published in May simply prohibited the reading of Colbert's work.[11] But in August, Tencin drew up a pastoral instruction of his own, longer and more important than his earlier letter

---

genitus: L'amitié de J. Soanen et de J. Colbert de Croissy," *Chroniques de Port-Royal*, No. 19 (1971), pp. 56-57, 62, 64.

[8] Several bishops reportedly even proposed that all relations with the appellants be entirely broken off, "un schisme ouvert," but a majority rejected the idea (see *NNEE*, June 29, 1733, p. 131).

[9] Fleury to Cardinal Corradini, April 13, 1733, AAE, M&D, Fonds divers (Rome), MS 74, fols. 27-29; on the discussions held between May and July 1733, see *ibid.*, fols. 65-78. See also the analysis in Sareil, p. 245. Strongest opposition to the convocation of a council apparently came from Chauvelin (see AAE, M&D, Fonds divers [Rome], MS 75, fol. 91, and Chauvelin to Saint-Aignan, Dec. 7, 1734, *ibid.*, MS 74, fol. 210).

[10] *Ibid.*, fol. 206.

[11] *Lettre pastorale et ordonnance de monseigneur l'archevêque d'Embrun, portant défense de lire un écrit intitulé: "Instruction pastorale de monseigneur l'évêque de Montpellier . . ."* (10 mai 1733).

and ordinance, in which he undertook a direct refutation of Colbert.[12]
All of these pieces were filled with what the *Nouvelles ecclésiastiques*
described as "indecent rantings," Tencin allegedly treating Colbert, his
archenemy since the Council of Embrun, "without any respect, like a
heresiarch."[13] He accused Colbert of attempting to weaken, if not destroy, the traditional conception of miracles, "the divine promises that
serve as the foundation of the Church of Jesus Christ."[14] Joining the
archbishop of Embrun in the onslaught against Colbert was Bishop La
Fare of Laon, who since 1731 had been the most outspoken and intemperate critic of the Pâris cult. In a *mandement* dated July 1, 1733, La
Fare condemned Colbert's "monstrous work" for authorizing an "outrageous fanaticism" and for "consecrating and canonizing . . . widespread disobedience toward the decisions of the Church."[15]

While La Fare's episcopal decree was eventually suppressed by an
arrêt du conseil of October 22, 1733,[16] both his work and those of
Tencin received considerable, if indirect, support from Rome when
Pope Clement XII likewise condemned Colbert's instruction, primarily
on doctrinal grounds. In a brief published on October 3, the pope,
conspicuously silent for more than a year on the matter of the Pâris
cult, denounced the pastoral instruction for containing propositions
which were "false, scandalous, seditious, outrageous, absurd, rash,
blasphemous, schismatic, erroneous, and notoriously heretical."[17]

Despite the formidable arsenal of royal *arrêt*, episcopal decrees, and
papal brief arrayed against him, Colbert was not prepared to give up
the battle without a hard fight. On July 26, 1733, the bishop addressed
a letter to the king, defending himself against the crimes which his
various detractors (including the *conseil d'état*) had imputed to him.[18]
Colbert insisted that he was perfectly justified, as successor to the
Apostles, in speaking out as he had "in order to warn my brothers of

---

[12] *Instruction pastorale de monseigneur l'archevêque-prince d'Embrun, dans
laquelle il réfute l'ouvrage qui a paru sous ce titre: "Instruction pastorale de
monseigneur l'évêque de Montpellier . . ."* (5 août 1733).

[13] Jan. 20, 1734, p. 15. [14] Cited *ibid.*, Sept. 15, 1734, p. 160.

[15] *Mandement de monseigneur l'évêque-duc de Laon au sujet de quatre imprimés, dont . . . le quatrième [a pour titre]: "Instruction pastorale de M. l'évêque
de Montpellier . . ."* (1 juillet 1733), p. 11.

[16] Cf. AAE, M&D, France, MS 1284, fols. 277-84. Tencin's two works were not
suppressed, suggesting that despite their violation of the declarations of silence,
his efforts may actually have had the approval of the government (see Sareil,
p. 213).

[17] Cited by Barbier, II, 499-500 (September 1734).

[18] *Lettre de monseigneur l'évêque de Montpellier au roi, au sujet de l'Arrêt
du Conseil d'Etat, du 25 avril 1733 . . .* (26 juillet 1733), in *Oeuvres*, II, 51-56.

the evils which may threaten us if we do not wake up."[19] He was particularly disturbed by the council's insinuation that he was somehow responsible for provoking "a revolution [within the Church] from which will emerge a new Church composed of those who resist the present one."[20] Though he was prepared to acknowledge the "revolutionary" character of his activities, Colbert denied that he or anyone else who believed as he did was undermining the Church or threatening it with imminent destruction. According to the bishop, this "revolution," far from subversive or intended to create a new Church, "will produce a renewal of piety, zeal, [and] charity in the members of the Church. . . ."[21] Indeed, Colbert argued, the continued incidence of miracles was an ongoing demonstration against the bull *Unigenitus*, proof that it was neither the work of the Church nor the work of God. The king, therefore, must needs respect the divine presence manifested in the miracles: "May Your Majesty have the goodness to weigh the force of this testimony," Colbert implored. "[You] will not be able to deny the evidence."[22] It was not to be the last time that the king would receive such a direct appeal on behalf of the Pâris cult and the *anticonstitutionnaire* cause. Like all the others, however, it fell on deaf ears. The *conseil d'état*'s condemnation was not lifted.

Colbert's replies to the pope and to the *constitutionnaire* bishops came several months later. His response to Clement XII was contained in the first part of a long pastoral letter addressed to the clergy and faithful of his diocese on April 21, 1734, and circulated throughout the kingdom.[23] He began by expressing his resentment at having to defend himself publicly against the unjust condemnation made without proof, and against the "flood of degrading epithets which the First of the Ministers of God applies to a [tract] intended to make known the very works of God."[24] The bishop went on to announce that, in any event, he had already obtained divine vindication of his position. On October 4, 1733, the very day after the publication of the papal condemnation, one of Colbert's faithful, a certain Marie Boissonnade, had experienced a miraculous cure through the intercession of Fran-

---

[19] *Ibid.*, pp. 6, 8.

[20] These words were drawn from the *arrêt* itself.

[21] *Lettre de [Colbert]*, p. 11.   [22] Cf. *NNEE*, Nov. 3, 1733, p. 224.

[23] *Lettre pastorale de monseigneur l'évêque de Montpellier, adressée au clergé et aux fidèles de son diocèse, pour leur notifier d'un miracle opéré dans son diocèse par l'intercession de M. François de Pâris, et les prémunir contre un bref de N. S.-P. le pape en date du 3 octobre 1733, et deux écrits de M. l'archevêque d'Embrun de la même année (21 avril 1734)*, in *Oeuvres*, II, 57-92.

[24] *Ibid.*, pp. 57-59; also cited in *NNEE*, Sept. 15, 1734, p. 159.

çois de Pâris.[25] "Thus," wrote the exultant bishop of Montpellier, invoking the miracle on his behalf, "God wishes to avenge me for this frightful decree."[26]

Having disposed of the papal condemnation, Colbert devoted the remainder of his pastoral letter to a response to Archbishop Tencin in which he was far more aggressive in tone.[27] Drawing support for his position from scriptural sources and the precedents of Church tradition, Colbert presented a stinging denunciation of his opponent which, like Tencin's, went well beyond the issue of the miracles to a consideration of the fundamental theological and ecclesiastical questions at stake between the *constitutionnaire* and *anticonstitutionnaire* parties. According to Barbier, who regretted the entire affair, Colbert "insult[ed] M. Embrun, treat[ed] him as ignorant, as a man barely versed in Scripture [and] of very questionable faith. . . ."[28] Though Colbert may have scored the debating points, Tencin and his party still had the government on their side.

On August 28, 1734, the *conseil d'état*, acting on the advice of Chancellor Daguesseau,[29] suppressed Colbert's pastoral letter for being "contrary to the respect owed to the Church and to the king and for tending to arouse controversy and to disturb public tranquility."[30] The council chose to ignore completely Colbert's impassioned letter to the king, in which the bishop had sought to defend himself against a variety of charges stemming from the publication of his first pastoral instruction on the miracles. Instead, the council attempted to justify its latest *arrêt* on rather familiar grounds, arguing that Colbert's recent pastoral decree had been written "in the same spirit" as the earlier one, and that it was "just as rash, perhaps even more dangerous than the first," that it was filled with rancor and enmity for the Bull, the pope, and all the bishops united to Rome, "without even sparing the Church itself." The *arrêt* further charged Colbert with "opposing . . . miracles to the infallible authority of the Church . . . [and with thereby] establishing principles capable of shaking the only solid foundation upon which the submission of the faithful was based." Finally, the council denounced him for seeking to alarm the faithful, in ominously

---

[25] *Oeuvres*, II, 59-62, *et passim*; *pièces justificatives* may be found in an appendix (*ibid.*, pp. 89-92). See also *NNEE*, Dec. 28, 1733, p. 260.

[26] Cited in Durand, p. 327. Cf. Jérôme-Nicolas de Pâris to Colbert, Nov. 5, 1733, AFA, P.R. 5455, and Colbert to [d'Etemare?], Nov. 23, 1733, BA, MS 5784, p. 54.

[27] *Oeuvres*, II, 70-88.

[28] Barbier, II, 500 (September 1734); cf. *NNEE*, Sept. 22, 1734, p. 161.

[29] Fleury to Vintimille, Aug. 17, 1734, BM, MS 2358, p. 397.

[30] BN, MSS Fr., MS 22091, fols. 170-71; cf. *NNEE*, Sept. 22, 1734, p. 168.

prophetic tones, about some supposed dangers threatening the Church from within.[31]

The *conseil d'état* was keeping itself busy, suppressing pastoral letters almost with a vengeance. Within less than a year and a half Colbert had twice fallen victim to the council's wrath.[32] The same fate befell Colbert's colleague, Bishop Caylus of Auxerre, who had joined the episcopal debate over the Pâris miracles during the previous year.[33] On December 26, 1733, despite considerable vocal opposition from a number of *curés* in his diocese, Caylus published a pastoral decree describing the sudden cure of a domestic named Edmée (or Aimée) Desvignes of Seignelay.[34] The decree was significant because the bishop himself had conducted an intensive investigation of the cure and duly authenticated it as miraculous. It was, in fact, the first of the Pâris miracles to have been juridically verified and formally published by a French bishop in accordance with rules laid down by the Council of Trent. However, the decree contained more than just a simple recitation of the miracle—a matter that was clearly the prerogative of the bishop. Strongly committed to the *anticonstitutionnaire* cause, Caylus drew for his flock the appropriate lessons about the bull *Unigenitus*, "lessons" which challenged the royal government and its official ecclesiastical policy. On March 28, 1734, therefore, after Chancellor Daguesseau had undertaken a careful examination of the pastoral decree, the *conseil d'état* issued yet another *arrêt*, emphatically suppressing the

[31] *Ibid*. Papal authorities were incensed at Colbert's latest pastoral letter, but the diplomatic efforts of the duc de Saint-Aignan apparently succeeded in preventing Clement XII from actually publishing a second decree, though one was drawn up (Saint-Aignan to Chauvelin, Oct. 23, 1734, AAE, M&D, Fonds divers [Rome], MS 64, fols. 183-86; Chauvelin to Saint-Aignan, Nov. 11, 1734, *ibid*., fols. 187-88; Saint-Aignan to Chauvelin, Nov. 12, 1734, *ibid*., fols. 189-90; Saint-Aignan to Chauvelin, Nov. 19, 1734, *ibid*., fols. 191-95; Chauvelin to Saint-Aignan, Dec. 7, 1734, *ibid*., fols. 195-98).

[32] To be sure, the council had also been busying itself suppressing *constitutionnaire* decrees and letters as well. The relative silence of the Parlement of Paris throughout much of this period may in fact have been bought as part of a *quid pro quo* accommodation (see Ch. VIII above).

[33] For a brief exchange of views between Fleury and Vintimille regarding Bishop Caylus, whom the archbishop of Paris described as an "insolent troublemaker," see: Vintimille to Fleury, March 21, 1734, Fleury to Vintimille, March 28, 1734, and Vintimille to Fleury, April 2, 1734, BM, MS 2358, pp. 331-32, 339. Cf. Léon Noël, "Une semonce du cardinal de Fleury à Monseigneur de Caylus," *Congrès de l'Association bourguignonne des sociétés savantes*, 31 (1960), pp. 265-69.

[34] *Mandement de monseigneur l'évêque d'Auxerre, à l'occasion du miracle opéré dans la ville de Seignelay, de ce diocèse, le 6 janvier 1733, jour de l'Epiphanie (26 décembre 1733)*. Cf. discussion in *NNEE*, April 23, 1734, pp. 71-72.

work, principally on the grounds of its attacks against the Bull.[35] At the same time, Caylus' report of the Seignelay miracle also provoked a brief flurry of polemical exchanges, beginning with an anonymous *constitutionnaire* tract which sought to discredit the bishop's entire investigation as well as to heap scorn upon him.[36]

Yet to be heard from in this series of public exchanges between appellant and *constitutionnaire* prelates was Archbishop Languet of Sens, the fierce, but capable polemicist, who had become one of Cardinal Fleury's principal advisers on ecclesiastical affairs. By the end of 1734, increasingly disturbed by the pastoral decrees of Colbert and Caylus[37] and angered by the unauthorized publication of allegedly miraculous cures within his own diocese, Languet rejoined the battle in earnest. On Christmas Day he published a long and sometimes intemperate three-part pastoral instruction, written with government approval and addressed not merely to the clergy and faithful of his own diocese, but to the entire Gallican Church.[38] The second and third parts dealt with both the miracles and the convulsions. In section two, Languet intended to show "that there was nothing in these [bizarre phenomena] which proved with certainty that God, and not the devil, was their author."[39] In section three, largely based on the infamous, error-filled *Journal des convulsions* of Mme. Duguet-Mol, the archbishop sought to

---

[35] See Fleury to Vintimille, March 28, 1734, BM, MS 2358, p. 332. Text of the decree cited in *NNEE*, April 23, 1734, p. 72. The *Nouvellistes* offered some caustic comments in response to this *arrêt*: "Si quelqu'un doutoit encore que ce soit un parti pris de la Cour de ne souffrir l'examen ou du moins la publication d'aucun miracle attribué à Monsieur de Pâris, quelqu'évidente qu'en soit d'ailleurs la certitude, il en sera apparemment convaincu lorsqu'il apprendra que le Mandement de M. l'Evêque d'Auxerre a été supprimé par un Arrêt du Conseil . . ." (*ibid.*).

[36] *Lettre d'Auxerre, du 18 mars 1734, contenant une relation fidèle de l'invention et de la publication du prétendu miracle opéré à Seignelay dans la personne d'Edmée Desvignes*. The reply was contained in a *Lettre d'Auxerre, du 20 avril 1734, où l'on réfute celle du 18 mars au sujet du miracle de Seignelay*. A counter-response followed: *Réfutation des moyens de défense de M. d'Auxerre publiées par un anonyme soi-disant Auxerrois, dans une Lettre du 20 avril 1734, pour servir de réponse au Supplément du 15 mars et à la Relation du prétendu miracle de Seignelay*. See also the *Courtes Réflexions d'un laïque, au sujet de l'Arrêt du Conseil contre le Mandement de M. d'Auxerre qui publie un miracle opéré dans son diocèse par l'intercession de M. de Pâris*. Cf. discussion in *NNEE*, June 18, 1734, p. 106.

[37] See long letter from Languet to [Chauvelin?], Aug. 6, 1734, AAE, M&D, France, MS 1289, fols. 334-35.

[38] *Instruction pastorale . . . au sujet des prétendus miracles du diacre de Saint-Médard et des convulsions arrivées à son tombeau (25 décembre 1734)*.

[39] Cited in *NNEE*, Jan. 28, 1735, p. 14.

demonstrate why "one must never listen to miracles to the prejudice of the body of bishops united with the pope," as well as to prove that the activities of the convulsionaries were exactly like those of the Camisard fanatics of the Cévennes.[40] But it was the first part, which dealt only with the question of the miracles, that provoked the greatest storm of protest. Languet denied the validity of the seventeen miraculous cures which the *curés* of Paris had announced in 1731 in their two petitions to Vintimille. He also declared the cures announced by Colbert, Caylus, and certain ecclesiastics in his own diocese of Sens to be "false, misleading, the wretched fruits of a manifest seduction; effects of the prejudice of some, the credulity of others, [and] the deceit of several: [they reflected the] intrigue, duplicity, fraud, delusion . . . in a word, the shame of the [Jansenist] party which is producing and praising them."[41] There was nothing particularly new about this kind of denunciation; other *constitutionnaires* had condemned the miracles in language and tone just as harsh as Languet's. Far more provocative, however, was the archbishop's disrespectful treatment and defamation of the Parisian *curés*. He charged them with having employed fraudulent measures in order to get the cures of M. Pâris authorized as miracles. He also accused them of being factious "sectaries" who were trying every means possible to "canonize their party."[42] Like Vintimille before him, Languet soon discovered that the sensitivity and influence of these priests were not to be taken lightly.

Indeed, it was as a direct consequence of Languet's pastoral instruction that the character of the public debate over the miracles, for almost two years primarily a duel of bishops, was dramatically altered. Once again serious questions of ecclesiastical prerogative had been injected into the controversy, and the *curés* of Paris, past masters at the game of religious politics, were quick to take up Languet's challenge. Disturbed both by the archbishop's contemptuous treatment of them and by his condemnation of the miracles, twenty-three *curés*, including five who had earlier signed the *Consultation contre les convulsions*,[43] presented the Parlement of Paris with a thirty-six-page *requête* asking to be received as *appelants comme d'abus* against the envenomed pastoral instruction.[44] They accused Languet of having committed a series of

---

[40] *Ibid.*, June 21, 1735, p. 97.   [41] *Ibid.*, Nov. 1, 1734, p. 185.
[42] *Ibid.*, p. 186.
[43] The five *curés* were Goy, Charpentier, Thomassin, Bence, and Secousse. The fact that they were signatories of both the *requête* and the *Consultation des Trente* is a rather significant indication that, for some *anticonstitutionnaires* at least, the miracles and convulsions had become entirely separate issues.
[44] *Requête présentée au parlement par vingt-trois curés de la ville, faubourgs et*

offenses. A "foreign prelate," he had interfered in matters of exclusive concern to the diocese of Paris and therefore beyond his jurisdiction.[45] He had presumed to question the legitimacy of the investigation which the abbé Achille Thomassin had conducted with the complete authorization of the late Cardinal-Archbishop Noailles.[46] Without any evidence, he had denounced as false and contrived cures which a juridical examination had demonstrated to be miraculous. Finally, he had opposed true facts and convincing proofs merely with "insidious reasoning, vague presumptions, odious conjectures, [and] obscure acts, born out of passion [and] originated by suspicious or discredited persons."[47] By way of rebuttal, the *curés* presented a detailed discussion of the four miracles which the Thomassin commission had investigated in 1728; they also made extensive references to the many others attributed to François de Pâris since then. But they were not finished.

What the *curés* found most intolerable about Languet's pastoral instruction was that the archbishop, not content with attempting to undermine the miracles, had directed "scandalous and defamatory remarks" against them.[48] Languet, they contended, had unjustly accused them of attempting to seduce their "credulous parishioners" with "criminal intrigues."[49] Even worse, he had gone so far as to suggest that Vintimille, who had never officially answered the *curés'* two *requêtes* of 1731, should now reply with an unequivocal denunciation of those petitions and announce that "the Church disregards the miracles of sectaries." The *curés* insisted that such a statement established beyond any doubt the abusive character of the pastoral instruction: "By this single expression both the late M. Noailles and the supplicants are stigmatized with the most odious epithet. . . . Can one listen without horror to such a libel? Has there ever been an action tending more overtly to schism and to agitating the supplicants' parishioners against their legitimate pastors?"[50]

A council of ten *avocats*[51] heard the complaints of the *curés*. In their

---

banlieue de Paris, contre l'Instruction pastorale de M. Languet . . . (5 mai 1735). Plans for a concerted response to Languet had already been under discussion since January (see Rochebouet to Colbert, Jan. 20, 1735, AFA, P.R. 5547). On this affair see also AAE, M&D, France, MS 1298, fols. 250-54.

[45] *Requête présentée au parlement,* p. 5.

[46] Thomassin's brother, it is worth noting, was one of the five *curés* who signed both the *requête* and the *Consultation des Trente.*

[47] Cited in *NNEE,* July 23, 1735, p. 116.

[48] *Requête présentée au parlement,* p. 32.

[49] *Ibid.,* p. 3.   [50] *Ibid.,* p. 36.

[51] These were the same *avocats*—Le Roy, Le Roy de Vallières, De La Vignes,

published *consultation*, composed by the Jansenist Aubry,[52] they agreed
that Languet had acted improperly in issuing a public censure of parish
priests over whom he had absolutely no jurisdiction, and that his instruction did indeed contain excessively provocative and needlessly
abusive language. They recommended, therefore, that the Parlement,
"always concerned to preserve the tranquility of the Church and the
State and to restrain all actions which tend toward schism," should
receive the *curés'* appeal.[53] As expected, the Parlement admitted the
requête and the accompanying legal report of the *avocats*. On May
5, 1735, with the abbé Pucelle acting as *rapporteur* in the case, the
Grand'Chambre issued an *arrêt* authorizing the *curés'* petition to be
forwarded to the *procureur-général* for further action.[54] The government, however, was anxious to avert another bitter struggle within
the Church and between bishops and magistrates. The king's council
thus forbade the court to hear the case or to pass any judgment on it.
The magistrates, after voicing their usual strenuous objections to this
latest interference with their duly constituted prerogatives, reluctantly
agreed to comply with the royal order.

Despite the government's refusal to permit the Paris Parlement to
pursue the *appel comme d'abus* and the magistrates' resigned acquiescence in that decision, the controversy over Languet's pastoral letter
abated only gradually. Agitation on the part of the *curés* continued
intermittently well into the fall. In addition, a number of tracts appeared which denounced the archbishop of Sens and applauded the
efforts of the *curés*.[55] By the end of the year, however, a good deal
of attention had begun to shift back once again to the archbishop of
Paris, as Msgr. Vintimille was forced to enter the fray himself. The
charges and countercharges exchanged between Languet and the Paris
curés involved matters that clearly belonged within Vintimille's pur-

---

Du Hamel, Prévost, Guillet de Blaru, Pothouin, Visinier, Aubry, and Le Roy,
fils—who were later to draw up the *consultations* for two of the convulsionaries
(Denise Regné and Charlotte de la Porte) prosecuted by the counselor Sévert
(see Ch. VIII above).

[52] *NNEE*, Dec. 19, 1739, p. 198. The *consultation* was published in conjunction
with the *curés'* petition to the Parlement.

[53] *Requête présentée au parlement*, p. 37.

[54] Journal of De Lisle, May 1735, AN, U-384.

[55] *Requête présentée à Momus par M. l'archevêque de Sens, au sujet d'un écrit
qui a pour titre: "Requête présentée par les curés de Paris . . . ,"* and *Lettre
écrite à Msgr. l'archevêque de Sens, par un clerc de son diocèse, au sujet de sa
conduite dans les affaires présentes de la religion (29 mai 1735)*. Cf. also *Réplique
à un écrit intitulé: "Requête présentée au parlement par 23 curés de la ville,
faubourgs et banlieue de Paris . . ."* (1736).

view. The continuation of the controversy over the miracles of François de Pâris, to which Vintimille had remained a mere spectator for
some time, could not help placing him in an increasingly untenable
position. As a result, after having stood aside from the debate for
nearly three years, Vintimille was finally prepared to break his long
silence—a silence which had been only partly self-imposed.

During a period extending all the way back to 1731—and as recently
as their latest petition to the Parlement—the *curés* of Paris had repeatedly reproached Vintimille for his refusal to respond to their two
requêtes on the miracles. They had even expressed a willingness to
cooperate in an episcopal examination and to furnish the diocesan authorities with all the relevant materials and evidence they could discover. But their appeals and suggestions fell on deaf ears. In the meantime, satirical songs and *estampes*, critical pamphlets and broadsides,
vicious libels and lampoons continued to taunt Vintimille for his silence and challenged him to order a juridical investigation into the
miracles.[56]

Despite the veil of official silence with which the archbishop had
apparently shrouded the question of the Pâris miracles, Vintimille had
by no means been ignoring the subject. On the contrary, preliminary
discussions concerning a proposed pastoral decree were already under
way as early as the beginning of 1733.[57] With advice and encouragement from Cardinal Fleury and others at Versailles, Vintimille and
his own council of theologians proceeded carefully, but steadily, to
sift through the *procès-verbaux* compiled for Cardinal Noailles in 1728,
as well as through other evidence gathered since then. They inspected
and studied all the available materials, weighing them in the light of
accepted doctrine on the nature of miracles. The task was a delicate
one, requiring not only painstaking care in the investigations but also
extreme caution in the wording of the eventual decree so as to avoid
unnecessarily offending the sensibilities of the Paris *curés* or inadvertently provoking the magistrates in the Parlement into renewed
hostilities with their archbishop. Cardinal Fleury even had a series of
guidelines—a "Plan de l'Ecrit que l'on peut faire sur les miracles"—
drawn up for Vintimille, which contained suggestions as to what points
the archbishop might include and what questions he ought to avoid.[58]

[56] 3ᵉ *Recueil des miracles opérés au tombeau de M. de Pâris*, p. 59; 4ᵉ *Recueil
des miracles* . . . , p. 32.

[57] Vintimille to Fleury, Feb. 5, 1733, BM, MS 2358, p. 28.

[58] The *mémoire* was dated May 28, 1733, AAE, M&D, France, MS 1283, fols.
105-107.

By late June, Vintimille had completed a draft of his decree and sent it on to Versailles. Although Fleury congratulated his friend on the work and acknowledged that it would be "very useful and important [if we are] to try to disabuse the foolish and the credulous of their faith in this supposed saint,"[59] several of the cardinal-minister's advisers, including Chauvelin and Joly de Fleury, had serious misgivings and recommended a delay in its publication.[60] They believed that there was no urgency about issuing the decree and only dangerous results to be expected from acting too precipitously. Out of a sense of "cautious prudence and moderation," and out of an abiding fear of exposing himself to additional *appels comme d'abus*, Vintimille agreed to postpone the publication of his *ordonnance*, at least for the moment.[61] In maintaining his silence, Vintimille hoped he might help restore a spirit of peace and harmony within the diocese.

While publication of his decree was temporarily suspended, Vintimille and his advisers continued to work on their project, which went through several more drafts in the following year.[62] But the representations of Cardinal Fleury and the archbishop's own apparent faint-heartedness combined to delay the promulgation of the decree for over two years. However, the appearance of Languet's pastoral instruction of December 1734 and the petition which twenty-three Paris *curés* subsequently presented to the Parlement served to arouse in Vintimille a sense of anger and frustration. Developments in 1735 awakened him to a realization that the *curés* had taken unfair advantage of his policy of moderation and accommodation and that as far as these disobedient priests were concerned, his continued silence would not serve the cause of peace and harmony for which he had been so ardently yearning all these years.[63] Since the *curés* had now forced

[59] June 25, 1733, BM, MS 2358, p. 157. See also Vintimille to Fleury, June 26, 1733, *ibid.*, p. 159.

[60] Chauvelin to abbé Couet, June 26, 1733, AAE, M&D, France, MS 1284, fol. 241; Chauvelin to Couet, July 2 and 6, 1733, *ibid.*, MS 1283, fols. 265-66; Chauvelin to Couet, Oct. 6, 1733, *ibid.*, MS 1284, fol. 90; and Joly de Fleury to Chauvelin, July 15, 1733, BN, J.F., MS 134, fol. 68.

[61] On Vintimille's timidity regarding the *curés* and the Parlement, see Fleury to Cardinal Corradini, April 13, 1733, AAE, M&D, Fonds divers (Rome), MS 74, fols. 27-29.

[62] Vintimille to Fleury, April 2, 1734, BM, MS 2358, pp. 339-40.

[63] Vintimille to Fleury, May 5, 1735, *ibid.*, p. 516. Cf. Vintimille to Fleury, Aug. 13, 1735, *ibid.*, pp. 578-79. According to the *NNEE*, Vintimille was also probably "secrètement jaloux de l'usurpation de M. de Sens" (March 10, 1736, p. 37). A longstanding, if unspoken, rivalry existed between the sees of Paris and Sens. Languet's "officious intrusion" in this matter may have reflected a continuing

his hand, the time had come for immediate and decisive action. Cardinal Fleury concurred.[64] Even so, Vintimille was forced to suffer another series of delays and postponements along with several rounds of consultations and revisions—in the archbishop's own best interests, if not always with his total consent.

In May it was recommended that Vintimille wait until at least after the forthcoming quinquennial Assembly of the Clergy, over which the archbishop would be presiding, had completed its work. Certain advisers were fearful that, in the event the *ordonnance* were published in advance of the Assembly and it happened to provoke the *curés* into presenting still another *appel comme d'abus* to the Parlement, such an appeal would prove embarrassing to Vintimille and seriously disrupt the ecclesiastical proceedings. Moreover, the "wicked Jansenists," adroit propagandists that they were, could be expected to take advantage of such a situation and provoke a bitter confrontation between Assembly and Parlement.[65]

In mid-August, with the Assembly just about to adjourn, there were further delays. Despite the growing sense of urgency conveyed in Vintimille's letters to Fleury, the cardinal-minister still recommended additional revisions. "In so delicate a matter," he contended, "one cannot be too cautious. . . . We have made numerous important and essential corrections, without which it would have perhaps been dangerous to publish the decree."[66] By August 13 Vintimille had incorporated the various suggestions in the work and returned the corrected draft to Fleury.[67] Two weeks later Fleury advised the archbishop to send a copy to Chancellor Daguesseau for his legal opinion.[68] Vintimille balked at first, arguing that the work was ready for publication and that the "restoration of [his] own personal sense of honor, dignity,

---

belief on the archbishop's part that he still possessed certain rights over Paris, elevated to an archbishopric and an ecclesiastical province in the early seventeenth century, but until then a diocese subordinate to the metropolitan in Sens. See Dent, "Changes in Episcopal Structure."

[64] Fleury to Vintimille, May 6, 1735, BM, MS 2358, p. 517.

[65] Abbé de Chabanne to [Chauvelin?], May 9, 1735, AAE, M&D, France, MS 1296, fols. 267-68.

[66] Aug. 10, 1735, BM, MS 2358, p. 577.

[67] Vintimille to Fleury, Aug. 13, 1735, *ibid.*, p. 578. "J'en ai osté toutes les questions qui pourroient aller au-delà des faits contre lesquels j'ai des preuves certaines, et qui pourroient donner la moindre atteinte aux maximes du Royaume ou soulever les esprits par raport au dogme" (*ibid.*). One of the things he agreed to omit was a series of passages which were harshly critical of Bishops Caylus of Auxerre and Colbert of Montpellier.

[68] Fleury to Vintimille, Aug. 25, 1735, *ibid.*, p. 583.

and worth" could brook no additional postponements; but finally he again consented.[69]

By late October, while Fleury and Daguesseau were reviewing the latest draft—presumably for the last time—Vintimille could abide the wait no longer. Exasperated, his spirit almost broken, the archbishop informed his friend, the cardinal-minister:

> All the difficulties that have been raised regarding my decree have convinced me that I was wiser to keep quiet than to speak and expose myself to possible contradictions or to the *appels comme d'abus* that everyone makes us fear so much. I swear to you, My Lord, that it is so humiliating for me, that without losing the will to do my duty I am losing the courage. . . .[70]

And yet the process of revising and correcting the *ordonnance*, down to even the most minute details, continued to drag on for several more weeks. By mid-November, Vintimille was almost desperate: "My conscience, and the duty I owe to my diocese and to the Church," he wrote Fleury on the 18th, "do not permit me to delay any longer issuing a statement on the miracles, unless I am willing to allow my silence to provide the *curés* and all posterity with the proof necessary to authorize them."[71] By nightfall Fleury had advised the archbishop that further revision would not be necessary and that he was free to go ahead with the publication of his *ordonnance*.[72] All the obstacles and reservations had now been disposed of—or so it must have seemed to all concerned.

Incredibly enough, however, although the work apparently went immediately to press, the *gens du roi* in the Paris Parlement now raised some new questions for Fleury to contemplate.[73] With the sovereign court about to reconvene after its annual recess, First President Portail expressed grave fears that Vintimille's *ordonnance* might arouse a storm of protest within "Jansenist" circles and among the "partisans of the convulsions," protests that could spread to the Palais de Justice.[74] Several weeks later, in a letter sent to Fleury, Daguesseau, and

[69] Vintimille to Fleury, Aug. 26, 1735, *ibid.*, p. 584. A copy of Daguesseau's detailed comments—"Réflexions générales sur le mandement de M. l'Archevêque de Paris" (undated)—may be found in BPR, L.P. 485, No. 18.

[70] Vintimille to Fleury, Oct. 23, 1735, BM, MS 2358, p. 609. Cf. Vintimille to Fleury, Oct. 30, 1735, *ibid.*, p. 613.

[71] Vintimille to Fleury, Nov. 18, 1735, *ibid.*, p. 624.

[72] Fleury to Vintimille, Nov. 18, 1735, *ibid.*, p. 625.

[73] Cf. Vintimille to Fleury, Dec. 17, 1735, and Fleury to Vintimille, Dec. 19, 1735, *ibid.*, pp. 641-43.

[74] Letter to Joly de Fleury, Nov. 1735, BN, J.F., MS 161, fol. 294.

Chauvelin, the *procureur-général* offered a somewhat more detailed scenario of the dangerous consequences that would attend the publication of the archbishop's decree at this time. He insisted that to do so would be "the most certain means of reuniting the anticonvulsionary doctors with the others [i.e., the proconvulsionary ones], of perhaps dampening the zealous hostility which is felt against the convulsionaries, of possibly provoking another *appel comme d'abus*, or at least of renewing the one which the *curés* had submitted against the archbishop of Sens and which we have been able to keep suspended until now."[75] While acknowledging the thoughtfulness of Joly de Fleury's observations, Cardinal Fleury was convinced that it was no longer possible or, for that matter, desirable to hold back on Vintimille's pastoral decree, copies of which were already in circulation. The archbishop, confronted by the public defiance of the *curés*, would be left in an untenable position if he were deprived of this opportunity to defend himself.[76] Chancellor Daguesseau, as responsible as anyone for delaying the pastoral instruction, was even more forceful in his defense of Vintimille's right to publish:

We must admit . . . that the archbishop of Paris is in an embarrassing situation, one in which he can neither speak nor remain silent. It is for him to weigh along with you and with the First President all the consequences of a decree in which he will be hard put to avoid the dangerous pitfalls which surround him. If we had paid as much attention to containing the *curés* as we have devoted to impeding their archbishop, there would have been nothing more to wish for. But while we give those of an inferior rank the liberty to do everything and print everything, we become alarmed only when their superior—whose silence they simultaneously reproach and abuse—is finally forced to speak out. I doubt that this is the best way of truly reestablishing tranquility. In the end, I am quite prepared to leave the matter entirely to his discretion and yours.[77]

[75] Dec. 19, 1735, *ibid.*, fol. 293; another draft of the letter to Chauvelin is in AAE, M&D, France, MS 1284, fol. 240. See also a second letter from Joly de Fleury to Fleury, Dec. 20, 1735, BN, J.F., MS 161, fol. 293.

[76] Fleury to Joly de Fleury, Dec. 20, 1735, *ibid.*, fol. 295.

[77] Letter to Joly de Fleury, Dec. 20, 1735, *ibid.*, fol. 296. Cf. Vintimille's somewhat pathetic letter to Fleury, Dec. 10, 1735, BM, MS 2358, pp. 636-37, which prompted the king, through Fleury, and the cardinal-minister himself to give the *ordonnance* their personal blessing and to add that, "Il y a lieu d'espérer que cet ouvrage aura l'effet que vous en attendez et je ne doute point aussi qu'il ne réussisse dans l'esprit public" (Fleury to Vintimille, Dec. 12, 1735, *ibid.*, p. 638). At the risk of straining the reader's credulity, one should add that Cardinal Fleury forced Vintimille to delay the distribution of his decree for yet another week,

Given these assurances, and with the interminable delays at last over, Vintimille was finally free to promulgate his *ordonnance*, which represented the archbishop's first official pronouncement on the Pâris miracles since his decree in the Anne Lefranc case more than four years earlier. The formal decree, which concerned itself exclusively with the cures investigated under Cardinal Noailles in 1728, was actually preceded by a long, two-part *requête*, or indictment, nominally issued by the *promoteur-général*, Nigon de Berty.[78] In the first part of his indictment the abbé de Berty sought to expose a series of procedural errors which the Thomassin commission had allegedly committed in the course of its inquest. Berty's account of the manner by which Thomassin had come to undertake his investigations and of the way in which he had drawn up the original *procès-verbaux* challenged the Jansenist version on a number of crucial points. The *promoteur* began by questioning whether the former vicegerent had ever received any direct or formal authorization from Noailles to conduct his investigations—a question which Vintimille himself had raised several times over the years. Neither the *vicaires-généraux* who had been members of Noailles' archdiocesan council in 1728 nor the late archbishop's own secretary could remember any such authorization. To be sure, M. Assolan, former undersecretary to Cardinal Noailles, recalled having seen a "letter of commission addressed to M. Thomassin that empowered him to gather information about some miracles which had supposedly been effected through the intercession of M. Pâris."[79] But he could not remember if Noailles had ever signed the letter. Nor was there any evidence to be found in the surviving secretarial records regarding a "commission" of this sort. As for the *procès-verbaux* Assolan admitted that he had been completely unaware of their existence. Still Thomassin insisted that Noailles had issued an actual ordinance charging him to examine the miracles—an assertion corroborated, as on previous occasions, by the abbé Isoard, *curé* of

---

while the authorities in Paris made plans to cope with any disturbances its appearance might occasion (see the two letters from M. Monglad, Fleury's secretary, to Vintimille, Dec. 13, 1735, *ibid.*, pp. 639-40). The *ordonnance* finally appeared on December 20—more than two and a half years after the initial draft had been completed!

[78] *Requête du promoteur général de l'archevêque de Paris*, published and bound together with Vintimille's *ordonnance*. This format was suggested by Chancellor Daguesseau (BPR, L.P. 480, No. 18). According to the *NNEE*, "Dom La Taste lui-même, si on en croit le bruit public, a été un des principaux fabricateurs de la requête" (March 10, 1736, p. 37).

[79] Cited in Bernard de Lacombe, *La résistance janséniste et parlementaire au temps de Louis XV: L'abbé Nigon de Berty* (Paris, 1948), p. 52.

Sainte-Marine and former *promoteur-général* under Noailles. The Oratorian priest Fouquet, who claimed that the *procès-verbaux* had been delivered to him for safekeeping, still refused (as before) to disclose the identity of the person from whom he had obtained them. According to Berty, these *anticonstitutionnaires* had a very weak case for their version of the story. The disappearance of essential documents, evasive responses to pointed questions, and contradictory or inconclusive testimony, he maintained, justified a dismissal of the entire dossier.[80]

But Berty's indictment went beyond a mere catalogue of alleged procedural irregularities. In the second part of the *requête* the determined *promoteur* endeavored to cast doubt on the validity of Thomassin's findings.[81] Drawing directly upon Languet's recent *Instruction pastorale*, Berty enunciated a series of principles that were said to be the ones by which the Church distinguished between real miraculous cures and apparent or contrived ones. According to his application of these rules to each of the supposed cures investigated under Thomassin, he was able to demonstrate that none of them was authentic or, consequently, worthy of publication. In the conclusion to his *requête*, Berty urged Vintimille to take immediate steps to condemn the alleged miracles of and cult to François de Pâris, "in order to warn the faithful against a dangerous credulity, whose pernicious effects we have deplored on many occasions."[82]

In a thirty-three-page "reply" to Berty's indictment, Vintimille addressed an *ordonnance* to the faithful, dated November 8, 1735, in which he followed quite closely the arguments set forth by his *promoteur*.[83] He declared that the *procès-verbaux* compiled in 1728 were "irregular and without authority," and he asserted that the alleged miracles investigated by the abbé Thomassin had been "brazenly published, devoid of proofs, and unworthy of any belief."[84] He explicitly forbade the publication not only of these "Noailles miracles," but also of the thirteen described in the *curés'* second petition of October 1731 and of all others attributed to the intercession of the deacon Pâris. In addition, without making any effort to examine the rest of

[80] *Requête du promoteur général*, p. 3; see also pp. 17-18.

[81] The documents used and cited by Berty are in BN, MSS Fr., MS 22245, fols. 1-204; fols. 206-209 contain an inventory of these pieces. Some of these same documents are reprinted as an appendix to Vintimille's *ordonnance*.

[82] *Requête du promoteur général*, p. 67.

[83] *Ordonnance de monseigneur l'archevêque de Paris, rendue sur la Requête du promoteur général de l'archevêché de Paris, au sujet des prétendus miracles attribués à l'intercession du sieur Pâris*.

[84] Cited in Lacombe, p. 57.

the *oeuvre* at first hand, he also denied the divine nature of the convulsions. Referring to the *Consultation des Trente* in his condemnation, he denounced the convulsionaries as dangerous and scandalous fanatics.[85]

Though intended ostensibly as a reply to the *curés* on the miracles, the decree gave Vintimille the opportunity to go well beyond a mere indictment of the Pâris cult to a reassertion of his archiepiscopal authority against "these arrogant and insubordinate parish priests" who had been such a problem to him ever since his arrival in Paris. "It is time to make use of our authority," he bluntly declared, to reestablish "the agreement, the union, the subordination which must, for the welfare of the flock, prevail between the bishops and the priests of the 'second order.'"[86] He denounced the *curés* for having attempted to undermine the hierarchy with public reproaches of their archbishop:

> There is nothing more irregular than such conduct. Priests league together in spite of the provision of the laws which forbid it; they dare publicly to approve a cult which their archbishop has prohibited in a solemn declaration; they make a demand of him which they themselves know can only end in a dangerous outburst, can only excite the public and increase the troubles which [already] agitate the diocese. The object of their demand is irrelevant to the functions of their ministry; but an ardent and imprudent zeal transforms them into *promoteurs*, and causes them to usurp a function which never belonged to them. Not content to criticize . . . our conduct, they prescribe to us the judgment which we must make, and seem to forbid us to examine the facts upon which they call for us to make a pronouncement. In these acts who will not recognize an enterprise contrary to all the laws of subordination and dependence?[87]

In short, Vintimille charged, the *curés* had been seeking to exploit the cult to M. Pâris in an effort to subvert the natural, established order of the Church; their archbishop announced that such behavior was utterly intolerable.

Vintimille's *ordonnance*, composed with the express approval of the government, seemed to have struck a hard blow at all of the parti-

---

[85] *Ordonnance*, pp. 83-85. Unlike the *consultants*, Vintimille noted that the convulsions had originated at the tomb of François de Pâris and used that fact to indict both the Pâris cult and the entire convulsionary movement. The convulsionists, of course, had drawn very different conclusions from their notion of the inseparability of miracles and convulsions.

[86] *Ibid.*, p. 75.   [87] *Ibid.*, p. 74.

sans of M. Pâris, whatever their position toward the convulsionaries. Not unexpectedly, the archbishop received warm messages of support and encouragement from some of his like-minded episcopal colleagues. The Sorbonne even sent a delegation to Vintimille's residence to convey the formal compliments of the Faculty of Theology.[88] At the same time, although Vintimille's condemnations inspired considerable protest from the *anticonstitutionnaires*, the reaction among the archbishop's principal antagonists, the magistrates in the Parlement and the dissident parish *curés*, was surprisingly restrained, the fears of the *gens du roi* thus proving groundless. In part this reaction may have been a result of the archbishop's decision not to order his decree to be formally announced from the parish pulpits—a precaution designed to avoid giving the opposition clergy still one more opportunity to flaunt their disrespect for his authority. Or perhaps the mild reaction was a reflection of the already considerable erosion of Vintimille's position of authority, so that his words may have been regarded as little more than empty threats. Whatever the reason—and the efforts of Fleury, Daguesseau, and the others who put the *ordonnance* through countless revisions should not be overlooked[89]—the *curés* did not even attempt their usual *appels comme d'abus*. A mood of relative calm prevailed at the Palais de Justice; the magistrates remained uncommonly silent, passing up an opportunity to attack a favorite target once again—a sign perhaps of the sovereign court's own growing disenchantment with the entire Pâris cult. There were others, however, who were determined to retaliate against Vintimille and his *promoteur-général*.

Within a few months of the archbishop's ordinance, the original papers authorizing the Thomassin commission, lost for so long, were suddenly "rediscovered." On the morning of March 8, 1736, a certain Jean-Claude Péret, canon from Saint-Honoré, deposited them with a notary at the Châtelet. According to Péret, "an unknown individual" had brought the documents to him the previous evening, along with the official *requête* for an investigation which the abbé Isoard, then *promoteur*, had originally drawn up. The papers were apparently authentic: Péret, another former *promoteur-général* in the archdiocese, recognized the handwriting of both M. Assolan, who had prepared the

[88] Vintimille to Fleury, Dec. 24, 1735, BM, MS 2358, p. 643, and Fleury to Vintimille, Dec. 27, 1735, *ibid.*, p. 644. See also Archbishop Languet's *Mandement et instruction pastorale* of March 1736.

[89] Cf. Daguesseau's extended "Remarques particulières sur le mandement," in which the chancellor sought to anticipate any objections which *curés* or *parlementaires* might have been expected to raise against Vintimille's pastoral instruction and to persuade the archbishop to revise his decree accordingly (BPR, L.P. 485, No. 18).

order, and Cardinal Noailles, whose signature was affixed to it.[90] The *Nouvelles ecclésiastiques* announced the news with great exultation.[91] By the end of April, Noailles' order and Isoard's *requête* were anonymously published and widely circulated.[92] Attempts on the part of Vintimille's office to deny the authenticity of these papers[93] were dismissed by the *Nouvellistes* as wholly insubstantial.[94]

In the ensuing weeks there appeared a series of anonymous lampoons, satirical verses, and pamphlets attacking Vintimille's pastoral decree and ridiculing the archbishop and his *promoteur*.[95] While these nameless pamphleteers and satirists were taking the Parisian ecclesiastical authorities to task, several persons intimately involved with the miracles, including one woman who had actually experienced a cure attributed to the deacon Pâris, came forward to challenge the archbishop's findings and to complain anew about his adamant refusal to accord the miracles a full and proper examination.[96] Finally, the episcopal supporters of the cult also joined in the attack. Bishop Varlet of

[90] Lacombe, pp. 57-58; see also *NNEE*, March 10, 1736, pp. 37-39.

[91] *Ibid.*, p. 39.

[92] BN, Salle des Imprimés, LD-4 2089. Cf. the "Acte de dépôt (avec expédition) de la commission pour informer des miracles de feu François de Pâris, diacre, donnée par L. A. Cardinal de Noailles, archevêque de Paris, à Thomassin, docteur de Sorbonne, vice-gérent de l'officialité de Paris, chez les notaires Marchand et Bricault à Paris par Jean-Claude Péret, chanoine de l'église collégiale et paroissiale de St.-Honoré de Paris (8 mars 1736)," in AFA, P.R. 6181.

[93] "Acte de dépôt fait par M. Péret de la requeste de M. Isoard et de l'ordonnance de M. le cardinal de Noailles au sujet des prétendus miracles de M. Pâris, avec des réflexions sur cet acte et sur lesdites requeste et ordonnance," p. 13.

[94] *NNEE*, July 21, 1736, pp. 113-15.

[95] See, in particular, the *Quatrième harangue des habitants de la paroisse de Sarcelles à Mgr. l'archevêque de Paris*, which appeared in numerous printed and manuscript versions (e.g., BN, MSS Fr., MS 25564). Also interesting: *Almanach du Diable contenant des prédictions très curieuses et absolument infaillibles pour l'année 1737*. Satirical songs and verses may be found in BN, MSS Fr., MSS 12634, 12707, 13662, and 15133, *passim*. In a much more serious vein was the *Second discours sur les miracles opérés au tombeau et par l'intercession de M. de Pâris, diacre, où l'on répond aux objections*, a tract attributed to Nicolas Le Gros (BPR, L.P. 482, No. 33).

[96] *Lettre de M. Chaulin, prêtre, docteur de Sorbonne, à Msgr. l'archevêque de Paris, en réponse à l'article de son Ordonnance, du 8 novembre 1735, qui concerne le miracle de punition arrivé en la personne de la veuve de Lorme, frappée de paralysie sur le tombeau de M. de Pâris, le 4 août 1731 (1 mai 1736)*; and *Lettre de Mlle. Mossaron à Msgr. l'archevêque de Paris, au sujet de ce qui est dit dans son Ordonnance, du 8 novembre 1735, contre le miracle de sa guérison subite et une paralysie de 18 mois, arrivé, le 26 juin 1728, au tombeau de M. de Pâris, diacre de sainte mémoire, inhumé a S.-Médard, et vérifié, le mois suivant, par ordre de M. le cardinal de Noailles (6 avril 1737)*.

Babylone, heretofore silent on the matter, responded to Vintimille's ordinance in a seventy-one-page "letter" to Bishop Colbert.[97] Colbert himself also denounced the abbé de Berty's indictment as "sophistical and unworthy of the Church of Jesus Christ."[98] There was, however, much more significant evidence than these various letters, pamphlets, and verses to indicate not only the low esteem in which the *anticonstitutionnaire* supporters of the Pâris cult held Vintimille, but also the weakened state of his authority. Blatantly, and with impunity, they flaunted his prohibition against the unauthorized publication of any alleged miracles. A tenth *Recueil des miracles*, printed in "Utrecht," was circulating in Paris by the middle of 1736.[99] Accounts of individual cures were still being published and widely distributed.[100] Sympathetic printers even went so far as to reissue copies of the Paris *curés'* two *requêtes* of 1731, which were published along with the various *recueils* that continued to appear at this time.[101]

Though far from ended,[102] the controversy over Vintimille's *ordonnance* receded into the background toward the end of 1736, when attention shifted back again to the irrepressible Archbishop Languet. It had become quite clear, at least to those Jansenists who had remained faithful to François de Pâris—and especially to those who still accepted

---

[97] *Lettre de monseigneur l'évêque de Babylone à monseigneur l'évêque de Montpellier, pour servir de réponse à l'Ordonnance de M. l'archevêque de Paris, rendue le 8 novembre 1735, au sujet des miracles opérés par l'intercession de M. de Pâris (12 mai 1736).* See discussion in *NNEE*, Aug. 4, 1736, p. 124.

[98] Cited *ibid.*, March 23, 1737, p. 46.

[99] With the publication of the tenth *recueil*, the *Nouvellistes* reported, there were "en tout 104 miracles mis sous les yeux du public: sans compter ceux dont les relations ont été données séparément; & un très grand nombre d'autres dont on se contente de s'édifier dans le secret, soit à Paris, soit ailleurs, & même hors du royaume" (July 28, 1736, p. 117).

[100] See, for example, the *Relation de la maladie de Mlle. Le Juge, fille de M. Le Juge, conseiller du roi, correcteur en la chambre des comptes de Paris; et de sa guérison miraculeuse, arrivée le 9 mars, au soir, de la présente année 1737.* The *Déclaration faite devant notaire, le 12 mai 1735, par Joseph Massy, ci-devant luthérien, de la guérison miraculeuse d'une espèce de lèpre, demandée à Dieu, par l'intercession du B. H. François de Pâris, en signe pour connoître si la vérité est du côté des appelants* tells of an Irish Protestant who was not only cured of leprosy but also converted to Catholicism through the "efforts" of M. Pâris; the conversion ceremony took place at the cathedral of Notre-Dame on Nov. 21, 1737.

[101] BN, Salle des Imprimés, LD-4 2077A and 2077B.

[102] See *L'Imposture confondue. Réponse à deux libelles intitulés, le premier: "Lettre de M. l'évêque de Babylone à M. l'évêque de Montpellier, pour servir de réponse à l'Ordonnance de M. l'archevêque de Paris . . ."; et le second: "Instruction pastorale de M. l'évêque de Montpellier . . ." (25 mars 1737).* This work was eventually suppressed by the authorities (see n. 154 below).

both the miracles and the convulsions—that the influential archbishop of Sens represented the greatest threat to their cause. The fiery prelate was as vitriolic as ever in his second major pastoral decree on the subject, which he issued in March 1736.[103] Far from limiting himself to diatribes against the miracles of Saint-Médard, Languet made yet another contribution to the smouldering debate over the convulsionaries and the *Consultation des Trente*.[104] However, it was his pronouncements on the miracles and his denunciations of the *anticonstitutionnaire* defenders of the Pâris cult that continued to evoke the sharpest and most frequent attacks. The previous August, Bishop Caylus, himself a confirmed anticonvulsionary, had spent almost the entire third part of an eighty-four-page episcopal decree replying to Languet's earlier attack on him and on the Seignelay miracle.[105] In November 1736 Colbert published another pastoral instruction on the miracles and "in defense of the Truth," devoting the first two sections of the very long and wide-ranging work to a detailed refutation of Languet, who had so viciously attacked and insulted him in his most recent *mandement*.[106] Colbert's instruction received the unqualified praise of numerous *anticonstitutionnaire* clergy, including Jean Soanen, who voiced his own enthusiastic support in a letter that was

103 *Mandement et instruction pastorale de monseigneur J.-Joseph Languet, archevêque de Sens, pour publier l'Ordonnance de monseigneur l'archevêque de Paris au sujet des prétendus miracles du sieur Pâris, diacre; comme aussi pour précautionner les fidèles contre un écrit intitulé: "Instruction pastorale de M. l'évêque d'Auxerre" du 8 août 1735; . . . et encore contre un autre écrit intitulé: "Requête de plusieurs curés de Paris, contre l'Instruction pastorale de monseigneur l'archevêque de Sens"* (25 *mars* 1736). Languet also received strong support from his fellow *constitutionnaire* bishops, including Tencin, who published yet another refutation of Colbert in a *Lettre pastorale et ordonnance* of Dec. 5, 1735.

104 Excerpts and comments upon the pastoral instruction may be found in *NNEE*, Dec. 1, 1736, pp. 189-90.

105 *Instruction pastorale de Mgr. l'évêque d'Auxerre, au sujet de quelques écrits et libelles répandus dans le public contre son Mandement, du 20 décembre 1733, à l'occasion du miracle opéré dans la ville de Seignelay; de ce diocèse (8 août 1735).* See discussion in *NNEE*, March 3, 1736, pp. 33-36. See also Caylus' letter of May 11, 1735 to the Paris *curés*, in which the bishop of Auxerre congratulated them on their appealing to the Parlement against Languet's "abusive pastoral decree" and on their continuing display of "zeal, firmness, and courage in defense of Truth and Justice" (AFA, P.R. 4770).

106 *Instruction pastorale de monseigneur l'évêque de Montpellier, adressée au clergé et aux fidèles de son diocèse, pour servir de réponse à l'Instruction pastorale de M. l'archevêque de Sens contre les miracles de M. Pâris (11 novembre 1736),* in *Oeuvres*, II, 93-214. See discussion in *NNEE*, March 16, 1737, pp. 41-43, March 23, 1737, pp. 46-48, March 30, 1737, pp. 49-52, and April 27, 1737, p. 66.

also sharply critical of Languet.[107] In early 1737 Caylus contributed yet one more reply to the archbishop of Sens,[108] thereby adding to the veritable torrent of pamphlets and episcopal pronouncements already raining down upon Paris from all over the kingdom. The most impressive refutation of Languet, however, and by far the most spectacular, came not from any of these bishops, but from a magistrate in the Parlement of Paris, Carré de Montgeron, whose work on behalf of the Pâris cult was reaching its culmination at this time.

The wealthy *parlementaire*, Louis-Basile Carré de Montgeron, counselor in the second chamber of *enquêtes*, had been for many years the leading protagonist and benefactor of the convulsionary movement. Montgeron's involvement in the cause of the Pâris cult had a most unusual beginning. Out of mere curiosity the magistrate, a professed deist and libertine, paid a visit to the cemetery of Saint-Médard on September 7, 1731. There, in the midst of the fervent devotions of innumerable pious faithful, he experienced a sudden, "miraculous" conversion at François de Pâris' tomb, on which he lay in a trance for some four hours. No sooner had he regained consciousness than he swore before God to devote himself almost entirely to the cult. From that day forward, aspiring to be the St. Paul of the Pâris cult, Montgeron worked with an indefatigable missionary zeal on behalf of the cause. Both inside and outside the Parlement, as counselor and as disciple, he undertook to convert relatives, colleagues, friends, and acquaintances.[109] He paid regular visits to the cemetery of Saint-Médard and, after it was closed, assiduously attended various convulsionary assemblies all over Paris, serving as a *secouriste* for a number of the brethren.[110] In his roles of *père nourricier* and *économe des pauvres*, as he was sometimes called,[111] Montgeron provided generous pensions to poor convulsionaries, protected many of them from arrest, and

---

[107] Letter to Colbert of March 30, 1737, reprinted *ibid.*, July 5, 1737, pp. 105-106. See also Rochebouet, *curé* of Saint-Germain-le-Vieux (Paris), to Colbert, Jan. 7, 1737, AFA, P.R. 5547.

[108] *Cinquième Lettre, ou Réponse de Mgr. l'évêque d'Auxerre au Mandement de monseigneur l'archevêque de Sens daté du 25 mars 1736 (13 mars 1737).*

[109] He was so successful with his father that the old man, after dismissing his *constitutionnaire* confessor and replacing him with the abbé Firmin Tournus, intimate friend and confessor to François de Pâris, enthusiastically fasted himself to death shortly after Easter in 1732.

[110] Montgeron to Soanen, Jan. 12, 1738, AFA, P.R. 6472; Montgeron to Colbert, Nov. 29, 1737, *ibid.*, P.R. 4935.

[111] See Montgeron to Soanen, Dec. 13, 1735, *ibid.*, P.R. 6472; see also Bontoux, "Paris janséniste au 18e siècle," p. 218.

visited and offered spiritual encouragement to the other, less fortunate *soeurs* and *frères* whom he was not able to save from imprisonment.[112] In addition, Montgeron helped finance the *Nouvelles ecclésiastiques*,[113] subsidized the publication of a variety of convulsionist works, and apparently even owned, or at least heavily supported, two or three clandestine printing establishments in Paris as well as others in the Auxerrois.[114]

Montgeron was thus a man whose financial independence, official position, and political connections afforded the convulsionary brethren and the entire *anticonstitutionnaire* party a significant degree of assistance, protection, and security. Great benefactor and protector that he was, apostle of the miracles and the convulsions, Montgeron never-

[112] BHVP, N.A., MS 125, I, 233; BN, J.F., MS 205, fols. 143-44; and Montgeron to Soanen, Dec. 13, 1735, AFA, P.R. 6472. The prisoners referred to him as "papa de Montgeron." Some of them had convulsions in his presence while he was paying them a visit. An adept *secouriste*, Montgeron assisted them in their seizures, occasionally calming them by putting his foot on their stomach (Ravaisson, XIV, 366). The convulsionary known as Soeur Pélagie (Mlle. Pélagie Rousseau) was apparently his chief protégée, obtaining shelter in the magistrate's own home (BA, MS 11268, fols. 138-68).

[113] Mlle. Bontoux notes that Montgeron also paid frequent visits to the *ateliers* of the *Nouvelles ecclésiastiques*, where he sometimes helped correct the page proofs. According to the governor of the Bastille, moreover, "c'est grâce à ce haut patronage que les imprimeurs ne furent pas poursuivis en justice. On ne pouvait faire leur procès sans faire celui du magistrat, et le lieutenant de police hésitait encore à inquiéter Montgeron" (cited by Bontoux, "Paris janséniste au 18ᵉ siècle," p. 218, from BA, MS 11366, fol. 200).

[114] On Montgeron's printing establishments in Paris, see BA, MSS 11329 and 11366. On his activities in the Auxerrois, where he owned a château at Ratilly that he gave over to the Jansenist abbé Terrasson in an act of pious charity, see *ibid.*, MS 11304, especially fols. 97-100. Mme. Duguet-Mol reported Montgeron's involvement in the maintenance of a regular network of *anticonstitutionnaire* correspondence and the exchange of manuscripts and printed tracts from Paris to Troyes and Auxerre (see her letter to [Hérault?], Nov. 4, 1737, *ibid.*, MS 11032). Of course, Montgeron's precise activities, although they must have obviously been considerable, remained fairly well obscured, since the beneficiaries of his largesse were careful to hide his name and his actions (Dedieu, "L'agonie du jansénisme," p. 204). A number of authors have nevertheless attempted to deal with Montgeron's various provincial activities. See, in particular, Raymond Escholier, "Survivances du Jansénisme à Auxerre," *Congrès de l'Association bourguignonne des sociétés savantes*, 31 (1960), pp. 227-35; Pierre Ordioni, *La résistance gallicane et janséniste dans le diocèse d'Auxerre, 1704-1760* (Auxerre, 1932), p. 100; Chanoine Grossier, "Correspondance entre le Cardinal de Fleury, ministre d'Etat et Mgr. Languet, Archevêque de Sens, sur le Jansénisme en Puisaye," *Congrès de l'Association bourguignonne des sociétés savantes*, 31 (1960), pp. 259-63; and Dedieu, "Un nouveau Port-Royal au diocèse d'Auxerre," *Le Correspondant*, 101 (September 1929), pp. 641-61.

theless believed that he had an even more crucial and fundamental task to perform: to demonstrate, dramatically and beyond all doubt, the divine character of the Pâris miracles. It was while in exile in 1732 that Montgeron, with the encouragement of the deposed Bishop Soanen, the theologian Nicolas Le Gros, and others, first decided to undertake this mammoth project.[115] For five years he spent much of his time and a substantial part of his large fortune in collecting and cataloguing all the evidence he could find to support the miracles; the convulsions, for the most part, he determined to leave for subsequent researches. He worked at his task with a sense of divinely inspired duty and an inexhaustible enthusiasm. Throughout this period he maintained a voluminous secret correspondence with sympathetic persons—priests, bishops, theologians, doctors, magistrates, lawyers, and notaries—all over France and even abroad,[116] soliciting documents and notarized depositions and seeking expert medical and theological opinions.[117] As sections of his manuscript were completed, he circulated them to many of these same people, incorporating some of their comments and observations in subsequent revisions. Some Jansenist theologians objected to his project, largely on the grounds that Montgeron lacked the necessary training or qualifications to deal with so important and complex a subject.[118] But Montgeron, buoyed by the continuous support he received from Bishops Soanen and Colbert and a host of other leading *anticonstitutionnaires*, managed to override their objections and to proceed with his undertaking.[119]

By 1735 the completion of his work took on a new urgency and a greater significance. In addition to the substantial defections from the *oeuvre* within Jansenist and parlementary ranks, Montgeron saw *constitutionnaires* like Languet, Vintimille, and La Taste stepping up their attacks on his beloved cult. On June 11, 1736, moreover, the police raided a number of clandestine printing shops with which Montgeron had been associated, including one in which he kept a substantial quantity of his papers, notes, and other materials, both manuscript and

[115] See Montgeron to Soanen, April 26, 1737, and June 17, 1737, AFA, P.R. 6472.

[116] Montgeron to Colbert, Oct. 9, 1733, and Nov. 10, 1733, *ibid.*, P.R. 4935. See also Dedieu, "L'agonie du jansénisme," p. 204, n. 81.

[117] See Colbert to Montgeron, Oct. 31, 1733, in *Oeuvres de Colbert*, III, 618-19.

[118] See Montgeron to Colbert, June 17, 1737, and Nov. 29, 1737, AFA, P.R. 4935. There were also specific criticisms of the style and contents of Montgeron's work in addition to the attacks on his general competence.

[119] He maintained a sporadic correspondence with both bishops during this entire period. Besides the letters cited above, see also the one he wrote to Colbert congratulating the bishop of Montpellier for his pastoral instruction of November 1736 (Feb. 18, 1737, AFA, P.R. 4935).

printed.[120] Among the ten people arrested was the abbé François Imbert (better known as Montigny), who had been working for some time on Montgeron's book. Although the police failed to discover the magistrate's various papers or any of the page proofs, which were all hidden under a mattress, the raid no doubt convinced Montgeron of the need to get his work immediately through the press.[121]

Having willingly sacrificed material interest to conviction and principle in this enterprise, and having overcome considerable opposition and various obstacles, Montgeron finally completed the publication of his book—*La Vérité des Miracles opérés à l'intercession de M. de Pâris & autres Appellans, démontrée contre M. l'Archevêque de Sens* —in late 1736 or early 1737. Although the first edition of the work appears to have been printed in Utrecht under the supervision of the abbé Nicolas Le Gros, another edition, following shortly thereafter, was printed clandestinely in Paris, probably on one of Montgeron's own secret presses.[122] Profusely illustrated with engravings by the noted artist, Jean Restout,[123] whom Montgeron had commissioned for the project, the huge 900-page work consisted of five parts of varying lengths. A brief "Avertissement," or foreword, and a thirty-two-page account of Montgeron's "miraculous conversion" formed the opening two sections of the book. By far the longest and most impressive section was the fourth, entitled "Démonstrations." It contained very elaborate and detailed discussions of eight of the cures effected through the intercession of François de Pâris, each of them supported by a massive collection of seemingly decisive *pièces justificatives*, including an impressive array of detailed medical observations.[124] These "demonstra-

---

[120] BA, MS 11307, fols. 245-365; Funck-Brentano, p. 263. See also Montgeron to Soanen, April 26, 1737, and June 17, 1737, AFA, P.R. 6472.

[121] The fact that the police were unable to find this secret cache, even though the papers were right under their very noses, struck Montgeron as a sure sign that divine providence was protecting his enterprise (Montgeron to Soanen, June 17, 1737, AFA, P.R. 6472).

[122] Armogathe, p. 137, n. 3. After the police raid in June 1736, the abbé Dubuisson (also known as Charles Lajus) took over at least some of the Montgeron printing operations and saw *La Vérité des Miracles* through the press (see *mémoire* of Dubut, July 8, 1740, BA, MS 11479, fols. 63 and 65; see also the "Papiers du magasin du Sr. Dubuisson," *ibid.*, MS 10222 as well as the rest of the carton in which the Dubut *mémoire* is found).

[123] See Gazier, "Jean Restout et les miracles du diacre de Pâris," pp. 117-30.

[124] "Relations, Déclarations par devant Notaires, Actes du dépôt, Certificats, Procès-Verbaux, Rapports, Consultations, Dissertations de Médecins & Chirurgiens, Lettres, &c." (*NNEE*, Sept. 14, 1737, p. 145). Montgeron's work exercised an extraordinary fascination upon the French medical world in the late nineteenth

tions," carefully argued and rigorously thorough, were designed to prove that the miraculous cures were incontrovertibly true. As the *Nouvelles ecclésiastiques* approvingly observed, "one needs only to open the book in order to see that this great adversary of the works of God [Languet] is refuted in a thousand ways, . . . convicted of lies proved and verified by authentic and formal acts."[125] In two other sections—the third, a short "Essai de Dissertation sur la Foi due au Témoignage," and the fifth, a twenty-eight-page discussion of the "Conséquences qu'on doit tirer des miracles, avec des Réponses aux objections qu'on y oppose"—Montgeron further developed the conclusions reached in his demonstrations on behalf of the truth and the divine character of M. Pâris' cures. To be sure, except for the sheer mass of evidence which he brought together in this book—and its importance and overwhelming abundance must not be minimized—Montgeron does not appear to have added anything particularly original to the debate, at least nothing by way of new arguments. But he had not conceived his work to be merely another collection of refutations directed against Languet and the other *constitutionnaires*, or just one more contribution to the long and now tiresome exchange of polemics. He had undertaken his project with a much grander purpose in mind than that. Indeed, as the third part of the work, an "Epître au Roi," clearly indicated, Montgeron intended to take the bold step of appealing directly to the king.[126]

On July 29, 1737, dressed in his magisterial vestments, Montgeron made his way to Versailles in order to present Louis XV with a magnificent gold-embossed and green leather-bound edition of *La Vérité des Miracles*.[127] He entered the palace and penetrated into the royal dining hall, unmolested. When dinner was over, he bowed respectfully and offered his book to the young king. While stunned members of

---

and early twentieth centuries. Psychologists and neurologists, in particular, including Pierre Janet, Jean-Martin Charcot, and many of the latter's disciples at the Salpêtrière, repeatedly testified to the "scientific" nature and the high quality of Montgeron's clinical descriptions.

[125] Sept. 14, 1737, p. 147.

[126] See Montgeron to Soanen, June 17, 1737, AFA, P.R. 6472. As he observed to Soanen, Montgeron's hopes of moving the king rested on a belief that Louis XV "ne combat la vérité que parce qu'il l'ignore" (*ibid.*).

[127] This beautiful volume is at present in the possession of the Bibliothèque de la Société des Amis de Port-Royal. For some details on how this copy became part of the library's holdings, see Gazier, *Histoire générale*, I, 282, n. 2. M. Gazier was himself a *bibliothécaire* at this library on the rue Saint-Jacques; his familial descendants still have charge of its excellent collection.

the court looked on in silent amazement,[128] Montgeron delivered a brief speech in the form of a harangue:

> Sire, the ardent zeal which I feel for your Majesty obliged me to compose this book in order to disclose several truths which are being kept hidden from you, though it is in your interest to be acquainted with them, and to reveal certain projects which are being secretly plotted against your authority.
>
> I know, Sire, that the action which I am taking is going to draw upon me the hatred of those who are employing all their efforts to prevent your Majesty and his principal ministers from being well informed about facts of which this book contains the proof; but I am not afraid to expose myself to their resentment, for it was a question of rendering the most essential of all services to your Majesty and to the promotion of true religion.[129]

The twenty-eight-page dedicatory "epistle to the king" expressed similar sentiments, though in a lengthier and more specific form. In justification of his action, Montgeron asserted that it was his duty as a magistrate in the sovereign court to instruct the king about the truth, for the king's religion, his glory, the salvation of his sacred person, and the very security of his throne were all at stake. He cautioned the monarch that the bull *Unigenitus* represented a dangerous encroachment on royal authority, a plot between Rome and the Jesuits, who were "the cause of all the troubles in [this] realm." Unlike these enemies of the crown and of the Gallican Church, who had long been deceiving the king, the appellants were his most faithful subjects and the party of truth, order, unity, and justice within the Church. If only the king would understand what a glorious honor it was for God to have chosen his reign as the age of miracles, as the time to make His presence visible to mankind, he would surely embrace the miracles of and the cult to M. Pâris, and the restoration of virtue and religious peace could be accomplished.[130] It was in fact Montgeron's ardent hope —and plea—that his extensive demonstrations and lengthy arguments might move the king and convince him of "la vérité des miracles."

Montgeron's hopes, and with them those of his supporters, were very shortly dashed. After successfully making his delivery to Louis

---

[128] "Régulièrement, à l'approche d'un homme inconnu vers la personne du Roi, comme on ne pénétre point l'intention, les officiers devoient se jeter sur lui & le repousser; mais à cette génuflexion imprévue, tout le monde demeurera étonné & dans l'inaction" (Barbier, III, 90 [July 1737]).

[129] "Avertissement," unpaginated; also cited by *NNEE*, July 30, 1737, p. 117.

[130] "Epître au roi," pp. ii-iii, xxvi-xxviii; see also *NNEE*, Aug. 13, 1737, p. 127.

XV and evading capture for this audacious act, Montgeron went next to Saint-Cloud, where he presented yet another copy of his book to the duke of Orléans. He then made his way back to Paris and delivered copies to First President Le Peletier of the Parlement, the *avocat-général* Gilbert de Voisins, and the *procureur-général* Joly de Fleury. At Versailles, in the meantime, Cardinal Fleury had already discovered Montgeron's identity[131] and issued orders for his arrest.[132] The cardinal-minister thoroughly relished this moment. For quite some time he had been well aware of and greatly disturbed by Montgeron's troublesome activities on behalf of the convulsionaries and the appellants, particularly his clandestine publishing ventures;[133] but until this point he had been reluctant to proceed against the magistrate for fear that Montgeron's fellow counselors would raise the cry of ultramontane persecution or protest against the government's violation of parlementary prerogatives.[134] Now, however, Montgeron had just committed an offense which placed him beyond the pale—"à l'abri de son corps"—and clearly warranted a *lettre de cachet*.[135] Only indirectly related to the issue of the Bull, his impertinent action could presumably be punished without running the risk of another serious confrontation between crown and Parlement. Shortly past midnight, therefore, soon after Montgeron had returned to his home, he was visited by two of Hérault's officers,[136] armed with a *lettre de cachet* ordering him to the

---

[131] The king had never seen him before, and Montgeron apparently left before anyone had gotten the chance to find out either from him or from the title page of his book who he actually was.

[132] AN, O^1 81, fols. 288-90.

[133] Archbishop Languet had been complaining to the royal government about Montgeron's activities for at least five years (see Languet to Fleury, Aug. 26, 1732, Bibliothèque municipale de Sens, Collection Languet, Vol. 34, No. 7). For a discussion of the official attitude toward Montgeron during this period, especially regarding his various undertakings outside of Paris, see: Dedieu, "Un nouveau Port-Royal au diocèse d'Auxerre," pp. 655-57; Grossier, pp. 260-63; and Escholier, pp. 227-28. See also BA, MS 11304, fols. 64-71, 91-123, *et passim*. Even after the mass arrests and confiscations of 1736, in which the police discovered abundant evidence of Montgeron's involvement in clandestine printing operations, the authorities had hesitated to take any steps against him for fear of "wounding the pride" of the Parlement (see BA, MS 11366, fol. 200).

[134] Fleury's attitude toward Montgeron, whom he regarded as more than a little insane, had long been rather contemptuous. Responding to a letter from Vintimille sent in early February 1735, Fleury observed that "Il ne faut pas prétendre guérir [M.] de Montgeron, et il faudroit un saint plus puissant que M. Pâris pour [lui] remettre la cervelle . . ." (Feb. 10, 1735, BM, MS 2358, pp. 469-70).

[135] BA, MS 11366, fol. 310.

[136] Duval, a *commandant du guet*, and Lepinay, a *commissaire du Châtelet*.

Bastille and commanding that all his papers—an enormous quantity of manuscripts and printed pieces—be impounded and sealed and all copies of his book be confiscated.[137]

The government's action provoked another controversy with the Parlement of Paris, though this one was to be notably mild by comparison with most previous ones since 1730. Later that very same day, July 30, the First President convoked the entire body of magistrates. Protesting the government's treatment of Montgeron, they agreed unanimously on the need to send a "solemn deputation" to the king.[138] Through the *gens du roi* Louis XV expressed his willingness to discuss the matter with representatives of the sovereign court, and on August 2 a small delegation of magistrates left for an audience at Versailles. The nature of their protest, already decided upon in Paris, was extremely revealing. It suggested, perhaps better than any other previous action taken by the Parlement as a body, the real motives behind the interest which most of the magistrates had displayed toward the Saint-Médard question from the very outset: namely, that their involvement had derived primarily, if not exclusively, from an abiding concern with the legal and judicial issues raised by the affair and with the protection of their precious jurisdictional and political prerogatives. In stating their objections to the king, they made absolutely no mention either of Montgeron's book or of the cult for which he had been crusading so ardently and so long. They were even willing to concede that Montgeron had failed to show the proper respect for the monarch's sacred person, and that he had thus committed "an excessively extravagant act."[139] In any event, their argument with the government was not that Montgeron should have been permitted to act with impunity. Rather, they based their protest exclusively on the grounds that the royal government, in proceeding against Montgeron, had committed several irregularities and had violated certain of his privileges as a magistrate. They argued, in the first place, that it was out of keeping with tradition for "a simple *commissaire* from the Châtelet" to have affixed the seal on papers belonging to a magistrate. Second, they claimed that as a member of the Parlement Montgeron had the right to be arrested "by an officer of the musketeers," not by a mere *guet*. Finally, and most important, they asserted that in cases of alleged

---

137 BA, MS 11366, fol. 321; Barbier, III, 89-91 (July 1737); and *NNEE*, July 30, 1737, pp. 117-18, and Aug. 7, 1737, p. 121.

138 Cited *ibid.*, July 30, 1737, p. 117. For much of what follows see: BN, J.F., MS 171, fols. 106-11; BN, NAFr., MS 8190, fols. 314-15, 329-30, and 332-34; and BN, MSS Fr., MS 10908, fols. 184-86.

139 Barbier, III, 91-92 (July 1737).

criminal conduct the sovereign court had the prerogative of judging a colleague first, before he was sent to the Bastille.[140] What they demanded, therefore, was that Montgeron be set free in order to be tried by his "natural judges."[141]

The ceremony with Louis XV did not last more than a few minutes. After hearing the speech of the First President, the impatient king, already dressed for the day's hunt, bluntly declared: "I was determined to punish a lack of respect which concerned my very person. If I deem [it] appropriate to go even farther, I will let you know of my intentions."[142] In elaboration of the monarch's extremely brief remarks, and in justification of the government's action, Chancellor Daguesseau added simply that there had not been enough time to follow ordinary forms and procedures. To have done so "would have delayed the punishment of an action so rash that the king could not regard it as that of a magistrate. As for the printed materials that were seized, . . . it was necessary to take this precaution in order to prevent them from being circulated among the public."[143]

After the session at Versailles, the magistrates were unusually compliant. Despite their initial resentment at the crown's alleged mistreatment of Montgeron, they were not eager to engage in another fierce or prolonged dispute with Fleury over their colleague. Presumably they did not consider the merits of his case sufficient to justify pursuing it with very much enthusiasm. Even before the meeting had taken place with the king, Barbier had astutely observed that "the Parlement will take steps only for form's sake, and that . . . [Montgeron,] the victim of the indiscretion of his zeal, . . . will remain in the Bastille."[144] Indeed, though not entirely satisfied with the royal verdict, the sovereign court duly registered it the very next day without much fuss.[145] However, before they all withdrew into their respective chambers, the magistrates did recommend that "the First President should continue his entreaties before the king on behalf of

---

[140] *Ibid.*, p. 92 (July 1737), and *NNEE*, Aug. 7, 1737, p. 121.

[141] A portion of the First President's remarks to the king may be found *ibid.*

[142] Cited *ibid.*; see also Barbier, III, 95 (August 1737). The nature of Louis' response to the delegation had been carefully prepared in advance, with Cardinal Fleury taking particular advantage of some valuable information which Hérault had obtained from police spies within the Parlement of Paris itself (see Fleury to Hérault, Aug. 1, 1737, BA, MS 11366, fol. 314).

[143] Cited in *NNEE*, Aug. 7, 1737, p. 121; see also Barbier, III, 95 (August 1737).

[144] *Ibid.*, p. 92 (July 1737). In a letter to Hérault, Fleury remarked that, "Si on faisoit justice à M. de Montgeron on le mettroit à St. Lazare," that is, in a house of detention for the insane (Aug. 1, 1737, BA, MS 11366, fol. 315).

[145] Barbier, III, 95 (August 1737).

M. de Montgeron."[146] With this mandate the First President and the Parlement in general embarked on a series of rather feeble efforts to obtain Montgeron's release. But in the face of the king's adamant refusal to hear their appeals, they did not even attempt to pursue their protests very far.

The only change in Montgeron's situation was his transfer during the sovereign court's annual recess, first in October from the Bastille to Saint-André-de-Villeneuve-Lès-Avignon.[147] Then, in November, when his "extravagant behavior" proved to be a source of embarrassment for the ardent *constitutionnaire* bishop of Avignon, Montgeron was moved from there to Viviers. The Parlement of Paris was somehow satisfied that Montgeron had been transferred not as a prisoner, but simply as an exile,[148] the magistrates perhaps believing that such a change in status might signal a softening in the government's treatment of their fellow counselor.[149] But it was at Viviers that Montgeron experienced yet another humiliation; the *constitutionnaire* clergy, regarding him as an excommunicate for his refusal to accept the bull *Unigenitus* as a rule of faith, publicly denied him the sacraments. He protested this outrageous treatment to his colleagues in the Paris Parlement, the only place "where it was still possible to find some people attached to the Truth," and implored them to make representations to the king on his behalf.[150] Despite a direct appeal made on June 4, 1738, and formal remonstrances delivered less than four weeks later, the magistrates failed to move the king or his government.[151] Nor were they prepared to pursue the matter any further, presumably satisfied that they had done all they could to assist him. It was clearer than ever that few of Montgeron's erstwhile colleagues had either the will or the interest to protect him or his cause with their former energy. Thus, as the *procès* of the convulsionaries had already demonstrated, as far as the Parle-

---

[146] *NNEE*, Aug. 7, 1737, p. 122.   [147] Barbier, III, 102 (October 1737).

[148] Montgeron's status as exile instead of prisoner allowed him certain privileges: "Il profita de cette situation pour fonder à Villeneuve des écoles gratuites dont il payait généreusement les maîtres et les maîtresses, et c'était lui qui fournissait les livres" (A. Gazier, *Histoire générale*, I, 285). It was precisely these activities, however, which enraged the bishop of Avignon.

[149] *NNEE*, Dec. 6, 1737, p. 193. See also De Lisle's report of the "Mercuriales du 27 novembre 1737," AN, U-388.

[150] Montgeron to Le Febvre de St.-Hilaire, April 1738, cited by Bluche, p. 255. His initial appeal was made in a letter to First President Le Peletier, Dec. 27, 1737, BA, MS 10222; another one, more urgent, was made on April 1, 1738, BPR, L.P. 461, No. 55. Cf. Barbier, III, 128-30 (April 1738).

[151] Flammermont, I, 362-73; BN, NAFr., MS 8191, fols. 480-81, 511, 590-91, 597-603, 640, 656-66, 673-74; Barbier III, 136-37 (June 1738).

384

ment of Paris was concerned, the noisy affair that had begun at Saint-Médard was just about over. Not even the continued enthusiasm and involvement of one of their fellow judges could change that fact.

Outside the Parlement, in the meantime, the reaction to the Montgeron episode had been considerably more passionate and intense. Montgeron had stirred up yet another lively controversy to add to the various issues already being fiercely contested. As expected, opinion was very sharply divided. Whatever their position on the Bull, the opponents of the Pâris cult and of the convulsionaries generally condemned Montgeron as much for his action at Versailles as for the religious message contained in his book. They congratulated the government for taking such prompt and stern measures against the magistrate, described by one anonymous polemicist as an "impious Figurist."[152] Numerous satires appeared which criticized and ridiculed Montgeron's efforts.[153] Some *constitutionnaires*, in an apparently oblique rejoinder to *La Vérité des Miracles*, rushed a second edition of Vintimille's July 1731 *mandement* (now dated August 13, 1737) through the presses and onto the streets of Paris. Another critic, more direct and intemperate, went so far as to claim that Montgeron's work offered unequivocal confirmation that the *anticonstitutionnaires*, like the Lutherans and the Calvinists, were representatives of Antichrist.[154]

[152] See the *Lettre à Msgr. ***, pour servir comme une réponse à ses Réflexions sur la démarche de M. de Montgeron*. See also the brief, but equally caustic, *Lettre d'un théologien, où l'on montre ce qu'on doit penser d'un petit écrit qui a pour titre: "Réflexions sur la démarche de M. de Montgeron"* as well as the *Lettres à un magistrat, sur la démarche de M. de Montgeron* and *Le Magistrat trompé, ou La victime du parti janséniste . . . (8 septembre 1737)*. The *Lettres à un magistrat* and a subsequent *Suite des lettres à un magistrat* were eventually suppressed by an *arrêt* of the Paris Parlement on Jan. 4, 1738.

[153] A large quantity and wide variety of ephemeral pieces—"chansons, vaudevilles, anecdotes, sonnets, épigrammes, vers libres, épitaphes, vers satiriques"—may be found in the following: BN, MSS Fr., MSS 12634, 12675, 12707-708, 13662, and 15133, *passim*.

[154] *L'Antéchrist démasqué et confondu dans le parti miraculiste des appelants de la bulle "Unigenitus," ou Continuation des traits de ressemblance que ces réfractaires ont avec la secte de l'Antéchrist. Pour servir de réfutation au livre de M. de Montgeron et à tous les libelles du parti en faveur de l'appel et des miracles du temps; . . . et pour confondre en même temps les Luthériens, les Calvinistes, les Déistes, les Athées et toutes les sectes hérétiques et schismatiques séparées de la communion de l'Eglise romaine*. The anonymous author demonstrated his point by showing that the Number of the Beast (666) could be found in all of the following: HAERETICUS FILIUS PERDITIONIS; LUTHER DOCTEUR HÉRÉTIQUE; PASQUIER QUESNEL INSIGNE JANSÉNISTE CHEF D'HÉRÉSIE; and FRANÇOIS DE PÂRIS VRAI JANSÉNISTE QUESNELISTE! Although neither the Parlement nor the royal government issued an *arrêt* formally

Those who supported Montgeron, however, went immediately to his defense. The *Nouvelles ecclésiastiques* wasted no time in printing the story of Montgeron's presentation to the king, which ran in its issue of July 30. The journal went on to devote the major portion of some seven or eight subsequent issues to excerpting his book and following the fortunes of his case.[155] The editor, who had already honored the magistrate by representing him on the frontispiece for 1737 in the act of writing his *magnum opus*, praised the work as a "solid, instructive, and edifying piece, . . . especially decisive and triumphant against the bull *Unigenitus*."[156] Bishops Soanen and Colbert both published long letters on Montgeron's behalf.[157] The anonymous author of the *Réflexions sur la démarche de M. de Montgeron* argued, in justification of the magistrate, that his action was supported by significant precedents dating back to the Apostolic church and all of them "inspired and hence authorized by the spirit of God."[158] Finally, there were the inevitable songs, odes, and satires, which extolled Montgeron's virtues and decried the malevolence of his detractors.[159]

The convulsionary faithful, especially those who had benefited from Montgeron's munificence, were reportedly much grieved over his imprisonment.[160] But his capture also served as a source of inspiration. Popular leaflets and pamphlets elevated him to the position of religious martyr; portraits depicted him standing heroically beneath the image

---

suppressing this work, the authorities did seize all copies they could find along with all copies of *Le Magistrat trompé* and *L'Imposture confondue* (Peltier ["fils de l'inspecteur des Brigades"]) to Joly de Fleury, Jan. 29, 1738, BN, J.F., MS 176, fols. 65-66).

[155] *NNEE*, July 30, 1737, pp. 117-18; Aug. 7, 1737, pp. 121-22; Aug. 13, 1737, pp. 127-28; Aug. 25, 1737, pp. 133-35; Aug. 31, 1737, pp. 137-40; Sept. 14, 1737, pp. 145-48; Oct. 5, 1737, pp. 157-60; and Dec. 6, 1737, pp. 193-94. When it is recalled that there was usually a delay of at least two weeks before a news item got into the journal, one can see what great importance the editor must have attached to the Montgeron case, as he kept his readers informed of events almost as they happened.

[156] *Ibid.*, Oct. 5, 1737, p. 159.

[157] *Justification et apologie de la démarche de M. Montgeron, par MM. les évêques de Senez et de Montpellier (14 août 1737)*. See also Soanen à M***, Aug. 12, 1737, in *Oeuvres*, II, 456-59. For a discussion see *NNEE*, Aug. 25, 1737, pp. 133-35, and Durand, p. 345.

[158] Cited by *NNEE*, Aug. 7, 1737, p. 122; see also *ibid.*, Aug. 25, 1737, p. 135. For pamphlets which attacked this one, see above, n. 152. Another anonymous work favorable to the magistrate was the *Réflexions en forme de lettre sur la démarche de M. de Montgeron*.

[159] BN, MSS Fr., MSS 12634, 12675, 12707-708, 13662, and 15133, *passim*.

[160] *NNEE*, July 30, 1737, p. 117.

of the Holy Spirit, symbolized in the form of a dove. Prayers were even composed in his name and on his behalf.[161]

Montgeron's case seemed also to have received support of a rather different kind. Just after the government began to burn copies of *La Vérité des Miracles*,[162] two serious and portentous fires broke out in Paris within three months of one another. The first occurred on August 2, the day of the Parlement's audience with the king; it gutted the Hôtel-Dieu and caused a substantial number of casualities.[163] The second, which began on October 26 at the Chambre des Comptes, raged out of control for three days, severely damaging that building and some adjoining ones and resulting again in several deaths.[164] The mysterious origins of both of these fires gave rise to suggestions that they represented divine retribution for Montgeron's punishment and even to some wild speculation linking them directly to the convulsionaries.[165] Nor was that the end of the mystery. One of the few apartments spared by the fire was occupied by Armand Arouet, Voltaire's convulsionary brother, who was *receveur des épices* in the Chambre des Comptes. Stranger still, as Gazier has observed, "Arouet was not arrested, harassed, dismissed, or called upon to sell his post, even though there was much 'Jansenism' in [the] affair."[166]

Despite all this "testimony" allegedly demonstrating the innocence of Montgeron and the truth and righteousness of his cause, and despite the considerable body of partisan and popular sympathy which he had received, his status as a prisoner—or "exile"—did not change. If anything, this widespread support made Cardinal Fleury more anxious than ever to keep him out of Paris and out of circulation. But Montgeron's incarceration did not mark the end of his activities on behalf

[161] BN, MSS NAFr., MS 1702, fols. 96-102; see also BN, Salle des Imprimés, LD-4 2151. Cf. *Almanach de Dieu pour l'année 1738. Dédié à M. Carré de Montgeron, conseiller au parlement de Paris.*

[162] Hérault had 5,000 copies of the work burned at the Bastille, under Montgeron's window. "Mais l'auteur," Gazier notes, "avait pris ses précautions; il en parut la même année, à Utrecht, une nouvelle édition vendue à très bas prix quoique fort belle, car les planches avaient été sauvées, et l'ouvrage fut aussitôt traduit en plusieurs langues" (*Histoire générale*, I, 285). The book was already circulating in Troyes and Auxerre by the fall (see Mme. Duguet-Mol to [Hérault?], Nov. 4, 1737, BA, MS 11032).

[163] Barbier, III, 93-94 (August 1737).   [164] *Ibid.*, pp. 103-106 (October 1737). [165] *Ibid.*, p. 105 (October 1737).

[166] Gazier, "Le frère de Voltaire," p. 630. According to some anonymous *Notes historiques* which Gazier quotes on the matter, several convulsionaries were supposed to have responded to the burning of Montgeron's book by publicly announcing: "Ils ont brûlé les papiers de Dieu, Dieu brûlera les leurs" (*ibid.*).

of the convulsionary cause.[167] Indeed, his work as benefactor and con-troversialist does not seem to have been very seriously curtailed. From the citadel of Valence to which he was finally (and secretly) trans-ferred in late June 1738—and where he died in 1754—he somehow still managed to dispense money to needy convulsionaries and to continue his extensive correspondence.[168] Even more significant, he was able to write and supervise the publication of two more enormous volumes, one appearing in 1741, the other in 1748, both of them strong apolo-getics for the complete *oeuvres des convulsions*.[169] Like *La Vérité des Miracles*, which the Roman Inquisition had already placed on the Index in February 1739, each of these later tomes was ultimately to become the center of still other heated controversies. By the 1740s, however, though the questions surrounding the miracles and convul-sions were not dead, they remained alive primarily as issues to be de-bated among theologians and philosophers.[170] They were no longer of much interest to the public or to the civil and ecclesiastical authorities, for whom the miracles of François de Pâris and the entire convulsion-ary movement had finally ceased to be a critical problem. In this respect, then, Montgeron had totally failed: not even the miracles,

[167] See, for example, Montgeron to d'Etemare, May 13, 1738, AFA, P.R. 2855.

[168] Montgeron's transfer from Viviers to Valence occurred just before the Parlement presented remonstrances on his behalf on June 29, 1737. The condi-tions of his imprisonment were theoretically restrictive, and he was supposed to be subject to close supervision (cf. d'Angervilliers [*secrétaire d'état* with re-sponsibility for the Dauphiné] to the Governor of Valence, June 23, 1738, AAE, M&D, Fonds divers [Rome], MS 65, fols. 319-21; see also Fleury to Vintimille, June 12, 1738, BM, MS 2358, p. 745). Evidence of his ongoing efforts in support of the *oeuvre* may be found in: BA, MS 11304, *passim*, and ibid., MS 11479, especially Dubut *mémoire* of July 8, 1740, fols. 63-65 and 72-73 ("M. Regina, greffier des états à Aix est un de ceux dont M. de Montgeron se sert pour recevoir les lettres et paquets qui lui sont envoyés de Paris . . . ," fol. 65).

[169] Both of these volumes were published in Holland. Whereas the first volume consisted essentially of clinical observations, the second and third were more theological in nature. Writing of the citadel at Valence, Gazier has observed that "Le major de cette place avait sans doute des ordres secrets, car il interna l'exile dans la citadelle, en lui faisant payer sa nourriture et son logement, et il ne lui laissa de liberté que celle de communier tous les dimanches dans la chapelle du château" (*Histoire générale*, I, 285-86). However, the fact that Montgeron was able to turn out two massive volumes and continue his extensive correspond-ence would suggest that the government's surveillance over him during his im-prisonment must have been minimal. Many of his letters, diverse notes, and the corrected manuscript of his third volume were preserved by Le Paige and may be found at the BPR, L.P. 479.

[170] See, for example, the abbé d'Etemare's "Notes sur les volumes de M. de Montgeron," AFA, P.R. 5969. Disputes among the *anticonstitutionnaires* over the contents of Montgeron's second volume may be followed in BPR, L.P. 490.

temporarily separated from the rest of the *oeuvre* for reasons of polemical strategy, had been accorded official recognition. What is more, by the time of his death, Montgeron's own wide-ranging and uncompromising defense of the convulsions, the *secours meurtriers*, and all the rest of the *oeuvre* had so thoroughly alienated most of the Jansenist theologians and pamphleteers, including the editor of the *Nouvelles ecclésiastiques*, that he did not even seem worthy of an obituary in the appellant gazette or a place in the various *anticonstitutionnaire* necrologies of the time.[171]

Montgeron's attempt to persuade the king was a final, last-gasp effort to turn the tide that had been running ever more strongly in favor of the *constitutionnaires* and the other enemies of the Pâris cult. It was a gesture of desperation and an exercise in futility. Even more frustrating, the king apparently did not get to read *La Vérité des Miracles*.[172] The government of Cardinal Fleury, with only an oblique reference to Montgeron's book and absolutely no public comment on the miracles themselves, had obtained the magistrate's permanent imprisonment. Although ostensibly it was not as a convulsionist or as a protagonist of the Pâris cult but as a perpetrator of *lèse-majesté* that Montgeron had been pursued and arrested, the effect was the same. His audacious act had precipitated an important, if brief, controversy, but it was the last significant episode in the decade-long religious and political struggle that had originated at Saint-Médard.

The loss of Montgeron's active and present support and protection was by itself a serious blow to the cause of M. Pâris.[173] But his imprisonment took on an even more critical aspect when death deprived the cult of still other influential supporters. Bishop Charles-Joachim Colbert de Croissy, one of the four original appellants and the most important episcopal spokesman for the Pâris miracles, died on April 3, 1738, after a long and distinguished career in the Gallican Church. His contributions to the cause of the appeal and the cause of Saint-Médard, and particularly his efforts to forge the link between the two, had been considerable. In his death the practitioners of the Pâris cult and the convulsionaries lost a great friend.[174] Two years later they lost another. On Christmas Day 1740 the pious nonagenarian Bishop Jean Soanen died at the abbey of Chaise-Dieu to which he had been exiled, as "martyr to the Truth," thirteen years earlier. From his remote moun-

---

[171] Cf. *NNEE*, Dec. 4, 1750, p. 196.   [172] Barbier, III, 96 (August 1737).

[173] Montgeron "séquestré pour toujours, . . . [le] parti janséniste . . . perd un chef et un appui dans le Parlement" (*ibid.*, p. 102 [October 1737]).

[174] See "Ode sur la mort de Msgr. Colbert" (1738), in Raunié, VI, 214-18. Cf. Barbier's encomium, III, 127 (April 1738).

tain retreat in the Auvergne the charismatic "prisoner of Jesus Christ" had remained an active source of inspiration to all *anticonstitutionnaires*. In the last years of his life, while maintaining a voluminous correspondence with friends and admirers all over France, Soanen had assumed the role of elder statesman and father confessor to his fellow Jansenists, many of whom made long pilgrimages to consult with him and receive his blessings.[175] During this period he had also continued to share with his colleague from Montpellier a position of first rank among the followers of François de Pâris in the capital as well as throughout the kingdom.[176] These two patriarchs, both longtime "ecclesiastical politicians" and spiritual leaders, veterans of the struggle which began with the promulgation of the bull *Unigenitus*, more recently protagonists in another related struggle which began with the death of an obscure deacon—they, too, were now dead.

Thus by the end of the 1730s the fortunes of the Pâris cult seemed bleak indeed. The convulsionary movement was no longer regarded as respectable—or, more important, supportable—by any politically significant or numerically substantial segment of French society. As a body, the magistrates in the Parlement of Paris had abandoned the cause for which only a few had ever had much direct personal involvement or enthusiasm in the first place.[177] The passing of Colbert and Soanen left few notable *anticonstitutionnaires* who were very strong advocates of either the miracles or the convulsions. Even the Parisian clergy had fallen rather silent on the whole matter. The various opponents of the cult, in the meantime, had grown stronger than ever. The miracles and convulsions, for lack of any influential backing, thus all but ceased to be an issue of religious politics.

However, although their cause was no longer at the center of political and ecclesiastical controversy (theological debates aside), the followers of François de Pâris still managed to sustain their movement and continued to attract new adherents all over France. Neither the

[175] Montgeron and Jérôme-Nicolas de Pâris were two of the most prominent to make the trek.

[176] Soanen had also tried—unsuccessfully—to serve as a moderating influence between the bitter rival factions in the dispute over the *secours*. Frequent appeals were made to him to try to restore calm and order (see Le Paige to Soanen, July 27, 1737, AFA, P.R. 6693).

[177] The Parlement's repudiation of the convulsionaries in no way reflects a shift in the court's fundamentally *anticonstitutionnaire* tendencies or an abandonment of the magistrates' commitment to defend persecuted members of the so-called *parti janséniste*. Events of the next three decades clearly belie such a conclusion. See *NNEE*, *passim*, esp. after the late 1740s, and Van Kley's book on the expulsion of the Jesuits.

imprisonment nor the death which had befallen their chief compatriots could deter the faithful from practicing their cult. Indeed, the loss of these *frères* and *soeurs* had a powerful inspirational impact, convincing some that the arrival of Elijah and the conversion of the Jews was indeed very close at hand.[178] What is more, no sooner had Msgr. Soanen died than he began to "perform" miracles in the manner of several saintly predecessors.[179] But even more impressive was the spectacle which had earlier greeted the death of Jérôme-Nicolas de Pâris.

On August 16, 1737, less than three weeks after Montgeron's arrest, the younger brother of the deacon, counselor in the first chamber of *enquêtes*, died from the effects of "nearly incredible austerities" to which he had subjected himself since his exile to Clermont in 1732.[180] Out of veneration for and in emulation of his late brother he gave over his remaining years to a life of extreme penitence and abstinence, devoted to the Pâris cult. However, except for his display of pique concerning Vintimille's defamation of his brother's memory and over the government's alleged mistreatment of François' body, the precise nature of his contribution to the *oeuvre* remains obscure.[181] Whatever

[178] Cf. the *Relations de deux apparitions du prophète Elie au Frère Alexandre Ottin, la première en 1730, la seconde en 1740.* The second "appearance" occurred at Port-Royal-des-Champs on Aug. 31, 1740; Ottin was accompanied by his father and five brothers.

[179] Invocations of the *bienheureux* had already produced eight alleged miracles while Soanen was still alive (*Vie et lettres*, Ch. 12). Two others accomplished posthumously were more fully documented (*ibid.*, Ch. 13). See also the *Relation du miracle arrivé en la personne de Marie-Anne Pollet, affligée depuis près de quatre années d'une complication de maux étranges, et guérie, le 4 mai de la présente année, par l'intercession de l'illustrissime seigneur Jean Soanen, de sainte mémoire, . . .* (1741).

[180] *NNEE*, Oct. 19, 1737, p. 165. A variety of instruments of mortification, including hairshirts and sharp-pointed crucifixes, were found in Pâris' apartment. A major influence on his later years was Bishop Soanen, whom he first met in November 1732 (see the letters from Pâris to Soanen, Jan. 26, 1733, March 24, 1734, and Dec. 24, 1736, AFA, P.R. 6785). Cf. excerpts of a manuscript biography of M. Pâris in BPR, L.P. 475.

[181] But see the extraordinary "Rêve (or "Songe") de M. Pâris," a vivid, phantasmagoric "dream" the magistrate was said to have had a few months before his death. The dream depicts a living tableau of the entire convulsionary movement, the whole thing set in the cemetery of Saint-Médard, with all the principal protagonists, *constitutionnaire* and *anticonstitutionnaire*, symbolized in biblical forms. The dream is actually a "figure" of the life of Christ. The deacon Pâris is represented as Jesus Himself, with a crown of thorns on his head and his body being flogged by René Hérault, lieutenant-general of police. Among the other *dramatis personae*: Cardinal Fleury, "très vicieux, faisoit Hérode et donnoit ordre de faire périr les innocents pour tâcher de détruire celui qu'il craignoit comme un obstacle à son règne et à sa puissance"; Vintimille "représentoit Pilate, se lavoit les mains,

specific part the magistrate may have played in convulsionary circles, his own reputation for saintliness must nonetheless have been considerable, if the reaction to his death is any indication. The news of his passing had hardly begun to spread when large crowds of people from every station in society flocked to his home "in search of some item which had belonged to him. . . . Piety and contemplation were painted on every face."[182] Nor was that all, for the next day, when the funeral was to take place at his parish church of Saint-Gervais, "public veneration was even more marked."[183] From the house to the church the streets were lined with spectators,[184] while others, "righteously curious," looked on from their windows. The area around Saint-Gervais was filled with so many carriages that "this spectacle resembled an entrance of an ambassador more than a funeral service."[185] It was May 3, 1727, all over again.

Jérôme-Nicolas de Pâris had specifically requested that he be buried in the cemetery of Saint-Gervais. However, Hérault issued orders to inter him in the church, in order to avoid the same disturbances that had begun to occur at the cemetery of Saint-Médard a decade earlier.[186] Yet despite the presence of police agents sent to ensure that tranquility prevailed, crowds of people continued to visit the site. As before with the magistrate's brother, they carried away dirt and pieces of the board on which the body had been placed.[187] There were even reports of posthumous miracles performed through Jérôme-Nicolas' intercession.[188]

---

et disoit si j'y consent ce n'est que par crainte de Cézar, car je pense autrement que je n'agis"; Carré de Montgeron, "qui faisoit l'aveugle-né et soutenoit sa guérison miraculeuse" and elsewhere "faisoit Saint-Paul"; and Jérôme-Nicolas, dressed in white, "se voyoit destiné à faire l'ange de la résurrection, quand il se réveilla en sursaut." Manuscript copies of the *rêve* may be found in numerous Parisian archives (e.g., BA, MS 6884, fols. 25-28). It has also been published—with commentary—by Prince de Cardé and J. Roubinovitch, *Contribution à l'étude de l'état mental des Jansénistes convulsionnaires* (Poitiers, 1902).

182 *NNEE*, Oct. 19, 1737, p. 166.   183 *Ibid.*

184 Barbier described it as "un monde étonnant" (III, 97 [August 1737]).

185 *NNEE*, Oct. 19, 1737, p. 166. The editor also offered his own evaluation of this popular reaction: "C'est ainsi que Dieu a permis que fût honoré après la mort celui qui s'étoit tant abbaissé pendant les dernières années de sa vie: ou plutôt, c'est ainsi que Dieu a voulu que fut honorée la pratique de la pénitence, si affoiblie & si ignorée de nos jours: c'est ainsi que la gloire du S. Diacre a déjà rejailli en quelque sorte sur un frère qui, malgré la censure & les contradictions, a jugé sainement que le moyen le plus assuré de se réunir à lui, étoit de le suivre dans le chemin étroit qu'il avoit, pour ainsi dire, frayé par sa vie pénitente" (*ibid.*).

186 Barbier, III, 98 (August 1737).   187 *Ibid.*

188 Colbert to Caylus, Oct. 8, 1737, in *Oeuvres de Colbert*, III, 842.

The spirit of François de Pâris was far from dead. Attendance was still considerable at the church of Saint-Médard as well. On May 1, 1737, for example, which was the tenth anniversary of the deacon's death, the number of people who crowded into the little church was as great as it had ever been.[189] Even though the civil disturbances of an earlier day were all but over, the police, as a precautionary measure, kept an agent stationed nearby.[190] As far as the convulsionary *séances* were concerned, developments since 1735 had made a severe impact, with many of the less devoted and more disillusioned brethren gradually deserting the movement. Nevertheless, a significant proportion of the convulsionaries remained undeterred by the threat of arrests which were still being made in substantial numbers well beyond 1737. Though the prisons were becoming filled with their fellow *frères* and *soeurs*,[191] they continued to attract new adherents and to meet in their clandestine assemblies. There were, in short, few signs to indicate that these people had even begun to forget their beloved deacon or to abandon the observances associated with his memory. Thus, despite the irreparable loss—through death, imprisonment, intimidation, or repudiation—of virtually all supporters of power or influence, despite its virtual demise as a *cause célèbre* where the authorities were concerned, despite the fact that politically its fate had been sealed, the cult to François de Pâris had managed to retain much of its vitality. In this respect, then, the persistent efforts of Vintimille, Fleury, and their innumerable

[189] *NNEE*, May 4, 1737, p. 69. Vintimille reported that there were fewer persons of distinction in attendance than in years past, but even he and Cardinal Fleury were forced to admit that the dedication and tenacity of those present remained undiminished (Vintimille to Fleury, May 4, 1737, BM, MS 2358, p. 669, and Fleury to Vintimille, May 8, 1737, *ibid.*, pp. 670-71). The frustrated archbishop also made it clear that he would take no further action regarding the devotions at Saint-Médard, abandoning virtually all responsibility in this matter to the civil authorities.

[190] Indeed, a police officer would continue until May 9, 1757, to write his daily accounts of events going on in and around the church, where restrictions on access long remained in force. According to the last report, "On a remarqué qu'il est venu plus de monde cette année que les précédents" (BA, MS 10202). Official concern about the well in the back of the house once occupied by François de Pâris likewise persisted well beyond the period covered in this book (see the extraordinary series of letters exchanged between Archbishop Christophe de Beaumont and the office of lieutenant-general of police, March-July 1751, *ibid.*).

[191] Fifty convulsionaries were sent to the Bastille in 1740 alone, more than in any other year (Funck-Brentano, p. 233). Police raids conducted between the late 1730s and the early 1760s disclosed the existence of dozens of active conventicles in Paris and vicinity alone (BA, MSS 11344, 11375, 11422, 11462, 11471, 11487, 11508, 11525, 11540, 11571, 11583, 11606, 11624, 11627, 11628, 11629, 11630, 11635, 11689, 11695, 11965, 12077).

constitutionnaire (and later even *anticonstitutionnaire*) allies to stifle these unauthorized devotions had been largely a failure. Returned to the level of popular religion whence it had originated, the cult would still be providing spiritual sustenance in Paris, indeed all over France, well into the nineteenth century.[192]

[192] On late eighteenth- and early nineteenth-century convulsionary millennialism, see esp. Clarke Garrett, *Respectable Folly: Millenarians and the French Revolution in France and England* (Baltimore, 1975); Claude Hau, *Le Messie de l'an XIII et les Fareinistes* (Paris, 1955); and Henri Desroche, *Dieux d'hommes: Dictionnaire des messianismes et millénarismes de l'ère chrétienne* (Paris, 1969), *passim*. An apparently strong attachment to the memory of François de Pâris survived, in fact, into the twentieth century. In 1901, when the *curé* of Saint-Médard prepared to have some repair work done around the sanctuary, rumors began circulating that he was actually engaged in secret excavations designed to disinter the remains of the deacon Pâris' body and to toss them into the Seine. At this point scrawled renderings of the famous couplet, "De par le roi . . . ," reappeared on buildings throughout the neighborhood. Nothing more came of the affair, however ("Notes, trouvailles, et curiosités: La fermeture du cimetière Saint-Médard en 1732," *L'intermédiaire des chercheurs et curieux*, 37 [1901], col. 998).

Conclusion

The bitter doctrinal and ecclesiastical quarrels associated with the bull *Unigenitus*—still left unresolved by the end of the 1730s—contributed in no small measure to a growing sense of religious confusion and uncertainty as well as to a gradual erosion of public faith and confidence in the authority and prestige of the clerical establishment. These prolonged and acrimonious controversies not only weakened and exhausted the Church but also brought considerable discredit to the institution, at a time when Enlightenment critics were already beginning to take the offensive and to point ever more accusingly at the antisocial and dysfunctional character of established religion in eighteenth-century France. On the eve of its confrontation with the philosophes, the Church, riven by deep dissension and discord, was widely (if somewhat unfairly) perceived as suffering from a kind of institutional sclerosis: dominated by an entrenched aristocratic caste, rigid in its defense of the hierarchical structure, incapable of accommodating new social or intellectual transfusions, unwilling to tolerate (but unable to prevent or to eradicate) variations in religious beliefs or practices, and unprepared to absorb the tensions in consciousness and sensibility between the old modes and the new. Such was the environment in which the Pâris cult and the convulsionary movement emerged and developed.

Although by no means an exclusively popular phenomenon, the convulsionaries appealed by and large to a politically unsophisticated, inexperienced, and inarticulate people who basically lacked any conventional or approved forms of communication of their own and who were permitted few formal means of protest or opportunities of self-assertion. For its adherents, the sect served as a significant vehicle not only for the expression of values, attitudes, and aspirations and for the exploration of an alternative religious experience, but also for the venting of inchoate feelings of discontent and alienation. Certainly, the convulsionaries' search for unsanctioned and unorthodox forms of religious nourishment already implied a certain level of dissatisfaction with the established religious order and with the vitality of the Church's worship, a certain sense of unfulfilled, if unspecified, spiritual needs. But official attempts to interfere with and stifle those aspirations by resort to force only intensified the convulsionaries' feelings of frustration and disaffection, while exacerbating their sense of estrangement from the hierarchy of the Gallican Church.

It is difficult, of course, to assess the cumulative impact of such experiences on the people of eighteenth-century France. Although the experience of the convulsionaries probably did not make for a general vision of social, political, or institutional change, it seems reasonable to conclude that their repeated confrontations with the architects and executors of official religious policy and their constant exposure to *anticonstitutionnaire* propaganda had taught many of the movement's adherents to recognize and denounce manifestations of royal and especially sacerdotal "despotism." These experiences also contributed to the development of a vague, but potentially important, political consciousness among certain segments of the Paris faithful, some of them ancestors of the artisans and journeymen from among whom the *sans-culottes* would emerge half a century later. To be sure, there is little evidence that the convulsionaries ever thought of themselves as anything other than the obedient subjects of the king, for whom they frequently professed their undiminished respect and loyalty. While some of them occasionally mouthed a vaguely antiestablishmentarian political rhetoric, their criticisms rarely encompassed a direct, outspoken, or very harsh attack on the monarch himself or on royal authority. As so often in the *ancien régime*, responsibility for the alleged injustice and the arbitrary methods with which the convulsionaries had been treated was generally laid at the door of His Majesty's ministers and their "Jesuit advisers." And yet, though most of the convulsionaries remained basically attached to the maintenance of monarchical authority and were not out to overturn or even to threaten the stability of the established order, to challenge the nature of existing political relationships, or to favor any fundamental institutional redistribution of power, some of their ideas seemed incompatible with —indeed, even potentially subversive of—many of the religious, political, and social conceptions so sacred to the *ancien régime*.

The Gallican Church, like the Bourbon monarchy, was based on time-honored principles of order, hierarchy, and corporate privilege —principles which the convulsionary world view and devotional innovations certainly seemed to call into question. While promoting the concept of spiritual renewal and redemption, the followers of the deacon Pâris were endeavoring to create a new sacral community modeled on the ancient ideals of Christian brotherhood, a fraternal and egalitarian society of *frères* and *soeurs* in full, voluntary association within the involuntary constraints of the established Church. In so doing, the convulsionaries were implicitly criticizing the very structure of the Church and its governing ideology and indirectly questioning the rigidly hierarchical and authoritarian character of the institution. The convulsionaries thus conveyed, though they did not fully develop, an ideal image of the Church as a participatory congregation of the faithful. Amid suggestions of an alternative ecclesiology that had already been enunciated in some Jansenist circles, they began to exalt the role of the laity and the "second order" of the clergy within the ecclesiastical polity. Yet however much they may have viewed the Church as an instrument of reaction and as an obstacle to salvation, their aim was not to leave the institution but to regenerate it from within. Even if their concept of spiritual liberation and the nature of their *séance* activities appeared to challenge the principle of exclusive sacerdotal access to the divine and to bypass, at least in part, the Church's formal liturgical framework, the convulsionaries had no intention of repudiating all ecclesiastical authority, of denying the legitimacy of the priestly functions, or of ignoring the Church's sacramental prescriptions. As with their attitude toward the crown, the followers of François de Pâris were not prepared to draw out the full implications of their spiritual and ecclesiastical position.

For all the efforts of *anticonstitutionnaire* magistrates and *curés* to exploit the Pâris miracles and the other charismatic manifestations to partisan advantage, the convulsionary movement never achieved great political significance as a serious challenge to bishops or throne. While many convulsionaries may have come to perceive their experiences—and their political universe—through the spectacles of the Jansenist party's theology and ecclesiology and begun to utter antipapal and antiepiscopal slogans, they never had any realistic hope or prospect of extending their vision of the proper religious order beyond their various scattered conventicles. Even so, the convulsionary movement was no mere ephemeral outburst. No matter how unrealistic or unattainable their objectives, no matter how modest their accomplishments, no matter how vague or undeveloped their positions on certain issues, for the better part of a decade and in the face of repeated setbacks, the followers of François de Pâris had managed to keep the authorities in both Church and State very much preoccupied with their pronouncements and their activities—activities which had not been easily isolated or disentangled from the intricate web of Parisian ecclesiastical politics.

But the impact of the Saint-Médard episode and of the religious disputes in which the miracles and convulsions became embroiled extended well beyond the 1730s, beyond the sphere of ecclesiastical politics, beyond even the borders of France. On January 11, 1750, John Wesley, the celebrated Methodist divine, made the following entry in his *Journal*:

> I read, to my no small amazement, the account given by Monsieur Montgeron, both of his own conversion and of the other miracles wrought at the tomb of Abbé Pâris. I had always looked upon the whole affair as a mere legend, as I suppose most Protestants do, but I see no possible way to deny these facts without invalidating all human testimony. I may full as reasonably deny that there is such a person as Mr. Montgeron or such a city as Paris in the world. . . . If it be said, "But will not the admitting of these miracles establish Popery?" Just the reverse. Abbé Pâris lived and died in open opposition to the grossest errors of popery, and in particular, to that diabolical bull *Unigenitus*, which destroys the very foundations of Christianity.[1]

More than a decade later, Wesley had occasion to refer once more to the "affair of the Abbé Pâris":

> . . . whoever will read over with calmness and impartiality but one volume of Monsieur Montgeron, will then be a competent judge. Meantime I would just observe, that if these miracles were real, they would strike at the root of the whole Papal authority, as having been wrought in direct opposition to the famous bull *Unigenitus*.[2]

Such a view of the relationship between the Pâris miracles and the Bull, though without the anti-Catholic bias, had of course been the position which most Jansenists had taken almost from the first, and it was precisely such a conclusion which had so discomfited the *constitutionnaires* from Paris to Rome.

While for Protestants like Wesley the Saint-Médard miracles demonstrated the utter bankruptcy of "popery," to his contemporaries among the philosophes, British as well as French, these phenomena raised a series of additional questions, chiefly of an epistemological nature. The philosophes' basically hostile treatment of the subject was part of a wide-ranging crusade against irrationality and superstition, part of a general skeptical attack on all allegedly supernatural manifestations—an attack that went to the very heart of the theologico-political system on which these phenomena rested. Although the

[1] Ed. Nehemiah Curnock, 8 vols. (London, 1909-16), III, 451.
[2] Letter to Bishop Warburton of Gloucester, Nov. 26, 1762, in *Works*, 14 vols. (London, 1872), IX, 127-28.

propagators of *lumières* had nothing but contempt for the activities ("grotesque, hysterical frenzies") of the convulsionaries, whom they scornfully dismissed as "ridiculous enthusiasts" or "deranged fanatics," they did treat the question of the miracles with a good deal of philosophical seriousness.[3] Indeed, by the 1740s the general problem of miracles had acquired a certain degree of intellectual topicality. Hume, in particular, dealt with the subject in the context of an overall assessment of the possibility of miracles and a discussion of the difficulties of evaluating testimonial evidence with empirically based critical canons. While he himself denied all miracles, the Scottish philosopher left the clear impression that he believed that the "miraculous" cures which had supposedly occurred at Saint-Médard were more probable and better attested than those of Jesus Christ and that the Jesuit theologians, in attacking the former, furnished an arsenal of arguments for attacking the latter as well. Hume was especially impressed by the extraordinary quantity and quality of the evidence that had been accumulated. "Many of the miracles," he observed, "were immediately proved upon the spot, before judges of unquestioned integrity, attested by witnesses of credit and distinction, in a learned age, and on the most eminent theater that is now in the world."[4]

In fact, orthodox defenders of the faith had been greatly embarrassed and unsettled by the amazingly strong evidence supporting the miraculous character of many of the Pâris cures. They sought to rescue the Gospel miracles and to counter the skeptics by denying all similarity or connection between the accomplishments of Jesus Christ and the prodigies attributed to François de Pâris. In the end, however, they could do so only by denying the evidence and by questioning the sufficiency and the reliability of all human testimony, thereby undermining their own attempts to establish empirical criteria with which to distinguish the authentic miracle from the counterfeit and unwittingly aiding the cause of the skeptics. Attempts to gainsay the miraculous nature of the Pâris cures on the grounds of the deacon's doctrinal unorthodoxy proved equally unsatisfactory and unconvincing. While the theologians, both Jansenist and Jesuit, continued to wrangle over their definitions and to search in vain for a universally

[3] Cf. Kathleen W. Wilkins, "The Treatment of the Supernatural in the *Encyclopédie*," *Studies on Voltaire and the Eighteenth Century*, 90 (1972), pp. 1,757-71; Robert R. Palmer, *Catholics and Unbelievers in Eighteenth-Century France* (Princeton, 1939), pp. 92-95, 99-102; and Kreiser, "The Attitude of the Philosophes Toward the Convulsionaries of Saint-Médard" (paper read at the 3rd International Congress on the Enlightenment, Nancy, July 1971).

[4] *An Inquiry Concerning Human Understanding*, ed. Charles W. Hendel (Indianapolis, 1955), pp. 132-35.

acceptable and incontrovertible set of criteria, the status of the miracle became increasingly precarious. Unfortunately for the Church, the debate—theological and philosophical—left most of the vexing questions unresolved. Thus, in one of the most significant, albeit unanticipated and unintended, consequences of the Saint-Médard episode, the miracles of François de Pâris had provided Enlightenment critics with a major weapon in their challenge to the edifice of orthodox religious belief.

In the last analysis, the many-sided ecclesiastical struggles of the 1730s, of which the convulsionary affair was but a part, struck at the heart of the question of authority in eighteenth-century France— authority in the Church, authority in the State, and the relationships beween the two. The Saint-Médard episode and the events associated with it revealed the extent of the interpenetration and overlapping of religious and secular authority and the confused, often chaotic jurisdictional tangles which the royal government proved unable (and perhaps unwilling) to straighten out. Developments in the 1730s also disclosed the degree of disunion and distrust which reigned in the sphere of religious politics, as the various contending forces, ever more strident in their demands on the monarchy, vied with one another at all levels. Forced by the complexities and contradictions of ecclesiastical affairs to act as mediator between competing groups and institutions with conflicting and virtually irreconcilable interests, the French crown followed a rather pragmatic approach, vacillating almost unpredictably and irresolutely from one equivocal expedient to another and evading disagreeable decisions which might have too drastically upset the status quo or disturbed the balance of forces the government sought to maintain. Although the administration of Cardinal Fleury had managed to avoid an actual breakdown of authority at this time and temporarily composed the conflict of rival jurisdictions, this enforced peace was achieved without relieving any of the underlying tensions.

The government's pursuit of the convulsionaries had, of course, been part of a much larger official ecclesiastical policy: the imposition of the bull *Unigenitus* as a law of Church and State and the establishment of religious tranquility and conformity throughout the kingdom. By the late 1730s the perseverant Fleury appeared to have blunted, deflected, or silenced most of the *anticonstitutionnaire* criticism which had greeted the controversial royal declaration of March 1730. Not only had he successfully played most of the contending forces against each other; he had also seen the excitement over the Pâris cult all but dissipated and the convulsionary affair virtually eliminated as a *cause célèbre* in contemporary ecclesiastical debate. Like many of his other "successes," however, Fleury's political victory in the matter of the convulsionary movement, accomplished largely through the intimidation of dissidents and nonconformists and through the eventual detachment from the sect of many of its adherents' erstwhile supporters, was not an unqualified triumph. As a result of the sometimes arbitrary and heavy-handed methods used against both lay and clerical opponents of *Unigenitus* and followers of M. Pâris, the Fleury administration was to leave a bitter legacy of suspicion, frustration, and hostility in many quarters. Indeed, the government's handling of the convulsionary episode, like its enforcement of the Bull and its disposition of the other problems which bore upon the Saint-Médard affair, may have served rather to diminish than to enhance the authority and prestige of the crown.

The Saint-Médard episode thus strikingly exemplifies, albeit in a limited domain, the growing plight of the eighteenth-century Bourbon monarchy. In a society where most authority, secular as well as ecclesiastical, was more apparent than real, and where the administrative machinery for developing and enforcing royal policy was often inadequate to the task, continued respect for the legitimacy of the established order—and the very coherence of that order—depended in large measure on a shared consensus of received values, symbols, and myths. But the supposed consensus which the Bourbon kings had long sought to promulgate and propagate was largely an illusory façade, from behind which the underlying divisions and disharmonies of early modern France occasionally broke through. It was just such a situation that obtained in Paris in the late 1720s and 1730s—a time of unsettled conditions and considerable ferment and indiscipline within the Church—when the *parti janséniste*, a makeshift political coalition uniting the antipapal, anti-Jesuitical Gallicanism and parlementary constitutionalism of magistrates and lawyers with the anti-hierarchical Richerism of appellant priests, showed the formidable resistance it could muster against official ecclesiastical policies. Though relative calm was to prevail in the ecclesiastical sphere for more than a decade, the stormy religious crisis of the 1730s, a prelude to the fratricidal *billets de confession* affair and the even more momentous confrontations of the 1750s, seems not only to have revealed but also to have exacerbated some of the fundamental ideological, cultural, constitutional, and institutional tensions of the *ancien régime* and portended serious trouble both for the integrity of the Gallican Church and for the very future of Bourbon absolutism.

Bibliography

I. Primary Sources

A. Manuscripts

1. Archives

ARCHIVES DE LA PREFECTURE DE POLICE, PARIS

MSS Aa 307, $E\frac{b}{68}$

ARCHIVES DE PARIS ET DE L'ANCIEN DEPARTEMENT DE LA SEINE

D. 4 AZ783, D. 4G¹

ARCHIVES DU MINISTERE DES AFFAIRES ETRANGERES, PARIS

Correspondance Politique, Rome
  MSS 720-31, 733, 740, 742-43
Correspondance Politique, Rome (Supplément)
  MS 18
Mémoires et Documents, Fonds divers (Rome)
  MSS 7, 21-22, 37, 41-66, 73-75, 92
Mémoires et Documents, France
  MSS 27, 78, 1260-71, 1274-79, 1282-84, 1289-90, 1296-98, 1302
Mémoires et Documents, Petits Fonds
  MSS 1557-58, 1599-601, 1645, 1671, 1688-89, 1735-36

ARCHIVES HISTORIQUES DE L'ARCHEVECHE DE PARIS

MSS 8° P 18 (4.297), 8° P 61-62 (4.421, 4.423), 8° PR 1-2 (4.337-38),
  8° PR 4-6 (4.340-42), 8° PR 8-11 (4.344-47), 8° PR 13 (4.349),
  4° PR 1-6 (4.351-56), 4° PR 8 (4.358)

ARCHIVES NATIONALES, PARIS

Série AD III
  Carton 22
Série AD XVII
  Cartons 5B, 6
Série E
  Volumes 2105, 2111-13, 2119-21, 2128-29, 2135-36, 2142-43, 2150-51, 2158-59, 2166-68

Série G⁸*
  Volumes 680-82
Série L
  Cartons 15, 19
Série M^{IV}
  Carton 746
Série O¹
  Volumes 75-77, 81, 377-80
Série U
  Volumes 242-54, 374-89, 877, 1163-80
Série X^{1A}
  Volumes 8453-65
Série X^{1B}
  Cartons 9690-93
Série X^{2B}
  Carton 1335
Archives Privées
  A.P. 257, Cartons 8, 14-19, 27

RIJKSARCHIEF, UTRECHT

Ancien Fonds d'Amersfoort
  P.R. 2855, 3025, 3037, 3182, 3367, 4156, 4665, 4690, 4712, 4737, 4750,
    4770, 4833, 4843, 4866, 4891, 4902, 4935, 5062, 5154, 5166, 5249,
    5448, 5455, 5505, 5547, 5606, 5622, 5732-86, 5898, 5961, 5969,
    5988, 6439, 6451, 6453, 6456, 6457, 6472, 6547, 6568, 6628-30,
    6685, 6693, 6785, 6863, 6882-84, 6967, 7002, 7023/24

2. *Libraries*

BIBLIOTHEQUE DE L'ARSENAL, PARIS

MSS 2054, 2056, 2107, 2483, 3053, 3128, 3893, 4852, 5345-46, 5351,
  5378, 5407, 5783-84, 5802-804, 6033, 6048, 6580-81, 6882-91,
  7896-7904
Archives de la Bastille
  MSS 10007-10008, 10028-32, 10136, 10161-66, 10170-71, 10173, 10178,
    10182-83, 10188-93, 10196-226, 10233, 10297, 10325-27, 11032-34,
    11097, 11140, 11151, 11154, 11160, 11164, 11167, 11173, 11179,
    11188-90, 11193, 11195, 11197, 11199, 11201, 11207, 11210-11,
    11217-19, 11223, 11225, 11229, 11236-37, 11241, 11244-45, 11249,
    11253, 11257, 11259, 11262, 11268-69, 11271, 11274-75, 11279,
    11283, 11285, 11287, 11289, 11296, 11299, 11304-307, 11310,
    11312-15, 11320-21, 11325, 11327-29, 11331, 11333, 11336, 11339,

11341, 11344, 11349, 11352, 11354-55, 11359, 11366, 11369, 11375, 11377, 11379, 11384-85, 11401-402, 11409, 11416, 11422, 11434, 11439-50, 11447, 11455, 11457-58, 11462, 11464-65, 11471-72, 11479, 11483, 11487-89, 11491, 11495, 11506, 11508-509, 11513-14, 11525, 11531, 11540, 11571, 11577, 11583, 11606, 11614, 11624, 11627-30, 11633, 11689, 11695, 11964-65, 12031, 12042, 12077, 12483-84, 12487-90, 12555-60, 12581, 12684, 12689-91, 12693

BIBLIOTHEQUE DE L'UNIVERSITE DE PARIS

MSS 233-36, 238-40, 242, 1266-67

BIBLIOTHEQUE DE LA CHAMBRE DES DEPUTES, PARIS

MSS 1421-23

BIBLIOTHEQUE DE LA SOCIETE DE L'HISTOIRE DU PROTESTANTISME FRANÇAIS, PARIS

MSS 116-17, 118 (1-3), 119, 121-23, 127-30, 196-97

BIBLIOTHEQUE DE LA SOCIETE DES AMIS DE PORT-ROYAL, PARIS

Collection Le Paige

MSS 17, 435, 444-50, 452-54, 461, 474-508, 493-646bis, 648-52, 905-11, 1227-34, 1541-45, 1566-74

BIBLIOTHEQUE DU SENAT, PARIS

MSS 543-51, 721, 732, 793

BIBLIOTHEQUE HISTORIQUE DE LA VILLE DE PARIS

MSS 559, 703, 719-21, 4321, 10988, CP 3481, CP 3501-13, CP 3521-22, CP 3622-24, CP 3689, NA 125-32, NA 135-36

BIBLIOTHEQUE MAZARINE, PARIS

MSS 2357-58, 3944

BIBLIOTHEQUE MUNICIPALE DE SENS

Volumes 32, 32[bis], 34, 37, 40-44

BIBLIOTHEQUE MUNICIPALE DE TROYES

MSS 771, 939-40, 945, 1009-15, 1017-19, 1050, 1052-53, 1055-56, 1058-62, 1065-66, 1073, 1104, 1122, 1134, 1190-91, 1194, 1197-98, 1277, 1281, 1338, 1567, 1572, 1577, 1585, 1587-88, 1640, 1642-45, 1648-49, 1650, 1653, 1658, 1660, 1663, 1665, 1670, 1672,

1674-78, 1789, 1793, 1798, 1803-1804, 1809-10, 1818-19, 1821-23, 1825, 1827, 1831, 1833, 2079, 2082, 2088, 2094, 2097-98, 2100, 2106, 2113-14, 2116, 2119-20, 2125-26, 2129-30, 2150, 2156, 2160, 2163, 2173-74, 2176, 2178, 2182, 2184, 2188, 2196, 2213-14, 2226-30, 2232-33, 2240, 2257, 2336-37, 2340, 2353, 2367, 2507, 2543, 2794

BIBLIOTHEQUE NATIONALE, PARIS

Collection Clairambault
 MSS 523, 526-27, 558-59
Collection Joly de Fleury
 MSS 12, 99-101, 103, 107, 111, 116-19, 124, 126-27, 129-30, 132, 134, 146-48, 150, 154-55, 158, 161-62, 164-65, 168-69, 171-72, 175-76, 180, 205-206, 223, 276, 284, 313, 368, 451, 474, 600, 1048, 1317, 1322, 1331, 1415, 1476-77, 1481, 1491, 1616, 1984, 2309, 2465
Collection Moreau
 MS 844
Fonds Français
 MSS 6791, 6822, 7039, 7043, 8050, 8053, 8089, 8989, 10232, 10600, 10908-909, 11356, 11431, 12632-35, 12674-75, 12699-708, 12800, 12803-804, 13071, 13661-62, 13811-12, 13833, 13918, 15801-804, 15132-33, 17090, 17714-15, 17767-69, 19667-69, 20115, 20958, 20972, 22090-91, 22139, 22175, 22245, 22326, 23441-58, 23495, 24044, 24073, 24414-15, 24444, 24876-77, 25000, 25541-42, 25564
Nouvelles Acquisitions Françaises
 MSS 1702, 1891, 1909, 2076-77, 3332-34, 3336, 3363, 4093-113, 4259, 4261-64, 4735, 5096, 6505, 8181-91, 10967, 10979, 11004-11008, 11067, 11382, 11402, 11635-36, 13165-76, 22139

BIBLIOTHEQUE SAINTE-GENEVIEVE, PARIS

MSS 713, 735, 1519-20, 1944, 1946, 2482, 2533, 2905, 2926-27, 2934-35, 3378

MULLEN LIBRARY, THE CATHOLIC UNIVERSITY OF AMERICA, WASHINGTON, D.C.

Clement XI Collection
Thousands of uncatalogued volumes and manuscripts; especially useful were those entitled *Miscellanea Relativa alla Bolla Unigenitus.*

NEWBERRY LIBRARY, CHICAGO, ILL.

MSS 3A, 17-19

B. Relics

MUSEE MUNICIPAL, ARGENTEUIL

The museum catalogue lists the following items associated with Fran-
çois de Pâris among its repository:
Terre de sa tombe
Fragments de sa robe de chambre et de sa culotte
Bois de son bureau et de son lit
Morceau d'une cuiller ayant appartenu au Diacre
Cheveux
Gousset
Cendres bénites
Etoffe de drap
Pierre du tombeau
Fragments de doublure d'habit et d'une planche de couchage
Herbe du cimetière Saint-Médard
Spécimens de son écriture
Morceaux du manteau de lit
In addition, the museum possesses:
Fragments de ceinture et chemise dans laquelle est mort Nicolas de
Pâris le 16-8-1737
Autre fragment de la même chemise

C. Printed Sources

*1. Religious Pamphlets, Ecclesiastical Histories, and Theological
Tracts Dealing with the Jansenist Controversy*

*Abrégé chronologique de l'histoire de Port-Royal des Champs: Office
et pèlerinage en l'honneur des saints et saintes qui ont habité ce saint
désert, pour l'utilité de ceux qui ont la dévotion de visiter les ruines
de ce célèbre monastère et les lieux où reposent les corps qui en ont
été exhumés.* N.p., 1760.
*Abrégé historique des détours et des variations du jansénisme, depuis
son origine jusqu'à présent.* N.p., 1739.
[Barral, Pierre]. *Appellants célèbres, ou Abrégé de la vie des personnes
les plus recommandables entre ceux qui ont pris part à l'appel interjeté contre la bulle Unigenitus.* N.p., 1753.
[———; Guibaud, Eustache; and Valla, Joseph]. *Dictionnaire historique, littéraire et critique, contenant une idée abrégée de la vie
et des hommes illustres en tout genre, de tout tems et de tout pays.*
6 vols. Avignon, 1758-59.
Bentivoglio, Cornelio. *Istoria della Costituzione Unigenitus.* Edited by
Raffaele Belvederi. 3 vols. Bari, 1968.

[Besoigne, Jérôme]. *Histoire de l'abbaye de Port-Royal.* 6 vols. Cologne, 1752.

[———]. *Juste milieu qu'il faut tenir dans les disputes de religion, ou Règles de conduite dans le temps de contestation, soit pour les théologiens qui disputent, soit pour les fidèles qui en sont spectateurs.* N.p., 1736.

Boursier, Laurent-François. *Explication abrégée des principales questions qui ont rapport aux affaires présentes. . . .* N.p., 1731.

———. *Recueil de diverses difficultés proposées par les théologiens de France, sur la constitution Unigenitus.* N.p., 1716.

[Cadry, Jean-Baptiste, and Louail, Jean-Baptiste]. *Histoire du livre des "Réflexions morales sur le Nouveau Testament" et de la constitution Unigenitus.* 4 vols. Amsterdam, 1723-39.

[Cerveau, René]. *Nécrologe des plus célèbres défenseurs et confesseurs de la vérité du 18e siècle.* 2 vols. N.p., 1760.

[———]. *Supplément au Nécrologe. . . .* 2 vols. N.p., 1763-64.

[Clémencet, Charles]. *Histoire générale de Port-Royal depuis la réforme de l'abbaye jusqu'à son entière destruction.* 10 vols. Amsterdam, 1755-57.

[Colonia, Dominique de]. *Bibliothèque janséniste, ou Catalogue alphabétique des principaux livres jansénistes.* 2 vols. Brussels, 1739.

[———, and Patouillet, Louis]. *Dictionnaire des livres jansénistes ou qui favorisent le jansénisme.* 4 vols. Antwerp, 1752.

[Dettey, abbé]. *La vie de M. de Caylus, évêque d'Auxerre.* 2 vols. Amsterdam, 1765.

Dialogue sur les affaires du temps, entre un ancien marguillier de la paroisse de Saint-Médard de Paris et un prêtre de la communauté de Saint-Sulpice, dans une voiture publique. N.p., n.d.

[Du Fossé, Pierre Thomas]. *Mémoires pour servir à l'histoire de Port-Royal.* Utrecht, 1739.

[Etemare, Jean-Baptiste Le Sesne des Ménilles d', and Boyer, Pierre]. *Les Gémissements d'une âme vivement touchée de la destruction du saint monastère de Port-Royal-des-Champs.* 3rd ed. N.p., 1734.

[———]. *4e Gémissement d'une âme vivement touchée de la Constitution de N.-S.-P. le Pape Clément XI.* N.p., 1714.

[Fontaine, Nicolas]. *Mémoires pour servir à l'histoire de Port-Royal.* 2 vols. Utrecht, 1736.

[Fouillou, Jacques]. *Mémoires sur la destruction de l'abbaye de Port-Royal des Champs.* N.p., 1711.

[Fourquevaux, Jean-Baptiste-Raymond de Pavie de]. *Catéchisme historique et dogmatique sur les contestations qui divisent maintenant l'Eglise.* 2 vols. The Hague, 1729-30.

[————, and Troya d'Assigny, Louis]. *Catéchisme historique et dogmatique sur les contestations qui divisent maintenant l'Eglise.* Rev. ed. 5 vols. Nancy, 1750-68.

[Gerberon, Gabriel]. *Histoire générale du jansénisme.* 3 vols. Amsterdam, 1700.

[Goujet, Claude-Pierre]. *Vie de M. Duguet.* N.p., 1741.

[Guilbert, Pierre]. *Mémoires historiques et chronologiques sur l'abbaye de Port-Royal des Champs.* 9 vols. Utrecht, 1755-59.

[Jouin, Nicolas]. *Le vrai recueil des Sarcelles: Mémoires, notes, et anecdotes intéressantes sur la conduite de l'archevêque de Paris et de quelques autres prélats français. Le Philotanus, et le Porte-feuille du diable.* 2 vols. Amsterdam, 1764.

[La Borde, Vivien de]. *Du témoignage de la vérité dans l'Eglise.* . . . N.p., 1714.

Lafitau, Pierre-François. *Histoire de la constitution Unigenitus.* 2 vols. Avignon, 1737.

Lebeuf, Jean. *Dissertation sur l'histoire ecclésiastique et civile de Paris.* 3 vols. Paris, 1739-43.

[Le Cerf de la Viéville, Jean-Philippe]. *Histoire de la Constitution Unigenitus en ce qui regarde la congrégation de Saint-Maur.* Utrecht, 1736.

[Le Clerc, Pierre]. *Vies intéressantes et édifiantes des religieuses de Port-Royal et de plusieurs personnes qui leur étoient attachées.* 4 vols. Utrecht, 1750-52.

[Le Gros, Nicolas]. *Abrégé chronologique des principaux événements qui ont précédé la constitution Unigenitus, qui y ont donné lieu, ou qui en sont les suites.* Utrecht, 1730.

[————]. *Discours sur les "Nouvelles ecclésiastiques."* N.p., 1735.

[————]. *Du renversement des libertés de l'église gallicane dans l'affaire de la constitution Unigenitus.* 2 vols. N.p., 1716.

[————]. *Entretiens d'un ecclésiastique et d'un laïc, au sujet de la constitution Unigenitus.* Utrecht, 1737.

[————]. *Mémoires sur les droits du second ordre du clergé.* . . . N.p., 1733.

[————]. *Recueil de divers ouvrages au sujet de la constitution Unigenitus, faits pour l'instruction et pour la consolation des fidèles qui sont touchés des maux de l'Eglise.* Utrecht, 1740.

[————]. *Suite du Catéchisme historique et dogmatique.* 2 vols. Utrecht, 1751.

[————, and Besoigne, Jérôme]. *Catéchisme sur l'Eglise pour les temps de trouble.* N.p., 1737.

Lettre d'un docteur de Paris à un ecclésiastique de province, concernant les "Nouvelles ecclésiastiques." N.p., 1732.

Lettre écrite à un curé de Paris par les fidèles de sa paroisse, au sujet du mandement de M. l'archevêque contre les "Nouvelles ecclésiastiques." N.p., 1732.

[Nivelle, Gabriel-Nicolas, ed.]. *La constitution Unigenitus déférée à l'Eglise universelle, ou Recueil général des actes d'appel interjetés au futur concile général . . . avec les arrêts et autres actes des parlements du royaume qui ont rapport à ces objets.* 3 vols. Cologne, 1757.

[———, ed.]. *Le Cri de la foi, ou Recueil des différents témoignages rendus par plusieurs facultés, chapitres, curés, communautés ecclésiastiques et réguliers au sujet de la constitution Unigenitus.* 3 vols. N.p., 1719.

[———, ed.]. *Les Hexaples, ou les Six colonnes sur la constitution Unigenitus.* 6 vols. Amsterdam, 1721.

[Petitpied, Nicolas]. *Examen pacifique de l'acceptation et du fond de la bulle Unigenitus.* 3 vols. Cologne, 1749.

[Pinault, Olivier]. *Histoire abrégée de la dernière persécution de Port-Royal.* 3 vols. N.p., 1750.

[Poulain de Nogent, Mlle.]. *Nouvelle histoire abrégée de l'abbaye de Port-Royal, depuis sa fondation jusqu'à sa destruction. . . .* 2 vols. Paris, 1786.

Preuves de la liberté de l'Eglise de France dans l'acceptation de la constitution Unigenitus, ou Recueil des ordres émanés de l'autorité séculière pour y faire recevoir cette Bulle. Amsterdam, 1726.

[Quesnel, Pierre]. *Abrégé historique et chronologique dans lequel on démontre par les faits depuis le commencement du monde jusqu'en l'année 1733 que la vraie religion a toujours été et sera toujours combattue. . . .* Frankfurt, 1732.

[———]. *Almanach du diable, contenant des prédictions très curieuses et absolument infaillibles. . . .* 2 vols. N.p., 1737-38.

[———]. *Le Calendrier ecclésiastique . . . , avec le nécrologe des personnes qui depuis un siècle se sont le plus distinguées par leur piété, leur attachement à Port-Royal, et leur amour pour les vérités combattues. . . .* 6 vols. Utrecht, 1735-57.

[———]. *Etrennes jansénistes, ou Journal des principaux faits de l'histoire du prétendu jansénisme depuis son origine et des miracles opérés par l'intercession du B. H. Pâris, en forme d'almanach pour l'année 1733.* N.p., 1733.

[Racine, Bonaventure]. *Abrégé de l'histoire ecclésiastique.* Rev. ed. 15 vols. Cologne, 1748-62.

Racine, Jean. *Abrégé de l'histoire de Port-Royal.* Edited by Augustin Gazier. 2nd ed. Paris, 1909.

Réflexions judicieuses sur les "Nouvelles ecclésiastiques" de l'année courante 1736. N.p., 1736.

Réponse raisonnée aux "Réflexions judicieuses. . . ." N.p., n.d.

Thuillier, Vincent. *Rome et la France: La seconde phase du jansénisme. Fragment de l'histoire de la constitution Unigenitus de Dom Vincent Thuillier.* Edited by A.-M.-P. Ingold. Paris, 1901.

[Villefore de Bourgoing, Joseph-François]. *Anecdotes ou mémoires secrètes sur la constitution Unigenitus.* 3 vols. Utrecht, 1734.

2. Works Dealing with the Miracles and Convulsions of Saint-Médard

Anecdotes aussi sûres que curieuses touchant la conduite tyrannique et barbare qu'on a exercée sur Denyse Regné à la Bastille. N.p., 1760.

Apologie de l'auteur des "Problèmes" contre le vain triomphe de l'auteur de l'Examen de la Consultation. N.p., 1736.

L'apothéose de l'abbé Pâris racontée en détail par le fidèle témoin Vifvinfros. N.p., n.d.

L'appel et les miracles du temps foudroyés par la "Consultation sur les convulsions" et par le parjure des Jansénistes. N.p., 1735.

[Asfeld, Jacques Vincent Bidal d']. *Vains efforts des mêlangistes ou discernants dans l'oeuvre des convulsions, pour défendre le système de mélange. . . .* N.p., 1738.

[Barbeau de la Bruyère, Jean-Louis]. *La vie de M. François de Pâris, diacre.* Paris, 1731.

[Bonnaire, Louis de]. *Examen critique, physique et théologique des convulsions et des caractères divins qu'on croit voir dans les accidents des convulsionnaires.* N.p., 1733.

[————]. *Observations apologétiques de l'auteur des Examens critique, physique et théologique des convulsions.* 2 vols. N.p., 1733.

[————]. *Réponses de l'auteur des trois Examens aux Lettres d'un ami.* N.p., 1734.

[Boucher, Philippe]. *Lettres de M. l'abbé de l'Isle à un ami de Paris, sur les miracles qui s'opèrent par l'intercession de M. de Pâris.* 2nd ed. Utrecht, 1732.

Bougeant, Guillaume-Hyacinthe. *La Femme docteur, ou la Théologie tombée en quenouille, comédie.* Liège, 1731.

————. *Les Quakres français, ou les Nouvelles trembleurs, comédie.* Utrecht, 1732.

————. *Relation des miracles de Mr. Pâris, avec un abrégé de sa vie et un dialogue sur les neuvaines.* Utrecht, 1732.

Bougeant, Guillaume-Hyacinthe. *Le Saint déniché, ou la Banqueroute des marchands de miracles, comédie.* The Hague, 1732.

[Boursier, Laurent-François]. *Mémoire théologique sur ce qu'on appelle les secours violents dans les convulsions.* N.p., 1743.

[Boyer, Pierre]. *L'autorité des miracles des appellants dans l'Eglise.* N.p., 1734.

[———]. *Pensées sur les prodiges de nos jours.* N.p., 1734.

[———]. *La vie de M. de Pâris, diacre.* Brussels, 1731.

Consultation sur les convulsions. N.p., 1735.

[Crêpe, P.]. *Notion de l'Oeuvre des convulsions et des secours.* N.p., 1788.

Défense de l'autorité et des décisions des merveilles que Dieu ne cesse point de faire en France depuis un grand nombre d'années. 2 vols. N.p., 1752.

[De Lan, François Hyacinthe]. *Défense de la "Dissertation théologique contre les convulsions."* N.p., 1734.

[———]. *Dissertation théologique contre les convulsions, adressée au laïc auteur des "Réflexions sur la Réponse au Plan général."* N.p., 1733.

[———]. *Réponse à l'écrit intitulé: "Plan général de l'oeuvre des convulsions."* N.p., 1733.

Démonstration de la vérité et de l'autorité des miracles des appelants suivant les principes de M. Pascal. N.p., 1737.

[Desessarts, Jean-Baptiste Poncet]. *De l'autorité des miracles et de l'usage qu'on en doit faire.* N.p., n.d.

[———]. *12e Lettre de M.*** à un de ses amis, au sujet de la Consultation contre les convulsions.* N.p., 1735.

[———]. *8e Lettre sur l'oeuvre des convulsions. . . .* N.p., 1733.

[———]. *Illusion faite au public par la fausse description que M. de Montgeron faite de l'état présent des convulsionnaires.* N.p., 1749.

[———]. *Lettres de M.* à un de ses amis, sur l'oeuvre des convulsions.* N.p., 1734.

[———]. *Lettres de M. P. au sujet de l'écrit intitulé: "Vains efforts des Mélangistes. . . ."* N.p., 1738-40.

[———]. *La possibilité du mêlange dans les oeuvres surnaturelles du genre merveilleux prouvée par l'Ecriture. . . .* N.p., n.d.

[———]. *13e Lettre de Monsieur P*** à un de ses amis sur les convulsions.* N.p., n.d.

[Des Voeux, Antoine Vinchon]. *Critique générale du livre de Mr. de Montgeron sur les miracles de Mr. l'abbé de Pâris, ou Nouvelles lettres sur les miracles.* 2 vols. Amsterdam, 1740.

[————]. *Dissertation sur les miracles que l'on attribue aux reliques de M. l'abbé Pâris.* Leiden, 1732.

[————]. *Lettres sur les miracles, où l'on établit les caractères distinctifs des vrais miracles en général, en particulier de ceux qui s'opèrent sur le corps-humain. . . .* Rotterdam, 1735.

Deux problèmes à résoudre sur l'oeuvre des convulsions, l'un pour la spéculation, l'autre pour la pratique. N.p., 1734.

Discours sur les miracles, par un théologien. N.p., 1732.

Dissertations sur les miracles. N.p., 1733.

[Doyen, Barthélemy]. *Vie de M. de Pâris, diacre du diocèse de Paris.* Paris, 1731.

[Duguet-Mol, Mme.]. *Journal historique des convulsions du temps.* N.p., 1733.

Elévation du coeur à Dieu sur les maux de l'Eglise, et sur les merveilles qui s'opèrent au tombeau du bienheureux de Pâris. N.p., n.d.

Entretiens sur les miracles des derniers temps, ou les Lettres de M. le chevalier***. N.p., n.d.

Essai d'un plan sur l'oeuvre des convulsions. N.p., n.d.

[Etemare, Jean-Baptiste Le Sesne des Ménilles d']. *Exposé de la manière de penser de M. l'abbé De*** touchant l'événement des convulsions. . . .* N.p., 1735.

[————]. *Lettre d'un ecclésiastique à un évêque.* N.p., 1733.

[————]. *Lettres de M. Détemare et de M. Gourlin à M. de La Boissière au sujet de son Traité des miracles. . . .* Paris, 1787.

Examen de l'écrit intitulé: "Exposé de la manière de penser de M. l'abbé d'E . . . touchant l'événement des convulsions." N.p., 1736.

Examen de la Consultation au sujet des convulsions. N.p., 1735.

Examen de la 3e Lettre contre les convulsions et de la théologie de son auteur sur les guérisons miraculeuses. N.p., 1733.

Examen du "Mémoire sur le terme d'Oeuvre des convulsions." N.p., 1736.

Exposition du sentiment de plusieurs théologiens, défenseurs légitimes de l'oeuvre des convulsions et des miracles, au sujet de la Consultation des docteurs. . . . N.p., 1735.

[Fouillou, Jacques]. *Dissertation sur les miracles, contre les impies.* N.p., 1742.

[————]. *Lettre à M.*** sur la nouvelle théologie des convulsionnaires.* N.p., 1734.

[————]. *Lettre à Madame*** sur le prétendu caractère prophétique des convulsions.* N.p., 1733.

[————]. *Nouvelles observations sur les convulsions. . . .* N.p., 1733.

[Fouillou, Jacques]. *Observations sur l'origine et le progrès des convulsions qui ont commencé au cimetière Saint-Médard.* N.p., 1733.

[Fronteau, Marie-Anne-Elisabeth (Soeur Holda)]. *Recueil de prédictions intéressantes faites depuis 1733, par diverses personnes, sur plusieurs événements importants.* 2 vols. N.p., 1792.

[Gennes, Julien-René-Benjamin de]. *Coup d'oeil, en forme de lettre, sur les convulsions.* N.p., 1733.

[———]. *Lettre . . . au sujet des convulsions.* N.p., 1733.

[———]. *Réclamation des défenseurs légitimes des convulsions et des secours. . . .* N.p., 1743.

[Gourlin, Pierre-Sébastien]. *Recherche de la vérité, ou Lettres sur l'oeuvre des convulsions.* N.p., 1733.

[Gudver, Abbé]. *Entretiens sur les miracles.* Brussels, 1732.

Histoire des miracles et du culte de M. Pâris, avec les persécutions suscitées à sa mémoire et aux malades qui ont eu recours à lui, pour servir de suite à la Vie de ce saint diacre. Rev. ed. 2 vols. N.p., 1734.

Hume, David. *An Enquiry Concerning Human Understanding and Other Essays.* Edited by Ernest C. Mossner. New York, 1963.

Jugement équitable sur les convulsions. N.p., 1733.

[La Boissière, Simon Hervieux de]. *Défense du "Traité des miracles."* N.p., 1769.

[———]. *Préservatif contre les faux principes et les maximes dangereuses établies par M. de Montgeron pour justifier les secours violents qu'on donne aux convulsionnaires.* 2nd ed. Paris, 1787.

[———]. *Traité des miracles.* 2 vols. Paris, 1763-64.

Languet de Gergy, Jacques-Joseph. *Instruction pastorale au sujet des prétendus miracles du diacre de Saint-Médard et des convulsions arrivées à son tombeau.* 2 vols. Paris, 1734-35.

La Taste, Louis-Bernard de. *Lettres théologiques aux écrivains défenseurs des convulsions et autres prétendus miracles du temps.* 2 vols. Paris, 1740.

Lettres adressées à un défenseur du mélange dans l'oeuvre des convulsions. N.p., 1738-40.

Lettres du chevalier*** . . . [qui] servent de réfutations aux Lettres de l'abbé De L'Isle sur les miracles de M. de Pâris, et à tous les écrits de cette nature qui ont paru et qui pourront paraître dans la suite, comme aussi au système fanatique des figuristes. N.p., 1734.

Mémoire sur le terme d'Oeuvre des convulsions, où l'on démêle les équivoques de ce terme et où l'on fixe le sens dans lequel il est légitimement appliqué à l'événement des convulsions. N.p., n.d.

Les miracles futurs de l'évêque d'Utrecht proposés par souscription. N.p., n.d.

Montgeron, Louis-Basile Carré de. *Continuation des démonstrations des miracles.* . . . *Observations sur l'oeuvre des convulsions et sur l'état des convulsionnaires.* 2 vols. N.p., 1741-48.

———. *La Vérité des Miracles opérés à l'intercession de M. de Pâris & autres Appellans, démontrée contre M. l'Archevêque de Sens.* Utrecht, 1737.

Nouveau plan des réflexions sur la consultation des docteurs contre les convulsions. N.p., 1735.

[Petitpied, Nicolas]. *Dissertation sur les miracles, et en particulier sur ceux qui ont été opérés au tombeau de M. de Pâris, en l'église de S.-Médard de Paris.* . . . N.p., 1731.

[Pilé, abbé]. *Idée de l'oeuvre des secours selon les sentiments de ses légitimes défenseurs.* N.p., 1786.

Plan de diverses questions sur un bruit répandu dans le public, qu'actuellement on fait signer une consultation sur les convulsions. N.p., 1735.

Plan général de l'Oeuvre des convulsions, avec des Réflexions d'un laïc en réfutation de la Réponse que M. l'abbé de L. a faite à ce Plan. N.p., 1733.

Préjugés légitimes pour les convulsions, en faveur des simples et pour servir de supplément à l'écrit qui a pour titre: "Avis aux fidèles." N.p., n.d.

Recueil de discours de plusieurs convulsionnaires. N.p., 1734.

Recueils des miracles opérés au tombeau de M. de Pâris. 3 vols. N.p., 1732-35.

Réflexions sur l'Ordonnance du roi du 17 février 1733. N.p., 1733.

Réflexions sur l'Ordonnance du roi en date du 27 janvier 1732. . . . N.p., 1732.

Réflexions sur le miracle arrivé à Moissy par l'intercession de M. Pâris. 2nd ed. Utrecht, 1742.

Réflexions sur les miracles que Dieu opère au tombeau de M. de Pâris et, en particulier, sur la manière étonnante et extraordinaire dont il les opère depuis six mois ou environ. N.p., n.d.

Réfutation d'un second écrit contre la Consultation, intitulé: "Exposition du sentiment de plusieurs théologiens, défenseurs légitimes de l'oeuvre des convulsions et des miracles." N.p., 1735.

Règle infaillible pour discerner les vrais des faux miracles. N.p., n.d.

Réponse succincte à un écrit intitulé: "Examen de la Consultation sur les convulsions." N.p., n.d.

Requête au bienheureux diacre Pâris, par MM. les appelants défenseurs des convulsions. N.p., 1735.

Reynaud, abbé. *Le secourisme détruit dans ses fondements.* N.p., 1759.

[Saint-Jean, abbé de]. *Lettre d'un ecclésiastique de province à un de ses amis, où il donne une idée abrégée de l'Oeuvre des convulsions.* N.p., 1733.

[————]. *Supplément à la "Lettre d'un ecclésiastique de province. . . ."* N.p., 1734.

Seconde lettre d'un ecclésiastique à un ami, au sujet du mandement de M. l'archevêque de Paris du 15 juillet 1731. N.p., 1731.

Suffrages en faveur des deux dernières tomes de M. de Montgeron. . . . Relations et preuves de quelques-unes des nouvelles merveilles que Dieu opère journellement depuis 1748 dans l'oeuvre des convulsions et des secours. N.p., 1749.

Le système des discernants dans l'oeuvre des convulsions, confondu par la doctrine des saints Pères. . . . N.p., 1736.

Le système du mélange dans l'oeuvre des convulsions, confondu par ses ressemblances avec le système des augustinistes, et par les erreurs et les défauts qu'il renferme. N.p., 1735.

Vintimille du Luc, Charles Gaspard Guillaume de. *Mandement . . . au sujet d'un écrit qui a pour titre: "Dissertation sur les miracles. . . ."* Paris, 1731.

————. *Ordonnance . . . rendue sur la requête du promoteur-général de l'archevêché de Paris, au sujet des prétendus miracles attribués à l'intercession du sieur Pâris. . . .* Paris, 1735.

3. Works of Figurist Exegesis

[Bonnaire, Louis de, and Boidot, abbé]. *Traités historiques et polémiques de la fin du monde, de la venue d'Elie et du retour des Juifs.* 3 vols. Amsterdam, 1737-38.

[Desessarts, Alexis]. *De l'avènement d'Elie.* 2 vols. N.p., 1734-35.

[Duguet, Jacques-Joseph]. *Explication du mystère de la Passion.* 2 vols. Paris, 1728.

[————]. *Règles pour l'intelligence des Saintes Ecritures.* Paris, 1716.

[Etemare, Jean-Baptiste Le Sesne des Ménilles d']. *Essai d'un parallèle du temps de Jésus-Christ et des nôtres, pour servir d'instruction et de consolation dans les grandes épreuves au milieu desquelles nous vivons.* N.p., n.d.

[————]. *Explication de l'Apocalypse.* Paris, 1866.

[————]. *Explication de quelques prophéties touchant la conversion future des Juifs.* N.p., 1724.

[————]. *Histoire de la religion représentée dans l'Ecriture sainte sous divers symboles.* 2 vols. Paris, 1862.

[————]. *Principes pour l'intelligence de l'Ecriture sainte.* Paris, 1865.

[Fourquevaux, Jean-Baptiste-Raymond de Pavie de]. *Introduction abrégée à l'intelligence des prophéties de l'Ecriture par l'usage qu'en fait S. Paul dans l'Epître aux Romains.* N.p., 1731.

[Gudver, abbé]. *Jésus-Christ sous l'anathème et l'excommunication.* Amsterdam, 1731.

[Joubert, François]. *Commentaire sur l'Apocalypse.* 2 vols. Avignon, 1762.

[————]. *De la connaissance des temps par rapport à la religion.* Utrecht, 1727.

[————]. *Lettres de M.*** sur l'interprétation des Saintes Ecritures.* N.p., 1744.

[————]. *Parallèle abrégé de l'histoire du peuple d'Israël et de l'histoire de l'Eglise.* N.p., 1723.

[Lambert, Bernard]. *Avertissement aux fidèles sur les signes qui annoncent que tout se dispose pour le retour d'Israël, et l'exécution des menaces faites aux Gentils apostats.* Paris, 1793.

[————]. *Exposition des prédictions et des promesses faites à l'Eglise pour les derniers temps de la gentilité.* 2 vols. Paris, 1806.

[Pâris, François de]. *Explication de l'épître aux Romains.* 3 vols. Paris, 1732.

[————]. *Plan de la religion.* N.p., 1740.

[————]. *Science du vrai, qui contient les principaux mystères de la foi.* N.p., 1733.

[Pilé, abbé]. *La vérité combattue et victorieuse, ou Prières et instructions sur l'état présent de l'Eglise.* N.p., 1779.

4. Works Dealing with Religious Ceremonies and Practices

Bernard, Jean-Frédéric, ed. *Cérémonies et coutumes religieuses de tous les peuples du monde, représentées par des figures dessinées de la main de Bernard Picart, avec une explication historique et quelques dissertations curieuses.* 11 vols. Amsterdam, 1723-43.

Lebrun, Pierre. *Histoire critique des pratiques superstitieuses qui ont séduit le Peuple, et embarrassé les Sçavans, avec la méthode et les principes pour discerner les effets naturels d'avec ceux qui ne le sont pas.* Rouen, 1701-1702.

————, and Thiers, Jean-Baptiste. *Superstitions anciennes et modernes: Préjugés vulgaires qui ont induit les peuples à des usages et à des pratiques contraires à la religion.* 2 vols. Amsterdam, 1733-36.

Lehoreau, René. *Cérémonial de l'église d'Angers.* Edited by François Lebrun. Paris, 1967.

Thiers, Jean-Baptiste. *Traité des superstitions selon l'Ecriture sainte, les décrets des conciles et les sentiments des saints et des théologiens.* 2nd ed. 4 vols. Paris, 1697-1704.

5. Newspapers and Periodicals

Almanach royal.

Bibliothèque raisonnée des ouvrages des savans de l'Europe.

Mémoires pour servir à l'histoire des sciences et des beaux-arts (Journal de Trévoux).

Nouvelles ecclésiastiques, ou Mémoires pour servir à l'histoire de la Constitution "Unigenitus."

Supplément des Nouvelles ecclésiastiques.

Tables raisonnées et alphabétiques des "Nouvelles ecclésiastiques" depuis 1728 jusqu'en 1760 inclusivement. Edited by abbé de Bonnemare. 2 vols. Paris, 1767.

6. Collections of Documents

Ceyssens, Lucien, ed. *La fin de la première période du jansénisme: Sources des années 1654-1660.* 2 vols. Brussels, 1963-65.

————, ed. *La première bulle contre Jansénius: Sources relatives à son histoire, 1644-1653.* 2 vols. Brussels, 1961-62.

————, ed. *Sources relatives aux débuts du jansénisme et de l'antijansénisme, 1640-1643.* Louvain, 1957.

Collection des procès-verbaux des assemblées générales du clergé de France depuis l'année 1560. Edited by A. Duranthon. 9 vols. Paris, 1767-68.

Corda, Augustin, and Trudon des Ormes, A., eds. *Catalogue des factums et d'autres documents judiciaires antérieures à 1790.* 10 vols. Paris, 1890-1936.

Flammermont, Jules Gustave, ed. *Remontrances du Parlement de Paris au 18ᵉ siècle.* 3 vols. Paris, 1888-98.

Funck-Brentano, Frantz, ed. *Les lettres de cachet à Paris.* Paris, 1903.

Isambert, François-André et al., eds. *Recueil général des anciennes lois françaises, depuis l'an 420 jusqu'à la Révolution de 1789.* 29 vols. Paris, 1822-33.

Mention, Léon, ed. *Documents relatifs aux rapports du clergé avec la royauté.* 2 vols. Paris, 1893-1903.

Raunié, Emile, ed. *Chansonnier historique du 18ᵉ siècle.* 10 vols. Paris, 1879-84.

Ravaisson, François, ed. *Archives de la Bastille.* 19 vols. Paris, 1866-1904.

Recueil des actes, titres, et mémoires concernant les affaires du clergé de France. Edited by Pierre Lemerre. 14 vols. Paris, 1768-71.

Recueil dit de Maurepas, pièces libres, chansons, épigrammes, et autres vers satiriques sur divers personnages des siècles de Louis XIV et Louis XV. 3 vols. Leiden, 1865.

Sibour, Marie-Dominique-Auguste, ed. *Actes de l'Eglise de Paris touchant la discipline et l'administration.* Paris, 1854.

7. *Memoirs, Journals, Correspondence, and Reports*

Aguesseau, Henri-François d'. *Oeuvres complètes.* Edited by Jean-Marie Pardessus. 16 vols. Paris, 1819.

Argenson, René-Louis de Voyer, marquis d'. *Journal et mémoires.* Edited by Edme-Jacques Rathery. 9 vols. Paris, 1859-67.

Barbier, Edmond-Jean-François. *Chronique de la Régence et du règne de Louis XV (1718-1763).* 8 vols. Paris, 1857.

Bérengier, Th., ed. *Une correspondance littéraire au 18ᵉ siècle entre Dom de la Rue, Bénédictin de la Congrégation de St.-Maur, et Mgr. d'Inguimbert, évêque de Carpentras.* Avignon-Paris, 1888.

Bernis, François Joachim de Pierre de. *Mémoires et lettres (1715-1758).* Edited by Frédéric Masson. 2 vols. Paris, 1878.

Buvat, Jean. *Journal de la Régence.* Edited by Emile Campardon. 2 vols. Paris, 1865.

Carra, Jean-Louis. *Mémoires historiques et authentiques sur la Bastille.* 3 vols. Paris, 1789.

[Charpentier]. *La Bastille dévoilée, ou Recueil de pièces authentiques pour servir à son histoire.* 2 vols. Paris, 1789-90.

Clark, Ruth, ed. *Lettres de Germain Vuillart, ami de Port-Royal à M. Louis de Préfontaine (1694-1700).* Geneva, 1951.

Colbert, Charles-Joachim. *Oeuvres.* 3 vols. Cologne, 1740.

Cottin, Paul, ed. *Rapports inédits du lieutenant de police René d'Argenson (1697-1715).* Paris, 1891.

Dangeau, Philippe de Courcillon, marquis de. *Journal.* Edited by Eudore Soulié *et al.* 19 vols. Paris, 1854-60.

Dorsanne, Antoine. *Journal . . . contenant ce qui s'est passé à Rome et en France dans l'affaire de la constitution Unigenitus.* 2 vols. Rome, 1753.

Dubuisson, Simon-Henri. *Mémoires secrètes du 18ᵉ siècle: Lettres du commissaire Dubuisson au Marquis de Caumont, 1735-41.* Edited by A. Rouxel. Paris, 1882.

Feydeau de Marville, Claude-Henri. *Lettres de M. de Marville, lieutenant général de police, au ministre Maurepas (1742-1747).* Edited by A. de Boislisle. 3 vols. Paris, 1896-1905.

Gaultier, Jean-B., ed. *La vie et les lettres de Messire Jean Soanen, évêque de Senez.* 2 vols. Cologne, 1750.

Gazier, Augustin, ed. "Fragment inédit des Mémoires du chancelier d'Aguesseau," *Bulletin philologique et historique (jusqu'à 1715) du Comité des travaux historiques* (1918), 24-58.

Goldmann, Lucien, ed. *Correspondance de Martin de Barcos, abbé de Saint-Cyran.* Paris, 1956.

Grimm, Friedrich Melchior. *Correspondance littéraire, philosophique et critique de Grimm et de Diderot depuis 1753 jusqu'en 1790*. 15 vols. Paris, 1829-31.

Halkin, Léon, ed. "Correspondance de dom Edmond Martène avec le baron G. de Crassier, archéologue liégeois," *Bulletin de l'Institut archéologique liégeois*, 27 (1898), 19-308.

Heeckeren, Émile de, ed. *Correspondance de Benoît XIV*. 2 vols. Paris, 1912.

Hénault, Charles-Jean-François. *Mémoires du Président Hénault*. Edited by François Rousseau. Paris, 1911.

Jadin, Louis, ed. *Le cardinal Thomas-Philippe d'Alsace, archevêque de Malines, et le Saint-Siège: Correspondance tirée des Archives du Vatican, 1703-1759*. Brussels-Rome, 1953.

Jordan, Charles-Etienne. *Histoire d'un voyage littéraire fait en 1733 en France, en Angleterre, en Hollande*. The Hague, 1735.

Lamoignon, Guillaume de. "Journal historique de Guillaume de Lamoignon, avocat-général au Parlement de Paris, 1713-1718." Edited by Henri Courteault. *Annuaire-Bulletin de la Société de l'histoire de France*, 47 (1910), 238-95.

Legendre, Louis. *Mémoires*. Edited by M. Roux. Paris, 1863.

Luynes, Charles-Philippe d'Albert, duc de. *Mémoires sur la cour de Louis XV (1735-1738)*. Edited by L. Dussieux and E. Soulié. 17 vols. Paris, 1860-65.

Marais, Mathieu. *Journal et mémoires sur la Régence et le règne de Louis XV (1715-1737)*. Edited by A. M. de Lescure. 4 vols. Paris, 1863-68.

[Maupoint, *avocat*]. *Calendrier historique, avec le Journal des cérémonies et usages qui s'observent à la Cour, à Paris, et à la Campagne*. Paris, 1737.

Mémoires du comte de Maurepas [apoc.]. 2nd ed. 4 vols. Paris, 1792.

Mercier, Louis Sebastien. *Tableau de Paris*. Rev. ed. 12 vols. Amsterdam, 1782-88.

Mercure ecclésiastique, ou Journal historique des ouvrages du tems, avec un examen critique de chaque ouvrage. Utrecht, 1733.

Narbonne, Pierre. *Journal des règnes de Louis XIV et Louis XV de l'année 1701 à l'année 1744*. Paris, 1866.

Nouvelles de la Cour et de la ville, 1734-1738. Edited by Edouard de Barthélemy. Paris, 1879.

Platelle, Henri, ed. *Journal d'un curé de campagne au 17ᵉ siècle*. Paris, 1965.

Pöllnitz, Karl-Ludwig von. *Lettres et mémoires*. 5 vols. Amsterdam, 1737.

Quesnel, Pasquier. *Un janséniste en exil: Correspondance de Pasquier*

Quesnel, sur les affaires politiques et religieuses de son temps. Edited by Mme. Albert Le Roy. 2 vols. Paris, 1900.

Rives, D.-B., ed. *Lettres inédites du Chancelier d'Aguesseau.* Paris, 1823.

Saint-Simon, Louis de Rouvroy, duc de. *Mémoires.* Edited by A. de Boislisle. 41 vols. Paris, 1879-1928.

Villars, Louis-Hector, duc de. *Mémoires.* 6 vols. Paris, 1884-1904.

[Walpole, Horatio]. *Memoirs of the Life and Administration of the Late Andrew-Hercules de Fleury.* 2nd ed. London, 1743.

8. Medical Works

Chastelain, Mathieu. *Traité des convulsions et des mouvements convulsifs qu'on appelle à présent vapeurs.* Paris, 1691.

Devillers, Charles. *Le colosse aux pieds d'argille.* Paris, 1784.

Hecquet, Philippe. *Lettres d'un médecin de Paris à un médecin de province, sur le miracle arrivé sur une femme du faubourg St.-Antoine.* N.p., 1725.

———. *La médecine, la chirurgie et la pharmacie des pauvres.* 2nd ed. 4 vols. Paris, 1749.

———. *Le naturalisme des convulsions, dans les maladies de l'épidémie convulsionnaire.* Soleure, 1734.

———. *Réponse à la "Lettre à un confesseur, touchant le devoir des médecins . . . au sujet des miracles et des convulsions."* N.p., 1733.

———. *La suçeuse convulsionnaire, ou la Psylle miraculeuse.* N.p., 1736.

[Lefebvre de Saint-Marc, Ch.]. *Vie de M. Hecquet.* Paris, 1749.

Lettre à un confesseur, touchant le devoir des médecins et chirurgiens au sujet des miracles et des convulsions. N.p., 1733.

Morand, Sauveur-François. *Opuscules de chirurgie.* Paris, 1768-72.

Observations de médecine sur la maladie appellée convulsion. Paris, 1732.

Procès-verbaux de plusieurs médecins et chirurgiens au sujet de quelques personnes soi-disantes agitées de convulsions. Paris, 1732.

*Réponse à la "Lettre d'un docteur en médecine de la Faculté de***."* N.p., 1736.

9. Dictionaries, Manuals, and Law Books, Civil and Ecclesiastical

[Boyer, abbé de]. *Principes sur l'administration temporelle des paroisses.* 2 vols. Paris, 1786.

Brillon, Pierre-Jacques. *Dictionnaire de jurisprudence et des arrêts.* Rev. ed. 7 vols. Lyon, 1781-88.

Brillon, Pierre-Jacques. *Nouveau dictionnaire civil et canonique de droit et de pratique.* Paris, 1697.

Desessarts, Nicolas Toussaint Lemoyne. *Dictionnaire universel de police.* . . . 8 vols. Paris, 1786-90.

Duperray, Michel. *Notes et observations sur les cinquante articles de l'édit de 1695 concernant la juridiction ecclésiastique.* Paris, 1718.

Durand de Maillane, Pierre Toussaint. *Dictionnaire de droit canonique et de pratique bénéficiale.* 2nd ed. rev. 4 vols. Lyon, 1770.

Du Rousseaud de la Combe, Guy. *Recueil de jurisprudence canonique et bénéficiale.* Rev. ed. Paris, 1755.

Ferrière, Claude-Joseph de. *Dictionnaire de droit et de pratique.* 3rd ed. rev. 2 vols. Paris, 1749.

Fleury, Claude. *Institution au droit ecclésiastique.* Rev. ed. 2 vols. Paris, 1767.

Fréminville, Edme de la Poix de. *Dictionnaire ou traité de la police générale des villes, bourgs, paroisses et seigneuries de la campagne.* Rev. ed. Paris, 1775.

Guyot, Pierre J.J.G. *Répertoire universel et raisonné de jurisprudence civile, criminelle, canonique et bénéficiale.* 36 vols. Paris, 1780-88.

———. *Traité des droits, fonctions, franchises, exemptions, prérogatives et privilèges.* 3 vols. Paris, 1786-87.

Héricourt du Vatier, Louis de. *Les loix ecclésiastiques de France dans leur ordre naturel et une analyse des livres du droit canonique conférés avec les usages de l'Eglise Gallicane.* Rev. ed. Paris, 1771.

Hurtaut, Pierre-Thomas-Nicolas, and Magny, A. *Dictionnaire historique de la ville de Paris et ses environs.* 4 vols. Paris, 1779.

Jousse, Daniel. *Commentaire sur l'édit du mois d'avril 1695, concernant la juridiction ecclésiastique.* 2 vols. Paris, 1764.

———. *Nouveau commentaire sur l'édit du mois d'avril 1695.* . . . 2 vols. Paris, 1770.

———. *Traité du gouvernement spirituel et temporel des paroisses.* Paris, 1769.

La Croix, Claude de. *Le parfait ecclésiastique, ou Diverses instructions sur toutes les fonctions cléricales.* Paris, 1665.

Lamare, Nicolas de. *Traité de la police.* 4 vols. Paris, 1705-38.

[Lambert, Joseph]. *La manière de bien instruire les pauvres, et en particulier les gens de la campagne.* Rouen, 1716.

Lebeuf, Jean. *Histoire de la ville et de tout le diocèse de Paris.* Edited by A. Augier and F. Bournon. 7 vols. Paris, 1883-93.

Le Maire, Jean-Baptiste-Charles. "La police de Paris en 1770." Edited by Augustin Gazier. *Mémoires de la Société de l'histoire de Paris et de l'Ile de France,* 5 (1878), 1-131.

[Mildmay, William]. *The Police of France.* London, 1763.

Sallé, Jacques-Antoine. *L'esprit des ordonnances de Louis XIV.* 2 vols. Paris, 1758.

——. *Nouveau code des curés.* 4 vols. Paris, 1778-80.

[Travers, Nicolas]. *Les pouvoirs légitimes du premier et du second ordre dans l'administration des sacrements et le gouvernement de l'Eglise.* N.p., 1744.

II. SECONDARY SOURCES

A. Books and Dissertations

Abercrombie, Nigel. *The Origins of Jansenism.* Oxford, 1936.

Abricossoff, Glafira. *L'hystérie aux 17e et 18e siècles.* Paris, 1897.

Adam, Antoine. *Du mysticisme à la révolte.* Paris, 1968.

Affre, P. *L'appel comme d'abus.* Paris, 1845.

Agulhon, Maurice. *La sociabilité méridionale: Confréries et associations dans la vie collective en Provence orientale à la fin du 18e siècle.* 2 vols. Aix-en-Provence, 1966.

Antoine, Michel. *Le Conseil du Roi sous le règne de Louis XV.* Geneva, 1970.

Appolis, Emile. *Entre Jansénistes et zelanti: Le tiers-parti catholique au 18e siècle.* Paris, 1960.

——. *Le jansénisme dans le diocèse de Lodève au 18e siècle.* Albi, 1952.

Ardoin, Paul. *La bulle Unigenitus dans les diocèses d'Aix, Arles, Marseille, Fréjus, Toulon.* 2 vols. Marseille, 1936.

Aubertin, Charles. *L'esprit public au 18e siècle.* Paris, 1873.

Avenel, Georges d'. *Les évêques et archevêques de Paris depuis Saint Denis jusqu'à nos jours.* 2 vols. Paris, 1878.

Azéma, Xavier. *Un prélat janséniste: Louis Fouquet, évêque et comte d'Agde, 1656-1707.* Paris, 1963.

Bachelier, Alcime. *Le jansénisme à Nantes.* Paris, 1934.

Back, Kurt W., and Kerckhoff, Alan C. *The June Bug: A Study of Hysterical Contagion.* New York, 1968.

Barkun, Michael. *Disaster and the Millennium.* New Haven, 1974.

Barroux, Marius. *Essai de bibliographie critique des généralités de l'histoire de Paris.* Paris, 1908.

Barthélemy, Edouard de. *Le Cardinal de Noailles.* Paris, 1886.

Batiffol, Pierre, *Histoire du Bréviaire romain.* 3rd ed. rev. Paris, 1911.

Bellanger, Claude et al. *Histoire générale de la presse française.* 5 vols. Paris, 1969-76.

Bellerose, Leo M. "The Ecclesiastical Theory of the Parlement of Paris in the 18th Century." Ph.D. Dissertation, Georgetown University, 1947.

Berlanstein, Lenard R. *The Barristers of Toulouse in the 18th Century, 1740-1793*. Baltimore, 1975.

Bertrand, Alexandre. *Traité du somnambulisme et des différentes modifications qu'il présente*. Paris, 1823.

Bertrand, Louis. *Bibliothèque sulpicienne, ou Histoire littéraire de la Compagnie de Saint-Sulpice*. 3 vols. Paris, 1900.

Bickart, Roger. *Les Parlements et la notion de souveraineté nationale au 18e siècle*. Paris, 1932.

Billy, André. *Rue Maudicte et à l'entour*. N.p., 1943.

Biot, René, ed. *Médecine et merveilleux*. Groupe lyonnaise d'études médicales, philosophiques et biologiques. Paris, 1956.

Bisson de Barthélemy, P. *Les Joly de Fleury, procureurs-généraux au Parlement de Paris au 18e siècle*. Paris, 1964.

Blanc, Hippolyte. *Le merveilleux dans le jansénisme*. Paris, 1865.

Blet, Pierre. *Les assemblées du clergé et Louis XIV de 1670 à 1693*. Rome, 1972.

———. *Le clergé de France et la monarchie: Etude sur les Assemblées générales du clergé de 1615 à 1666*. 2 vols. Rome, 1959.

Blewett, Peter F. "The Gallicanism of Louis-Ellies Du Pin." Ph.D. Dissertation, Boston College, 1969.

Bloch, Marc. *Les rois thaumaturges: Etude sur le caractère surnaturel attribué à la puissance royale*. Strasbourg, 1924.

Bluche, François. *Les magistrats du Parlement de Paris au 18e siècle (1715-1771)*. Paris, 1960.

———. *L'origine des magistrats du Parlement de Paris au 18e siècle*. Paris, 1956.

———. *La vie quotidienne de la noblesse française au 18e siècle*. Paris, 1973.

Blunt, John H., ed. *Dictionary of Sects, Heresies, Ecclesiastical Parties, and Schools of Religious Thought*. London, 1874.

Boinet, Amédée. *Les églises parisiennes*. 3 vols. Paris, 1948-64.

Bollème, Geneviève. *Les almanachs populaires aux 17e et 18e siècles: Essai d'histoire sociale*. Paris, 1969.

———, ed. *La bibliothèque bleue: Littérature populaire en France du 17e au 19e siècle*. Paris, 1971.

Bonniot, Joseph de. *Le miracle et ses contrefaçons*. 5th ed. Paris, 1895.

Bontoux, Françoise. *'Nouvelles ecclésiastiques,' parlement de Paris et parlementaires (1730-1762)*. Diplôme d'études supérieures d'histoire, University of Paris, 1955.

Boulard, Fernand. *Premiers itinéraires en sociologie religieuse.* 2nd ed. Paris, 1966.

Boullée, A. A. *Histoire de la vie et des ouvrages du chancelier d'Aguesseau.* 2 vols. Paris, 1835.

Bourlon, J. *Les Assemblées du clergé et le jansénisme.* Paris, 1909.

Bournet, Léon. *La querelle janséniste.* Paris, 1924.

Bourneville, Désiré Magloire, and Voulet, Paul. *De la contracture hystérique permanente.* Paris, 1872.

Bournon, Fernand. *Histoire générale de Paris: La Bastille.* Paris, 1892-94.

Bouteiller, Marcelle. *Chamanisme et guérison magique.* Paris, 1950.

———. *Médecine populaire d'hier et d'aujourd'hui.* Paris, 1966.

Boutry, Maurice. *Une créature du cardinal Dubois: Intrigues et missions du cardinal de Tencin.* Paris, 1902.

Bouvier, Henri. *Histoire de l'église et de l'ancien archidiocèse de Sens.* 3 vols. Paris, 1906-11.

Braudel, Fernand, and Labrousse, Ernest, eds. *Histoire économique et sociale de la France moderne, 1660-1789.* Paris, 1970.

Brémond, Henri. *Histoire littéraire du sentiment religieux en France depuis la fin des guerres de religion jusqu'à nos jours.* 11 vols. Paris, 1916-33.

Brewer, Ebenezer C. *A Dictionary of Miracles, Imitative, Realistic, and Dogmatic.* Philadelphia, 1884.

Briquet, Pierre. *Traité clinique et thérapeutique de l'hystérie.* Paris, 1859.

Brochard, Louis. *Saint-Gervais: Histoire de la paroisse.* Paris, 1950.

Brongniart, Marcel. *La paroisse Saint-Médard au faubourg Saint-Marceau.* Paris, 1951.

Broutin, Paul. *La réforme pastorale en France au 17e siècle: Recherches sur la tradition pastorale après le concile de Trente.* 2 vols. Paris, 1956.

Bruggeman, J., and Van de Ven, A. J. *Inventaire des pièces d'archives françaises se rapportant à l'abbaye de Port-Royal-des-Champs et son cercle et à la résistance contre la bulle Unigenitus et à l'appel (Ancien Fonds d'Amersfoort).* The Hague, 1972.

Burns, Robert M. "David Hume and Miracles in Historical Perspective." Ph.D. Dissertation, Princeton University, 1971.

Burridge, Kenelm. *New Heaven, New Earth: A Study of Millenarian Activities.* Oxford, 1969.

Buteau, Henry. *L'ordre des avocats, ses rapports avec la magistrature: Histoire, législation, jurisprudence.* Paris, 1895.

Cagnac, Moïse. *De l'appel comme d'abus dans l'ancien droit français.* Paris, 1906.

Cahen, Léon. *Le grand bureau des pauvres de Paris au milieu du 18ᵉ siècle.* Paris, 1904.

———. *La paroisse Saint-Germain-l'Auxerrois (1715-1745).* Diplôme d'études supérieures, University of Paris, 1895.

———. *Les querelles religieuses et parlementaires sous Louis XV.* Paris, 1931.

———, and Letaconnoux, J., eds. *La vie parisienne au 18ᵉ siècle. Leçons faites à l'Ecole des Hautes Etudes Sociales.* Paris, 1914.

Callahan, Marie T. "The Gallicanism of Claude Fleury." Ph.D. Dissertation, Boston College, 1970.

Calmeil, Louis F. *De la folie.* 2 vols. Paris, 1845.

Calvet, Jean. *La littérature religieuse de François de Sales à Fénelon.* Paris, 1938.

Candel, Jules. *Les prédicateurs français dans la première moitié du 18ᵉ siècle.* Paris, 1904.

Cans, Albert. *L'organisation financière du clergé de France à l'époque de Louis XIV.* Paris, 1909.

Cardé, Prince de, and Roubinovitch, Dr. J. *Contribution à l'étude de l'état mental des Jansénistes convulsionnaires.* Poitiers, 1902.

Carré, Henri. *La France sous Louis XV (1723-1774).* Paris, 1891.

———. *La noblesse de France et l'opinion publique au 18ᵉ siècle.* Paris, 1920.

Carreyre, Jean. *Le Jansénisme durant la Régence.* 3 vols. Louvain, 1929-33.

Carrier, Hervé. *The Sociology of Religious Belonging.* Translated by Arthur J. Arrieri. London, 1965.

Carrière, Victor, ed. *Introduction aux études d'histoire ecclésiastique locale.* 3 vols. Paris, 1934-40.

Carson, John W. "The Social Position of a French Lawyer (1718-1763): An Appraisal of the Advocate Barbier." Ph.D. Dissertation, University of Nebraska, 1957.

Charcot, Jean-Martin. *Les démoniaques dans l'art.* Paris, 1887.

Charrier, Jules. *Histoire du jansénisme dans le diocèse de Nevers.* Paris, 1920.

Chassaigne, André. *Des lettres de cachet sous l'ancien régime.* Paris, 1903.

Chassaigne, Marc. *La Lieutenance-Générale de Police de Paris.* Paris, 1906.

Chatelin, Philippe. *Contribution à l'étude du régime des aliénés et anor-*

maux aux 17ᵉ et 18ᵉ siècles: L'élimination des "anti-sociaux." Le donjon de Vincennes et ses prisonniers. Paris, 1921.

Chénon, Emile. *Histoire des rapports de l'Eglise et de l'Etat.* 2nd ed. Paris, 1913.

————. *Histoire générale du droit français public et privé des origines à 1815.* 2 vols. Paris, 1926-29.

Chéruel, Pierre A. *Dictionnaire historique des institutions, moeurs et coutumes de la France.* 5th ed. 2 vols. Paris, 1880.

Chételat, Paul. *Etude sur Duguet.* Paris, 1879.

Chill, Emanuel S. "The Company of the Holy Sacrament, 1630-1666: Social Aspects of the French Counter-Reformation." Ph.D. Dissertation, Columbia University, 1960.

Christ, Yvan. *Eglises parisiennes actuelles et disparues.* Paris, 1947.

Clark, Ruth. *Strangers and Sojourners at Port-Royal.* Cambridge, Eng., 1932.

Clément, Pierre. *La police sous Louis XIV.* 2nd ed. Paris, 1866.

Cobb, Richard. *The Police and the People: French Popular Protest, 1789-1820.* Oxford, 1970.

Cocatre-Zilgien, André. *Les doctrines politiques des milieux parlementaires dans la seconde moitié du 18ᵉ siècle ou les avocats dans la bataille idéologique prérévolutionnaire.* Lille, 1963.

Cognet, Louis. *Claude Lancelot, Solitaire de Port-Royal.* Paris, 1950.

————. *La crépuscule des mystiques.* Tournai, 1958.

————. *Le jansénisme.* Paris, 1961.

————. *Les origines de la spiritualité française au 17ᵉ siècle.* Paris, 1949.

————. *La réforme de Port-Royal, 1591-1618.* Paris, 1950.

————. *La spiritualité moderne.* Vol. I: *L'essor, 1500-1650.* Paris, 1966.

Cohn, Norman. *The Pursuit of the Millennium.* 3rd ed. New York, 1970.

Collin de Plancy, Jacques. *Dictionnaire critique des reliques et des images miraculeuses.* 3 vols. Paris, 1821-22.

Coudy, Julien. *Les moyens d'action de l'ordre du clergé au Conseil du Roi (1561-1715).* Paris, 1954.

Coulanges, A. de. *La chaire française au 18ᵉ siècle.* Paris, 1801.

Couly, Auguste. *Les fabriques avant la Révolution française.* Toulouse, 1910.

Coynart, Charles de. *Le chevalier de Folard (1669-1752).* Paris, 1914.

Cragg, Gerald R. *The Church and the Age of Reason (1648-1789).* Baltimore, 1960.

Cross, Whitney R. *The Burned-Over District: The Social and Intel-*

lectual History of Enthusiastic Religion in Western New York, 1800-1850. Ithaca, 1950.

Crousaz-Crétat, Paul de. L'Eglise et l'état ou les deux puissances au 18e siècle (1715-1789). Paris, 1893.

———. Paris sous Louis XIV. 2 vols. Paris, 1922-23.

Cutten, George Barton. Speaking with Tongues: Historically and Psychologically Considered. New Haven, 1927.

Daoust, Joseph. Dom Martène: Un géant de l'érudition bénédictine. Abbaye S. Wandrille, 1947.

Daumard, Adeline, and Furet, François. Structures et relations sociales à Paris au milieu du 18e siècle. Paris, 1961.

Davis, Natalie Z. Society and Culture in Early Modern France. Stanford, 1975.

Declareuil, Joseph. Histoire générale du droit français des origines à 1789. Paris, 1925.

De Felice, Philippe. Foules en délire. Extases collectives: Essai sur quelques formes inférieures de la mystique. Paris, 1947.

Degert, A. Histoire des séminaires français jusqu'à la Révolution. 2 vols. Paris, 1912.

Dejean, Etienne. Un prélat indépendant au 17e siècle: Nicolas Pavillon, évêque d'Alet (1637-1677). Paris, 1909.

Delarc, Odon Jean Marie. L'Eglise de Paris pendant la Révolution française, 1789-1801. 3 vols. Paris, 1895-97.

Delumeau, Jean. Le Catholicisme entre Luther et Voltaire. Paris, 1971.

Dent, Cynthia A. "The French Church and the Monarchy in the Reign of Louis XIV: An Administrative Study." Ph.D. Dissertation, University of London, 1967.

D'Erceville, S.-M. De Port-Royal à Rome: Histoire des Soeurs de Sainte-Marie. Paris, 1956.

Desautels, Alfred. Les "Mémoires de Trévoux" et le mouvement des idées au 18e siècle, 1701-34. Rome, 1956.

Desdevises du Dézert, Georges N. L'Eglise et l'Etat en France, 1598-1906. 2 vols. Paris, 1907-1908.

Desmaze, Charles A. Le Parlement de Paris. Paris, 1859.

Desnoiresterres, Gustav Le Brisoys. La comédie satirique au 18e siècle. Paris, 1885.

Desroche, Henri. Dieux d'hommes: Dictionnaire des messianismes et millénarismes de l'ère chrétienne. Paris, 1969.

Deyon, Pierre. Amiens, capitale provinciale: Etude sur la société urbaine au 17e siècle. Paris, 1967.

DiCorcia, Joseph N. "Parisian Society, 1740-1763: A Cross-Sectional Analysis." Ph.D. Dissertation, Duke University, 1973.

Dictionnaire des églises de France, Belgique, Luxembourg, Suisse. 5 vols. Paris, 1966-71.

Dingwall, Eric J. *Some Human Oddities: Studies in the Queer, the Uncanny and the Fanatical.* New York, 1962.

Dollinger, Philippe, and Wolff, Philippe. *Bibliographie d'histoire des villes de France.* Paris, 1967.

Dubreuil, Auguste. *Etude historique et critique sur les Fareinistes ou Farinistes.* Lyon, 1908.

Ducros, Louis. *La société française au 18e siècle, d'après les mémoires et les correspondances du temps.* Paris, 1922.

Dufey, Pierre-Joseph-Spiridion. *Histoire, actes, et remontrances des parlements de France, chambres des comptes, cours des aides, et autres cours souveraines, depuis 1461 jusqu'à leur suppression.* 2 vols. Paris, 1826.

Dufour, Valentin. *Bibliographie historique, artistique et littéraire de Paris avant 1789.* Paris, 1882.

Dulaure, Jacques-Antoine. *Histoire physique, civile et morale de Paris.* 6th ed. 8 vols. Paris, 1837-39.

Dumas, Georges. *Histoire du journal de Trévoux depuis 1701 jusqu'à 1762.* Paris, 1936.

—————. *Le surnaturel et les dieux d'après les maladies mentales (Essai de théogénie pathologique).* Paris, 1946.

Dumolin, Maurice, and Outardel, Georges. *Les Eglises de France: Paris et le Seine.* Paris, 1936.

Dupront, Alphonse. *Les lettres, les sciences, la religion and les arts dans la société française de la deuxième moitié du 18e siècle.* 2 vols. Paris, 1965.

Durand, Valentin. *Les évêques au 18e siècle en Languedoc.* Montpellier, 1907.

—————. *Le jansénisme au 18e siècle et Joachim Colbert, évêque de Montpellier.* Toulouse, 1907.

Egret, Jean. *Louis XV et l'opposition parlementaire, 1715-1774.* Paris, 1970.

Ehrard, Jean. *L'idée de nature en France dans la première moitié du 18e siècle.* 2 vols. Paris, 1963.

Elie le prophète selon les Ecritures et les traditions chrétiennes. Paris, 1956.

Escholier, Marc. *Port-Royal.* Paris, 1965.

Esmein, Adhémar. *Cours élémentaire du droit français public et privé, des origines à 1815.* Paris, 1929.

Esmonin, Edmond. *Etudes sur la France des 17e et 18e siècles.* Paris, 1964.

Eymard d'Angers, Julien. *L'humanisme chrétien au 17ᵉ siècle: S. François de Sales et Yves de Paris.* The Hague, 1970.

Fayard, Ennamond-Dominique-Nicolas. *Aperçu historique sur le Parlement de Paris.* 3 vols. Paris, 1878.

Febvre, Lucien. *Combats pour l'histoire.* Paris, 1953.

Feret, Pierre. *La faculté de théologie de Paris et ses docteurs les plus célèbres. Epoque moderne.* 7 vols. Paris, 1900-10.

Ferté, Jeanne. *La vie religieuse dans les campagnes parisiennes (1622-1695).* Paris, 1962.

Ferté, Louis Henri. *Rollin, sa vie, ses oeuvres, et l'Université de son temps.* Paris, 1902.

Festinger, Leon; Riecken, Henry W.; and Schachter, Stanley. *When Prophecy Fails.* Minneapolis, 1956.

Figuier, Louis. *Histoire du merveilleux dans les temps modernes.* 4 vols. Paris, 1860-61.

Flammermont, Jules Gustave. *Les Jésuites et les Parlements au 18ᵉ siècle.* Paris, 1885.

Ford, Franklin L. *Robe and Sword: The Regrouping of the French Aristocracy after Louis XIV.* Cambridge, Mass., 1953.

Fosseyeux, Marcel. *Les écoles de charité à Paris sous l'ancien régime et dans la première partie du 19ᵉ siècle.* Paris, 1912.

———. *L'Hôtel-Dieu de Paris au 17ᵉ et au 18ᵉ siècles.* Paris, 1912.

Foster, Michael. *Lectures on the History of Physiology during the 16th, 17th, and 18th Centuries.* Cambridge, Eng., 1901.

Foucault, Michel. *Histoire de la folie à l'âge classique.* 2nd ed. Paris, 1972.

Fournel, Jean-François. *Histoire des avocats au Parlement et du barreau de Paris depuis S. Louis jusqu'au 15 octobre 1790.* 2 vols. Paris, 1813.

Franjou, Edmond. *La querelle janséniste à Joigny et dans le Jovinien au 18ᵉ siècle.* Auxerre, 1970.

Frank, Jerome. *Persuasion and Healing: A Comparative Study of Psychotherapy.* Rev. ed. Baltimore, 1973.

Frêche, Georges, and Sudreau, J. *Un chancelier gallican: Daguesseau et un cardinal diplomate: François-Joachim de Pierre de Bernis.* Paris, 1969.

Friedmann, Adrien. *Paris: Ses rues, ses paroisses du Moyen Age à la Révolution.* Paris, 1959.

——— et al. *Paris, fonctions d'une capitale.* Paris, 1962.

Gagnol, P. *Le jansénisme convulsionnaire et l'affaire de la Planchette.* Paris, 1911.

Gaillard, Jean. *Un prélat janséniste: Choart de Buzenval, 1651-1679.* Paris, 1902.

Garrett, Clarke. *Respectable Folly: Millenarians and the French Revolution in France and England.* Baltimore, 1975.

Gaudry, Joachim-Antoine-Joseph. *Histoire du barreau de Paris depuis son origine jusqu'à 1830.* 2 vols. Paris, 1864.

Gaxotte, Pierre. *Paris au 18e siècle.* Paris, 1968.

Gazier, Augustin. *Histoire générale du mouvement janséniste depuis ses origines jusqu'à nos jours.* 2 vols. Paris, 1922.

————. *Une suite à l'histoire de Port-Royal d'après des documents inédits: Jeanne de Boisgnorel et Christophe de Beaumont (1750-1782).* Paris, 1906.

Gazier, Cécile. *Après Port-Royal: L'ordre hospitalier des Soeurs de Sainte-Marthe de Paris, 1713-1918.* Paris, 1923.

————. *Ces Messieurs de Port-Royal.*

————. *Histoire de la Société et de la Bibliothèque de Port-Royal.* Paris, 1966.

————. *Histoire du monastère de Port-Royal.* Paris, 1929.

Genestal, Robert. *Les origines de l'appel comme d'abus.* Paris, 1950.

Gérin, Charles. *Recherches historiques sur l'assemblée du clergé de France de 1682.* 2nd ed. Paris, 1870.

Germain, Elisabeth. *Langages de la foi à travers l'histoire. Mentalités et catéchèse: Approche d'une étude des mentalités.* Paris, 1972.

Gilardoni, Camille. *La bulle 'Unigenitus' et la fin du jansénisme en Champagne.* Vitry-le-François, 1892.

————. *Un curé janséniste à Vitry au 17e siècle.* Vitry-le-François, 1887.

Gilles de la Tourette, Georges. *Traité clinique et thérapeutique de l'hystérie.* 2 vols. Paris, 1891.

Girault de Coursac, P. *Education d'un roi.* Paris, 1972.

Glasson, Ernest. *Le Parlement de Paris: Son rôle politique depuis le règne de Charles VII jusqu'à la Révolution.* 2 vols. Paris, 1901.

Godard, Philippe. *La querelle des refus de sacrements (1730-65).* Paris, 1937.

Godart, Justin. *Le jansénisme à Lyon: Benoît Fourgon (1687-1773).* Paris, 1934.

Golden, Richard M. "Godly Rebellion: Parisian *Curés* and the Religious Fronde, 1652-1662." Ph.D. Dissertation, The Johns Hopkins University, 1974.

Goldmann, Lucien. *Le dieu câché: Etude sur la vision tragique dans les Pensées de Pascal et dans le théâtre de Racine.* Paris, 1955.

Goodman, Felicitas. *Speaking in Tongues: A Cross-Cultural Study of Glossolalia.* Chicago, 1972.

Gorce, Jean-Denys-Bernard. *L'oeuvre médicale de Prospero Lambertini (Pape Benoît XIV), 1675-1758.* Bordeaux, 1915.

[Gosselin, Louis Léon Théodore]. *Le mysticisme révolutionnaire: Robespierre et la "Mère de Dieu."* 11th ed. Paris, 1926.

Gourdon de Genouillac, Nicolas-Jules-Henri. *Les compagnons de la Marjolaine.* Paris, 1881.

———. *Les convulsionnaires.* 2 vols. Paris, 1860.

———. *Les convulsionnaires de Paris.* Paris, 1881.

———. *Paris à travers les siècles: Histoire nationale de Paris et des Parisiens depuis la fondation de Lutèce jusqu'à nos jours.* 5 vols. Paris, 1879-80.

Grand-Carteret, John. *Les almanachs français. Bibliographie, iconographie . . . , 1600-1895.* Paris, 1896.

Greenbaum, Louis S. *Talleyrand: Statesman-Priest. The Agent-General of the Clergy and the Church of France at the End of the Old Regime.* Washington, D.C., 1970.

Grégoire, Henri. *Histoire des sectes religieuses.* 2 vols. Paris, 1814.

———. *Les ruines de Port-Royal des Champs en 1809, année séculière de la destruction de ce monastère.* Paris, 1809.

Groethuysen, Bernard. *Origines de l'esprit bourgeois en France: L'Eglise et la bourgeoisie.* Paris, 1927.

Guariglia, Guglielmo. *Prophetismus und Heilserwartungs-Bewegungen als völkerkundliches und religionsgeschichtliches Problem.* Horn-Wien, 1959.

Gueranger, Prosper. *Institutions liturgiques.* 2nd ed. 4 vols. Paris, 1878-85.

Guettée, René. *Histoire de l'Eglise de France.* 12 vols. Paris, 1847-56.

Guide des recherches dans les fonds judiciaires de l'ancien régime. Paris, 1958.

Guillaume, Paul. *Essai sur la vie religieuse de l'Orléanais de 1600 à 1789.* 2 vols. Orléans, 1957.

Guitton, Georges. *Le Père de la Chaize, confesseur de Louis XIV.* 2 vols. Paris, 1959.

Hallays, André. *Le pèlerinage de Port-Royal.* Paris, 1925.

———. *Les solitaires de Port-Royal.* Paris, 1927.

Hamscher, Albert. "The Relations Between the Parlement of Paris and the Crown after the Fronde, 1653-1673." Ph.D. Dissertation, Emory University, 1973.

Hardy, Georges. *Le Cardinal de Fleury et le mouvement janséniste.* Paris, 1925.

Hardy, James. *Judicial Politics in the Old Régime: The Parlement of Paris during the Regency*. Baton Rouge, 1967.

Hargreaves, Kevin J. "Cornelius Jansenius and the Origins of Jansenism." Ph.D. Dissertation, Brandeis University, 1974.

Hatin, Eugène. *Histoire politique et littéraire de la presse en France*. 3 vols. Paris, 1859.

Hau, Claude. *Le Messie de l'an XIII et les Fareinistes*. Paris, 1955.

Hauterive, Ernest d'. *Le merveilleux au 18e siècle*. Paris, 1803.

Havinga, Jan Christiaan Adolf. *Les "Nouvelles Ecclésiastiques" dans leur lutte contre l'esprit philosophique*. Amersfoort, 1925.

Haynes, Renée. *Philosopher King: The Humanist Pope, Benedict XIV*. London, 1970.

Hecker, J.F.C. *The Dancing Mania of the Middle Ages*. Translated by B. G. Babington. London, 1844.

Henry, Marthe. *Les origines de l'élimination des antisociaux et de l'assistance aux aliénés chroniques: La Salpêtrière sous l'ancien régime*. Paris, 1922.

Hertzberg, Arthur. *The French Enlightenment and the Jews*. New York, 1968.

Hillairet, Jacques. *Les 200 cimetières du vieux Paris*. Paris, 1958.

———. *Evocation du vieux Paris*. Paris, 1951.

Hitchcock, James F. "Popular Religion in Elizabethan England." Ph.D. Dissertation, Princeton University, 1965.

Hoffer, Paul. *La dévotion à Marie au déclin du 17e siècle. Autour du jansénisme et des "Avis salutaires de la B. V. M. à ses dévots indiscrets."* Paris, 1938.

Honigsheim, Paul. *Die Staats- und Sozial-Lehren der französischen Jansenisten im 17. Jahrhundert*. Darmstadt, 1969.

Hufton, Olwen. *The Poor of 18th-Century France, 1750-1789*. Oxford, 1974.

Ingold, Augustin-Marie-Pierre. *Essai de bibliographie oratorienne*. 2 vols. Paris, 1880-82.

———. *L'Oratoire et le jansénisme*. Paris, 1887.

Jacomet, Pierre. *Vicissitudes et chutes du Parlement de Paris*. Paris, 1954.

Jager, Jean-Nicolas. *Histoire de l'église catholique en France*. 21 vols. Paris, 1862-76.

Jahan, René-François. *Etude historique sur l'appel comme d'abus*. Laval, 1888.

James, E. D. *Pierre Nicole, Jansenism, and Humanism: A Study of His Thought*. The Hague, 1973.

Janet, Pierre. *Psychological Healing: A Historical and Clinical Study.* Translated by E. and C. Paul. 2 vols. New York, 1925.

Jansen, Paule. *Le Cardinal Mazarin et le mouvement jansénsite français, 1653-1659.* Paris, 1967.

Jarrin, Ch. *Le Fareinisme.* Bourg, 1881.

Jauffret, F. *Lutte doctrinale entre Monseigneur de Belsunce, évêque de Marseille, et le jansénisme.* Marseille, 1882.

Jean, Armand. *Les évêques et les archevêques de France depuis 1682 jusqu'à 1801.* Paris, 1891.

Jervis, W. Henley. *The Gallican Church: A History of the Church of France from the Concordat of Bologna, A.D. 1516, to the Revolution.* 2 vols. London, 1872.

Jette, Marie-Henri. *La France religieuse au 18ᵉ siècle.* Paris-Tournai, 1956.

Jobez, Alphonse. *La France sous Louis XV (1715-1774).* 6 vols. Paris, 1864-73.

Jourdain, Charles-M.-G.-B. *Histoire de l'Université de Paris au 17ᵉ et au 18ᵉ siècles.* Paris, 1862-66.

Kaplow, Jeffry. *The Names of Kings: The Parisian Laboring Poor in the 18th Century.* New York, 1972.

Kemp, Eric W. *Canonization and Authority in the Western Church.* London, 1948.

Kildahl, John P. *The Psychology of Speaking in Tongues.* New York, 1972.

Knox, Ronald A. *Enthusiam: A Chapter in the History of Religion, with Special Reference to the 17th and 18th Centuries.* Oxford, 1951.

Kolakowski, Leszek. *Chrétiens sans église: La conscience religieuse et le lien confessionel au 17ᵉ siècle.* Paris, 1969.

Kural, Roxanne. *Contribution à l'histoire des mentalités de l'Occident pré-industriel: Etude de deux manuscrits de convulsionnaires jansénistes du milieu du 18ᵉ siècle.* Mémoire de maîtrise, University of Paris, 1970-71.

Lacombe, Bernard de. *La résistance janséniste et parlementaire au temps de Louis XV: L'abbé Nigon de Berty (1702-72).* Paris, 1948.

Lacombe, Paul. *Bibliographie parisienne: Tableaux de moeurs (1600-1880).* Paris, 1887.

Laehr, Heinrich. *Die Literatur der Psychiatrie, Neurologie, und Psychologie von 1459-1799.* 3 vols. Berlin, 1900.

Lafforgue, Abbé. *Histoire des fabriques des églises de France sous l'ancien régime.* Paris, 1923.

Laignel-Lavastine, Maxime, and Vinchon, Jean. *Les maladies de l'esprit et leurs médecins du 16ᵉ au 19ᵉ siècle.* Paris, 1930.

434

Lanternari, Vittorio. *The Religions of the Oppressed: A Study of Modern Messianic Cults*. Translated by Lisa Sergio. New York, 1963.

Laporte, Jean. *La doctrine de Port-Royal*. 2 vols. Paris, 1923.

Latreille, André; Delaruelle, Etienne; and Palanque, Jean-Rémy. *Histoire du Catholicisme en France*. 3 vols. Paris, 1957-62.

Laurent, Benoît. *En Forez: Les Béguines*. Saint-Etienne, 1944.

Le Bras, Gabriel. *Etudes de sociologie religieuse*. 2 vols. Paris, 1955-56.

———. *Institutions ecclésiastiques de la Chrétienté médiévale*. 2 vols. Paris, 1959.

Lebrun, François. *Les hommes et la mort en Anjou aux 17ᵉ et 18ᵉ siècles: Essai de démographie et de psychologie historiques*. Paris, 1971.

Leclercq, G. *Zeger Bernard van Espen et l'autorité ecclésiastique*. Zurich, 1964.

Leclercq, Henri M. *Histoire de la Régence pendant la minorité de Louis XV*. 3 vols. Paris, 1922.

Lee, Umphrey. *The Historical Background of Early Methodist Enthusiasm*. New York, 1931.

Lefrançois, Philippe. *Paris à travers les siècles*. 10 vols. Paris, 1948-56.

Legier-Desgranges, Henri. *Du jansénisme à la Révolution: Madame de Moysan et l'extravagante affaire de l'Hôpital Général, 1749-1758*. Paris, 1955.

Le Goff, Jacques, ed. *Hérésies et sociétés dans l'Europe pré-industrielle, 11ᵉ-18ᵉ siècles*. Paris, 1968.

Lekai, Louis Julius. *The Rise of the Cistercian Strict Observance in 17th-Century France*. Washington, D. C., 1968.

Lemaire, André. *Les lois fondamentales de la monarchie française d'après les théoriciens de l'ancien régime*. Paris, 1907.

Lemontey, Pierre-Edouard. *Histoire de la Régence et de la minorité de Louis XV jusqu'au ministère du cardinal de Fleury*. 2 vols. Paris, 1832.

Lepaysant, P. *Le Port-Royal de Normandie: Saint-Himer-en-Auge et son prieur, Henri de Roquette, 1699-1789*. Paris, 1926.

Lepointe, Gabriel. *L'organisation et la politique financières du clergé de France sous le règne de Louis XV*. Paris, 1924.

———. *Les rapports de l'Eglise et de l'Etat en France*. Paris, 1964.

———, and Vandenbossche, André. *Eléments de bibliographie de l'histoire des institutions et des faits sociaux (987-1875)*. Paris, 1958.

Le Roy, Albert. *Le Gallicanisme au 18ᵉ siècle: La France et Rome de 1700 à 1715*. Paris, 1892.

Lestocquoy, Jean. *La vie religieuse en France du 7ᵉ au 20ᵉ siècle*. Paris, 1964.

Lewis, Ioan M. *Ecstatic Religion: An Anthropological Study of Spirit Possession and Shamanism*. Harmondsworth, 1971.

Lhermitte, Jean. *Le problème des miracles*. 7th ed. Paris, 1956.

———. *True and False Possession*. Translated by P. J. Hepburne-Scott. New York, 1963.

Lieutaud, Victor. *Le jansénisme à Senez en 1728*. Digne, 1905.

Lottin, Alain. *Vie et mentalité d'un Lillois sous Louis XIV*. Lille, 1968.

Loyson, Jules-Théodore. *L'Assemblée du Clergé de France de 1682*. Paris, 1870.

Lucius, Henriette. *La littérature "visionnaire" en France du début du 16ᵉ au début du 19ᵉ siècle: Etude de sémantique et de littérature*. Paris, 1970.

Mahieu, Léon. *Jansénisme et antijansénisme dans les diocèses d'Arras et de Cambrai*. Lille, 1944.

———. *Jansénisme et antijansénisme dans les diocèses de Boulogne-sur-Mer et de Tournai*. Lille, 1948.

Mandrou, Robert. *De la culture populaire aux 17ᵉ et 18ᵉ siècles: La Bibliothèque bleue de Troyes*. Paris, 1964.

———. *La France aux 17ᵉ et 18ᵉ siècles*. Paris, 1967.

Manuel, Frank. *The 18th Century Confronts the Gods*. Cambridge, Mass., 1959.

Marion, Marcel. *Dictionnaire des institutions de la France aux 17ᵉ et 18ᵉ siècles*. Paris, 1923.

Martène, Edmond. *Histoire de la Congrégation de Saint-Maur*. Edited by G. Charvin. 4 vols. Paris, 1928-43.

Martimort, Aimé-Georges. *Le Gallicanisme*. Paris, 1973.

———. *Le Gallicanisme de Bossuet*. Paris, 1953.

Martin, Henri-Jean. *Livre, pouvoir et société à Paris au 17ᵉ siècle (1598-1701)*. 2 vols. Geneva, 1969.

Martin, Victor. *Le Gallicanisme politique et le clergé de France*. Paris, 1929.

Mathieu, Pierre-François. *Histoire des miraculés et des convulsionnaires de Saint-Médard*. Paris, 1864.

McManners, John. *French Ecclesiastical Society under the Ancien Régime: A Study of Angers in the 18th Century*. Manchester, 1960.

Mellor, Alec. *Histoire de l'anticléricalisme français*. Paris, 1966.

Mercier, Roger. *La réhabilitation de la nature humaine*. Villemonble, 1960.

Méric, Elie. *Le clergé sous l'ancien régime*. Paris, 1890.

Meurgey, Jacques. *Histoire de la paroisse Saint-Jacques-de-la-Boucherie.* Paris, 1926.

Meyer, Albert de. *Les premières controverses jansénistes en France (1640-1649).* Louvain, 1919.

Meyer, Jean. *La noblesse bretonne au 18ᵉ siècle.* 2 vols. Paris, 1966.

Mirville, Jules-Eudes de. *Des esprits et de leurs manifestations fluidiques.* Paris, 1853.

Miscellanea Jansenistica offerts à Lucien Ceyssens, O.F.M., à l'occasion de son 60ᵉ anniversaire. Héverlé-Louvain, 1963.

Molho, Raphaël. *L'ordre et les ténèbres, ou la naissance d'un mythe du 17ᵉ siècle chez Sainte-Beuve.* Paris, 1972.

Monin, H. *L'Etat de Paris en 1789: Etudes et documents sur l'ancien régime à Paris.* Paris, 1889.

Monnier, Francis. *Le chancelier d'Aguesseau: Sa conduite et ses idées politiques et son influence sur le mouvement des esprits pendant la première moitié du 18ᵉ siècle.* Paris, 1860.

Monod, Albert. *De Pascal à Chateaubriand: Les défenseurs français du Christianisme de 1670 à 1802.* Paris, 1916.

Montbas, Hugues de. *La police parisienne sous Louis XVI.* Paris, 1949.

[Mouffle d'Angerville]. *Vie privée de Louis XV, ou principaux événemens, particularités et anecdotes de son règne.* 4 vols. London, 1781.

Mousnier, Roland. *Les institutions de la France sous la monarchie absolue.* Paris, 1974.

——. *Paris au 17ᵉ siècle.* Paris, 1961.

——. *La plume, la faucille et le marteau: Institutions et société en France, du Moyen Age à la Révolution.* Paris, 1970.

—— et al. *Le conseil du roi, de Louis XII à la Révolution.* Paris, 1970.

Mousset, Albert. *L'étrange histoire des convulsionnaires de Saint-Médard.* Paris, 1953.

Namer, Gérard. *L'abbé Le Roy et ses amis: Essai sur le jansénisme extrémiste intramondain.* Paris, 1964.

Neveu, Bruno. *Un historien à l'école de Port-Royal: Sebastien Le Nain de Tillemont (1637-1698).* The Hague, 1966.

——. *Sébastien Joseph du Cambout de Pontchâteau (1634-1690) et ses missions à Rome.* Paris, 1969.

Newton, William Ritchey. "Port-Royal and Jansenism: Social Experience, Group Formation and Religious Attitudes in 17th-Century France." 3 vols. Ph.D. Dissertation, University of Michigan, 1974.

Nuttinck, Michel. *La vie et l'oeuvre de Zeger-Bernard van Espen:*

Un canoniste janséniste, gallican et régalien à l'Université de Louvain. Louvain, 1969.

O'Keefe, Cyril B. *Contemporary Reactions to the Enlightenment (1728-1762).* Paris-Geneva, 1974.

Olivier-Martin, François Jean Marie. *Histoire de droit français des origines à la Révolution.* Paris, 1951.

————. *L'organisation corporative de la France d'ancien régime.* Paris, 1938.

Orcibal, Jean. *Jean Duvergier de Hauranne, abbé de Saint-Cyran, et son temps (1581-1638).* Paris, 1948.

————. *Louis XIV contre Innocent XI: Les appels au futur concile de 1688 et l'opinion française.* Paris, 1949.

————. *Port-Royal entre le miracle et l'obéissance: Flavie Passart et Angélique de St.-Jean Arnauld d'Andilly.* Paris, 1957.

————. *Le premier Port-Royal: Réforme ou contre-réforme.* Paris, n.d.

————. *Saint-Cyran et le jansénisme.* Paris, 1961.

————. *La spiritualité de Saint-Cyran, avec ses écrits de piété inédits.* Paris, 1962.

Ordioni, Pierre. *La résistance gallicane et janséniste dans le diocèse d'Auxerre, 1704-1760.* Auxerre, 1932.

————. *La survivance des idées gallicanes et jansénistes en Auxerrois de 1760 à nos jours.* Auxerre, 1933.

Owen, Alan R. G. *Hysteria, Hypnosis, and Healing: The Work of J.-M. Charcot.* New York, 1971.

Palmer, Robert R. *Catholics and Unbelievers in 18th-Century France.* Princeton, 1939.

Paquier, Jules. *Le Jansénisme.* Paris, 1909.

Parquez, Jacques. *La bulle "Unigenitus" et le Jansénisme politique.* Paris, 1936.

Pastor, Ludwig von. *The History of the Popes.* 40 vols. London, 1891-1953.

Pensa, Henri. *Sorcellerie et religion: Du désordre dans les esprits et dans les moeurs aux 17ᵉ et 18ᵉ siècles.* 2nd ed. Paris, 1935.

Pérouas, Louis. *Le diocèse de La Rochelle de 1648 à 1724: Sociologie et pastorale.* Paris, 1964.

Phipps, Frances. "Louis XV: A Style of Kingship, 1710-1757." Ph.D. Dissertation, The Johns Hopkins University, 1973.

Picot, Michel-Joseph-Pierre. *Mémoires pour servir à l'histoire ecclésiastique pendant le 18ᵉ siècle.* 3rd ed. 7 vols. Paris, 1853-57.

Pitsch, Marguerite. *La vie populaire à Paris au 18ᵉ siècle.* 2 vols. Paris, 1949.

Platelle, Henri. *Les chrétiens face au miracle: Lille au 17ᵉ siècle*. Paris, 1968.

Plongeron, Bernard. *Conscience religieuse en Révolution: Regards sur l'histoire religieuse de la Révolution française*. Paris, 1969.

———. *Théologie et politique au siècle des lumières (1770-1820)*. Geneva, 1973.

———. *La vie quotidienne du clergé français au 18ᵉ siècle*. Paris, 1974.

———, and Pannet, Robert, eds. *Le christianisme populaire: Les dossiers de l'histoire*. Paris, 1976.

Pluquet, François. *Dictionnaire des hérésies, des erreurs et des schismes*. 2 vols. Paris, 1847.

Poète, Marcel. *Répertoire des sources manuscrites de l'histoire de Paris*. 3 vols. Paris, 1915-16.

———. *Une vie de cité: Paris de sa naissance à nos jours*. 3 vols. Paris, 1924-31.

Pomeau, René. *La religion de Voltaire*. 2nd ed. rev. Paris, 1969.

Préclin, Edmond. *Les jansénistes du 18ᵉ siècle et la constitution civile du clergé*. Paris, 1929.

———. *L'union des Eglises gallicane et anglicane. Une tentative au temps de Louis XV: P.-F. Le Courayer (de 1681 à 1732) et Guillaume Wake*. Paris, 1928.

———, and Jarry, Eugène. *Les luttes politiques et doctrinales aux 17ᵉ et 18ᵉ siècles*. Vol. xix of *Histoire de l'Eglise depuis les origines jusqu'à nos jours*. Edited by J.-B. Duroselle and Eugène Jarry. 2 vols. Paris, 1955-56.

Prévost, Arthur-Emile. *Le diocèse de Troyes: Histoire et documents*. 3 vols. Dijon, 1923-26.

Prunel, Louis. *La renaissance catholique en France au 17ᵉ siècle*. Paris, 1921.

Puyol, Pierre-Edouard. *Edmond Richer: Etude historique et critique sur la rénovation du Gallicanisme au commencement du 17ᵉ siècle*. 2 vols. Paris, 1876.

Quicherat, Jules. *Histoire de Sainte-Barbe, collège, communauté, institution*. 3 vols. Paris, 1860-64.

Ravitch, Norman. *Sword and Mitre: Government and Episcopate in France and England in the Age of Aristocracy*. The Hague, 1966.

Raybaud, Léon Pierre. *Papauté et pouvoir temporel sous les pontificats de Clément XII et Benoît XIV (1730-1758)*. Paris, 1963.

Rea, Lilian. *The Enthusiasts of Port-Royal*. London, 1912.

Regnault, Emile. *Christophe de Beaumont, archevêque de Paris (1703-1781)*. 2 vols. Paris, 1882.

Reik, Theodor. *Dogma and Compulsion: Psychoanalytic Studies of Religion and Myths.* Translated by Bernard Miall. New York, 1951.

Remacle, Louis. *Ultramontains et Gallicans au 18ᵉ siècle: Honoré de Quiqueran de Beaujeu, évêque de Castres, et Jacques de Forbin-Janson, archevêque d'Arles.* Marseille, 1872.

Réthoré, Edmond. *Argenteuil et son passé.* 2 vols. Saint-Gratien, 1968.

———. *Du jansénisme et de sa longue survivance à Argenteuil.* Sannois, n.d.

Richer, Paul. *Etudes cliniques sur la grande hystérie ou hystéroépilepsie.* 2nd ed. rev. Paris, 1885.

Richter, Jean Beatrice. "Currents of Spirituality in 18th-Century France: Nuns, Sisters, and Philosophes." Ph.D. Dissertation, University of Wisconsin, 1972.

Riley, Philip F. "Moral Rigorism in the Character of Louis XIV: A Study of the Sun King's Interest in the Moral Behavior of Frenchmen between 1683 and 1715." Ph.D. Dissertation, University of Notre Dame, 1971.

Rivière, Ernest M. *Corrections et additions à la Bibliothèque de la Compagnie des Jésus: Supplément au "De Backer-Sommervogel."* Toulouse, 1911.

Rochegude, Félix, and Clébert, Jean-Paul. *Les rues de Paris.* 2 vols. Paris, 1958.

Rocquain, Félix. *L'esprit révolutionnaire avant la Révolution, 1715-1789.* Paris, 1878.

Rose, Louis. *Faith Healing.* Harmondsworth, 1971.

Rosen, George. *Madness in Society: Chapters in the Historical Sociology of Mental Illness.* Chicago, 1968.

Rousselet, Marcel. *Histoire de la magistrature française des origines à nos jours.* 2 vols. Paris, 1957.

Sainte-Beuve, C.-A. *Port-Royal.* Garnier ed. 3 vols. Paris, 1953-55.

Saint-Germain, Jacques. *La Reynie et la police au grand siècle.* Paris, 1962.

Salgues, Jacques-Barthélemy. *Des erreurs et des préjugés répandus dans les 18ᵉ et 19ᵉ siècles.* 2 vols. Paris, 1828.

Samoyault, Jean-Pierre. *Les bureaux du Secrétariat d'Etat des affaires étrangères sous Louis XV: Administration, personnel.* Paris, 1971.

Sareil, Jean. *Les Tencin: Histoire d'une famille au 18ᵉ siècle.* Geneva, 1969.

Sargant, William. *Battle for the Mind: A Physiology of Conversion and Brainwashing.* Garden City, N.Y., 1957.

Sars, Maxime de. *Le Cardinal de Fleury: Apôtre de la paix.* Paris, 1942.

Schimmelpenninck, Mary Anne. *Narrative of the Demolition of the Monastery of Port Royal des Champs.* London, 1816.

Schmitt, Thérèse-Jean. *L'organisation ecclésiastique et la pratique religieuse dans l'archidiaconé d'Autun de 1650 à 1750.* Autun, 1957.

Schoenher, Pierre. *Histoire du séminaire de Saint-Nicolas du Chardonnet, 1612-1908.* 2 vols. Paris, 1909-11.

Séché, Léon. *Les derniers jansénistes, depuis la ruine de Port-Royal jusqu'à nos jours, 1710-1870.* 3 vols. Paris, 1891-93.

Semelaigne, René. *Les pionniers de la psychiatrie française avant et après Pinel.* 2 vols. Paris, 1930-32.

Serbat, Louis-Emile. *Les assemblées du clergé de France.* Paris, 1906.

Shennan, J. H. *The Parlement of Paris.* Ithaca, 1968.

Sicard, Augustin. *L'ancien clergé de France.* 3 vols. Paris, 1893-1903.

Silvy, Louis. *La vérité de l'histoire ecclésiastique rétablie par des monuments authentiques.* Paris, 1814.

Smelser, Neil J. *Theory of Collective Behavior.* New York, 1971.

Sommervogel, Carlos, ed. *Bibliothèque de la Compagnie de Jésus.* 11 vols. Paris, 1890-1932.

———. *Dictionnaire des ouvrages anonymes et pseudonymes publiés par des religieux de la Compagnie de Jésus depuis sa fondation jusqu'à nos jours.* Paris, 1884.

Sonnino, Paul. *Louis XIV's View of the Papacy (1661-1667).* Berkeley, 1966.

Soriano, Marc. *Les contes de Perrault: Culture savante et traditions populaires.* Paris, 1968.

Stone, Bailey S. "Crisis in the Paris Parlement: The Grand-Chambriers, 1774-1789." Ph.D. Dissertation, Princeton University, 1972.

Suaudeau, René. *L'Evêque inspecteur administratif sous la Monarchie absolue.* 2 vols. Paris, 1940.

Symes, Joseph J. "The Contrary Estimation of Saint Vincent de Paul on the Abbé de Saint-Cyran." Ph.D. Dissertation, St. John's University, 1973.

Tackett, Timothy. *Priest and Parish in Eighteenth-Century France.* Princeton, 1977.

Tans, J.A.G. *Pasquier Quesnel et les Pays-Bas.* Paris, 1960.

Tapié, Victor-Lucien *et al. Retables baroques de Bretagne et spiritualité du 17e siècle: Etude sémiographique et religieuse.* Paris, 1972.

Taveneaux, René. *Le jansénisme en Lorraine, 1640-1789.* Paris, 1960.

———. *Jansénisme et politique.* Paris, 1965.

———. *La vie quotidienne des jansénistes.* Paris, 1973.

Temkin, Owsei. *The Falling Sickness: A History of Epilepsy from the Greeks to the Beginnings of Modern Neurology.* Baltimore, 1945.

Thibout, Marc. *Saint-Médard*. Paris, 1946.

Thomas, Jacques-François. *Essai sur la morale de Port-Royal*. Paris, 1942.

———. *La querelle de l'Unigenitus*. Paris, 1949.

Thomas, Keith. *Religion and the Decline of Magic*. New York, 1971.

Thrupp, Sylvia, ed. *Millennial Dreams in Action: Studies in Revolutionary Religious Movements*. New York, 1970.

Thuillet, Louis. *Gabriel Nicolas de la Reynie, premier lieutenant général de police de Paris*. Limoges, 1930.

Tonquedec, Joseph de. *Introduction à l'étude du merveilleux et du miracle*. 3rd ed. Paris, 1923.

———. *Les maladies nerveuses ou mentales et les manifestations diaboliques*. Paris, 1938.

———. *Merveilleux métapsychique et miracle chrétien*. Paris, 1955.

Trégelles, S. P. *The Jansenists: Their Rise, Persecutions by the Jesuits, and Existing Remnant*. London, 1851.

Trénard, Louis. *Lyon, de l'Encyclopédie au Préromantisme: Histoire sociale des idées*. 2 vols. Paris, 1958.

Tucker, Susie I. *Enthusiasm: A Study in Semantic Change*. Cambridge, Eng., 1972.

Turner, Victor W. *The Ritual Process: Structure and Anti-Structure*. Chicago, 1969.

Vaissière, Pierre de. *Curés de campagne de l'ancienne France*. Paris, 1933.

Van Kley, Dale. *The Jansenists and the Expulsion of the Jesuits from France, 1757-1765*. New Haven, 1975.

Vaucher, Alfred-Félix. *Une célébrité oubliée: Le P. Manuel de Lacunza y Diaz (1731-1801)*. Collonges-sous-Salève, Haute-Savoie, 1941.

Veith, Ilza. *Hysteria: The History of a Disease*. Chicago, 1965.

Verlaque, Victor. *Histoire du cardinal de Fleury et de son administration*. Paris, 1878.

Vié, Jacques. *Les aliénés et les correctionnaires à Saint-Lazare au 17ᵉ et au 18ᵉ siècles*. Paris, 1930.

Vimont, Maurice. *Histoire de l'église et de la paroisse Saint-Leu-Saint-Gilles*. Paris, 1932.

Viollet, Paul. *Droit public: Histoire des institutions politiques et administratives de la France*. 3 vols. Paris, 1890-1903.

———. *Le roi et ses ministres pendant les trois derniers siècles de la monarchie*. Paris, 1912.

Vovelle, Michel. *Mourir autrefois: Attitudes collectives devant la mort aux 17ᵉ et 18ᵉ siècles*. Paris, 1974.

————. *Piété baroque et déchristianisation en Provence au 18ᵉ siècle.* Paris, 1973.

Vulliaud, Paul. *La fin du monde.* Paris, 1952.

Vulliod, A. *La femme docteur: Mme Gottsched et son modèle français Bougeant, ou Jansénisme et Piétisme.* Lyon-Paris, 1912.

Wattine, Adolphe. *Magistrats célèbres du 18ᵉ siècle.* Paris, 1941.

Weaver, F. Ellen. "The Inner History of a Reform that Failed: The Monastery of Port-Royal (1647-1684)." Ph.D. Dissertation, Princeton University, 1973.

Wilhelm, Henry. *Nouveau supplément à l'Histoire littéraire de la Congrégation de Saint-Maur.* Edited by Dom Ursmer Berlière, Dom Antoine Dubourg, and A.M.P. Ingold. 2 vols. Paris, 1908.

Willaert, Léopold. *Bibliotheca janseniana belgica.* 3 vols. Paris, 1949-51.

————. *Les origines du jansénisme dans les Pays-Bas catholiques.* Gebloux, 1948.

Williams, Alan John. "The Police of Paris, 1718-1789." Ph.D. Dissertation, Yale University, 1974.

Williams, William H. "The Priest in History: A Study in Divided Loyalties in the French Lower Clergy from 1776 to 1789." Ph.D. Dissertation, Duke University, 1965.

Wilson, Arthur M. *French Foreign Policy during the Administration of Cardinal Fleury, 1726-1743.* Cambridge, Mass., 1936.

Wilson, Bryan. *Religious Sects: A Sociological Study.* London, 1970.

Zaretzky, Irving I., and Leone, Mark P., eds. *Religious Movements in Contemporary America.* Princeton, 1975.

B. Articles

Abse, D. Wilfred. "Hysterical Conversion and Dissociative Syndromes and the Hysterical Character," in *American Handbook of Psychiatry.* Edited by Silvano Arieti. 2nd ed. rev. 6 vols. New York, 1974, III, 155-94.

Adhemar d'Alès, Alphonse. "La théologie du diacre Pâris," *Recherches de science religieuse,* 10 (1920), 373-87.

Adler, Nathan. "The Antinomian Personality: The Hippie Character Type," *Psychiatry,* 31 (1968), 325-38.

Amann, Emile. "Autour de l'histoire du gallicanisme," *Revue des sciences religieuses,* 21 (1947), 17-52; 22 (1948), 9-26.

Antoine, Michel. "Le Conseil des Dépêches sous le règne de Louis XV," *Bibliothèque de l'Ecole des Chartes,* 111 (1953), 158-208; 112 (1954), 126-81.

"Apocalypse et idée de fin de temps," *La Table ronde,* No. 110 (February 1957).

Appolis, Emile. "A travers le 18ᵉ siècle catholique. Entre jansénistes et constitutionnaires: Un tiers parti," *Annales: Economies, Sociétés, Civilisations,* 6 (1951), 154-71.

————. "La collaboration de Soanen aux 'Nouvelles ecclésiastiques,'" *Revue d'histoire de l'Eglise de France,* 30 (1944), 96-99.

————. "Une controverse autour d'un 'miracle' janséniste," *Monspeliensis Hippocrates,* 44 (1969), 20-28.

————. "L'histoire provinciale du jansénisme au 18ᵉ siècle," *Annales: Economies, Sociétés, Civilisations,* 7 (1952), 87-92.

————. "Les 'miracles' jansénistes dans le Bas-Languedoc (1732-45)," *Annales du Midi,* 67 (1955), 269-79.

————. "Un prélat philojanséniste sous la Régence: Honoré de Quiqueran de Beaujeu, évêque de Castres," in *La Régence.* Paris, 1970, pp. 238-45.

Armogathe, Jean-Robert. "A propos des miracles de Saint-Médard: Les preuves de Carré de Montgeron et le positivisme des Lumières," *Revue de l'histoire des religions,* 180 (1971), 135-60.

————. "Les catéchismes et l'enseignement populaire en France au 18ᵉ siècle," in *Images du Peuple au 18ᵉ siècle.* Colloque, Aix-en-Provence, 1969. Paris, 1973, pp. 103-21.

Arnaud d'Agnel, G. "Les convulsionnaires de Pignans," *Annales du Midi,* 19 (1907), 206-20.

Aubert, Félix. "Le Parlement et les prisonniers," *Bulletin de la Société de l'histoire de Paris et de l'Ile de France,* 20 (1893), 101-14.

Barry, Alfred. "Bossuet and the Gallican Declaration of 1682," *Catholic Historical Review,* 15 (1929), 143-53.

Bassieux, F. "Théorie des libertés gallicanes du parlement de Paris au 18ᵉ siècle," *Nouvelle revue historique de droit français et étranger,* 30 (1906), 330-50.

Berger, Peter L. "The Sociological Study of Sectarianism," *Social Research,* 21 (1954), 467-85.

Bernier, H. "Etude sur le jansénisme," *Revue de l'Anjou et du Maine,* 2 (1854), 101-15, 355-87.

Berthelot du Chesnay, Charles. "Le clergé diocésain français au 18ᵉ siècle et les registres des insinuations ecclésiastiques," *Revue d'histoire moderne et contemporaine,* 10 (1963), 241-69.

————. "Le clergé séculier français du second ordre d'après les insinuations ecclésiastiques," *Bulletin de la Société d'histoire moderne,* 62 (1963), 2-5.

————. "La spiritualité des laïcs," *17ᵉ siècle,* Nos. 62-63 (1964), 30-46.

Besnier, R. "Les synodes du diocèse de Paris de 1715 à 1790," in *Etudes d'histoire du droit canonique dédiées à Gabriel Le Bras.* 2 vols. Paris, 1965, I, 33-40.

Besson, M. "La rue Mouffetard et son histoire," *Bulletin de la Montagne Sainte-Geneviève et ses abords* (January 1955), 2-8.

Bibolet, Françoise. "Le fonds janséniste de la Bibliothèque de Troyes," *Chronique de Port-Royal*, Nos. 17-18 (1969), 59-67.

Bindet, J. "Quelques aspects du jansénisme dans l'ancien diocèse d'Avranches (17ᵉ and 18ᵉ siècles)," *Revue de l'Avranchin et du pays de Granville*, 46 (1969), 249-71.

Blet, Pierre. "Innocent XI et l'Assemblée du Clergé de France de 1682: La rédaction du Bref 'Paternae charitati,'" *Archivum Historicae Pontificiae*, 7 (1969), 329-63.

————. "Jésuites gallicans au 17ᵉ siècle? A propos de l'ouvrage du P. Guitton sur le P. de La Chaize," *Archivum Historicum Societatis Iesu*, 29 (1960), 55-82.

————. "Une légende tenace: Colbert et la déclaration du clergé de 1682," *Revue des travaux de l'Académie des sciences morales et politiques*, 4th ser., 124 (1972), 25-45.

————. "L'ordre du clergé au 17ᵉ siècle," *Revue d'histoire de l'Eglise de France*, 54 (1968), 5-26.

Bliard, Pierre. "Un couvent janséniste au 18ᵉ siècle," *Etudes*, 109 (1906), 362-67.

Boisen, Anton T. "Economic Distress and Religious Experience: A Study of the Holy Rollers," *Psychiatry*, 2 (1939), 185-94.

————. "The Sense of Isolation in Mental Disorders: Its Religious Significance," *American Journal of Sociology*, 33 (1927-28), 555-67.

Bollème, Geneviève. "Littérature populaire et littérature de colportage au 18ᵉ siècle," in *Livre et société dans la France du 18ᵉ siècle*. Paris, 1965, pp. 61-92.

Bontoux, Françoise. "Paris janséniste au 18ᵉ siècle: Les Nouvelles ecclésiastiques," *Mémoires de la Fédération des Sociétés historiques et archéologiques de Paris et de l'Ile de France*, 7 (1955), 205-20.

Borel, A. "Les convulsionnaires et le diacre Pâris," *L'évolution psychiatrique*, 4 (1935), 3-24.

Bost, Charles. "Les prophètes des Cévennes," *Revue d'histoire et de philosophie religieuses*, 5 (1925), 401-30.

————. "Les prophètes du Languedoc en 1701 et 1702," *Revue historique*, 136 (1921), 1-36; 137 (1921), 1-31.

Bourloton, Edgar. "Les jansénistes en 1895," *Vie contemporaine* (August 1, 1895), 267-84.

Bouwsma, William J. "Gallicanism and the Nature of Christendom," in

Renaissance Studies in Honor of Hans Baron. Edited by Anthony Molho and John A. Tedeschi. Dekalb, Ill., 1971, pp. 809-30.

Brancolini, Julien, and Bouyssy, Marie-Thérèse. "La vie provinciale du livre à la fin de l'ancien régime," in *Livre et société dans la France du 18ᵉ siècle.* 2 vols. Paris, 1965-70, II, 3-37.

Bülau, Friedrich. "Condamine und die Convulsionnäre," in *Geheime Geschichten und Räthselhafte Menschen.* 12 vols. Leipzig, 1850-64, I, 402-10.

Buisard, Augustin. "Le jansénisme en Touraine, d'après le journal d'un curé de Tours (1713-1749)," *Bulletin de la société archéologique de Touraine,* 14 (1903-1904), 283-300, 313-80, 488-516.

Cahen, Léon. "Les idées charitables à Paris au 17ᵉ et au 18ᵉ siècles," *Revue d'histoire moderne et contemporaine,* 2 (1900), 5-22.

———. "La population parisienne au milieu du 18ᵉ siècle," *Revue de Paris,* 26 (September 1919), 146-70.

Carreyre, Jean. "Le Concile d'Embrun (1727-1728)," *Revue des questions historiques,* 14 (1929), 47-106, 318-67.

———. "La doctrine janséniste," in *Introduction aux études d'histoire ecclésiastique locale.* Edited by Victor Carrière. 3 vols. Paris, 1934-40, III, 513-39.

———. "Le Jansénisme pendant les premiers mois de la Régence," *Revue d'histoire ecclésiastique,* 21 (1925), 479-509; 22 (1926), 759-96.

———. "Les luttes du Jansénisme," *Revue d'histoire de l'Eglise de France,* 10 (1924), 441-60.

———. "Quesnel et le Quesnellisme," *Dictionnaire de théologie catholique.* Edited by A. Vacant and E. Mangenot. Vol. XIII², cols. 1,460-1,535.

———. "Unigenitus (Bulle)," *ibid.* Vol. XV², cols. 2,061-2,162.

Carter, A. Barham. "A Physician's View of Hysteria," *Lancet,* No. 7789 (December 9, 1972), 1,241-43.

Cauchie, Alfred. "Les assemblées du clergé sous l'ancien régime: Matériaux et origines," *Revue des sciences philosophiques et théologiques,* 2 (1908), 74-95.

———. "Le gallicanisme en Sorbonne, d'après le correspondance de Bargellini, nonce en France de 1668 à 1671," *Revue d'histoire ecclésiastique,* 3 (1902), 972-85; 4 (1903), 39-54, 448-69.

———. "La paix de Clément IX (1668-1669)," *Revue d'histoire et de littérature religieuses,* 3 (1898), 481-501.

Certeau, Michel de. "Crise sociale et réformisme spirituel au début du 17ᵉ siècle: Une 'nouvelle spiritualité' chez les Jésuites français," *Revue d'ascétique et de mystique,* 41 (1965), 339-86.

———. "Cultures et spiritualités," *Concilium,* No. 19 (1966), 7-25.

―――. "De Saint-Cyran au jansénisme: Conversion et réforme," *Christus*, 10 (1963), 399-413.

―――. "L'histoire religieuse du 17ᵉ siècle: Problèmes de méthodes," *Revue des sciences religieuses*, 57 (1969), 231-50.

―――. "Le jansénisme hier et aujourd'hui: A propos d'un livre récent," *Revue d'ascétique et de mystique*, 46 (1970), 449-56.

―――. "Une mutation culturelle et religieuse: Les magistrats devant les sorciers du 17ᵉ siècle," *Revue d'histoire de l'Eglise de France*, 55 (1969), 300-19.

Ceyssens, Lucien. "Les cinq propositions de Jansénius à Rome," *Revue d'histoire ecclésiastique*, 66 (1971), 449-501, 821-86.

―――. "Le côté juridique des premières difficultés jansénistes," in *Reformata reformanda: Festgabe für Hubert Jedin*. Edited by Erwin Iserloh. 2 vols. Münster-Westf., 1965, II, 401-13.

―――. "Le jansénisme: Considérations historiques préliminaires à sa notion," *Analecta gregoriana*, 71 (1952), 3-32.

―――. "Les papiers de Quesnel saisis à Bruxelles et transportés à Paris en 1703 et 1704," *Revue d'histoire ecclésiastique*, 44 (1949), 508-51.

Charcot, Jean-Martin. "La foi qui guérit," *Revue hebdomadaire*, 7 (December 1892), 112-32.

―――, and Marie, Pierre. "Hysteria," in *A Dictionary of Psychological Medicine*. Edited by D. Hack Tuke. 2 vols. Philadelphia, 1892, I, 627-41.

Charlot, E., and Dupâquier, J. "Mouvement annuel de la population de la ville de Paris de 1670 à 1821," *Annales de démographie historique* (1967), 511-19.

Chatelus, Jean. "Thèmes picturaux dans les appartements de marchands et artisans parisiens au 18ᵉ siècle," *18ᵉ siècle*, 6 (1974), 309-24.

Chaunu, Pierre. "Le 17ᵉ siècle religieux: Réflections préalables," *Annales: Economies, Sociétés, Civilisations*, 22 (1967), 279-302.

―――. "Une histoire religieuse sérielle: A propos du diocèse de La Rochelle (1648-1724), et sur quelques exemples normands," *Revue d'histoire moderne et contemporaine*, 12 (1965), 5-34.

―――. "Jansénisme et frontière de catholicité (17ᵉ et 18ᵉ siècles)," *Revue historique*, 227 (1962), 115-38.

Chauvet, Paul. "Compagnons imprimeurs et imprimeries clandestines à Paris sous le règne de Louis XV," *Revue d'histoire économique et sociale*, 26 (1940-47), 40-46, 151-72.

Chenu, Marie-Dominique. "Orthodoxie et hérésie: Le point de vue du théologien," *Annales: Economies, Sociétés, Civilisations*, 18 (1963), 75-80.

Chodoff, Paul. "The Diagnosis of Hysteria: An Overview," *American Journal of Psychiatry*, 131 (1974), 1,073-78.

———, and Lyons, Henry. "Hysteria, the Hysterical Personality and 'Hysterical' Conversion," *American Journal of Psychiatry*, 114 (1958), 634-40.

Church, William F. "The Decline of French Jurists as Political Theorists, 1660-1789," *French Historical Studies*, 5 (1967), 1-40.

Cleghorn, R. A. "Hysteria: Multiple Manifestations of Semantic Confusion," *Canadian Psychiatric Association Journal*, 14 (1969), 539-51.

———. "Hysterical Personality and Conversion: Theoretical Aspects," *Canadian Psychiatric Association Journal*, 14 (1969), 553-67.

Cognet, Louis. "La dévotion mariale à Port-Royal," in *Maria: Etudes sur la Sainte Vierge*. Edited by Hubert Du Manoir. 8 vols. Paris, 1949-71, III, 119-51.

———. "La direction de conscience à Port-Royal," *Supplément de la vie spirituelle*, 8 (1955), 289-305.

———. "Etat présent des études Port-Royalistes," *Critique*, 8 (1952), 689-702.

———. "L'état présent des travaux sur Port-Royal et le jansénisme," *L'information littéraire*, 9 (1957), 139-46.

———. "Le jansénisme, drame gallican," *L'Année canonique*, 10 (1965), 75-83.

———. "Les jansénistes et le Sacré-Coeur," *Etudes carmélitaines*, 29 (1950), 234-53.

———. "Le mépris du monde à Port-Royal et dans le jansénisme," *Revue d'ascétique et de mystique*, 41 (1965), 387-402.

———. "Note sur Quesnel et sur l'ecclésiologie de Port-Royal," *Irenikon*, 21 (1948), 326-32, 439-46.

———. "Les Petites Ecoles de Port-Royal," *Cahiers de l'Association internationale des études françaises*, 3-5 (1953), 19-29.

Cohn, Norman. "Réflexions sur le millénarisme," *Archives de sociologie des religions*, 3 (1958), 103-107.

Constant, Gustave. "Une source trop négligée de l'histoire paroissiale: Les registres des marguilliers," *Revue d'histoire de l'Eglise de France*, 24 (1938), 170-83.

"Les convulsionnaires à la Bastille (1732)," *Revue retrospective*, 10 (1889), 140-41.

Coste, P. "Les détenus de Saint-Lazare aux 17e et 18e siècles," *Revue des études historiques*, 92 (1926), 275-90.

Cousin, Bernard. "Deux cents miracles en Provence sous Louis XIV," *Revue d'histoire de la spiritualité*, 52 (1976), 225-44.

Crehan, F. J. "The Bible in the Roman Catholic Church from Trent to the Present Day," in *The Cambridge History of the Bible*. Edited by S. L. Greenslade. 3 vols. Cambridge, Eng., 1900, III, 199-237.

Cruickshanks, Evelyn. "Public Opinion in Paris in the 1740s: The Reports of the Chevalier de Mouhy," *Bulletin of the Institute of Historical Research*, 27 (1954), 54-68.

Dagens, Jean. "Le 17ᵉ siècle, siècle de Saint-Augustin," *Cahiers de l'Association internationale des études françaises*, 3-5 (1953), 31-38.

Dainville, François de. "La carte du jansénisme à Paris en 1739 d'après les papiers de la Nonciature," *Bulletin de la Société de l'histoire de Paris et de l'Ile de France*, 96 (1969), 113-24.

Darnton, Robert. "The Memoirs of Lenoir, Lieutenant de Police of Paris, 1774-1785," *English Historical Review*, 85 (1970), 532-59.

———. "Reading, Writing, and Publishing in 18th-Century France: A Case Study in the Sociology of Literature," in *Historical Studies Today*. Edited by Felix Gilbert and Stephen R. Graubard. New York, 1972, pp. 238-80.

Darricau, Raymond. "Lumières nouvelles sur l'histoire du clergé de France sous Louis XIV," *Revue d'histoire ecclésiastique*, 69 (1974), 93-102.

Davis, Natalie Z. "Some Tasks and Themes in the Study of Popular Religion," in *The Pursuit of Holiness in Late Medieval and Renaissance Religion*. Edited by Charles Trinkaus with Heiko A. Oberman. Vol. x of *Studies in Medieval and Reformation Thought*. Leiden, 1974, pp. 307-36.

Dedieu, Joseph. "L'agonie du jansénisme," *Revue d'histoire de l'Eglise de France*, 14 (1928), 161-214.

———. "Le désarroi janséniste pendant la période du quesnellisme," in *Introduction aux études d'histoire ecclésiastique locale*. Edited by Victor Carrière. 3 vols. Paris, 1934-40, III, 541-89.

———. "Un nouveau Port-Royal au diocèse d'Auxerre," *Le Correspondant*, 101 (September 1929), 641-61.

Delooz, Pierre. "Pour une étude sociologique de la sainteté canonisée dans l'Eglise catholique," *Archives de sociologie des religions*, 7 (1962), 17-43.

Delumeau, Jean. "Au sujet de la déchristianisation," *Revue d'histoire moderne et contemporaine*, 22 (1975), 52-60.

———. "Ignorance religieuse et mentalité magique sous l'ancien régime." Paper presented before the annual meeting of the Society for French Historical Studies. Ottawa, March 1972.

———. "Les Réformateurs et la superstition," in *Colloque l'Amiral de Coligny et son temps* (Paris, 1972). Paris, 1974, pp. 451-87, 518-24.

———. "Résistance du paganisme," *Christus*, 19 (1972), 480-94.

Denis, Paul. "Les Bénédictins de Saint-Germain-des-Près et la cour de Rome en 1735," *Revue Mabillon*, 4 (1908-1909), 324-66.

———. "Le Cardinal de Fleury, Dom Alaydon et Dom Thuillier," *Revue bénédictine*, 26 (1909), 325-70.

———. "Un procureur-général de Cluny, agent secret à Rome de Philippe d'Orléans (1717-1718)," *Revue Mabillon*, 6 (1910-11), 381-436.

———. "Quelques lettres de dom Louvard, prisonnier à la Bastille," *Revue Mabillon*, 4 (1908-1909), 498-525.

Dent, Cynthia A. "Changes in the Episcopal Structure of the Church of France in the 17th Century as an Aspect of Bourbon State-Building," *Bulletin of the Institute of Historical Research*, 48 (1975), 214-29.

———. "The Council of State and the Clergy During the Reign of Louis XIV: An Aspect of the Growth of French Absolutism," *Journal of Ecclesiastical History*, 24 (1973), 245-66.

De Rosa, Gabriele. "Santeté, clergé et peuple dans le Mezzogiorno italien au milieu du 18e siècle," *Revue d'histoire de la spiritualité*, 52 (1976), 245-64.

Desjardins, G. "Le fonds du Conseil d'Etat de l'Ancien Régime aux Archives nationales," *Bibliothèque de l'Ecole des Chartes*, 59 (1898), 5-55.

Desroche, Henri. "Autour de la sociologie dite 'des sectes,'" *L'Année sociologique*, 3rd ser. (1955-56), 395-421.

———. "'Heavens on Earth': Micromillénarismes et communautarisme utopique en Amérique de Nord du 17e au 19e siècle," *Archives de sociologie des religions*, 2 (1975), 57-92.

———. "Sociologie des sectes," *L'Année sociologique*, 3rd ser. (1952), 393-429.

Deyon, Pierre. "Mentalités populaires, un sondage à Amiens au 17e siècle," *Annales: Economies, sociétés, civilisations*, 17 (1962), 448-58.

———. "Perspectives et limites d'une 'sociologie' du jansénisme," *Annales: Economies, Sociétés, Civilisations*, 21 (1966), 428-34.

Dillay, Madeleine. "Les 'registres secrets' des Chambres des Enquêtes et des Requêtes du Parlement du Paris," *Bibliothèque de l'Ecole des Chartes*, 108 (1950), 75-123.

Dolhagary, B. "Curés," in *Dictionnaire de théologie catholique*. Edited by A. Vacant and E. Mangenot. Vol. III², cols. 2,429-53.

Dominique, Pierre. "Port-Royal et les Jésuites, ou les desseins politiques de deux siècles," *Ecrits de Paris* (February 1966), 26-33.

Dreyfus, F.-G. "Jansénisme, romantisme et antiromantisme au 18e siècle," *Revue d'histoire et de philosophie religieuses*, 42 (1962), 45-55.

Dubruel, Marc. "La cour de Rome et l'extension de la Régale," *Revue d'histoire de l'Eglise de France*, 9 (1923), 161-84, 456-92.

———. "Les origines de l'agence janséniste à Rome à la fin du 17ᵉ siècle: La première mission de l'abbé de Pontchâteau, 1677-1678," *Etudes*, 188 (1926), 400-20.

———. "La querelle de la régale sous Louis XIV: Le premier heurt (1673-1676)," *Revue des questions historiques*, 97 (1922), 257-311.

Dudon, Paul. "Le Fareinisme," *Bulletin de la Société Gorini*, 5 (1908), 117-25, 316-33, 345-68; 6 (1909), 66-88; 7 (1910), 67-83; 10 (1913), 113-27, 237-53, 399-413.

Dufour, Valentin. "Etat du diocèse de Paris en 1789," *Bulletin du Comité d'histoire et d'archéologie du diocèse de Paris*, 1 (1883), 20-60, 197-212, 314-53, 416-33; 2 (1884), 229-69.

Dumont, François. "Les 'prélats administrateurs' au 18ᵉ siècle en France," in *Etudes d'histoire du droit canonique dédiées à Gabriel Le Bras*. 2 vols. Paris, 1965, 1, 513-21.

———. "Royauté française et monarchie absolue au 17ᵉ siècle," *17ᵉ siècle*, Nos. 58-59 (1963), 3-29.

Dupront, Alphonse. "Formes de la culture de masses: De la doléance politique au pèlerinage panique (18ᵉ-20ᵉ siècles)," in *Niveaux de culture et groupes sociaux*. Paris, 1967, pp. 149-70.

———. "Problèmes et méthodes d'une histoire de la psychologie collective," *Annales: Economies, Sociétés, Civilisations*, 16 (1961), 3-11.

Durengues, abbé. "Monsieur Boileau de l'archevêché (1649-1735)," *Recueil des travaux de la Société d'agriculture, science et arts d'Agen*, 15 (1908), 1-334.

"L'Eglise Saint-Médard," *Le Magasin pittoresque*, 13 (1845), 307-309.

Egret, Jean. "Note d'orientation de recherches sur les cours souveraines, particulièrement au 18ᵉ siècle," *Bulletin de la section d'histoire moderne et contemporaine du Comité des travaux historiques et scientifiques*, fasc. 5 (1964), 44-53.

Ehrard, Jean. "Histoire des idées et histoire sociale en France au 18ᵉ siècle: Réflexions de méthode," in *Niveaux de culture et groupes sociaux*. Paris, 1967, pp. 171-88.

Engel, George L. "Conversion Symptoms," in *Signs and Symptoms: Applied Pathologic Physiology and Clinical Interpretation*. Edited by Cyril M. MacBryde and Robert S. Blacklow. 5th ed. Philadelphia, 1970, pp. 650-68.

———. "'Psychogenic' Pain and the Pain-Prone Patient," *American Journal of Medicine*, 26 (1959), 899-918.

Escholier, Raymond. "Survivances du Jansénisme à Auxerre," *Congrès de l'Association bourguignonne des sociétés savantes*, 31 (1960), 227-35.

Estrée, Paul d'. "Un journaliste policier: Le chevalier de Mouhy," *Revue d'histoire littéraire de la France*, 4 (1897), 195-238.

Ey, Henri. "Introduction à l'étude actuelle de l'hystérie (Historique et analyse du concepte)," *La revue du praticien*, 14 (1964), 1,416-31.

Febvre, Lucien. "La dévotion en France au 17ᵉ siècle," *Revue de synthèse*, 3 (1932), 199-202.

Feret, Pierre. "Une négociation secrète entre Louis XIV et Clement XI en 1715," *Revue des questions historiques*, 85 (1909), 108-45.

Ferguson, Wallace K. "The Place of Jansenism in French History," *Journal of Religion*, 7 (1927), 16-42.

Finucane, R. C. "The Use and Abuse of Medieval Miracles," *History*, 60 (1975), 1-10.

Fosseyeux, Marcel. "L'Assistance aux prisonniers à Paris sous l'ancien régime," *Mémoires de la Société de l'histoire de Paris et de l'Ile de France*, 48 (1925), 110-29.

———. "Le budget de la charité à Paris au 18ᵉ siècle," *Revue des études historiques*, 85 (1919), 253-64.

———. "Le Cardinal de Noailles et l'administration du diocèse de Paris (1695-1729)," *Revue historique*, 114 (1913), 261-84; 115 (1914), 34-54.

———. "Inventaire sommaire des papiers de Louis Antoine de Noailles conservés aux archives de l'Assistance publique," *Bibliographie moderne*, 16 (1912), 7-66.

Friedmann, Adrien. "Les circonscriptions paroissiales de Paris avant la Révolution: Méthode de recherche. Résultats acquis," *L'Année canonique*, 7 (1962), 33-44.

Frijhoff, Willem. "La fonction du miracle dans une minorité catholique: Les Provinces-Unies au 17ᵉ siècle," *Revue d'histoire de la spiritualité*, 48 (1972), 151-77.

Froelschlé-Chopard, Marie-Hélène. "Les dévotions populaires d'après les visites pastorales: Un exemple, le diocèse de Vence au début du 18ᵉ siècle," *Revue d'histoire de l'Eglise de France*, 60 (1974), 85-100.

Funck-Brentano, Frantz. "La Bastille d'après ses archives," *Revue historique*, 42 (1890), 38-73, 278-316.

Furet, François. "Pour une définition des classes inférieures à l'époque moderne," *Annales: Economies, Sociétés, Civilisations*, 18 (1963), 459-75.

G. S. R. "Questionnaire sur les Messianismes et Millénarismes," *Archives de sociologie des religions*, 3 (1958), 88-90.

Gadille, J. "Histoire du catholicisme moderne et contemporaine," *Revue historique*, 244 (1970), 125-48, 387-440.

Gangneux, Gérard. "Le bas clergé sous l'ancien régime: L'exemple d'un curé aux 17ᵉ et 18ᵉ siècles," *Annales: Economies, Sociétés, Civilisations*, 14 (1959), 745-49.

Gaston, Jean. "L'assemblée de MM. les curés de Paris au 17ᵉ siècle," *Revue du clergé français*, 59 (1909), 676-79.

Gay, Jean-Lucien. "L'administration de la Capitale entre 1770 et 1789: La tutelle du Royauté et ses limites," *Mémoires de la Fédération des Sociétés historiques et archéologiques de Paris et de l'Ile de France*, 8 (1956), 299-370; 9 (1957-58), 283-363; 10 (1959), 181-247; 11 (1960), 363-403; 12 (1961), 135-218.

Gazier, Augustin. "La Bastille en 1743," *Mémoires de la Société de l'histoire de Paris et de l'Ile de France*, 7 (1880), 11-36.

————. "Les Christs prétendus jansénistes," *Revue de l'art chrétien*, 60 (1910), 77-94.

————. "Les écoles de charité du faubourg Saint-Antoine, école normale et groupes scolaires, 1713-1887," *Revue internationale de l'enseignement*, 51 (1906), 217-37, 314-26.

————. "François Boucher et le Bréviaire de 1736," *Revue de l'art chrétien*, 61 (1911), 121-30.

————. "Le frère de Voltaire (1685-1745)," *Revue des deux mondes*, 32 (1906), 615-46.

————. "Pascal et les écrivains de Port-Royal," in *Histoire de la langue et de la littérature française des origines à 1900*. Edited by Louis Petit de Julleville. 8 vols. Paris, 1896-99, IV, 560-627.

————. "Restout et les miracles du diacre Pâris," *Revue de l'art chrétien*, 62 (1912), 117-30.

Gazier, Cécile. "Une amie des derniers jours de Port-Royal: Françoise-Marguerite de Joncoux (1668-1715)," *Revue de Paris*, 36 (April 1929), 827-59.

————. "Un apôtre oublié du 17ᵉ siècle: Claude Bernard et le Séminaire des Trente-Trois," *Le Correspondant*, 314 (1929), 896-911.

————. "Les sources de Sainte-Beuve," *La revue bleue*, 64 (July 1926), 436-40.

Gazin-Gossel, J. "Henry de Thiard, cardinal de Bissy: Essai d'action commune de l'épiscopat français en 1735," *Revue d'histoire de l'Eglise de France*, 2 (1911), 539-53, 679-701.

Geertz, Hildreth. "An Anthropology of Religion and Magic, I," *Journal of Interdisciplinary History*, 6 (1975), 71-89.

Gérin, Charles. "Le pape Alexandre VIII et Louis XIV d'après des documents inédits," *Revue des questions historiques*, 22 (1877), 135-210.

Germain, A. "Les Multipliants: Episode de l'histoire de Montpellier, 1721-1723," *Revue catholique de Bordeaux*, 4 (1845), 266-80, 333-67.

Gilles de la Tourette, Georges. "Le miracle opéré sur Marie-Anne Couronneau le 13 juin 1731," *Nouvelle iconographie de la Salpêtrière*, 2 (1889), 241-50.

———. "Le sein hystérique," *Nouvelle iconographie de la Salpêtrière*, 8 (1895), 107-21.

Godefroy, Jean. "Le chevalier de Folard et les Bénédictins de Saint-Germain-des-Près," *Revue Mabillon*, 26 (1936), 114-33, 154-66.

Goldmann, Lucien. "Remarques sur le jansénisme: La vision tragique du monde et la noblesse de robe," *17ᵉ siècle*, No. 19 (1953), 177-95.

Golliet, Pierre. "Pasquier Quesnel et les destinées du jansénisme," *Revue d'histoire littéraire de la France*, 64 (1964), 455-62.

Goodman, Felicitas. "Glossolalia and Hallucination in Pentecostal Congregations," *Psychiatric Clinic*, 6 (1973), 97-103.

Gorce, Agnès de la. "Joute d'évêques à Embrun en 1727," *Miroir de l'histoire*, No. 38 (March 1953), 167-72.

Grisselle, Eugène. "Vers la paix de l'Eglise de France d'après des lettres inédites du négociateur, le cardinal de Polignac (1725-1732)," *Revue d'histoire de l'Eglise de France*, 2 (1911), 271-95, 404-20.

Grossier, Chanoine. "Correspondance entre le Cardinal Fleury, ministre d'Etat et Mgr. Languet, Archevêque de Sens, sur le Jansénisme en Puisaye," *Congrès de l'Association bourguignonne des sociétés savantes*, 31 (1960), 259-63.

Grünebaum-Ballin, P. "Grégoire convertisseur? ou la croyance au 'Retour d'Israël,'" *Revue des études juives*, 121 (1962), 383-98.

Guillaume, Joseph. "Comment concevoir une Monographie paroissiale?" *Revue d'histoire de l'Eglise de France*, 9 (1923), 369-88, 493-523.

Guitton, Georges. "Le Père François de la Chaize au milieu des intrigues jansénistes," *Nouvelle revue théologique*, 74 (1952), 160-80.

Guizard, abbé Louis. "L'ancienne législation synodale du Diocèse de Paris," *La semaine religieuse de Paris*, 204 (1956), 1,325-26; 205 (1957), 23-25.

Gurian, Waldemar. "L'influence de l'Ancien Régime sur la politique religieuse de la Révolution," *Revue internationale d'histoire politique et constitutionnelle*, 6 (1956), 259-77.

Gutton, Jean-Pierre. "Les mendiants dans la société parisienne au début du 18ᵉ siècle," *Cahiers d'histoire*, 13 (1968), 131-41.

Hallays, André. "Le dernier des Port-Royalistes: Augustin Gazier et son apologie du jansénisme," *Revue des deux mondes*, 7th ser., 14 (March 1923), 441-58.

Hamilton, Earl J. "Prices and Wages at Paris under John Law's System," *Quarterly Journal of Economics*, 51 (1936-37), 42-70.

Hanotaux, Gabriel. "Théories du gallicanisme," in *Sur les chemins de l'histoire*. 2 vols. Paris, 1924, I, 53-172.

Hardy, Georges. "Le cardinal de Fleury et le mouvement philosophique," *Annales historiques de la Révolution française*, 2 (1925), 513-27.

Hau, Claude. "Un faux messie contre Napoléon," *Miroir de l'histoire*, No. 114 (June 1959), 806-16.

Himelfarb, Hélène. "Saint-Simon et le jansénisme des Lumières," *Studies on Voltaire and the 18th Century*, 88 (1972), 749-68.

Holland, R. F. "The Miraculous," in *Religion and Understanding*. Edited by D. Z. Phillips. New York, 1967, pp. 155-70.

Hutt, Maurice G. "The Curés and the Third Estate: The Ideas of Reform in the Pamphlets of the French Lower Clergy in the Period 1787-1789," *Journal of Ecclesiastical History*, 8 (1957), 74-92.

———. "The Role of the Curés in the Estates-General of 1789," *Journal of Ecclesiastical History*, 6 (1955), 190-220.

"Incendie des archives de l'assistance publique à Paris," *Bibliothèque de l'Ecole des Chartes*, 32 (1871), 223-25.

"Incendie des archives de la Préfecture de police," *Bibliothèque de l'Ecole des Chartes*, 32 (1871), 225-26.

Jaloustre, Elie. "Un janséniste en exil: Jean Soanen, évêque de Senez à l'abbaye de la Chaise-Dieu. Sa rétraction, sa mort, son crâne," *Bulletin historique et scientifique de l'Auvergne*, 2nd ser., Nos. 6-7 (June-July 1902), 192-224, 228-71.

Join-Lambert, Michel. "La pratique religieuse dans le Diocèse de Rouen de 1707 à 1789," *Annales de Normandie*, 5 (1955), 35-49.

———. "La pratique religieuse dans le Diocèse de Rouen sous Louis XIV (1660-1715)," *Annales de Normandie*, 3 (1953), 247-74.

Judge, H. G. "Church and State under Louis XIV," *History*, 45 (1960), 217-33.

———. "The Congregation of the Oratory in France in the Late 17th Century," *Journal of Ecclesiastical History*, 12 (1961), 46-55.

Juge-Chapsal, Charles. "L'épiscopat de Jean Soanen," *Bulletin historique et scientifique de l'Auvergne*, 75 (1955), 33-67.

———. "Les origines de Jean Soanen, évêque et seigneur de Senez," *Bulletin de la Société scientifique et littéraire des Basses-Alpes*, 29 (1943), 97-121.

Julia, Dominique. "Le clergé paroissial dans le diocèse de Reims à la fin du 18ᵉ siècle," *Revue d'histoire moderne et contemporaine*, 13 (1966), 195-216.

———. "La crise des vocations, essai d'analyse historique," *Les Etudes* (1967), 238-51.

———. "Le prêtre du 18ᵉ siècle: La théologie et les institutions," *Recherches de science religieuse*, 58 (1970), 521-34.

———. "Problèmes d'historiographie religieuse," *18ᵉ siècle*, 5 (1973), 81-88.

———, and Frijhoff, Willem. "Le prêtre français à l'époque moderne," *Concilium*, No. 47 (1969), 123-31.

Kaplow, Jeffry. "The Culture of Poverty in Paris on the Eve of the Revolution," *International Review of Social History*, 12 (1967), 277-91.

———. "La population flottante de Paris à la fin de l'ancien régime," *Annales historiques de la Révolution française*, 39 (1967), 1-14.

Köbben, A.J.F. "Prophetic Movements as an Expression of Social Protest," *International Archives of Ethnography*, 49 (1960), 117-64.

La Barre, Weston. "Materials for a History of Studies of Crisis Cults: A Bibliographic Essay," *Current Anthropology*, 12 (1971), 3-44.

Labriolle, Chanoine de. "Le concile d'Embrun de 1727, révélateur de la société du 18ᵉ siècle," *Bulletin de la Société d'études des Hautes-Alpes* (1966), 143-56.

Lacombe, Bernard de. "L'opposition religieuse au début du 18ᵉ siècle," *Le Correspondant*, 215 (April 1904), 3-28.

Langlois, Marcel. "Madame de Maintenon et le Saint-Siège," *Revue d'histoire ecclésiastique*, 25 (1929), 32-72.

Laporte, Jean. "Pascal et la doctrine de Port-Royal," *Revue de métaphysique et de morale*, 30 (1923), 247-306.

Latreille, André. "Innocent XI, Pape 'janséniste,' Directeur de conscience de Louis XIV," *Cahiers d'histoire*, 1 (1956), 9-39.

———. "Les nonces apostoliques en France et l'église gallicane sous Innocent XI," *Revue d'histoire de l'Eglise de France*, 41 (1955), 211-34.

———. "Pratique, piété, et foi populaire dans la France moderne au 19ᵉ et 20ᵉ siècles," in *Popular Beliefs and Practices*. Edited by G. J. Cuming and Derek Baker. Volume 8 of *Studies in Church History*. Cambridge, Eng., 1972, 277-90.

Latreille, C. "Les Illuminés de Fareins," *Mercure de France*, 81 (October 1909), 561-82.

Lauras, André. "Symptomes et critères diagnostiques de l'hystérie," *La revue du praticien*, 14 (1964), 1,442-57.

Laurent, Marcel. "Deux évêques contre la bulle Unigenitus: L'amitié de J. Soanen et de J. Colbert de Croissy," *Chroniques de Port-Royal*, No. 19 (1971), 37-76.

―――. "Jean Soanen, évêque de Senez, devant le 'Concile' d'Embrun (1727)," *Revue d'Auvergne*, 82 (1968), 95-112.

Lavaquery, Eugène. "Les sources manuscrites de l'histoire religieuse de la France aux Archives des Affaires étrangères," *Revue d'histoire de l'Eglise de France*, 11 (1925), 53-72.

Leblanc, Yves. "L'abbé de Roquette, prieur de Saint-Himer, fut-il oui ou non, janséniste?" *Chroniques de Port-Royal*, Nos. 15-16 (1966), 27-44.

Le Bras, Gabriel. "Déchristianisation: Mot fallacieux," *Cahiers d'histoire*, 9 (1964), 92-97.

―――. "Notes sur le droit et les institutions de l'Eglise de France au 17ᵉ siècle," *17ᵉ siècle*, Nos. 58-59 (1963), 73-104.

―――. "Pour l'histoire du jansénisme dans l'Orléanais," *Revue d'histoire de l'Eglise de France*, 18 (1932), 189-96.

―――. "La vitalité religieuse de l'Eglise de France," *Revue d'histoire de l'Eglise de France*, 31 (1945), 277-306.

Lebrun, Jacques. "Bulletin d'histoire de la spiritualité: L'époque moderne," *Revue d'histoire de la spiritualité*, 50 (1974), 57-79.

Lecler, Joseph. "Qu'est-ce que les libertés de l'Eglise Gallicane?" *Recherches de science religieuse*, 23 (1933), 385-410, 542-68; 24 (1934), 47-85.

Lecomte, Maurice. "Les deux derniers procureurs des bénédictins à Rome: Dom Conrade et Dom Maloët (1716-1735), d'après leur correspondance," *Revue Mabillon*, 4 (1908-1909), 367-79.

Lecotté, R. "Méthodes d'enquêtes pour les cultes populaires," *Revue de synthèse*, 78 (1957), 367-89.

Leflon, Jean, and Godel, Jean. "La pratique et la vie religieuses en France aux 18ᵉ, 19ᵉ et 20ᵉ siècles dans une paroisse ou un groupe de paroisses," *Bulletin de la Section d'histoire moderne et contemporaine du Comité des travaux historiques et scientifiques*, fasc. 9 (1975), 17-27.

Lévy-Schneider, Léon. "L'autonomie administrative de l'épiscopat français à la fin de l'ancien régime," *Revue historique*, 151 (1926), 1-33.

Loevenbruck, L. "Convulsionnaires," *Dictionnaire de théologie catholique*. Edited by A. Vacant and E. Mangenot. Vol. III², cols. 1,756-62.

Lowe, Warner L. "Group Beliefs and Socio-Cultural Factors in Religious Delusions," *Journal of Social Psychology*, 40 (1954), 267-74.

―――. "Psychodynamics in Religious Delusions and Hallucinations," *American Journal of Psychotherapy*, 7 (1953), 454-62.

Mahieu, Bernard. "Les archives de l'Eglise catholique en France," *Archivum*, 4 (1954), 89-103.

Mandrou, Robert. "La fille aînée de l'Eglise," in *La France au temps de Louis XIV*. Paris, 1966, pp. 181-99.

———. "Littérature de colportage et mentalités paysannes aux 17ᵉ et 18ᵉ siècles," *Etudes rurales*, No. 15 (1964), 72-85.

———. "Spiritualité et pratique catholique au 17ᵉ siècle," *Annales: Economies, Sociétés, Civilisations*, 16 (1961), 136-46.

———. "Tragique 17ᵉ siècle: A propos de travaux récents," *Annales: Economies, Sociétés, Civilisations*, 12 (1957), 305-13.

Manneville, Charles-Henri. "Une vieille église de Paris: Saint-Médard," *Bulletin de la Montagne Sainte-Geneviève et ses abords*, 4 (1903-1904), 3-298.

Maricourt, André de, and Firmin-Didot, Georges. "Les Convulsionnaires," *La Nouvelle revue*, 3rd ser., 54 (October 1908), 356-68.

Marie, Auguste. "Les convulsionnaires de Saint-Médard," *Aesculape*, 14 (1924), 29-33, 54-58, 86-88.

Martimort, Aimé-Georges. "Comment les français du 17ᵉ voyaient le pape," *17ᵉ siècle*, Nos. 25-26 (1955), 83-101.

Martin, Victor. "L'adoption du gallicanisme politique par le clergé de France," *Revue des sciences religieuses*, 6 (1926), 305-44, 453-98; 7 (1927), 1-51, 181-225, 373-401, 545-78; 8 (1928), 1-23, 173-95, 361-97.

Mathiez, Albert. "Cathérine Théot," *Revue de Paris*, 8 (April 1901), 857-78.

Maury, Alfred. "Les Assemblées du clergé en France sous l'ancienne monarchie," *Revue des deux mondes*, 31 (1879), 754-96; 32 (1879), 509-55; 35 (1879), 265-300; 40 (1880), 621-67.

Mazoyer, Louis. "Les origines du prophétisme cévenol," *Revue historique*, 197 (1947), 23-55.

McManners, John. "Jansenism and Politics in the 18th Century," in *Church, Society and Politics*. Edited by Derek Baker. Oxford, 1975, pp. 253-73.

Messelet, Jean. "Jean Restout (1692-1768)," *Archives de l'art français*, 19 (1938), 97-188.

Méthivier, Hubert, "L'action catholique dans la société française du 17ᵉ siècle," *L'information historique*, 29 (1967), 16-19.

———. "Ferveurs et controverses spirituelles dans la France catholique du 17ᵉ siècle, "*L'information historique*, 28 (1966), 185-92.

Métraux, Alfred. "Dramatic Elements in Ritual Possession," *Diogenes*, No. 11 (1955), 18-36.

Meuvret, Jean. "Les aspects politiques de la liquidation du conflit gallican, 1691-92," *Revue d'histoire de l'Eglise de France*, 33 (1947), 257-70.

————. "La situation matérielle des membres du clergé séculier dans la France du 17e siècle: Possibilités et limites des recherches," *Revue d'histoire de l'Eglise de France*, 54 (1968), 47-68.

Mews, Stuart. "Reason and Emotion in Working-Class Religion, 1794-1824," in *Schism, Heresy, and Religious Protest*. Edited by Derek Baker. Cambridge, Eng., 1972, pp. 365-82.

Millenarian Change: Movements of Total Transformation. Special number edited by Michael Barkun. *American Behavioral Scientist*, 16 (November-December 1972).

Montegre, de. "Convulsionnaires," *Dictionnaire des sciences médicales*. Edited by C.L.F. Panckoucke. Vol. VI, cols. 568-96.

Morey, Adrian, and Landor, Anthony. "Lorenzo Casoni and Papal Policy for the Church in France, 1682-1689," *Journal of Ecclesiastical History*, 4 (1953), 77-84.

Morrison, Denton F. "Some Notes Toward Theory on Relative Deprivation, Social Movements, and Social Change," *American Behavioral Scientist*, 14 (1971), 675-90.

Morsier, G. de. "La 'Grande hystérie de Charcot': Essai sur les causes d'une erreur médicale et judiciaire. Doctrine et perception," *Revue médicale de la Suisse Romande*, 89 (1969), 177-203.

Mousset, Alfred. "Un vent de folie au 'siècle des lumières': Les 'miracles' du cimetière Saint-Médard," *Historia*, No. 127 (June 1957), 567-74.

Nau, Paul. "A l'origine des encycliques modernes: Un épisode de la lutte des évêques et des parlements, 1755-1756," *Revue historique de droit français et étranger*, 34 (1956), 225-67.

Nemiah, John C. "Hysterical Neurosis, Conversion Type," in *Comprehensive Textbook of Psychiatry*. Edited by Alfred M. Freedman, Harold I. Kaplan, and Benjamin J. Sadock. 2nd ed. 2 vols. Baltimore, 1975, I, 1,208-20.

Neveu, Bruno. "Politique ecclésiastique et controverses doctrinales à Rome de 1683 à 1705," *Bulletin de la Société d'histoire moderne*, 74 (1974-75), 11-19.

N[icod], E[mmanuel]. "Le diacre Pâris," *Revue historique, archéologique, littéraire et pittoresque du Vivarais illustrée*, 21 (1913), 282-84.

Noir, Julien. "La foi qui guérit à Saint-Médard. A propos d'un portrait du diacre Pâris," *Bulletin de la Montagne Sainte-Geneviève et ses abords*, 6 (1909-12), 69-82.

"Notes, trouvailles, et curiosités: La fermeture du cimetière Saint-

Médard en 1732," *L'intermédiaire des chercheurs et curieux*, 37 (1901), cols. 998-1,000.

Noyon, Augustin. "Un miracle du diacre Pâris: La guérison de l'abbé de Becherand (1731-1732)," *Etudes*, 156 (1918), 412-32.

Orcibal, Jean. "L'idée d'église chez les catholiques du 17ᵉ siècle," *Relazioni del X. Congresso internazionale di scienze storiche*, 4 (1955), 111-35.

——. "Martin de Barcos (1600-1678), abbé de Saint-Cyran et sa correspondance," *Revue d'histoire ecclésiastique*, 52 (1957), 877-99.

——. "Les origines du jansénisme d'après les récentes publications du R. P. Lucien Ceyssens," *Revue d'histoire ecclésiastique*, 53 (1958), 830-38.

——. "Qu'est-ce que le jansénisme?" *Cahiers de l'Association internationale des études françaises*, 3 (1953), 39-53.

——. "La signification du miracle et sa place dans l'ecclésiologie pascalienne," *Chroniques de Port-Royal*, Nos. 20-21 (1972), 83-95.

Péronnet, M. "Police et religion à la fin du 18ᵉ siècle," *Annales historiques de la Révolution française*, 42 (1970), 375-97.

Pérouas, Louis. "La diversité religieuse de l'Ouest aux 17ᵉ et 18ᵉ siècles," *L'information historique*, 28 (1966), 162-65.

——. "Missions intérieures et missions extérieures françaises pendant les premières décennies du 17ᵉ siècle," *Parole et mission*, 7 (1964), 644-59.

——. "Le nombre des vocations sacerdotales, est-il un critère valable en sociologie religieuse historique aux 17ᵉ et 18ᵉ siècles?" *Actes du 87ᵉ Congrès national des sociétés savantes. Section d'histoire moderne et contemporaine*. (Poitiers, 1962), 35-40.

——. "La pastorale liturgique au 17ᵉ siècle," *Mélanges de science religieuse*, 23 (1966), 30-44.

Peter, Jean-Pierre. "Une enquête de la Société royale de médecine: Malades et maladies à la fin du 18ᵉ siècle," *Annales: Economies, Sociétés, Civilisations*, 22 (1967), 711-51.

Pillorget, René, and Viguerie, Jean de. "Les quartiers de Paris aux 17ᵉ et 18ᵉ siècles," *Revue d'histoire moderne et contemporaine*, 17 (1970), 253-77.

Pillorget, Suzanne. "René Hérault de Fontaine, procureur-général au Grand Conseil (1718-1722) et lieutenant-général de police de Paris (1725-1739): Histoire d'une fortune," *Actes du 93ᵉ Congrès national des sociétés savantes. Section d'histoire moderne et contemporaine*. 3 vols. (Tours, 1968), II, 287-311.

Plongeron, Bernard. "L'histoire de l'Eglise au carrefour des sciences religieuses," *Concilium*, No. 57 (1970), 47-58.

―――. "Une image de l'Eglise d'après les *Nouvelles ecclésiastiques* (1728-1790)," *Revue d'histoire de l'Eglise de France*, 53 (1967), 241-68.

―――. "Recherches sur l'*Aufklärung* catholique en Europe occidentale (1770-1830)," *Revue d'histoire moderne et contemporaine*, 16 (1969), 555-605.

―――. "Regards sur l'historiographie religieuse de la Révolution: La déchristianisation," *Annales historiques de la Révolution française*, 40 (1968), 145-205.

―――. "Spiritualité et pauvreté monastique au 18e siècle," *Revue d'histoire de l'Eglise de France*, 52 (1966), 87-111.

Pommier, Jean. "Tricentenaire d'un miracle: Port-Royal et la Sainte-Epine," *Mercure de France*, 326 (March 1956), 437-57.

Portefaix, Jean. "Les événements judiciaires du règne de Louis XV," *Miroir de l'histoire*, No. 42 (July 1953), 681-91; No. 43 (August 1953), 839-48; No. 44 (September 1953), 973-82.

Préclin, Edmond. "Les conséquences sociales du jansénisme," in *Introduction aux études d'histoire ecclésiastique locale*. Edited by Victor Carrière. 3 vols. Paris, 1934-40, III, 592-638.

―――. "Edmond Richer (1559-1631): Sa vie, son oeuvre, le richérisme," *Revue d'histoire moderne*, 5 (1930), 241-69, 321-36.

―――. "L'influence du jansénisme français à l'étranger," *Revue historique*, 182 (1938), 24-71.

Raison, abbé Louis. "Le mouvement janséniste au diocèse de Dol," *Bulletin et mémoires de la Société archéologique du département d'Ille-et-Vilaine*, 56 (1930), 1-98.

―――. "Le mouvement janséniste au diocèse de Rennes," *Annales de Bretagne*, 39 (1931), 539-73; 40 (1932), 36-63, 213-70; 46 (1938), 7-52; 47 (1940), 185-261; 48 (1941), 1-62, 211-83; 49 (1942), 1-101; 50 (1943), 1-68; 51 (1944), 1-87.

―――. "Le mouvement janséniste au diocèse de Saint-Malo," *Mémoires de la Société d'histoire et d'archéologie de Bretagne*, 11 (1930), 5-121.

Rech, Gilbert. "Daguesseau et le jansénisme," in *Le Chancelier Henri-François Daguesseau, 1668-1751*. Limoges, 1953, pp. 119-30.

Regnault, Félix. "Des béguins," *Bulletin de la Société d'anthropologie de Paris*, 4th ser., 1 (1890), 662-80; 2 (1891), 785-92.

―――. "L'hypnotisme dans la génèse des miracles," *Revue de l'hypnotisme*, 8 (1894), 270-77.

Réjalot, Dom Thierry. "Le jansénisme à l'abbaye d'Orval, 1674-1764," *Annales de l'Institut archéologique du Luxembourg*, 63 (1932), 57-196.

461

Rémond, René. "La déchristianisation: Etat présent de la question et des travaux en langue française," *Concilium*, 7 (1965), 131-36.

Rétif, André. "Histoire étrange du mot 'Secouriste,'" *Vie et langage*, No. 217 (April 1970), 223-27.

Risso, Michèle. "Misère, magie, et psychothérapie: Une communauté magico-religieuse de l'Italie méridionale," *Confinia psychiatrica*, 14 (1971), 108-32.

Rocquain, Félix. "Les refus de sacrements, 1752-1754," *Revue historique*, 5 (1877), 241-64.

Rogister, J.M.J. "New Light on the Fall of Chauvelin," *English Historical Review*, 83 (1968), 314-30.

Rosen, George. "Emotion and Sensibility in Ages of Anxiety: A Comparative Historical Review," *American Journal of Psychiatry*, 124 (1967), 771-84.

———. "Psychopathology in the Social Process: A Study of the Persecution of Witches in Europe as a Contribution to the Understanding of Mass Delusions and Psychic Epidemics," *Journal of Health and Human Behavior*, 1 (1960), 200-11.

———. "Social Change and Psychopathology in the Emotional Climate of Millenarian Movements," *American Behavioral Scientist*, 16 (1972), 153-67.

Sainte-Beuve, Charles-Augustin. "Rollin," in *Causeries du Lundi*. 3rd ed. 15 vols. Paris, 1857-72, VI, 261-82.

Salmon, J.H.M. "The King and His Conscience: The Religious Problems of Louis XIV," *History Today*, 15 (1965), 240-48.

Salzman, Leon. "The Psychology of Religious and Ideological Conversion," *Psychiatry*, 16 (1953), 177-87.

———. "Spiritual and Faith Healing," *Journal of Pastoral Care*, 11 (1957), 146-55.

Saouter, G. "L'esprit de Saint-Maur et le jansénisme convulsionnaire," *Vieux St.-Maur*, 49 (1971), 158-60.

Sauzet, Robert. "Miracles et Contre-Réforme en Bas-Languedoc sous Louis XIV," *Revue d'histoire de la spiritualité*, 48 (1972), 179-91.

———. "Pèlerinage panique et pèlerinage de dévotion: Notre-Dame de Rochefort au 17e siècle," *Annales du Midi*, 77 (1965), 375-97.

Serent, Antoine de. "Les Frères Mineurs en face du Jansénisme (1607-1754)," *Etudes franciscaines*, 2 (1951), 213-28, 321-32.

Sérieux, Paul. "Le Parlement de Paris et la surveillance des maisons d'aliénés et de correctionnaires aux 17e et 18e siècles," *Revue historique de droit français et étranger*, 4th ser., 17 (1938), 404-59.

———. "Le traitement des maladies mentales à la Bastille," *Archives internationales de neurologie*, 41¹ (January-May 1922), 137-50, 177-86; 41² (June-December 1922), 12-23, 51-62, 96-107, 121-30, 161-80.

———. "Le traitement des maladies mentales dans les maisons d'aliénés du 18ᵉ siècle," *Archives internationales de neurologie*, 43 (June-December 1924), 97-119, 145-54, 191-204; 44 (January-May 1925), 21-31, 50-64, 90-105, 121-33.

———, and Goulard, Roger. "Le personnel médical de la Bastille," *Bulletin de la Société française de l'histoire de la médecine*, 20 (1926), 178-98.

———. "Le service médicale de la Bastille," *Bulletin de la Société française de l'histoire de la médecine*, 20 (1926), 117-34, 218-23.

———, and Libert, Lucien. "Un asile de sûreté sous l'ancien régime," *La France médicale*, 58 (1911), 438-40, 458-60; 59 (1912), 18-29, 38-40.

———. "La Bastille et ses prisonniers: Contributions à l'étude des asiles de sûreté," *L'encéphale*, 6 (July-December 1911), 18-31, 112-26, 223-44, 366-78, 392-93.

———. "Les lettres de cachet: 'Prisonniers de famille' et 'placements volontaires,'" *Bulletin de la Société de médecine mentale de Belgique*, No. 159 (December 1911), 356-78; No. 160 (February 1912), 38-64.

———. "Le régime des aliénés en France au 18ᵉ siècle," *Annales médico-psychologiques*, 10th ser., 6 (1914-15), 43-76, 196-219, 311-23, 470-97, 598-627; 7 (1916), 74-98.

Shackleton, Robert. "Jansenism and the Enlightenment," *Studies on Voltaire and the 18th Century*, 57 (1967), 1,388-96.

Shennan, J. H. "The Political Role of the Parlement of Paris, 1715-1723," *Historical Journal*, 8 (1965), 179-200.

———. "The Political Role of the Parlement of Paris under Cardinal Fleury," *English Historical Review*, 81 (1966), 520-42.

Sigal, Pierre-André. "Maladies, pèlerinage et guérisons au 12ᵉ siècle: Les miracles de saint Gibrien à Reims," *Annales: Economies, Sociétés, Civilisations*, 24 (1969), 1,522-39.

Smith, Marian W. "Towards a Classification of Cult Movements," *Man*, 59 (1959), 8-12.

Smith-Rosenberg, Carroll. "The Hysterical Woman: Sex Roles and Role Conflict in 19th-Century America." *Social Research*, 39 (1972), 652-78.

"Sur une brochure intitulé: *Vues sur le second avènement de Jésus-Christ*," *L'ami de la religion et du roi*, 25 (1820), 145-52, 177-84.

Talmon, Yonina. "Millenarian Movements," *Archives européennes de sociologie*, 7 (1966), 159-200.

Talmon, Yonina. "Pursuit of the Millennium: The Relation between Religious and Social Change," *Archives européennes de sociologie*, 3 (1962), 125-48.

Tans, J.A.G. "Les idées politiques des jansénistes," *Neophilologus*, 40 (1956), 1-18.

———. "L'influence des jansénistes français en Hollande," *Revue des sciences religieuses*, 39 (1965), 268-84.

Tauriac, A. "Suite aux 'Convulsions de Saint-Médard.' Une incarnation du Saint-Esprit, rue des Gobelins," *Bulletin de la Montagne Sainte-Geneviève et ses abords*, 12 (March 1956), 2-10; 13 (April 1956), 1-7.

Taveneaux, René. "Les foyers jansénistes de l'Argonne et de ses bordures," *Actes du 88ᵉ Congrès national des sociétés savantes. Section d'histoire moderne et contemporaine*. (Clermont-Ferrand, 1963), 49-63.

———. "Le jansénisme dans le diocèse de Verdun au début du 18ᵉ siècle," *Annales de l'Est*, 5th ser., 1 (1950), 15-33.

———. "Jansénisme et vie sociale en France au 17ᵉ siècle," *Revue d'histoire de l'Eglise de France*, 54 (1968), 27-46.

———. "Note d'orientation de recherches sur le jansénisme français au 18ᵉ siècle," *Bulletin de la Section d'histoire moderne et contemporaine du Comité des travaux historiques et scientifiques*, fasc. 4 (1962), 43-47.

———. "Port-Royal ou l'héroïsme de la sainteté," in *Héroïsme et création littéraire sous les règnes d'Henri IV et de Louis XIII*. Edited by Noémi Hepp and Georges Livet. Paris, 1974, pp. 99-109.

———. "Un projet de retraite de Pasquier Quesnel à Sénones, 1716-1717," *Annales de l'Est*, 5th ser., 13 (1962), 107-25.

———. "La vie religieuse en France de l'avènement d'Henri IV à la mort de Louis XIV (1598-1715)," *Bulletin de la Société des Professeurs d'histoire et de géographie de l'enseignement public*, No. 200 (October 1966), 119-30.

Thomas, Keith. "An Anthropology of Religion and Magic, II," *Journal of Interdisciplinary History*, 6 (1975), 91-109.

Thompson, Edward P. "Anthropology and the Discipline of Historical Context," *Midland History*, 1 (1971-72), 41-55.

Tinayre, Marcelle. "Une journée de Port-Royal des Champs (1654)," *Revue de Paris*, 9² (1902), 809-34.

Trénard, Louis. "Le catholicisme au 18ᵉ siècle, d'après les travaux récents," *L'information historique*, 26 (1964), 53-65.

———. "L'histoire des mentalités collectives. Les pensées et les hommes. Bilans et perspectives," *Revue d'histoire moderne et contemporaine*, 16 (1969), 652-62.

————. "La vie religieuse au 17ᵉ siècle," *L'information historique*, 31 (1969), 23-29, 66-72.

————, and Hilaire, Yves-Marie. "Idées, croyances et sensibilité religieuses du 18ᵉ siècle au 19ᵉ," *Bulletin de la Section d'Histoire moderne et contemporaine du Comité des travaux historiques et scientifiques*, fasc. 5 (1964), 7-27.

Ultee, J. Maarten. "The Suppression of *Fêtes* in France, 1666," *Catholic Historical Review*, 62 (1976), 181-99.

Vaissière, Pierre de. "L'état social des curés de la campagne au 18ᵉ siècle, d'après la correspondance de l'Agence Générale du Clergé aux Archives nationales," *Revue d'histoire de l'Eglise de France*, 19 (1933), 23-53.

Valet, Paul. "Le diacre Pâris et les convulsionnaires de Saint-Médard," *Bulletin de la Montagne Sainte-Geneviève et ses abords*, 1 (1896), 343-420.

Vallet, R. "La participation volontaire dans la conduite hystérique," *L'évolution psychiatrique*, 28 (1963), 467-91.

Veer, Albert C. de. "Le 'Grand recueil' dans les papiers de Quesnel saisis à Bruxelles et transportés à Paris en 1703 et 1704," *Revue d'histoire ecclésiastique*, 46 (1951), 187-91.

Venard, Marc. "Une histoire religieuse dans une histoire totale: 'Les paysans de Languedoc,' " *Revue d'histoire de l'Eglise de France*, 53 (1967), 35-47.

Ventre, abbé L. "A propos d'un centenaire, 1740-1940: Jean Soanen, évêque janséniste de Senez," *Bulletin de la Société scientifique et littéraire des Basses-Alpes*, 28 (1940-41), 7-50, 181-95, 291-316; 29 (1942), 40-53, 158-65.

Vial, Paul. "L'Eglise de France vue par le nonce en 1766," *Cahiers d'histoire*, 8 (1963), 107-24.

Viguerie, Jean de. "Prédication et théologie populaire au temps de Grignion de Montfort," *L'information historique*, 36 (1974), 210.

Vinchon, Jean. "Les convulsionnaires de Saint-Médard, ont-ils dépassé les limites des pouvoirs humains?" *Etudes carmélitaines*, 32 (1953), 39-47.

Vinot-Préfontaine, Jean. "Beauvais janséniste. Le culte de Nicolas Choart de Buzenval," *Revue des questions historiques*, 103 (1925), 408-22.

Viollet, Paul. "Communication au Conseil d'administration," *Bulletin de la Société de l'histoire de Paris et de l'Ile de France*, 17 (1890), 97-98.

Virieux, Maurice. "Jansénisme et molinisme dans le clergé du diocèse de Grenoble au début du 18ᵉ siècle," *Revue d'histoire de l'Eglise de France*, 60 (1974), 297-322.

Vovelle, Michel. "Entre baroque et jansénisme: Mentalités collectives dans la Provence au temps de la peste," in *La Régence*. Paris, 1970, pp. 215-20.

———. "Etude quantitative de la déchristiansation au 18ᵉ siècle: Débat ouvert, tabou ou dépassé?" *18ᵉ siècle*, No. 5 (1973), 163-72.

———. "Vue nouvelle sur l'histoire des mentalités: 'La sociabilité méridionale au 18ᵉ siècle,' " *Revue d'histoire de l'Eglise de France*, 53 (1967), 48-54.

Waffelaert, G.-J. "Convulsionnaires," *Dictionnaire apologétique de la foi catholique*. Edited by Alphonse Adhemar d'Alès. Vol. 1, cols. 705-13.

———. "Les démoniaques de la Salpêtrière et les vrais possédés du Démon," *Science catholique*, 2 (1887-88), 273-87, 352-69, 496-507, 571-93.

Wallace, Anthony F. C. "Revitalization Movements: Some Theoretical Considerations for Their Comparative Study," *American Anthropologist*, 58 (1956), 264-81.

———; Voget, Fred W.; and Smith, Marian W. "Toward a Classification of Cult Movements: Some Further Contributions," *Man*, 59 (1959), 25-28.

Weber, Max. "The Social Psychology of the World Religions," in *From Max Weber: Essays in Sociology*. Translated and edited by Hans H. Gerth and C. Wright Mills. New York, 1946, pp. 267-301.

Weis, Eberhard. "Jansenismus und Gesellschaft in Frankreich," *Historische Zeitschrift*, 214 (1972), 42-57.

Wickersheimer, Ernest. "Les guérisons miraculeuses du cardinal Pierre de Luxembourg (1387-1390)," *Comptes rendus du 2ᵉ congrès international de l'histoire de la médecine* (Evreux, 1922), 371-89.

Widlöcher, D. "La personnalité des hystériques," *La revue du praticien*, 14 (1964), 1,432-41.

Wilkins, Kay S. "The Treatment of the Supernatural in the *Encyclopédie*," *Studies on Voltaire and the 18th Century*, 90 (1972), 1,757-71.

Williams, William H. "Voltaire and the Utility of the Lower Clergy," *Studies on Voltaire and the 18th Century*, 58 (1967), 1,869-91.

Wilson, Bryan R. "An Analysis of Sect Development," *American Sociological Review*, 24 (1959), 3-15.

———. "Millennialism in Comparative Perspective," *Comparative Studies in Society and History*, 6 (1963), 93-114.

Wright, A. D. "The People of Catholic Europe and the People of Anglican England," *Historical Journal,* 18 (1975), 451-66.

Yardeni, Myriam. "L'ordre des avocats et la grève du barreau parisien en 1602," *Revue d'histoire économique et sociale,* 44 (1966), 481-507.

Index

Avocats (cont.)
case, 135-39; go on strike, 186-87, 206-207; popularity of, 187; and legal defense of convulsionaries, 336-37, 338, 361-62n. *See also Appel comme d'abus*; Parlement of Paris

Barbier, Edmond-Jean-François, 67, 112n, 168, 169n, 187, 206n, 238n, 241, 321n, 324, 325, 353, 357, 383
Barchman, Corneille-Jean, 79
Barneville, Mathieu de, 339n
Bastille: *anticonstitutionnaires* incarcerated in, 34n, 48, 305; convulsionaries incarcerated in, 204, 279-81, 282, 294, 299n, 306n, 307, 308n, 321n, 376n, 393; interrogations of convulsionaries at, 209-12, 215; Carré de Montgeron incarcerated in, 382-84, 387n
Bayle, Pierre, 4n
Beast of the Apocalypse, 303, 304, 306, 318, 385n
Beaumont, Christophe de, 393n
Belle-Isle, Charles-Louis-Auguste Fouquet, Count de, 213n
Belsunce, Henri-Xavier de, 77, 225
Berruyer, Isaac-Joseph, 229n
Berty, Simon Nigon de. *See* Nigon de Berty, Simon
Bérulle, Pierre de, 7
Bescherand de la Motte, abbé, 174-75, 176n, 177-79, 202, 208, 213, 286, 319
Besoigne, Jérôme, 293n
Bibliothèque bleue, 147
Bibliothèque de la Société des Amis de Port-Royal, 269n, 379n
Bigot, Cathérine, 174
Bissy, Henri Thiard, Cardinal de, 114n, 185n, 192n, 229n, 354
Blondel, Pierre, 160
Boileau, Etienne, 333nn
Boindin de Boisbessin, 156
Boissonnade, Marie, 356
Bougeant, Guillaume-Hyacinthe, 176n
Bouhier, Jean, 275n
Bouillerot family (*marguilliers* at Saint-Médard), 162-66
Boulogne, 78
Boulogne, bishop of, 108

Bourbon, Louis-Henri, Duke de, 39
Boursier, Laurent-François, 51n, 132, 293n, 343n
Boyer, Pierre, 82n, 193n, 256n, 314n, 326-28, 329
Brussels, 10
Buzenval, Nicolas Choart de, 72

Cabalists, Renaissance, 247n
Calendrier mystérieux pour l'année 1733, 303-305, 306, 318, 332, 335
Camisards, 286, 360
Capitation, 22-23
Carré de Montgeron, Louis-Basile. *See* Montgeron, Louis-Basile Carré de
Catholic Reformation, 141-45, 147
Causse, Jeanne (Soeur Félicité, Soeur Noir, Soeur Robert), 309, 333
Causse, Jean-Robert (Frère Augustin), 332, 333, 334, 336, 338; background of, 309; religious claims of, 309-11, 312, 326-28; extravagant ritual behavior attributed to, 309, 311, 312, 313, 315; as shadowy, elusive figure, 311, 330, 332, 333n, 339, 340; and La Restan, 313, 328, 340; charges made against, 313-14, 315, 317, 333n; *anticonstitutionnaire* detractors of, 314-17, 326-28, enmity of, toward "Jansenist doctors," 315, 327-28, 332; and Pierre Boyer, 316n, 326-28, 329; and Frère Athanase, 328, 329; repudiates Augustiniste "system," 340n. *See also* Augustinistes
Caylus, Daniel-Charles-Gabriel de, 289n, 341n, 358-59, 365n, 374, 375
Cellier, Suzanne (Soeur Roch), 253n
Celoron, Claude, 78-79, 81
Censorship, royal, 37, 40, 45, 46, 47, 50, 52, 53, 110-11, 229, 323, 342, 357-58, 386n, 387
Chaise-Dieu, 47, 316, 389-90
Chambre des Comptes, 387
Charcot, Jean-Martin, 261n, 379n
Charpentier (*curé* of Saint-Leu), 193n
Châtelet, 351, 371, 382
Chaulin, François, 157, 372n
Chauvelin, Germain-Louis de, 80, 108n, 114n, 195, 199; and Pâris cult and miracles, 95, 196n, 197n, 220n, 243n,